ENCYCLOPEDIA OF
WORLD CONSTITUTIONS

❧

Volume III

ENCYCLOPEDIA OF WORLD CONSTITUTIONS

Volume III

(Oman to Zimbabwe)

EDITED BY GERHARD ROBBERS

An imprint of Infobase Publishing

Encyclopedia of World Constitutions

Facts On File, Inc.
An imprint of Infobase Publishing
132 West 31st Street
New York NY 10001

Library of Congress Cataloging-in-Publication Data
Encyclopedia of world constitutions / edited by Gerhard Robbers.
p. cm.
Includes index.
ISBN 0-8160-6078-9
1. Constitutions. 2. Constitutional law. 3. Comparative law. I. Robbers, Gerhard.
K3157.E5E53 2006
342.02—dc22   2005028923

Facts On File books are available at special discounts when purchased in bulk quantities for businesses, associations, institutions, or sales promotions. Please call our Special Sales Department in New York at (212) 967-8800 or (800) 322-8755.

You can find Facts On File on the World Wide Web at http://www.factsonfile.com

Text design by Erika K. Arroyo
Cover design by Dorothy M. Preston

Printed in the United States of America

VB Hermitage 10 9 8 7 6 5 4 3 2 1

This book is printed on acid-free paper.

Contents

Entries O to Z

OMAN

At-a-Glance

OFFICIAL NAME
Sultanate of Oman

CAPITAL
Muscat

POPULATION
3,001,583 (2005 est.)

SIZE
82,031 sq. mi. (212,460 sq. km)

LANGUAGES
Arabic (official)

RELIGIONS
Ibadhi Muslim 75%, Sunni Muslim and Shia Muslim 12.5%, Hindu 5.6%, Christian 4.9%, Buddhist 0.8%, other 1.2% (2000 est.)

NATIONAL OR ETHNIC COMPOSITION
Arab 48.1%, South Asian (Bangladeshi 4.4%, Pakistani [mostly Baluchi] 15%, Tamil 2.5%) 31.7%, other Arab 7.2%, Persian 2.8%, Zanzibari 2.5%, other 7.7% (2000)

DATE OF INDEPENDENCE OR CREATION
1650 (expulsion of the Portuguese)

TYPE OF GOVERNMENT
Monarchy

TYPE OF STATE
Unitary state

TYPE OF LEGISLATURE
Bicameral advisory body

DATE OF CONSTITUTION
November 6, 1996

DATE OF LAST AMENDMENT
No amendment

Oman is a hereditary monarchy. Parliament does little more than advise the sultan. The judiciary is declared by the constitution to be independent. The constitution guarantees fundamental rights. Islam is the state religion.

CONSTITUTIONAL HISTORY

Islam was introduced in the seventh century C.E. along with the political rule of the early caliphs. One hundred years later, the Ibadite strain of the new religion arrived, and the preexisting tribal society was politically unified by the Ibadite imams. The Ibadite state was headed by an elected imam who served as the political and religious leader of the country.

Hereditary dynasties competed with the imams for centuries. The Nabhanid dynasty controlled the interior of Oman from the mid-12th century until 1406. The Portuguese sacked the city of Muscat in 1507 and established their rule in the area, but in 1650 the Ya'rubid dynasty recaptured Muscat; the sultans established a maritime empire that stretched south to the east African coast. The Persian ruler Nadir Shah invaded the country in 1737.

Sultan Said Ibn Taymor succeeded to the sultanate in 1932; by then it was a British protectorate. The sultan kept Oman isolated from most of the world, maintaining diplomatic relations only with the United States, the United Kingdom, and India. The sultan did little to develop the country and was overthrown by his son, Quaboos bin Said, in 1970. The new sultan opened the country to the outside world and liberalized the government. He issued the basic law of Oman on November 6, 1996.

FORM AND IMPACT OF THE CONSTITUTION

The constitution of Oman is contained in a single written document, called the Basic Law of the State. Laws and procedures that have the force of law must conform to the provisions of the basic law. No one in the state may issue regulations, decisions, or instructions that contravene the existing laws and decrees or international treaties and agreements that constitute part of the law of the country.

BASIC ORGANIZATIONAL STRUCTURE

Oman is a unitary state subdivided into five regions and three governorates.

LEADING CONSTITUTIONAL PRINCIPLES

The Sultanate of Oman is a fully sovereign Arab Islamic state. The religion of the state is Islam and the Islamic sharia is the basis of legislation. The system of government is a hereditary sultanate. Rule in the sultanate must be based on justice, equality, and consultation with the Shura Council. The constitution sets out further principles concerning the political, economic, social, cultural, and security policies of the state.

CONSTITUTIONAL BODIES

The main constitutional bodies are the sultan, the Council of Ministers, the Oman Council, and the judiciary.

The Sultan

The sultan is the head of state and the supreme commander of the armed forces. His person is inviolable and must be respected, and his orders must be obeyed. The sultan is the symbol of the national unity as well as its guardian and defender. Succession to the sultan passes to a male descendent of Sayyid Turki bin Said bin Sultan. The male who is chosen to rule should be an adult Muslim of sound mind and a legitimate son of Omani Muslim parents.

The sultan guides the general policy of the state, represents the state both internally and externally in all international relations, and presides over the Council of Ministers or appoints a person to serve in that position. The sultan appoints and dismisses high-ranking officials such as cabinet ministers and senior judges. The sultan declares the state of emergency or war, issues and ratifies laws, and signs international treaties and agreements.

The sultan is assisted in drafting and implementing the general policy of the state by the Council of Ministers and specialized councils.

The Council of Ministers

The Council of Ministers is the body entrusted with implementing general state policies. It submits recommendations to the sultan on economic, political, and social as well as executive and administrative matters. It proposes draft laws and decrees and discharges any other competencies vested in it by the sultan or conferred upon it by the provisions of the law.

The sultan can appoint a prime minister and define his or her functions and powers. Prime ministers, deputy prime ministers, and cabinet ministers must be of Omani nationality by birth and at least 30 years old. The sultan himself can fulfill the functions of prime minister.

Specialized councils can be established in accordance with royal decrees that also define their powers and members.

The Oman Council

The Oman parliament consists of the Shura Council (Majilis ash-Shura) and the Council of State (Majilis ad-Dawls). The law specifies the powers of each of these councils, the length of their terms, the frequency of their sessions, and their rules of procedure.

The Shura Council consists of 83 members. They are elected by universal suffrage for four-year terms. They represent the regions of the country and discuss legislative measures. Women can serve on the council.

The Council of State comprises 58 members appointed by the sultan. It acts as an upper house of the Oman Council and discusses policy issues.

The Lawmaking Process

It is the sultan only who decides on the laws. The chambers of the Oman Council have mostly advisory functions. The Shura Council does have a limited right to propose legislation.

The Judiciary

The judicial power is independent and vested in the courts of law. There is no power over the judges in their rulings except the law. Judges can only be dismissed in cases specified by the law. The jurisdiction of military courts is restricted to military crimes committed by members of the armed forces and the security forces. A special Administrative Causes Court adjudicates administrative disputes. Islamic courts decide personal status cases.

THE ELECTION PROCESS

The constitution does not refer to any election procedures. Ordinary law provides for universal suffrage for the Shura Council.

POLITICAL PARTIES

The constitution does not expressly discuss political parties. In practice there are none.

CITIZENSHIP

Nationality is regulated by the law. It may not be forfeited or withdrawn except within the limits of the law.

FUNDAMENTAL RIGHTS

The constitution guarantees a number of fundamental rights such as personal freedom and protection against arbitrary imprisonment. No person may be subjected to torture or humiliating treatment. It is not permitted to perform any medical or scientific experiment on any person without his or her freely given consent. Dwellings are inviolable. Freedom of opinion and expression is guaranteed within the limits of the law. Freedom of press is guaranteed in accordance with the conditions and circumstances defined by the law.

There are also basic duties expressed in the constitution, such as respect for the law and the observance of public order and public morals.

Impact and Functions of Fundamental Rights

The constitution guarantees classic rights such as freedom of opinion and protection against unfair arrest. Fundamental principles obligate the state to provide social and cultural services such as education and public health. Family is declared the basis of society.

Limitations to Fundamental Rights

Many of the fundamental rights are guaranteed only within the limits of the law. For some rights further limitations are specifically established. This applies, for example, to the freedom of the press: It is prohibited to print or publish material that leads to public discord, violates the security of the state, or abuses a person's dignity and his or her rights.

ECONOMY

The constitution sets out certain basic economic principles: The national economy must be based on justice, and its chief pillar is constructive and fruitful cooperation of the public and private sectors. The constitution establishes a free economy within the limits of the law and the public interest. Public property is inviolable; private property is protected.

RELIGIOUS COMMUNITIES

The religion of the state is Islam. The freedom to practice religious rites is protected in accordance with recognized customs provided that it does not disrupt public order or conflict with accepted standards of behavior.

MILITARY DEFENSE AND STATE OF EMERGENCY

The sultan is supreme commander of the armed forces. It is the sultan who declares a state of war or emergency. In the case of martial law the jurisdiction of military courts can be extended to others than members of the armed forces and security forces. In the case of martial law, the provisions of the basic law can be suspended.

AMENDMENTS TO THE CONSTITUTION

The basic law can only be amended in the same manner in which it was promulgated. This means that only the sultan can, by decree, amend the constitution.

PRIMARY SOURCES
Constitution in English. Available online. URL: http://www.oefre.unibe.ch/law/icl/mu00000_.html. Accessed on July 19, 2005.

SECONDARY SOURCES
Bureau of Public Affairs, U.S. Department of State, "Background Note and Country Reports on Human Rights Practices and International Religious Freedom Report 2004." Available online: URL: http://www.state.gov/g/drl/rls/irf/2004/35505.htm. Accessed on June 27, 2006.

Helem Chapin Metz, ed., *Oman: A Country Study.* Washington, D.C.: U.S. Library of Congress, 1993. Available online. URL: http://memory.loc.gov/frd/cs/omtoc.html. Accessed on September 19, 2005.

United Nations Development Programme. "Constitutions of the Arab Region." Available online. URL: http://www.pogar.org/themes/constitution.asp. Accessed on September 26, 2005.

Gerhard Robbers

PAKISTAN

At-a-Glance

OFFICIAL NAME
Islamic Republic of Pakistan

CAPITAL
Islamabad

POPULATION
150,694,740 (2005 est.)

SIZE
310,401 sq. mi. (803,940 sq. km)

LANGUAGES
Urdu (national), English (official), Punjabi, Sindhi, Pushto, Baluchi (local)

RELIGIONS
Muslim (Sunni 77%, Shia 20%) 97%, Christian, Hindu, other 3%

NATIONAL OR ETHNIC COMPOSITION
Punjabi, Sindhi, Pashtun (Pathan), Baluch, Muhajir (immigrants from India and their descendants)

DATE OF INDEPENDENCE OR CREATION
August 14, 1947

TYPE OF GOVERNMENT
Parliamentary democracy

TYPE OF STATE
Federal state

TYPE OF LEGISLATURE
Bicameral parliament at the center, unicameral legislature in the provinces

DATE OF CONSTITUTION
August 14, 1973

DATE OF LAST AMENDMENT
January 20, 2004

Pakistan is a parliamentary democracy with separation of executive, legislative, and judicial powers. It is a federation of four provinces with a strong federal government at the center. The constitution provides for a number of fundamental rights, which include various human rights and civil liberties recognized internationally. These fundamental rights are enforceable through the courts.

The president is the head of state and enjoys substantial powers in relation to certain executive and legislative functions. The prime minister is the chief executive of the federal government and is elected by the members of the National Assembly, the lower house of the Parliament. The members of the National Assembly and the provincial assemblies are elected through direct elections. A number of political parties participate in the elections.

The constitution declares Islam a state religion but allows freedom of religion to the members of other faiths. The economic system is based on a market economy. The people of Pakistan are diverse, consisting of various ethnic groups speaking different languages and with different cultures. The constitution stipulates that Pakistan should live in peace with all countries in the world and provides for a special relationship with other Muslim countries.

CONSTITUTIONAL HISTORY

Pakistan emerged as a separate independent state on August 14, 1947, after the departure of British rulers from India. Prior to independence, the areas that would become Pakistan formed part of British India. On independence, British India was divided into the Dominions of India and Pakistan under the 1947 Indian Independence Act.

Muslims arrived in India with the invasion of Sindh, a Pakistani province, in 712 C.E. Waves of Muslim conquerors followed until Delhi fell to the Muslims under Muhammad Ghori in 1192. The Delhi Sultanate was founded by Qutubuddin Aibak in 1206, and Muslim power continued to expand until it reigned supreme over the entire Indian subcontinent. Sultans of five Turkish and Afghan dynasties ruled Delhi until 1526.

Mughal rule began in 1526, when the empire's founder, Babur, conquered Delhi. The great Mughal emperors (1526–1707) are known for laying the foundation of modern administration and introducing a system of agricultural revenue administration that still prevails in India and Pakistan. The Mughals ruled by decrees, each emperor concentrating all executive, legislative, and judicial powers in himself. No written constitutions are known to have existed during the Muslim rule of India from 1206 to 1857. The governments during this period followed a pattern of hereditary monarchy.

The Mughal Empire fell into decline after 1707. The British, who had entered India as traders, gradually extended their control over India at the expense of the Mughals. British expansionism continued unabated, and in 1857 the last of the Mughal emperors, Bahadur Shah Zafar, was defeated by the forces of the British East India Company. The Mughal emperor was exiled to Rangoon in Burma and the British government took direct administrative control of India under the 1858 Government of India Act.

From 1858 onward, the British government in India faced an increasingly strong local opposition movement, first favoring self-government and later complete independence. The British government allowed the people of India some degree of self-government from time to time, until the British Parliament passed the 1935 Government of India Act, giving India a constitutional framework. The act allowed autonomy to the provinces and enlarged the participation of Indians at the center of the government. The act made Sindh a separate province.

General elections were held under the 1935 act. In the provincial elections, the Congress Party (mainly representing Hindus in India) won a majority of seats in eight provinces and consequently formed governments in those provinces. The victory at the polls was regarded by the Congress Party as a mandate to deal with the British on behalf of all Indians. Muslims felt they were not treated equitably in Congress-controlled provinces and became convinced they should seek a separate homeland for themselves. The All India Muslim League, which represented most of the Muslims in India, passed a resolution in Lahore on March 23, 1940, now known as the Pakistan Resolution, in which they demanded that areas in which Muslims were numerically the majority, particularly in the northwestern and eastern zones of India, should be assembled to constitute an independent and sovereign state. This resolution constituted a formal demand for an independent state for Muslims in India and was the starting point of the Pakistan movement.

British Prime Minister Attlee announced on February 20, 1947, that full self-government would be granted to India by June 1948 at the latest. On June 3, 1947, the British government accepted the proposed partition of India and undertook to extend dominion status to the successor governments of India and Pakistan by August 15, 1947.

In the Muslim majority provinces of Bengal, Punjab, and Sindh, the choice of whether to join Pakistan or India was left to the members of the provincial legislative assemblies. However, in Bengal (with a Muslim majority of 55 percent) and Punjab (with a Muslim majority of 57 percent), the assemblies were themselves in effect partitioned. Representatives of districts with a Muslim majority voted as one part, while representatives of Hindu or non-Muslim majority districts voted as another. If either part voted in favor of provincial partition, the province would be provisionally divided on the basis of Muslim majority and non-Muslim majority districts. Thereafter, a boundary commission would divide each province on the basis of contiguous majority areas of Muslims and non-Muslims.

It was on the basis of this constitutional scheme that Bengal and the Punjab were partitioned by the boundary commission; as a result the eastern part of Bengal and the western portion of the Punjab, with Muslim majority districts, formed part of Pakistan. The legislative assembly of Sindh voted in favor of joining Pakistan. In the North-West Frontier, the result of a referendum favored joining Pakistan. Thus Pakistan came into existence on August 14, 1947, as an independent sovereign state.

Under the provisions of the 1947 Indian Independence Act, the 1935 Government of India Act became, with certain necessary adaptations, the working constitution of Pakistan. The 1947 Pakistan (Provisional Constitution) Order established the federation of Pakistan with the provinces of East Bengal, West Punjab, Sindh, North West Frontier Province (NWFP), and Baluchistan. Karachi became the capital of the federation. The Constituent Assembly of India, elected in 1946 before partition, was split in two; the members elected from the areas forming part of Pakistan formed the Constituent Assembly of Pakistan. This Constituent Assembly was assigned the task of framing a permanent constitution for Pakistan.

One of the first constitutional acts of the Constituent Assembly was to pass the Objectives Resolution in March 1949. It emphasized the democratic character of the state by pronouncing that the state would exercise its powers and authority through the chosen representatives of the people of Pakistan. It provided for a guarantee of fundamental rights and aimed to safeguard the legitimate interests of the minorities and backward classes, secure the independence of the judiciary, and provide autonomy for the provinces. This resolution was intended to establish guidelines for the future constitution of Pakistan.

The Constituent Assembly of Pakistan took a long time to draft the constitution. Pakistan was divided into two parts, or wings: East Pakistan with 55 percent of the population on 15 percent of the land area, and West Pakistan with 45 percent of the population on 85 percent of the land area. The two wings of the country were separated by more than 1,000 miles of Indian territory, or approximately 3,000 miles by sea. Four issues remained subjects of contention: national language, proportion of representation of the regions in Parliament, provincial autonomy, and the form of the electorate.

After more than seven years of debate and deliberation, these issues were resolved. Both Urdu and Bengali were declared national languages. Representation in the lower house of Parliament would be determined on the basis of population, and representation in the upper house would be equal for each province or federating unit. The question of whether the electorate would be joint or separate was left open. The federation was allocated authority over a number of important subjects, such as defense, foreign policy, currency, and communications; the remaining subjects were left to the provinces. With these provisions, the draft of the constitution was finalized by the Constituent Assembly in October 1954. Its adoption was postponed to a future session.

On October 24, 1954, Ghulam Muhammad, governor-general of Pakistan, who had been offended by certain provisions passed by the Constituent Assembly curtailing his powers, ordered dissolution of the Constituent Assembly on the pretext that it had taken too long to frame the constitution, and that its members had lost their representative character. This act led to a series of legal battles. In a decision by the Federal Court, the governor-general was advised to hold an election for a successor Constituent Assembly that could then frame and adopt a constitution for Pakistan.

The second Constituent Assembly was elected in June 1955 and adopted the draft constitution on February 29, 1956. The constitution went into force on March 23, 1956. The second Constituent Assembly adopted most of the provisions of the draft constitution finalized by the first Constituent Assembly in October 1954. The provinces of West Pakistan were merged into a single province called West Pakistan and the province of East Bengal was renamed East Pakistan.

The 1956 constitution could have established democracy in Pakistan had it been enforced properly and with sincerity of purpose. Most of its provisions were identical to the provisions of the constitution of India, implemented in January 1950, which has been instrumental in establishing sustainable democracy in India. However, no elections were held under the 1956 constitution. General elections were announced for February 1959, but while the political parties were busy with the campaign, President Sikandar Mirza proclaimed martial law throughout the country on October 7, 1958, and abrogated the constitution. He appointed General Ayub Khan, commander in chief of the Pakistan army, as chief martial law administrator. Ayub Khan soon overthrew President Mirza. After exiling Mirza, he assumed the office of president.

The 1962 constitution drafted under Ayub's control provided for a highly centralized system with a presidential form of government. All the powers of the state were concentrated in the hands of the president, who could even legislate in times of emergency by issuing ordinances, without any approval from the Parliament.

This 1962 constitution did not last long. It was seen by the people of Pakistan as an instrument to allow a military ruler to preserve his position of power. Countrywide

political agitation forced Ayub to resign in March 1969. He was succeeded by General Yahya Khan, commander in chief of the Pakistan army. Yahya proclaimed martial law throughout the country and abrogated the 1962 constitution. He promised to hold free and fair general elections on the basis of adult franchise.

General elections for the national and provincial assemblies were held in December 1970. The results were very lopsided. The Awami League, led by Sheikh Mujib, won 167 of the 169 seats allocated to East Pakistan. In West Pakistan, the Peoples' Party, led by Zulfiqar Ali Bhutto, won 60 percent of the 144 seats. This led to a confrontation between the two regions. Yahya, in this complex political situation, refused to transfer power to the Awami League, which had the absolute majority in the National Assembly. When he postponed the meeting of the National Assembly after having summoned it, a revolt broke out in East Pakistan. When negotiations for a political settlement failed, Yahya made the fateful decision to suppress the political uprising through military action, and on March 25, 1971, Mujib was arrested and taken to West Pakistan. The resulting military insurrection in East Pakistan was supported by the Indian government. Ultimately, Indian armed forces invaded East Pakistan, and the Pakistan army surrendered at Dhaka on December 16, 1971. East Pakistan seceded from the Union of Pakistan and became Bangladesh, an independent sovereign country.

After deliberations lasting more than a year, the National Assembly, acting as the Constituent Assembly, adopted a new permanent constitution. The new constitution went into force on August 14, 1973.

As many as seven amendments to the constitution were passed within four years of implementation, effectively diluting the guarantees of fundamental rights and curtailing the jurisdiction and powers of the judiciary. In general elections to the national and provincial assemblies held in March 1977, the opposition made serious allegations of vote rigging and electoral fraud by Bhutto and his Peoples' Party. Political agitation led to the overthrow of the Bhutto government on July 5, 1977, by a military junta headed by General Zia, the army's chief of staff. He imposed martial law and suspended the constitution. Bhutto was arrested, tried for the murder of a political opponent, sentenced to death, and executed in April 1979. General elections were not held until February 1985; the constitution was restored the following month after extensive amendments under Zia's direction.

On October 12, 1999, the federal government, then headed by Prime Minister Nawaz Sharif, was sacked by military generals headed by General Parvez Musharraf, the army's chief of staff. Musharraf did not impose martial law but assumed the powers as chief executive of the federal government and appointed military governors in the provinces. He suspended the constitution and introduced a provisional constitution order. Musharraf also suspended Parliament and the provincial assemblies. Once again, the Supreme Court upheld the military takeover on the basis of the doctrine of state necessity and conferred on Musharraf the power to amend the constitution.

Musharraf later removed President Rafiq Tarar in June 2001 and assumed the office himself. He held a referendum on April 30, 2002, that backed his continuation as president whatever the outcome of general elections scheduled for October. As a further guarantee, he made extensive changes to the constitution on August 21, 2002, giving primacy to the office of the president. As before, the president has the power to dissolve national and provincial assemblies at his or her discretion and to dismiss the federal and provincial governments. He or she may also appoint important constitutional officeholders such as the chiefs of the armed forces, the chief election commissioner, and provincial governors. The amendments were validated by the new Parliament with only minor modifications in December 2003.

FORM AND IMPACT OF THE CONSTITUTION

The 1973 constitution, a written constitution codified in a single document, has been repeatedly and comprehensively amended to meet the interests of the military rulers and preserve their positions of power. Thus, it has been altered beyond recognition. Its basic structure of parliamentary democracy has been changed. It is dominated instead by presidential powers, and other constitutional institutions matter very little. The prime minister and the cabinet are weak and subordinate to the will of the president. The Parliament has been undermined and most legislation is implemented through presidential ordinances, which Parliament then rubber-stamps. Parliamentary traditions and conventions have not developed because of the extended periods of military rule during which legislatures were nonexistent.

The credibility of other important constitutional institutions, such as the judiciary and the election commission, has been seriously impaired. The constitution has lost its sanctity and importance as the basic law of the country as a result of its repeated abrogation, suspension, and alteration.

BASIC ORGANIZATIONAL STRUCTURE

Pakistan is a federation of four provinces. Punjab is the most populous province with more than 55 percent of the total population of the country. Baluchistan has the largest land area with more than 40 percent of the entire territory of Pakistan, but it has less than 5 percent of the total population. Sindh and NWFP, the remaining provinces, both have substantial populations. Karachi is Pakistan's largest city with a population of more than 10 million people.

The constitution created provincial legislatures and executives as replicas of the institutions at the national level. The federal structure has shown a marked tendency toward centralized control and authority, in part through exploitation of the constitutional duty of the federal government to protect each province against external aggression and internal disturbance. Provincial governments are obliged to exercise their executive authority in such a way as to ensure compliance with federal laws.

The subjects under the legislative and executive authority of the federation include foreign affairs, defense, currency, citizenship, foreign and interprovincial trade and commerce, census, taxes, excise duties and customs, the central bank, postal and all forms of telecommunication, and minerals, including oil and gas. The provincial authority controls subjects such as land revenue, taxes on agricultural income, urban property tax, health, education, and local government. There is a concurrent list of subjects on which both Parliament and provincial assemblies can legislate. In these realms, if there is any inconsistency between the federal and provincial laws on the same subject, the federal law prevails to the extent of inconsistency. The concurrent list includes civil and criminal law, family law, bankruptcy, arbitration, trusts, transfer of property, population planning, drugs, terrorism, and trade unions.

LEADING CONSTITUTIONAL PRINCIPLES

In principle, Pakistan is a federal parliamentary democracy with a division of executive, legislative, and judicial powers. The constitution provides for a unified system of courts: the provincial courts, high courts, and subordinate courts, and the federal court—the Supreme Court of Pakistan—all exercising jurisdiction under all laws, federal, provincial, and local. The judiciary is supposed to be an independent organ of the state, separate from the legislature and the executive.

The constitution enumerates "directive principles of policy" that both the federal and the provincial legislatures and governments must follow. These include preservation of Islamic values among the Muslims in Pakistan; prevention of concentration of wealth in the hands of a few; promotion of social justice by ending illiteracy, by providing free secondary education, and by ensuring inexpensive and expeditious justice; protection of legitimate rights of non-Muslim minorities; participation of women in all spheres of life; strengthening of the bonds of unity among Muslim countries; and advancing of peace and goodwill toward the peoples of the world.

CONSTITUTIONAL BODIES

The predominant executive bodies provided for in the constitution include the president, the prime minister, and the cabinet, consisting of federal ministers and ministers of state. The legislature consists of two houses, the upper house referred to as the Senate, headed by a chair, and the lower house, the National Assembly, headed by a speaker. At the provincial level the governor, the chief minister, and the cabinet, consisting of provincial ministers, are the principal executive bodies. Each province has a provincial assembly headed by a speaker. The judiciary consists of the Supreme Court of Pakistan and the high courts, one for each province. Other important constitutional officeholders include the chief election commissioner, the comptroller and the auditor general, the attorney general, and the advocates general.

The Federal President

The president is the head of state of the Islamic Republic of Pakistan. The office of president under the original 1973 constitution was a ceremonial office with very little power. Today, after several amendments, the office of the president is the most powerful under the constitution. The president has the power to dissolve the National Assembly at his or her discretion and can instruct a governor to dissolve the provincial assembly of a province. The president can thus dismiss the federal administration and have the provincial administration dismissed. The president also appoints the chief election commissioner and the chiefs of armed forces at his or her discretion. The president can appoint governors in nonbinding consultation with the prime minister. The president appoints the judges of the Supreme Court and the high courts on the advice of the prime minister and in consultation with the chief justices. The president appoints all executive officers, such as ambassadors and civil servants, on the advice of the prime minister.

The president is elected for a period of five years and can be reelected. The electoral college that elects the president consists of both houses of Parliament and the four provincial assemblies. The president must be a Muslim, a citizen of Pakistan, and at least 45 years of age. The president must be qualified to be elected as a member of the National Assembly. The office of president is part of the Parliament, as the president must assent to any bill passed by Parliament in order for it to become law. The president can return a bill with comments for reconsideration. If it is again passed with or without amendment the president cannot withhold assent. The president has the power to legislate through ordinances when Parliament is either dissolved or not in session. However, such presidential ordinances are temporary laws, which expire after four months unless approved by the Parliament within such time.

The Federal Cabinet

Under the constitution, the federal cabinet dominates the government in Pakistan. It is headed by the prime minister, the chief executive of the government. The prime minister runs the federal administration through the cabinet, which consists of the federal ministers and ministers of state. The prime minister selects the cabinet members.

In the first meeting of the National Assembly after general elections, the prime minister is elected by a majority of the total members of the National Assembly. The prime minister can only be removed by a vote of no confidence by a majority of the total members of the National Assembly. The prime minister and the cabinet can be removed by the president after dissolution of the National Assembly, at the president's discretion.

Under the original constitution, the prime minister was to be the dominant figure of Pakistani politics. From 1973 to July 1977, Prime Minister Zulfiqar Ali Bhutto was indeed the dominant political figure in the country. Once again, from the death of Zia in August 1988 to the military takeover by Musharraf in October 1999, Benazir Bhutto and Nawaz Sharif, each serving two terms as prime ministers, were the dominant political figures in the politics of Pakistan. However, when the office of the president is held by a military ruler, the prime ministers have been politically eclipsed.

The Parliament

The Parliament consists of the president and two houses, the Senate and the National Assembly. The members of the National Assembly are elected on the basis of population from territorial constituencies carved by the election commission. The candidate who secures the most votes in that constituency is elected. The National Assembly is elected for a period of five years, but it can be dissolved earlier by the president for one of three reasons: if the president is so advised by the prime minister; if it appears that no member of the National Assembly can command the confidence of the majority of its members; or if it appears that the federal government cannot be carried on in accordance with the provisions of the constitution and an appeal to the electorate has become necessary. This provision has been abused repeatedly by various presidents.

The members of the Senate are elected for a term of six years by the provincial assemblies. Every three years, half of the members of the Senate retire and elections are held for their seats. All provinces, regardless of their size or population, have an equal number of representatives in the Senate. The Senate is a permanent house and cannot be dissolved. Its chairperson, who is elected for a three-year term, succeeds as acting president in case the office of president is vacated as a result of death or resignation.

The Lawmaking Process

The main function of the Parliament is legislation. Bills are generally introduced by the federal cabinet through the prime minister or the relevant committee. Even individual members of Parliament can introduce legislation through what is called a private member's bill.

Any legislation can originate in either of the houses of Parliament except the finance bill (the federal budget), which originates in the National Assembly. In case of differences between the two houses on any legislation, a joint sitting is called by the president and the legislation is passed in the joint sitting by a majority of those present and voting.

The Judiciary

The constitution requires the judiciary in Pakistan to be independent of the executive and the legislature. The Supreme Court is the highest court in the country. It exercises jurisdiction over all disputes—constitutional, civil, criminal, administrative, and others. The decisions of the Supreme Court are binding on all courts and administrative authorities in Pakistan. All executive and judicial authorities throughout the country are required to act in aid of the Supreme Court to ensure execution and implementation of its decisions, decrees, orders, directives, or writs.

The Supreme Court is the chief interpreter of the constitution. It hears appeals from the provincial high courts and has original jurisdiction in disputes between the federation and a province or among the provinces. It has special original jurisdiction in cases of public importance to issue writs against any violation of fundamental rights.

A high court is the highest court of appeal in a province. It exercises all kinds of jurisdictions under federal as well as provincial laws except in matters of the civil service. It has constitutional jurisdiction to issue writs to the judicial and administrative authorities throughout the province.

The Supreme Court and the high courts have authority to declare any law, federal or provincial, unconstitutional if it is repugnant to the fundamental rights under the constitution or inconsistent with any other provision of the constitution. A judge of a high court or of the Supreme Court cannot be removed before the age of retirement unless recommended by the Supreme Judicial Council, consisting of five senior judges.

The record of the Supreme Court in exercise of its constitutional jurisdiction is mixed and controversial. It has handed down some positive judgments relating to the enforcement of fundamental rights. In contrast, it also has a record of upholding and legitimizing military regimes relying on the doctrine of state necessity. Such judgments have eroded its credibility among the people of Pakistan.

THE ELECTION PROCESS

All citizens of at least 18 years of age are entitled to cast their votes in the elections. Every citizen above 25 years can contest an election to a seat in the National Assembly or a provincial assembly. The minimal age for a candidate to the Senate is 30 years. The elections of the president, houses of Parliament, and provincial assembly are conducted by the Election Commission of Pakistan.

POLITICAL PARTIES

Every citizen of at least 18 years of age has a fundamental right to form or join a political party. Pakistan has a number of political parties that participate in elections. The law requires every political party to have a democratic internal structure and to submit its accounts periodically to the Election Commission.

The federal cabinet may ban a political party if it is of the opinion that the party is working against the sovereignty or integrity of Pakistan. The federal cabinet is obliged to send a reference of any such order to the Supreme Court, and the matter is then subject to the court's judgment. In only one instance has the Supreme Court upheld such an order.

Political parties in Pakistan are weak. In contradiction to the legal requirements, they lack democratic internal structures. Repeated military takeovers have caused immense harm to the development of political parties and the political process in the country. The military regimes have destabilized the political parties in order to perpetuate their own rule.

CITIZENSHIP

Citizenship in Pakistan is acquired either by birth or through nationalization. All persons who entered Pakistan on or before 1951 became citizens of Pakistan by operation of law.

FUNDAMENTAL RIGHTS

The chapter of the constitution on fundamental rights includes a number of human rights and civil liberties. The principal fundamental rights guaranteed by the constitution are as follows: All citizens are equal before the law and are entitled to equal protection of law, no person can be deprived of life or liberty except in accordance with the law, no person can be punished for an act that was not punishable when committed, and there should be no discrimination on the basis of race, religion, caste, sex, or place of birth. All forms of slavery and forced labor have been banned; all torture and cruel or inhuman treatment or punishment are illegal. Every person has a right to acquire, hold, and dispose of property in any part of Pakistan, subject to reasonable restrictions under the law. The dignity of human beings and the privacy of the home have been declared inviolate. Protection is provided against double jeopardy and self-incrimination. All citizens are guaranteed freedom of speech, expression, and press; freedom to assemble peacefully; freedom of association; and freedom to move throughout Pakistan and to reside in any part of the country. Freedom of conscience and the right to profess, practice, and propagate any religion and establish, manage, and maintain religious institutions are also guaranteed. Every citizen has the right to enter into any lawful profession or professions or to conduct any lawful trade or business.

Impact and Functions of Fundamental Right

Pakistan has a history of very inconsistent enforcement of fundamental rights. Since the first constitution of 1956, fundamental rights have been suspended for a total of about 30 years. Since the constitution of 1973, fundamental rights have been enforceable through the courts for a total of about 15 years. The military regimes have been hostile to fundamental rights, and even the civilian governments have displayed a tendency to suspend or discourage the enforcement of fundamental rights.

Nevertheless, the superior courts have made progressive and liberal judgments regarding the enforcement of fundamental rights, particularly relating to preventive detention, human dignity, forced labor, freedom of association, freedom of movement, and equality before law. In addition, civil society organizations are becoming increasingly aware of fundamental rights and are spreading their awareness to the larger population. It will nevertheless take some time before the general citizens of Pakistan will have faith and place credibility in the process of enforcement of fundamental rights.

Limitations on Fundamental Rights

Fundamental rights are subject to limitations and reasonable restrictions under the law. Such limitations can be imposed in the interest of public order or morality. For example, freedom of speech is subject to restrictions relating to public order and morality, contempt of court, the glory of Islam, or defamation. Similarly, the freedoms of profession, occupation, trade, or business are subject to professional regulations, laws against monopolies, and the licensing of trades or professions. The right to equality and equal protection of the laws has been held to be subject to reasonable classification.

The purpose of such limitations is to ensure that rights are not abused. However, a fundamental right cannot be curtailed or denied on the pretext of regulation, because a fundamental right is not subordinate to an ordinary law. It should be regulated in such a manner that the legitimate enjoyment of the right is not in any way curtailed.

ECONOMY

The constitution does not specify any particular economic system. However, Article 3 provides for the elimination of all forms of exploitation and promotes equitable distribution of economic resources in keeping with individual ability and work performed. The directive principles of policy include securing the economic well-being of the people; preventing the concentration of wealth and the means of production in the hands of a few; providing the basic necessities of life; providing food, clothing, housing, education, and medical relief for citizens incapable of earning their livelihood because of unemployment, sickness, or similar reasons. The right of property has been made subject to a number of constitutional restrictions. Thus, no law that provides for the acquisition of property for providing housing, education, and the maintenance of sick, old, and infirm people is regarded as unconstitutional.

Despite the initial socialist bias of the constitution, the economy has been managed so that the constitutional objectives stated have not been achieved. There is an acute concentration of wealth and resources in the hands of a few individuals. The economy of Pakistan can be described as a market economy.

RELIGIOUS COMMUNITIES

Article 2 of the constitution declares Islam as the state religion of Pakistan. Muslims form 97 percent of the total population. Among the religious minorities, Christians make up the largest percentage. They include both Catholics and Protestants. There are freedom of religion and freedom to maintain religious institutions in Pakistan. The relationship between Muslims and other religious communities has generally been peaceful.

MILITARY DEFENSE AND STATE OF EMERGENCY

It is the duty of the state to maintain armed forces to protect Pakistan against external aggression and internal disorder. The military can also be called in aid of civil authorities in cases of civil commotion or disturbances threatening public peace.

Pakistan maintains a large military machine because of threats from India and instability in Afghanistan, its two chief neighbors. More than one-third of the total budget is allocated for military spending. The military budget cannot be discussed in Parliament. All this makes the presence of the military overwhelming in the affairs of Pakistan.

There are a number of provisions in the constitution relating to proclaiming a state of emergency. The president can declare an emergency if the country is threatened by war or external aggression or by internal disturbances beyond the power of provincial governments to control. Emergency can also be proclaimed in case of a breakdown of the constitutional machinery in a province. The president is also empowered to proclaim a financial emergency when there is a serious threat to the financial stability or credit of Pakistan. During the period of emergency, the operation of certain fundamental rights, such as the freedoms of movement, assembly, trade and business, speech and the press, and property rights, are suspended.

The history of Pakistan is replete with proclamations of emergency. Time and again, it appears, emergencies were declared not primarily for the stated reasons, but with the aim of depriving the people of their political rights and civil liberties.

AMENDMENTS TO THE CONSTITUTION

The constitution, or any of its provisions, can be amended by an act of Parliament; it needs the votes of not less than two-thirds of the total number of members of the National Assembly and the Senate, voting separately as two houses. No amendment of a constitutional provision affecting the borders of a province can be made unless such an amendment has been approved by a resolution of the provincial assembly of that province by not less than two-thirds of the total members of that assembly.

PRIMARY SOURCES

Constitution in English. Available online. URL: http://www.pakistani.org/pakistan/constitution/. Accessed on September 20, 2005.

SECONDARY SOURCES

Amita Shastri and A. Jeyaratnam Wilson, *The Post-colonial States of South Asia: Political and Constitutional Problems.* London: Taylor & Francis, 2001.

Hamid Khan

PALAU

At-a-Glance

OFFICIAL NAME
The Republic of Palau

CAPITAL
Koror

POPULATION
20,016 (July 2004 est.)

SIZE
177 sq. mi. (458 sq. km) Nine principal islands and more than 300 smaller islands lying about 850 km southeast of the Philippines

LANGUAGES
English, Palauan, Sonsoralese, Tobi, Angaur, and Japanese

RELIGIONS
Christian (Roman Catholic, Seventh-Day Adventist, Jehovah's Witnesses, Assembly of God, Latter-day Saints) 65%, Modekngei 25%, other 10%

NATIONAL OR ETHNIC COMPOSITION
Palauan 70%, Asian (Filipinos, Chinese, Taiwanese, Vietnamese) 28%, White 2%

DATE OF INDEPENDENCE OR CREATION
October 1, 1994

TYPE OF GOVERNMENT
Constitutional republic in free association with the United States

TYPE OF STATE
Federal state

TYPE OF LEGISLATURE
Bicameral congress (Olbiil Era Kelulau)

DATE OF CONSTITUTION
January 1, 1981

DATE OF LAST AMENDMENT
Four amendments to the constitution approved November 2, 2004

Palau is a constitutional republic based on the rule of law. The constitution creates a clear division of powers among the executive, legislative, and judicial branches. The constitution also adopts a modified federal system of government. Under the constitution, government responsibilities are shared by the national government and 16 state governments. All powers that are not expressly delegated to the states or denied to the national government are powers of the national government. The national government also may delegate powers to the state governments by legislation.

CONSTITUTIONAL HISTORY

The islands of Palau first were settled by immigrants from Southeast Asia about 2500 B.C.E. Regular contact with Europeans began in the 18th century. In 1886, Pope Leo XIII awarded Spain sovereignty over the islands. After its defeat in the Spanish-American War in 1899, Spain sold

Palau to Germany, which administered the islands until 1914, when Japan took control. After the end of World War II (1939–45), the United Nations authorized the United States to administer Palau, along with the other Micronesian islands, as part of the Trust Territory of the Pacific Islands. Palau achieved limited self-government in 1981 with the adoption of the Constitution of the Republic of Palau. In 1985, Palau and the United States signed a Compact of Free Association. However, because of internal debate over provisions of the compact, it was not approved by a constitutionally required referendum until 1993. In 1994, Palau became an independent republic in free association with the United States.

FORM AND IMPACT OF THE CONSTITUTION

Palau has a written constitution that entered into force on January 1, 1981. Article 2 of the constitution makes the document "the supreme law of the land." No law, act of the government, or agreement to which the government is a party may conflict with the constitution.

BASIC ORGANIZATIONAL STRUCTURE

Palau is a federal republic consisting of a national government and 16 states. In addition, each state has its own constitution, governor, and legislature.

LEADING CONSTITUTIONAL PRINCIPLES

The constitution provides that Palau is a republic with a democratically elected government. Under the constitution, government responsibilities are shared by the national government and the states. The rule of law is essential to the Palaun constitution, and there is an extensive list of human rights.

CONSTITUTIONAL BODIES

The main constitutional organs are the president, the National Congress, the judiciary, and the Council of Chiefs.

The President

Palau has a presidential form of government. Under Article 8 of the constitution, the executive branch is headed by the president and the vice president, who are elected for four-year terms. The president and vice president must be at least 35 years old and have been a resident of Palau for the five years preceding the election. A 2004 amendment to the constitution requires that candidates for the offices of president and vice president be elected jointly. The president may not serve for more than two consecutive terms. The president and vice president may be impeached for treason, bribery, or other serious crimes by a vote of at least two-thirds of the members of each house of the Olbiil Era Kelulau. The president and vice president may be removed from office by a recall referendum.

National Congress

Article 9 of the constitution places the legislative power of the national government in the bicameral Olbiil Era Kelulau, which consists of the House of Delegates and the Senate. Among the powers given to the National Congress under the constitution are those to enact laws, impose taxes, regulate commerce, and ratify treaties. Although both houses are equal under the constitution, the Senate has the power to advise and consent to presidential appointments.

The House of Delegates consists of one delegate from each of Palau's 16 states. The number of senators is determined by the Congressional Reapportionment Commission. Currently, there are nine senators. Members of both houses are elected by the people for a four-year term. However, a 2004 amendment to the constitution provides that no person may serve more than three terms as a member of the Olbiil Era Kelulau.

The Lawmaking Process

To adopt a law, both chambers of the Olbiil Era Kelulau must consent.

The Judiciary

Article 10 of the constitution places the judicial power of Palau in a judiciary consisting of a Supreme Court, a National Court, and inferior courts of limited jurisdiction that are established by law. At present, these consist of the Court of Common Pleas and the Land Court. All judges hold office on condition of their good behavior. The Supreme Court consists of a Trial Division and an Appellate Division. It is composed of a chief justice and three to six associate justices. A justice of the Supreme Court may be impeached for cause (i.e., treason, bribery, high crimes, or inability to carry out the functions of the office) by a two-thirds vote of the members of each house of the Olbiil Era Kelulau. Judges of the National Court and the inferior courts may be impeached for cause by a majority vote of the members of each house of the Olbiil Era Kelulau.

The judicial power extends to all matters and to all persons physically within Palau. There are no state courts.

Council of Chiefs

Traditional Palaun culture has undergone change as a result of years of control by Spain, Germany, Japan, and the United States. Although the clan and the system of chiefs still are important, these traditional sources of authority have been superseded by that of elected officials. Article 5 of the constitution attempts to preserve traditional culture by prohibiting the government from interfering with those customary functions of traditional leaders that are not inconsistent with the constitution. It also establishes a Council of Chiefs consisting of the highest traditional chiefs from each of Palau's 16 states. The council advises the president on matters of traditional law and custom. A number of the state constitutions also provide for a council of traditional chiefs to promote traditional ways of life.

The States

Article 11 of the constitution provides that the "structure and organization of the state governments must follow democratic principles, traditions of Palau, and shall not be inconsistent with the constitution." Although the population of Palau's states varies from a few hundred to more than 11,000, each of the 16 states elects a governor and state legislature.

THE ELECTION PROCESS AND POLITICAL PARTICIPATION

Article 7 of the constitution provides that all Palauans over the age of 18 have the right to vote in national and state elections. The Olbiil Era Kelulau establishes the residency requirements for national elections while the state sets the requirements for state elections.

POLITICAL PARTIES

Although there have been political parties in the past in Palau, none currently is active in the republic.

CITIZENSHIP

Palaun citizenship is governed by Article 3 of the constitution and the Citizenship Act. Anyone who was a citizen of the Trust Territory immediately prior to January 1, 1981, and had at least one parent of "recognized Palaun ancestry" is a citizen of Palau. A person born of parents one or both of whom are citizens of Palau is also a Palaun citizen. A 2004 amendment to the constitution permits Palauan citizens to become citizens of the United States and other nations without renouncing their Palauan citizenship. A citizen of another country may become a naturalized Palaun citizen only if one or both of the person's parents are of "recognized Palaun ancestry" and the person renounces citizenship in the other country.

FUNDAMENTAL RIGHTS

Article 4 of the constitution contains an extensive statement of fundamental rights. These are freedom of conscience and philosophical and religious belief; freedom of expression and the press; freedom of peaceful assembly, association, and the petition of the government for redress of grievances; and the right to be secure in person, house, papers, and effects against entry, search, and seizure. The constitution also guarantees equality under the law, equal protection, and freedom from discrimination based on sex, race, place of origin, language, religion or belief, social status or clan affiliation; freedom from the deprivation of life, liberty, or property without due process of law; protection against the taking of private property except for a "recognized public use" and for just compensation; and freedom from criminal liability for an act that was not a legally recognized crime at the time of its commission.

There are freedom from double jeopardy for the same offense; a prohibition on the impairment of contracts by legislation; no imprisonment for debt; a requirement that a warrant for search and seizure be issued only by a judge on a showing of probable cause; a presumption of innocence in criminal cases until proof of guilt is established beyond a reasonable doubt; and the right of an accused to be informed of the nature of the accusation, to have a speedy trial, to examine all witnesses, and to be protected against self-incrimination. Further fundamental rights concerning the judiciary are the right to counsel and to reasonable bail, a recognition of the writ of habeas corpus that cannot be suspended, the liability of the national government for damages for unlawful arrest or damage to private property, and the right of a victim of a criminal offense to compensation by the government, or at the discretion of a court.

The constitution prohibits torture; cruel, inhumane, or degrading treatment or punishment; excessive fines; and slavery and involuntary servitude. Citizens have the right to examine any government document and to observe the official deliberations of any government agency. Men and women are guaranteed equality in marital and related parental rights, privileges, and responsibilities.

Impact and Functions of Fundamental Rights

The fundamental rights guaranteed in the constitution generally are respected and remedies lie with the courts for violations. The U.S. Department of State Report on Human Rights Practices—2003 found that the government respected the human rights of its citizens. In particular, it found no reports of arbitrary or unlawful deprivation of life committed by the government or its agents, no political prisons and no reports of politically motivated disappearances, no torture or other cruel treatment of prisoners, no arbitrary arrest or detention and no forced exile, and respect for freedom of the press, assembly, association, and the Internet. A number of domestic and international human rights groups operate without government restraint and government officials are cooperative and responsive.

Limitations to Fundamental Rights

The provisions for fundamental rights in Article 4 of the constitution contain no words about limitations. Many of the sections begin, "The government shall take no action to…." The only limitations on fundamental rights could arise through Section 14 of Article 8, which concerns the state of emergency.

ECONOMY

Although the Palaun constitution does not create a specific economic system for the republic, Article 4 guarantees that a person cannot be deprived of property without due process of law. It also prohibits the taking of private property except for a "recognized public use" and for just compensation.

The Palaun government employs about half of the republic's employed workers. The other principal economic activities are agriculture, fishing, and tourism. There are a large number of foreign workers in the country, principally Filipino.

Under the Compact of Free Association, Palau will receive more than U.S. $450 million over 15 years and be eligible to participate in more than 40 programs of the federal government in the United States.

RELIGIOUS COMMUNITIES

The Palaun constitution provides for freedom of religion, and the government respects the rights of people to practice their religion. About 40 percent of the population are Roman Catholic, 25 percent are Protestant (mainly Seventh-Day Adventists, Jehovah's Witnesses, the Assembly of God, the Liebenzell Mission, and Latter-day Saints), 25 percent belong to the Modekngei religion (indigenous to Palau), and the remaining 10 percent belong to other religions.

MILITARY DEFENSE AND STATE OF EMERGENCY

Palau has no military forces. Under the Compact of Free Association between Palau and the United States, defense is the responsibility of the United States and the United States military is granted access to the islands for 50 years.

Palau has a national police force under the supervision of the minister of justice. It also has a Marine Law Enforcement Division, which patrols the country's borders with the assistance of the Australian government.

Article 8 of the constitution provides that in the event that war, external aggression, civil rebellion, or natural catastrophe threatens the life or property of the people of Palau, the president may declare a state of emergency and temporarily assume legislative powers. However, the president first must be given approval by the Olbiil Era Kelulau for the state of emergency and may not assume emergency powers for more than 10 days without the further approval of the Olbiil Era Kelulau.

AMENDMENTS TO THE CONSTITUTION

Under Article 14 of the constitution, an amendment to the constitution may be proposed by a constitutional convention, by a popular initiative signed by 25 percent of the voters, or by a resolution adopted by at least three-fourths of the members of the Olbiil Era Kelulau. An amendment proposed by one of these methods is adopted if it obtains a majority of the votes cast in a general election.

PRIMARY SOURCES
Constitution in English. Available online. URL: http://www.paclii.org/pw/legis/consol_act/cotrop359/. Accessed on June 27, 2006.

SECONDARY SOURCES
Bob Aldridge and Ched Myers, *Resisting the Serpent: Palau's Struggle for Self-Determination*. Baltimore: Fortkamp, 1990.
William J. Butler, *Palau, a Challenge to the Rule of Law in Micronesia*. New York: American Association for the International Commission of Jurists, 1988.
"Constitution of the Republic of Palau." In *Constitutions of the Countries of the World*, edited by Gisbert H. Flanz. Dobbs Ferry, N.Y.: Oceana, 1996.
Arnold H. Leibowitz, *Embattled Island: Palau's Struggle for Independence*. Westport, Conn.: Praeger, 1996.
Sue R. Roff, *Overreaching in Paradise: United States Policy in Palau since 1945*. Juneau, Alaska: Denali Press, 1991.

Bruce Ottley

PALESTINE

At-a-Glance

OFFICIAL NAME
Palestine

CAPITAL
East Jerusalem

POPULATION
3,512,062 (2005 est.)

SIZE
2,338 sq. mi. (6,055 sq. km)

LANGUAGES
Arabic

RELIGIONS
Muslim 97.8%, Christian 2.1%, other 0.01%

NATIONAL OR ETHNIC COMPOSITION
Arab

DATE OF INDEPENDENCE OR CREATION
Still under occupation; Palestinian Authority established May 4, 1994

TYPE OF GOVERNMENT
Constitutional democracy

TYPE OF STATE
Central authority

TYPE OF LEGISLATURE
Unicameral parliament

DATE OF CONSTITUTION
May 29, 2002

DATE OF LAST AMENDMENT
March 19, 2003

The Palestinian Authority was created in the West Bank and Gaza Strip on May 4, 1994, as a result of the Oslo Accords for Peace between Israel and the Palestine Liberation Organization (PLO). On January 27, 1996, the legislative body of the Palestinian Authority, known as the Palestinian Legislative Counsel, was elected in the first general political elections, both presidential and legislative, in the West Bank and Gaza. The outcome of the elections was that Arafat was elected president of the Palestinian Authority and 88 members of parliament were elected. The Palestinian Authority has an institutional design permitting the existence of a mixed system of governance headed by the president and an appointed prime minister. The Palestinian political system is based on the principle of separation of powers as stated in the Declaration of Independence (1988), which calls for a parliamentary system of government and the independence of the judiciary.

The Palestinian Legislative Counsel adopted its first draft constitution (the Basic Law) in 1997; it was ratified, in its third draft form, by the president only on May 29, 2002. The Basic Law, as the interim constitution, was subject to several amendments in the process of its transformation into a state constitution.

The Palestinian constitution is still in its draft form, with the expectation that it is to be finalized prior to the long-awaited independence. The Palestinian state will eventually adopt a constitution not different from the current draft, possibly with small modifications reflecting domestic and international demands.

CONSTITUTIONAL HISTORY

Palestine, as have most other states, will adopt the constitution that reflects its particular history and its connectedness to the rest of the world.

Although formulating a constitution is a rare occurrence in the history of a state, Palestine has had a long experience with constitutions and constitutional reform because of its peculiar historical experience. The constitutional legacy starts with the colonial constitution of 1922 enacted by the British mandate authorities. This constitution was still in use in 1948 when the first of a series of Arab-Israeli wars took place. The war ended with the establishment of the state of Israel and Jordanian and Egyptian control over the West Bank, including East Jerusalem, and the Gaza Strip, respectively. After that war, the 1952 Jordanian constitution was introduced; it aimed at integrating the West Bank and East Jerusalem into the Hashemite Kingdom of Jordan. Meanwhile, Gaza was under Egyptian military control and in 1955 witnessed the adoption of the Basic Law to act as a precursor to the full constitution of the Palestinian state. Palestinians remained without their own state and constitution with the advent of Israeli occupation in 1967, which put the Palestinian territory under military occupation, a situation that still prevails.

FORM AND IMPACT OF THE CONSTITUTION

Palestine has a written draft constitution, codified in a single document, the Constitution of the State of Palestine. Currently, the constitution is in its revised third draft, ratified by the president. The constitution states that it will take precedence over all other laws in Palestine. In addition, the constitution states that Palestine abides by the charters of the United Nations and Arab League. The absence of effective sovereignty and the presence of Israeli settlements and military occupation forces in Palestine preclude the possibility of enforcing the rule of law under the Palestinian constitution on all residents of the Palestinian territory. As a guiding principle, the constitution will take precedence over all law within the Palestinian state.

BASIC ORGANIZATIONAL STRUCTURE

Palestine is a centralist state, with two disconnected territories: the West Bank, including East Jerusalem, and the Gaza Strip. Palestine comprises 16 districts, five in the Gaza Strip and 11 in the West Bank, East Jerusalem one of them.

LEADING CONSTITUTIONAL PRINCIPLES

Palestine's system of government is a constitutional parliamentary representative democracy, with mixed attributes of both the parliamentary and the presidential systems. There is no effective separation or division of powers, and the lines are more than blurred. The constitution stipulates that Palestine shall be a republic and a democracy with a clear separation of powers and have an independent judiciary, but the reality does not conform to this ideal. Many Palestinians believe that the rule of law is absent, and the Palestinian citizen has most of his or her rights denied by the Israeli military occupation. Islam is a main source of legislation, although the rights of other monotheistic religions are preserved by the constitution.

CONSTITUTIONAL BODIES

The main bodies provided for in the constitution are the president, the parliament, the administration, and the judiciary.

The President

The president of the state is the head of the republic, the defender of the constitution and the unity of the people. The president is responsible for the continuity of the state and its national independence and for maintenance of law and order in public life.

The Parliament

The parliament, which is called the House of Representatives, is the legislative branch. Its seat is Jerusalem. According to the constitution, the house shall be composed of 150 members.

The Lawmaking Process

The government or any member of the House of Representatives may propose a law, and laws approved are published in *The Palestinian Gazette*. They enter into force 30 days after their publication.

The Administration

The constitution also enumerates the administration as well as the cabinet ministers as the executive branch of the state. The cabinet is headed by the prime minister. The House of Representatives must approve the appointment of the cabinet ministers and the program of the administration.

The Judiciary

The Constitutional Court and the Supreme Council represent the judicial branch of the state. These two independent bodies monitor and hold accountable the executive. The Supreme Council by tradition is responsible for all the institutions of the judiciary. The office of the attorney general takes cases of public interest to court in the name of the people in accordance with the law.

THE ELECTION PROCESS AND POLITICAL PARTICIPATION

According to the Election Law of 1996, all Palestinian citizens age 18 or older who are formally registered in the electoral list have the right to vote. Palestinian citizens age 35 or older who are resident in Palestine are eligible to stand for presidential office. In all the electoral regulations, the right to vote and stand for office is universal for all Palestinians regardless of religion, ethnicity, or gender.

POLITICAL PARTIES

Palestine enjoys a pluralistic electoral system in which several recognized registered parties compete.

CITIZENSHIP

The legal definition of Palestinian citizenship states that a Palestinian citizen is one who is born within the border of Mandatory Palestine or had legal citizenship status during the same period or one whose ancestors or spouses have been Palestinian citizens. Palestinian citizenship is inalienable and is transmitted from ancestors to offspring.

FUNDAMENTAL RIGHTS

The state of Palestine abides by the Charter of the United Nations and the Universal Declaration of Human Rights. Citizens are equal before the law, and the state is committed to safeguarding their civil, political, social, and economic rights. The track record of Palestine leaves much to be desired in the protection of fundamental rights and liberties, and the Israeli occupation exacerbates conditions.

The constitution stipulates that all citizens enjoy fundamental rights and freedoms including the right to life safeguarded and protected by law without discrimination. All traditional human rights and fundamental freedoms, whether religious, civil, political, economic, social, or cultural, are guaranteed by the state.

Impact and Functions of Fundamental Rights

This adherence to human rights and fundamental freedoms in the constitution will be enforced once a Palestinian state is established. Currently, an intensive debate is taking place in the Palestinian civil society with the aim to ensure that no provision of the constitution will jeopardize the status of fundamental freedom, especially women's rights.

Limitations to Fundamental Rights

It is not permitted to impose any limitation on fundamental rights and freedoms except to the extent necessary to preserve public order and only in a case of emergency, threat of war, or natural disaster.

ECONOMY

The economic system in Palestine is based on the principles of a free market economy, and the state is charged with the task of providing the regulatory framework and the protection of private property. Public companies can be established without prejudice to the aforementioned principles.

RELIGIOUS COMMUNITIES

Palestine is a pluralistic society composed of Muslims, Christians, and Jews, and the constitution guarantees equality in rights and duties to all religious communities. However, the principle of equidistance between the state and the different religious communities is compromised by the fact that the constitution states that "the principles of Islamic sharia" are a major source of legislation. Nonetheless, the constitution reaffirms that Christianity and all other monotheistic religions are accorded sanctity and respect.

MILITARY DEFENSE AND STATE OF EMERGENCY

The state is responsible for the security of person and property. Defending the nation is the duty of the state as well. A state of emergency can be declared for a period of 30 days after consultations of the president, prime minister, and speaker of the House of Representatives Council. This state of emergency can be renewed only once.

AMENDMENTS TO THE CONSTITUTION

The Palestinian constitution is currently in its third draft, ratified by the president on May 4, 2003. The president of the state, the prime minister, or one-third of the members of the House of Representatives Council may request an amendment to the constitution.

PRIMARY SOURCES
Basic Law in English. Available online. URL: http://www. jmcc.org/documents/palestineconstitution-eng.pdf. Accessed on September 3, 2005.
Basic law in Arabic. Available online. URL: http:// lawcenter.birzeit.edu/. Accessed on August 17, 2005.

SECONDARY SOURCES
Nathan J. Brown, *The Third Draft Constitution for a Palestinian State: Translation and Commentary.* Ramallah: Palestinian Center for Policy and Survey Research, 2003.
Central Elections Commission, *Democracy in Palestine: The Palestinian Public Elections to the President of the Palestinians Authority and Members of Legislative 1996.* 2d ed. Ramallah: Palestinian Central Elections Commission, 2002.

Samir A. Awad

PANAMA

At-a-Glance

OFFICIAL NAME
Republic of Panama

CAPITAL
Panama City

POPULATION
3,000,463 (July 2004 est.)

SIZE
30,193 sq. mi. (78,200 sq. km)

LANGUAGES
Spanish (official)

RELIGIONS
Roman Catholic 85%, Protestant 15%

NATIONAL OR ETHNIC COMPOSITION
Mestizo (mixed Amerindian and white) 70%, Amerindian and mixed (West Indian) 14%, white 10%, Amerindian 6%

DATE OF INDEPENDENCE OR CREATION
November 3, 1903

TYPE OF GOVERNMENT
Presidential democracy

TYPE OF STATE
Unitary state

TYPE OF LEGISLATURE
Unicameral assembly

DATE OF CONSTITUTION
October 11, 1972

DATE OF LAST AMENDMENT
November 15, 2004

Panama is a unitary, republican, and democratic state built on the principle of separation of powers. The country is organized territorially into provinces and *comarcas* (indigenous reservations), most subdivided into districts and *corregimientos* (administrative divisions within districts). Fundamental rights are guaranteed. Judicial remedies exist for protecting those rights, including a special remedy for ensuring international human rights. The preamble calls for Central American regional integration and respect for human dignity. Private initiative in a free market is the cornerstone of the economy, but the state may regulate the economy for purposes of social justice. Panama banned armed forces in 1994. The Panama Canal is declared an inalienable national patrimony. The constitution is difficult to change but offers a so-called parallel constitutional assembly as an amendment method.

In practice, institutional trust has been at times undermined by apparently self-serving decisions of the authorities. Political parties are seen as dominated by elites.

The inefficient state administration does not favor efficient market conditions or wealth distribution. Despite several reforms, the constitution of 1972 is still associated with dictatorship. Initiatives are still under way to promote a constitutional convention to adopt a new constitution that would promote the consolidation of a modern and citizen-oriented democracy.

CONSTITUTIONAL HISTORY

With the arrival of Rodrigo de Bastidas in 1501, the Spanish conquest and settlement of the Panamanian territory began, crushing the indigenous population. Since then, Panama has been seen mostly as a convenient path between the Atlantic and Pacific Oceans, perceived as a strategic area by global powers.

Panama separated from Spain on November 28, 1821. It joined the Gran Colombia, a union that comprised Ecuador, Venezuela, and Colombia and lasted until 1830.

On several occasions during the 19th century, Panama tried to separate from Colombia; it gained federal state status within Colombia in 1855. After the Colombian senate rejected a treaty with the United States for building the Panama Canal, Panamanian leaders, with the support of the Americans, declared Panama's independence in 1903.

The Panamanian state began under U.S. tutelage. The constitution of 1904, the first Panamanian constitution in the 20th century, gave the United States the right of intervention. The 1941 constitution removed that right; its sponsor, the authoritarian leader Arnulfo Arias, was later deposed. In 1946, a constitutional convention adopted a constitution that was considered democratic and forward-looking for its time. The democratic era ended in 1968 when the general Omar Torrijos seized power; he later issued the dictatorial 1972 constitution to legitimize his coup.

After the 1977 Panama Canal treaties modernized the colonial relationship between Panama and the United States, an integral constitutional reform took place in 1983. It was welcomed by many, because it eliminated the dictatorial aspects of the 1972 constitution. Nevertheless, the military continued to be influential. In 1987, a clash between the United States and Manuel Noriega's regime ended with the United States invading Panama in 1989. Guillermo Endara, who had won the elections annulled by Manuel Noriega earlier that year, took over the nation's struggling democratization process. Voices for a new constitution began to grow louder.

Despite its several reforms, the 1972 constitution is still associated with the past dictatorship. Panamanian political culture is moving toward more democracy and transparency, and a new constitution able to induce citizens' loyalty seems to many to be the necessary next step.

FORM AND IMPACT OF THE CONSTITUTION

Panama has a written codified constitution of more than 300 articles. Its length is the by-product of the mistrust of the legislature—citizens perceive that representatives sometimes act solely according to their narrow interests. The constitution prevails over all other laws, with the Supreme Court responsible for constitutional review. Yet inconsistent constitutional jurisprudence has weakened it. Finally, universal norms of international law form part of the domestic order.

BASIC ORGANIZATIONAL STRUCTURE

Panama is divided into nine provinces. Governors appointed by the president direct each. Provinces differ in geographical area, population size, and economic strength. Within provinces are municipalities, governed by locally elected mayors.

LEADING CONSTITUTIONAL PRINCIPLES

Panama is a unitary, republican, democratic, and representative state. According to the principle of separation of powers, there is a division of the executive, legislative, and judicial powers. The constitution guarantees fundamental rights.

CONSTITUTIONAL BODIES

The main constitutional bodies are the president, the National Assembly, and the Supreme Court.

The President

The president is the head of state, elected in direct free elections for five years. The president cannot be reelected for two consecutive terms. The president coordinates all public administration, conducts foreign relations, ensures public order, and has regulatory powers. The National Assembly has the authority to impeach the president.

The president appoints and dismisses his or her state secretaries, called ministers. The president chairs the Cabinet Counsel, a consultative body composed of the vice president and the secretaries of state. Among other powers, the cabinet appoints the justices of the Supreme Court and decrees a state of emergency. The National Assembly can censure the state secretaries.

The National Assembly

The National Assembly is the representative body of the people. Its 71 members are elected for five years in direct elections and can be reelected. They enjoy immunity and procedural privileges, but the Supreme Court can investigate them for common crimes. The political parties and the electors can revoke their mandates.

The Lawmaking Process

Organic laws can be proposed by permanent committees of the National Assembly and by state secretaries, with authorization of the Cabinet Council. The Supreme Court, the attorney general, and the electoral court may also propose organic laws, in certain matters related to their roles. Ordinary laws can be proposed by any member of the legislature, a state secretary, or a provincial council president.

All laws must be discussed and approved in three debates. Organic laws must be approved by the absolute majority of the members of the assembly, ordinary laws, by the majority of the representatives in attendance. The president may approve a bill or may veto it on policy or constitutional grounds. In that case, he or she sends the bill back to the assembly, which can approve it by two-thirds of all its members. If the president vetoes a bill as unconstitutional and the National Assembly insists on its approval, the president sends the bill to the Supreme Court, which makes the final decision.

The Judiciary

The Supreme Court is the highest judicial body. The Cabinet Council, with the ratification of the National Assembly, appoints the justices to a 10-year term. The Supreme Court is organized into four chambers according to the following jurisdictions: civil, criminal, administrative and labor, and general subject matter. Apart from dealing with issues in their respective chambers, all members of the Supreme Court decide constitutional review cases jointly.

THE ELECTION PROCESS

Panamanians over the age of 18 have both the right to stand for and the right to vote in elections. The vote is free, equal, universal, secret, and direct. An independent electoral court of three justices oversees the freedom and honesty of the elections. Each of the traditional state powers—executive, legislative, and judicial—appoints one electoral justice for 10 years.

POLITICAL PARTIES

Political parties are essential for forming the popular will and expressing political pluralism. Parties enjoy public financing and almost monopolize nominations for the National Assembly and the presidency. No political party based on gender, race, religion, or undemocratic doctrines can be organized.

CITIZENSHIP

Panamanian citizenship is acquired by birth to Panamanian parents or by birth on Panamanian territory, regardless of the nationality of the parents. A foreign child who is adopted before he or she is seven years old becomes Panamanian. Citizenship can also be acquired through naturalization by complying with residency requirements. Citizens by birth from Spain or other Latin American countries enjoy reciprocity for naturalization.

FUNDAMENTAL RIGHTS

The constitution guarantees fundamental rights. It ensures a traditional set of liberal human rights and civil liberties such as freedom of speech, freedom of religion, equality before the law, freedom of movement, and due process. In addition, it recognizes social rights concerning family, labor, culture, social assistance, public health, and environment. Other fundamental rights inferable from the constitution can be recognized and thus protected. Fundamental rights are binding on all authorities. Social rights, however, are not in general judiciable; instead, they are meant to guide state policymaking.

Impact and Functions of Fundamental Rights

Along with the judicial protection of fundamental rights, protection of fundamental rights in general is paramount. There is a specialized process for protecting fundamental rights. In addition, an ombudsperson oversees the protection of these rights. Nonetheless, Supreme Court decisions have shown inconsistencies that have promoted mistrust.

Limitations to Fundamental Rights

Fundamental rights may have constitutional limitations, and laws may regulate their exercise. The authorities are constitutionally required to protect the fundamental rights of the inhabitants within the Panamanian jurisdiction.

ECONOMY

Panama has a market economy balanced with principles of social justice. Economic initiative is protected for private persons, but the state can intervene to achieve social justice, for example, by establishing minimal wages. The constitution guarantees the classical liberal rights needed for a free market. The wide array of social rights speaks for a social state.

RELIGIOUS COMMUNITIES

The constitution guarantees religious freedom within no other limitation than respect of Christian morals and public order. It also protects the autonomy of religious associations. No official church exists, but the constitution acknowledges that most Panamanians are Catholic. The state must treat members of all religions equally; however, the Catholic Church's influence on public opinion is noticeable.

MILITARY DEFENSE AND STATE OF EMERGENCY

The constitution bans all armed forces. A police force is charged with providing public security services. There is no military service in Panama, but the constitution proclaims the duty of all Panamanians to defend the integrity of the national territory.

AMENDMENTS TO THE CONSTITUTION

The National Assembly, the Cabinet Council, and the Supreme Court have the power to propose constitutional amendments. The process takes place over a period of two successive terms of the National Assembly with an election in between. An absolute majority is needed in both assemblies, and the versions must be identical. In addition, one National Assembly can amend the constitution, after approving the change in two different legislative sessions by absolute majority and referring it to a national referendum for the citizens' approval. Finally, a "parallel constitutional convention" can be convened, either by the executive with the support of the National Assembly or by a citizens' initiative supported by 20 percent of voters. This convention cannot alter the terms of elective offices or take retroactive measures.

PRIMARY SOURCES

1972 Constitution in Spanish (as amended 2004). Available online. URLs: http://www.oas.org/juridico/mla/sp/pan/sp_pan-int-text-const.pdf; http://www.organojudicial.gob.pa/contenido/organizacion/normas/constitucion_2004.htm. Accessed on September 23, 2005.

Instituto de Investigaciones Jurídicas de la Universidad Autónoma de México (UNAM), "Navegador Jurídico Internacional, Gobierno de Panamá." Available online. URL: http://info.juridicas.unam.mx/navjus/gob/pm.htm (1995–2003). Accessed on July 17, 2005.

SECONDARY SOURCES

Bureau of Democracy, Human Rights, and Labor, U.S. Department of State, *Country Reports on Human Rights Practices—2003, Panama.* Released February 25, 2004. Available online. URL: http://www.state.gov/g/drl/rls/hrrpt/2003/27907.htm. Accessed on August 22, 2005.

Jorge Fábrega, ed., *Estudios de Derecho Constitucional Panameño.* Panamá: Editora Jurídica Panameña, 1987.

Salvador Sánchez González, *Panamá, en Justicia Constitucional en Iberoamérica.* Madrid: Instituto de Derecho Público Comparado, Universidad Carlos III de Madrid. Available online. URL: http://www.uc3m.es/uc3m/inst/MGP/JCI/02-panama.htm. Accessed on September 23, 2005.

"Latin American Network Information Center (LANIC), Panama." Available online. URL: http://lanic.utexas.edu/la/ca/panama/. Accessed on August 28, 2005.

Miguel González Marcos, "Specialized Constitutional Review in Latin America: Choosing between a Constitutional Chamber and a Constitutional Court." *Verfassung und Recht in Übersee* 36 (2003): 164–205.

Carlos Bolívar Pedreschi, *De la Protección del Canal a la Militarización del País.* San José, Costa Rica: Litografía e Imprenta Lil, 1987.

César Quintero, *Evolución Constitucional de Panamá.* 2d ed. Bogotá: Universidad Esternado de Colombia, 1988.

*Miguel González Marcos and
Salvador Sánchez González*

PAPUA NEW GUINEA

At-a-Glance

OFFICIAL NAME
Independent State of Papua New Guinea

CAPITAL
Port Moresby

POPULATION
5,190,786 (2005 est.)

SIZE
178,704 sq. mi. (462,840 sq. km)

LANGUAGES
English, Pidgin, Motu, over 820 other languages

RELIGIONS
Roman Catholic 22%, Lutheran 16%, Presbyterian/
Methodist/London Missionary Society 8%, Anglican
5%, Evangelical Alliance 4%, Seventh-Day Adventist
1%, other Protestant 10%, indigenous beliefs 34%

NATIONAL OR ETHNIC COMPOSITION
Papua New Guinea is made of diverse cultures with
Papuan 84%, Melanesian 15%, and other 1%

DATE OF INDEPENDENCE OR CREATION
September 16, 1975

TYPE OF GOVERNMENT
Parliamentary democracy

TYPE OF STATE
Quasi-federal state

TYPE OF LEGISLATURE
Unicameral parliament

DATE OF CONSTITUTION
September 16, 1975

DATE OF LAST AMENDMENT
January 20, 2004

Papua New Guinea was formerly a colony of Great Britain and Germany, and later of Australia. It became an independent state in 1975. At independence, it became a parliamentary democracy based on the Westminster model of government. This system of government was adopted from the country's former colonial ruler, Australia. There are three arms of government—the legislature, the executive, and the judiciary, which are separate and independent of each other and, in principle, function in a coordinated manner. The country has a quasi-federal system of government.

Papua New Guinea is a constitutional monarchy. Its head of state is Queen Elizabeth II and her heirs. The queen is represented in the country by the governor-general, who is elected by the parliament and holds office for a six-year period. The executive arm of the government is made up of the head of state and the National Executive Council, which is headed and appointed by the prime minister.

The constitution of Papua New Guinea is the supreme law of the land. All legislative, judicial, and administrative acts are subject to the constitution. Any legislation or judicial decision or administrative action that is contrary to the constitution is deemed null and void. Papua New Guinea has entrenched in its constitution fundamental human rights and freedoms. The constitution provides very stringent procedures for amending fundamental rights and freedoms or any part of the constitution itself. Several human rights and freedoms can only be amended by a three-quarters majority of votes in parliament. The judiciary, perceived as the custodian of the constitution, is very independent, strong, and vibrant. The courts are accessible to victims of human rights abuses, who can easily obtain appropriate redress.

CONSTITUTIONAL HISTORY

Papua New Guineans sighted the first Europeans as early as the 15th century. Formal contact was not, however, established until 1884, with the colonization of the country by the British and the Germans. The southern half of the country became British New Guinea; the northern part, German New Guinea. The British and Germans introduced their laws, which they imposed on the people. It is imperative to note, however, that both the Germans and the British enacted laws that protected the rights of indigenous people to their land and to the practice of their customs in local communities. This legal protection remained until independence in 1975. The diversity of cultures in Papua New Guinea and the prominent role of customary law in local communities today can be attributed to the strong protection given to traditional land, communities, and cultures by the Germans and the British, and later by the Australians.

German New Guinea was controlled through the German New Guinea Company until 1917. After Germany was defeated in World War I (1914–18), German New Guinea became a trust territory of the League of Nations and later the United Nations until independence in 1975. British New Guinea was controlled directly by the British until 1901, when it was transferred to Australia, when that country itself became independent. In 1905, the name of the territory was changed to Papua. Papua remained a colony of Australia until 1975.

In 1949, both territories began to have a single administration controlled by the Australians. The legal and political structure of the colonial administration was regulated under the Papua and New Guinea Act 1949–75, which was considered the constitution of the two territories. Under the colonial administration, political decisions and laws were made in Canberra and applied in Papua and New Guinea.

In 1964 the first elections were held in Papua New Guinea. Two subsequent elections were held (1968 and 1972) prior to independence in 1975. Each of these elections put more Papua New Guineans in the House of Assembly. After the 1972 elections, the first Papua New Guinean chief minister, Sir Michael Somare, was appointed to run the affairs of the two territories. Papua New Guinea became self-governing in 1973, and on September 16, 1975, it became an independent state.

In the period between 1964 and 1972, three parliamentary Constitutional Commissions were established to ascertain whether the country was ready for independence. The 1964 and 1968 Constitutional Commissions both concluded that the country was not yet ready. The 1972 Constitutional Commission, called the Constitutional Planning Committee, reached two significant conclusions: First, it reported to the House of Assembly that the country was ready for independence and that independence from Australia should be sought sooner rather than later. Second, it recommended to the legislature the adoption of a draft constitution that it had prepared. The constitution was adopted on August 15, 1975, a month before independence, and it took effect when the country became independent on September 16. In its first 30 years of independence, the constitution was amended 29 times, the latest amendment on January 20, 2004.

FORM AND IMPACT OF THE CONSTITUTION

The constitution of Papua New Guinea is a written document and is supplemented by organic laws and acts of parliament. The constitution is an exhaustive blueprint, one of the longest written constitutions in the world. The Papua New Guinea constitution is also programmatic: It sets out in detail the development goals and aspirations of the people of Papua New Guinea. These development programs are described in the National Goals and Directive Principles.

The constitution is the supreme law of the land. All laws of the parliament, provincial governments, and local governments, as well as administrative and judicial decisions, must comply with the constitution. Moreover, international law must meet the criteria stipulated in Section 117 of the constitution to be applicable in Papua New Guinea.

BASIC ORGANIZATIONAL STRUCTURE

Papua New Guinea is a quasi-federal state. It has 19 provincial governments and 297 local governments. The provincial and local governments have very little administrative and financial autonomy. Their lawmaking power is also restricted.

The central government has control over the bureaucracy and finances.

Bougainville (an island province) rebelled in 1988, seeking to secede from Papua New Guinea. After a long and protracted struggle, peace was eventually restored on the island in the late 1990s. One of the key demands of the Bougainvilleans was greater political, legal, and financial autonomy. In 2002, the government agreed to this demand by amending the constitution. This preferential treatment has triggered a move by some of the other provincial governments also to seek more legislative, administrative, and financial powers.

LEADING CONSTITUTIONAL PRINCIPLES

The Papua New Guinea constitution is itself the basic legal principle. It is accepted by the people, state institutions, and judicial officials. The rule of law takes center stage. Section 37 of the constitution declares that no one is above the law and that everyone has the right to the protection of the law. The courts are mandated by the constitution to ensure that the rule of law is strengthened and promoted at all levels of government.

The constitution also promotes other principles such as democracy, with its two tenets of responsible government and representative government; separation of powers; principles of natural justice, equality, and participation; and political, social, and religious freedoms. These principles are firmly embedded in the constitution and are zealously guarded by a strong and independent judiciary. Public officials are required by law to ensure that these principles are taken into consideration in their deliberations. An aggrieved party can confidently raise these principles to obtain a remedy from the courts.

CONSTITUTIONAL BODIES

There are two categories of institutions established by the constitution. In the first category are the usual state institutions. These would include the legislature, the executive, and the judiciary and their various instrumentalities such as the head of state, the prime minister, the chief justice, provincial and local governments, and the government departments. The second category of constitutional bodies are what is called constitutional offices. These offices are creatures of the constitution and are independent; they are not subject to the direction and control of the government. These bodies include the ombudsperson commission, the office of the public prosecutor, the office of the public solicitor, the electoral commission, the auditor general, the electoral boundaries commission, the judicial and legal services commission, and the public service commission. Their primary function is to keep a check on the government to ensure that the constitutional principles, and particularly the rule of law, are applied fairly in the operations of government.

The persons who hold constitutional offices must have high integrity, strong character, and an unblemished personal record. These constitutional officeholders are appointed by a bipartisan committee of the parliament. There are stringent rules provided by the constitution for the appointment and removal of constitutional officeholders.

The Head of State

Queen Elizabeth II is the head of state of Papua New Guinea. She is represented in Papua New Guinea by the governor-general, who is elected by parliament in a secret ballot. Once elected, the governor-general holds office for a period of six years and is eligible for reappointment. The head of state may act only upon the instructions of the government. He or she has no legal capacity to act independently. This peculiar role of the head of state has been described by the courts as being a "rubber stamp."

The governor-general can be easily dismissed by a simple vote of the National Executive Council, after informing Her Majesty, Queen Elizabeth II. The dismissal of the head of state is then ratified by parliament.

The head of state appoints the prime minister after his or her election by the parliament and the members of the National Executive Council upon the advice of the prime minister. The head of state also appoints the constitutional officeholders and the heads of state departments and agencies, upon the advice of the appointing authority. It is also the function of the head of state to call for national elections on the advice of the electoral commissioner. After a national election, it is the duty of the head of state to open a new parliamentary term.

The National Administration

The head of state is a member of the national executive. The principal policymaking authority is the National Executive Council, chaired by the prime minister. The members of the National Executive Council hold office at the pleasure of the prime minister. The prime minister thus wields extensive political power. It is the prime minister who determines the number of cabinet posts as well as who should fill them. The prime minister also endorses the appointment of heads of government departments, statutory bodies, and public institutions.

The prime minister is elected into office at the first sitting of parliament after a national election. After the first 18 months in office, a prime minister can be removed through a vote of no confidence. When a prime minister is thus removed, the administration loses office and a new administration is installed. Since independence in 1975, this mechanism has been utilized several times successfully by the opposition parties to remove the incumbent. The no confidence provision of the constitution has been criticized over the years as a major cause of political instability in the country. Several attempts have been made, so far unsuccessful, to extend the 18-month grace period of a new government to 24 or 36 months. These attempts have been attacked as a ploy to keep a rogue government in office.

The National Parliament

The National Parliament is the pinnacle legislative body in Papua New Guinea. There are 109 elected members, who hold office for a period of five years.

From 1964, members of parliament were elected through the "first-past-the post" electoral system, meaning the candidate with a simple plurality of votes could win an election. However, since 2003, a new voting system has been introduced, limited preferential voting. Several by-elections using the new system have been conducted. The 2007 national election will be conducted by the limited preferential voting system.

The Lawmaking Process

The power to make laws is vested in the National Parliament. According to the constitution the parliament's lawmaking power can be transferred to another body or authority. Under the auspices of this provision, provincial and local governments have now been given legislative powers. Provincial and local government laws must be consistent with the constitution, organic laws, and acts of parliament in order to be enforceable; they are also applicable only in the province or the local government area.

The parliament is empowered by the constitution to make laws for the peace and good order of the country. Laws originate in the form of a government bill or a private member's bill. The bill goes through three readings and, if passed by parliament, becomes law. The constitution makes it clear that a law cannot take force until it has either been certified by the speaker of parliament or complied with a caveat in the law that provides for the manner in which it will go into force.

The Judiciary

The judiciary is made up of the Supreme Court, the National court, district courts, local courts, and village courts. The Supreme Court is the highest court in Papua New Guinea. There are also three specialized courts: the land court, the family court, and the juvenile or children's court.

The judges of the National court and the Supreme Court are appointed by the judicial and legal services commission. The chief justice, on the other hand, is appointed by the National Executive Council. A judicial appointment is not permanent, but subject to review every 10 years. Magistrates of the district and local courts are also appointed and removed by the judicial and legal services commission. Magistrates of the district and local courts also sit as magistrates of land, family, and juvenile courts.

The national court and Supreme Court are the only courts that have the power to deal with human rights issues. All constitutional matters fall within the jurisdiction of the Supreme Court.

THE ELECTION PROCESS

Elections in Papua New Guinea are held every five years. Every Papua New Guinean has the right to vote at age 18 and to stand for public office at age 25.

Elections to the parliament and local governments are supervised by the National Electoral Commission. Since 2003, elections to parliament have been conducted through the limited preferential voting system.

POLITICAL PARTIES

Papua New Guinea is a thriving democracy. It has a pluralistic system of political parties. The constitution provides that every citizen has the right to form an association or political organization and to be a member of an association or a political party. This freedom under Section 47 has provided the impetus for the creation of political parties. In the 2002 national election, more than 40 political parties were registered with the office of the registrar of political parties.

Since independence in 1975, no one political party has enjoyed a majority in parliament. Administrations have been formed and dissolved by coalitions of parties. A political party can be deregistered if it does not meet certain conditions under the law. A politician who is a member of a political party that does not comply with the requirements of the law can be removed from parliament.

CITIZENSHIP

Papua New Guinean citizenship can be acquired in two ways: through birth in the country or through naturalization. All persons born in Papua New Guinea to a Papua New Guinean parent or resident are citizens of the country.

A foreign adult who wishes to become a naturalized citizen must have lived continuously in Papua New Guinea for more than eight years to be eligible for consideration for citizenship. Dual citizenship is prohibited. A naturalized citizen must renounce his or her former citizenship.

FUNDAMENTAL RIGHTS

There are three traditional layers of basic rights. The first layer relates to first-generation rights. These rights comprise civil and political rights. The second set of rights consists of economic, social, and cultural rights. These two sets of rights have close association with the United Nations Universal Declaration of Human Rights. The third layer of rights, these third-generation rights, is centered on collective or fraternity rights.

The constitution gives prominence to first-generation rights. Second- and third-generation rights have not been explicitly adopted by the constitution. The constitution does, however, provide for the creation of other rights, which may implicitly encompass second- and third-generation rights.

Among the classical political, social, and economic rights and freedoms guaranteed by the constitution are freedom from slavery and forced labor, freedom from inhumane treatment, and the right to the protection of property. Also protected are freedom of thought, conscience, and religion; freedom of speech; freedom of peaceful assembly and association; freedom of employment; and the right to privacy.

Functions and Impact of Fundamental Rights

All government agencies and officials and private persons are exhorted by the constitution to give effect to and protect these rights and freedoms. Section 57 of the constitution compels the judiciary and law officers to investigate violations of fundamental rights either on their own initiative or through an application by a private person. Section 58 of the constitution provides for compensation when breaches of basic rights are proved in a court of law. Interestingly, the constitution also permits the courts and law officers to take preemptive action to prevent the infringement of basic rights if they perceive that an act or omission will result in breaches of such rights.

Limitations of Fundamental Rights

Several of the fundamental rights and freedoms can be limited in only one situation—a declared state of emergency such as a natural disaster, war, or civil strife. The limitation must be clearly spelled out in an act of parliament and can apply only during a state of emergency. At the end of the emergency, full rights and freedoms are restored. An important caveat included in the constitution is that during emergencies human rights and fundamental freedoms can only be restricted and not prohibited or repealed. Thus, the executive or the legislature cannot use the pretext of an emergency to abrogate the rights and freedoms of the people.

ECONOMY

Among the national goals of the country declared in the preamble of the constitution are that the country be politically and economically independent, and the country's economy be self-reliant. The strategy for achieving this objective is provided in Goal 3 of the constitution, which calls for the strict control of the economy by the state. State intervention in foreign investments and the economy was perceived as the means by which Papua New Guineans could achieve self-reliance. Papua New Guineans were called upon to use their profits in economic activities for national development.

The underpinning of the constitution is that Papua New Guinea is a social state. The state is required to provide the resources and facilities to enable the people to enhance their capacities to generate economic gains for themselves and the country.

Over the last 20 years, it has become apparent that the state did not have the capacity to provide the opportunities for Papua New Guineans to enhance their economic well-being. As a result of mismanagement of the economy, deteriorating infrastructure, and lack of government services in the rural areas, Papua New Guinea has been forced by multilateral financial organizations to adopt new economic models to resuscitate the economy. This new approach has meant the abandonment of the socialist principles of the constitution and the adoption of free market economic ideals. The introduction of this new economic model has meant that the 85 percent of the people who live in the rural areas now have to pay for goods and services that were in the past provided free by the state.

RELIGIOUS COMMUNITIES

Papua New Guinea is a predominantly Christian country; the preamble of the constitution declares it to be a Christian country. Respect for other religions including traditional pagan beliefs is, however, protected by the constitution. Freedom of thought, conscience, and religion is guaranteed. There is a clear demarcation between the church and the state. Public officials are free to exercise their faith but are required by the constitution to apply and promote fairness in the conduct of their official duties.

The Christian churches have historically played a pivotal role in the development of the country. They continue to be heavily involved in providing basic health and education and other services to the people, especially those in the remote areas of the country, where there is no government presence. Given the important role the churches play in the development process, the state considers the church as a strategic ally. In this regard, the state supports the efforts of the churches through financial assistance provided through the annual national budget.

MILITARY DEFENSE AND STATE OF EMERGENCY

The military in Papua New Guinea is controlled by the civilian government. There is no commander in chief. Section 98 of the constitution expressly states that the military is directly responsible to the National Executive Council through the minister of defense. The National Executive Council has the power to appoint and remove the commander of the defense force. The Papua New Guinea military is a small force, and, thus, enlistment in the defense force is voluntary. There is no general conscription in the country.

The main function of the defense force is to protect the country against military attack. In peacetime, the military is actively involved in civic duties such as assisting civil servants in the conduct of national elections, in relief work in times of natural disasters, in building of roads and bridges, and in assisting the police in states of emergency.

A state of emergency can only be declared by the governor-general on the advice of the National Executive Council. Once a state of emergency is declared, the parliament is required to meet within 15 days either to approve or to revoke the declaration. The same provision in unequivocal terms transfers the power to supervise and control the emergency to the parliament. The parliament exercises this function through a bipartisan parliamentary committee. Two critical institutions are prohibited by the constitution from taking control of the emergency—the National Executive Council and the military. During a state of emergency, the parliament through the bipartisan committee and the police force are given the mandate to control and supervise the emergency. This provision is meant to prevent the usurpation of power by the executive or the military.

AMENDMENTS TO THE CONSTITUTION

The constitution can only be amended by the parliament. The constitution itself provides an elaborate set of rules for amending its provisions. Section 17 specifies three different categories of provisions that may be changed, and three corresponding sets of voting rules. The first relates to critical provisions of the constitution, which require a three-quarter majority of votes to effect an amendment. These include primarily the fundamental human rights and freedoms provisions. The second category of provisions require a two-third majority of votes to change. The third category of provisions require only an absolute majority of votes to change.

A proposal to amend the constitution, if approved at the first reading, must pass through a second vote two months after it was introduced in parliament. The two-month interval is designed to enable the members of parliament as individuals and through parliamentary committees to consider the proposed amendment in detail. When the proposed amendment bill is read the second time and passed by parliament, it goes into force and the relevant provision or provisions of the constitution are deemed amended. If the proposed amendment bill is rejected at the second reading, it cannot be reintroduced into parliament.

PRIMARY SOURCES

Constitution in English. Available online. URL: http://www.paclii.org./pg/legis/consol_act/cotisopng534/. Accessed on September 24, 2005.
"The Papua New Guinean Legal Information Network." Available online. URL: http://www.niumedia.com/pnginlaw. Accessed on August 27, 2005.

SECONDARY SOURCES

Eric L. Kwa, *Constitutional Law of Papua New Guinea.* Sydney: Law Book Company, 2001.
Eric L. Kwa et al., eds., *The Development of Administrative Law in Papua New Guinea.* New Delhi: UBSPD and UPNG Law School, 2000.
Anthony J. Regan, Owen Jessep, and Eric L. Kwa, eds., *Twenty Years of the Papua New Guinea Constitution.* Sydney: Law Book Company, 2001.

Eric L. Kwa

PARAGUAY

At-a-Glance

OFFICIAL NAME
Republic of Paraguay

CAPITAL
Asunción

POPULATION
6,191,368 (2005 est.)

SIZE
157,047 sq. mi. (406,750 sq. km)

LANGUAGES
Spanish, Guaraní

RELIGIONS
Catholic 90%, Protestant 10%

NATIONAL OR ETHNIC COMPOSITION
Mestizo (mixed Spanish and Amerindian) 95%,
Indian and European 5%

DATE OF INDEPENDENCE OR CREATION
May 14, 1811 (from Spain)

TYPE OF GOVERNMENT
Constitutional republic

TYPE OF STATE
Unitary state

TYPE OF LEGISLATURE
Bicameral parliament

DATE OF CONSTITUTION
June 20, 1992

DATE OF LAST AMENDMENT
No amendment

Paraguay is a representative, participatory, and pluralistic democracy founded on the recognition of human dignity, where the constitution is the supreme law. The state is unitary, but also decentralized. The national territory is divided into 17 departments and one capital city, Asunción. The departments have political, administrative, and regulatory autonomy.

The government is exercised through executive, legislative, and judicial authorities. These three branches are, according to the constitution, independent, balanced, and coordinated. A system of checks and balance is also established.

The constitution provides for far-reaching guarantees of human rights. Constitutional remedies are established and enforceable by the judicial power, which includes a Supreme Court of Justice that, through its constitutional chamber, is responsible for hearing and resolving cases of unconstitutionality of laws and decisions.

The federal president is both the head of state and the head of the administration. The people, by a simple majority of voters, directly elect the president and vice president. A pluralistic system of political parties has intense political impact.

Religious freedom is guaranteed, and state and religious communities are separated. The economic system can be described as a market economy with a large informal sector such as thousands of microenterprises and urban street vendors. The military force is subject to the state and must abide by the constitution and the law. By constitutional law, Paraguay is obliged to contribute to the search for peace.

CONSTITUTIONAL HISTORY

Paraguay as a political entity emerged in 1811, when its independence from Spain was declared. Internal political instability and the threat of a takeover by Argentina prevented the state from promulgating a constitution. A series of documents were drafted, but they were not constitutions in a formal sense: Their subject was merely the organization of the postrevolution government.

In 1813, a general congress was held, the first of its kind in Latin America. Over 1,000 representatives were elected by universal male suffrage. The congress proclaimed the Paraguayan Republic. José Gaspar Rodríguez de Francia (1766–1840), one of the most important figures in the history of Paraguay, was the first consul. Fulgencio Yegros was the second.

The 1814 general congress named Francia the supreme dictator of the republic; in 1816, he was named dictator for life. Despite the inherent violence of the dictatorship, Francia, almost on his own, succeeded in building a strong, prosperous, safe, and independent nation at a time when Paraguay's continued existence as an independent country seemed unlikely.

In 1840 Francia died without a successor, and in the following few years, many ruling juntas and consuls governed Paraguay. Nevertheless, it was a creative period. On November 25, 1842, independence was ratified by an extraordinary congress. Until then, there had not been a single document that registered the political and legal existence of Paraguay as an independent country. According to the 1842 Independence Act, the objective of the new country was a free and independent nation under the republican system, with a strong connection to the Catholic Church. An 1842 resolution prohibited the existence or tolerance of other religions or the freedom of belief and worship.

Carlos Antonio López (1787–1862) became first consul in 1841, and president of the republic in 1844. At his initiative the first effective constitution of Paraguay was promulgated that same year. This constitution established a basic outline of a division of powers dominated by the executive. Congress had the authority to elect the president of the republic. The 1844 constitution established equality before the law, even equality of rich and poor; the right to move about from place to place; and the right to be heard by the government. The slave trade was prohibited.

On November 11, 1864, under the government of Francisco Solano López (1826–70), son and successor of Carlos Antonio López, the war of the Triple Alliance began. Paraguay's attempt to become a third force between Brazil and Argentina had placed the country against the combined forces of Argentina, Brazil, and Uruguay. The war ruined Paraguay; it lost large territories to Brazil and Argentina, and modernization was dramatically stopped. In 1864, there had been 406,000 people in Paraguay; by the end of the war only 231,000 were left, mostly women, children, and the elderly.

On November 25, 1870, a new constitution was adopted. It guaranteed freedom of belief and worship, but Catholicism remained the official religion. Shipping on the rivers of Paraguay—one of the causes of the war—was opened to all countries. A good number of fundamental rights were established, such as the right to work, freedom of the press, and freedom of association. Slavery was completely abolished.

The 1870 constitution remained in force until 1940, when, after a revolution by soldiers of the Chaco War (1932–33), veterans, students, and workers, a new constitution was promulgated on July 10, 1940. This constitution had a clearly social orientation and was intended to address the social and economic problems of Paraguay. For example, the constitution clearly stated that private interests should never prevail over public interests. Health care and social assistance were established as fundamental duties of the state. The executive remained far more powerful than the other powers, providing a legitimate basis for an open dictatorship.

After further years of political and social unrest, Paraguay suffered a new coup d'état on August 15, 1954, as Alfredo Stroessner, a Chaco War hero, seized power. Continued instability ensued, even including guerrilla fighting. In August 1967, a new constitution was promulgated, giving Stroessner unlimited lifetime power.

After a 35-year dictatorship, another coup d'état in 1989 ended the regime of Alfredo Stroessner and started the process of redemocratization. On June 26, 1992, the current constitution was promulgated. It was the start of a new Paraguay, committed to democratic values and effective guarantees for human rights.

FORM AND IMPACT OF THE CONSTITUTION

Paraguay has a written constitution; codified in a single document, called the Constitution of the Republic of Paraguay (Constitución de la República del Paraguay), it takes precedence over all other national law. International law must be in accordance with the constitution to be applicable within Paraguay.

The constitution is the supreme law of Paraguay. The citizens have the right to resist usurpers' seizing public power contrary to the constitution by any means available to them. The hierarchy of norms is established by the constitution itself. Listed in descending order, the constitution; international treaties, conventions, and agreements that have been approved and ratified by congress; laws promulgated by congress; and other legal provisions of lesser rank make up the national legal system.

In addition to its normative function, the constitution represents values and objectives for rebuilding and maintaining government and society.

BASIC ORGANIZATIONAL STRUCTURE

Paraguay is a unitary, indivisible, and decentralized state. The national territory is divided into 17 departments (*departamentos*), municipalities, and the capital city of Asunción, which is a municipality independent of any department. The municipalities enjoy, within the limits of the constitution and the law, political, administrative, and regulatory autonomy regarding their own affairs. They exercise independence in collecting and investing their resources.

Each department is headed by a governor and by a departmental board. The governor represents the executive power and is responsible for implementing national policy. The departments are only administrative entities without any legislative and judicial authority, or even without much executive authority, of their own. Municipalities are local government organizations with legal status. The municipal government is managed by a mayor and by a council elected directly by legally qualified voters.

LEADING CONSTITUTIONAL PRINCIPLES

Paraguay's system of government is a presidential democracy. There is a strong division of the executive, legislative, and judicial powers, based on a system of checks and balances. The judiciary is independent and includes a constitutional court, the Supreme Court of Justice.

The Paraguayan constitutional system is defined by a number of leading principles: Paraguay is a representative, participatory, and pluralistic democracy. It is a unitary, indivisible, and decentralized state. It is a republic and a social state based on the rule of law. In Article 1 the constitution states: "The Republic of Paraguay is and always will be independent. It is constituted as a social state of law, which is unitary, indivisible, and decentralized as prescribed by this constitution and the laws." According to Article 1, the Republic of Paraguay is a democracy founded on the recognition of human dignity.

Suffrage is the main instrument of democracy and is based on universal, free, equal, and secret voting. Political participation is rather strictly shaped through an indirect, representative democracy. Direct democracy is very limited. According to Article 122, certain questions cannot be submitted to a referendum, such as international relations, expropriations, national defense, taxes, the national general budget, or the conduct of national, departmental, or municipal elections.

Human dignity is a leading principle of the constitution. The preamble affirms the principles of representative, participatory, pluralistic republican democracy; national sovereignty and independence; and participation in the international community.

Other principles are contained in the constitution implicitly, such as the value of life, environmental protection, religious neutrality, and equality. There is a strong concern for human rights, including the recognition of the Indian peoples and ethnic groups and of their right to preserve and develop their ethnic identity in their respective territories.

CONSTITUTIONAL BODIES

The predominant bodies provided for in the constitution are the president and the Council of Ministers; the bicameral congress (*Congreso*), consisting of the Senate and the Chamber of Deputies; and the judiciary including the Constitutional Court. A number of other bodies complete this list such as the public defender, responsible for the defense of human rights.

The President

The president is the head of state and the head of the administration of the Republic of Paraguay, responsible for the general administration of the country internally and the foreign representation of the state, including the power to negotiate and sign international treaties. The president has the duty to observe and enforce the constitution and the law and can also issue decrees. The president participates in the lawmaking process by proposing draft legislation to congress and by promulgating laws, ordering their publication, regulating them, and ensuring their enforcement. The president has the right to pardon or alter sentences imposed by judges or courts of the republic.

Although the constitution establishes a division of powers, the president has great visibility and political power. He or she is the chief of the federal administration and of the armed forces. The president is assisted by the cabinet or Council of Ministers, a constitutional body subordinated to the president and responsible for the conduct and management of public business.

The president of the republic is directly elected by the people for a five-year term, by a simple majority of voters, and can be in no way reelected. The president must be a natural Paraguayan national at least 35 years of age.

The president can be removed from office in case of disability, leave of absence, or misdeeds. In the latter case, the president may be forced to undergo impeachment proceedings for malfeasance in office, crimes committed in office, or common crimes (Article 225). The Chamber of Deputies has the authority to press the charges by a two-thirds majority. The Senate then conducts a public trial and can declare the president guilty and remove him or her from office by a two-thirds absolute majority vote. In cases of common crimes, the records of these procedures are then sent to the appropriate regular court.

The Congress (Senate and Chamber of Deputies)

The legislative power is exercised by the Congress, consisting of the Senate and the Chamber of Deputies. Senators and deputies are jointly and directly elected for a term of five years. Reelection is allowed.

Congress has broad authority. With both chambers present, congress administers the oath of office to the president of the republic, the vice president, and the justices of the Supreme Court of Justice. It can also authorize the entry of foreign armed forces into the national territory. Congress has the authority to ensure the observation of the constitution and the laws, and to pass codes and other laws.

The chambers may create joint investigating committees on any matter of public interest or on the conduct of their members, although the activities of such committees do not affect the exclusive powers of the judiciary nor violate the rights and guarantees granted by the constitution. Any conclusions they reach are not binding on the courts; and their findings are conveyed to an appropriate regular judge.

A member of either chamber may lose his or her seat when there is tangible evidence of improper use of office or a violation that would make the member ineligible for or incompatible with the office according to the constitution.

The Chamber of Deputies

The Chamber of Deputies represents the country's territorial departments. It consists of at least 80 members elected directly by the people in departmental electoral districts. The number of deputies is determined by the Supreme Electoral Court before each election, taking into consideration the number of voters in each department. To be elected as deputy, the candidate must be a Paraguayan natural citizen at least 25 years old.

The Chamber of Deputies has the exclusive power to initiate draft laws concerning departmental or municipal matters or to authorize state intervention in departmental or municipal governments.

The Senate

The Senate consists of at least 45 members elected directly by the people in each district. As the number of voters increases, the number of senators increases in the same proportion. To be elected as a senator, a candidate must be a Paraguayan natural citizen who is at least 35 years old.

Under the Paraguayan constitution, former presidents of the republic who were democratically elected and were not removed from office by impeachment enjoy lifetime membership in the national Senate. However, they do not count toward a quorum.

The Senate has the exclusive power to initiate draft laws concerning the approval of treaties and international agreements and to appoint or propose the appointment of magistrates and officials as provided in the constitution.

The Lawmaking Process

One of the main duties of the Congress is to pass legislation. The right to introduce a bill is possessed by every member of the Senate and the Chamber of Deputies, by the administration, by the people, and by the Supreme Court of Justice. In some cases, this power is restricted exclusively to one chamber or to the administration. For example, the administration introduces legislation on the national general budget.

When a bill has been approved by the chamber where it was proposed, it is immediately submitted to the consideration of the other chamber. If the other chamber approves it, and if the executive power subsequently approves it, the new law is promulgated and published within five days.

The president may veto the bill. In that case, the bill returns for further discussion to the originating chamber. The veto can be overridden by an absolute majority. If it is overridden, the bill is sent to the reviewing chamber, which must also consider the president's objections. If the reviewing chamber overrides the veto by an absolute majority, the original version of the law is approved.

The Judiciary

The judiciary is independent of the executive and legislative branches and is a powerful factor in legal life. The constitution declares that the judicial power is the guardian of the constitution. It interprets the constitution, complies with it, and orders its enforcement.

The judicial branch is responsible for administering justice. Administration is exercised by the Supreme Court of Justice, and by appellate and lower courts as established by the constitution and the laws. There are special courts for civil and criminal cases, courts for tax issues, and a court for external audit, which is part of the judicial power.

The highest court in Paraguay is the Supreme Court of Justice. It ranks above the other branches of the judiciary and has exclusive powers to resolve constitutional disputes. Although the authority to hear and decide cases of unconstitutionality is the most important responsibility of the Supreme Court of Justice, it also serves as a court of final appeals, supervises all branches of the judiciary, and resolves conflicts of jurisdiction and authority in accordance with the law. The Supreme Court of Justice consists of nine members and is divided into two chambers, one of which hears constitutional matters.

To become a member of the Supreme Court of Justice, one must be a natural Paraguayan national, 35 years old, hold a doctorate in law, and enjoy an honorable reputation. Additionally, one must have practiced law, held a court office, or held a teaching job at a law school for at least 10 years. The members of the Supreme Court of Justice are chosen by the Senate with the concurrence of the administration from a list of three candidates proposed by the Council of Magistrates.

The importance of the court arises from the fact that every exercise of state power must be in compliance with the constitution. The Supreme Court of Justice can declare acts of parliament void on grounds of unconstitutionality. Petitions of unconstitutionality may be filed directly before the chamber, or by way of a defense before any other court, and at any moment during a case. In such cases, the respective files are submitted to the Supreme Court.

THE ELECTION PROCESS

All Paraguayan citizens over the age of 18, residing in the national territory, have both the right to stand for election and the right to vote in the election. Foreigners who have permanent residence papers have the same right in municipal elections.

The president and vice president of the republic are elected jointly and directly by the people, by a simple majority of votes, in general elections held 90 to 120 days before the expiration of the ongoing constitutional term. Senators and deputies and their respective alternates are chosen in elections held simultaneously with that of the president.

The departmental governors and departmental boards are elected directly by the citizens residing in the respective departments through elections held simultaneously with the national general elections.

POLITICAL PARTIES

Paraguay has a pluralistic political party system. The multiparty system is a basic structure of the constitutional order, defined as a pluralistic democracy.

The political parties constitute a fundamental element of public life in the Republic of Paraguay. According to the constitution, the parties must reflect pluralism; participate in nominating and preparing elective officials; provide guidance for national, departmental, and municipal policies; and participate in the civic training of citizens (Article 124). The parties are legal organizations subject to public law; their democratic nature is ensured by the law.

Other forms of political participation are the referendum and the initiative of the people.

CITIZENSHIP

Paraguayan nationality is primarily acquired by birth. A combination of the principles of *ius sanguinis* and *ius soli* is applied. A child acquires Paraguayan nationality if he or she is born in the territory of the republic, or if the child is born abroad, one or both of the child's parents is a Paraguayan national in the service of the republic, or one or both of the parents is a Paraguayan national, and the child decides to reside permanently in Paraguay. Naturalization is possible.

Every Paraguayan national over the age of 18 years is a citizen, as well as every naturalized Paraguayan national two years after obtaining his or her naturalization.

FUNDAMENTAL RIGHTS

The constitution defines fundamental rights at the very beginning of its second title. In doing so, the framers of the constitution have emphasized the fundamental importance of the rights of the individual.

The Paraguayan constitution guarantees the traditional, classic set of human rights and guarantees social human rights, such as the right to work, labor rights, the right to education, the right to health, and even the right to a healthy environment, which is an aspect of the third generation of fundamental rights. The Indian peoples have their fundamental rights guaranteed in the same section of the constitution. In sum, the constitution guarantees a large number of fundamental rights that have great importance in Paraguay.

The starting point for human rights in the constitution is the guarantee of the right to live. Article 4 states: "The right to live is inherent to the human being. Its protection is guaranteed, in general, after the time of conception. The death penalty remains abolished. Each individual's physical and psychological integrity as well as his or her honor and reputation will be protected by the State. The law will regulate the freedom to dispose of ones own body, but only for scientific or medical purposes."

Human dignity is not guaranteed as a fundamental right, but it is a principle that is expressly stated by the constitution. According to the preamble of the constitution, the Paraguayan people recognize human dignity for the purpose of ensuring freedom, equality, and justice. Article 1, Title 1 (about basic principles), also says: "The Republic of Paraguay adopts as its system of government a representative, participatory, and pluralistic democracy, which is founded on the recognition of human dignity." Establishing human dignity is thus one of the most important general principles in the constitution, which also specifically guarantees numerous rights. The basic rights set out in the constitution are binding on the legislature, the executive, and the judiciary, as directly applicable law. Thus they are binding for all public authorities in any circumstances in which they act.

Article 7 establishes the right to a healthy environment: "Everyone has the right to live in a healthy, ecologically balanced environment. The preservation, recovery, and improvement of the environment, as well as efforts to reconcile these goals with comprehensive human development, are priority objectives of social interest. The respective laws and government policies will seek to meet these objectives."

Chapter 2 deals with rights relating to personal freedoms. Article 9, regarding individual freedom and security, declares that "everyone has the right to have his or her freedom and security protected. No one may be forced to do anything that is not mandated by law, and no one may be prevented from doing something that is not prohibited by law." The general equal treatment clause is contained in Article 46, which guarantees that all residents of the republic are equal before the law. This fundamental right is stated as a catch-all provision and then expanded by a number of specific provisions such as a guarantee of equality of men and women and of equal access to justice. A special rule related to affirmative action is provided in Article 46 (2): "Guarantees aimed at preventing unfair inequalities will not be considered discriminatory, but egalitarian factors."

The constitution distinguishes between human rights, which apply to every human being, and those fundamental rights reserved for Paraguayans only. Examples of general human rights are the right to live and the right to freedom; examples of Paraguayans' rights are the freedom of movement, the freedom to reside where one chooses, and the right to equal treatment.

Impact and Functions of Fundamental Rights

The 1992 constitution was promulgated after a dictatorship that lasted 34 years. During this period, there were no limitations on the executive power, which dominated the legislative and the judiciary powers. The 1992 constitution represents a new, modern, and democratic Paraguay.

The provisions on fundamental rights were particularly meaningful to Paraguayans, immediately after a dictatorship, as a symbol of redemocratization. The new state would consider all the people—the Indian peoples were explicitly recognized—and the minimal rights that make possible a dignified existence. In addition to the classic fundamental rights, social and solidarity rights were guaranteed, in order to allow their effective exercise.

Fundamental rights have a strong impact in public life. The state shall respect and protect these rights in the lawmaking process, the application of the law, and its interpretation. The fundamental rights shall, however, also be respected by individuals because these rights represent a choice of values that is valid even in private life.

However, the rights and guarantees provided are more symbolic than effective. The Amnesty International Report 2003 states that during the year 2002 there were instances in which the security forces were guilty of excessive force, failure to investigate killings, torture, ill treatment of conscripts, and recruitment of minors.

Limitations to Fundamental Rights

The fundamental rights specified in the constitution are not absolute, but have limitations established by the constitution itself. The limits relate to the specific needs of the public and the rights of others.

For example, Article 109 guarantees the right to private property. However, the constitution requires that private property have a socioeconomic function: Its use should contribute to the commonweal.

ECONOMY

The Paraguayan constitution establishes principles concerning the economic system (Articles 176–180), which must be respected by the state and its agencies. The fundamental goal of the state's economic policy must be the promotion of socioeconomic and cultural development.

The state is mandated to promote orderly, sustained economic growth through the rational use of available resources, in order to create new sources of jobs, to increase

the national wealth, and to ensure the well-being of the people. Comprehensive programs are to be devised to coordinate and guide national economic activities.

Rights provisions protect the freedom to own property, the right to be fully employed without discrimination, and the right to form associations and trade unions. Additional economic rights, such as free competition, free circulation of goods, and intellectual property rights, are also protected.

Paraguay is defined by constitutional law as a social state, providing for minimal social standards. Taken as a whole, the Paraguayan economic system can be described as a social market economy, according to the constitution. However, in practical terms the economy is marked by a large informal sector with thousands of microenterprises and urban street vendors.

RELIGIOUS COMMUNITIES

Freedom of religion, ideology, worship, and belief, which is guaranteed as a fundamental right, also involves rights for the religious communities. According to the Paraguayan civil code, the churches are legal entities (Article 91).

There is no established official religion, and public authorities are required to be strictly neutral in their relations with religious communities. The independence of all religious denominations is limited only by the restrictions imposed by the constitution and the law.

The constitution guarantees that no one may be disturbed, questioned, or forced to give testimony by reason of his or her religion, beliefs, or ideology. The right to conscientious objection for ethical or religious reasons is recognized in those cases in which the constitution and the law permit it.

Freedom of religion is also guaranteed by the constitution for the Indian peoples, who have the right to pursue their customary religious practices freely. In its provisions on education and culture, the constitution guarantees the right to have a religious education.

Despite the essential separation of religion and the state, there are many areas in which they cooperate. For example, the churches receive subsidies from the state.

All past Paraguayan constitutions have stressed the connection between the state and the Catholic Church. The Catholic religion was, until the 1967 constitution, the official religion.

The 1992 constitution clearly states that relations between the state and the Catholic Church are based on independence, cooperation, and autonomy. Nevertheless, the influence of the Catholic Church in social and public life is very strong. The church strives to act as the representative and defender of the people against poverty, when the state fails to do so. It also intervenes in issues of public health and personal relationships, for example, protesting the adoption of the "morning-after" pill, a current issue of public debate in Paraguay.

MILITARY DEFENSE AND STATE OF EMERGENCY

The federal government is responsible for creating and maintaining the armed forces. The commander in chief of the armed forces is the president of the republic; this office may not be delegated.

The constitution calls the armed forces a national institution, organized as a permanent, professional, nondeliberative, and obedient force (Article 173), subordinated to the state, the constitution, and the law. Its mission is to safeguard the integrity of the national territory and to defend the legitimately constituted authorities. The constitution also provides for the existence of military courts with exclusive jurisdiction to hear crimes and disciplinary violations of a military nature, committed by military personnel on active duty. If there is doubt about the nature of the violation, it is considered a civilian violation.

According to Article 129, every Paraguayan must be prepared for, and must complete, service in the armed defense of the country, not to exceed 12 months in times of peace. This obligation is not mandatory for women, Indians, or conscientious objectors. Women may be required to serve, in an auxiliary capacity, only if necessary during an international armed conflict.

The law currently requires all men over the age of 18 to perform basic service. In addition, there are professional soldiers who serve for fixed periods or for life. Conscientious objectors can file a petition to be excluded from military service; they must then provide services to benefit the civilian population in aid centers designated by the law, under civilian jurisdiction. The constitution bans punitive treatment of conscientious objectors or heavier burdens than those imposed on conscripts. The constitution prohibits personal military service that is not determined by law or is set up for the benefit of private citizens or organizations.

The constitution outlines in detail the state of emergency (Article 288). It is said to exist in cases of international armed conflict, whether formally declared or not. A state of emergency also exists in cases of serious internal upheaval that poses an imminent threat to the constitution or to the regular functioning of the organizations created by it. The powers of the civil authorities remain essentially intact; there are no significant increase in the powers of the military and no martial law even in the exceptional case of a state of defense. Nor may fundamental rights be limited. The only exceptions are that the executive branch may order the detention of persons suspected of participating in these events and their transfer from one place to another within Paraguay. The suspect always has the option of leaving the country. The executive may also prohibit public meetings or demonstrations at these times.

AMENDMENTS TO THE CONSTITUTION

The constitution has been designed to be difficult to change. Amendments can be initiated by a quarter of the members of either of the two chambers of the Congress, by the president of the republic, or by any 30,000 voters through a signed petition. Approval by an absolute majority of both chambers is required. After that approval, the amendment is submitted to the Superior Electoral Court, which must call a referendum. If the referendum approves the amendment, it is considered approved, promulgated, and part of the constitution. If the amendment repeals any constitutional provision, no other amendment on the same subject may be proposed for three years.

Certain fundamental provisions are not subject to normal amendment, although they can be reformed by a National Constituent Assembly directly elected for this purpose (Article 289). Such provisions are those affecting the election, composition, term in office, or powers of any of the three branches of government. Also entrenched are provisions regarding life and the environment, freedom, equality, and family rights.

The Constituent Assembly can also draft, approve, and promulgate a new constitution. However, the difficulty of the amendment process protects the essential identity of the constitution from slow degradation or creeping subversion.

PRIMARY SOURCES

Constitution in English. Available online. URL: http://www.oefre.unibe.ch/law/icl/pa00000_.html. Accessed on August 8, 2005.

Constitution in Spanish. Available online. URL: http://www.pdba.georgetown.edu/Constitutions/Paraguay/para1992.html. Accessed on June 27, 2006.

SECONDARY SOURCES

Carlos Q. Mateo Balmelli, *Las actuales discusiones constitucionales en América Latina: Paraguay, Chile, Argentina.* Asunción: Editorial Don Bosco, 1991.

Conrado Pappalardo Zaldívar, *Paraguay: itinerario constitucional.* Asunción: Intercontinental Editora, 1993.

Vivianne Geraldes Ferreira

PERU

At-a-Glance

OFFICIAL NAME
Republic of Peru

CAPITAL
Lima

POPULATION
27,544,305 (2005 est.)

SIZE
496,226 sq. mi. (1,285,220 sq. km)

LANGUAGES
Spanish, Quecha (official), Aymara, many minor Amazonian languages

RELIGIONS
Catholic 85%, Evangelical 7%, other (mainly native religions) 8%

NATIONAL OR ETHNIC COMPOSITION
Amerindian 45%, mestizo (mixed Amerindian and white) 37%, white 15%, black, Japanese, Chinese, and other 3%

DATE OF INDEPENDENCE OR CREATION
July 28, 1821

TYPE OF GOVERNMENT
Democratic republic

TYPE OF STATE
Unitary state

TYPE OF LEGISLATURE
Unicameral parliament

DATE OF CONSTITUTION
December 31, 1993

DATE OF LAST AMENDMENT
October 4. 2005

Peru is a democratic republic under the rule of law. There is a clear division of executive, judiciary, and legislative powers. The tough Peruvian geography has marked its government structure. The existence of huge desert areas, high mountain regions, and the endless Amazon jungle has encouraged a tendency toward centralist government, to protect against invasions of national territory. The most important duties that the constitution establishes for the state are to protect national autonomy, guarantee human rights, protect the safety of its people. and promote the general well-being in accordance with justice and an integral and balanced development of the nation.

The president is the chief of state and represents the country. He or she is elected by the people in direct elections every five years and can be reelected of the end of the term of office. The president is the head of the executive power and manages this power with the help of cabinet ministers he or she chooses. The cabinet ministers have the political responsibility for the administration. The parliament not only passes laws but also performs important control duties.

The constitution is the main law that directs and guarantees the development of Peru as a nation.

CONSTITUTIONAL HISTORY

The first constitution of Peru was made when its territory was still under Spanish rule. It was known as the Constitution of Cádiz and was issued on March 19, 1812, in the city of Cádiz, Spain. It was liberal for its time, and several English and French thinkers took part in its creation. It has been a model and a reference for subsequent constitutions.

The country has seen 21 different constitutions since 1812. A variety of cultural, geographical, and ethnic factors contributed to this large number, and to the resulting legal instability. The most important reason is a tradition of strong leadership. Democratic governments have often been usurped by powerful individuals, who then installed nominal governments. These individuals then sought legitimacy by summoning constitutional congresses.

The origins of Peru can be found in the great civilizations that inhabited its current territory for more than 7,000 years, such as the Chavin de Huantar, Chimz, Mochica, Paracas, and Nazca. At the beginning of the 14th century C.E. one of these civilizations, the Inca culture, dominated much of South America from its chief site at Cuzco; it created a great empire.

After 100 years, when the empire had entered a decadent period, a Spanish military force invaded and took over all its territory. This began a long difficult process of Europeanization of South America that lasted for over 400 years. This period ended as a consequence of liberal ideas that were introduced to America through the Spanish Constitution of Cádiz.

Peru declared its independence of Spain in Lima on July 28, 1821. The first task of the new independent government was to complete the war of liberation still taking place in some parts of the national territory. This warlike government was a direct precedent of the kind of leadership that has made democracy precarious in Peru.

The most difficult task, however, was to convince the people of Peru that independence did not mean betraying their most basic religious beliefs. During the 400-year-long Spanish supremacy, Spanish jurists had been successful in teaching that the Spanish king was the ruler God chose to govern America; to deny this meant teaching against the church. They had created a normative doctrinal framework known as Regio Vicariat, according to which to be Catholic in America it was necessary to be subject to the Spanish king, and to be a subject of the Spanish king it was necessary to be Catholic.

True national feeling began to emerge as a result of two important historical events: the final division of the country into two independent states of Peru and Bolivia (1837–39) and the Pacific War among Chile, Peru, and Bolivia (1879–82). Facing these two events, Peru started its long and yet unfinished process of obtaining its own national identity.

The beginning of this process is best visible in the 1856 constitution, soon replaced by the 1860 constitution. This 1856 constitution is a key reference for understanding the Peruvian constitutional system.

After the first century of independence, an important liberal movement prevailed. It had been launched by the former president Manuel Pardo y Lavalle (1834–78) and drew support from opposition to the military leadership that had devastated the country during its first 100 years of independence. Don Augusto B. Leguma, a civilian president, called a National Assembly to give Peru a new constitution on January 18, 1920. After President Leguma was overthrown by a military coup, a long series of constitutions were enacted before the current one, implemented in 1993.

FORM AND IMPACT OF THE CONSTITUTION

The Peruvian constitution is a written law enacted in a single document. It is the most important law of the country, and all other legal acts must conform to it. The constitution can be enacted only by an assembly specially summoned for this purpose, taking into account all the country. It aspires to consolidate the country as a nation and to organize it as a state, trying to build a bridge connecting its past, present, and future. It names the human being as the raison d'être of a legally organized society, whose principal duty is to protect the individual and facilitate his or her healthy development. The constitution states the basic rights of the human being and establishes mechanisms to respect and protect them. International treaties and agreements signed by Peru must be in accordance with the constitution's basic principles and rules.

In a culturally, ethnically, and geographically heterogeneous country such as Peru, the constitution works as a way to integrate society. However, this diversity means that different segments of the Peruvian people perceive the constitution in different ways. For Peruvians with a European background, the constitution fulfills the role that has been assigned to it, but for other parts of the population it remains little more than an indication that they are in some way a part of a society whose governmental workings remain unclear. Nevertheless, the document serves as a reference point that becomes more important every day in the effort to create a Peruvian identity.

BASIC ORGANIZATIONAL STRUCTURE

Peru has a centralized government, with its seat in the city of Lima. The government is structured in regions, departments, provinces, and districts, whose borders reflect the administrative structures created by the Spanish viceroyalty, which in turn followed the demarcation of ecclesiastical dioceses. Decentralizing power in Peru is an old dream not yet fulfilled. Although the authorities of regions, departments, provinces, and districts are chosen by direct popular election, the authorities are still struggling against the centralistic inertia left by the Spanish regime, and against bureaucratic obstruction.

Decentralization is more real in the economic than in the legal, social, or political arena. Peruvian society is characterized by a permanent struggle between the more liberal, somewhat Americanized urban population and the more conservative, closed rural population. Thus, decentralization must take on deeper challenges than a simple division of the national budget.

LEADING CONSTITUTIONAL PRINCIPLES

By its constitution, Peru is a democratic, social, independent, and sovereign republic. The power arises from the people and is exercised according to the constitution. The constitution clearly states that no one must obey a usurping government or anyone who publicly violates the constitution or the law. It is a recognized right of the civil population to revolt in order to protect the constitutional order when it is violated.

CONSTITUTIONAL BODIES

The constitution states as constitutional bodies the executive power under the leadership of the president, who works with the cabinet, the congress, and the judiciary.

The President and the Cabinet

The exercise of power is centralized in the president of the republic, who enforces the law established by Congress. This duty is controlled by the Congress. The president must act together with the cabinet, composed of the state ministers.

The cabinet's main duty is to coordinate the work of all of the cabinet ministers. It also serves as a link between the president and Congress. Within 30 days after assuming office, the president of the cabinet, along with all the cabinet ministers, must present their general policies to Congress, along with the most important measures for implementing them. The cabinet then needs a vote of confidence from Congress. The cabinet ministers are subject to the censure of Congress.

The Congress

Peru has a one-chamber Congress whose duty is to pass laws and to supervise the performance of the president. The Congress has 120 members, elected by direct popular election for a term of five years.

Although the Peruvian constitutional system centralizes the exercise of power in the president, it also creates a control system designed to prevent the personal or arbitrary use of the power. It has been broadly discussed whether Peru has a parliamentary or a presidential regime. The current constitution has created a mixture of both systems. However, the tendency of the people of Peru is to grant to the president all the tasks of the supreme state order. Therefore, there is a strong presidential power.

The Lawmaking Process

Legislation lies with the Congress, Organic laws, which are those laws that regulate certain key issues such as the structure and functioning of government organs, require a majority of more than one-half of the total members of Congress. Other laws are passed with a relative major-

ity. Bills can be introduced by the president of the republic and by the members of Congress. A number of other bodies enumerated in the constitution, such as the governments of local communities, can introduce bills that relate to their own matters. The president can veto a law but he or she has to promulgate the law when the veto is overriden by parliament.

The Judiciary

The judiciary is headed by a Supreme Court, acting as the highest judicial body. Below the Supreme Court, superior courts sit in the major cities of the country. Below these rank the Courts of First Instance.

The lowest courts are very important because they administer justice in a local and direct way. They are elected by the people and demonstrate an effort to provide access to state justice for the most remote and almost forgotten settlements. The Peruvian constitution also recognizes special organs of customary jurisdiction in the peasant and native communities that enforce customary law, as long as the fundamental rights of human beings are not violated. Thus the Peruvian legal structure accommodates the legal systems of the indigenous cultures that have maintained rules and principles since ancient times, even in the face of 500 years of European cultural presence. It is a bold effort to counteract Peruvian cultural and social upheaval.

Two other important constitutional bodies are the Academy of Judges, which is in charge of the education and training of judges, and the National Council of Judges, which appoints and dismisses judges and determines their terms of office according to personal evaluations. There are seven members of this council. One is chosen by the Supreme Court, one by the Board of Supreme Public Prosecutors, one by the faculty of the law school, two by other professional schools, one by the presidents of national universities, and one by the presidents of private universities.

The Public Ministry is another important organ of the Peruvian constitution. It is an autonomous entity headed by the national prosecutor. It has a mandate to promote the law and the public interest, to protect the independence of state powers, and to represent the people in court.

Furthermore, there is an autonomous organ called the Defensoría del Pueblo (Council for the Defense of the People), headed by the ombudsperson, who is elected by a two-thirds majority of the Congress. It protects the constitutional and fundamental rights of human beings and of the community and supervises the actions of the state administration and the services it provides the citizens.

THE ELECTION PROCESS AND POLITICAL PARTICIPATION

Any Peruvian citizen over the age of 18 has the right to vote in elections and to be elected. The suffrage is universal and compulsory until the age of 70. Members of the military may not vote.

POLITICAL PARTIES

Peru is a country of leaders and not of parties. Peruvian law has tried to encourage the development of democratic political parties, but a stable party system has not emerged.

CITIZENSHIP

Citizenship is acquired at the age of 18; it is a formal requirement to be registered in the national registry office.

FUNDAMENTAL RIGHTS

The constitution starts by guaranteeing the fundamental rights and freedoms of the human being. It does so in full accordance with the 1948 Universal Declaration of Human Rights, approved in Peru in 1959. It states that protection of human beings and respect for their dignity are the basic purposes of society and the state.

The constitution provides procedural guarantees for human rights, such as the action of unconstitutionality and popular action. All laws, decrees, and individual acts of government that are contrary to the constitution can be annulled. There is a Court of Constitutional Guarantees; the constitution also grants the right to turn to international courts or organizations of which Peru is a member.

Limitations of Fundamental Rights

Peruvian constitutional jurisprudence recognizes that rights and freedoms are limited by the rights of others and by the needs of public order, which is viewed as the fundamental condition for life in society.

ECONOMY

The constitution guarantees the free pursuit of private enterprise within a social market economy under a regime of economic pluralism. It explicitly guarantees the freedom to work and the freedom of enterprise, commerce, industry, and competition. Monopolies and the abuse of leading positions are banned. The right to free hiring is guaranteed. National and foreign investments are placed under the same conditions. Free possession and disposition of foreign currency are protected. The right to property is inviolable, and the state has a duty to protect this inviolability. However, this right can be abrogated as a result of national security or public necessity with a previous compensation payment in cash that includes damages.

RELIGIOUS COMMUNITIES

Until the 1920 constitution, Peruvian identity and Catholicism were synonymous. In accordance with the long history of the Spanish Regio Vicariate, the state considered religion part of its legal competence. The Catholic Church was a state structure, and the clerics were government employees.

The church in effect helped create the Peruvian nation. In the most remote locales, when a Catholic missionary arrived, the Peruvian identity arrived as well; where a church was established, a Peruvian flag was planted. Today, in the multicultural and multiethnic complex reality of Peru, the Catholic religion is a link that unifies the country. Therefore, the state considers it necessary to recognize the church in constitutional law.

Much of this structure lasted until the 1979 constitution, when a regime of autonomy and cooperation was established between state and church. A new agreement between the Holy See and the Peruvian government went into force, as a reflection of its major role in the historical, cultural, and moral formation of Peru.

Under the current constitution, religious freedom and equality coexist with the regime of special cooperation with the Catholic Church. The state respects other religions and can establish forms of cooperation with them. Everybody has freedom of conscience and religion individually or in community with others. There is no persecution due to ideas or beliefs. The public exercise of all faiths is free, unless it offends morality or impacts public order.

MILITARY DEFENSE AND STATE OF EMERGENCY

The president exercises supreme leadership of the armed forces. The armed forces must not take part in political affairs.

The constitution states that all persons and legal entities are obliged to participate in the military defense of the country. The purpose of the army is to guarantee the independence and territorial integrity of Peru. The national police guarantee, maintain, and reestablish internal order.

The president, with the consent of the cabinet, has the power to declare "states of exception": A state of exception must have a definite term, and the president must inform congress of such a declaration. The state of emergency is declared in the case of disruption of peace or public disorder, catastrophe, or other serious circumstances. In these cases, the exercise of several personal rights is suspended. The state of siege is declared in the case of invasion by foreign troops, civil war, or the imminent possibility of such events. In these cases, the rights that are to be suspended must be specifically enumerated.

AMENDMENTS TO THE CONSTITUTION

Amendments to the constitution must be passed by the Congress with a majority of all its members. They must then be ratified by national referendum. The referendum is not needed if the amendment is passed in two ordinary sessions of parliament with the consent in both cases of two-thirds of the members.

PRIMARY SOURCES

Constitution in English. Available online. URL: http://www.idio.int/texts/leg6577.pdf. Accessed on June 27, 2006.

Constitution in Spanish. Available online. URL: http://www.congreso.gob.pe/ntley/ConstitucionP.htm. Accessed on September 21, 2005.

SECONDARY SOURCES

Constituciones políticas de los países del Pacto andino: Bolívia, Colombia, Ecuador, Perú, Venezuela. 2d ed. Bogotá: Secretaria Ejecutiva del Parlamento Andino, 1991.

United Nations, "Core Document Forming Part of the Reports of States Parties: Peru" (HRI/CORE/1/Add.43/Rev.I), 27 June 1995. Available online. URL: http://www.unhchr.ch/tbs/doc.nsf. Accessed on August 1, 2005.

Carlos Valderrama Adriansén

PHILIPPINES

At-a-Glance

OFFICIAL NAME
Republic of the Philippines

CAPITAL
Manila

POPULATION
86,536,700 (2005 est)

SIZE
115,831 sq. mi. (300,001 sq. km)

LANGUAGES
Filipino (Tagalog), English

RELIGIONS
Catholic 83%, Protestant 9%, Muslim 5%, Buddhist and other 3%

ETHNIC COMPOSITION
Malay 95.5%, Chinese 1.5%, other 3%

DATE OF INDEPENDENCE OR CREATION
July 4, 1946

TYPE OF GOVERNMENT
Presidential democracy

TYPE OF STATE
Unitary state

TYPE OF LEGISLATURE
Bicameral parliament

DATE OF CONSTITUTION
February 2, 1987

DATE OF LAST AMENDMENT
No amendment

The Republic of the Philippines is a constitutional democracy. The model of presidential government as well as the comprehensive powers and role of the Supreme Court display a clear similarity to U.S. constitutional law. The similarities root in the colonial history of the country, which after centuries of Spanish sovereignty was governed by the United States for nearly half a century before gaining independence.

That said, the overall constitution is far from being a copy of the U.S. model. Instead, it reveals a strong belief in social engineering and the mandate of the state to steer the development of the economy and society. Furthermore, since overcoming the authoritarian regime of Ferdinand Marcos, the Philippines have become famous for exercising "peoples' power," adding another element to a rather unique constitutional experience.

The president is the dominating political figure. Legislative, executive, and judicial powers are separated. Fundamental rights are guaranteed.

CONSTITUTIONAL HISTORY

The islands of the Philippines were not united as one state before the time of Spanish colonialism. In the pre-Spanish period the typical unit of government in this region was the *barangay,* which was also the word for the boats that carried the early Malay immigrants to the islands. The *barangay* was a unit consisting of about 30 to 100 families, headed by an individual ruler who had executive, legislative, and judicial power. There is evidence of written laws at that time, but information is sparse.

Unification of the islands occurred with Spanish rule, which was established soon after the explorer Ferdinand Magellan "planted the sword and cross" in 1521. During this period the Philippines were administered from afar, first by the Spanish colonial authorities in Mexico, and after 1821 directly from Spain. Whereas most parts of the Philippines were gradually transformed by the influx of Spanish language and culture and by the Roman Catholic state religion, the small Muslim areas, where Spanish control was thin, remained culturally separate.

A constitutional history of the Philippines must begin in the early 18th century, when the colony was for three short periods granted representation in the Spanish Cortes, an early form of parliament. Starting in 1872, drafts for a Philippine constitution were debated, but Spain missed the opportunity for reform. The revocation of Philippine representation in the Cortes combined with other causes sparked revolts at the end of the 19th century. A Filipino nationalism emerged among intellectuals called *illustrados* (enlightened ones).

Revolutionary forces gained control over most parts of the Philippines, declared independence, and convened a constitutional assembly. Drawing on the constitutions of France, Belgium, and to some degree the United States, the assembly promulgated the Malolos Constitution, on January 21, 1899. It was a democratic constitution, emphasizing sovereignty of the people and containing a bill of rights. However, by this time the tide had already turned against the revolutionaries, as Spain ceded the Philippines to the United States in the Treaty of Paris of December 10, 1898. The United States, which refused to accept independence of the Philippines, gained control of the country, using overwhelming military force against the Filipino nationalists.

In the first half of the 20th century, the United States increased self-government in the Philippines step by step: A Philippine assembly convened for the first time in 1907, a Philippine Autonomy Act was adopted in 1916, and a Philippines Independence Act (Tydings-McDuffie Law) was enacted in 1934, providing a precise road map to sovereignty.

The first effective constitution was drafted by a (Filipino) Constitutional Convention and approved by the U.S. Congress in 1935. Using both the U.S. Constitution and the Malolos Constitution of 1899 as sources, it provided for a presidential form of government and contained a bill of rights. This constitution remained in force after independence was attained in 1946, although it was amended in important respects—introducing a bicameral system, decreasing the term of the president, creating an independent Commission on Elections, and guaranteeing certain business rights to U.S. citizens. A constitution adopted under Japanese occupation in 1943 and briefly implemented had no lasting effect on the development of Philippine constitutionalism.

The democratic development of the Philippines was interrupted when the elected president, Ferdinand Marcos, transformed the system into authoritarianism in the early 1970s. In January 1973, shortly after imposing martial law, Marcos held a referendum on a new constitution. The new constitution provided for a unicameral parliamentary system, under which the president was the symbolic head of state with some significant powers but was not head of the executive administration. However, Marcos filled the positions of president and prime minister simultaneously, practicing an authoritarian style of government. The Philippines remained under martial law rule until 1982.

Dissatisfaction with Marcos's leadership and economic crisis led to increasing political oppression in the early 1980s. Disaffection intensified after the assassination of the major opposition politician, Ninoy Aquino, in 1983 and culminated in 1986 after allegedly widespread fraud in the presidential elections. Widespread demonstrations, which took place mainly on one of Manila's main highways, finally forced Marcos to accept an offer of the United States for exile in Hawaii.

The opposition leader, Corazon C. Aquino, was proclaimed the first woman president of the Philippines on February 25, 1986. From the constitutional perspective it is important that the new government did not take office according to the rules of the 1973 constitution. Instead, Aquino declared a revolutionary government; Proclamation No. 3 explicitly stated that "the new government was installed through a direct exercise of the power of the Filipino people assisted by units of the New Armed Forces of the Philippines." Proclamation No. 3 promulgated a provisional "Freedom Constitution." A 48-member Constitutional Commission was charged with drafting a new democratic constitution.

The commission relied on the traditions established by the 1935 constitution, while also undertaking to deal with current problems and reflect recent experiences; its deliberations were widely reported. The new supreme law was approved by a national referendum and took effect on February 2, 1987. It has been in force since, without amendment.

FORM AND IMPACT OF THE CONSTITUTION

The Philippine constitution is a single comprehensive document. In comparison to the short Constitution of the United States, it is an extensive text. It provides for the basic institutions of government and fundamental rights but also contains binding directives for state policies in many fields, thus serving as both basic law and political program.

The constitution is the supreme source of law in the Philippines. Laws and any other state action can be declared void by the Supreme Court if they do not conform to its provisions. As with the traditional U.S. approach, which from the outset strongly influenced Philippine constitutional law, the famous dictum applies: The constitution is what the judges say it is.

BASIC ORGANIZATIONAL STRUCTURE

The Philippines, despite consisting of a great number of islands, has during its constitutional history traditionally mostly been a unitary state without much respect for a vertical balancing of powers. However, the realization of substantial local autonomy is now recognized in the constitution to be basic state policy; the basic structure and functions of local government are outlined in some detail. Further details were provided in the Local Government Code of 1991.

The constitution also provides for "autonomous regions" in Muslim Mindanao and in the Cordilleras, which are given legislative powers in certain fields; this has been put into effect so far only in Mindanao. In this respect, the constitution can be described as an example of asymmetrical federalism, which can also be seen in Tanzania, where Zanzibar has a similar special status.

LEADING CONSTITUTIONAL PRINCIPLES

The constitution does not include a catalogue of leading principles that, could, for example, be protected against amendment. However, Article 2 contains a Declaration of Principles and State Policies. Democracy, republicanism, fundamental rights, social justice, separation of church and state, supremacy of civil authority, control of public powers, local autonomy, and peacefulness in foreign affairs may be identified as leading principles of the constitution. The Constitutional Commission described it colorfully as "pro-life, pro-poor, pro-Filipino, and anti-dictatorship." The president of the commission, Cecilia Muñoz-Palma, said: "This is a nationalist constitution which prohibits foreign military bases beyond 1991, except under certain conditions, and which outlaws the stationing of nuclear weapons on our soil. It carries the mandate for social justice, including land reform and labor rights, beyond the limits of previous constitutions. It empowers the people to amend the constitution and to pass their own laws, if desired. It devolves the powers of imperial Manila to the provinces and cities in over-centralization. It raises family solidarity to the level of a constitutional policy. It demilitarizes the police. By restricting martial law powers, the constitution made this draconian option unattractive for any government."

CONSTITUTIONAL BODIES

The principal constitutional bodies are the president and the administration; the Congress, consisting of the House of Representatives and the Senate; and the judiciary, including a Supreme Court responsible for safeguarding the constitution. Constitutional commissions—the Civil Service Commission, Commission on Elections, and Commission on Audit—are significant as well. The "people" itself may in some respect be seen as a "constitutional body" in the Philippine constitution.

The President

The presidency of the Philippines is the dominant constitutional organ, and the president is usually the dominant figure in the political life of the country. All executive power is vested in the president, who controls all executive departments, bureaus, and offices and acts as commander in chief of all armed forces. The president is elected by direct vote and serves for a six-year term. Candidates must be citizens of the Philippines by birth, residents for at least 10 years at the time of the election, and a minimum of 40 years old.

As a result of the experience of Ferdinand Marcos, who systematically abused and extended his powers as president and prime minister, respectively, the constitutional system of 1987 focuses intensively on controlling the executive. However, in regard to the powers of the president the Supreme Court has opted for a generous interpretation, asserting the existence of "residual powers" not specifically mentioned in the constitution (*Marcos v. Manglapus*, 1989).

The most significant limitation to the presidential office is the strict limit of one term, which is exceptional in comparative constitutional law. During his or her term, the president may be impeached for violating his or her duties. Although this procedure had not been finalized, President Estrada, after allegedly accepting illegal payoffs from the gambling industry, was ousted from office by "people's power" in 2001. The Supreme Court subsequently upheld the legality of the events by interpreting Estrada's behavior as effective resignation (*Joseph Estrada v. Gloria Macapagal-Arroyo*, 2001).

The Executive Administration

Besides the president, who has overall responsibility for the executive branch, there is a vice president, who is directly elected in a separate vote and who therefore may be a member of a different political party. The president nominates the candidates to head government departments and ministries, who form the cabinet. The Commission of Appointments, composed of 24 members of Congress, votes on the nominations. Executive officials must strictly avoid any conflict of interests.

Congress (House of Representatives and Senate)

The Constitutional Commission, after heavy discussion, opted in favor of bicameralism by a vote of 23 to 22. The constitution states: "The legislative power shall be vested in the Congress of the Philippines which shall consist of a Senate and a House of Representatives, except to the extent reserved to the people by the provision on initiative and referendum."

The House of Representatives is the first chamber (lower house) of Congress. It consists of a maximum of 260 members, 208 directly elected and 52 indirectly elected from party lists. Members have to be "natural born citizens" of the Philippines of at least 25 years of age and can serve a maximum of three consecutive terms. They have to disclose all financial and business interests, and they may not serve in any other government or government-related offices during their term. They have a right to a salary to be determined by law and the right to immunity.

The Senate consists of 24 senators, who are selected by direct vote for six-year terms. Candidates have to be natural-born citizens of the Philippines at least 35 years of age; each senator can serve a maximum of two consecutive terms. Individual rights and obligations in office are mostly identical to those of the members of the House of Representatives.

The powers of Congress are classified as follows: (1) general legislative power, (2) specific powers attributed by the constitution, (3) implied powers that are essential or necessary to the effective exercise of the powers expressly granted, and (4) inherent powers that result from sovereignty of parliament. However, Philippine constitutionalism does not follow the English tradition of an absolute parliamentary sovereignty. In recent Philippine history, the congressional powers of impeachment and investigation have played important roles.

The Lawmaking Process

Congress has in an overall view the typical rights and duties of a modern legislature. As the Philippines are not a federal state, there was no need to circumscribe the topics of legislation. Instead, Congress is generally the competent constitutional organ for legislation. In order to ensure appropriate discussion and reflection on the law, three readings in each house are required. Inappropriate "deals" are discouraged by a requirement that each law have only one topic. Thus, the general tendency of the constitution to establish procedures as a guarantee against abuse of power is also applied to Congress.

Other organs can also interfere in the legislative process. The president can use the veto power, which can raise the approval quorum to two-thirds in both houses. Furthermore, the people themselves can use the instruments of initiative and referendum (Article 7, Sections 1 and 32), as another example of Philippines "people power."

The Judiciary

The judicial system of the Philippines is the topic of a specific provision in the constitution. Basically, only the Supreme Court is addressed in this article, and the structure and jurisdiction of the courts in general are subject to special legislation. It is fair to say that the Supreme Court, highlighted as it is in the constitution, is itself a constitutional organ. This characterization is also supported by the precise language used to emphasize the court's role in protecting the constitution.

However, the Supreme Court of the Philippines is not a special constitutional court in the German-Austrian tradition, but in structure a Supreme Court comparable to that of the United States. It consists of a chief justice and 14 associate judges. Similarly to that in the United States the position of a Supreme Court judge is not limited by term, but there is a compulsory retirement age of 70 years. The impact of this court on the constitutional and legal system of the contemporary Philippines is profound. Also in this sense the Philippines are probably the most "American" of the Asian constitutional systems.

"People Power"

It has been academically suggested in the Philippines that the constitution "deinstitutionalizes" democracy by recognizing the right of the people to intervene directly to a significant extent. Perhaps this is an exaggeration, but it is evident that the Philippine constitution contains strong elements of "direct democracy." In this it differs from the model of the U.S. constitution, although some state U.S. constitutions offer some parallels. In the Philippine constitution, "people's organizations" are explicitly embraced as part of the political structure. Furthermore, the people have the power to propose or repeal laws by referendum, to recall local government officials, and to propose amendments to the constitution. All these articles are references to the peaceful revolution by "people power" that paved the way for the current Philippine constitution, some years before such revolutions started to be routine in worldwide constitutional development.

THE ELECTION PROCESS

Suffrage is the topic of a special article of the constitution. All citizens of the Philippines from the age of 18 have the right to vote, as long as they are not disqualified by law. The right to be elected to the Senate or the House of Representatives is restricted to natural born citizens from the age of 35 and 25, respectively. Residency and literacy requirements also apply. Senators are elected by direct vote. In the House of Representatives a fifth of the representatives are elected from party lists on the basis of proportionality; the other members are also elected by direct vote.

POLITICAL PARTIES AND "PEOPLE'S ORGANIZATIONS"

The Philippines do not have an established system of traditional political parties. Political parties were basically the power forums for leading personalities under the two-party system that prevailed between 1946 and 1972, before a one-party system emerged under the domination of Ferdinand Marcos. Redemocratization introduced rediversification of the party political landscape, but parties are still widely considered to be platforms for prominent politicians (including, as in the United States, famous movie stars), rather than programmatic political institutions in their own right.

The constitution does not contain provisions regulating political parties, but it acknowledges in general the importance of an empowered people (civil society) for the political process. The role and rights of "independent people's organizations" are described in some detail. They are defined as "bona fide associations of citizens with demonstrated capacity to promote the public interest and with identifiable leadership, membership, and structure." Their right to participate in social, political, and economic decision making may not be abridged, and Congress is obliged to provide adequate mechanisms for consultation.

CITIZENSHIP

As the Philippines emphasize sovereignty of the country, citizenship is of major importance. However, naturalization after birth does not facilitate political ambitions, as only born citizens may run for Congress or the presidency. Citizenship by birth is based on the principle of *ius sanguinis,* meaning the nationality of mother or father is the relevant factor, rather than place of birth.

FUNDAMENTAL RIGHTS

The protection of fundamental rights can be regarded as one of the central topics of the constitution of the Philippines. It is cited in the Declaration of Principles and State Policies, and it is highlighted via the extensive Bill of Rights; furthermore, social justice and human rights are the subject of additional substantive and procedural regulation.

The Bill of Rights basically consists of classical liberal first-generation rights. The most important single provision is Article 3, Section 1: "No person shall be deprived of life, liberty, or property without due process of law, nor shall any person be denied the equal protection of the laws." A remarkable detail is the equal protection of "the life of the mother and the life of the unborn from conception" (Article 2, Section 12). Also named rights are freedom of speech and assembly, access to bail and legal assistance, public information, freedom from detention without due process of law, and freedom from torture, loss of property without compensation, or religious tests for public offices. The overall purpose of the catalogue of fundamental rights is to protect human beings against the abuse of power. To safeguard the rights such measures as the inadmissibility of evidence and penal as well as civil sanctions are also constitutional guarantees.

Apart from the liberal fundamental rights the constitution provides for many social and economic rights across all sectors, specified especially in Article 13. Social justice is a fundamental value of the constitution, which clearly is intended to be able to justify certain restriction of individual rights of property. The protection of labor, rural and urban land reform, housing, health, and women's rights is part of the attempt to make social justice a reality not only for the wealthy, but also for the large number of poor people in Philippine society. Educational rights, the protection of scientific and artistic activities, and protection of family life are also elements of a comprehensive constitutional framework, which consistently links policy goals with the rights of the individuals concerned. Neither "small fishermen" nor "urban or rural dwellers" are forgotten by the constitution.

Impact and Functions of Fundamental Rights

The fundamental rights have a substantial impact on the legal system of the Philippines. The Supreme Court has the responsibility to decide on the constitutionality of legislation, which includes its conformity to fundamental rights. As preceding constitutions also listed fundamental rights, the Supreme Court can nowadays build on a substantial historical tradition in interpreting fundamental rights, although its history has not been completely successful in the defending (or at least attempting to defend) human rights. The court in its decisions also relies heavily on the jurisprudence of the courts in the United States, especially the federal Supreme Court.

The direct applicability of the Bill of Rights provisions cannot be doubted and the courts act accordingly. Concerning the many social and economic rights there is intensive discussion about the question of the extent to which they are "self-enforcing" and can be directly relied on by the judiciary. The Supreme Court has applied some of these clauses but on the other hand has also emphasized the primary responsibility of the legislature to effect them. Strong dissenting opinions in the relevant Supreme Court decisions indicate the importance of this question to the development of Philippine constitutionalism.

In order to protect fundamental rights, the constitution does not exclusively refer to judicial mechanisms; in recognition of the massive human rights problems under the Marcos regime, it also provides for an independent Commission on Human Rights with substantial investigative, monitoring, educational, and advocacy responsibilities. The Supreme Court has curbed the role of this commission in some respects; it is, however, still an important instrument of constitutional human rights policy. It also plays an important role in the participatory mechanism for human rights planning by governmental and nongovernmental organizations to develop a National Human Rights Plan.

The Philippines have ratified all major universal human rights treaties. Furthermore, the Philippines are the only member of the Association of South-East Asian Nations (ASEAN) to allow individual communications under the first additional protocol to the International Covenant on Civil and Political Rights. It seems noteworthy that this Human Rights Commission shall also monitor the Philippine government's compliance with international treaty obligations on human rights, which is an indication that the constitution's commitment to fundamental rights also encompasses the international sources in this field.

Limitations to Fundamental Rights

As everywhere, personal freedom is not absolute under the Philippine constitution, but is subject to restrictions. Most notably the police power of the state has been a constitutional justification for many minor and major restrictions of personal liberty. The power of eminent domain and taxation additionally provide justification for interference. All these powers are themselves not absolute and entail various limitations. Fundamental rights provisions are explicitly limited in relation to legislative regulation. Somewhat obscurely, the abolition of the death penalty was combined with the authorization of the legislature to reintroduce it; as a result it was reinstated in 1993, but it was again abolished in 2006.

The scope of fundamental rights in real life is practically limited in various regards. Where the constitution provides for social and economic rights, these promises do not extinguish poverty or unemployment. Where it prohibits cruel, degrading, or inhuman punishment, this has not prevented prisons from being extremely overpopulated. Where it guarantees freedom from discrimination, it does not automatically prevent discriminatory activities within private entities, and where it guarantees freedom of expression, it does not prevent a significantly high number of killed or kidnapped journalists. Poverty and violence remain major problems in Philippine society that have not yet been solved by a very ambitious constitutional set of guarantees and policies.

ECONOMY

The constitution of the Philippines contains a lengthy chapter, National Economy and Patrimony, and a wide range of provisions relevant to labor, property, trade unions, and other economics-related subjects. Taken as a whole, the system envisaged by the constitution may be qualified as a social market economy, based on a strong belief in the ability of the state to steer economic development in order to generate wealth and overcome poverty.

A significant characteristic legacy of anticolonial struggles is the protectionist approach ("Filipino First Policy") of the constitution, which provides for discrimination against foreign competitors in practically relevant ways in some of its aspects (*Manila Prince Hotel v. Government Service Insurance System*, 1997). However, the accession of the country to the World Trade Organization has not been blocked on constitutional grounds as a result of this "economic nationalism" (*Tanada v. Angara*, 1997), and in 2004 the Supreme Court strengthened the power

of the legislature to define the details of the extent of a foreign investment policy.

RELIGIOUS COMMUNITIES

The people of the Philippines are predominantly Roman Catholic (more than 90 percent of the population), and the preamble of the constitution implores the aid of the almighty God for the sovereign people. However, religious freedom is guaranteed and the constitution provides, in the tradition of the policy followed since early constitutionalism in the Philippines, for strict separation of church and state. A strong Muslim population has traditionally lived in the south of the country. In Mindanao Muslim law is partly recognized and applied by special Muslim courts to the extent that it does not conflict with constitutional values.

MILITARY DEFENSE AND STATE OF EMERGENCY

The constitution of the Philippines renounces war as an instrument of national policy and describes the role of the military as follows: "Civilian authority is, at all times, supreme over the military. The armed forces of the Philippines is the protector of the people and the State. Its goal is to secure the sovereignty of the State and the integrity of the national territory." The president is the commander in chief of all armed forces. Consequently, in pursuing the approach of not overemphasizing the role of the military, the constitution does not elaborate details in a special article, but only provides for some provisions within the General Provisions in Article 16. Military service in the Philippines is voluntary. The sole power to declare a state of war lies with the Congress, which has to vote on this question with a two-thirds majority in joint session.

Considering the background of years under martial law during the authoritarian regime of Ferdinand Marcos, it is not surprising that the constitution attempts to install safeguards against the illegitimate abuse of emergency powers. The president can still declare martial law, but his or her activities are to be controlled by Congress and—in a proceeding that can be filed by any citizen—by the Supreme Court. In general, the constitution shall not cease to be operative after the imposition of martial law.

AMENDMENTS TO THE CONSTITUTION

In recent history the Philippines have become famous for exercising "people power," ousting first President Ferdinand Marcos in 1986 and then President Josef Estrada in 1999. Both events were accepted by the Supreme Court, the first as justified by revolution, the latter more legalistically as an interpretation of the president's escape as resignation. Considering these events and in addition the "takeover" by Ferdinand Marcos, which also had been accepted by the Supreme Court, it could be argued that constitutional provisions do not play a decisive role when it comes to regime change in the Philippines. Some analysts even argue that the people's right to revolt is accepted by the current constitution, which explicitly acknowledges the sovereignty of the people. It is undeniable, however, that the constitution of the Philippines provides, as do most constitutions in the world, a procedure for its amendment. These provisions demand respect; therefore, it is true from the legal perspective that the constitution can only be amended in accordance with these provisions. When the Supreme Court in 1997 rejected the attempt to amend the constitution in order to allow reelection of President Ramos ("Pirma cases"), one of the judges explicitly declared as a task of the court that it never again be used as a legitimizing tool for those who wish to perpetuate their own power.

The power to amend the constitution lies with the Congress, which must vote with a three-quarters majority in both houses; with a Constitutional Convention; and with a plebiscite. Despite this variety of procedural options for constitutional amendment, the constitution of 1987 has not been amended to date.

PRIMARY SOURCES

Constitution in English. URL: http://www.gov.ph/aboutphil/constitution.asp. Accessed on August 2, 2005.

"The 1998 Constitution (and All Major Historic Constitutional Documents of the Philippines since the Malolos-Constitution of 1899)." In *Constitutionalism in the Philippines,* edited by Rufus B. Rodriguez. Manila: Rex Book Store, 1997.

SECONDARY SOURCES

Joaquin G. Bernas, *The Intent of the 1987 Constitution Writers.* Quezon City: Rex Book Store, 1995.

———, *The 1987 Constitution of the Republic of the Philippines: A Commentary.* Manila: Rex Book Store, 2003.

Teresa Burke, "Philippine Constitution." *Harvard International Law Journal* 28 (1988): 568.

Hector S. De Leon, *Textbook on the Philippine Constitution.* Manila: Rex Book Store, 2002.

Jörg Menzel

POLAND

At-a-Glance

OFFICIAL NAME
Republic of Poland

CAPITAL
Warsaw

POPULATION
38,100,000 (2005 est.)

SIZE
120,728 sq. mi. (312,685 sq. km)

LANGUAGES
Polish

RELIGIONS
Catholic 95%, Christian Orthodox 1.5%, Protestant
0.3%, unaffiliated or other 3.2%

NATIONAL OR ETHNIC COMPOSITION
Polish 96%, German 2.4%, other (largely Ukrainians,
Byelorussians, Lithuanians, Jews, Roma) 1.6%

DATE OF INDEPENDENCE OR CREATION
November 11, 1918

TYPE OF GOVERNMENT
Parliamentary democracy

TYPE OF STATE
Unitary state

TYPE OF LEGISLATURE
Bicameral parliament

DATE OF CONSTITUTION
October 17, 1997

DATE OF LAST AMENDMENT
No amendment

The Republic of Poland, defined as the common good of all its citizens, is a democratic state ruled by law that implements the principles of social justice. The system of government is based on the separation of, and balance among, legislative, executive, and judicial powers. Poland is organized as a decentralized, unitary state. The constitution of the republic provides for guarantees of individual freedoms and rights. In case of an infringement of those rights, there are effective remedies enforceable by an independent judiciary or by a Constitutional Tribunal.

The president is the head of state. The function of the president is mainly representative, and the president does not formulate state policy. The central political figure is the prime minister as head of the executive. The prime minister is politically accountable to the Sejm as the representative body of the people. Free, equal, general, direct, and proportional elections of the members of the Sejm are guaranteed, as is as a pluralistic system of political parties.

Religious freedom is protected. The relationship between the state and the religious organizations is based on the principle of respect for the autonomy and mutual independence of each in its own sphere. The economic system can be described as a social market economy. The armed forces are obliged to observe neutrality in political matters and are subject to civil and democratic control. The Republic of Poland respects international law as binding upon it.

CONSTITUTIONAL HISTORY

The Polish state was established in central Europe in the second half of the 10th century, as a union of the principal Polish Slavic tribes under the baptized Christian ruler Mieszko I of the Piast dynasty. From the 12th until the 14th century, Poland went through a period of feudal fragmentation. In 1385 Poland and Lithuania were united under one crown. After the unification of the kingdom, provincial assemblies composed of the knights of Little and Great Poland emerged. In the year 1493, the first Polish Diet (Sejm) was convened. The laws passed by its deputies were to be observed throughout the entire state. Twelve years later the Polish king accepted the Sejm's *nihil novi* law, which is sometimes considered the country's first constitution. According to this act, in the future nothing new was to be enacted without a joint consensus of the senators and deputies.

In the second half of the 16th century, the nobility decided that the kingship was to be an elected position; the monarch would be elected for life at a general convention. Upon his election each king had to confirm certain basic laws, known as the Henrician Articles and *pacta conventa*, which guaranteed religious tolerance and the right to refuse allegiance to the king, and which banned the imposition of new taxes without the consent of the Sejm.

As a result, the royal power became limited. Nevertheless, in the 17th century the Sejm divided into assorted factions and failed to exploit its strong constitutional position. Its sessions frequently dissolved for procedural reasons, the Sejm gradually disintegrated and the state was seriously weakened.

In 1772 Russia, Prussia, and Austria imposed the first partition of Poland, annexing about 30 percent of Polish territory. Fearing an impending catastrophe, on May 3, 1791, a group of patriotic deputies gathered in the Sejm together with the king to enact the Government Law, which was the first real constitution in Europe. The law created a new legal order in the state, based on the principles of the sovereignty of the nation and the separation of powers. It recognized the Sejm as a legislative and supervisory body and vested executive authority in the king and the Guard of Law (the cabinet of ministers), accountable to the Sejm. The decisions of the king required the countersignature of the appropriate minister.

These reforms constituted the greatest accomplishment in the history of Polish parliamentarianism, but Russia and Prussia reacted quickly. In the course of the next few years, as a result of the second (1793) and the third (1795) partitions, the sovereign state of Poland was erased from the map of Europe for 123 years.

Poland regained its independence in 1918. On March 17, 1921, the Sejm enacted a new constitution, which guaranteed civil liberties and introduced a parliamentary cabinet system. From the legal point of view the March constitution was one of the most modern legislative acts in the contemporary world. However, the political forces were not able to solve the numerous social and ethnic problems inherited from the era of partition. In May 1926, Marshal Józef Piłsudski carried out a military coup d'état. The constitution was amended with the aim of strengthening the executive. This trend culminated with the constitution of April 1935, which rejected the parliamentary cabinet system and considerably extended the powers of the president.

In September 1939, German and Soviet troops attacked Poland. The country was occupied until 1945, but the Polish government in exile continued to operate on the basis of the 1935 constitution. In postwar Poland the Communists seized power, and in 1952, the Sejm passed the constitution of the Polish People's Republic. It established numerous institutions bearing such adjectives as *democratic* or *people's,* but the totalitarian nature of the system was obvious.

The creation of the independent trade union Solidarity in 1980 revived hopes for democratization. They were shattered by the Declaration of Martial Law in December 1981. However, in 1989 Poland became the first post-Communist country to start the process of democratic transformation. The roundtable discussions of government and Communist Party officials, on one side, and the revived Solidarity Trade Union, on the other, led to an agreement on fundamental reform of the 1952 constitution. Partly democratic elections to the Sejm followed, along with completely free elections to the reinstated Senate.

The June 1989 elections were a great success for Solidarity. Candidates from its list won 99 seats of 100 in the Senate and all seats open to democratic competition (35%) in the Sejm. As a result, the democratic opposition was able to form the first non-Communist government in postwar Poland, although the Communist leader, Wojciech Jaruzelski became president.

In December 1989, parliament adopted an important constitutional reform: Poland ceased to be "a socialist state" and became "a democratic state ruled by law." The principle of the leading role of the Communist Party was abolished; in its place, freedom to create and operate political parties was proclaimed. A free market, based on full protection of ownership, replaced the Communist economic system. In 1990 the Solidarity leader, Lech Walesa, was elected president, and in 1991, free elections to both chambers of parliament were held. Further constitutional reforms were gradually implemented, including the so-called Little Constitution of October 1992. On October 17, 1997, a new, comprehensive constitution entered into force; it had been passed by joint chambers of parliament on April 2 that year and subsequently approved by national referendum on May 25.

On May 1, 2004, Poland became a member of the European Union. Poles had high hopes of participating in shaping a prosperous and peaceful future for the continent.

FORM AND IMPACT OF THE CONSTITUTION

Poland has a written constitution, codified in a single document, which is the supreme law of the land. Ratified international agreements are sources of universally binding law of the republic. The law of the European Union has precedence over Polish law.

The constitution of Poland is based on respect for freedom and justice, cooperation among public powers, and social dialogue. The principle of subsidiarity (meaning that the smaller entity should decide as long as it reasonably can) is affirmed, in an attempt to strengthen the powers of citizens and local communities. All laws must comply with the provisions of the constitution. The Constitutional Tribunal controls the constitutionality of statutes and can examine the conformity of all legal enactments with those of higher rank. The present constitution is the expression of modern legal thought; it is also an important tool helping to create a society composed of self-conscious citizens.

BASIC ORGANIZATIONAL STRUCTURE

Poland is a unitary state divided into communes, districts, and *voivodeships* (regions), with the commune the basic unit of local self-government. The *voivode,* who can be seen as a regional president, represents the Council of Ministers locally. Following the principle of decentralization, self-government exists on all levels of territorial division. Local self-government performs public tasks not reserved by the constitution or statutes to the organs of other public authorities. Within the limits established by statute, units of local self-government may set the level of local taxes and charges. Members of a self-governing community may decide matters concerning their community by means of a referendum. Citizens have the right to elect representatives to organs of local self-government and to revoke those organs, which are established by direct election.

LEADING CONSTITUTIONAL PRINCIPLES

The constitution establishes a parliamentary system of government, defined in doctrine as rationalized parliamentarism. There is a balance of the legislative, executive, and judicial powers, with a certain tendency to diminish the dependence of the executive upon parliament, characteristic of a classical parliamentary system. The courts and tribunals, including the Constitutional Tribunal, are independent of other branches of power.

Several leading principles characterize the Polish constitutional system. They are intended to guide the interpretation of specific provisions of the constitution.

According to Article 4, the supreme, sovereign power is vested in the nation, understood as a politically, rather than ethnically, based entity. That power is exercised mostly through the mechanism of elections, but there also exist certain forms of direct democracy, particularly the referendum.

A nationwide referendum may be held to resolve matters of particular importance to the state. A referendum may also be used in amending the constitution or in ratifying agreements on joining supranational organizations. In addition, the constitution provides for the procedure of a people's initiative, by means of which any 100,000 voters may submit a bill to the Sejm.

The principle of a state ruled by law, expressed in Article 7, requires that the organs of public authority function on the basis of, and within, the limits of the law. In a broader sense, it comprises the following attributes: constitutionalism, statutes as fundamental sources of the law, separation of powers, and constitutional regulation of fundamental rights and freedoms. The Constitutional Tribunal has developed several additional rules, including "the principle of citizen's confidence in the State."

The principle of civil society is not formally proclaimed by the constitution. However, basic elements of this concept are present in numerous provisions, particularly those that guarantee political pluralism and protect political parties, trade unions, and other associations. Freedom of the mass media and freedom of conscience and religion are recognized in Poland as constitutive elements of civil society.

The principle of a social market economy is proclaimed in Article 20, which specifies that basic components of that economy are freedom of economic activity, private ownership, solidarity, and dialogue and cooperation among social partners. The right to property and the right of inheritance are protected. Expropriation may be allowed solely for public purposes and for just compensation.

For the first time in Polish constitutional history the principle of the inherent dignity of the person is made explicit. Article 30 reads, "The inherent and inalienable dignity of the person shall constitute a source of freedoms and rights of persons and citizens." The whole system of constitutional norms is subordinated to the realization of this principle.

CONSTITUTIONAL BODIES

The structure of state authorities is established according to the concept of separation of, and balance among, powers. Executive power is vested in the president and the Council of Ministers; legislative power is vested in parliament, composed of the Sejm and the Senate; and judicial power is vested in the courts and tribunals. A number of other organs complete the list, such as the Supreme Chamber of Control, the Commissioner for Citizens' Rights, and the National Council of Radio Broadcasting and Television.

The President of the Republic

The president performs the function of head of state and guarantor of the continuity of state authority. The president ensures observance of the constitution, is the supreme commander of the armed forces, and safeguards the sovereignty and security of the state, as well as the inviolability and integrity of its territory. The president appoints the Council of Ministers after approval by the Sejm.

The president, a Polish citizen who is at least 35 years of age, is elected in universal, equal, and direct elections, for a five-year term of office and may be reelected for only one additional term. The president may be held accountable before the Tribunal of State for an infringement of the constitution or statute or for committing of an offense.

The president promulgates statutes, but before signing a bill may refer it to the Constitutional Tribunal for a ruling on its conformity with the constitution. The president may also refuse to sign the bill and refer it, with reasons given, to the Sejm for reconsideration. If the bill is again passed by the Sejm by a three-fifths majority vote, the president must sign it.

The president represents the state in foreign affairs and ratifies international agreements, in certain cases after prior consent granted by statute. The president formally confers military ranks and appoints judges for indefinite periods on the motion of the National Council of the Judiciary. The president has the right to pardon criminal offenders. In the event of a direct external threat to the state, the president may, at the request of the prime minister, order a general or partial mobilization and deployment of the armed forces in defense of the republic.

The political position of the president is not very strong. Not charged with formulating state policy, the president instead acts as a political arbiter in situations of threats to the constitutional order or when top state authorities have failed to operate properly.

The Council of Ministers

The Council of Ministers is composed of the prime minister and two categories of cabinet ministers. The first category of ministers (or heads of committees specified in statutes) consists of those who direct a particular branch of government administration. The second category comprises ministers who perform tasks assigned to them by the prime minister. Deputy prime ministers may also be appointed. The prime minister plays a leading role, particularly in the process of appointing cabinet ministers and in the construction of the Council of Ministers.

The Council of Ministers conducts the internal affairs and foreign policy of the state. It has the right to initiate legislation, issue regulations, ensure the implementation of statutes, coordinate the work of all bodies of government administration, and conclude international agreements.

The members of the Council of Ministers are collectively and individually responsible to the Sejm. The constitution provides for the so-called constructive vote of no confidence, whereby persons who introduce a draft resolution requiring a vote of no confidence in the council must at the same time propose a candidate for a new prime minister.

The Parliament

The Polish parliament is composed of two chambers, the Sejm and the Senate. The Sejm consists of 460 deputies elected in universal, equal, direct, and proportional elections. The Senate consists of 100 senators elected in universal and direct elections. Members of both chambers are elected for a four-year term of office.

Members of parliament cannot be held accountable for their activity performed within the scope of their mandate either during their term or after its completion. A member of parliament cannot be detained or arrested without the consent of the respective chamber, except in cases when he or she has been apprehended in the commission of an offense. However, even then the marshall (speaker) of the chamber may order an immediate release of the parliament member.

The president's right to dissolve parliament is limited to two situations. The president is obliged to shorten the term of the Sejm in case of failure to form an administration. The president may optionally shorten the Sejm's term of office if it fails to pass the budget bill within four months of its receipt. Apart from this, parliament may dissolve itself as a result of a Sejm decision, leading to new elections. Any shortening of the term of office of the Sejm also entails a shortening of the term of office of the Senate.

The Sejm enjoys a considerably stronger position than the Senate. Only the Sejm adopts bills, although the Senate may propose amendments to them. Control over the Council of Ministers is exercised exclusively by the Sejm. Equal rights are conferred to both chambers only with respect to amending the constitution and ratifying an international agreement to transfer authority to a supranational organization.

The Lawmaking Process

Legislation is the most important task of parliament. The constitution enumerates in Article 87 the sources of universally binding law, among them statutes. According to Polish constitutional doctrine a statute is an act of parliament, which has a normative character and is of the highest rank as a source of law, subordinate only to the constitution, with unlimited scope of regulation. Some matters may be regulated only by means of a statute or only with an explicit statutory authorization.

The right of legislative initiative belongs to the deputies, the president, the Council of Ministers, and the Senate. The Council of Ministers may classify a bill it introduces as urgent, in which case the period for consideration and signing is shortened. The constitution also provides for popular legislative initiative; any group of 100,000 citizens who have the right to vote in elections to the Sejm may introduce legislation. This does not apply to budgetary bills and bills on the amendment of the constitution.

The Sejm considers bills in the course of three readings and passes them by a simple majority vote. A bill passed by the Sejm is submitted to the Senate, which may adopt it outright, adopt it with amendments, or reject it completely. The Senate's rejection or amendments can be overruled by an absolute majority vote of the Sejm in the presence of at least half of the statutory number of deputies.

The president may also reject a bill. The Sejm can overrule a presidential veto with a three-fifths majority. When the president signs a bill, he or she orders its promulgation in the *Journal of Laws*.

The Judiciary

The judiciary in Poland is independent of other branches of government power. Administration of justice is implemented by the Supreme Court, the common courts, administrative courts, and military courts. Extraordinary courts or summary procedures may be established only during a time of war.

Judges are appointed for an indefinite period by the president on the recommendation of the national Council of the Judiciary. They cannot be removed from office and within the exercise of their office are subject only to the constitution and statutes. Judges cannot belong to a political party or trade union; they must not engage in public activities incompatible with the principle of independence of the courts and judges.

The constitution contains extensive guarantees of the rights of defendants in criminal processes, such as the right to defense and presumption of innocence.

The Supreme Court reviews the decisions of common and military courts on appeal. The Chief Administrative Court and other administrative courts exercise control over the performance of the public administration.

The function of constitutional review is performed by the Constitutional Tribunal. It examines the conformity of legal enactments with enactments of higher rank in accordance with a hierarchy of the sources of law specified by the constitution.

The Constitutional Tribunal can act at the request of various authorized bodies. Any court may refer a question of law to it, for a ruling as to whether a normative act conforms to the constitution, a ratified international agreement, or a statute, if the ruling could determine an issue currently examined before that court. The constitution has established the institution known as the constitutional complaint: Any person who believes that his or her constitutional freedoms or rights have been infringed upon can appeal to the Constitutional Tribunal. The complaint must relate to a specific legal provision on the basis of which a court or public body made a final decision against the complainant.

The constitution has also established the Tribunal of State, which adjudicates questions regarding the constitutional accountability of officeholders such as the president, members of the Council of Ministers, and members of parliament.

THE ELECTION PROCESS

All Polish citizens who on the day of an election have attained 18 years of age have the right to vote in that election. Qualification for eligibility depends on the kind of election—18 years of age for elections to local councils, 21 years of age for elections to the Sejm, and 30 years of age for elections to the Senate.

Parliamentary Elections

The constitutional provisions relating to elections are very general and are complemented by election statutes, or *ordynacja wyborcza*. A total of 460 deputies are elected to the Sejm on the basis of proportional representation in multimember constituencies from lists of candidates. Only those lists that have gained at least 5 percent of the total number of votes validly cast nationwide are taken into account in the allocation of seats. The list proposed by the election coalitions is taken into account in the allocation of seats only if it has gained at least 8 percent of the total number of votes cast nationwide. The 5 percent threshold may be waived in regard to election committees of national minorities.

One hundred senators are elected on the basis of majority vote in multimember constituencies.

POLITICAL PARTIES

Poland has a pluralistic system of political parties. The right to form and maintain political parties is among the political freedoms of citizens. According to Article 11 of the constitution, political parties should be founded on the principle of voluntary membership and the equality of Polish citizens. Their purpose should be to influence the formulation of state policy by democratic means. The financing of political parties is open to public inspection.

The constitution in Article 13 forbids political parties whose programs are based upon totalitarian methods and the modes of activity of Nazism, fascism, and communism. The same applies to political parties that sanction racial or national hatred, use violence to obtain power or influence state policy, or maintain secrecy in their membership structure. The Constitutional Tribunal has the authority to ban any party that falls under the Article 13 restrictions.

CITIZENSHIP

Polish citizenship is primarily acquired by birth to parents who are Polish citizens; the principle of *ius sanguinis* is applied. A foreigner who wants to obtain Polish citizenship must live in Poland for at least five years and submit the appropriate application to the president.

FUNDAMENTAL RIGHTS

The constitution defines fundamental rights in its second chapter, immediately after the basic principles of the republic. This precedence reflects the intentions of the framers, who wanted to ensure the superior position of individual rights.

The constitution distinguishes three categories of individual freedoms and rights: personal, political, and economic-social-cultural. The source of all these freedoms and rights is the inherent, inalienable, and inviolable dignity of the person. The protection of individual rights and freedoms is the obligation of public authorities.

The constitution declares that all persons are equal before the law and no one may be discriminated against in political, social, or economic life for any reason whatsoever. Polish citizens who are members of national or ethnic minorities are free to maintain and develop their own language, to maintain customs and traditions, and to develop their own culture.

The constitution adopts as a general rule that anyone under the authority of the Polish state enjoys the freedoms and rights ensured by the constitution. However, some fundamental freedoms and rights are reserved for Polish citizens, such as the right of access to public office and the right to participation in national elections or referendums.

Impact and Functions of Fundamental Rights

According to Polish legal thought, personal and political rights and freedoms are of fundamental importance. Constitutional regulation in this field takes into account international law binding upon Poland, as well as constitutional standards existing in other democratic states. In principle, the state should refrain from interfering with the legally protected autonomy of the individual unless there is a lawful reason to do so. State authorities are bound, however, actively to create adequate institutional guarantees, such as judicial protection, so that the content of constitutional norms is in fact implemented. Among the means for the defense of freedoms and rights, the constitution provides for the individual constitutional complaint and the right to apply to the commissioner for citizens' rights, for assistance in protecting his or her freedoms or rights from infringement by organs of public authority.

More problematic are economic, social, and cultural rights and freedoms. It is often held in constitutional doctrine that because of their programmatic nature, these rights and freedoms are difficult to implement. The framers included this group of rights and freedoms in the constitution but divided them into two categories.

To the first category belong rights that are judicially protected and may be exercised directly on the basis of constitutional norms. This applies to the right of owner-

ship, other property rights, the right of inheritance, the freedom to choose and to pursue one's profession and to choose one's place of work, the right to social security, the freedom to teach, and the freedom to enjoy the products of culture.

The second category of rights and freedoms may be asserted subject to limitations defined by statute. The constitution imposes on public authorities an obligation to pursue specified policies, such as ensuring the ecological security of current and future generations or satisfying the housing needs of citizens.

Limitations to Fundamental Rights

The fundamental freedoms and rights specified in the constitution have certain limits, but any such limitation may be imposed only by statute, and only when necessary in a democratic state for the protection of its security or public order, or of the natural environment, health or public morals, or the freedom or rights of other persons. Such limitations must not violate the essence of freedoms and rights.

Limitations on constitutional freedoms and rights may be imposed in a state of martial law, emergency, or natural disaster. However, the constitution also identifies rights and freedoms that cannot be limited by any statute. These include the dignity of the person, citizenship, protection of life, humane treatment, ascription of criminal responsibility, access to a court, personal rights, freedom of conscience and religion, the right to petition, and the protection of family and children.

ECONOMY

The constitution in Article 20 describes the Polish economic system as a social market economy. The same provision imposes on the state the obligation to mitigate the social effects of market mechanisms.

The economic system must respect rights of different actors who participate in the market, on the basis of comprehensive protection of the right to ownership and freedom of economic activity. The protection guaranteed by the constitution refers to every form of property, and limitations upon the freedom of economic activity may be imposed only by means of statute, and only for important public reasons.

Work is protected and the state is obliged to supervise working conditions. The constitution does not guarantee the right to work but only protects the freedom to choose and to pursue one's occupation and to choose one's place of work. The constitution proclaims the principle that the family farm should be the basis of the agricultural system of the state, but without infringing upon the right to ownership and freedom of economic activity.

The social aspect of the system is visible in such constitutional requirements as solidarity, dialogue, and cooperation among social partners; statutory regulation of minimum wages; and the right to social security whenever one is incapacitated for work by reason of sickness or invalidism, as well as when one reaches the age of retirement.

RELIGIOUS COMMUNITIES

The constitutional status of religious communities in Poland may be defined according to principles enumerated in Article 25. This provision stipulates that churches and other religious organizations have equal rights and public authorities should be impartial in matters of personal conviction. The relationship between the state and churches is based on the principle of respect for their autonomy and the mutual independence of each in its own sphere, as well as on the principle of cooperation for the individual and common good.

With respect to the Roman Catholic Church, Article 25 stipulates that relations between that church and the state should be determined by international treaty concluded with the Holy See. Accordingly, in 1998 Poland ratified the Concordat with the Holy See signed five years earlier.

The relations between the state and other churches and religious organizations are determined by statutes adopted pursuant to agreements concluded between their appropriate representatives and the Council of Ministers. Pursuant to statutory provisions in force citizens are entitled to create religious communities, take part in religious activities and ceremonies, and proclaim their religion or convictions.

MILITARY DEFENSE AND STATE OF EMERGENCY

The principal constitutional obligations of the Polish armed forces are to safeguard the independence and territorial integrity of the state and to ensure the security and inviolability of its borders. In the event of a direct external threat to the state, the president, on request of the prime minister, orders a general or partial mobilization and deployment of the armed forces in defense of the state.

The armed forces must observe neutrality in political matters and are subject to civil and democratic control. The Council of Ministers exercises general control in the field of national defense and annually specifies the number of citizens who are required to perform active military service. Any citizen whose religious convictions or moral principles do not allow him to perform military service may be obliged to perform substitute service.

In situations of particular danger, if ordinary constitutional measures are inadequate, appropriate extraordinary measures may be introduced: martial law, a state of emergency, or a state of natural disaster. Martial law may be declared only in the case of external threats to the state, acts of armed aggression against Polish territory, or an obligation of common defense against aggression that arises by virtue of international agreement. The state of emergency may be introduced in the case of threats to the constitutional order of the state, to the security of the citizenry, or to public order.

The powers of the state bodies remain essentially intact during these periods. Only if the Sejm is unable to assemble is the president authorized to issue regulations that have the force of statute.

AMENDMENTS TO THE CONSTITUTION

A bill to amend the constitution must be adopted in the Sejm by a majority of at least two-thirds of the votes, and in the Senate by an absolute majority of the votes. However, if a bill to amend the constitution relates to principles of fundamental significance for the republic (Chapter 1); the freedoms, rights, and obligations of persons and citizens (Chapter 2); or the amendment procedure (Chapter 12), a confirmatory referendum may be held.

PRIMARY SOURCES

Constitution in English: *The Constitution of the Republic of Poland*. Warsaw: Sejm, 1999. Available online. URL: http://www.sejm.gov.pl/prawo/konst/angielski/kon1.htm. Accessed on June 27, 2006.

Constitution in Polish: *Konstytucja Rzeczypospolitej Polskiej*. Warsaw: Wydawnictwo Sejmowe, 2003. Available online. URL: http://www.sejm.gov.pl/prawo/konstytucja/kon1.htm. Accessed on July 16, 2005.

SECONDARY SOURCES

J. Gutkowski, *The Polish Sejm*. Warsaw: Sejm Publishing Office, 1997.

Polish Constitutional Law: The Constitution and Selected Statutory Materials. Warsaw: Bureau of Research, Chancellery of the Sejm, 2000.

The Principles of Basic Institutions of the System of Government in Poland. Warsaw: Sejm Publishing Office, 1999.

Krzysztof Wójtowicz

PORTUGAL

At-a-Glance

OFFICIAL NAME
Portuguese Republic

CAPITAL
Lisbon

POPULATION
10,356,117 (2005 est.)

SIZE
37,312 sq. mi. (96,631 sq. km)

LANGUAGES
Portuguese

RELIGIONS
Catholic 92.9%, Christian Orthodox 0.22%,
Protestant and other Christian 2.16%, Muslim 0.15%,
Hindu and other non-Christian 0.18%, Jewish 0.02%,
without religion 4.33%, other 0,04%

NATIONAL OR ETHNIC COMPOSITION
Portuguese 96.1%, other (largely Cape Verdean,
Brazilian, Eastern European immigrants) 3.9%

DATE OF INDEPENDENCE OR CREATION
1143 C.E.

TYPE OF GOVERNMENT
Parliamentary democracy

TYPE OF STATE
Centralist state

TYPE OF LEGISLATURE
Unicameral legislature

DATE OF CONSTITUTION
April 2, 1976

DATE OF LAST AMENDMENT
August 12., 2005

The Portuguese constitution of 1976 is the lasting product of the revolution of April 25, 1974, which overthrew the fascist regime that had followed the military coup of 1926 and had interrupted a series of liberal constitutions that began in 1822.

The Portuguese Republic is defined in the constitution as a democratic state based upon the rule of law, the sovereignty of the people, the pluralism of democratic expression and democratic political organization, respect and effective guarantees for fundamental rights and freedoms, and the separation and interdependence of powers. Portugal has as its aims the achievement of economic, social, and cultural democracy and the deepening of participatory democracy.

At the time of its approval, the Portuguese constitution recognized more rights than any other country. They included social, economic, and cultural ·rights, which were harmonized with civil and political rights as far as possible.

The system of government is mixed parliamentary and presidential. The president of the republic and the parliament are separately and directly elected by the people for different terms of office: five and four years, respectively. The president chooses the prime minister with due regard for the results of the parliamentary election, since the government is dismissed if parliament rejects a vote of confidence in its program or approves a motion of censure. The president may dismiss the prime minister and dissolve the parliament, but the administration is autonomous and may initiate legislation. The president does not initiate legislation, but has limited veto power. Political pluralism is ensured by the political parties and by the right of political minorities to form an opposition.

Portugal is a unitary state with two autonomous regions, the archipelagoes of Azores and Madeira. Church and state are separated. The state recognizes international law, interprets human rights in harmony with the Universal Declaration of Human Rights, and may accept limitations on sovereignty imposed by the European Union and the International Criminal Court.

CONSTITUTIONAL HISTORY

Portugal became independent in 1143 C.E., when the emperor of León and Castile recognized the kingdom under Afonso Henriques. There was at first no ethnic or linguistic differentiation from Galicia, which is now part of northern Spain, and a common literature flourished until the 14th century.

The reconquest against the Muslims, who at the time ruled the Iberian Peninsula, was completed with the taking of Algarve in 1267, which gave the state its current boundaries (with minor corrections). The war was a common enterprise of the king, the aristocracy, the clerical leadership, the military orders, and the enfranchised municipalities. It strengthened the royal power and contributed to an early feeling of national identity. This feeling was expressed during the dynastic crisis that followed the death of King Ferdinand through popular support of John I, an illegitimate brother of Ferdinand, against John I of Castile, his son-in-law. After the Portuguese John won the Battle of Aljubarrota (1385), the country concentrated its energies in trade with Flanders and the Mediterranean; in the conquest of Ceuta, Tangier, and Arzila; and above all in the discoveries and consequent trade with the Orient.

The Portuguese state in the Middle Ages was part of Western Christianity as a religious, cultural, and political entity. Afonso Henriques had entered a feudal relationship with the pope as a vassal in 1143; in 1245 Pope Innocent IV deposed the Portuguese king, Sancho II, and passed the kingdom to his brother, Afonso III.

Portuguese discoveries in the 15th century dramatically changed the history of the country and the world. Between 1418 and 1488, the west coast of Africa south of Morocco was systematically discovered, mapped, and opened to world trade. With the rounding of the Cape of Good Hope, the way was cleared into the Indian Ocean. In 1494 the pope divided the world between Portugal and Spain in the Treaty of Tordesillas (1494) for the purposes of trade and expansion. In the following years Portugal established a wide-ranging economic-military-political system with three main strong points (Goa in western India, Ormuz at the entry to the Persian Gulf, and Malacca between the the Indian Ocean and the South China Sea). A string of fortresses was built in ports along the coast of East Africa, the Persian Gulf, and the shores of India and Ceylon. Farther east less fortified settlements were built with the consent of the local rulers from Bengal to China, securing the trade of the Orient to Portugal for nearly a century. The king of Portugal added to his title both shores of the South Atlantic in Africa and America. He navigated, traded, and conquered in Ethiopia, Arabia, Persia, and India.

In 1580, the Portuguese Crown was inherited by King Philip II of Spain, who was accepted as King Philip I of Portugal by the Cortes (the Portuguese parliament, which included nobility, clergy, and commoners). This led to a progressive annexation by Spain. The enemies of Spain became enemies of Portugal. The Dutch, soon followed by English and French ships, put an end to the Portuguese trade monopoly in Asia and even invaded a part of Brazil.

A nationalist revolution in 1640 gave the Crown to John IV, and peace was made with Spain in 1668. To win the war of independence Portugal renewed its traditional alliance with the English monarchy, and Charles II of England married John's daughter, Catherine of Braganza, in return for a large dowry, which included Bombay and Tangier. The decay of the Portuguese empire in the 18th century was somewhat compensated for by the exploitation of gold and diamonds in Brazil.

When the Napoleonic army invaded Portugal in 1807, the Portuguese monarchy was absolute; the king held supreme legislative, executive, and judicial powers. The Crown was the monarch's personal right, inherited from the founder of the monarchy, Afonso Henriques. True, there were fundamental laws of the kingdom that could not be changed except by agreement of the king and the Cortes, including the (apocryphal) Proceedings of the Cortes de Lamego, which recorded ancient custom, and the laws made in the Cortes of 1674, 1679, and 1698 about the institution of the Crown, the regency, and the marriage of princes. But they included nothing about the correlative rights and duties of subject and king and therefore could not be characterized as having the elements of a constitution.

The royal family and court fled from the French to Brazil escorted by English vessels, and an English army landed in Portugal to fight the French. When peace finally ensued, a constitutionalist revolution in 1820 seized power from the English military command, and a constituent assembly was elected and drew up a democratic constitution for the monarchy in 1822. According to this constitution, the sovereignty is vested in the nation, from which the hereditary king receives authority.

King John VI had declared Brazil a kingdom united with Portugal in 1815, and the 1822 constitution endorsed his decision. But after John VI returned to Portugal, his son, Pedro, declared Brazilian independence and became emperor of Brazil in 1822. When John died in 1826, Pedro, as Pedro IV of Portugal, granted the country a constitutional charter providing for a parliamentary regime. His brother, Miguel, launched a civil war from 1828 to 1834 to restore the absolutist regime, but Pedro's charter was later restored, and it remained in force, with a brief interruption by a more democratic constitution between 1838 and 1842, until 1910.

At the end of 19th century, a bad financial situation, combined with national humiliation at the hands of the English over Africa territorial demands, gave momentum to the Republican Party, which established a republic through the revolution of 1910.

The republican constitution of 1911 was clearly individualistic. Its list of liberal rights included prohibition of the death penalty, habeas corpus, equality of all religions, and judicial review. The political system was parliamentary: The bicameral parliament controlled the administration and could not be dissolved. Political life was characterized by weak, short-lived administrations and a continuous repression of the Catholic Church by the state. The Portuguese expeditionary force in World War I was insufficiently supported and was decimated in the Battle of Lys, leading to resentment of the regime in the armed forces. Poverty and structural difficulties in the economy continued unabated.

A revolt in 1926 established a military regime. Professor António de Oliveira Salazar became minister of finance in 1928 and prime minister in 1932. Salazar ushered in a new constitution in 1933, approved by plebiscite and modified in 1945, 1951, 1959, and 1971. The constitution established a "corporative" state with an elected Assembly of the Republic and a Corporative Chamber, which participated in preparing laws and, after 1959, in indirectly electing the president of the republic. The regime was in fact a one-party system and a personal dictatorship, with censorship of published opinion and a strong political police.

Before 1959 the president of the republic was directly elected, and in turn appointed the prime minister. Threatened by the election success of General Delgado in 1958, Salazar changed the constitution to make the election indirect.

The overseas colonies had long been considered provinces of the unitary state of Portugal when nationalist rebellions broke out in 1961 in Angola and later in Guinea and Mozambique. Salazar suffered a brain injury in 1968 and was replaced by Marcelo Caetano, who was unable to change the regime and to put an end to the colonial war. He was deposed by the revolution of 1974.

The revolution of April 25, 1974, began as a bloodless military coup of the secret Armed Forces Movement, which immediately gained widespread support among the people. It was followed by a transitional period until a new constitution was approved and applied. The transition was characterized by social, political, and military turmoil, during which agreements leading to the independence of most of Portugal's old colonies were reached; the very large agrarian estates were expropriated; and banking, insurance, and large industrial enterprises were nationalized (to be privatized only after 1989).

Elections to the Constituent Assembly on April 25, 1975, gave a large majority to a coalition of the Socialist Party (38%) and the Popular Democratic Party (26.4%), which supported a liberal constitution and social democratic policies. The system of government was negotiated by the military (represented by the president of the Revolutionary Council) and the political parties and the Platform of Constitutional Agreement on February 26, 1976, was produced. The constitution was approved on April 2 that year and entered into force on April 25. A transition period, during which the Revolutionary Council maintained political and legislative powers in military matters and controlled violations of the constitution, ended with the amendments of 1982, which created a Constitutional Court and subordinated the armed forces to democratic civil power.

Other constitutional revisions occurred in 1989, 1992, 1997, 2001, and 2004. Perhaps the most important changes were those of 1989, which limited sovereignty as part of the development of the European Union and allowed for the privatization of nationalized property.

The constitution of 1976 was an original document that advanced the definition of the rule of law and especially of the rights of human beings. In this it was influenced by the German Grundgesetz, by the Italian constitution, by the International Declaration of Human Rights, and by the European Convention. The definition of the social, cultural, and economic rights was influenced by the United Nations Covenant and by the Italian constitution, which again influenced the definition of the autonomous regions of Madeira and Azores. The ombudsperson concept was imported from Scandinavia. French *semi-présidentialisme* and preventive control of constitutionality were influential. The economic constitution and the definition of some economic rights may have been influenced by the Programme Commun of the French Left and by Communist constitutions of Eastern Europe, since some of those articles resulted from combined votes of the Socialist and the Communist Parties. It is difficult to identify influences, because almost every proposed article was changed in consequence of discussion.

The Portuguese constitution influenced the Spanish and other later European constitutions, as well as the constitutions of the former Portuguese colonies, which became, with Portugal and Brazil, member states of the Community of the Portuguese Speaking Countries (CPLP).

FORM AND IMPACT OF THE CONSTITUTION

The Portuguese constitution is a single document. Amendments are inserted in their appropriate place through substitutions, deletions, and additions.

The validity of the laws and other actions of the state, the autonomous regions, local governments, and any other public bodies depends upon their compliance with the constitution. Courts may not apply any rules that contravene the provisions of the constitution or the principles contained therein.

The rules and principles of general or customary international law are an integral part of Portuguese law. Rules made by the competent organs of international organizations to which Portugal belongs apply directly in national law to the extent that the constitutive treaty provides. International treaties that are unconstitutional, in substance or form, but have been duly ratified may be applied as part of Portuguese law, provided that the provisions are applied as part of the law of the other treaty party, unless the unconstitutionality arises from the contravention of a basic principle.

The provisions of the treaties instituting the European Union and the norms that emanate from their organs apply internally according to European Union law, with regard to the basic principles of the democratic state under the rule of law. With a view to securing international justice and to promotion of respect for human and people's rights, Portugal accepts the jurisdiction of the International Criminal Court under the conditions established in the corresponding treaty.

Outside the legal domain, the constitution is widely accepted in society and often used as an argument in public discussion—apart from the phrase in the original preamble about the people's decision to open the way to socialism.

BASIC ORGANIZATIONAL STRUCTURE

Portugal is a unitary state that nevertheless recognizes the self-governing system of the islands, the principles of subsidiarity, the autonomy of local authorities, and the democratic decentralization of the public service. The archipelagoes of the Azores and Madeira are autonomous regions with their own political and administrative statutes and their own institutions of self-government. As such, they have the power to legislate, in compliance with the fundamental principles of the general laws of the republic, on such matters of specific interest to the regions as are not within the exclusive powers of parliament or the administration.

Local authorities on the mainland include parishes, municipalities, and administrative regions. Every local authority includes an elected assembly with powers of deliberation and a corporate executive body responsible to it. Local authorities have their own assets and financial resources and may have tax-levying powers, in accordance with the law.

LEADING CONSTITUTIONAL PRINCIPLES

In Article 1 of the constitution, the state is denominated the Portuguese Republic and defined as "a sovereign Republic that is based upon the dignity of the human person and the will of the people and is committed to building a free and just society united in its common purposes." This definition is developed in Article 2, which says that "the Portuguese Republic is a democratic State that is based upon the rule of law, the sovereignty of the people, the pluralism of democratic expression and democratic political organization, and respect and effective guarantees for fundamental rights and freedoms and the separation and inter-dependence of powers, and that has as its aims the achievement of economic, social and cultural democracy and the deepening of participatory democracy." It is therefore possible to distinguish the leading constitutional principles as follows: (1) the republican principle, (2) the rule of law, (3) the democratic principle, and (4) the social justice principle.

The republican principle includes negatively the repudiation of any form of monarchy, autocracy, or dicta-

torship and of hereditary or other privileges, offices, or honors that are not equally accessible to all citizens on a basis of merit, election, or luck—but not money. The republican ideal is linked positively to the sovereignty of the people and to the principles of equality, liberty, pluralism, autonomy, participation, solidarity, and responsibility that contribute to the configuration of other principles.

The rule of law governs the operations of all state institutions and their relations to each other and to individuals, but it is also defined as including the fundamental rights and freedoms and their judicial guarantees. One of these is the right of each party in a judicial process to appeal to the Constitutional Court by invoking a violation of the constitution.

The laws are hierarchically ordered according to the bodies that created them. The rule of law thus also includes the principle of constitutionality of all state acts, including laws and constitutional changes. Constitutionality presupposes the existence of legislative and constitutional reservations, that is, of matters that can only be ruled by laws (for example, crimes and punishments, taxation, and other restrictions on rights) or by the constitution (for example, the powers of government organs). The principle of legality presupposes the separation of legislative, executive-administrative, and judicial powers, and their interdependence. For example, laws must be promulgated and can be vetoed by the president of the republic, who can also involve the Constitutional Court on questions of their constitutionality. The overall reason for the principle of separation and interdependence of powers is the protection of rights. Rights, in a broad sense, and the human dignity ensured by them, are the supreme content and justification of the rule of law.

The democratic principle is developed through the different ways of ensuring the sovereignty of the people: that is, the supremacy of the will of the people in the resolution of national and local problems. These ways may be expressed by subprinciples, such as the majoritarian principle (collective decisions are made by majority of votes), the principle of suffrage (power holders are chosen through universal, equal, direct, secret, and periodic elections), the principle of political participation (all citizens have the right to hold public office and to contribute to the formation of political will, either directly through referendum and popular initiatives or indirectly through representatives associated in political parties), and the principle of political pluralism (both majority and minorities may express themselves and associate, and the minority has the right to opposition).

The social justice principle expresses the constitution's goals of achieving economic, social, and cultural democracy and deepening participatory democracy. In this context, the constitution recognizes individual and collective economic, social, and cultural rights. The state has the duty to promote the welfare and quality of life of the people and actual equality between Portuguese in their enjoyment of economic, social, cultural, and environmental rights (welfare state principle). The social program of the constitution has some normative content; according to the jurisprudence of the Constitutional Court, no institution aimed at social justice can be eliminated without substituting another with the same scope.

Churches and religious communities shall be separated from the state and are free to determine their own organization and to perform their own ceremonies and worship.

CONSTITUTIONAL BODIES

The constitutional bodies that have supreme authority (organs of sovereignty) are the president of the republic (and the Council of State), the Assembly of the Republic, the administration, and the courts.

The President of the Republic

The president of the republic represents the Portuguese Republic and guarantees the independence of the nation, the unity of the state, and the proper functioning of democratic institutions. He or she also is commander in chief of the armed forces.

The president has the power to dissolve the Assembly of the Republic, to appoint the prime minister, to dismiss the administration under certain conditions, to grant pardons, and to commute sentences, after receiving the opinion of the administration.

The president of the republic has the authority to promulgate and publish laws, decree laws, and regulative decrees and to sign resolutions of the Assembly of the Republic approving international agreements and the other decrees of government. The president has the power to ask the Constitutional Court to review the constitutionality of laws, decree laws, and international conventions.

Within 20 days of receiving a draft law approved by the assembly, or after the Constitutional Court rules that the draft is constitutional, the president of the republic must either promulgate the law or ask the assembly, on the basis of substantial grounds, to reconsider it. If the assembly confirms its vote by an absolute majority of the members entitled to vote—or by two-thirds of the deputies present in certain matters—the president must promulgate the law.

With respect to international relations, the president has the power to declare war in the case of actual or imminent aggression or to make peace, on the proposal of the administration, after receiving the opinion of the Council of State and with the authorization of the Assembly of the Republic.

The president of the republic is elected for a term of five years of office by universal, direct, and secret suffrage. Portuguese citizens who are entitled to vote and are at least 35 years of age are eligible for election. Any president who has served two consecutive terms must wait at least five years before seeking another term.

The Council of State

The Council of State advises the president of the republic, who presides over its meetings. It consists of the president, the president of the Assembly of the Republic, the prime minister, the president of the Constitutional Court, the ombudsperson, the presidents of the regional governments, former presidents of the republic, five citizens appointed by the president of the republic for the period corresponding to the president's term of office, and five citizens elected by the Assembly of the Republic, by a system of proportional representation, for the period corresponding to the legislative term.

The Assembly of the Republic

The Assembly of the Republic is the representative body of the people. Deputies are expected to represent the whole country, rather than the electoral district for which they were elected.

The assembly has the powers to amend the constitution, to enact legislation on any subject other than those in the exclusive powers of the administration, to delegate to the administration power to legislate, and to approve international agreements. The assembly has authority to keep the administration and the public service under review. Members of the administration must attend prearranged sessions to answer questions or receive requests for information from deputies.

The assembly debates the administration's program and can vote on motions of confidence or censure. A vote of no confidence or censure leads to the dismissal of the administration.

The Assembly of the Republic has not fewer than 180 and not more than 230 deputies, as provided in the electoral law. The legislative term lasts for four years.

Deputies are not subject to civil, criminal, or disciplinary proceedings in respect of their voting or opinions expressed in the performance of their duties. They may not testify at a trial or be a defendant and may not be detained or arrested without the permission of the assembly. Permission shall be obligatory when there is strong evidence that a serious crime has been committed.

The Lawmaking Process

Legislation includes laws, decree laws made by the administration, and regional legislative decrees. Laws and decree laws have equal force, subject to the subordination of decree laws published under legislative authority and those that develop the basic principles of the legal system. Both require promulgation by the president of the republic, as described previously.

The power to initiate laws lies with deputies, parliamentary groups, the administration, and groups of electing citizens. The power to initiate laws in the autonomous regions lies with the appropriate regional legislative assembly.

The Administration

The administration conducts the general policy of the country and is the highest organ of public administration. The prime minister is appointed by the president of the republic on the advice of the parties represented in the assembly and with due regard for the results of the general election. The other members of the administration are appointed by the president of the republic on the recommendation of the prime minister.

The administration has legislative powers: to make decree laws on matters not within the exclusive powers of the assembly, to make decree laws on matters delegated to it by the assembly, and to make decree laws amplifying laws that state basic principles of the legal system. The administration has exclusive legislative powers in matters concerning its own structure and operation. The administration also has power to make regulative decrees necessary for the proper enforcement of the laws. Decree laws and regulative decrees must be promulgated by the president of the republic.

The administration is dismissed when the assembly rejects its program, fails to support a motion of confidence, or supports a motion of censure. The president of the republic may, after hearing the opinion of the Council of State, dismiss the administration when necessary to safeguard the proper functioning of democratic institutions.

The Judiciary

The courts are independent and subject only to the law. There are the following categories of courts, in addition to the Constitutional Court: the Supreme Court of Justice and the courts of law of first instance and of second instance, which have general jurisdiction in civil and criminal matters; the Supreme Administrative Court and other administrative and fiscal courts; and the Court of Audit. Maritime courts, arbitration courts, and judgeships of peace may be established.

The Constitutional Court has the specific power to administer justice in matters involving questions of constitutional law. It is composed of 13 judges, 10 chosen by the Assembly of the Republic; each candidate must receive the support of two-thirds of those voting (provided that amounts to an absolute majority of deputies). The remaining three judges are chosen by the first 10. Six of the 13 members must be judges; the remainder must be lawyers. Judges of the Constitutional Court hold office for nine years and cannot be reappointed. The president of the republic may ask the Constitutional Court to review the constitutionality of any provision of any law or decree he or she has been asked to promulgate.

Such a ruling may also be requested by the ombudsperson, the attorney general, one-tenth of the assembly deputies, or other authorities specified in the constitution. The court may also make such a ruling on its own initiative after three identical decisions of the court on individual appeals. The court may also overturn laws or decrees on grounds that they violate superior law and may invalidate regional laws that it believes exceed the limits of legislative authority of the national or regional authorities. All the Constitutional Court's rulings are generally binding.

The Constitutional Court also has jurisdiction to hear constitutional appeals against lower court decisions. In any case, appeals may only be made on questions of the unconstitutionality or illegality of the law. The appealed court, if censured, must then review the facts of the case on the basis of the decision of the Constitutional Court.

The Constitutional Court also has the authority to decide whether there has been a failure to enact legislation that is necessary to implement the constitution. The initiative for such a ruling must be that of the president of the republic, the ombudsperson, or, in a case when the rights of an autonomous region have been contravened, the presidents of the regional legislative assemblies.

Finally, the Constitutional Court controls the constitutionality and legality of referendums, is the supreme electoral court, decides appeals against loss of parliamentary seats or appeals related to elections in the Assembly of the Republic, and has certain powers of control over political parties (verifying the legality of their constitutions, dissolving them, reviewing their financial accounts, and deciding appeals from internal disciplinary and other decisions). The latter powers have been added through constitutional amendments or laws and demonstrate the high regard the Court enjoys.

The decisions of the Constitutional Court have had considerable impact on the legal, political, and social life of the country and contribute to making the constitution a living element in the public sphere. The court has managed to show evenhanded restraint; for example, it ruled that a referendum on abortion could proceed, as either outcome would be constitutional. It has also shown boldness; for example, it overturned a minimal age limit of 25 for receiving income benefits, proclaiming a right to a minimal living standard based on the principle of respect for human dignity.

THE ELECTION PROCESS AND POLITICAL PARTICIPATION

All citizens over the age of 18 have the right to vote and to be elected. The elections are conducted in accordance with the principle of proportional representation.

Binding referendums may be called by the president of the republic on the proposal of the assembly or the administration. A referendum may also be held on the initiative of citizens. The only subjects for a referendum are matters of national interest otherwise lying within the authority of the assembly or the administration—that of the approval of laws or international conventions. Amendments to the constitution may not be submitted to a referendum.

All citizens have the right to submit, individually or jointly with others, petitions, representations, claims, or complaints to any authority. They must be informed, within a reasonable time, of the result of the claim. Everyone, personally or through associations, enjoys the right of *actio popularis,* to help prevent, suppress, or prosecute offenses against public health, consumer rights, the quality of life, the preservation of the environment, and the cultural heritage.

POLITICAL PARTIES

The political parties are the means to organize and express the will of the people. They are obliged to respect the principles of national independence, the unity of the state, and political democracy.

Political parties that are represented in the assembly but not in the administration have the right to be informed regularly and directly by the government on the progress of the principal matters of public interest. All political parties must register with the Constitutional Court, which reviews their constitution and their finances and has the power to dissolve them, especially if they adopt a fascist ideology.

CITIZENSHIP

Portuguese citizens are all persons who are regarded as such by Portuguese law or international conventions. According to nationality law, individuals born in Portugal are Portuguese citizens; there are also ways of acquiring citizenship by application.

FUNDAMENTAL RIGHTS

The Portuguese constitution recognizes a very comprehensive set of fundamental rights, including liberties or negative rights against the state; rights of political participation; economic, social, and cultural rights that characterize a social state; and fourth-generation rights, such as the right to a good environment. The constitution distinguishes three categories: personal rights, freedoms, and guarantees; rights, freedoms, and guarantees of political participation; and rights, freedoms, and guarantees of workers. Other economic, social, and cultural rights are also recognized.

In principle, aliens and stateless persons temporarily or habitually resident in Portugal enjoy the same rights and are subject to the same duties as Portuguese citizens. This does not apply to political rights, to the performance of nontechnical public functions, or to rights and duties explicitly restricted to Portuguese citizens. Citizens of Portuguese-speaking countries may, by international convention and provided that there is reciprocity, be granted rights not otherwise conferred on aliens, except the right to become president of the republic, president of the assembly, prime minister, or president of a supreme court, or to serve in the armed forces or in the diplomatic service. Provided that there is reciprocity, the law may confer upon aliens who reside in the national territory the right to vote for and to stand for election as members of the organs of local authorities.

Impact and Functions of the Fundamental Rights

The constitutional provisions relating to rights, freedoms, and guarantees are directly applicable to, and binding on, both public and private entities. It is a basic responsibility of the state to guarantee fundamental rights and freedoms.

Limitations to Fundamental Rights

In a provision (Article 18) adopted from the German constitution, the Portuguese constitution states that rights, freedoms, and guarantees may be restricted by law only in matters expressly provided for in the constitution, and only to the extent necessary to safeguard other rights or interests protected by the constitution. Laws restricting rights, freedoms, and guarantees must be general and abstract in character, must not have retroactive effect, and must not limit the essential content of the right in question.

ECONOMY

The so-called economic constitution within the Portuguese constitution covers 38 articles, including an entire section on economic organization, and chapters on workers rights, liberties, and guarantees and economic rights. Such a comparative weight is due to the revolutionary context of the first version. However, the constitutional amendments of 1982 and of 1989 have eliminated the socialist trend of the first version, especially the irreversibility of nationalizations.

Among the basic principles of economic organization are the coexistence of public, private, cooperative, and social sectors in the ownership of the means of production; freedom of business initiative and organization; and government economic plans in the framework of a mixed economy. These principles are linked to the aim of achieving economic democracy, as an element of the social justice principle of the constitution.

RELIGIOUS COMMUNITIES

Freedom of conscience, religion, and worship is inviolable. The right to conscientious objection is guaranteed according to law, not only in respect of military service but also in general. This is an important innovation in constitutional history, introduced by amendment in 1982.

Churches and religious communities are separate from the state, are free to determine their own organization, and are permitted to perform their own ceremonies and worship. The separation of churches from the state is a basic principle that cannot be changed through constitutional amendment.

MILITARY DEFENSE AND STATE OF EMERGENCY

The armed forces are obliged to obey the civilian authorities. They have the responsibility to provide military defense of the republic, to satisfy the country's international obligations of a military character, and to participate in humanitarian and peace missions undertaken by the international organizations that include Portugal. The armed forces may be used to perform civil protection missions, to help meet basic needs, to improve the quality of life of the people, and to support technical and military cooperation initiatives.

A state of siege or a state of emergency may be declared in all or any part of the national territory, but only in the event of actual or imminent aggression by foreign forces, of serious threat to or disturbance of the democratic constitutional order, or of a public disaster. A declaration of a state of emergency or a state of siege must in no case affect the rights to life, personal integrity and identity, civil capacity, and citizenship of the person; the nonretroactivity of criminal law; the defense rights of accused persons; and the freedom of conscience and religion. A declaration of a state of siege or a state of emergency may not affect the powers and operation of the organs of sovereignty and of self-government of the autonomous regions, nor the rights and immunities of their members.

The constitutional amendment of 1997 removed the requirement of compulsory military service. A 1999 law put peacetime military service on a voluntary basis. The right to conscientious objection is a fundamental right.

AMENDMENTS TO THE CONSTITUTION

The Assembly of the Republic may revise the constitution five years after the date of the previous amendment. It may also, by a majority of four-fifths of all deputies, assume special powers to revise this constitution at any time. Amendments must be approved by a majority of two-thirds of all deputies.

No amendments can change national independence and the unity of the state; the republican form of government; the separation of the churches from the state; the rights, freedoms, and guarantees of citizens; the rights of workers, workers' committees, and trade unions; the coexistence of public, private, cooperative, and social sectors in the ownership of the means of production; the role of economic plans within the framework of a mixed economy; universal, direct, secret, and regular suffrage for the election of members of the organs of sovereignty, the autonomous regions, and local government and a system of proportional representation; pluralism in expression and political organization, which shall include political parties and the right of democratic opposition; separation and interdependence of the organs of sovereignty; judicial review of norms for positive unconstitutionality and unconstitutionality by omission; independence of the courts; autonomy of local authorities; and political and administrative autonomy of the archipelagoes of the Azores and Madeira.

PRIMARY SOURCES

Constitution in English and in Portuguese. Available online. URLs: http://www.parlamento.pt/ingles/cons_leg/crp_ing/index.html; http://www.parlamento.pt/const_leg/crp_port/index.html. Accessed on August 22, 2005.

Constitution in English: *Constitutions of Europe: Texts Collected by the Council of Europe Venice Commission.* Vol. 2. Leiden/Boston: Martinus Nijhoff, 2004.

Portuguese Constitution in Portuguese (official publication): "Lei Constitucional no. 1/2004 de 24 de Julho." *Diário da República* 1 série-A, 24, no. 7 (2004): 4,650–4,693.

SECONDARY SOURCES

Kenneth R. Maxwell and Scott C. Mouge, eds., *Portugal: The Constitution and the Consolidation of Democracy 1976–1989.* New York: Camões Center Special Report 2, 1991.

Howard J. Wiarda and Margaret McLeish Mott, *Catholic Roots and Democratic Flowers: Political Systems in Spain and Portugal.* Westport, Conn.: Praeger, 2001.

José de Sousa e Brito

QATAR

At-a-Glance

OFFICIAL NAME
State of Qatar

CAPITAL
Doha

POPULATION
840,290 (2004), 80% noncitizens

SIZE
4,399 sq. mi. (11,437 sq. km)

LANGUAGES
Arabic

RELIGIONS
Sunni Muslim 77%, Shiite Muslim 16%, Hindu or
other 7%

NATIONAL OR ETHNIC COMPOSITION
Qatari 20%, South Asian 33%, other Arab 25%, Iranian
17%, other (Europeans, Japanese, Americans) 5%

DATE OF INDEPENDENCE OR CREATION
September 3, 1971

TYPE OF GOVERNMENT
Constitutional hereditary monarchy

TYPE OF STATE
Unitary state

TYPE OF LEGISLATURE
Unicameral Advisory Council

DATE OF CONSTITUTION
April 19, 1972 (provisional)
June 8, 2004 (ratification)
June 9, 2005 (in force)

DATE OF LAST AMENDMENT
No amendment

The emirate of Qatar is a constitutional, hereditary monarchy. The emir is head of state and has in the past enjoyed almost absolute authority. Since 1995, Qatar has undergone a process of political transformation initiated by the new emir, Sheikh Hamad bin Khalifa Al Thani, aimed at modernizing the state apparatus and implementing the rule of law. A permanent constitution, which was accepted in a public referendum in 2003 and ratified in June 2004, went into force on June 9, 2005, replacing the provisional constitution from 1972.

The political system of Qatar does not, and will not, include political parties. Free elections took place for the first time in 1999, when the Central Municipal Council was formed.

The law is based on Islamic principles.

Qatar's national income is primarily derived from oil and natural gas exports. Qatar is a social welfare state; however, social welfare provisions do not apply to the huge number of non-Qatari, who make up some four-fifths of the population.

CONSTITUTIONAL HISTORY

The Al Thani family has ruled the Qatar peninsula since the late 19th century. Threatened by the Ottoman Empire, the emir of Qatar signed a protection agreement with the British in 1916. After the withdrawal of the British military forces from east of Suez in 1968, a plan for a federation emerged, uniting Qatar with Bahrain and seven other states of the region. During the federal negotiations, Qatar drafted a provisional statute, which was promulgated on April 2, 1970. After independence in 1971, the statute was revised; a provisional constitution was developed and entered into force on April 19, 1972. It provided for the confirmation of the Al Thani family as the ruling dynasty, the establishment of a Council of Ministers, and the creation of an Advisory Council. The Advisory Council, the function of which was to advise the ruler on legal and financial matters, was established in 1972.

After the 1990–91 Gulf crisis, leading citizens demanded wider participation in political affairs. Political liberalization did not, however, begin until the new emir, Hamad bin Khalifa Al Thani, ascended to power in 1995. He set up a committee in 1999 to draft a permanent constitution. Accepted in 2003 via public referendum and ratified by the emir in 2004, the new permanent constitution took effect on June 9, 2005.

FORM AND IMPACT OF THE CONSTITUTION

The permanent constitution (ad-dustur) is codified in a single document. It provides for public participation in governance for the first time in Qatari history. Although this participation is limited, it is hoped to have a future impact on internal control mechanisms and help overcome troubled alliances within the large Al Thani family. The Advisory Council still has only modest powers. Any progress toward democracy will require constitutional revisions to expand parliamentary power.

BASIC ORGANIZATIONAL STRUCTURE

Qatar is a constitutional, hereditary monarchy with a centralized government.

LEADING CONSTITUTIONAL PRINCIPLES

Qatar's political system is described as democratic (Article 1). The constitution provides for the separation of powers, whereby executive and legislative powers remain largely under the authority of the emir while the judiciary is independent. The Islamic sharia is a principal source of legislation, although it is not the only source.

The people of Qatar see themselves as belonging to the Arab nation (al-umma al-arabiyya).

CONSTITUTIONAL BODIES

The predominant bodies provided for in the constitution are the emir, the Council of Ministers, the Advisory Council, and the judiciary.

The Emir

The emir is head of state. Assisted by the Council of Ministers and the Advisory Council, he holds both executive and legislative power. The emir is also commander in chief of the armed forces and minister of defense.

Rule in Qatar is hereditary in the reigning Al Thani family. According to the permanent constitution, power is to be handed down from father to son. In the event that the reigning emir is no longer able to act as such, the Council of the Ruling Family makes this fact public.

The Council of Ministers

The Council of Ministers (Majlis al-Wuzara) is the highest executive organ. It controls internal and external affairs in accordance with the constitution and the law, proposes draft laws to the Advisory Council, and administers the finances of the state.

The emir appoints all ministers including the prime minister. Currently 11 ministers are in office, including one female minister. Ministers can be removed from office with a two-thirds majority vote of the Advisory Council.

The Advisory Council

The Advisory Council (Majlis as-Shura) is the legislative body. Laws are debated in the council; government policy and the budget need its approval. Resolutions of the Advisory Council are passed by an absolute majority of the members in attendance. Council sessions are open to the public.

Council members have a four-year term of office. According to the new constitution, two-thirds of the 45 council members are elected by direct, general, and secret ballot, and one-third is appointed by the emir.

The council can remove a minister with a two-thirds majority vote. This can be difficult to reach if the appointed members vote to retain the minister, because all of the elected members must then vote for the removal.

The emir can dissolve the Advisory Council, but he must justify this act, and the council cannot be dissolved twice for the same reason. When it is dissolved, the election for a new council must take place within six months. Until a new council is elected, the emir, with the assistance of the Council of Ministers, holds the power of legislation.

The Lawmaking Process

The Advisory Council debates draft laws proposed by the Council of Ministers. A law takes force after it has been ratified by the emir and promulgated via publication in the official gazette. If the emir refuses ratification, the law is returned to the Advisory Council. Should the Advisory Council pass the bill again with a two-thirds majority, the emir is obliged to ratify it.

The Judiciary

The judiciary acts independently.

Qatar had a dual court system up until 2004, in which the Islamic sharia courts and the civil courts (mahakim al-adliyya) had different functions. The sharia courts were under the jurisdiction of the Ministry of Awqaf and Islamic Affairs, while the civil courts, according to codified law, were supervised by the Ministry of Justice.

With the new judicial system introduced in 2004, all courts were united under one judicial body. A court of cassation (final appeal), a court of appeal, and a court of first instance were formed. A Supreme Judicial Council, presided over by the head of the court of cassation, was established. The Supreme Judicial Council is now the highest authority in the judiciary of Qatar.

In early 2005 Qatar set up a Shiite personal law court. The new constitution makes no provision for court restrictions on executive authority.

THE ELECTION PROCESS

All citizens of Qatar, male and female, have the right to vote in elections at age 18 and to stand for election at age 30.

POLITICAL PARTIES

Qatar does not have organized political pluralism. Political parties do not exist.

CITIZENSHIP

Qatari citizenship is patrilineal: The child of a Qatari father acquires citizenship by birth.

FUNDAMENTAL RIGHTS

The permanent constitution defines public rights and duties. It guarantees equality before the law regardless of sex, race, language, or religion. Personal freedom, freedom of expression, freedom of assembly, and freedom of the press, of printing, and of publication are guaranteed in accordance with the law.

Impact and Functions of Human Rights

Since the process of political transformation in Qatar only began in 1999, judging the impact of newly established rights is difficult. However, the individual liberties anticipated for Qatari citizens seem in the process of fulfillment. In May 2004, for example, a law permitting the introduction of trade unions was passed.

Limitations to Fundamental Rights

The constitution distinguishes between basic rights for all and special rights for citizens. Only those who have Qatari citizenship enjoy freedom of assembly and the right to establish organizations. The same is true of free access to education.

Most special rights, such as freedom of the press, are guaranteed only in accordance with the law. The founding of the satellite television channel Al Jazeera in 1996, for example, was a significant step in the direction of genuine freedom of the press and has had an enormous local and translocal impact. However, as with other media in Qatar, criticism of the ruling family is still strictly avoided.

ECONOMY

The permanent constitution does not stipulate a particular economic system. The state guarantees freedom of economic enterprise based on social justice and balanced cooperation of private and public activity. It further encourages investment, providing the necessary guarantees and facilities.

RELIGIOUS COMMUNITIES

Freedom to practice religion is guaranteed. Religious communities do not have explicit rights.

MILITARY DEFENSE AND STATE OF EMERGENCY

According to Article 71, the emir can declare a war of defense; a war of aggression is prohibited. He can also declare martial law in a state of emergency, but that declaration must be approved by the Advisory Council.

AMENDMENTS TO THE CONSTITUTION

The permanent constitution can be amended only by a two-thirds majority of the Advisory Council. Certain fundamental provisions, such as the hereditary rule and functions of the emir, cannot be changed. Furthermore, no article of the permanent constitution may be proposed for amendment within 10 years of entry into force.

PRIMARY SOURCES
Constitution in English. Available online. URL:http://english.mofa.gov.qa/details.cfm?id=80. Accessed on June 27, 2006.
Constitution in Arabic. Available online. URL: http://www.mofa.gov.qa/details.cfm?id=206. Accessed on July 16, 2005.

SECONDARY SOURCES
Nathan J. Brown, *Constitutions in a Nonconstitutional World: Arab Basic Laws and the Prospects for Accountable Government.* Albany, N.Y.: State University of New York Press, 2002.
———, *The Rule of Law in the Arab World: Courts in Egypt and the Gulf.* Cambridge: Cambridge University Press, 1997.
Michael Herb, "Parliaments in the Gulf Monarchies: A Long Way from Democracy." *Arab Reform Bulletin* 2, no. 10 (2004): 7.
Rosemarie S. Zahlan, *The Making of the Modern Gulf States.* Reading, U.K.: Ithaca Press, 1998.

Bettina Gräf

ROMANIA

At-a-Glance

OFFICIAL NAME
Romania

CAPITAL
Bucharest

POPULATION
21,680,900 (2005 est.)

SIZE
92,043 sq. mi. (238,391 sq. km)

LANGUAGES
Romanian

RELIGIONS
Orthodox 86.8%, Catholic 4.7%, Protestant 4.7%,
other 3.8%

NATIONAL OR ETHNIC COMPOSITION
Romanian 89.5%, Hungarian 6.6%, Roma 2.5%,
German 0.3%, Ukrainian 0.3%, other 4.2%

DATE OF INDEPENDENCE OR CREATION
December 1, 1918

TYPE OF GOVERNMENT
Semipresidential democracy

TYPE OF STATE
Unitary state

TYPE OF LEGISLATURE
Bicameral parliament

DATE OF CONSTITUTION
December 8, 1991

DATE OF LAST AMENDMENT
October 19, 2003

Romania is a semipresidential republic, founded on the principles of democracy, the rule of law, and division of powers. It is a unitary state, divided into 40 administrative entities. The constitution is a written document that guarantees fundamental human rights.

The head of state is the president, elected by equal, universal, and direct vote. The legislative branch is represented by parliament, which is bicameral.

State and church are separated in Romania. The economic system can be described as an emerging market system.

CONSTITUTIONAL HISTORY

In Romania, the constitution appeared later than in other European countries, such as France or Italy.

For centuries, the Romanian territories were under Ottoman domination. During the 18th century, after a series of treaties, Romanian entities obtained the right to trade freely, which facilitated the flourishing of capitalism.

An important moment in constitutional history was the unification of two Romanian territories—Muntenia and Moldova—in 1859, under the rule of Alexandru Ioan Cuza. Cuza initiated a reform process and, in 1864, two documents were adopted—Cuza's Statute and the electoral law—that together represented the first Romanian constitution. According to the statute, the ruler (*domnitorul*) and a bicameral parliament exercised state powers. The statute dealt with the lawmaking process and the operations of government. The electoral law attached to the statute specified electoral rights and regulations and eligibility to vote and stand for office.

Cuza abdicated in February 1866, and the German prince Carol of Hohenzollern-Sigmaringen was designated to rule the country. A constitution was adopted the same year. It regulated issues such as the Romanian territory, the rights of Romanians, the powers of the state, finances, and the army. Special attention was given to the right to property, which was considered sacred and inviolable. The legislative power was collectively exercised by the king and the legislature, which comprised a Senate and a Chamber of Deputies. The executive power rested with the ruler. The 1866 constitution was amended several times and remained in force for over half a century.

The second half of the 19th century was characterized by industrial development and agricultural reform. In terms of political evolution, an important event was the independence war of 1877, which gained Romania recognition as a sovereign state. At the end of World War I (1914–18), after the dissolution of the Austro-Hungarian and Russian Empires, Transylvania, Bukovina, and Bessarabia became part of Romania. A new constitution was needed to sanction these changes.

This new constitution was adopted in 1923 and represented a liberal project. Although similar in many respects to its predecessor, the 1923 constitution was more democratic, as it guaranteed wider rights and freedoms, especially electoral ones.

The historical circumstances of the year 1938 triggered the imposition of a royal dictatorship by King Carol II, who imposed a new constitution, subjected to plebiscite on February 24 and promulgated a few days later. The most important change was the concentration of state powers in the hands of the king, who was declared "head of the state" and was given both legislative and executive powers. The universal vote was abolished.

In 1940, King Carol II was forced to abdicate in favor of his son. The new constitution was suspended, the legislature dissolved, royal prerogatives reduced, and the president of the Council of Ministers was vested with full dictatorial powers. In 1944, as Romania faced defeat in World War II (1939–45), the constitution of 1923 was partially reinstated. Several normative acts of a constitutional nature were adopted in the next few years, with the aim of reinforcing democratic rule.

On December 30, 1947, the monarchy was abolished and a republic proclaimed. As a consequence, the constitution of 1923 was abrogated, and in April 1948 a new constitution was adopted. It characterized Romania as a unitary, independent, and sovereign state, emerging from the fight of the people against fascism and imperialism.

The new constitution stipulated that all powers emanated from and belonged to the people; as a consequence all natural resources and communication media were declared public property. Article 11 created the legal framework for the subsequent nationalization of the economy, by stipulating that the means of production, banks, and insurance companies in private hands could become state property when required by the general interest.

Between 1948 and 1952, Romanian economic life was revolutionized under pressure from the Soviet military occupation. A new constitution, adopted in September 1952, regulated both the state power and the national economy. Three social-economic modes were recognized: socialist, small merchandise production, and capitalist.

The state was reorganized along Leninist principles of centralism. Article 80 put an end to political pluralism, as Romania became a one-party state.

The next decade was characterized by the dissolution of private property and the strengthening of the leading role of the Communist Party. In 1965, another constitution was adopted. It maintained the principle of a single-party state but also enumerated fundamental rights and obligations of citizens.

The revolution of December 1989 generated fundamental changes in Romanian society and triggered radical constitutional reform. In 1991, a new constitution was adopted and approved by referendum. It was amended in 2003 and is currently in force. Romania's new polity is based on principles such as the republican form of government, the division of powers, the rule of law, political pluralism, the bicameral structure of parliament, freedom and democracy, respect for human rights, and the responsibility and removability of those who hold government power.

FORM AND IMPACT OF THE CONSTITUTION

Romania has a written constitution, which consists of a single document. It takes precedence over national law as well as over the treaties ratified by the parliament. Therefore, in order to prevent situations of noncompliance with Romania's international obligations, a treaty that is contrary to the constitution can be ratified only after a constitutional amendment.

The constitution has a significant impact in Romanian society, given that all the other laws must comply with it.

BASIC ORGANIZATIONAL STRUCTURE

Romania is a unitary state; it has one constitution, one system of laws, one parliament, one head of state, and a single judicial system with nationwide jurisdiction.

The territory is divided into 40 territorial-administrative entities called counties (*judete*). Each has an elected county council, competent to decide upon local issues.

LEADING CONSTITUTIONAL PRINCIPLES

According to Article 1 of the constitution, Romania is a democratic and social state, governed by the rule of law, in which human dignity, citizen's rights and freedoms, the free development of human personality, justice, and political pluralism represent supreme values. These values are said to be guaranteed in the spirit of the democratic traditions of the Romanian people and the ideals of the revolution of December 1989.

The leading constitutional principles are the rule of law, the democratic and social state, and the division of powers. The rule of law sets limits on the power exercised by the government. In other words, in Romania no one is above the law; free access to justice has a crucial role.

Romania is a democratic state where legitimacy of the public authorities is based on the will of the people, as revealed by free and fair elections. Among other characteristics of the Romanian state one can include a pluralist political system, the political responsibility of the government to parliament, and the independence of the judiciary.

In Romania, education, public health, and social protection are fundamental values guaranteed by the constitution. Public education is free of charge. Moreover, the state grants scholarships to children or young people of disadvantaged families. Similarly, the state is committed to take the necessary measures to ensure public hygiene and health. Last but not least, the state promotes economic development and social protection with a view to ensuring a decent living standard for the people. Citizens have the right to pensions, paid maternity leave, medical care in public health centers, unemployment benefits, and other forms of public social security and assistance.

The state is organized on the basis of the principle of the separation and balance of powers—legislative, executive, and judicial—within the framework of constitutional democracy.

CONSTITUTIONAL BODIES

The most important constitutional bodies are the parliament, the president, the administration, the judiciary, and the Constitutional Court.

The Parliament

The parliament, the supreme representative body of the Romanian people and the sole legislative authority of the country, exercises political control over the executive. It is bicameral, consisting of a Chamber of Deputies and a Senate. Both chambers are elected by universal, equal, direct, secret, and free suffrage for a term of four years.

Article 72 grants members of the two chambers parliamentary immunity; they cannot be held judicially accountable for the votes cast or the political opinions expressed while exercising their office. Deputies and senators can only be prosecuted by the prosecutor's office attached to the High Court of Cassation and Justice and cannot be searched, detained, or arrested without the consent of their chamber and only after they are heard.

The Lawmaking Process

Making laws is the most important function of the parliament. In theory, parliament is the sole legislative au-

thority in the country; in practice, however, it shares this function with the executive, which has legislative initiative, as do the administration and citizens.

The administration exercises this initiative by introducing bills to whichever chamber has the right to decide first on the bill as indicated in the constitution. The chamber has 45 days to debate and adopt the bill. For codes and other complex laws, the time limit is 60 days. If the time limit is exceeded, the draft law is deemed adopted. After the first chamber adopts or repeals the draft law, it is submitted to the other chamber, which makes the final decision.

Once a law has been adopted by parliament, it is submitted to the president of the republic to be promulgated within 20 days. The president can return the law to the parliament for reexamination, but he or she may do so only once. After promulgation, the law is published in the *Official Gazette of Romania* and takes force three days after the publication or on a subsequent date specified in its text.

The President

The president of Romania is the head of state and is elected by universal, equal, direct, secret, and free suffrage. This process confers a special political status: as representative of the Romanian state in international relations, protector of national independence, and guardian of the constitution and of the proper functioning of public authorities. The president also acts as a mediator between the state powers as well as between state and society.

The term of office of the president used to be four years. Starting with the presidential elections of 2004, the term of office is five years.

The president designates a candidate for the office of prime minister and appoints the rest of the administration after a vote of confidence in parliament. The president promulgates the laws and concludes international treaties negotiated by the government. The president is also the commander in chief of the armed forces. Among other powers, the president appoints civil servants, including judges, and grants individual pardons for criminal offenses.

The Administration

The administration consists of the prime minister and the ministers. Its role is to ensure the implementation of the domestic and foreign policy of the country and exercise general management of public administration. The candidate for the office of prime minister is designated by the president, but in order for the administration to be appointed, parliament must pass a vote of confidence on its program and its members. Only the parliament can dismiss the government; it does so by a vote of no confidence.

The Judiciary

In Romania, justice is administered by the High Court of Cassation [final appeal] and Justice and the other courts set up in conformity with the law. The right to appeal a judicial decision before a higher court is guaranteed.

According to Article 124 of the constitution, judges are independent and subject only to the law.

The Constitutional Court is charged with guaranteeing the supremacy of the constitution. It consists of nine judges appointed for a term of office of nine years. Its main role is to decide the constitutionality of laws. The court can be asked to decide a matter by an ordinary court, at the request of one of the parties or on its own initiative.

One of the most important decisions the Constitutional Court has made regarded the fundamental right of access to justice. The court interpreted the provisions of the Code of Criminal Procedure as guaranteeing the right of the interested party to challenge a decision of the prosecutor before the court, even though the code did not stipulate such a right or provide procedures for such a challenge.

THE ELECTION PROCESS AND POLITICAL PARTICIPATION

Every citizen at least 18 years old has the right to vote for the president, members of the parliament, and local authorities (mayors and members of county and local councils). Article 36, however, denies the vote to mentally deficient persons, declared as such by a final court decision, and convicted felons, who are temporarily deprived of their electoral rights.

In order to stand for elections, candidates must have the right to vote and have their domicile in Romania. Those officials who are not allowed to join a political party—judges of the Constitutional Court, people's advocates, magistrates, active members of the armed forces, police, and certain other civil servants—cannot stand for office unless they resign from their post. Persons younger than 23 years old cannot be elected to the Chamber of Deputies; the cutoff age is 33 for the Senate and 35 for the presidency.

The Chamber of Deputies and the Senate are elected in districts, by universal, equal, direct, secret, and freely expressed suffrage, on the basis of a party list system and independent candidatures, according to the principle of proportional representation. The electoral threshold is 5 percent of the votes for political parties and between 8 percent and 10 percent for political alliances formed of two or more political parties.

POLITICAL PARTIES

According to Article 8 of the constitution, political pluralism represents a condition and a guarantee of constitutional democracy in Romania. Political parties contribute to the definition and expression of the political will of the people. However, not all political views can be freely ex-

pressed; Article 40 stipulates that political parties that, by their aims or activity, militate against political pluralism, the rule of law, or the sovereignty, integrity, or independence of Romania are unconstitutional. The unconstitutionality of a political party can only be determined by the Constitutional Court.

Political parties have four main sources of financing: membership fees, donations, income generated by party activities, and public funds.

CITIZENSHIP

Romanian citizenship is primarily acquired by birth. The principle of *ius sanguinis* prevails. A child is a Romanian citizen if at least one of his or her parents is a Romanian citizen. The child's birthplace, and the parents' residence, are not relevant.

FUNDAMENTAL RIGHTS

The Romanian constitution defines fundamental rights extensively in its second chapter (Articles 15–54), Fundamental Rights, Freedoms and Duties. It recognizes several categories of rights. The first are generically called "Inviolabilities"; they ensure respect for life, freedom of movement, and physical and psychological safety. This category also includes the interdiction of torture and inhuman or degrading treatment, the interdiction of the death penalty, the right to individual freedom and safety, the right to defense and representation in court, and respect for one's private life, family life, and domicile.

The second category includes the so-called social and economic rights, which are designed to ensure the social and material conditions of life including education. They include the right to study, the right to health protection, the right to work, the right to certain social conditions of work, the right to strike, the right to property, the right to marriage, the right to a healthy environment, the right to decent living conditions, and the right of children and disabled persons to special social protection.

A third category includes exclusively political rights, which may only be exercised by Romanian citizens, for the purpose of governing the country. These include the right to vote, the right to be elected, and the right to be elected to the European Parliament.

The fourth category consists of social and political rights and freedoms that are needed by citizens for the purpose of governing or achieving their social and spiritual goals. These rights include freedom of conscience, freedom of expression, the right to information, freedom of association, the right to assembly, and the inviolability of correspondence.

The fifth category consists of two fundamental rights known as guarantee rights: the right to petition and the right of a person injured in the exercise of his or her fundamental rights by a public authority to obtain reparation.

The Romanian constitution also contains, in Article 18, the right to asylum. This grants certain foreign citizens or those without any citizenship the right to live in the country.

A general equal treatment clause contained in Article 16 guarantees that all persons are equal before the law and public authorities. It also includes some specific equality provisions, such as the equality of men and women and the interdiction of discrimination.

These fundamental rights and freedoms stem from several international instruments to which Romania is a party, such as the Universal Declaration of Human Rights. In fact, Article 20 states that the rights provisions in the constitution must be interpreted in accordance with the Universal Declaration of Human Rights and other treaties to which Romania is a party. In case of a difference between the constitution and the treaties, the latter are to prevail, unless the Romanian constitution or law is more favorable than the international law, it which case it is applied.

Impact and Functions of Fundamental Rights

In the Romanian constitutional system, fundamental rights are primarily defensive rights, which imply the nonintervention of the state in the exercise of the right. However, the state also has a positive obligation to create the necessary legal and administrative means to ensure the proper exercise and protection of these rights.

Fundamental rights apply not only in relations between individuals and state authorities but also in those between individuals. Inviolabilities such as the right to physical integrity or the respect of one's private life, family life, and domicile must be upheld in all circumstances.

Limitations to Fundamental Rights

Article 49 of the Romanian constitution lists cases in which the exercise of a right or freedom can be limited. However, the limitation must be made via an explicit law and can be imposed only for the purpose of protecting national security, order, public health and morals, the rights and freedoms of others, and criminal investigation or of responding to natural hazards or disasters.

The enumeration is limitative and cannot be extended. Furthermore, the restriction of the right or freedom is submitted to certain conditions: Namely, any restriction must be necessary to the functioning of a democratic society (a criterion largely developed by the European Court of Human Rights), proportional with the situation that has generated it (the principle of proportionality), and nondiscriminatory, and it must not affect the very existence of the right or freedom.

The Romanian constitution does not contain provisions aimed at punishing the abuse of fundamental rights. However, there are a number of internal laws, such as the Civil Procedure Code or the Penal Code, that contain interdictions and punishments for certain types of rights abuse.

ECONOMY

The Romanian constitution specifies, in Title 4, Economy and Public Finances, that Romania has a market economy founded on independent entrepreneurial initiative and free competition. The state is obliged to guarantee free trade, protect against unfair commercial practices, and create circumstances favorable to the improvement of living standards.

The right to property and the right to inheritance are mentioned in the chapter concerning fundamental rights, as are the right of assembly and the right to form trade associations, both crucial to a market economy. Private property and public property enjoy equal protection. Expropriation is limited by strict conditions such as just reparation. Nationalization on the basis of discriminatory criteria is forbidden. To prepare for membership in the European Union, recent amendments to the constitution allow persons who have foreign citizenship or no citizenship to own and inherit land in Romania.

In sum, Romania can be said to have an emerging market economy.

RELIGIOUS COMMUNITIES

Freedom of religion or belief is guaranteed as a human right, as are the rights of religious communities. State and church are separate, and there is no established state church. Religious communities are independent of the state, but they enjoy support through chaplaincies in the army, hospitals, penitentiaries, asylums, and orphanages.

Dominant religions, by number of adherents, are the Orthodox and Catholic Churches.

Religious communities enjoy financial independence from the state and conduct their activity on the basis of collections from the adherents. In order for them to benefit from state funds, a government decision must be issued with this purpose. Religious communities administer their activities according to their own statutes, which must, however, respect applicable laws.

MILITARY DEFENSE AND STATE OF EMERGENCY

Military service is one of the elements included in Chapter 3, Title 2, of the Romanian constitution, Fundamental Duties. Citizens can be subject to military conscription between the ages of 20 and 35. Since the revision in 2003, the Romanian constitution no longer conceives military service as compulsory for men. Both men and women may volunteer for military service.

Romania has obliged itself, as party to international treaties, not to produce atomic, biological, or chemical weapons.

A state of defense or state of emergency is declared by the president, who must submit the declaration for the approval of the Parliament within five days. If Parliament is not in session, it must be convened and must continue to work throughout the state of defense or state of emergency.

During these states, the exercise of some fundamental rights and freedoms can be restricted upon agreement from the minister of justice. The restrictions must be in strict proportion to the needs of the situation.

The ministry of internal affairs coordinates the measures taken during these periods. Civil authorities essentially maintain their powers intact but also gain new responsibilities related to the state of defense or emergency.

AMENDMENTS TO THE CONSTITUTION

The Romanian constitution can be amended on the initiative of the president, the administration, at least one-quarter of the number of deputies or senators, or 500,000 citizens who hold the right to vote.

The draft of the amendment must be adopted by the Chamber of Deputies and by the Senate by a majority of at least two-thirds of the number of members in each chamber. It must also be approved by the citizens, through a referendum held no later than 30 days from the date of passing the draft.

No amendment can be made to any constitutional provision affecting the national, independent, unitary, and indivisible character of the Romanian state; its republican form of government; its territorial integrity; its official language; the independence of its judiciary; or its political pluralism. Likewise, no revision shall be made if it results in the suppression of citizens' fundamental rights and freedoms, or of the safeguards thereof. The constitution also cannot be revised during a state of siege, emergency, or war.

PRIMARY SOURCES

Basic Law in English. Available online. URL: http://www.ccr.ro/default.aspx?lang=EN. Accessed on September 12, 2005.

Basic Law in Romanian: *Constituția României*. Bucarest: All Beck, 2003. Available online. URL: http://www.cdep.ro/. Accessed on August 10, 2005.

SECONDARY SOURCES

Patricia Ionea, "Free Access to a Court—Special Aspects Arising from the Case-Law of the Constitutional Court and of the European Court of Human Rights." *Constitutional Court's Bulletin* no. 7 (May 2004). Available online. URL: http://www.ccr.ro/default.aspx?page=publications/buletin/7/ionea. Accessed on February 6, 2006.

Cristian Ionescu, *Instituții Politice și de drept constituțional*. Bucharest: Economica, 2002.

Ioan Muraru, *Drept Constituțional și Instituții Politice*. Bucharest: Actami, 1998.

Nicolae Popa, "The Constitutional Court of Romania, Twelve Years of Activity, 1992–2004: Evolutions over the Last Three years." *Constitutional Court's Bulletin* no. 7 (May 2004). Available online. URL: http://www.ccr.ro/dcfault.aspx?page=publications/buletin/7/popa. Accessed on February 6, 2006.

Vladimir Tismaneau and Gail Kligman, ed., "Romania after the 2000 Elections." *East European Constitutional Review* 10, no. 1. (2001). Available online. URL: http://www.law.nyu.edu/eecr/vol10num1/index.html.

Laurentiu D. Tanase, Ruxandra Pasoi, and Ioana Dumitriu

RUSSIA

At-a-Glance

OFFICIAL NAME
The Russian Federation, or Russia

CAPITAL
Moscow

POPULATION
145,200,000 (2005 est.)

SIZE
137,821 sq. mi. (357,021 sq. km)

LANGUAGES
Russian

RELIGIONS
Christian Orthodox 50%, Muslim 13%, Buddhist 1.5%, Jewish 0.5%, unaffiliated or other 35%

NATIONAL OR ETHNIC COMPOSITION
Russian 79.8%, Tatarian 3.8%, Ukrainian 2%, Bashkirian 1.2%, Chuvash 1.1%, other (about 155 nationalities) 13.3%

DATE OF INDEPENDENCE OR CREATION
June 12, 1990

TYPE OF GOVERNMENT
Presidential democracy

TYPE OF STATE
Federal state

TYPE OF LEGISLATURE
Bicameral parliament

DATE OF CONSTITUTION
December 12, 1993

DATE OF LAST AMENDMENT
June 6, 2001

The Russian Federation is a democratic, federal, law-based state with a republican form of government. All citizens of Russia have the right to participate in forming the country's legislature, the Federal Assembly, and to elect its head of state, the president of Russia, by free democratic elections.

The Russian state is a federation uniting 89 entities: 21 republics, six territories, 49 regions, two cities of federal importance, 10 autonomous areas, and one autonomous region. The governmental bodies of the federation carry out their powers within the limits set up by the constitution. At the same time, significant powers are exercised directly by federal bodies: the president, the Federal Assembly, and the executive administration. The president has extensive powers, heads the system of government bodies, and is the guarantor of the observance of the federal constitution. The president is the central political figure in Russia.

Russia is an emerging democratic state. All modern political rights and forms of participation, such as free-dom of speech, assembly, processions, and demonstrations, are given to all Russians, who may use them to influence state internal affairs.

Russia has a multiparty system. Religious freedom is guaranteed, and state and religious communities are separated. The Russian economic model can be characterized as a market economy subject to bureaucratic intervention by the state. Russia has military forces, whose supreme commander is the president. The military doctrine of Russia has a defensive character, combining adherence to world peace with a firm determination to protect national interests and to guarantee the military safety of Russia and its allies.

CONSTITUTIONAL HISTORY

Most historians see Russian history as beginning in the mid-ninth century. However, the history of the Russian *people* began much earlier. Their ancestors the Slavs have been present in Europe since antiquity.

Russian annals say that the Slavs who lived to the north of Novgorod were constantly at odds among themselves and invited Scandinavian Varyags (Vikings) to install order. It is doubtful whether there is historical truth to this; in any case, Vikings invaded many countries without invitation. The historical fact is that Rurik, the famous Varyag leader, entered the area with his forces, occupied Novgorod, and reigned from 862. This event is conventionally considered to be the foundation of the Russian state.

At the beginning of the 10th century Prince Oleg united the separate Slavic states, including Novgorod and Kiev, in an association of Slavic tribes called Kievskaja Rus. Kiev, "mother of Russian cities," became the center of the country. Under Prince Vladimir, Kievskaja Rus accepted Orthodox Christianity from the Byzantines in 988, and the blossoming of the Kievan state began.

During this feudal era, Russia faced continuous struggle against its neighbors. In the 13th century a Mongolian nomad state called the Golden Horde appeared in East Asia. In 1235, Mongolian armies led by Khan Batyj appeared in the Ural Mountains. After defeating the Volga Bulgars and destroying their capital, the nomads turned to Russia, destroying and burning cities and inflicting immense losses on the population. The following year, Khan Batyj moved against the Kievskaja Rus; Kiev was burned in 1240. The Mongolian yoke remained over Russia for about two centuries, influencing the course of all subsequent Russian history.

During the Mongolian occupation, Kievskaja Rus lost its former strength. The little-known city of Moscow became the power center of Russia thanks to the skillful politics of the Moscow princes. By the end of the 14th century, the Moscow state had become so strong that Grand Duke Dimitry Donskoy was able to oppose the Golden Horde openly. Donskoy inflicted a decisive defeat on the armies of Khan Mamaj in 1380 on the Kulikovo field, near the river Don. According to historians, the Moscow state was born on the Kulikovo field.

In 1480, Ivan III refused to render tribute to the Mongolians. Soon after that, the Golden Horde fell apart and Mongolian power in Russia ended. The grandson of Ivan III, Ivan IV (The Terrible), accepted a new title, czar and grand duke of all Russia. Ivan's rule marked the beginning of a new period in the development of Russian statehood: a monarchy tempered with representation for the nobility. After Ivan's death Russia was ruled de facto by the boyar (high-ranking noble) Boris Godunov, who, after the death without issue of Ivan's son, Feodor, was elected the new czar by the Zemskiy Sobor, the representative body of Russia. The first years of his rule were successful, but after 1600, chaos reigned during a 13-year Time of Troubles. Polish forces took advantage of this anarchy, and in 1610 they occupied Moscow. In 1612, the Russian national militia freed Moscow, where in 1613 representatives of the Russian people gathered from all regions of the country and elected Michael Romanov czar via the Zemskiy Sobor. The house of Romanov ruled Russia for the next 300 years.

In 1689, Peter I acceded to the throne. He transformed the backward Moscow state into the Russian Empire, which entered the family of European states as a great power. Through many wars, he won control of the east coast of the Baltic Sea. In 1721 he proclaimed himself czar of all Russia; at that moment the Russian state became an absolute monarchy. The most significant reforms were actually carried out by Catherine II (1762–96) and Alexander II (1855–81). Catherine decentralized the empire and established the beginning of local self-government; Alexander abolished serfdom, introduced local self-government in the zemstvas (regions) and cities, and carried out judicial reform.

The crucial reform of the regime of absolute monarchy took place early in the 20th century under the pressure of ceaseless revolutionary activity. By the Manifest of October 17, 1905, Czar Nicholas II gave legislative powers to the newly created legislative body, the State Duma. Together with the State Council created earlier by Alexander I, the legislature had been formed in Russia. The position of prime minister was also created.

In February 1917, in the third year of World War I (1914–18), famine in Saint Petersburg led to disorder. Up to 200,000 soldiers stationed in the city, and now opposed to the war, joined workers in a revolt. The czar and his government were arrested and replaced by the so-called Provisional Government formed by deputies of the State Duma. Thus, Russia became a bourgeois-democratic republic.

However, thanks to indecision and inaction in the Provisional Government, the influence of the radical Communists (Bolsheviks) increased significantly. In mid-October 1917 the Bolsheviks under Vladimir Lenin launched their own revolution. On October 25 they arrested all members of the Provisional Government and, facing hardly any resistance, occupied all governmental agencies in Saint Petersburg. Thus, the authority of the Soviets (Bolshevik-controlled workers' councils) was established in Russia. When the Bolsheviks lost nationwide elections to the Constituent Assembly, they disbanded the body by force and fashioned their own institutions.

The first constitution of Russia was passed in 1918, for the Russian Soviet Federative Socialist Republic (RSFSR). It declared the sovereignty of the Russian state, the class domination of workers and peasants (under Communist Party leadership), and the establishment of a socialist regime. During the next 70 years, new constitutions were adopted three times (1925, 1937, and 1978) for Russia.

The same also happened for the Union of Soviet Socialist Republics (USSR) in 1924, 1936, and 1977. This federal union was formed in 1922 after Russia reconquered various parts of the old Russian Empire and set up local soviet republics. Each new constitution proclaimed a new stage of development of the Soviet state and ostensibly established new foundations for human rights and new state mechanisms to defend the interests of the people. However, typical of all the Soviet constitutions was the monopolistic power of the Communist Party, Marxist ideological context, and the denial of the internationally recognized principle of the difference and interaction between state and society.

All Soviet constitutions had a fictitious character: Human rights were proclaimed, but were never realized in practice. This tension inevitably led to a crisis in Soviet constitutional doctrine, which began in the 1980s. The answer to this crisis was a declaration by the first Congress of People's Deputies of the RSFSR of June 12, 1990, On the State Sovereignty of the RSFSR. This was rapidly followed by the collapse of Soviet society and the Soviet state, and the rapid disintegration of the USSR.

In 1993, President Boris Yeltsin started the process of drafting a new constitution. In a situation of sharp sociopolitical confrontation, the Communist-dominated Supreme Soviet of Russia blocked all attempts to pass the new constitution. On September 21, in contradiction to the norms of the 1978 constitution, Yeltsin dissolved the Congress of People's Deputies of Russia as well as all Soviet government bodies. On December 12, 1993, the people adopted the new constitution, opening a new period in the history of the political system of Russia.

FORM AND IMPACT OF THE CONSTITUTION

Russia has a written constitution, codified in a single document. The supremacy of the constitution and of federal laws throughout the territory of Russia is the legal expression of the country's sovereignty. The constitution has a dual legal nature: It is the law of the federation, regulating the conduct of its territorial subunits, and it is the law of the society established by the people, aimed at protecting society from an arbitrary state.

The federal constitution and laws, by virtue of their predominance, do not require any endorsement by the various subunits of the federation; they apply directly in all of the territory of the state. Hence, if any local laws or other legal actions of the territorial members of the Russian Federation conflict with the constitution of Russia or with federal laws, all courts and administrative bodies are obliged to apply the federal constitution and federal laws directly.

Russia is a founding member of the United Nations Organization and a permanent member of its Security Council.

BASIC ORGANIZATIONAL STRUCTURE

Russia is a federation with 89 territorial members that are equal in rights. There are 21 republics, six territories, 49 regions, two cities of federal importance, 10 autonomous areas, and one autonomous region. However, there is a trend to streamline the number of members of the federation, through the association of territories. For example, from December 1, 2005, onward, the Perm area and the Comi-Permyatskiy autonomous region are united into a new entity—the Perm territory.

Each of the 21 "republics" is considered to be a state within the structure of Russian federalism and has the right to adopt its own constitution and laws. The territories, regions, cities of federal importance, autonomous region, and the autonomous areas are territorial formations. Each has a basic constituent document, a charter, and laws.

The federal structure of Russia is based on the principle of state integrity and the equality and self-determination of the diverse peoples in the federation. In relation to the federal bodies of state authority, all members of the Russian Federation are equal. Russia guarantees the rights of indigenous peoples according to universally recognized principles and the norms of international law, and in accordance with treaties and agreements signed by Russia.

The distribution of powers between the center and the members remains the most important problem in their relationship. The constitution defines the jurisdiction of Russia, the powers of the federation members, and their joint jurisdiction. The members possess full state power unless an issue is assigned by the constitution to the federation or to joint jurisdiction.

The official language is Russian, but republics have the right to establish their own official languages, which are used alongside Russian. Local self-government is recognized, guaranteed, and independent within the limits of its authority. Local taxes exist separately from the state budgets and state taxes.

LEADING CONSTITUTIONAL PRINCIPLES

The constitution proclaims certain basic characteristics of Russia. It is federal, democratic, and law-bound with a republican form of government.

In a multinational state such as Russia the federal form of government is perhaps the most appropriate, as it allows a blending of the general interests of all people of Russia with the interests of each specific nation within the state.

The principles of government stated in the constitution correspond to the best practices of state construction in foreign countries, considering the historical and national features of Russia. They are designed to create an optimal realization of political, economic, and other freedoms. The principle of division of powers between the federal organs of government supports the democratic transformation of Russia and prevents the concentration of powers in the hands of one person in an authoritative regime.

The idea of a state founded on the rule of law is critically important. However, today this principle has not yet been implemented in fact. Instead it should be seen as one of the important goals that may be accomplished as Russian governmental institutions are reformed and a prosperous society arises.

Russia by its constitution is also a social state, which aims to create conditions for a life of dignity for all and for the free development of the person. Undoubtedly, the complexities of the current period have limited the resources available to the state to spend on social policy. Only if the economy of Russia improves considerably would it be possible to count on appropriate social help from the state.

Russia is a secular state. No religion can be established as a state religion or as an obligatory belief. Religious associations are separate from the state and are equal before the law.

CONSTITUTIONAL BODIES

Government in Russia is exercised by the following federal bodies: the president as head of state; the Federal Assembly, consisting of the Federation Council and the State Duma, as the legislature; the administration as the executive authority; and the judiciary, consisting of the Constitutional Court, the Supreme Court, the Higher Court of Arbitration, and other federal courts.

As Russia is a federal state, government functions are carried out not only by nationwide bodies, but also by government bodies within the members of the federation, which display a variety of government structures and functional organization. The federal constitution accepts such variety. These government systems are established independently, though they must follow the general principles of representative and executive government established by federal law.

The President

The constitution gives the president primary responsibility for maintaining the operation and the interaction of government authorities. The president defines the basic directions of external and internal policy; these policies need to be realized in corresponding laws passed by parliament, which are then accepted by the state authorities at all levels. According to the constitution, the president is the guarantor of the constitution and of the rights and freedoms of human beings and citizens.

The president is also the head of state. He or she represents Russia inside the country and on the international level. All diplomatic representatives are accredited with the president, who in turn appoints or dismisses Russia's diplomatic representatives to foreign states and international organizations. The president also exercises the right of pardon.

The president is the supreme commander in chief of the military forces. As such he or she appoints all commanders of the military forces and approves the military policy of Russia. The president can declare martial law, within the limits of federal constitutional law.

The president can initiate legislation and can veto laws. The president appoints a prime minister, with the consent of the State Duma, and approves the structure of the executive government on the suggestion of the prime minister.

The Federal Assembly (Parliament)

At the federal level, the Federal Assembly is the legislature of Russia. It consists of two chambers: the Council of the Federation and the State Duma.

As a rule, the chambers sit separately, and joint sessions are rare. The deputies of the State Duma represent all citizens of Russia. The Council of the Federation comprises representatives of the federation's territorial subunits.

Legislative activity is concentrated mainly in the State Duma. Bills are initiated only there; the Council of the Federation can approve or disapprove Duma laws within certain limits.

The Federal Assembly has only limited control over the administration. Both chambers of parliament have the right to control the execution of the federal budget. The State Duma also has the power to vote no confidence in the administration, which must then resign.

The Federal Executive Administration

The federal administration is the supreme executive body. It presides over the social and economic transformations of the country and over the implementation of state economic policy. The administration develops the draft federal budget and reports on its execution; it manages federal property; provides uniform financial, credit, and monetary policy; and carries out state support of culture, science, and public services.

Basic functions of the executive government are the implementation of federal laws and the supervision of the workings of all administrative bodies. It exercises its powers by adopting regulations on strategic and current issues of public administration, and by using the right of legislative initiative.

The Lawmaking Process

The right of initiative is vested in the president, the Council of the Federation and its members, deputies of the State Duma, the executive administration, and the legislative bodies of the members of the federation. This power also belongs to the Constitutional Court, the Supreme Court, and the Higher Arbitration Court, but only on issues within their sphere of authority.

Bills are submitted to the State Duma. Those introducing or abolishing taxes and other financial bills can be submitted only with the approval of the executive administration.

A federal law is adopted by the State Duma by a majority of its members. The Duma then sends it to the Council of the Federation within five days. The federal law is considered approved if the council either approves the bill by more than half of its members or fails to consider it within 14 days (except in certain matters in which the constitution requires its consideration). If the council tries to alter the bill, the chambers can create a conciliatory commission; or the State Duma can approve the original bill by a two-thirds majority and bypass the council.

An adopted federal law goes to the president for signing and publishing. If within 14 days of receiving the law the president rejects it, the State Duma and the Council of the Federation must reconsider it. If both chambers approve the law by two-thirds majorities, the president has to sign and publish the law.

Besides federal laws, the State Duma can adopt federal constitutional laws, as stipulated in the constitution. Such laws require approval by a three-fourths majority of the members of the council and a two-thirds majority of the deputies of the State Duma. The president cannot reject an adopted federal constitutional law.

The Judiciary

The judiciary is separate from the legislative and the executive bodies. According to the constitution, its particular attributes are independence, exclusiveness, and legality. Its main purposes are the protection of human rights and basic freedoms of the constitutional regime of Russia and the assurance of the legality of government actions.

The judiciary's exclusiveness entails that no other government body has the right to take up the functions or powers of the courts. Only they can declare a person guilty or impose criminal punishment. The legality of judicial power ensures that all judicial bodies and judges are bound by the constitution and federal laws.

The judiciary in Russia consists of the Constitutional Court, the Supreme Court, the Higher Arbitration Court, and other federal courts. The constitution also includes the office of procurator-general within the structure of the judiciary. The procurator-general of Russia is appointed by the Council of the Federation; he or she heads all bodies of state prosecution. The procurator-general is responsible for criminal prosecution and representation of the government in court proceedings.

THE ELECTION PROCESS

Free elections are defined in the constitution as the supreme direct expression of the power of the people. The will of the people, as expressed in elections, actually allows the democratic organization of authority in Russia. All representative bodies within Russia, the members of the federation, and local government are formed by elections. According to federal law, the president is also an elected position.

Only citizens of Russia have the right to vote; each citizen can exercise this right after having reached the age of 18 years. The minimal ages for election to federal and local government bodies are established by federal or regional laws. Anyone declared by a court to be incapacitated or imprisoned on a court verdict has no right to vote or be elected.

Presidential Elections

All citizens of Russia elect the president every four years. The president must be a citizen of Russia, at least 35 years old, and must have lived continuously in Russia for a minimum of 10 years before the elections. The president cannot serve more than two consecutive terms. Presidential elections are performed in two rounds: If no candidate receives more than 50 percent of the vote in the first round, the two candidates who receive the greatest number of votes run in a second, final round.

Parliamentary Elections

Elections to the State Duma take place every four years. Any citizen of Russia who is 21 years old and has the right to vote in elections can be elected as a deputy of the 450-member State Duma. Exactly half of the deputies are elected in a proportional system from lists submitted by federal parties. The other half are elected in single-mandate districts by relative majorities. As a result of the 2005 constitutional reform, from 2007 onward all deputies will be elected by the proportional system.

POLITICAL PARTIES

Ideological pluralism is guaranteed in Russia. No ideology can be established as a state or obligatory ideology. Associations are equal before the law. Ideological pluralism is understood as the right of persons, social groups, political parties, and associations to develop theories, views, and ideas concerning the economic, political, legal, and other aspects of Russia, foreign states, and the world as a whole; to propagate these views and ideas; and to conduct activities introducing these ideologies in practical life.

Parties have the right to propose candidates for elective offices including preelection campaigns. Political parties may not receive financial and other material aid from foreign states, organizations, or citizens. Currently, four leading political parties are represented in the State Duma.

Public associations, including political parties, are barred if they aim to promote violent change of the fundamental principles of the constitutional system, to infringe the integrity of Russia, to undermine the safety of the state, to create armed units, or to instigate social, racial, national, or religious strife. The party system is still in a formative stage in Russia.

CITIZENSHIP

Citizenship of Russia is acquired and terminated according to federal law. It is acquired by birth if at least one parent is a Russian citizen; by admission to citizenship of Russia; by restoration of citizenship for persons who were citizens of Russia but have lost their citizenship; and by other grounds as stated in federal law or international treaty. Russia also encourages those who live in the territory of Russia to acquire Russian citizenship.

Citizenship of Russia is equal irrespective of the way it was acquired. No one can be deprived of citizenship or of the right to change it. Citizenship cannot in any way be limited on the basis of social, racial, national, language, or religious differences. Citizenship is not terminated if a citizen resides outside Russia.

FUNDAMENTAL RIGHTS

According to the Russian constitution, the rights and freedoms of every human being are the supreme value. The recognition, observance, and protection of the rights and freedoms of all citizens and residents are the obligation of the state.

The specific human rights are listed in special clauses of the constitution, but the source and the basis of these rights are outside the sphere of the state, meaning that the state has to respect and protect them, but does not create them. They are inviolable and indestructible. The state must not only abstain from intervention against rights and freedoms, it is also obliged to protect them and actively create the conditions for their realization. In addition, the declaration of the protection of human rights imposes a duty on the state to create special institutions for their protection. The constitution, for example, establishes the office of an ombudsperson.

Emphasis on human rights as the supreme value recognized, respected, and protected by the state does not diminish the state in any way. On the contrary, this state duty considerably raises the influence of the state on the activity of society and on economic and cultural life.

Impact and Functions of Fundamental Rights

The majority of the rights and freedoms guaranteed in the Russian constitution are enjoyed by every resident, including foreign citizens and those without any citizenship. However, the constitution explicitly reserves certain rights and freedoms to citizens; for example, some rights and freedoms are predominantly political and thus pertain only to citizens of Russia. On occasion the constitution specifically addresses the rights of foreign citizens and those who have no citizenship.

Russia has assumed a duty to protect rights and freedoms from any illegal intervention or restriction. This does not mean that the state abstains completely from the sphere of rights. The state requires that no one may abuse his or her rights or freedoms, and no one may infringe upon the rights and freedoms and legitimate interests of other persons.

The state by law defines the maintenance, range, and limits of rights and freedoms; the means to guarantee their observance; and the duties of each person in Russia, such as the payment of taxes, the preservation of the environment, and the provision of military service. Human rights and freedoms can sometimes conflict. Society and the state must resolve these contradictions according to constitutional principles.

The Russian constitution reflects all the categories of rights accepted in modern legal theory: civil rights, political rights, economic rights, social rights, cultural rights, and ecological rights.

Civil rights are understood to entail a person's freedom to make decisions independently of the state. The spiritual and physical freedom from state control evolved historically before other freedoms, in the form of freedom of worship, freedom of speech and belief, and freedom of movement. Since being charged with a crime is often connected with imprisonment, the rights in this sphere historically also evolved early. Among them are the right to be considered innocent before an independent court can find otherwise, and the invalidity of evidence gained through torture.

Political rights allow citizens to participate in the formation of government institutions and to engage in political activity. Economic rights are basically connected with property rights; they include the freedom to engage in manufacturing, exchange, and distribution and consumption of goods and services. Social rights evolved later in the 20th century. They primarily concern wages, freedom to enter into labor contracts, the right to rest, and the right to a pension. Cultural rights are associated with the freedom of access to the spiritual and material assets created by the human community.

In the second half of the 20th century a new category appeared—ecological rights. These have resulted from the conflict between scientific and technical developments, on the one hand, and the requirements of a healthy environment, on the other.

Limitations to Fundamental Rights

The Russian constitution allows restrictions on fundamental rights under certain conditions, derived from the condition that the individual lives in a society in which personal freedom is exercised in interaction with other people. Everyone has duties to other people, society, and the state.

According to the constitution, fundamental rights can be limited only by special federal law, and only with the aim of protecting fundamental constitutional principles, morals, health, the rights and the legitimate interests of other persons, the maintenance of the defense of the country, and the safety of the state. No restriction must exceed what is necessary to achieve its legitimate aim.

The first requirement is quite clear. Only the legislature, by means of federal law, can establish any restriction; the president, the federal administration, and the members of the federation all lack such powers.

The other conditions are formulated in a rather general manner. The security of rights may depend on a correct estimation by the legislature of the danger menacing fundamental constitutional principles or public morals.

ECONOMY

The constitution guarantees the free movement of goods, services, and financial assets. It obliges the government to support fair economic competition, recognizes a general freedom of economic activity, and guarantees property rights for all people. Equal protection is accorded private, state, municipal, and other forms of ownership in Russia. The constitution does not contain a special section about the economic basis of the state; it also does not establish any "leading" pattern of ownership and does not provide any restrictions on other forms of ownership. The constitution obliges the state to engage in certain economic activities; however, the state may not establish any monopolies and must prevent unfair competition.

The constitution aims to encourage a market economy as the economic basis of Russian society. State bodies and institutions of local self-government are not allowed to draw income or benefits from the exercise of their powers.

The constitution's economic provisions have not been completely implemented in Russia. In practice, both large and small enterprises depend on administrative influence within the government. Such sectors as gas, electricity, pipelines, municipal services, railway transportation, and seaports are still directly supervised by the state. The judicial system also is under the influence of the state. The right to own real estate is essentially limited; thus the local bureaucracy has the opportunity to pressure businesses. At the same time, most of the gross national product is created by the private sector, and in many fields of industry sharp market competition does exist.

RELIGIOUS COMMUNITIES

Russia is a multidenominational state where people of various creeds live, including Orthodox Christians, Muslims, Buddhists, Catholics, Lutherans, Jews, and pagans. Christianity, Islam, Buddhism, and other religions of the Russian people form an integral part of its historical heritage. Freedom of worship assumes freedom of activity for religious associations on the basis of the principle of equality.

As a secular state, Russia does not render preference to any religion and does not forbid any religious activity as long as the law is respected. State bodies do not interfere with the internal affairs of religious associations. This position of the state is based on the loyalty of religious associations to the state and its laws. The procurator-general supervises the execution of the laws concerning freedom of worship and religious associations. To suppress illegal extremist activity, the government can forbid separatist religious associations, but such decisions may be adopted only by means of a court decision.

According to the federal law on the freedom of worship and religious associations, religious associations in Russia are created in the form of religious groups and religious organizations. A religious group is a voluntary association of citizens, carrying out its activities without registration by the authorities and without the status of a legal person. A religious organization is an association of citizens of Russia or other persons who constantly and lawfully live in Russia with a common creed, registered as a legal person or entity. In the beginning of 2003, there were 21,500 religious organizations registered in Russia.

The state has the power to deny registration to religious groups that infringe on human rights and commit crimes. The state limits the activities of religious associations or individual believers only when necessary to protect fundamental constitutional principles, morals, health, or the rights and legitimate interests of other persons. The state opposes proselytizing activity, which is incompatible with the laws and exercises a wrongful influence on the people.

According to the constitution, religious associations are separate from the state, and they may not be financed by the state budget. They are also barred from participation in political life. The state has no right to assign any state functions to religious associations. Religious associations and their hierarchies are not included in the system of the government and of local self-government; they must not influence state decisions.

Religious organizations may not be formed within state organs, institutions of local self-government, or public educational institutions. Civil servants have no right to use their positions to pursue the interests of religious associations. They may, however, participate in religious ceremonies as ordinary believers. In public buildings, religious symbols must not be exhibited.

Although religious associations are separated from the state, they are not separated from society. Therefore, the state is compelled to reckon with the opinions of the religious public. Religious organizations may own property, run mass media, and engaged in charities. They can also receive certain financial privileges from the state.

Separation of religious associations from the state requires that the character of education is secular. At the same time, however, the churches can have educational institutions for the preparation of their clerics.

MILITARY DEFENSE AND STATE OF EMERGENCY

Martial law in Russia can be imposed by the president, who must immediately inform both chambers of the Federal Assembly. The decree must immediately be broadcasted by radio and television, and officially published. The Council of the Federation must consider the decree within 48 hours; unless a majority of council members vote in favor, the decree expires on the following day.

The president must also notify the secretary-general and member states of the United Nations about the introduction of martial law and about the deviation from the obligations of Russia under international treaties entailed by the restrictions of human rights. The same kind of information is given after the cancellation of martial law.

The state of emergency establishes a special legal regime for government bodies, institutions of local self-government, and officials, organizations, and public associations as specified in the federal constitutional law on the state of emergency. The law prescribes restrictions on the rights of individuals and associations and imposes additional duties on them.

The state of emergency can be declared only if there is a real, extreme, and unpreventable threat to the safety of citizens or to the fundamental constitutional principles of Russia, and only if elimination of this threat is impossible without emergency measures.

The state of emergency is declared by a decree of the president, who immediately informs the Council of the Federation and the State Duma. A decree that is not approved by the Council of the Federation becomes invalid 72 hours after the moment of its promulgation. The validity of the state of emergency entered in the entirety of Russia cannot exceed 30 days, and it cannot exceed 60 days if it is declared in separate districts. After this time limit, the state of emergency is considered terminated. If the circumstances forming the basis are eliminated before the expiration date, the president cancels it.

AMENDMENTS TO THE CONSTITUTION

The constitution of Russia is rigid from the point of view of the amending process. The Federal Assembly may not revise provisions of Chapters 1 (Fundamental Constitutional Principles), 2 (Human Rights), and 9 (Constitutional Amendments and Review of the Constitution).

If a proposal to review any provisions of these chapters is supported by three-fifths of the members of the Council of the Federation and the deputies of the State Duma, a Constitutional Assembly must be convened. This assembly either confirms the existing text of the constitution or drafts a new constitution, which must be adopted by the Constitutional Assembly by two-thirds of its members or submitted to a referendum. In case of a referendum, the new constitution is considered adopted if more than half of the electorate participates in the referendum and over half of those who vote support it.

Amendments to other chapters can be adopted by two-thirds of the members of the State Duma and three-quarters of the members of the Council of the Federation. They go into force after they have been approved by the bodies of legislative power of at least two-thirds of the members of the federation.

Proposals for amendments may be submitted by the president of the republic, the executive administration, the legislative bodies of the members of the federation, and groups of at least one-fifth of the members of the Council of the Federation or the State Duma.

PRIMARY SOURCES

Constitution in English. Available online. URL: http://constitution.ru/en/10003000-01.htm. Accessed on July 31, 2005.

Constitution in Russian. Available online. URL: http://www.constitution.ru/index.htm. Accessed on June 27, 2006.

SECONDARY SOURCES

John T. Ishiyama and Ryan Kennedy, "Superpresidentialism and Political Party Development in Russia, Ukraine, Armenia and Kyrgyzstan." *Europe-Asia Studies* 53, no. 8 (2001): 1177–1191.

A. K. Kroupchenco, *Contemporary Law in Russia.* 2004.

V. N. Lopatin, *Human Rights in Russia and Legal Protection Activity of the State.* Saint Petersburg: Yuridicheskiy Tcentr Press, 2003.

Rett R. Ludwikowski, *Constitution-Making in the Region of Former Soviet Dominance.* Durham and London: Duke University Press, 1996.

Russia—A Country Study. Washington, D.C.: United States Government Printing Office, 1998.

Raymond Zickel, ed., *Soviet Union—A Country Study.* Washington, D.C.: United States Government Printing Office, 1992.

Nickolay Peshin

RWANDA

At-a-Glance

OFFICIAL NAME
Republic of Rwanda

CAPITAL
Kigali

POPULATION
7,954,013 (2005 est.)

SIZE
10,169 sq. mi. (26,338 sq. km)

LANGUAGES
Kinyarwanda (official), French (official), English (official), Kiswahili

RELIGIONS
Catholic 56.5%, Protestant 26%, Adventist 11.1%, Muslim 4.6%, indigenous beliefs 0.1%, unaffiliated or other 1.7%

NATIONAL OR ETHNIC COMPOSITION
Hutu 84%, Tutsi 15%, Twa 1%

DATE OF INDEPENDENCE OR CREATION
July 1, 1962

TYPE OF GOVERNMENT
Republic; presidential, multiparty system

TYPE OF STATE
Unitary, decentralized

TYPE OF LEGISLATURE
Bicameral parliament

DATE OF CONSTITUTION
June 4, 2003

DATE OF LAST AMENDMENT
No amendment

The constitution of Rwanda establishes a presidential system based on the rule of law and premised on the separation of executive, legislative, and judicial powers. Organized as a centralist state with a decentralized public administration, Rwanda is made up of 12 provinces (French, *préfectures*) with local governments and a strong central government.

The constitution provides for far-reaching guarantees of human rights. It is still early to determine whether the public authorities respect the fundamental rights theoretically protected; an independent judiciary is, in principle, entrusted to be the guardian of the listed rights and freedoms and ensure respect for them. Because of Rwanda's long-standing history of ethnic conflict and violence, the cardinal principles of the constitution are national unity, reconciliation, and the eradication of divisions.

The president of the republic is the head of state and the central political figure. As both head of the executive and guardian of the constitution, the president is granted extensive powers. Democratic principles are generally recognized and entrenched in the constitution, including regular elections of members of parliament and a pluralistic system of political parties.

Religious freedom is guaranteed and state and religious communities are separated. The economic system can be described as a social market economy. By law, the military is subject to the civil government. By constitutional law, Rwanda is obliged to contribute to international peace.

CONSTITUTIONAL HISTORY

Rwanda emerged as a single kingdom in central Africa in the middle of the 15th century C.E. and maintained its independence until the middle of the 19th century C.E. In 1895, Rwanda became part of German East Africa along with Burundi and Tanganyika. After the defeat of Germany in World War I (1914–18), the Versailles Treaty of 1919 assigned Ruanda-Urundi to Belgian rule; in 1923, Rwanda became a mandate territory of the League of Nations under the administration of Belgium.

In 1959, three years before independence from Belgium, government power was transferred from a Tutsi-dominated monarchy to a Hutu elite in what was known as the social revolution. The year 1959 triggered broader constitutional and political developments. Over the next several years, a wave of political violence left several thousand Tutsi dead, and thousands more driven into exile in neighboring countries.

On July 1, 1962, Rwanda was granted independence. It adopted its first constitution as an independent state on November 24, 1962. The constitution abolished the Mwami regime (a functional monarchy) and established a "democratic, social, and sovereign Republic." In 1973, Major-General Juvénal Habyarimana gained power after a successful military coup d'état. The second republic adopted a new constitution on December 17, 1978. This document decreed that political life was to be organized under a single party; the president of the ruling party was the only candidate eligible for the presidency of the republic; every Rwandan was, by law, a member of the party.

In October 1990, the Rwandese Patriotic Front (RPF), a liberation movement of mostly Tutsi refugees, began a civil war. Despite the ongoing conflict, Rwanda adopted a new constitution on June 10, 1991, officially authorizing the country to function as a pluralistic democracy.

The Rwandan government and the RPF then engaged in political talks, which culminated in the signing of the Arusha Peace Accords on August 4, 1993, an agreement guaranteeing power sharing by the two factions and officially ending the civil war. In April 1994, the plane carrying President Habyarimana of Rwanda and President Ntaryamira of Burundi was shot down in Rwanda.

Within hours of the plane crash, Hutu militia and elements in the army went on a rampage, killing in the ensuing 100 days about 1 million people and displacing more than double that number. Tutsi and Hutu alike were suspected of supporting the RPF. The RPF ended the killings by gaining power in a military victory in July 1994. The new regime adopted a transitional constitution, consisting of the June 10, 1991, constitution; the 1993 Arusha Accords; and the declarations of political parties.

On June 4, 2003, after a referendum, Rwanda adopted a new constitution, marking the end of a nine-year transition period. The framers of the constitution tried to ensure that genocide, divisions, discrimination, and dictatorship would never happen again.

The Republic of Rwanda is a founding member state of the African Union.

FORM AND IMPACT OF THE CONSTITUTION

Rwanda has a written constitution, codified in a single document, called the Constitution of the Republic of Rwanda. The constitution is the supreme law of the republic and takes precedence over all other national law. In principle, international law must be in accord with the constitution to be applicable within Rwanda. In general, the law in Rwanda complies with the constitution.

BASIC ORGANIZATIONAL STRUCTURE

Rwanda is a centralist state with a decentralized public administration made up of 12 provinces, each with its own local government. The provinces differ considerably in geographical area, population size, and economic strength. Federal laws govern the degree of administrative and financial autonomy allowed to the provinces.

LEADING CONSTITUTIONAL PRINCIPLES

Rwanda's system of government is presidential. There is a separation of executive, legislative, and judicial powers, complemented by checks and balances. The judiciary is independent.

The Rwandan constitutional system is defined by a number of leading principles: eradication of any divisions among Rwandans; promotion of national unity, dialogue, and consensus; pluralistic democratic government; equality of all Rwandans; and a social and secular republic based on the rule of law.

Emerging at a critical historical conjuncture in the political development of Rwanda, the constitution shapes political participation in light of the country's political and social history. For example, while representative democracy is recognized, the constitution stipulates that only two-thirds of the representatives in the Chamber of Deputies are elected by direct universal suffrage. The rule of law is entrenched in the constitution and safeguarded by a variety of mechanisms: an independent judiciary, a human rights commission, and an ombudsperson. Religious neutrality is explicitly contained in the constitution.

CONSTITUTIONAL BODIES

The predominant bodies provided for in the constitution are the president of the republic and the cabinet ministers, the bicameral parliament, and the Supreme Court.

The President and Cabinet

The president is head of the executive, guardian of the constitution, and guarantor of national unity. The constitution stipulates that executive power is vested in the president of the republic and the cabinet. The president appoints and dismisses the prime minister and, on the prime minister's recommendation, appoints and dismisses other ministers. In principle, members of the cabinet are appointed on the basis of their representation in parliament; however, no political party may hold more than 50 percent of the seats in the cabinet.

The cabinet implements national policy as agreed upon with the president. The cabinet is accountable to both the president and parliament.

The president of the republic can appoint and promote executive officers, senior officers in the army, and the police. As the commander in chief of the armed forces, the president has authority to declare war. The president is also the dominant political figure in Rwandan politics.

The president is elected by simple majority through direct universal suffrage for a seven-year term and can be reelected only once.

The Parliament

The Rwandan parliament is the central representative organ of the people, with power to make laws and to oversee the executive. It consists of two chambers: the Chamber of Deputies, whose members are elected for a five-year term, and the Senate, whose members serve a nonrenewable term of eight years.

Only two-thirds of the delegates in the Chamber of Deputies are elected in a general, direct, free, equal, and secret balloting process. One-third of the seats are reserved for women, who are chosen through indirect elections by local governments. Each local government in the 12 provinces elects a senator; the other members of the Senate are appointed by the president of the republic, by political organizations, and by academic institutions.

The Lawmaking Process

The right to initiate legislation is vested in each representative and in the cabinet. Certain bills of special importance can only become law with the Senate's assent. The president of the republic may raise objections to laws passed by parliament, but if these are rejected by parliament, the bill can pass into law.

The president of the republic may call a referendum on proposed laws of general national interest. The president can also issue presidential and executive orders and can promulgate legislation adopted by the cabinet when parliament is unable to convene. Such decree laws must be approved by parliament at its next session. The cabinet may exercise control over the agenda of parliament by using its priority rights: Upon its request, cabinet bills are always given priority over all other matters on the agenda.

The Judiciary

The judiciary is independent and separate from the legislative and executive branches of government.

The highest Rwandan court is the Supreme Court, consisting of a president, a vice president, and 12 appointed judges. It ranks above the high court of the republic and all provincial, district, municipality, and town courts. Generally, the Supreme Court hears appeals against decisions of the high court of the republic and the military high court, as well as constitutional disputes and criminal cases against high public officials. The Supreme Court also provides authentic interpretation of custom in cases in which the written law is silent.

Authentic interpretation of the law, however, is vested in parliament; the Supreme Court may only provide an opinion. Generally, judges are elected by the Senate on the basis of a list submitted by the president of the republic, who is required to consult the cabinet and the Superior Council of the Judiciary. The constitution also establishes a traditional system of justice, called Gacaca, specifically designed to hear cases against lower-level participants in the crimes committed in 1994.

THE ELECTION PROCESS

All Rwandans over the age of 18 have the right to vote in elections. Candidates must be over 21 to be elected to the Chamber of Deputies, and over 40 to be elected to the Senate.

POLITICAL PARTIES

The constitution of Rwanda recognizes a pluralistic system of political parties. Because of the country's recent political history and the role played by political parties in the genocide of 1994, activities of political organizations are closely regulated. For example, political parties are prohibited from recruiting their members on the basis of any discriminatory ground, including religion; two political parties (Christian Democrat and Islamist) had to change their name as a result. In addition, political parties must constantly reflect the unity of Rwandans, as well as gender equality at all levels.

The constitution also entrenches a forum of political parties meant to ensure consensus and promote national unity. The Senate may lodge a complaint against a political organization, and the organization can be banned by a decision of the high court of the republic or by the Supreme Court on appeal. Just what constitutes "divisionism" or discrimination is disputed in Rwandan politics. A resolution of these questions would be a critical indication that the government is promoting adherence to the rule of law, including freedom of expression, opinion, and association, to the fullest extent possible.

CITIZENSHIP

Rwandan citizenship is primarily acquired by birth; a child acquires Rwandan citizenship if one of his or her parents is a Rwandan citizen. It is of no relevance where a child is born.

FUNDAMENTAL RIGHTS

The constitution defines fundamental rights and duties of the citizens in its second chapter, directly after the provisions on the state and national sovereignty. The constitution guarantees the traditional set of liberal human rights and civil liberties. An equality clause prohibits discrimination of "whatever kind."

The constitution imposes an absolute obligation to respect, protect, and defend the human person and contains numerous references to the vital importance of human rights. The constitution enumerates many fundamental rights and freedoms and makes specific reference to the various international human rights instruments to which Rwanda adheres, including the African Charter on Human and People's Rights.

The constitution also enumerates duties. It draws on the treatment of "duties" in the African human rights convention, signaling the importance attached to this instrument.

The fundamental rights set out in the constitution have binding force on the legislature, the executive, and the judiciary as directly applicable law.

Impact and Functions of Fundamental Rights

Still suffering the consequences of the 1994 genocide, Rwanda in its human rights discourse focuses on the principle of equality and the prohibition of discrimination in all its manifestations.

Limitations to Fundamental Rights

Some limitations to fundamental rights have been introduced with the specific aim of preventing the recurrence of past abuses. For example, the constitutional freedoms of association, assembly, opinion, and the press are subject to ordinary legislation.

ECONOMY

The Rwandan constitution does not specify a particular economic system. However, certain basic decisions set by the framers of the constitution, such as the freedom of property, the freedom of occupation or profession, and the right to form associations, indicate a preference for a free-market system. The constitution also defines Rwanda as a social state. Taken as a whole, the Rwandan economic system can be described as a social market economy, which combines aspects of social responsibility with market freedom.

RELIGIOUS COMMUNITIES

While there is no established state church, freedom of religion or belief, which is guaranteed as a human right, involves rights of religious communities. Religious communities regulate and administer their affairs independently within the limits of the laws that apply to all associations.

MILITARY DEFENSE AND STATE OF EMERGENCY

Creation and maintenance of armed forces for defense are responsibilities of the government. Apart from defending the territorial integrity of the republic, the armed forces may only be used for special purposes that are specifically listed in the constitution, such as participating in humanitarian activities in the event of disasters, collaborating with other security organs in safeguarding public order, or participating in international peacekeeping and humanitarian assistance missions.

Ordinary legislation controls national service, whether civil or military.

The military is subject to civil government. The Republic of Rwanda ratified the Chemical Weapons Convention in 2004.

AMENDMENTS TO THE CONSTITUTION

The constitution can only be changed at the initiative of the president of the republic upon the cabinet's proposal, and if two-thirds of the members of both chambers of parliament vote in favor. The amendment then requires the support of three-quarters of the members of each chamber of parliament.

Certain fundamental provisions, including the term of office of the president of the republic, political pluralism, and the constitutional regime, can be amended only via a referendum. The amending clause itself is rigid and may not be changed.

PRIMARY SOURCES
Constitution of Rwanda of June 4, 2003, in English. Available online. URLs: http://www.rwandaparliament. gov.rw/; http://www.rwandaparliament.gov.rw/rapport/ constitution.pdf. Accessed on September 26, 2005.

Idi Gaparayi

SAINT CHRISTOPHER AND NEVIS (ST. KITTS AND NEVIS)

At-a-Glance

OFFICIAL NAME
Federation of Saint Christopher and Nevis; Federation of Saint Kitts and Nevis

CAPITAL
Basseterre

POPULATION
46,710 (2005 est.)

SIZE
101 sq. mi. (261 sq. km)

LANGUAGES
English

RELIGIONS
Anglican 25%, Methodist 25%, Pentecostal 8%, Moravian 8%, other Protestant 12%, Roman Catholic 7%, Hindu 2%, other 13%

NATIONAL OR ETHNIC COMPOSITION
Black African origin 90.4%, mulatto 5%, Indo-Pakistani 3%, British, Portuguese, and Lebanese 1%, other 0.6%

DATE OF INDEPENDENCE OR CREATION
September 19, 1983

TYPE OF GOVERNMENT
Constitutional monarchy

TYPE OF STATE
Federal state

TYPE OF LEGISLATURE
Unicameral parliament plus Nevis Island legislature in specified matters

DATE OF CONSTITUTION
September 19, 1983

DATE OF LAST AMENDMENT
No amendment

St. Kitts and Nevis is a federal state that adheres to the form of the British Westminster style parliamentary system of government. The uniqueness of its 1983 constitution derives from the provisions for the autonomy of the island of Nevis with regard to certain "specified matters" and the establishment of the separate Nevis Island Assembly (legislature) to address these local concerns. Both versions of the name—Saint Christopher and Nevis as well as Saint Kitts and Nevis are—official, although Saint Kitts and Nevis is preferred.

As a constitutional monarchy within the British Commonwealth of Nations, Saint Kitts and Nevis recognizes Queen Elizabeth II or her successors as the titular head of government. The British monarch is represented by a governor-general, who resides in Basseterre. Although legally responsible for the government of both islands, the gover-

nor-general appoints a deputy to represent him or her on Nevis. As the highest executive authority on the islands, the governor-general appoints the prime minister, the deputy prime minister, other ministers of the government, the leader of the opposition in parliament, and members of the Public Service Commission and the Police Service Commission. The governor-general may prorogue (adjourn) or dissolve the parliament at any time. In the judicial sphere, the governor-general has the power of pardon.

As in most Commonwealth countries, however, the apparently sweeping nature of the governor-general's powers is restricted by the requirement that the he or she act only in accordance with the advice of the prime minister. In Saint Kitts and Nevis, the governor-general is permitted to act without consultation only when the prime minister cannot be contacted because of absence or illness.

The federal government of Saint Kitts and Nevis is directed by a unicameral parliament known as the National Assembly, established by the 1983 constitution to replace the House of Assembly. The island of Nevis elects representatives both to the National Assembly and to its own Nevis Island Assembly. The focus of effective power in the federal government is the cabinet of ministers, which consists of the prime minister and other ministers.

The constitution of Saint Kitts and Nevis provides for far-reaching guarantees of human rights.

CONSTITUTIONAL HISTORY

Christopher Columbus visited Saint Kitts and Nevis on his second voyage in 1493 and found it inhabited by warlike Carib. He named it Saint Christopher for his patron saint. Divided during the 17th century between warring French and English colonists, Saint Kitts was given to Britain by the 1713 Treaty of Utrecht; although the French captured Brimstone Hill in 1782, the island was restored to Great Britain by the 1783 Treaty of Versailles. Nevis was also sighted by Columbus in 1493. The island's name derives from Columbus's description of the clouds atop Nevis peak as *las nieves,* or "the snows." It was settled by the English in 1628 and soon became one of the most prosperous of the Antilles.

The islands of Saint Kitts, Nevis, and Anguilla were united as a "presidency" within the Leeward Islands Federation by a federal act in 1882, a status it retained until 1956. The three-island grouping participated in the West Indies Federation from 1958 to 1962 and took part in the unsuccessful negotiations of the so-called Little Eight (Antigua and Barbuda, Barbados, Dominica, Montserrat, Saint Kitts-Nevis-Anguilla, Saint Lucia, and Saint Vincent and the Grenadines) that broke off in 1966. When these efforts failed, Saint Kitts-Nevis-Anguilla, along with most of the other small Caribbean colonies, accepted the British offer of associated statehood on February 27, 1967. The islands were granted full internal self-government, with the United Kingdom retaining responsibility for defense and foreign affairs. The Anguilla Act of July 1971 placed Anguilla directly under British control. On February 10, 1976, Anguilla was granted a constitution and its union with Saint Kitts and Nevis was formally severed in 1980.

A constitutional conference was held in London in 1982. In spite of disagreement over special provisions for Nevis, Saint Kitts and Nevis became independent on September 19, 1983. In August 1998, a vote in Nevis on a referendum to separate from Saint Kitts fell short of the two-thirds majority needed.

FORM AND IMPACT OF THE CONSTITUTION

Saint Kitts and Nevis has a written constitution, codified in a single document—the Constitution of Saint Christopher and Nevis of June 23, 1983. It is the supreme law of the state and makes void any inconsistent legal provision.

International law does not find explicit regulation within the constitutional body.

BASIC ORGANIZATIONAL STRUCTURE

The state is divided into 14 parishes. The constitution provides for a Constituency Boundaries Commission that has the task of reviewing the number and the boundaries of the constituencies and to report accordingly at certain intervals to the governor-general. It can recommend a modification of the existing administrative structure, and the National Assembly makes the final decision.

The Nevis Island Assembly is a separate eight-member body (five elected, three appointed) charged with regulating local affairs. The Nevis Island Assembly is subordinate to the National Assembly only with regard to external affairs and defense, and in cases in which similar but not identical legislation is passed by both bodies. The guidelines for legislative autonomy in Nevis are contained in the "specified matters," areas of local administration for which the Nevisian legislature may amend or revoke provisions passed by the National Assembly. There are 23 specified matters, including agricultural regulations, the borrowing of funds or procurement of grants for use on Nevis, water conservation and supply, Nevisian economic planning and development, housing, utilities, and roads and highways. These restrictions on Kittian control over internal Nevisian concerns appear to have been one of the major concessions (along with a local legislature and the right of secession) made by the People's Action Movement (PAM) to the Nevis Reformation Party (NRP) in order to maintain the two-island union after independence.

Nevisian secession from the federation would require a two-thirds vote in the Nevis Island Assembly and the approval of two-thirds of the voters in a referendum. Saint Kitts has no corresponding right of secession, reflecting the desire of the smaller island to protect itself from possible exploitation by its larger neighbor. The government of Nevis closely parallels the structure of the federal government and has a premier analogous to the prime minister, an assembly incorporating both elected and appointed members, and a body functioning as a local cabinet, the Nevis Island administration, which includes the premier plus two or more members of the Nevis Island Assembly. Disputes between the Nevis Island Administration and the federal government must be decided by the High Court.

Discussions continue on how the political relationship between the two islands can be improved, including review of the present constitution.

LEADING CONSTITUTIONAL PRINCIPLES

The Federation of Saint Christopher and Nevis is an independent Commonwealth realm with Queen Elizabeth II as head of state, represented in Saint Kitts and Nevis by a governor-general, who acts on the advice of the prime minister and the cabinet. The legislative, executive, and judicial branches are distinct and independent; none of these branches may delegate the exercise of its proper functions. Those who hold public office must take an oath to observe and comply with the constitution and the laws and to bear true allegiance to Her Majesty Queen Elizabeth II.

CONSTITUTIONAL BODIES

The predominant bodies provided for in the constitution are the parliament, which includes both the National Assembly and the Nevis Island Assembly and Administration; the governor-general; the prime minister; and the cabinet ministers. The constitution also provides for a supervisor of elections and a director of audit.

The National Assembly

The National Assembly is unicameral and comprises 14 members. Eleven members are elected to represent single-member constituencies (three of whom are from the island of Nevis) and three members are appointed by the governor-general—two on the advice of the prime minister and one on the advice of the leader of the opposition. The 11 members are elected by universal suffrage. The three appointed members are known as senators, although they do not form a separate house of parliament. The term of office for all 14 members of parliament is five years. The constitution provides for one standing committee, the Advisory Committee on Prerogative of Mercy; parliament is free to set up additional nonstanding committees. The cabinet of ministers is collectively responsible to the parliament.

The Nevis Island Assembly, Nevis Island Administration

The Nevis Island Legislature can make laws, which are called ordinances, for the peace, order, and good government of the island of Nevis with respect to the "specified matters." A law made by the Nevis Island Legislature that exceeds the specified matters and is inconsistent with a provision enacted by parliament is void.

The functions of the Nevis Island Administration are to advise the governor-general in the government of the island of Nevis. The administration is collectively responsible to the assembly.

The Governor-General, the Prime Minister, and Cabinet Ministers

The executive authority of Saint Kitts and Nevis is vested in Her Majesty Queen Elizabeth II. In practice, it is exercised on behalf of her majesty by the governor-general.

The governor-general appoints as prime minister the person who appears likely to command the support of the majority of the representatives. The prime minister and the cabinet conduct the affairs of state and are responsible for the general direction and control of the executive. The cabinet is collectively responsible to the National Assembly. The prime minister must keep the governor-general regularly and fully informed.

The Supervisor of Elections

The governor-general designates a supervisor of elections who exercises general supervision over the registration of voters and the conduct of elections of representatives. The supervisor of elections is in turn supervised in the performance of his or her functions by a three-member Electoral Commission.

The Director of Audit

The constitutional body in charge of the oversight of public finances is the director of audit, who is appointed by the governor-general acting in accordance with the recommendation of the Public Service Commission. The director of audit is a public office and enjoys full functional and administrative independence.

The Lawmaking Process

Any question proposed for decision in the National Assembly is decided by a majority of the votes of the members present and voting. The power of parliament to make laws is exercised by bills passed by the National Assembly and assented to by the governor-general. When the governor-general assents to a bill, the bill becomes law as soon as it is published in the *Gazette* as law.

The Judiciary

The judiciary is independent; it is part of the eastern Caribbean legal system, with the Eastern Caribbean Supreme Court based in Saint Lucia. Any person who alleges that any provision of the constitution has been or is being contravened can, if he or she has a relevant interest, apply to the High Court for a declaration and relief. The right to apply for a declaration and remedies in respect of such an alleged contravention is additional to any other legal action with respect to the same matter. There is a possibility of appeal to the Court of Appeals, and, further, to her majesty in council.

THE ELECTION PROCESS

Every Commonwealth citizen 18 years or older who meets the residence qualifications in Saint Kitts and Nevis is entitled to be registered as a voter in one constituency.

A person is qualified to be elected or appointed as a member of the National Assembly if he or she is a citizen of the age of 21 years or older, and at least one of his or her parents was born in Saint Kitts and Nevis. The candidate must also be domiciled there at the date of his or her nomination for election and appointment.

POLITICAL PARTIES

The politics of Saint Kitts and Nevis is based on a multiparty system.

CITIZENSHIP

Citizenship of Saint Kitts and Nevis is obtained by birth or by naturalization. Every person born in Saint Kitts and Nevis who was a citizen of the United Kingdom and colonies on September 19, 1983, or later, became a citizen on that day. The same rule applies to every person born outside Saint Kitts and Nevis if either of his or her parents or any one of his or her grandparents was born therein or was registered or naturalized while resident in Saint Kitts and Nevis. The constitution provides for dual citizenship, meaning that a citizen cannot be denied a passport on grounds of entitlement to apply for nationality in another country.

FUNDAMENTAL RIGHTS

The constitution establishes the fundamental rights of all persons, whatever their race, place of origin, birth, political opinions, color, creed, or sex may be, but subject to respect for the rights and freedoms of others and for the public interest. The right to life is guaranteed; no person can be deprived of life intentionally, save in execution of the sentence of a court in respect of a criminal offense of treason or murder of which the person has been convicted.

In addition, the constitution acknowledges the right to personal liberty, protection from slavery and forced labor, protection from inhuman treatment, protection from deprivation of property, and protection of persons or property from arbitrary search or entry. It also includes a provision securing protection of the law and of freedom of conscience, of expression, of assembly and association, and of movement, and protection from discrimination on the grounds of race, sex, or other factor.

ECONOMY

The constitution protects the right to private property. No property of any description can be taken except in accordance with the provisions of the law and for the payment of fair compensation within a reasonable time.

Saint Kitts and Nevis was the last sugar monoculture in the eastern Caribbean. In recent years the govern-ment has instituted a program of investment incentives to diversify its economy and has particularly promoted tourism.

RELIGIOUS COMMUNITIES

The constitution provides for freedom of religion, and the government respects this right in practice. All groups are free to maintain links with coreligionists in other countries. The government is secular; it does not take any steps to promote interfaith understanding. Relations among the various religious communities are generally amicable. The local Christian council conducts activities to promote greater mutual understanding and tolerance among adherents of different denominations within the Christian faith.

MILITARY DEFENSE AND STATE OF EMERGENCY

The Royal Saint Kitts and Nevis police force has approximately 370 members and includes a 50-person Special Services Unit. There are also a coast guard and a small, newly formed defense force.

The governor-general can declare a state of emergency for a period of seven days during a session of parliament, and for a maximum of 21 days in any other case unless the National Assembly has approved the state of emergency by resolution.

AMENDMENTS TO THE CONSTITUTION

Parliament may alter any of the provisions of the constitution by a vote of two-thirds of the representatives. Additional requirements for changing certain provisions are specified in Article 38.

PRIMARY SOURCES
Constitution in English. Available online. URL: http:// www.georgetown.edu/pdba/Constitutions/Kitts/ kitts83.html. Accessed on September 20, 2005.

SECONDARY SOURCES
Henry L. Stogumber Browne, *Law, Power and Government in St. Kitts, Nevis and Anguilla: Politics and Ambition Clash in a Mini-State.* St. Kitts: H. L. S. Browne, 1980.
International Business Publications, *St. Kitts and Nevis Foreign Policy and Government Guide.* International Business Publications, USA, 2004.

Lasia Bloß

SAINT LUCIA

At-a-Glance

OFFICIAL NAME
Saint Lucia

CAPITAL
Castries

POPULATION
164,213 (2005 est.)

SIZE
239 sq. mi. (619 sq. km)

LANGUAGES
English, French patois

RELIGIONS
Roman Catholic 90%, Anglican 3%, other Protestant 7%

NATIONAL OR ETHNIC COMPOSITION
Black 90%, mixed 6%, East Indian 3%, white 1%

DATE OF INDEPENDENCE OR CREATION
February 22, 1979

TYPE OF GOVERNMENT
Parliamentary democracy

TYPE OF STATE
Unitary state

TYPE OF LEGISLATURE
Bicameral parliament

DATE OF CONSTITUTION
December 20, 1978

DATE OF LAST AMENDMENT
No amendment

Saint Lucia gained independence in 1979 after being ruled by Britain since 1815. Since then it has been a parliamentary monarchy within the British Commonwealth.

Saint Lucia is a parliamentary democracy. The country is divided into 11 quarters. The legal system is based on the English common law. The British monarch is head of state and is represented by the governor-general. The preamble to the constitution professes faith in fundamental rights and freedoms, respect for the principles of social justice, and commitment to democracy—the principle of a government freely elected on the basis of universal adult suffrage—as well as to the rule of law. The government generally respects fundamental rights and freedoms. Religious freedom is guaranteed. There are no provisions addressing military forces in the constitution.

The economic system can be described as an agrarian market-based economy.

Saint Lucia is a full and participating member of the Caribbean Community (CARICOM).

CONSTITUTIONAL HISTORY

Saint Lucia is the second-largest island of the British Lesser Antilles, located roughly in the center of the Windward Island chain. Arawak Amerindians first settled on the island in the third century C.E., and the Carib later took over. The island was sighted by the Spanish in the first decade of the 16th century. After early failed attempts to settle there, it remained uncolonized until the mid-17th century, when it was ceded by the king of France to the French West India Company in 1642. In the following decades and centuries Saint Lucia alternately fell under the control of France and Britain 14 different times. Saint Lucia was finally ceded from the French to the British in 1815 and administered as a British Crown colony from 1838 until 1885, when it became administered as part of the British Windward Islands. The island was a province of the short-lived West Indian Federation from 1958 to 1962. The island was granted self-government in 1967 and achieved full independence on February 22, 1979.

FORM AND IMPACT OF THE CONSTITUTION

Saint Lucia has a written constitution, codified in one main document with three annexed schedules. The constitution is the supreme law of Saint Lucia and prevails over other legal provisions. Laws that are inconsistent with the constitution are void insofar as they are inconsistent.

BASIC ORGANIZATIONAL STRUCTURE

Saint Lucia is a unitary state divided into 11 quarters as administrative divisions.

LEADING CONSTITUTIONAL PRINCIPLES

The head of state (the monarch) is bound by the constitution and does not, with some exceptions, take part in the daily business of the state. The judiciary is independent, and the rule of law is manifested in the preamble of the constitution, enhanced by the country's subordination to the Eastern Caribbean Supreme Court.

CONSTITUTIONAL BODIES

The predominant bodies provided for in the constitution are the governor-general and the parliament, which is composed of the Senate and the House of Assembly, and the administration or cabinet. There is also a parliament commissioner.

The Governor-General

The governor-general represents the sovereign, who appoints him or her. The duties of the governor-general include appointing the prime minister and deputy prime minister and appointing the cabinet minister on the advice of the prime minister.

The Parliament

According to the constitution, the parliament of Saint Lucia consists of the queen, the Senate, and the House of Assembly. It is the legislative body of Saint Lucia.

The House of Assembly

The House of Assembly consists of 17 members elected for five-year terms in single-seat constituencies. The prime minister is normally the head of the party that wins the most votes in elections for the House of Assembly.

The Senate

The Senate has 11 appointed members. Six members are appointed on the advice of the prime minister, three on the advice of the leader of the opposition, and two after consultation with religious, economic, and social groups.

The Prime Minister and the Cabinet

The governor-general appoints a member of the House of Assembly who has the support of the majority of the members of the house to be prime minister. The governor-general also appoints, on the prime minister's recommendation, members of Parliament from the ruling party as cabinet ministers. The cabinet advise the governor-general on its activities and is responsible to the parliament for any advice given to the governor-general and for every action taken by a minister in the execution of office. The prime minister and cabinet can be removed by a no confidence vote.

The Parliament Commissioner

The parliament commissioner is not an elected member of the parliament and is appointed by the governor-general for a term not exceeding five years. The duties of the parliament commissioner are to investigate any action, decision, or recommendation made by any administration department or authority that appeared to be a result of faulty administration or injustice, not including proceedings in a court.

The Lawmaking Process

One of the main duties of the government is to make laws for the peace, order, and good government of Saint Lucia. The House of Assembly and the Senate pass bills for the governor-general's assent; they are afterward published in the official gazette as laws. In some specially defined cases it suffices that a bill be passed only by the House of Assembly before being presented to the governor-general.

The Judiciary

The two-level court system includes the Courts of Summary Jurisdiction (Magistrate's Courts) and the High Court, both of which have civil and criminal authority. The lower courts accept civil claims up to approximately $1,850 (EC$5,000) and criminal cases that are generally classified as "petty." The High Court has unlimited authority in both civil and criminal cases. All cases may be appealed to the Eastern Caribbean Court of Appeal, which is the highest court of Saint Lucia. Cases also may be appealed to the Privy Council in London as the final court of appeal. A family court handles child custody, maintenance, support, domestic violence, juvenile affairs, and related matters.

THE ELECTION PROCESS

Under the constitution, general elections must be held at least every five years by secret ballot. They may be held earlier at the discretion of the executive government in power. The right to vote in the election is granted to all citizens who are 21 years of age or above. If the administration so decides, the voting age can be lowered to 18 years. All citizens, except senators and members of the police forces, who are at least 21, literate, and not bankrupt have the right to stand for election to the House of Assembly.

POLITICAL PARTIES

Saint Lucia has three main political parties. Freedom of assembly and association is provided for by the constitution as a protected right. However, the constitution does not explicitly recognize political parties; nor is their formation required for participation in elections.

CITIZENSHIP

Upon the date of independence, February 22, 1979, citizenship was granted to citizens of the United Kingdom and Colonies (UKC) who were born, naturalized, or registered in Saint Lucia. A person born in the territory of Saint Lucia after February 22, 1979, regardless of the nationality of the parents, is also granted citizenship, as is a child born abroad, before or after independence, of which at least one of whose parents is a citizen or was eligible for citizenship at the time of independence.

Those foreigners or Commonwealth citizens who reside in Saint Lucia for seven years or who are married to a citizen of Saint Lucia, either living or deceased, may request citizenship. This request, however, is subject to the approval of the government. Dual citizenship is recognized.

FUNDAMENTAL RIGHTS

The constitution defines fundamental rights and their protection in its first chapter. The constitution guarantees the traditional set of liberal human rights and civil liberties but does not address economic or social rights.

Impact and Functions of Fundamental Rights

The constitution is the supreme law of Saint Lucia and prevails over other legal provisions. Laws that are inconsistent with the constitution, including the fundamental rights it guarantees, are void to the extent that they are inconsistent.

Limitations to Fundamental Rights

The fundamental rights specified the constitution are subject to limitations intended to ensure that the enjoyment of the rights and freedoms by any person does not prejudice the rights and freedoms of others or the public interest.

ECONOMY

There is no specific economic system defined in the constitution, but it contains provisions that must be met while structuring the economic system. The first chapter of the constitution protects against deprivation of property without compensation, and the privacy of the home and other property. The country has been a primarily agrarian, market-based economy but has been able to attract foreign business and investment, especially in its offshore banking and tourism industries.

RELIGIOUS COMMUNITIES

The first chapter of the constitution protects freedom of conscience, including freedom of thought and of religion, as a fundamental right and freedom. This provision also involves the religious communities. The government generally respects this right in practice and does not tolerate its abuse, either by governmental or private actors. It maintains a close relationship with the Christian Council.

MILITARY DEFENSE AND STATE OF EMERGENCY

The Royal Saint Lucia Police has 704 officers, including a 35-officer special services unit, which has some paramilitary training, and a coast guard unit. The civilian authorities maintain effective control of the security forces.

AMENDMENTS TO THE CONSTITUTION

There are different provisions concerning alterations or amendments to the constitution. The core provisions of the constitution can only be changed by the votes of three-quarters of the members of parliament. Other provisions can be changed by the votes of two-thirds of the members of parliament.

PRIMARY SOURCES
Constitution in English. Available online. URLs: http://www.stlucia.gov.lc/saint_lucia/saintluciaconstitution/the_saint_lucia_constitution.htm; http://www.georgetown.edu/pdba/Constitutions/Luciae/Luc78.html. Accessed on July 26, 2005.

SECONDARY SOURCES
Associated States: The Saint Lucia Constitution Order 1967. London: H.M.S.O., 1967.
Saint Lucia: the St. Lucia Constitution Order, 1978. London: H.M.S.O., 1978.
U.S. Department of State, St. Lucia. Available online. URL: http://www.state.gov/r/pa/ei/bgn/2344.htm. Accessed on June 27, 2006.

Bettina Bojarra

SAINT VINCENT AND THE GRENADINES

At-a-Glance

OFFICIAL NAME
Saint Vincent and the Grenadines

CAPITAL
Kingstown

POPULATION
121,000 (2005)

SIZE
150 sq. mi. (389 sq. km)

LANGUAGES
English, some French

RELIGIONS
Anglican 47%, Methodist 28%, Roman Catholic 13%, other (including Protestant denominations, Seventh-Day Adventist, and Hindu) 12%

NATIONAL OR ETHNIC COMPOSITION
African descent 66%, mixed 19%, East Indian 6%, Carib Indian 2%, other 7%

DATE OF INDEPENDENCE OR CREATION
October 27, 1979

TYPE OF GOVERNMENT
Parliamentary democracy

TYPE OF STATE
Independent sovereign state within the Commonwealth

TYPE OF LEGISLATURE
Unicameral

DATE OF CONSTITUTION
October 27, 1979

DATE OF LAST AMENDMENT
review in process

Saint Vincent and the Grenadines is a parliamentary democracy based on the rule of law with a clear division of executive, legislative, and judicial powers. The country is organized as six districts spread over the island of Saint Vincent and the 30 islands constituting the Grenadines.

The constitution provides for guarantees of human rights. These are widely respected by the public authorities; however, some human rights problems remain, such as excessive use of force by police, poor prison conditions, and an overburdened court system. If a violation of the constitution occurs, there are remedies enforceable by an independent judiciary, including the Eastern Caribbean Supreme Court—known in the country as the Saint Vincent and the Grenadines Supreme Court—as a high court and court of appeals. The constitution is currently undergoing a review carried out by a commission with public participation.

The British queen, Elizabeth II, is the formal head of state; she is represented by a governor-general, who has predominantly ceremonial functions. The prime minister, as the elected head of the executive government, is the central political figure but is dependent upon the parliament.

Religious freedom is guaranteed, and state and religious communities are separated. The economy depends to a large extent on agricultural products, construction, and tourism; it is burdened by periodic destruction by tropical weather. The country continues to suffer from unemployment and low per capita gross domestic product. The economy is based on a market system. Saint Vincent maintains no military force except a paramilitary unit within the police.

CONSTITUTIONAL HISTORY

Saint Vincent and the Grenadines was discovered by Christopher Columbus in 1498. It became a British colony in 1763 and remained—except during four-year French rule that began in 1779—under the British through various stages of colonial status until its independence in 1979. A representative assembly was authorized in 1776, a Crown colony government installed in 1877, and a legislative council created in 1925. From 1838 Saint Vincent was part of the federal colony of the Windward Islands. In 1958, it became part of the British West Indies with an internal self-government. Four years later, Saint Vincent became a separate British dependency, restyled in 1969 in an associated state. As of October 27, 1979, Saint Vincent is an independent state within the British Commonwealth.

Similarly to other former British colonies, Saint Vincent is a constitutional parliamentary monarchy. Saint Vincent and the Grenadines maintains close relations with the United States, Canada, and the United Kingdom; it cooperates with regional organizations, such as the Organization of Eastern Caribbean States (OECS) and the Caribbean Community and Common Market (CARICOM); it is a member of the United Nations, the Commonwealth of Nations, the Organization of American States, the Association of Caribbean States (ACS), and other international organizations.

FORM AND IMPACT OF THE CONSTITUTION

Saint Vincent and the Grenadines has a written constitution, codified in a single document, called the Constitution. It is the supreme law of the land and takes precedence over all other national law. Some human rights are not enshrined in the constitution but provided by ordinary law.

BASIC ORGANIZATIONAL STRUCTURE

Saint Vincent and the Grenadines is a state made up by the island of Saint Vincent and a number of smaller islands, islets, and cays referred to as the Grenadines. The central government administers the law in all parts of the country.

LEADING CONSTITUTIONAL PRINCIPLES

The system of government of Saint Vincent and the Grenadines is a parliamentary democracy. There is a division of the executive, legislative, and judicial powers, based on checks and balances. The judiciary is independent.

Political participation is shaped as an indirect, representative democracy; in certain instances referenda may be held. The rule of law is applied.

CONSTITUTIONAL BODIES

The predominant bodies provided for in the constitution are the governor-general, the cabinet of ministers, and the House of Assembly.

The Governor-General

Formally, the British queen or king is the head of state. She or he appoints the governor-general as her or his representative, "who shall hold office during Her Majesty's pleasure"; no term of office is specified in the constitution. The governor-general exercises executive authority on behalf of her majesty but must act in accordance with the advice of the cabinet of ministers. The governor-general appoints senators, the prime minister, and the leader of the opposition and may at any time prorogue (adjourn) or dissolve the parliament.

A deputy may be appointed to represent the office in cases of absence or other reasons of unavailability.

The Executive Administration and Cabinet of Ministers

The executive administration consists of the governor-general, the prime minister, and a number of ministers determined by parliament. Considered together, the prime minister and other ministers are referred to as the cabinet of ministers. Its function is to advise the governor-general. All ministers are appointed by the governor-general from among the members of the House of Assembly; they are collectively responsible to the house; the prime minister is subject to a no confidence vote by the parliament.

The House of Assembly (Parliament)

The parliament of Saint Vincent consists of her majesty and the House of Assembly. The house consists of representatives elected in constituencies in a general election (currently 15, as established by a Boundary Commission in accordance with the Constitution), six senators appointed by the governor-general or the advice of the prime minister and the leader of the opposition, the attorney general, and the speaker of the house if he or she is not a member of the parliament. Representatives and senators vacate their seats every time parliament is dissolved, and senators may be required to step down by the governor-general. The normal term of office is five years.

The parliament is the central body that makes laws for the peace, order, and good government of Saint Vincent. It may oust the prime minister by a vote of no confidence, which requires an absolute majority of all the representatives.

The Supervisor of Elections

The supervisor of elections supervises general elections. He or she also conducts referenda for the approval of an amendment to the constitution.

The Lawmaking Process

One of the main duties of the parliament is the passing of legislation. This is done in cooperation with other constitutional organs. Generally, a decision is made by a majority of the votes of the members present and voting. Bills passed by the parliament must be assented to by the governor-general and be published in the *Official Gazette* to become law. Restrictions to the lawmaking power of the parliament apply with regard to certain financial measures.

The Commissions

The Vincentian constitution makes provision for a number of commissions, such as the Public Service Commission, the Judicial and Legal Services Commission, and the Police Service Commission, which, with the cooperation of the governor-general, exercise control over the administration and the executive.

The Public Service Board of Appeal

The Public Service Board of Appeal hears appeals against disciplinary measures within the administration.

The Judiciary

The judiciary is independent of the administration. The High Court has original jurisdiction in questions relating to the constitution. Lower courts may in proceedings before them refer to the High Court questions as to the constitutionality of a given measure as they arise. Decisions by the High Court may be appealed before the Court of Appeals and Supreme Court; decisions of the latter in certain matters may be taken for appeal to her majesty in council.

The Eastern Caribbean Supreme Court, established by a number of Caribbean countries, has unlimited jurisdiction in accordance with the Supreme Court Act. It acts as the Court of Appeals for Saint Vincent and the Grenadines.

THE ELECTION PROCESS

All Vincentians over the age of 18 have the right to vote in elections. Commonwealth citizens of 21 upward who have resided in Saint Vincent for 12 months before the election may qualify to be elected a representative. The election process is supervised by the supervisor of elections in accordance with the constitution.

POLITICAL PARTIES

Saint Vincent and the Grenadines has a pluralistic system with two major political parties. Of them, the Unity Labor Party (ULP) won 12 of the 15 seats in parliament in the 2001 elections; the New Democratic Party (NDP) holds the remaining seats.

CITIZENSHIP

Every person born in Saint Vincent becomes a citizen at the date of his or her birth except when the parents belong to the diplomatic corps of a foreign country. Persons born outside Saint Vincent may become citizens if one of their parents is a citizen. A Commonwealth citizen may be registered as a citizen of Saint Vincent; citizenship can also be acquired through marriage to a citizen.

FUNDAMENTAL RIGHTS

The 1979 constitution defines fundamental rights in its first chapter, in which it guarantees the traditional set of human rights and civil liberties.

The protection of the right to life is the starting point; it does not, however, prevent the execution of a death sentence where permitted by law and reasonably justifiable in respect of a criminal offense. The constitution guarantees numerous specific rights. The human rights set out in the constitution have binding force for the legislature, the executive, and the judiciary as directly applicable law; thus, they are binding for all public authority.

The right to personal liberty and the protection from discrimination may be suspended in cases of emergency.

Impact and Functions of Fundamental Rights

Human rights are a centerpiece of the Vincentian legal system. Redress can be sought before the High Court for a violation of fundamental rights in the constitution, irrespective of any other lawful action. In addition, any court may in any proceedings before it refer a question as to the contravention of the fundamental rights to the High Court.

Limitations to Fundamental Rights

The fundamental rights are limited explicitly in the constitution by respect for the rights and freedoms of others and by the public interest, but no fundamental right may be disregarded completely: even the derogation in cases of emergency may only happen via reasonably justifiable measures for dealing with the situation.

The protection of fundamental rights is limited for members of a disciplined force, such as the military, police, or prison service.

ECONOMY

The Vincentian constitution does not specify a specific economic system. Yet, as in other constitutions, some provisions can be interpreted as providing a general economic framework in terms of a free-market system, such as the protection of property, the freedom to form associations, and the protection from slavery or forced labor.

RELIGIOUS COMMUNITIES

Freedom of religion or belief, which is guaranteed as a human right, also involves rights for religious communities. There is no established state church. The state may provide financial assistance for places of education established and maintained by religious communities; otherwise the public authorities remain neutral in their relations with religious communities, and religions must be treated equally.

The right to freedom of religion is reflected in practice. The government is secular, does not interfere with individuals' religious rights, and administers a policy that contributes to the generally free practice of religion. The government maintains a close relationship with the Christian Council, which comprises the Anglican, Roman Catholic, Salvation Army, and Methodist denominations. In public schools pupils receive nondenominational religious instruction on a voluntary basis.

MILITARY DEFENSE AND STATE OF EMERGENCY

Saint Vincent and the Grenadines maintains the Royal Saint Vincent Police. It is the only security force in the country and includes a coast guard and a small special services unit with some paramilitary training.

The police forces remain under the effective control of the civilian authorities. However, some human rights abuses committed by police forces have been reported.

The governor-general may declare a state of emergency in times of war, as a result of volcanic eruption or other natural disaster, or when action by any person constitutes a danger to public safety. A declaration of emergency generally elapses after seven days.

AMENDMENTS TO THE CONSTITUTION

Parliament may generally amend the constitution. However, certain sections, including the chapter containing fundamental rights, may only be submitted to the governor-general for assent if the alteration has been approved in a referendum by two-thirds of the valid votes. The constitution is currently undergoing a review.

PRIMARY SOURCES

Constitution. Available online. URL: http://www.pdba. georgetown.edu/Constitutions/Vincent/stvincent79. html. Accessed on June 27, 2006.

SECONDARY SOURCES

Bureau of Public Affairs, U.S. Department of State, "Background Note and Country Reports on Human Rights Practices and International Religious Freedom Report 2004." Available online. URL: http://www. state.gov/r/pa/ei/bgn/2345.htm. Accessed on June 27, 2006.
"The CIA World Fact Book." Available online. URL: http://www.cia.gov/cia/publications/factbook/geos/ vc.html. Accessed on August 17, 2005.
"The Eastern Caribbean Supreme Court." Available online. URL: http://www.eccourts.org/. Accessed on June 27, 2006.
Election World, "Country Reports." Available online. URL: http://www.electionworld.org/. Accessed on July 30, 2005.
Freedom House, Country Ratings, Available online. URL: http://www.freedomhouse.org/. Accessed on July 27, 2005.

Florian Wegelein

SAMOA

At-a-Glance

OFFICIAL NAME
Independent State of Samoa

CAPITAL
Apia

POPULATION
177,714 (2005 est.)

SIZE
1,137 sq. mi. (2,944 sq. km)

RELIGIONS
Christian

LANGUAGES
Samoan and English (official)

NATIONAL OR ETHNIC COMPOSITION
Samoan 92.6%, other 7.4%

DATE OF INDEPENDENCE OR CREATION
January 1, 1962

TYPE OF GOVERNMENT
Republic

TYPE OF STATE
Unitary state

TYPE OF LEGISLATURE
Unicameral parliament

DATE OF CONSTITUTION
January 1, 1962

DATE OF LAST AMENDMENT
March 2, 2001

Samoa is a parliamentary democracy organized on the basis of a cabinet headed by a prime minister. Its constitution was enacted in 1962, after a constitutional convention that ended the administration by the New Zealand Government of Western Samoa as a United Nations Trust Territory.

The constitution heralded the creation of Samoa as an independent state. Fundamental rights are guaranteed. Samoa has a growing market economy. The constitution is founded on Christian principles. Freedom of religion is guaranteed. Samoa does not have a military.

CONSTITUTIONAL HISTORY

After international claims by the British, German, and American governments, the control of Samoa (also known at that time as the Navigator Islands) was settled by treaty in 1899. The treaty granted the United States control of the eastern islands and Germany control of the western islands.

At the outbreak of World War I (1914–18), New Zealand forces took Western Samoa for the British govern-ment. At the end of the war, Western Samoa became a League of Nations Mandate and New Zealand was desig-nated as the administrative power. The New Zealand administration lasted until 1962.

The period of New Zealand governance was not free of political troubles. Traditional Samoan leaders did not willingly accept New Zealand administration. The Mau, a nonviolent opposition movement, became very popular. Increasing opposition generated repression and consider-able civil unrest.

During the New Zealand colonial administration, ba-sic government institutions were provided by the 1921 Sa-moa Act. There was no representation of Samoan people until the act was amended in 1923. This amendment gave recognition to the Fono a Faipule (meeting of traditional chiefs) as a council of advisers to the administrator. An amendment of the Samoa Act in 1926 established local representation in the Legislative Council.

After World War II (1939–45) Western Samoa became a United Nations Trust Territory. In 1947, New Zealand be-gan to consider self-government for Samoa and undertook a series of reforms of colonial government institutions. The Samoa Amendment Act of 1947 extended the legislative powers of the assembly and increased its members to 14, 12 of whom were elected by the Fono a Faipule. In 1953, a constitutional convention representing all sections of the Samoan population was called to produce a constitution for Western Samoa, which was not completed until 1960.

In 1957, the Samoa Act was amended again to abolish the Fono a Faipule, to enlarge the assembly with directly elected members, and to redefine the powers of the assembly. The assembly consisted of three official members, five European members, and 41 Samoan members who were elected by a limited suffrage.

By the end of 1960, the constitutional convention had approved a draft constitution. On the advice and under the supervision of the United Nations, a plebiscite took place on May 9, 1961, at which the Samoan people chose independence and approved the constitution. This was the first time Samoans had voted according to adult universal suffrage.

Samoa became an independent state and the constitution entered into force on January 1, 1962. The constitution was influenced by post–World War II human rights philosophy and was based on the legal structures introduced by New Zealand in the colonial period.

FORM AND IMPACT OF THE CONSTITUTION

The constitution is one document. It has 117 articles with key portions on fundamental rights, the head of state, the executive, parliament, the judiciary, public service, finance, land, and titles.

The constitution has proved to be very stable. At the time of its enactment it envisaged representation through chiefs (*matai*). Only *matai* could be elected to the Legislative Assembly and only *matai* could vote. This form of representation was accepted by the United Nations as satisfying the requirements of democracy because *matai* were the chosen representatives of their relevant family groups.

In 1962, parliament had 47 members. Of these 45 members represented territorial constituencies (whose electors were holders of *matai* title), and two represented individual voters who were citizens of non-Samoan origin.

The constitution has high political relevance and is the dominant set of rules for the government of Samoa. It is supplemented by and, to a degree, depends on the operation of Samoan custom (Faa Samoa).

The constitution is at the top of the hierarchy of norms. Next in order are legislation enacted by the Legislative Assembly, then subordinate legislation, and finally custom. English common law and equity are also sources of law in Samoa.

BASIC ORGANIZATIONAL STRUCTURE

The state is relatively small and centralized. Local government is conducted in a traditional way by each village.

The authority of each village is recognized by the Village Fono Act 1990, which confirms an executive, legislature, and judicial authority in the village leadership.

LEADING CONSTITUTIONAL PRINCIPLES

The preamble of the constitution explicitly recognizes the role of God and Samoan custom. These principles are important for the interpretation of the constitution and of human rights issues.

The constitution provides for the basic principles of democracy. Important rules are also contained in the Electoral Act 1963, in which provisions are made for the right to vote and the right to stand for election in parliament. There was a change of the electoral system in 1991 to provide for universal adult suffrage rather than *matai* suffrage. This significant change was made without changing the constitution.

The constitution is the supreme law of Samoa. The Supreme Court has the power to determine constitutionality. The doctrine of separation of powers is indicated by Parts 4, 5, and 6, which deal with the executive, legislature, and judiciary, respectively.

CONSTITUTIONAL BODIES

The main constitutional organs are the head of state, the cabinet, parliament, the judiciary, and the Public Service Commission.

Head of State

The constitution establishes that the head of state is known as O le Ao le Malo. The key local leaders at the time of passing the constitution—Tupua Tamasese and Malietoa Tanumafili II—became joint heads of state for life; Tupua died in 1963. Upon the death of Malietoa, the head of state will be elected by the Legislative Assembly for the five-year term provided by the constitution.

The executive power is vested in the head of state, who must act on the advice of the cabinet or the appropriate minister.

Cabinet

The cabinet consists of at least eight, but no more than 12, members of parliament, appointed by the head of state acting on the advice of the prime minister. The prime minister, who is also appointed by the head of state, presides over the cabinet and must command the confidence of a majority of the members of parliament.

Parliament

Parliament consists of the head of state and the Legislative Assembly. The Legislative Assembly is unicameral and has 49 seats. Their members are elected by popular vote for a term of five years.

The Lawmaking Process

Lawmaking follows the English practice of three readings of a law proposal, followed by signature of the head of state.

The Judiciary

The system of courts for Samoa comprises the Fa'amasino Fesoasoani Court, the Magistrates' Court, the Supreme Court, and the Court of Appeal. Judges are appointed by the head of state acting on the advice of the Judicial Service Commission. The chief of justice is appointed by the head of state on the advice of the prime minister.

The Land and Titles Court is a special court that has jurisdiction of matters relating to customary land and traditional Samoan title. It operates in accordance with its own rules of procedure without the presence of lawyers and independently of the general court system. This court has significant jurisdiction because the *matai* plays an important role in the political system and because 80 percent of Samoan land is held in customary title.

The Public Service Commission

The head of state, acting on the advice of the prime minister, appoints the members of the Public Service Commission. Its main function is to provide for planning, management policy, monitoring, and evaluation of human resources in the public service. It also acts as an advisory body to the cabinet in matters relating to "appointments, grading, salaries, promotions, transfer, retirement, and terminations of appointments, dismissals, and discipline."

THE ELECTION PROCESS

General elections to the Legislative Assembly are carried out within three months of dissolution of the previous assembly, as the head of state appoints.

A person is qualified to stand for election to the Legislative Assembly if he or she is a citizen of Samoa and is not disqualified by any law of Samoa. The Electoral Act of 1963 provides that 47 of the 49 seats are reserved for *matai* title holders and two seats are reserved for citizens not of Samoan heritage.

All Samoan citizens over the age of 21 are entitled to vote.

POLITICAL PARTIES

The Human Rights Protection Party (HRPP) and the Samoan National Development Party (SNDP) are both represented in parliament. The HRPP is the dominant party.

CITIZENSHIP

Every person born in Samoa is a Samoan citizen by birth. A person who is born outside Samoa whose father or mother is a citizen of Samoa at the time of his or her birth is a Samoan citizen by descent.

FUNDAMENTAL RIGHTS

The constitution provides for the protection of fundamental rights including the right to life, the right to personal liberty, freedom from inhuman treatment, freedom from forced labor, the right to a fair trial, and rights concerning criminal law.

Impact and Functions of Fundamental Rights

There is a continuing tension between the village authorities, acting on behalf of customary rights, and individuals. The village communities still tend to give preference to the community's interest over that of individuals. Failure to comply with a village order may, for example, lead to an order of banishment against the offender and his or her family. Such an order is also frequently accompanied by destruction or confiscation of the offender's property.

Limitations to Fundamental Rights

Some restrictions of rights are allowed in the public interest, including freedom of speech, assembly, association, movement, and residence. Fundamental rights may also be restricted by emergency orders made during declared states of emergency.

ECONOMY

The constitution establishes a treasury fund that must receive all money raised by Samoa. It has provisions relating to appropriated and unauthorized expenditure. Although there is no specific provision in the constitution regarding the economy, the Samoan economy has in recent times developed rapidly and along market lines not dissimilar to those of New Zealand. There has been a pattern of corporatization of government departments and activities, with a declared goal of privatization. The Samoan economy has been supported by substantial international aid.

RELIGIOUS COMMUNITIES

The constitution is declared to be founded on Christian principles, but freedom of conscience and belief is protected.

MILITARY DEFENSE AND STATE OF EMERGENCY

Samoa does not have a military force. The constitution provides that the head of state, in consultation with the cabinet, can declare a state of emergency for a limited time. Emergency orders can restrict constitutional rights and freedoms but are laid before parliament and are subject to its control.

AMENDMENTS TO THE CONSTITUTION

The constitution can be altered by an act of parliament passed with the special majority of two-thirds of the total membership. Amendments to Article 102 (relating to the alienation of customary land) also require the support of two-thirds of the national electorate voting in a poll.

PRIMARY SOURCES

Constitution in English. Available online. URL: http://www. paclii.org/ws/legis/consol_act/cotisows1960535/. Accessed on July 30, 2005.

SECONDARY SOURCES

Frederica M. Bunge and Melinda W. Cooke, eds., *Oceania: A Regional Study,* Area Handbook Series (Melanesia, Micronesia, Polynesia, Guam, American Samoa). Washington, D.C.: United States Government Printing Office, 1985.

T. Malifa, "The Franchise in the Constitution of Western Samoa: Towards a Theory of the Constitution." LL.M. Thesis, Harvard University, 1988.

Lauofo Meti, *Samoa: The Making of the Constitution.* Lepapaigalagala, Samoa: National University of Samoa: 2002.

Tony Angelo

SAN MARINO

At-a-Glance

OFFICIAL NAME
Republic of San Marino

CAPITAL
San Marino

POPULATION
29,300 (2005 est.)

SIZE
24 sq. mi. (61 sq. km)

LANGUAGES
Italian

RELIGIONS
Roman Catholic

NATIONAL OR ETHNIC COMPOSITION
Sammarinese, Italian

DATE OF INDEPENDENCE OR CREATION
301 C.E.

TYPE OF GOVERNMENT
Parliamentary democracy

TYPE OF STATE
Unitary state

TYPE OF LEGISLATURE
Unicameral parliament

DATE OF CONSTITUTION
1600 (statutes); July 8, 1974 (Declaration of Rights)

DATE OF LAST AMENDMENT
February 26, 2002

The Republic of San Marino is a parliamentary democracy. The form of government has specific features deriving from the constitutional and political history of the republic. The dominant role of parliament (Consiglio Grande e Generale) in the decision-making process works against the principle of separation of powers; however, the assembly itself has always been a collegial and republican body.

The parliament has lawmaking powers, policymaking functions, the power of appointment, as well as judicial and administrative functions. All the constitutional bodies are elected by the parliament.

The two capitani reggenti, elected by the parliament for six-month terms, combine the functions of head of state, head of the executive (Congresso di Stato), and speaker of the parliament. The executive, made up of members of the parliament and presided over by the head of state, has only recently obtained more autonomy and explicit functions of government and policymaking.

The Republic of San Marino has an uncodified constitution composed of a series of different laws and documents. One of the most important documents is the 1974 Declaration of the Rights of the Citizens and the Fundamental Principles of the Order of San Marino, which has a primary role in the hierarchy of legal sources. It contains several provisions showing characteristics of an entrenched constitution. The document contains provisions on the relation between citizens and the government, the protection of human rights, and the main principles concerning the organization of the state.

CONSTITUTIONAL HISTORY

The main feature of San Marino's constitutional history is its continuity. Its constitutional organization is ultimately based on statutes (Leges Statutae), going back to the 13th century and codified in 1600 C.E. Most of these statutes are still binding.

According to tradition, San Marino was founded in 301 C.E., when a Christian stonemason named Marinus hid on the peak of Mount Titano to escape from the anti-Christian Roman emperor Diocletian. He founded a small community of people who followed Christian beliefs.

Undoubtedly, the oldest body was the Arengo, the Assembly of the Heads of Families, which held all legislative and judicial powers. This created a type of government that can be described as a direct patriarchal democracy, tailored to a small close-knit community.

The transformation from direct to representative democracy took place in the 16th century when the powers of the Arengo were transferred to the parliament (Consiglio Grande e Generale). The latter was appointed by the Arengo from among its most distinguished members.

The most important day in the constitutional history of San Marino was March 25, 1906, when the Arengo passed a constitutional reform giving all citizens the right to vote in parliamentary elections. The form of government thus changed from an oligarchy to a democracy. This change was strengthened by a series of subsequent political developments, interrupted only during the period 1923–43, when San Marino was under fascist rule. The 1974 Declaration of Rights can be seen as the culmination of this process.

FORM AND IMPACT OF THE CONSTITUTION

San Marino does not have a written constitution. However, as the 1974 Declaration of Rights formalized certain constitutional matters, it occupies the high position in the hierarchy of legal sources typical of a rigid constitution. Some of the historical Leges Statutae, which continue to have some legal standing, have constitutional content.

Article 1 of the Declaration of Rights refers to the European Convention on Human Rights and other international treaties concerning human rights. These treaties prevail over conflicting domestic legislation.

BASIC ORGANIZATIONAL STRUCTURE

San Marino is a unitary state.

LEADING CONSTITUTIONAL PRINCIPLES

San Marino has a parliamentary democracy. The dominant role of parliament is strictly connected to the political traditions of a small, homogeneous, and conservative community.

The republican form of government, the protection of civil and political rights, and the principle of collegiality at all levels of the political system are constant features in the history of San Marino. Consequently, separation of powers is not needed as an instrument to protect fundamental rights. There is a strong overlap between legislative and administrative functions.

The population of San Marino enjoys social and cultural rights typical of a welfare state.

CONSTITUTIONAL BODIES

The constitutional bodies fixed in the 1974 Declaration of Rights are the head of state (capitani reggenti), the executive (Congresso di Stato), the parliament (Consiglio Grande e Generale), and the judiciary, including the Constitutional Court (Collegio dei Garanti), which was introduced by the Constitutional Reform of 2002.

The Head of State (Capitani Reggenti)

The capitani reggenti carry out the functions of a head of state collegially. They are elected by parliament in a secret ballot requiring an absolute majority. According to a constitutional convention, the capitani reggenti are chosen from among the members of parliament. Their mandate lasts for half a year (they begin office on April 1, and October 1, every year). They cannot be reelected for at least three years after a previous mandate. They preside over the parliament and the executive (Congresso di Stato). Collegiality and a short mandate prevent a shift toward authoritarianism.

The Executive (Congresso di Stato)

The executive (Congresso di Stato) is elected by the parliament from among its members. It is politically responsible to the parliament and carries out government and administrative activities; however, there is no explicit relationship of confidence between the executive and the parliament.

The Parliament (Consiglio Grande e Generale)

The parliament (Consiglio Grande e Generale) is composed of 60 members elected through universal and direct suffrage. It exercises legislative, political, and supervisory functions. The peculiarity of the parliament of San Marino lies in its administrative functions and powers of appointment. Therefore, the form of government is decidedly parliamentarian.

The Lawmaking Process
According to the standard procedure for approving a law, a bill must be included in the order of the day of parliament, which then assigns it to the relevant committee. After the committee has scrutinized the bill, it is sent back to the parliament for final debate and approval. A bill is approved by a majority of those voting. Constitutional amendments or laws have to be approved by a qualified majority of two-thirds of the assembly; if it fails to reach that threshold, but does win an absolute majority, a referendum can be held. Finally, organic laws (*leggi qualificate*) have to be approved by an absolute majority of the members of parliament.

The Judiciary

Until 2003, parliament appointed all the ordinary judges (who had to be from outside the country). The Consiglio dei Dodici (Council of Twelve), chosen by parliament from among its members and presided over by the head of state (capitani reggenti), was a third instance court in civil and administrative proceedings.

Since 2003, there has been one first instance court, organized as two benches, one civil and one administrative. Judges are now selected through a public examination system and can be from San Marino. This reform guarantees independence and freedom of the judiciary, as called for in the 1974 Declaration of Rights.

The Constitutional Court (Collegio dei Garanti) is composed of three sitting members and three deputies, elected by parliament by a majority of two-thirds of the members. The court carries out constitutional review of laws, acts having force of law, and customary laws. Furthermore, the Constitutional Court decides on the admissibility of referendums, resolves jurisdictional disputes of constitutional bodies, and pursues inquiries concerning the head of state.

THE ELECTION PROCESS

All citizens at least 18 years old can vote. All citizens who are at least 21 years old on the day of the elections can be elected.

POLITICAL PARTIES

The Republic of San Marino has a multiparty political system, with a proportional electoral system.

CITIZENSHIP

The primary way to become a citizen of the Republic of San Marino is by birth. The parliament can accord naturalization in special cases provided for by law.

FUNDAMENTAL RIGHTS

Historically, the principles of equality, personal freedom, freedom of expression, and freedom of assembly are part of the political and legal heritage of the Republic of San Marino. Article 5 of the 1974 Declaration of Rights states that "human rights are inviolable." The subsequent articles (6 to 11) enumerate the most important of these.

In some cases, the Declaration of Rights merely recognizes preexisting rights such as personal freedom, freedom of domicile, freedom of assembly, freedom of association, freedom of conscience, and freedom of creed. It also recognizes the right to vote, to be elected, and to join political parties and trade unions.

The document also contains a series of so-called social rights. They include the right to free education, social security, and a clean and safe environment, as well as protection of the historical and culture heritage.

Impact and Functions of Fundamental Rights

The basic rights set out in the Dichiarazione (Declaration) have binding force for all constitutional bodies.

Limitations to Fundamental Rights

Article 5 of the 1974 Declaration of Rights declares human rights as inviolable.

ECONOMY

The constitution of San Marino does not prescribe any particular economic system. Nevertheless, the country shows the typical features of a social market economy.

RELIGIOUS COMMUNITIES

Freedom of religion in San Marino encompasses both beliefs and practices. There is no established state church.

MILITARY DEFENSE AND STATE OF EMERGENCY

The army of the Republic of San Marino is staffed on a voluntary basis and is responsible to the head of state. In cases of internal or international states of emergency the parliament can call up all citizens between the ages of 16 and 60.

AMENDMENTS TO THE CONSTITUTION

Amendments to the 1974 Declaration of Rights have to be approved by a qualified majority of two-thirds of the Grand and General Council. If they are approved by only an absolute majority, a referendum is held.

PRIMARY SOURCES

The *"Dichiarazione dei diritti dei cittadini e dei principi fondamentali dell'ordinamento sammarinese,"* and all other laws of the Republic of San Marino are available in Italian. Available online. URL: www.consigliograndeegenerale.sm. Accessed on July 17, 2005.

SECONDARY SOURCES

A. Barbera, "La dichiarazione dei diritti dei cittadini e dei principi fondamentali (legge 59/74) nell'ordinamento di San Marino." In G. Guidi, ed., *Un collegio garante della costituzionalità delle norme in San Marino*. Rimini: Maggioli, 2000.

G. Guidi, "Repubblica di San Marino." In G. Guidi, ed., Piccolo Stato, *Costituzione e connessioni internazionali*, 121–170. Torino: Giappichelli, 2003.

L. Lonfernini, "Origine ed evoluzione storica dello Statuto Sammarinese (III secolo–XVI secolo)." In *Gli antichi Statuti della Repubblica di San Marino*, 19–35. San Marino: AIEP, 2002.

E. Spagna Musso, "L'ordinamento costituzionale di San Marino." In *Archivio Giuridico F. Serafini* (1986): 1–78.

Licia Califano

SÃO TOMÉ AND PRÍNCIPE

At-a-Glance

OFFICIAL NAME
Democratic Republic of São Tomé and Príncipe

CAPITAL
São Tomé

POPULATION
151,000 (2005 est.)

SIZE
380 sq. mi. (1,001 sq. km)

LANGUAGES
Portuguese (official language), Bantoues, Portuguese Creole (Crioulo)

RELIGIONS
Roman Catholic 82%, Protestant 15%, small animist minority 3%

NATIONAL OR ETHNIC COMPOSITION
Descendants of African slaves (Servicais, Forras, Angolares) 80%, Mestizo 10%, Europeans 2%, other 8%

DATE OF INDEPENDENCE
July 12, 1975

TYPE OF GOVERNMENT
Presidential democracy

TYPE OF STATE
Unitary state

TYPE OF LEGISLATURE
Unicameral parliament

DATE OF CONSTITUTION
September 10, 1990

DATE OF LAST AMENDMENT
January 29, 2003

A tiny island state facing a high degree of poverty and low economic development, São Tomé and Príncipe is one of Africa's most open and pluralistic democracies. Within the limits of a restrained budget, the rule of law and fundamental rights are fairly well respected. The constitutional system is based on the model of presidential democracy.

CONSTITUTIONAL HISTORY

São Tomé and Príncipe were two uninhabited islands until Portuguese sailors arrived on the day of Saint Thomas (Portuguese, São Tomé) in 1470. It fell under the Portuguese Crown in the 16th century and saw considerable development as a port of transshipment in the slave trade and later as an exporter of sugar and cocoa. Slave labor was formally abolished in 1876, but forced paid labor continued until the middle of the 20th century and gave rise to social conflicts.

With decolonization beginning in Africa in the 1950s, a liberation front called Movimento de Libertação de São Tomée Príncipe (MLSTP) was formed abroad. When the Portuguese dictatorship was overturned in 1974, the new Portuguese government negotiated transition to independence, which was achieved on July 12, 1975.

The MLSTP established one-party rule following Marxist doctrine. In 1990 São Tomé and Príncipe became one of the first African countries to introduce multiparty rule. The constitution dating from 1975 was revised in 1990, but not completely replaced. The recent constitutional revision of 2003 has constituted an additional step of development toward constitutional democracy and has devolved some power to subnational entities.

FORM AND IMPACT OF THE CONSTITUTION

Despite the economic hardship the country faces, it has successfully followed the path of democracy and respect for the rule of law over the last two decades. Two unsuccessful coup attempts were made since 1990, the second in 2003. However, order was quickly restored by nonviolent means.

A regular transition from the first democratic president to the second was achieved in 2001. The constitution appears to have considerable impact, and the country is one of the freest in Africa.

BASIC ORGANIZATIONAL STRUCTURE

São Tomé and Príncipe is a unitary state and a presidential republic. The island of Príncipe has some autonomy.

LEADING CONSTITUTIONAL PRINCIPLES

The 1990/2003 constitution has important features taken from the Portuguese presidential type of government, with an even more powerful position of the president of the republic. There is a division of powers among the legislature, the judiciary, and the executive, under the supervision of the president. Rule of law and fundamental rights are enshrined in the constitution. The socialist past still is visible in the text of the constitution.

São Tomé and Príncipe is a secular state. It aims at promoting peaceful relations with neighboring countries and countries of Portuguese language and proclaims its adherence to the values of the United Nations (UN) and the African Union. International treaty law takes precedence over national legislation, but not over the constitution.

CONSTITUTIONAL BODIES

The main constitutional bodies are the president of the republic, the executive administration, the Council of State, the National Assembly, the Constitutional Tribunal, and the Supreme Court of Justice.

The President of the Republic

The president is the most powerful figure in the constitutional life of São Tomé, as the head of state and supreme commander of the armed forces. The president guarantees national independence and ensures the proper functioning of the institutions.

The president is directly elected for five years. There is in principle no limit to reelection. No person can, however, be elected for three *consecutive* terms. In order to be eligible, candidates must have São Toméan nationality and be of São Toméan descent, with no other citizenship; they must have lived permanently on the national territory at least three years before their candidacy and must be older than 35.

The president may not hold any other office. He or she must notify the National Assembly of any absence from the national territory; its assent is required for absence of more than five days or travel on official duty. If the necessary assent is not sought, the president is removed from office without further steps. In case of incapacity, the president is replaced by the president of the National Assembly.

The president appoints the prime minister and the council of ministers and can demand the resignation of the prime minister at any time. The president also has the power to dissolve the National Assembly after a favorable vote in the Council of State.

The president may veto a law voted in the National Assembly. The veto can be overridden by a qualified majority.

The president is responsible to the Supreme Court for crimes committed while in office when acting in official duty. The accusation must first be approved by two-thirds of the members of the National Assembly, acting upon a proposal by one-fifth of its members. Other crimes are tried before ordinary courts, after the term of office ends.

The Executive Administration

The executive administration is composed of the prime minister, the cabinet ministers, and the secretaries of state. It is appointed by the president of the republic, taking into consideration the results of parliamentary elections. A new administration has to be formed after every election. The prime minister must be of São Toméan descent and may not possess another citizenship. The administration is politically responsible before the assembly. Holding of executive governmental posts is incompatible with holding any other post in public and private institutions.

The executive administration convened in the Council of Ministers appoints high civil and military officers. It also disposes of extensive regulatory power and has the power to initiate laws.

The Council of State

The Council of State is a consultative organ for the president of the republic. It is composed of the president of the National Assembly, the prime minister, the president of the Constitutional Court, the attorney general of the republic, the president of the regional government of the autonomous region of Príncipe, the former presidents of the republic, three distinguished citizens chosen by the president for the duration of the president's term of office, and three citizens chosen by the National Assembly for the term of the legislature on the basis of proportional representation of political forces. The Council of State may make recommendations on dissolution of the National Assembly, declaration of war and peace, and other matters.

The National Assembly (Parliament)

Members of the National Assembly are elected by universal suffrage for four-year terms with the possibility of reelection. The constitution affirms the principle that each member represents the whole nation, not his or her constituency.

The size of the assembly is determined by law; it currently has 55 members. Parliamentary activity is limited to two biannual sessions. A Permanent Committee assures continuity between these two sessions.

The constitution provides for parliamentary immunity. A member of parliament can be removed from the assembly by a secret vote of two-thirds of the members of the assembly, in cases of grave disrespect for his or her duties.

The National Assembly can remove the administration by a motion of censure. It has the power to appoint the judges of the Supreme Court.

The Lawmaking Process

The National Assembly disposes of the power of lawmaking. The division between parliamentary lawmaking power and governmental regulatory power is determined by a catalog in the constitution.

The Judiciary

There is a single jurisdiction for civil, criminal, and administrative affairs. It is formally independent, and the independence of individual judges is constitutionally protected. The Supreme Court is at the apex of the judiciary.

The judiciary decides matters related to the respect for fundamental rights. The judiciary has ruled against both the executive administration and the president, but it apparently is still subject at times to influence and manipulation. The court system is overburdened, understaffed, inadequately funded, and plagued by long delays in hearing cases.

The Constitutional Tribunal

The Constitutional Tribunal is composed of five members, three of them members of the judiciary, the other two jurists of other professions. The tribunal has the power to review the constitutionality of legal norms, whether statutes or international agreements; it rules on whether the president is incapacitated; it reviews the electoral process and referenda; and it decides on the legality and constitutionality of political parties.

THE ELECTION PROCESS

Elections are open, universal, direct, equal, and secret. Elections have produced changing majorities in parliament and have replaced a president from one party with a successor from another. A recent constitutional revision introduced popular referendums. The National Assembly or the Council of Ministers can propose referendums on matters within their purview; other issues to be decided by referendum are specified in the constitution or the law.

Since the latest constitutional revision, foreign nationals may participate in local government elections on condition of reciprocity.

POLITICAL PARTIES

São Tomé and Príncipe has become a multiparty state. The MLSTP, the only party admitted until 1990, still has considerable power in the political process, though not enough to obstruct political change. The current president of the republic is of the opposition Ação Democrática Independente (ADI) party.

CITIZENSHIP

Citizenship is acquired either by descent from a São Toméan father or mother, regardless of the country of birth, or by birth on São Tomé and Príncipe. Naturalization is possible on condition of five years of residence and renunciation of former citizenship. Naturalization is subject to certain conditions, among others "good morality" and sufficient means of support. São Toméan citizens may keep their nationality when they acquire a foreign one.

FUNDAMENTAL RIGHTS

The constitution enshrines a vast catalogue of fundamental rights, including an elaborated list of social rights. Their exercise may be restricted during a state of emergency.

The general human rights record is good. However, there are problems in some areas, in part caused by the lack of resources for public institutions. Security forces have on occasion beaten and abused detainees, although the constitution prohibits torture and degrading treatment; they have also on occasion violently dispersed demonstrations. Prison conditions are harsh, and the judicial system is inefficient. Violence and discrimination against women are widespread, child labor remains a problem, and labor practices on plantations are harsh.

The police force is ineffective and widely viewed as corrupt. Police officers have successfully been held responsible for human rights abuses in court. Government and international donors are trying to improve the living conditions of security agents, to reduce the temptation for corruption.

Defense rights are constitutionally protected. However, they find their limits in the underequipped court system.

Freedom of press is recognized. Although permitted by law, there is no private radio or TV. Opposition parties receive free airtime. Freedom of association and assembly is also in principle respected, although police sometimes mishandle political demonstrations. Although equality of men and women is far from realized, a woman was recently appointed prime minister.

The death penalty has been abolished by the constitution. No person may be extradited to a country that applies the death penalty for the crime in question.

ECONOMY

The constitution provides for a mixed economic system. Private, public, and cooperative property is constitutionally protected; the right to join a labor union is recognized.

RELIGIOUS COMMUNITIES

Although predominantly Roman Catholic, São Tomé and Príncipe is a secular republic. Freedom of religion is guaranteed.

MILITARY DEFENSE AND STATE OF EMERGENCY

The president of the republic is the commander in chief of the armed forces. Military service is compulsory, and the defense of the country the "honor and supreme duty" of every citizen. It appears that the defense forces have not acquired any lethal weapons since 1990.

Declarations of war need parliamentary approval, as does any participation by the armed forces in foreign military operations or any presence of foreign troops on the national territory.

A state of emergency can be declared by the president, but it requires parliamentary authorization. The constitution does not specify any additional conditions on the exercise of emergency powers.

AMENDMENTS TO THE CONSTITUTION

Amendments to the constitution may be initiated by three-quarters of the members of the National Assembly, and approved by two-thirds of the members. The president of the republic may call a popular referendum on an amendment at the proposal of the National Assembly, but has no veto power in the matter.

Limits to constitutional revision have been recently introduced. A revision may not impact the independence and the territorial integrity of the country, the secular and republican form of government, fundamental rights, the separation of powers, the guarantee of free elections, the autonomy of regional and local government, the independence of the courts, or political pluralism.

No new constitutional revision may be approved until five years have passed since the previous revision. No constitutional revisions are allowed during a state of emergency.

PRIMARY SOURCES

Constitution in English (extracts). Available online. URL: http://www.chr.up.ac.za/hr_docs/constitutions/docs/Sao%20Tome(english%20summary)(rev).doc. Accessed on July 24, 2005.

SECONDARY SOURCES

Bureau of Public Affairs, U.S. Department of State, "Background Note and Country Reports on Human Rights Practices and International Religious Freedom Report 2004." Available online. URL: http://www.state.gov/r/pa/ei/bgn/5434.htm. Accessed on June 27, 2006.

Malte Beyer

SAUDI ARABIA

At-a-Glance

OFFICIAL NAME
Kingdom of Saudi Arabia (Al Mamlakah al Arabiya as Suudiyah)

CAPITAL
Riyadh

POPULATION
25,795,938 (2005 est.)

SIZE
829,995 sq. mi. (2,149,690 sq. km)

LANGUAGES
Arabic

RELIGIONS
Muslim 93.7%, Christian 3.7%, Hindu 1.1%, other 1.5%

NATIONAL OR ETHNIC COMPOSITION
Arab 90%, Afro-Asian and other 10%

DATE OF INDEPENDENCE OR CREATION
September 23, 1932

TYPE OF GOVERNMENT
Monarchy

TYPE OF STATE
Centralist unified state with 13 provinces

TYPE OF LEGISLATURE
Council of Ministers that enacts laws (subject to royal veto); Consultative Council (Majlis al-Shura; appointed by monarch and advisory only)

DATE OF CONSTITUTION
Basic Law of March 1, 1992

DATE OF LAST AMENDMENT
No amendment

The Kingdom of Saudi Arabia is a unitary state under the hereditary monarchy of the al-Saud family. Saudi Arabia's Basic Law of Governance, promulgated by King Fahd in 1992, declares that the Quran (the words revealed to the Prophet Muhammad) and the *sunnah* (traditions from the life of Muhammad) are the constitution of Saudi Arabia and that the state shall be governed in accordance with sharia (Islamic law). The Basic Law provides that the king, who is also the prime minister, shall rule the kingdom in accordance with sharia and that he will choose his successor from among the direct descendants of the founder of the al-Saud dynasty. The king chooses the members of his Council of Ministers, which acts as the principal lawmaking body of the state, but whose decisions are subject to royal veto.

Although the Basic Law effectively provides that the king is the ultimate political authority in the state, high Islamic religious leaders, collectively known as the Ulema, have significant influence over the king and the other political institutions. The exact nature and degree of the influence of the Ulema are debated, but it is commonly believed that the king, despite all of the power vested in him by tradition and through the Basic Law, would be unable to govern without *ijma* (consensus) and *shura* (consultation). It is generally believed that the influence proceeds in both directions between the king and the Ulema and that each is to some extent dependent on the other for its legitimacy and influence.

Saudi Arabia is not a democracy, and citizens do not have the right to vote. The Basic Law states that citizens shall have rights in accordance with sharia. It is widely believed that the judicial system of Saudi Arabia is not free and does not operate in an independent manner, and therefore that laws may be inconsistently applied to the benefit of the state, the royal family, or other influential persons. In the early 21st century, the Saudi government began to take some limited steps to introduce elections of officials at the local level.

CONSTITUTIONAL HISTORY

The Kingdom of Saudi Arabia first became a unified and independent political entity in 1932 under King Abdul-Aziz ibn Abdelrahman al-Saud (who is generally called ibn Saud outside Saudi Arabia and Abdul-Aziz inside Saudi Arabia), who conquered rival tribes and united the different regions of the modern-day kingdom. During the 20th century, Saudi Arabia was transformed from a poor desert kingdom largely populated by warring Bedouin tribes and coastal merchants and fishermen into one of the richest countries in the world, holding the world's largest known oil reserves.

The constitutional history of modern Saudi Arabia may reasonably be said to have begun during the lifetime of the Prophet Muhammad in the sixth and seventh centuries C.E. The Prophet lived in the holy cities of Mecca and Medina, where he received revelations that culminated in the creation of the Quran, the holiest text for Muslims and the basis for much of sharia (Islamic law), which is recognized as being the underlying law of the modern Saudi state. The traditions of Muhammad's life constitute the *sunnah,* which is recognized as the second most important source of sharia and is also recognized as law in Saudi Arabia. (The *sunnah* are collected and recorded in stories and quotations known as *ahadith.*) Saudi Arabia is particularly marked by the fact that the two most sacred sites of Islam, the mosques of Mecca and Medina, are on its soil. The official title of the king of Saudi Arabia is Custodian of the Two Holy Mosques.

Throughout much of its history after the seventh century, the Arabian Peninsula—modern-day Saudi Arabia, Yemen, and other Gulf states—was the scene of ongoing struggles among warring clans. Traditionally, the two most important competing geographical regions were the Hijaz and Nejd. The Hijaz, which is located along the western coast of the peninsula, contained the important trading, transportation, and religious centers of Mecca, Medina, and Jeddah. The geographical center of Arabia is the desert region of the Nejd, the site of the modern-day capital, Riyad. Traditionally, the Hijaz has been the more cosmopolitan, literate, and sophisticated part of Arabia, and the Nejd populated by less educated desert Bedouin. These perceived regional differences, though sometimes exaggerated and sometimes downplayed, continue to have social and political significance within Saudi Arabia.

European powers began to attempt to control portions of the Arabian Peninsula in the 16th century. The Turkish Ottoman Empire conquered parts of the peninsula, including Mecca and Medina, in the 17th century but was never able to overcome the enormous logistical difficulties posed by the huge desert regions at the center.

The modern history of Saudi Arabia may be said to have begun in the 18th century with the fortuitous alliance of two figures from the Nejd: Muhammad ibn Abd al-Wahhab (1703–92), the founder of the Wahhabist interpretation of Islam that prevails in Saudi Arabia, and Abdul-Aziz ibn Muhammad ibn Saud, the founder of the current ruling al-Saud family. As a young man, al-Wahhab traveled to and studied in the great centers of Islamic learning, including Baghdad, Damascus, Isfahan, Jerusalem, Cairo, and Mecca. He was particularly influenced by the writings of the 14th-century scholar Taqi al-Din ibn Taimiya, who has recently become recognized as one of the leading sources for contemporary Islamist extremism.

Upon his return to Arabia, al-Wahhab began to preach what is often (though controversially) called Wahhabism, an interpretation of the Quran that generally is recognized as the strictest form of Islam. He argued that most Muslims were practicing forms of Islam that contained unacceptable innovations (*bida*) that deviated from the original teachings of the Prophet Muhammad. He relentlessly and often violently attacked the symbols and practices he found offensive. He believed that many Muslims were wrongly paying homage to saints, scholars, the Prophet's companions, and even the Prophet himself—rather than exclusively to Allah.

Al-Wahhab destroyed shrines and tombstones of revered Islamic leaders, including those dedicated to the Prophet's companions. He refused to allow celebration of the Prophet's birthday, a major holiday throughout the Islamic world. He advocated a strict return to the laws of the Quran, including death by stoning for adultery and beheading for other grave offenses. The early followers of these teachings saw their role as that of purifying Islam, a goal that could not help but be offensive to other Muslims, who believed that they were worshiping and practicing correctly. Al-Wahhab's teachings and practices were gradually seen as too extreme for his community, and he was forced to flee his home.

The place to which al-Wahhab fled for safety was only a few miles to the south in Ad Dariyah, a small community under the rule of Muhammad ibn Saud. Ibn Saud, and his son afterward, had the ambition to extend the power of their family throughout the Arabian Peninsula. The arrival of al-Wahhab, with his zealotry, energy, and willingness to use force to achieve his religious goals, was seen as providing a religious impetus that could stimulate holy warriors to further the al-Saud family's political ambitions. In 1745, al-Wahhab and ibn Saud entered into an agreement to join forces to spread both the worldly ambitions of the house of Saud and a strict interpretation of Islam.

Al-Wahhab provided a religious rationale for the al-Saud family to suppress their political opponents. He declared that Islam requires Muslims to obey political authorities; any revolts against the emirs should be punished with violence. Thus the house of Saud could use religiously sanctioned force to suppress opponents to its political ambitions, and the Wahhabist understanding of Islam became the state orthodoxy. This agreement from 1745, renewed in the 20th century, is the basis for Saudi Arabian political legitimacy.

The al-Saud family collapsed in the 19th century, and the Arabian Peninsula fell again into the hands of rival factions and the Ottoman Empire. The Wahhabist interpretation of Islam, however, remained strong.

In January 1902, the young Abdul-Aziz ibn Abdelrahman al-Saud, a descendant of the 18th-century king Ibn Saud, and 15 warriors scaled the walls of Riyadh and captured its fort. This event, which is now widely celebrated in Saudi Arabia as having launched the new state, was the first step in a 30-year campaign that ultimately reacquired the territory of Ibn Saud's ancestors, including the important towns of Mecca, Medina, and Jeddah.

In the early years Abdul-Aziz's campaign to reunite the kingdom lacked broad-based support in the center of the country, where devotion to the teachings and practices of al-Wahhab remained strong. In order to accomplish his political aims, Abdul-Aziz, as his predecessors had, made common cause with a group of religious zealots and warriors, this time with the Ikhwan (Brethren), who were followers of al-Wahhab. One of their principal leaders was Abdallah of the Al al-Shaikh family, a descendant of Abd al-Wahhab. According to one historian, these white-robed Ikhwan became "the white terror" of Arabia. With their support, however, Abdul-Aziz conquered many of the Bedouin tribes, who in turn converted to the teachings of al-Wahhab and became new warriors to assist the ambitions of Abdul-Aziz and the Ikhwan. In 1924, Abdul-Aziz and the Ikhwan decided to liberate and purify the holy cities of Mecca and Medina, then ruled by the Ottoman Turks. In 1932, Abdul-Aziz formally announced the establishment of the Kingdom of Saudi Arabia, a land that was at that time desperately poor.

One of the first and most significant problems Abdul-Aziz faced with his reunited kingdom was the hostile relationship between the newly conquered Ulema of the cultured towns of Mecca and Medina and the warriorlike Wahhabist Ikhwan from the Nejd; one can imagine the resentment of the learned Ulema when being told by the desert Ikhwan that they did not understand true Islam.

Consistently with the teachings of al-Wahab, the Ikhwan destroyed several sites in Mecca and Medina that were considered by other Muslims to be among the holiest shrines of Islam, including the memorial at the Prophet's birthplace, the house of Abu Bakr (the first caliph after Muhammad), and the tombs of the early followers of the Prophet. The tension that such destruction caused was exacerbated by the Ikhwan's treatment of some pilgrims on the hajj, who were insulted and attacked when playing music. Abdul-Aziz tried to mediate such conflicts in order to maintain the support from the Ikhwan but not so strongly as to bring down the wrath of the Islamic world on him. (Before the discovery of oil, tourism in the sense of Muslims' visiting the holy cities was a principal source of Saudi revenue.)

Abdul-Aziz sought to placate his Ikhwan supporters by introducing strict religious laws, but he also sought to rein in the enforcement of the laws by individual Ikhwan. He thereupon created the religious police known as the *mutawwa'in* (Committee for the Propagation of Virtue and Prevention of Vice). Abdul-Aziz placed at the head of this new organization two Ulema from the Al al-Shaikh family, descendants of al-Wahhab.

The 1745 pact between the first Ibn Saud and al-Wahhab, and the understanding between the "second" Ibn Saud (Abdul-Aziz) and the Ikhwan, have had a powerful shaping force on the ethos, laws, and religious positions of the current Saudi state. Although the contemporary "arrangement" of the house of Saud and the Ulema has been variously called sacred, cynical, or hypocritical, it remains of vital importance.

In 1953, on the death of Abdul-Aziz, his son, King Saud, established the Council of Ministers, which acted as both a legislative and an executive body. In 1992, after calls for reform in Saudi Arabia that followed the first Gulf War, King Fahd issued the Basic Law of Governance, which may properly, if loosely, be considered to be the constitution of Saudi Arabia.

FORM AND IMPACT OF THE CONSTITUTION

The 1992 Basic Law of Governance is the legal text that most closely approximates a constitution for Saudi Arabia, even though the law itself declares that the country's constitution is the Quran and *sunnah*. The Basic Law was promulgated by the king and may effectively be amended or repealed on the authority of the king (presumably acting through the Council of Ministers, the members of which he may appoint or terminate at will).

The Basic Law provides that laws, treaties, international agreements, and concessions need to be issued and modified by royal decree to be effective, but that the laws of the kingdom must not violate international agreements. Saudi Arabia has ratified several international conventions, but not the International Convention on Civil and Political Rights or the International Convention on Economic, Social, and Cultural Rights.

BASIC ORGANIZATIONAL STRUCTURE

The Kingdom of Saudi Arabia is a unified central state with 13 regional provinces that are governed by the king. The laws, state officials, and courts are centralized under the ultimate authority of the king. The kingdom is not a democracy, and citizens do not have the general right to vote. In 2003, limited proposals were made to begin a process of allowing some local officials to be elected, and elections to municipal council have been held.

LEADING CONSTITUTIONAL PRINCIPLES

There are three dominant constitutional principles in Saudi Arabia: first, the governing authority of Islamic law and values; second, the political authority of the king; and third, the values of consensus and consultation. In addition to these dominant principles, several other values are identified in the Basic Law.

1. Islamic law and values: The Basic Law repeatedly identifies Islam, the Quran, *sunnah,* and sharia as forming the underlying values and principles of the Saudi state and the law that must be followed there. Article 1 of the Basic Law identifies the Holy Quran and the *sunnah* as the constitution of Saudi Arabia, and the Basic Law repeatedly speaks of sharia as the law of the state.

   sharia is an Arabic word that referred originally to a path, such as a path one would take to find water. Over time it began to mean "the right path" or "the right guide," including all the divine laws to be followed by Muslims, from prescriptions on prayer, to rules on marriage and divorce, and including criminal prohibitions.

   In addition, the state is required to "protect the Islamic Creed," "enjoin good and forbid evil," and "undertake the duties of the call to Islam." It is responsible for maintaining and guaranteeing the security of the Two Holy Mosques and for promoting Islamic culture. Article 1 identifies the state religion as Islam, declares the religious feasts of Eid Al-Fitr and Eid Al-Ad-ha to be the two national holidays, and identifies its article of faith as "There is no God but Allah, Muhammad is Allah's Messenger."

2. The authority of the king: The Basic Law designates the king as "the point of reference" for all political authorities, effectively giving him the power to control the political and legal system both through his own authority and through the power to name and replace political and judicial officials. Although the king is constrained by principles of Islamic law, he ultimately has a great deal of power to interpret the ways that law shall be applied.

3. Consensus and consultation: The Basic Law also acknowledges, albeit briefly, the importance of consensus and consultation in adopting and enforcing laws. This consensus and consultation, though fundamental to the governance of the Saudi state, are difficult to describe accurately because so much is based upon personal relationships, family connections, and wealth.

4. Other: The Basic Law identifies several other principles of the Saudi state, though informed observers differ on the extent to which they are merely rhetorical or taken seriously by the state and its officials. Among these values are family, the basic needs of individuals, and the unity of the state.

CONSTITUTIONAL BODIES

Under the Basic Law of 1992, there are three authorities in the state: the judicial, executive, and regulatory, though the king is the ultimate source of all these authorities. The major organs are the king, the Council of Ministers, the Consultative Council, the judiciary, and the Ulema.

The King

The king, who is also designated as prime minister, supreme commander of the armed forces, and custodian of the Two Holy Mosques, is the dominant political figure in the Saudi state. According to the Basic Law, the king is the head of state and is responsible for appointing (and replacing at will) all senior government and judicial officials. For example, the king appoints and replaces the members of the Council of Ministers, the body that serves as both the executive cabinet of the king and the lawmaking body of the Saudi state.

Though the king's authority technically is constrained by sharia, he is the person principally responsible for interpreting and applying sharia. There is no constitutional means of appealing a decision of the king.

The second most important constitutional figure is the crown prince, who is selected by the king from among the direct descendants of King Abdul-Aziz. The king may revoke the designation and replace the crown prince with another descendant of Abdul-Aziz. The king may delegate authority to the crown prince, as reportedly happened after King Fahd suffered a stroke in 1995 and effectively delegated his powers to Crown Prince Abdullah, who effectively ruled Saudi Arabia, even before his own accession to the throne in 2005.

The Council of Ministers

The Council of Ministers acts as both the legislative and the executive power under the authority of the king. Any decision of the Council of Ministers becomes law within 30 days unless vetoed by the king. By tradition, most of the members of the Council of Ministers are descendants of King Abdul-Aziz.

The Majlis al-Shura (Consultative Council)

Saudi Arabia also has the Majlis al-Shura (Consultative Council), now consisting of approximately 120 members, to advise the king. The king appoints and replaces members of the Majlis at will.

The Lawmaking Process

The Council of Ministers is the lawmaking body of the Saudi state. The king may veto any law adopted by the Council of Ministers.

The Judiciary

The Basic Law provides that the judiciary shall be independent, though the head of the judiciary is the minister of justice, who traditionally is either a member of the royal family or a descendant of al-Wahhab. The first minister of justice was also the grand mufti. The Ministry of Justice itself handles administrative matters for the court. The Supreme Judicial Council handles appeals and judicial supervision.

Judges are appointed and replaced at will by the king, who is responsible for implementing and enforcing judicial decisions. Courts are required to apply the sharia to the legal disputes brought before them.

The principal court system is known as the sharia courts, which have courts of first instance (limited courts and General Courts), Courts of Appeals (in Riyadh and Mecca), and a Supreme Judicial Council. Although a litigant technically can appeal a decision of the Supreme Judicial Council to the king or crown prince, it is said that as a matter of practice the royal family does not interfere with decisions of the courts. By default, all cases, whether civil or criminal, are handled by the sharia courts unless there is a specific law that directs the subject matter to another type of tribunal. The sharia courts, of course, apply the law of sharia, which consists of the writings of the Quran and *sunnah*. These courts are under the administrative supervision of the Ministry of Justice.

The personnel who serve in the Supreme Judicial Council, Ministry of Justice, and Supreme Council of Ulema often rotate among the positions and sometimes serve concurrently as president of more than one entity. The king always retains the authority to appoint and terminate a judge. The Shia minority is given limited rights to operate its own court system in matters of personal or family law. In addition to the sharia courts, there are parallel courts that are responsible for non-sharia matters, including many commercial and labor disputes. These courts are likely to be involved particularly when international businesses are involved.

Although some argue that the judiciary is in fact constrained by strict interpretations of sharia, others complain that judges are susceptible to political and even financial influence of Saudi officials, the royal family, and other Saudi elites. The courts also appear to be influenced by fatwas (legal opinions) issued by the grand mufti of Saudi Arabia.

The Ulema

Despite the overwhelming authority that the Basic Law grants to the king, the Saudi state to some extent operates on the basis of *ijma* (consensus) and *shura* (consultation). There is a vital but unarticulated religiopolitical understanding between the Ulema (chief religious leaders), the most important of whom are frequently descendants of al-Wahhab, and the descendants of King Abdul-Aziz. The Ulema play a critical role in the operation of the Saudi state, though they are not governmental officials per se. The grand mufti is now the head of all Ulema.

THE ELECTION PROCESS AND POLITICAL PARTICIPATION

As noted, Saudi Arabia is not a democracy, and citizens do not have the right to vote. In 2003, the government began limited efforts to establish elections for some posi-

tions at the local level. Though this may be the beginning of a significant change in the Saudi political and constitutional system, the proposals thus far are minor. Half of the members of 178 municipal councils in the kingdom's 13 regions were elected in 2005; the other half were appointed by the government.

POLITICAL PARTIES

There are no political parties in Saudi Arabia.

CITIZENSHIP

The Basic Law provides that citizenship rules will be established by law. In 2004, Saudi Arabia enacted a new citizenship law that includes a variety of complex rules on ways citizenship may be obtained and lost. It is noteworthy that a female child born in Saudi Arabia of a Saudi mother and non-Saudi father cannot obtain citizenship unless she marries a Saudi man. A male child born to a Saudi mother and non-Saudi father is a Saudi from birth, as are both males and females of Saudi fathers and non-Saudi mothers (unless they take the citizenship of their mother). Under the Basic Law, citizens are obligated to defend the Islamic faith.

FUNDAMENTAL RIGHTS

The Basic Law provides that the state shall protect human rights, but only in accordance with sharia. It further provides that the law shall be administered with justice, consultation, and equality. Personal dwellings should be inviolate, and privacy is to be respected. Individuals are not to be arrested, tried, or imprisoned except in conformity with sharia. The law also recognizes rights of ownership, private property, and rights of capital and labor.

Impact and Functions of Fundamental Rights

Outside observers are deeply skeptical about the extent to which fundamental rights are in fact recognized and respected by the state, particularly when the interests of the royal family conflict with those of others.

Limitations to Fundamental Rights

Fundamental rights are subject to the limitations imposed by sharia.

ECONOMY

The Basic Law provides that the natural resources that God has deposited underground, above ground, and in territorial waters are the property of the state. The significance of this provision is immediately apparent with the recognition that Saudi Arabia has the world's largest oil reserve—which is sometimes estimated as one-fourth of all known oil reserves. Once again, however, many outsiders believe that state ownership largely translates to ownership by members of the royal family. The division between the state and the royal family is not clear, and Saudi officials do not make any effort to resolve this potentially blatant conflict of interest.

RELIGIOUS COMMUNITIES

Saudi Arabia is overwhelmingly Islamic and officially follows Sunni Islam and the strict teachings of the school of al-Wahhab. The state is both directly and indirectly involved in matters of religion. Women are required to wear veils covering their faces and bodies. Alcohol is prohibited, and strict punishments are meted out for many offenses. There is active discrimination even against Shia Muslims; non-Islamic religious adherents are prohibited from worshiping in public and can be under threat even for worshiping in private. The United States Department of State, which issues reports on freedom of religion in most countries of the world, states pointedly that freedom of religion does not exist in Saudi Arabia.

MILITARY DEFENSE AND STATE OF EMERGENCY

The king is the supreme commander of the armed forces, and he has the power to declare states of emergency and mobilization for war.

AMENDMENTS TO THE CONSTITUTION

The Basic Law was originally promulgated by the king. Since the legislative body, the Council of Ministers, is effectively under the control of the king, the law can be changed at his will as well (perhaps modified by the requirement of consensus and consultation). Amendments can be made through the will of the king as issued by his Council of Ministers.

PRIMARY SOURCES

Basic Law of Governance in English. Available online. URL: http://www.saudiembassy.net/Country/government/law%20of%20governance.asp. Accessed on September 3, 2005. (official Saudi site)

SECONDARY SOURCES

Madawi al-Rasheed, *A History of Saudi Arabia*. Cambridge: Cambridge University Press, 2002.
Alexei Vassileiev, *The History of Saudi Arabia*. New York: New York University Press, 2000.
Frank E. Vogel, *Islamic Law and Legal System: Studies of Saudi Arabia*. Leiden: Brill, 2000.

T. Jeremy Gunn

SENEGAL

At-a-Glance

OFFICIAL NAME
Republic of Senegal

CAPITAL
Dakar

POPULATION
11,126,832 (2005 est.)

SIZE
75,749 sq. mi. (196,190 sq. km)

LANGUAGES
French (official), Wolof, Pulaar, Jola, Mandinka, Serer, Soninke (national languages)

RELIGIONS
Muslim 94%, indigenous beliefs 1%, Christian (mostly Roman Catholic) 5%

NATIONAL OR ETHNIC COMPOSITION
Wolof 43.3%, Pular 23.8%, Serer 14.7%, Jola 3.7%, Mandinka 3%, Soninke 1.1%, European and Lebanese 1%, other 9.4%

DATE OF INDEPENDENCE OR CREATION
April 4, 1960

TYPE OF GOVERNMENT
Semipresidential democracy

TYPE OF STATE
Decentralized unitary state

TYPE OF LEGISLATURE
Unicameral parliament

DATE OF CONSTITUTION
January 7, 2001

DATE OF LAST AMENDMENT
June 19, 2003

Senegal has a representative, liberal, and pluralistic form of government. It is based on the rule of law with a clear separation of executive, legislative, and judicial powers. It is also a decentralized unitary state with local communities that have administrative and financial autonomy. The Senegalese constitution proclaims and guarantees human rights. The constitution is respected by all public authorities. An independent judiciary decides cases of violations of its provisions.

The central figure of the state is the president of the republic, who is officially head of state. Free, equal, general, and direct elections of the president and of the parliament are guaranteed. A pluralist system of political parties has a certain impact on the political regime. Freedom of religion is guaranteed and the state and religion are separated. The existing economic system of this underdeveloped country is that of a market economy subject to government interventions. The armed forces are subordinate to the civil government.

CONSTITUTIONAL HISTORY

Senegal was partly or completely integrated in the medieval empires of Ghana, Mali, and Songhaï. On today's territory of Senegal there were at different times numerous kingdoms such as Tekrour, Djolof, Cayor, Sine, and Walo.

Some students of precolonial Wolof society in Senegal have detected a separation between religion and the state, and a separation between the executive and the legislative powers. The king exercised all except religious and legislative functions. Laws were determined by tradition and custom.

The king had a general protective and pacifying function, maintaining internal and external peace by using the armed forces at his disposal. He was the supreme arbiter of the country, administering justice by himself or delegating his authority. He also exercised fiscal functions. He was supported by a government with ministerial specialization: The grand *jaraaf* played the role of prime minister, the grand *farba* headed the police, the *fara séf* was minister of defense, and so on.

The king could also summon a superior council for all matters requiring serious decisions (such as defense of the kingdom and declaration of war). A council of grand electors, presided over by the grand *jaraf,* was charged with the election of the king. Despite the important powers of the king there was no endeavor to limit the royal power. The exterior event of colonization deeply disrupted Wolof and other local societies.

In the 15th century the Portuguese became the first Europeans to set foot on Senegalese soil, well before the English and the French. By the middle of the 17th century colonial trading posts were established, as a prelude to full colonial domination.

Senegal did not become a colony until the 18th century, after a struggle among the various colonial powers marked by several military expeditions and the signing of numerous treaties. In 1763, France lost possession of Senegal in the Treaty of Paris but regained the colony in the 1783 Treaty of Versailles. In 1809 Britain seized the colony again, then returned it to France in 1818. From 1854 to 1864, the French undertook several military expeditions and achieved the conquest of most of today's Senegal over the vigorous resistance of the Senegalese at Walo, Fouta, Cayor, and other sites. In 1886, Ziguinchor, today a regional capital in southern Senegal, was ceded to France. In 1889, a treaty between France and Britain drew the territorial borders between Senegal and The Gambia.

The inhabitants of four local communities were granted French citizenship as early as the 19th century, but the status of the colony did not differ significantly from that of other colonies. During the whole colonial period there was but one single power: the colonial state based in Paris.

Under the 1946 French constitution Senegal became an overseas territory, that is, an integral part of France. It was integrated into what at the time was called the French Union. Administrative institutions were created, and in 1946 a territorial assembly replaced the colonial council. The assembly remained under the supervision of the Grand Council of French-Occidental Africa, a superior assembly. On May 7, 1948, the law Lamine Gueye conferred French citizenship on all residents.

On June 23, 1956, a framework law (Gaston Defferre) granted administrative and political autonomy to the colony and installed universal suffrage. A reform modified the distribution of powers among the French state, the federation of French West Africa, and Senegal. With the adoption of the 1958 French constitution by referendum Senegal voted in favor of this project.

Thus, on November 15, 1958, the Territorial Assembly of Senegal adopted a resolution establishing the Republic of Senegal as a member of the French Community. The new state, in accordance with the 1958 French constitution, did not enjoy all the internal or international powers a state normally has.

The first Senegalese constitution dates from January 24, 1959. It provided for a unicameral parliamentary regime with a preponderance of the executive. At that time Senegal supported a federation with three other francophone states: (French) Sudan, Dahomey, and Upper Volta (today's Mali, Benin, and Burkina Faso, respectively), but Dahomey and Upper Volta refused to take part.

The federation of Senegal and Sudan adopted the name of Mali. In September 1959, the federation demanded its independence under Article 78 of the French constitution. On December 13, General de Gaulle promised that France would recognize the Federation of Mali. On April 4, 1960, treaties organizing the transfer of powers were concluded between France and Mali. A federal constitution was adopted on June 18, 1960, and on June 20 the independence of Mali was proclaimed.

On August 20, even before the institutions of government could be set up, the Federation of Mali broke apart, and its two components became independent states. Sudan maintained the name Mali. Senegal adopted a new constitution on August 26, 1960.

Since then, three constitutions have followed each other: one on August 26, 1960, installing a parliamentary system; another on March 7, 1963, installing a presidential regime, which underwent profound evolution; and another on January 22, 2001, which is still in effect.

FORM AND IMPACT OF THE CONSTITUTION

Senegal has a written constitution, codified in a single document that takes precedence over all other national law. International law must be compatible with the constitution to be applicable in Senegal. The law of supranational organizations into which Senegal integrates has precedence over the Senegalese constitution if it does not contradict its basic principles.

BASIC ORGANIZATIONAL STRUCTURE

Senegal is a decentralized unitary state. There is one single center of political decision, but there also are many (441) local communities, of which 320 are rural communities, 110 municipalities, and 11 regions. The local communities are recognized by the constitution of Senegal, which proclaims the principle of citizens' participation in public affairs through decentralized communities and the principle of free administration of local communities through councils elected by universal suffrage.

LEADING CONSTITUTIONAL PRINCIPLES

In the 2001 constitution there is no reference to any ideology. The preamble proclaims respect for and consolidation of the rule of law, in which government and citizens are subject to the same legal provisions under the control of an independent and impartial judiciary.

Article 1 states: "The Republic of Senegal is laïque [secular], democratic, and social. It guarantees the equality before the law for all citizens without distinction of origin, race, gender or religion. It respects all creeds." Article 1 also characterizes the principle of the republic as government of the people, by the people, and for the people.

National sovereignty belongs to the people, who exercise it through their representatives and through referenda (Article 2). The universality, equality, and secrecy of suffrage are guaranteed. The principle of separation of powers is affirmed. The constitution also enshrines the multiparty principle (Article 3).

CONSTITUTIONAL BODIES

The president of the republic, the administration, the National Assembly, the Constitutional Council, the State Council, the Cassation Court, and the courts and tribunals, and also the Council of the Republic for Economic and Social Affairs constitute the institutions of the republic (Article 5). The Council of the Republic for Economic and Social Affairs also plays an important role.

The President of the Republic

The president is elected for a term of five years and can be reelected indefinitely. The office of president of the republic is incompatible with all other public and private functions. The president enjoys penal immunity for any actions performed in the exercise of presidential functions. The president is not responsible to parliament except in the case of high treason (not defined in the constitution). In that case the president can be impeached by the National Assembly after a secret vote with a majority of three-fifth of all members; he or she is then tried by the High Court of Justice. The president enjoys particular protection against insults and disparagement.

If a president dies, becomes definitively incapacitated, or refuses to accept the election results, new elections must be organized within 60 days.

Until a new president is elected, the president of the National Assembly substitutes for him or her for three months. The substitute may not submit any bill to a referendum and may not submit any proposal to amend the constitution.

The president determines the policy of the nation, deciding on the general outlines of national and international policies and activities of the state. The president ensures that the prime minister and the ministers implement directives given to them in their respective domains. The ministers can exercise regulatory powers only if explicitly permitted by law, and only within organizations and functions under their specific authority. The president can delegate certain powers to the prime minister and the ministers, excluding the right to pardon, to call for referendums, or to initiate amendments to the constitution. The president presides over the Council of Ministers, which meets each week to discuss the most important questions, such as proposed bills and decrees, appointments to high office, and general directives.

The president is vested with extensive powers of appointment, covering all officials and state employees, though he or she may delegate this power to the prime minister or other ministers. The president also signs decrees and regulations.

The president of the republic receives the ambassadors and extraordinary envoys of foreign powers. The president directs the diplomatic service of Senegal and appoints all its foreign representatives. It is the president who determines the fundamental options of foreign policy; the minister of foreign affairs only exercises the presidential directives. The president negotiates, ratifies, and approves international engagements; however, treaties involving peace, commerce, or international organizations require ratification by the legislature.

According to the Senegalese constitution the president of the republic is the guarantor of the national independence and territorial integrity. The president is responsible for the national defense and is the commander in chief of the armed forces, which are at his or her disposal. The president appoints all military officers and chairs the Superior Council of the National Defence.

The president of the republic appoints magistrates, with the advice of the Superior Council of the Magistracy, which the president also chairs. The president has the right to pardon.

The president can also appeal to the Constitutional Council in cases of conflict with the parliament, especially in order to seek a declaration of unconstitutionality of a law passed by parliament.

The Executive Administration (Government)

The administration of the Republic of Senegal is directed by the prime minister. The administration coordinates and conducts the national policy determined by the president.

Members of the administration cannot serve in parliament or engage in any other public or private professional activity. They are responsible under criminal law for any acts performed in the exercise of their functions and qualified as crimes or offenses at the moment they are committed. They are charged by the National Assembly and tried by the High Court of Justice.

After his or her nomination, the prime minister presents a general declaration of policy to the National Assembly. The prime minister can ask the National Assembly to express its confidence in him or her.

The prime minister is the head of the executive and the civil servants, and he or she can appoint certain civil servants according to the law. The prime minister is responsible for the application of the law. The prime minister can delegate certain power to the minister and exercises regulatory powers.

The National Assembly

Currently the National Assembly has 142 members, called deputies. Their term of office is five years. A deputy whose ineligibility becomes apparent after the election or during the course of office is dismissed by the Supreme Court at the request of the National Assembly.

The office of a deputy is incompatible with a cabinet post, or with the exercise of any public or elective function in Senegal or any other state or organization. A deputy may not belong to the Economic and Social Council, except as its president.

A deputy may not help direct any enterprise with financial aims, unless the deputy held this office before being elected. However, members of the teaching staff of the University of Dakar, medical doctors in public hospitals, and persons charged with temporary missions of up to six months by the executive can be deputies.

Deputies cannot be tried for opinions or activities expressed or carried out in the exercise of their office. They cannot be the object of criminal prosecution nor be arrested for crimes and offenses except if caught in the act. Only the National Assembly while in session or its office when the assembly is not in session can authorize criminal prosecution of a deputy and lift parliamentary immunity. If convicted, the deputy loses the parliamentary mandate.

According to the constitution the assembly alone has power to make law; however, it can delegate this power to the commission of delegations that it can form. The domain of the law is limited to a number of matters stated in the constitution (Article 67).

The National Assembly can authorize the president of the republic to take measures that normally have to be passed by an ordinary law. The president can also circumvent the assembly entirely by submitting proposed laws to a referendum. Furthermore, the president can in the case of emergency make laws, which the assembly has the power to ratify or to overturn within 15 days after their adoption.

The assembly must vote on the budget within 60 days of its presentation. If no vote is taken within this time, the president can pass the budget by decree. All bills and proposed amendments proposed by the deputies that entail increases in public expenditure or decreases in public income must be accompanied by suggestions on means to rectify the imbalance.

Only the National Assembly has the power to declare war. Certain international treaties need the ratification or the approval of the assembly, including treaties of peace, commerce, and international organizations, if they are relevant to state finances, modify legal provisions, concern the status of persons, or concern the ceding, exchange, or acquisition of territory.

The National Assembly can pass amnesty laws. It participates extensively in the organization and functioning of the High Court of Justice and appoints the members of that court from among the deputies. It can charge the president of the republic for high treason by a majority of three-fifths of its members.

The Lawmaking Process

Laws can be initiated by the president of the republic (projects of law) or by the deputies (propositions of law). In practice, the vast majority of bills originate from the president.

The bills are prepared by permanent or special committees, who are aided in their work by the state ministers and state secretaries. The committee's report serves as a basis for plenary discussion, which begins with a general debate on the report. Then, there are discussion and vote article by article, including any amendments submitted during the first debate. The assembly may refer suggested modifications back to the committee.

The assembly finally votes the complete project. A relative majority is required except for organic laws, which require an absolute majority. If the president of the republic sends back the bill for reconsideration, a majority of three-fifths is required for renewed passage. The adopted law is promulgated by the president of the republic.

The Judiciary

According to the constitution the judiciary consists of the Constitutional Council, the Council of State, the Cassation Court, the Court of Appeal, and the various courts and tribunals. The judiciary power is the guardian of the rights and freedoms.

The independence of the judiciary is enshrined in the constitution, as are the means of guaranteeing this independence—for example, judges are not removable and there is a superior council of the magistrates. Judges are subject in the exercise of their functions only to the authority of the law.

The Constitutional Council can rule on the constitutionality of laws, at the appeal of the president of the republic or of one-tenth of the members of parliament. The Council of State can make a similar appeal concerning administrative matters; the Cassation Court can make an appeal concerning civil, commercial, and penal matters; and the Court of Appeals can appeal concerning matters of private law and administrative. The Constitutional Council also rules on electoral disputes and questions of the distribution of powers between the executive and the legislature.

The Council of the Republic for Economic and Social Affairs

The 2003 constitutional reform created a new consultative body: the Council of the Republic for Economic and Social Affairs. It is composed of 100 members: a quarter of them representing societal organizations, another quarter appointed by the president of the republic, and the remaining half elected by local communities. Its task is to give advice to the president of the republic, the administration, and the National Assembly in matters of economic, social, cultural, and institutional development. It can also play a role as mediator in social conflicts. The Council of the Republic ensures the participation of different societal forces and local communities in the development of national economic and social policy.

THE ELECTION PROCESS
The Presidential Elections

According to the constitution the president of the republic is elected by universal and direct suffrage by majority vote in two rounds. The first round takes place between 45 and 30 days before the expiration of the president's term, or within 60 days of a vacancy in the office. Election procedures are determined by law.

Candidates must be citizens of Senegal at least 35 years old and must enjoy civil and political rights. They must be presented by a legally constituted political party, and each party can only present one candidate. The Constitutional Court verifies that the candidates comply with the law and publishes the list of candidates. The election campaign begins 21 days before the first round and ends a day before elections. If there is a second round, the campaign is opened on the day the candidates are announced and ends at midnight before election day.

The Constitutional Council supervises the lawfulness of the electoral campaign and the elections and the acceptability of the candidates' propaganda. It decides on all urgent appeals and takes immediate action if needed to restore equality. It can even issue injunctions to the administrative authorities.

To be elected in the first round the candidate needs the absolute majority of votes. If this requirement is not met, a second round follows two weeks later, between the two candidates with the most votes. In the second round the candidate who has the relative majority succeeds.

The Legislative Elections

Deputies are elected by universal and direct suffrage. Half of them are elected by a majority from lists within each department, and half of them by proportional representation from national lists.

Any voter at least 25 years of age who has complied with the rules of military service is eligible to be a candidate. Naturalized foreigners and those who have obtained citizenship by marriage are not eligible for six years. The election campaign follows rules similar to those that apply to presidential elections.

The Constitutional Council proclaims the results and declares the candidates provisionally elected. Candidates can contest the results within five days before the council. However, any challenge that manifestly cannot influence the results of the election is declared unacceptable. If the court accepts a challenge, a new election is organized within 21 days.

POLITICAL PARTIES

The multiparty system has been a permanent feature of the political life of Senegal, except during a period of one-party rule between 1966 and 1974. The system has always been organized and structured, and is a key to understanding the functioning of the Senegalese political system.

Currently, nearly 80 political parties compete for power. This so-called political opening to a multiplicity of players is a recent phenomenon, but party-based political life has existed since the colonial era.

The political parties must follow certain rules. Respect for the constitution, national sovereignty, and democracy must be enshrined in their statutes. Parties may not conduct activities that endanger the security of the state or territorial integrity. Political parties may not identify themselves with one race, ethnicity, gender, religion, belief, language, or region. The political parties can be freely constituted with a declaration and registration. A decree of dissolution of a political party is an administrative act that can be appealed to the Supreme Court.

CITIZENSHIP

Senegalese citizenship is acquired by birth (*ius sanguinis*) or marriage. A child acquires Senegalese citizenship if one of his or her parents is a Senegalese citizen. The place of birth is irrelevant.

FUNDAMENTAL RIGHTS

The preamble of the Senegalese constitution makes reference to the 1789 Declaration of the Rights of Man and the Citizen, the 1948 Universal Declaration of Human Rights, the 1966 International Pacts Relative to Human Rights, the international instruments adopted by the United Nations relating to the rights of women and children, and the African Charter of Human and Peoples' Rights. The preamble then affirms the nation's respect for the fundamental liberties and rights of citizens and guarantees all citizens, without discrimination, an opportunity to exercise power at all levels, as well as access to public services. All forms of injustice, inequality, and discrimination are explicitly rejected. Title 2 of the constitution explicitly affirms these various rights. Statutory law provides the specific guarantees for and limits of these rights and freedoms.

The constitution recognizes civil and political rights, economic rights, social and cultural rights, and communal rights.

Impact and Functions of Fundamental Rights

Among civil and political rights are the sacred and inviolable character of the human person; the right to life, liberty, and security, and to the free development of the personality; protection for the integrity of the body, especially mutilation (the constitutional basis of prohibition of sexual mutilation). The constitution also guarantees freedom of assembly, freedom of expression, freedom of the press, freedom of association, freedom of opinion, freedom of movement, freedom to demonstrate, freedom of conscience (which includes the right to profess and to practice a religion of one's choice), and the right to privacy of communications and correspondence.

Among economic, social, and cultural rights are the right to own property; the right to work; the freedom to form trade unions; the right to strike; the right to health, education, and pluralist information; and the right to a healthy environment.

The constitution recognizes specific women's rights: the right to own real estate, the right to have and administer one's own property, nondiscrimination in employment, equality in salary and taxes, and prohibition of forced marriage. Family rights include the right to decent living conditions and the right of the young for protection against drugs.

Limitations to Fundamental Rights

All these freedoms and rights must be exercised under the conditions provided for by law. In order to promote and protect these freedoms, the state must punish all attacks against them and against their proper exercise. The rights and freedoms are guaranteed by the national and international judiciary and by independent administrative authorities.

ECONOMY

The Senegalese constitution does not indicate a specific economic system. Certain provisions, however, relate to the economy. There are a fundamental right to own property, a right to free enterprise, a right to work, a right of workers to participate in the determination of working conditions by their representatives, a right to transparency in public matters, and the principle of good governance. The constitution also provides for economic planning laws, which determine the objectives of the government's economic and social activities. The law also determines the rules for nationalization of enterprises, and conversely for the transfer of ownership from the public to the private sector.

RELIGIOUS COMMUNITIES

Despite proclaiming the principle of secularity, the constitution gives a very important place to religious communities, in a nod to national reality. Senegal is home to several important Muslim communities, whose influence extends beyond the spiritual field into temporal matters. Religious institutions and communities have the right to develop without interference, and they are protected by the state. They regulate and administer their affairs autonomously. The constitution also recognizes the right of religious institutions and communities to offer education. Freedom of conscience, freedom of religion and religious practice, and the profession of religious teaching are all recognized within the limits of public order.

MILITARY DEFENSE AND STATE OF EMERGENCY

The president of the republic is the commander in chief of the armed forces and is responsible for the national defense. The president appoints all members of the military. The president of the republic can decree a state of emergency or a state of siege for 12 days for all or part of the national territory, in three cases: dangers resulting from grave attacks on public order, subversive menaces against internal security, and public calamity (natural disaster). During the 12 days the National Assembly must convene if it is out of session. Only the assembly can prolong (through a law) the state of emergency or siege, for a time and territory that it determines itself.

In case of emergency the civil authorities remain in power, but their powers are considerably extended, and they can sharply limit the rights and freedoms of citizens. In a state of siege all powers are transferred to the military authority, which can take the same measures allowed in a state of emergency. A siege can be declared only in case of imminent danger to the internal or external security of the state. The military authority can confine itself to exercise only a part of the powers and leave the other part to the civil authorities.

A state of "exceptional powers" is also provided for in the constitution, in response to a grave and direct menace to public institutions, national independence, territorial integrity, or the execution of international duties, or to an interruption of the regular functioning of public powers. If these conditions are met, the president of the republic informs the nation by a message and starts the procedure.

The president can take all measures aiming at reestablishing the regular functioning of public powers and assuring the protection of the nation, thus exercising quasi-dictatorial powers. However, he or she may not propose a constitutional revision during this period.

During a period of exceptional powers the National Assembly remains in full session. If the president promulgates laws, the assembly must decide within 15 days on their ratification. If they are not passed to the office of the assembly in time, these measures become void. Finally, the president, when exercising exceptional powers, cannot prevent the Supreme Court from exercising its constitutional functions.

AMENDMENTS TO THE CONSTITUTION

The president of the republic and the members of the National Assembly have the right to introduce bills amending the constitution. The amendment must be adopted by the assembly and approved by a referendum. The president of the republic can decide not to submit the amendment to a referendum. In that case, the amendment needs the approval of a three-fifths majority in the assembly. The republican form of government cannot be amended.

PRIMARY SOURCES

Constitution in English (extracts). Available online. URL: http://www.chr.up.ac.za/hr_docs/constitutions/docs/ SenegalC%20(english%20summary)(rev).doc; http:// www.gouv.sn/textes/constitution.pdf. Accessed on July 23, 2005.

Constitution in French. Available online. URL: http://www. gouv.sn/textes/constitution.html. Accessed on August 18, 2005.

SECONDARY SOURCES

Bureau of Public Affairs, U.S. Department of State, "Background Note and Country Reports on Human Rights Practices and International Religious Freedom Report 2004." Available online. URL: http://www. state.gov/r/pa/ei/bgn/2862.htm. Accessed on June 27, 2006.

Human Rights Committee, *Fourth Periodic Reports of States Parties Due in 1995: Senegal.* November 1996. Available online. URL: http://www.unhchr.ch/tbs/doc.nsf, (CCPR/C/103/Add.1). Accessed on June 27, 2006.

Demba Sy

SERBIA AND MONTENEGRO

At-a-Glance

OFFICIAL NAME
State Union of Serbia and Montenegro

CAPITAL
Belgrade

POPULATION
10,600,000 (2005 est.)

SIZE
39,518 sq. mi. (102,350 sq. km)

LANGUAGES
Serbian

RELIGIONS
Christian Orthodox 84.97%, Catholic 5.48%, Muslim 3.19%, Protestant 1.07%, Jewish 0.01%, Asian religions 0.007%, other religions 0.25%, believers of no confession 0.005%, atheists 0.53%, unknown 4.488%

NATIONAL OR ETHNIC COMPOSITION
Serb 64.5%, Montenegrin 6.5%, Hungarian 3.1%, Albanian 14.5%, other 11.4%

DATE OF INDEPENDENCE OR CREATION
July 13, 1878

TYPE OF GOVERNMENT
Parliamentary democracy

TYPE OF STATE
State union of two member states

TYPE OF LEGISLATURE
Unicameral parliament

DATE OF CONSTITUTION
February 4, 2003

DATE OF LAST AMENDMENT
No amendments

Serbia and Montenegro is a state union of two equal states—Serbia and Montenegro, with a unique type of parliamentary system. It is a democratic community, based on fundamental rights and freedoms, rule of law, and social justice, where it is permitted to do anything that is not forbidden by the constitution and laws. The state is neither a federation nor a confederation, but appears closest to a real union. The state union is a contractual creation with a three-year term. With the expiry of that period, member states have the right to initiate proceedings in order to break away from the union. This decision is to be made by a referendum. The Republic of Montenegro declared its independence on June 3, 2006. A new constitution is in the making.

Four institutions that have been established in Serbia and Montenegro are rather atypical of a classic federal state. These, in fact, represent common bodies of the member states, rather than authentic bodies of the state union. They are as follows: Assembly of Serbia and Montenegro, president of Serbia and Montenegro, Council of Ministers, and Court of Serbia and Montenegro.

The Constitutional Charter of Serbia and Montenegro is not a constitution in the typical meaning of the word. Numerous solutions contained in this constitutional act are so specific that they cannot be compared to the provisions of constitutions in other contemporary states. However, a multiparty system has been established in Serbia and Montenegro, freedom of religion is guaranteed, the church is separated from the state, and a market economy and freedom of enterprise have been established as well. The army is placed under democratic and civilian control with defense as its main aim.

CONSTITUTIONAL HISTORY

The nations that form the present states of Serbia and Montenegro formed the feudal states of Raska and Duklja between the late seventh and the early ninth centuries C.E. Raska lived on as feudal Serbia in the period of the Nemanjić dynasty, which joined the former Duklja to their state. Nemanjić Serbia was a powerful monarchy limited only by its feudal lords. In those times, both rulers and state councils enforced numerous legal acts that regulated the rights and prerogatives of certain classes, the organization of power, courts and their procedures, crime and punishment, and property rights.

When Serbia won independence for its church from the Ecumenical Patriarch in Byzantium (Istanbul) in 1219 C.E., Sava Nemanjić became its first archbishop. Early church legal texts contained secular as well as religious regulations. Among the most famous of these law books is Sava's Nomocanon, also known as Krmchija, used in Russia and Bulgaria as well. The Serbian Orthodox Church was elevated to the level of a patriarchy in 1346 with its seat in Pec, in Kosovo and Metohija, during the rein of Czar Dushan. This Serbian ruler is remembered for the famous law code of 1349. In those times, enactment of a law code for an entire state was rare in Europe.

After the fall of Byzantium in 1453 and the fall of Smederevo, the last independent Serbian city-state, the Serbian state and church fell under Turkish rule for several centuries. The Serbian Church became the main keeper of Serbian identity and Serbian national traditions for several centuries. The liberation process began with the first Serbian uprising in 1804 led by the Serbian hero Karadjordje, founder of the Karadjordjevic dynasty, which ruled under Turkish overlords. The liberation process formally ended with the Treaty of Berlin in 1878 when both Serbia and Montenegro became independent.

Serbia enacted its first constitution in 1835, extracted from the illiterate Prince Milosh. It was influenced by the 1791 French constitution and the 1814 French Constitutional Charter. After opposition from Austria, Russia, and Turkey the constitution was withdrawn before having been applied. It was followed by the 1838 constitution (the Turkish constitution) and the 1869 constitution, considered the start of the "constitutional period." The most important Serbian constitution was enacted in 1888, after full independence was won. It introduced a parliamentary system into Serbia. King Alexander Karadjordjevic suspended this progressive constitution in favor of a new one in 1901, but the resulting turmoil ended in his assassination and the reenactment of the 1888 constitution in 1903.

In Montenegro, constitutional life advanced with the establishment of a central authority by the end of the 19th century. In 1905, under the influence of Montenegrin intellectuals educated abroad and the example of Serbia, Montenegro received its first constitution.

After World War I (1914–18) and the fall of the Austro-Hungarian Empire, a new state of South Slavic peoples was formed on December 1, 1918, called the Kingdom of Serbs, Croats, and Slovenians. It included the former kingdoms of Serbia and Montenegro as well as parts of the former Austro-Hungarian Empire with Slavic populations. The state was proclaimed a constitutional monarchy under the reign of the Serbian Karadjordjevic dynasty. Two constitutions were enacted, in 1921 and 1931, but neither had significant influence. In 1929, this state changed its name to the Kingdom of Yugoslavia.

Yugoslavia was invaded by both Germany and Italy during World War II (1939–45). Two major resistance movements were formed in the country; one supported the monarchy while the other, led by Josip Broz Tito, leaned toward the Soviet Union. Tito acquired stronger international support and gained power in the fall of 1945.

The Federal People's Republic of Yugoslavia was proclaimed. A socialist society started to develop under socialist constitutions. The first, enacted in 1945 under significant influence of the Russian Stalinist constitution, was followed by numerous constitutional documents whose common characteristic was the ideological independence of Yugoslav socialism. With the introduction of the principle of self-governance of economic enterprises in 1950, Yugoslavia broke away from the other socialist countries toward a policy of nonalignment with either of the two powerful political blocs. By the 1963 constitution, Yugoslavia changed its name to Socialist Federal Republic of Yugoslavia; it was the first socialist country to introduce a constitutional court.

The last socialist constitution, proclaimed in 1974, evidenced a profound crisis within the Yugoslav federation and a significant level of independence of its six federal states. Tito died in 1980. His socialist state disappeared in the bloody ethnic conflicts and civil wars, most pitting Serbia, still ruled by a Communist successor party, against the other republics and ethnicities within the old federation.

Serbia and Montenegro were unwilling to abandon the Federal Republic of Yugoslavia, proclaimed in the 1992 constitution. However, the difficulties of living in a federation whose two remaining members differed so immensely in size, population, and material resources prompted Serbia and Montenegro to change the very nature of their union. In February 2003, the Federal Republic of Yugoslavia ended its existence and a new State Union of Serbia and Montenegro was created. The republics, which were until then federal units, became states. The act providing the legal framework does not represent a constitution by either its name or contents, but a constitutional charter with a three-year time limit. The Republic of Montenegro declared its independence on June 3, 2006. Since June 28, 2006, Montenegro has been an independent member of the United Nations.

FORM AND IMPACT OF THE CONSTITUTION

The State Union of Serbia and Montenegro has a written constitutional document called the Constitutional Charter. The text of the Constitutional Charter is largely disproportionate to its significance in both its modest volume and its nonnormative manner of writing. The Charter on Human and Minority Rights and Fundamental Freedoms forms an integral part of the Constitutional Charter. The provisions of international treaties on human and minority rights and civil freedoms that apply to the territory of Serbia and Montenegro are enforceable directly. The charter stipulates the precedence of international law over the law of Serbia and Montenegro and the laws of the member states.

The charter specifies that the member states shall amend their constitutions or adopt new constitutions in order to harmonize them with the Constitutional Charter within six months of the date of its adoption. The Court of Serbia and Montenegro is competent to adjudicate compatibility of the constitutions of the member states with the Constitutional Charter, compatibility of the laws of Serbia and Montenegro with the Constitutional Charter, as well as compatibility of the laws of the member states with the law of Serbia and Montenegro. Up to the present day, with the six-month period long past, neither Serbia nor Montenegro has carried out the necessary amendments to its constitution.

BASIC ORGANIZATIONAL STRUCTURE

Since the State Union of Serbia and Montenegro was born in 2003, constitutional theorists have discussed the question of its legal nature. The majority believe that it is neither a federation nor a confederation. It is closest to a real union, showing certain similarities to the former Austro-Hungarian Empire (1867–1918). Since the union of states does not itself represent a state, each member state within the union has a complete and independent state organization of its own. The only attribute the union possesses is its international personality, the representation of which is shared by the two member states. The union represents a contractual creation with a three-year duration, after which each member state may vote to break away in a referendum.

The member states are equal. Each member state has its own constitution. Basically, the state union represents a simple sum or connection of its two member states.

LEADING CONSTITUTIONAL PRINCIPLES

In their constitutions of 1990 and 1992, both Serbia and Montenegro introduced hybrid systems of government by including some of the institutions and principles of a presidential system into a parliamentary context. Similarly, the State Union of Serbia and Montenegro allocates limited legislative authority to both the executive and the judicial authorities.

In light of provisions contained in the constitutions of the member states, the state union is a democratic state based on fundamental rights and freedoms, on the rule of law and social justice, where anything not forbidden by law is allowed. Each member of the state union has a republican structure with power belonging to the citizens, who exercise it directly and through freely elected representatives.

One of the basic aims of the state union is to advance respect for the principles and standards of the European Union (EU), with the goal of joining European organizations, particularly the EU.

CONSTITUTIONAL BODIES

Four key institutions exist in the framework of the state union, all of them mutual bodies of the member states rather than bodies of the state union. They are the Assembly of Serbia and Montenegro, the president of Serbia and Montenegro, the Council of Ministers, and the Court of Serbia and Montenegro.

Assembly of Serbia and Montenegro

The Assembly of Serbia and Montenegro is the legislative body of the state union, constrained by the modest reach of the union's authority. Some of its actions are subject to the preliminary approval of the assemblies or other bodies of the member states, such as the declaration and termination of a state of war and the membership of the state union in international organizations. Any decision by the assembly regarding the delimitation of the borders of the state union is subject to the preliminary approval of the assembly of the member state in whose territory the border in question is located.

The assembly elects the president of Serbia and Montenegro as well as its Council of Ministers. According to Article 19 of the charter, it enacts laws and other instruments governing military issues and defense, immigration policy, the granting of asylum, the visa regime, and integrated border management in line with the standards of the European Union. It also approves international treaties and agreements of Serbia and Montenegro.

The Assembly of Serbia and Montenegro is a unicameral body made up of 126 deputies having a four-year term of office. The deputies, among whom 91 are from Serbia and 35 from Montenegro, are elected directly in each member state. From among its deputies, the assembly elects its president and vice president, who may not be from the same member state. Also, the president of the Assembly of Serbia and Montenegro and the president of Serbia and Montenegro may not be from the same member state. The assembly makes decisions by a majority vote—but that must include the majority of the total number of deputies from each member state.

The Lawmaking Process
The legislative initiative is entrusted to the deputies of the Assembly of Serbia and Montenegro, the Council of Ministers, and the assemblies of the member states. Laws are passed by dual majority vote; the president of Serbia and Montenegro then proclaims the laws by a declarative act.

The President of Serbia and Montenegro

The president of Serbia and Montenegro is the head of state of the state union, as well as the head of the executive administration, in his or her capacity as chair of the Council of Ministers. As head of state the president represents Serbia and Montenegro at home and abroad, proclaims the laws passed by the assembly and the regulations passed by the Council of Ministers, receives diplomats' credentials, and recalls the chiefs of diplomatic and consular missions. The president of Serbia and Montenegro is a member of the Supreme Command Council, but not its president ex officio. The president nominates the members of the Council of Ministers (for approval by the Assembly) and can dismiss them.

A candidate for the president of the State Union has to be a citizen of the state union, above 18 years of age, and in possession of full civil capacity. The president and the vice president of the Assembly of Serbia and Montenegro jointly propose the candidate, who is chosen by the deputies by open ballot. A majority of the total number of deputies from each member state is needed. The president has a four-year term of office and may not be from the same member state for two consecutive terms. The president's term of office may cease prematurely by resignation, relief of duty, or the dissolution of the Assembly of Serbia and Montenegro.

The Council of Ministers

The Council of Ministers in the state union performs the duties of the administration in a state. It consists of the president of Serbia and Montenegro and five ministers. The term of office depends on the confidence of the deputies of the assembly and may last up to four years. It has three global executive duties: (1) charting and pursuing the policy of Serbia and Montenegro; (2) passing by-laws, decisions, and other general enactments for enforcement of the laws of Serbia and Montenegro; and (3) coordinating the work of the ministries.

The Court of Serbia and Montenegro

The Court of Serbia and Montenegro adjudicates conflicts of authority between the state union and the member states, between the member states, as well as between the institutions of the state union. It also adjudicates constitutional disputes and administrative disputes.

The Court of Serbia and Montenegro is made up of eight judges, four from each of the member states, elected by the Assembly of Serbia and Montenegro for a period of six years. It was formed only after a significant delay.

THE ELECTION PROCESS

Every citizen of the State Union of Serbia and Montenegro older than 18 has the right to vote and to be elected to local self-governing authorities, member state authorities, and state union institutions.

Parliamentary Elections

After an initial period of two years after the adoption of the Constitutional Charter, the deputies of the Assembly of Serbia and Montenegro are to be elected by direct ballot. Ninety-one Serbian and 35 Montenegrin deputies will be elected on the basis of the laws of the member states. The Assembly of Serbia and Montenegro will in turn elect all the institutions of the state union.

At the first elections for the Assembly of Serbia and Montenegro, deputies were elected indirectly, from among the deputies of the National Assembly of the Republic of Serbia, the Assembly of the Republic of Montenegro, and the Federal Assembly of the former Federal Republic of Yugoslavia.

POLITICAL PARTIES

Citizens of the state union cannot express their will in the union, but only within the member states. Therefore, the Constitutional Charter does not discuss forms of organized expression of the political will of the citizens. Such matters are regulated by the constitutions and laws of the member states, which both have multiparty systems regulated by state laws.

The Charter on Human and Minority Rights and Fundamental Freedoms that is part of the state union's Constitutional Charter guarantees everyone freedom of association, including the right not to be a member of an organization. Political parties, trade unions, and other organizations are formed without prior license, by entry into the register with the competent authority. The right to freedom of association may be restricted by the laws of the member states, only if necessary for the protection of public safety, public health or morals, national security, or the protection of rights of others. Organizations whose activities are aimed at forceful destruction of the constitutional system, or abolition of guaranteed human rights, or creation of racial, national, ethnic, or religious hatred may be prohibited by a court decision.

After living under a one-party system in the long period of socialism, citizens of the state union have expressed considerable interest in political involvement, forming over 300 political parties. Only 10 percent of these parties have any political influence.

CITIZENSHIP

A child born on the territory of Serbia and Montenegro, according to the recognized principle of *ius sanguinis*, has the right to hold its citizenship, unless he or she has another citizenship. A citizen of the State Union of Serbia and Montenegro may not be deprived of citizenship, expelled from the state union, or extradited outside its territory, save in accordance with international obligations of the state union.

FUNDAMENTAL RIGHTS

A distinct Charter on Human and Minority Rights and Fundamental Freedoms is an integral part of the Constitutional Charter. It not only grants all classic, traditional, and generally accepted human rights, but also accommodates the latest demands for the democratization of society.

Article 1 states that human dignity is inviolable and that every person is obliged to protect it. Every person is granted the right to free development of the personality, provided that it does not violate the rights of others guaranteed by this charter, and every person is obliged to respect the human and minority rights of others. All persons are equal before the law; therefore, any discrimination is prohibited on any ground such as race, color, sex, national or social origin, birth, religion, political or other opinion, property status, culture, language, age, or mental or physical disability.

A particular part of the charter includes rights of persons who are members of national minorities. The State Union of Serbia and Montenegro has thus demonstrated the significance it attributes to the harmonious life of its citizens of various nationalities, providing them with equal living and working conditions. Members of national minorities enjoy the freedom to express their national identity and the right to maintain their particularity, as well as a range of other rights. Discrimination, forcible assimilation, and instigation of racial, ethnic, and religious hatred are prohibited.

Impact and Functions of Fundamental Rights

Human and minority rights guaranteed by the charter are exercisable directly in accordance with the Constitutional Charter and are directly regulated, provided for, and protected by the constitutions, laws, and policies of the member states. The charter lists not only rights but also respectful duties, whose fulfillment guarantees freedom and security to individuals as well as stability and continuity to institutions of the authority.

Limitations to Fundamental Rights

The guaranteed human and minority rights may only be limited by the equal extent of the rights of others. These rights may only be restricted on the basis of the limitations prescribed by the Constitutional Charter of the State Union of Serbia and Montenegro, the Charter on Human and Minority Rights, the constitutions of the member states, or a generally applicable law. Human and minority rights may only be restricted to the extent required in an open and free democratic society for achieving the stated aim. The restrictions shall not be imposed for any other purposes except those for which they have been prescribed and shall in no way infringe upon the essence of the guaranteed right.

ECONOMY

Among the key aims of Serbia and Montenegro, as stated in the Constitutional Charter, are to create a market economy based on free enterprise, competition, and social justice, as well as to establish and ensure the smooth operation of the common market on its territory. This is to be done by coordinating and harmonizing the economic systems of the member states in line with the principles and standards of the European Union.

Eminent economists have raised doubts regarding the economic continuation of the union. The Constitutional Charter attempts to harmonize two distinct economic systems, a goal that seems almost impossible to achieve. They have different currencies, individual central banks, individual customs areas and policies, and individual fiscal systems.

The State Union of Serbia and Montenegro has neither property of its own nor a common economic area. It does not dispose of foreign currency funds or a state budget. There is no national currency or central bank.

The Charter on Human and Minority Rights and Fundamental Freedoms guarantees the right to property and right of inheritance. The right to work is also guaranteed, and the member states are obliged to create the conditions in which everyone can live from his or her work. Everyone has the right to free choice of work, to fair and adequate working conditions, and in particular to fair compensation for his or her work. Employed persons have the right to go on strike in accordance with the law. Every person residing in the State Union of Serbia and Montenegro has the right to social welfare and social security.

RELIGIOUS COMMUNITIES

In the State Union of Serbia and Montenegro, everyone has the right to freedom of religion. This right includes the freedom to change religion at one's own choice and the free expression of one's religion: the freedom to manifest religion in worship, teaching, professing, practicing, and observance. The law may limit these freedoms only in order to protect public safety, morals, health, or the rights of others.

Religious communities are separate from the state and are equal. They are free to regulate their internal organization independently as well as to exercise their religious activities and rites freely. With the purpose of spreading and explaining their teachings, religious communities may establish religious schools or charity organizations in accordance with the law.

The state union recognizes conscientious objection to military service.

MILITARY DEFENSE AND STATE OF EMERGENCY

Serbia and Montenegro has an army whose supreme commander is the Supreme Command Council, which includes the president of the state union and the presidents of the member states. The Supreme Command Council decides on the use of the army and makes decisions by consensus. Military theorists have questioned the practical value of a collective supreme command, which violates the elementary military principle of subordination to a single superior.

The army of Serbia and Montenegro is under democratic and civilian control, and its fundamental duty is to defend Serbia and Montenegro in line with the Constitutional Charter and the principles of international law that regulate the use of force. The Assembly of Serbia and Montenegro has authority to adopt a defense strategy in accordance with the law.

Conscripts perform their military service in the territory of the member state whose citizenship they hold unless they freely decide to do so on the territory of the other member state. The military term lasts nine months and includes all men over 18 years of age. Conscientious objectors may perform civilian service. Women may participate in the professional army as officers, noncommissioned officers, and contract soldiers.

AMENDMENTS TO THE CONSTITUTION

In comparison to the constitutions of the two member states, which belong to the category of rigid, inflexible constitutions and are not easily amended, the Constitutional Charter of the State Union of Serbia and Montenegro is classified as a flexible, fluid constitution.

The charter was introduced under the procedure for a regular law. The draft was adopted by simple majority in the assemblies of the former member republics and delivered for adoption and promulgation by the Federal Assembly of the former Federal Republic of Yugoslavia, which had no power to influence the final text. Article 62 of the Constitutional Charter simply states that the charter can be changed under the procedure and in the manner in which the Constitutional Charter was adopted.

PRIMARY SOURCES

Constitution in English. Available online. URL: http://www. mfa.gov.yu/Facts/const_scg.pdf. Accessed on June 27, 2006.

SECONDARY SOURCES

United Nations, "Core Document Forming Part of the Reports of States Parties: Yugoslavia" (HRI/CORE/1/ Add.40), 22 July 1994. Available online. URL: http:// www.unhchr.ch/tbs/doc.nsf.

Organization for Security and Co-operation in Europe, "Mission to Serbia and Montenegro." Available online. URL: http://www.osce.org/. Accessed on July 25, 2005.

Olivera Vučić

SEYCHELLES

At-a-Glance

OFFICIAL NAME
Republic of Seychelles

CAPITAL
Victoria

POPULATION
80,832 (2005 est.)

SIZE
455 sq. mi. (1,178 sq. km)

LANGUAGES
Creole, English, French (all official)

RELIGIONS
Catholic 86.6%, Anglican 6.8%, other Christian 2.5%, other 4.1%

NATIONAL OR ETHNIC COMPOSITION
Creole, mix of European, African, and Asian

DATE OF INDEPENDENCE OR CREATION
June 29, 1976

TYPE OF GOVERNMENT
Parliamentary democracy

TYPE OF STATE
Unitary state

TYPE OF LEGISLATURE
Unicameral parliament

DATE OF CONSTITUTION
June 18, 1993

DATE OF LAST AMENDMENT
May 31, 2000

Seychelles is a parliamentary democracy based on the rule of law with a division of executive, legislative, and judicial powers. The national government is headed by a president, who is the central figure in political life and has complete control over the security apparatus.

The constitution provides for various guarantees of human rights, which are on the whole respected by the public authorities. There are enforceable remedies if a violation occurs.

Free, equal, general, and direct elections of the president and the members of parliament are guaranteed. A pluralistic system of political parties was established in 1991. Since then, the former ruling party has remained in power by a vast majority in parliament.

Religious freedom is guaranteed, and state and religious communities are separated. The economic system is tending to a free-market economy based on growing tourism.

CONSTITUTIONAL HISTORY

Seychelles is a group of 115 Indian Ocean islands about 1,000 miles east of Kenya. In 1756 the islands were formally claimed by France, which named them in honor of the French finance minister Jean Moeau de Séchelles. The possession of the islands altered several times between France and the United Kingdom between 1794 and 1814, when Britain won exclusive control via the Treaty of Paris. The Seychelles were then administered as a dependency of Mauritius until their separation in 1903, when the islands became a British Crown colony.

Britain granted more political participation to the Seychellois in 1948, mostly to adult male property owners, who were allowed to elect a council of four members to advise the governor.

In the early 1960s, two new political parties emerged to replace the existing parties: One favored integration into the United Kingdom; the other demanded full independence. In 1967, the first universal elections were held, and a new governing council was elected.

In 1970, a new constitution took effect. The United Kingdom allowed almost full self-government of the Seychelles, except in matters of foreign affairs, until independence was achieved in 1975. One year after independence, on June 29, 1976, a one-party system was imposed. It lasted until 1991, when registration of political parties was once more allowed. With the introduction of the 1993 constitution, the formal transition to a multiparty democratic system was achieved, and general elections were held in 1993.

FORM AND IMPACT OF THE CONSTITUTION

Seychelles has a written constitution, codified in a single document, which takes precedence over all other national law. The 1993 constitution marks a clear break from the former undemocratic, one-party rule; it is regarded as the start of a new political era in Seychelles.

BASIC ORGANIZATIONAL STRUCTURE

Seychelles is a unitary state and a republic. There are an executive administration, a parliament, and a judicial system. The country is divided into 23 administrative districts.

LEADING CONSTITUTIONAL PRINCIPLES

The system of government is a parliamentary democracy. There is a division of the executive, legislative, and judicial powers, enforced by checks and balances. The Seychelles' constitutional system is defined by a number of leading principles: It is a democracy and a republic, and it is based on the rule of law.

CONSTITUTIONAL BODIES

The predominant bodies provided for in the constitution are the president, the cabinet ministers, and the national parliament.

The President

The president is both the head of state and the head of the executive administration. In addition, the president is the commander in chief of the armed forces. The president is elected directly by popular vote for a five-year term and is not allowed to serve more than three terms. The president has the authority to set the guidelines for governmental policy and thus has generally been the dominant figure in Seychellois politics.

After the amendment of the constitution in 1996, the position of a vice president was established.

The Administration

The executive administration comprises a council of ministers, which serves as a cabinet. The president appoints the members of the cabinet, which consists of a minimum of seven and a maximum of 14 ministers. The ministers' task is to advise the president on policy.

The National Assembly

The National Assembly (L'Assemblée Nationale) is a unicameral body with legislative, supervisory, and political powers. Its members are elected by universal suffrage and hold office for five-year terms. It consists of 34 members, 25 of them elected directly in their constituencies and nine allocated on a representative basis to parties that win at least 10 percent of the votes. The National Assembly can be dissolved by the president under certain circumstances.

The leader of the opposition is elected by those members of the parliament who do not belong to the party that nominated the president.

The Lawmaking Process

One of the main duties of the National Assembly is the passing of legislation. Certain bills can become law only if the president assents. If the assent is refused, the parliament can submit the case to the Constitutional Court for a decision.

The Judiciary

The judicial power of the Seychelles consists of the Court of Appeal (the highest court), the Supreme Court, and other subordinate courts and tribunals. The Supreme Court has original jurisdiction relating to the constitution as well as civil and criminal matters. The Court of Appeal has jurisdiction to decide appeals from a judgment of the Supreme Court. The Court of Appeal is therefore the highest judicial authority to decide on the application, violation, or interpretation of the constitution.

The constitution declares that the judiciary is separated from other governmental powers and independent of the administration. However, the president has the right to appoint judges to the Court of Appeal and the Supreme Court, on the proposal of a three-member Constitutional Appointments Authority. One member is appointed by the president, one by the leader of the opposition, and a third by the president on the recommendations of the first two appointees. This procedure leaves a high risk of patronage and executive interference with judicial independence.

THE ELECTION PROCESS

All Seychellois over the age of 17 have both the right to stand for election and the right to vote in the elections.

POLITICAL PARTIES

Since 1991, Seychelles has had a pluralistic system of political parties. Despite the transition to a multiparty system, the former ruling party still controls the government and political life. However, there are no longer any legal obstacles restricting opposition parties.

CITIZENSHIP

Seychellois citizenship is primarily acquired by birth. A child acquires Seychellois citizenship if at least one parent is a citizen; place of birth is irrelevant.

FUNDAMENTAL RIGHTS

After the transition to democracy, it was highly important to the Seychelles to create a new constitution with an emphasis on human rights. The constitution of Seychelles explicitly guarantees a large number of fundamental rights to its citizens. Among them are the right to life and dignity, freedom from slavery and compulsory labor, the right to liberty and property, and freedom of expression. In addition, there are a series of social rights, among them the right to health care, work, education, and social security. The right to a clean, healthy, and ecologically balanced environment is guaranteed. Women enjoy the same legal, political, and social rights as men.

Impact and Functions of Fundamental Rights

In general, fundamental rights are respected in Seychelles. There are reported infringements, particularly in the course of fighting crime and in the rights of women or foreigners.

Limitations to Fundamental Rights

The fundamental rights are not without limits. For example, freedom of speech or of the press may be limited "for protecting the reputation, rights and freedoms of private lives of persons" or "in the interest of defense, public order or public morality."

These constitutional provisions may easily be interpreted in a way that allows far-reaching limitations to fundamental rights. However, the constitution also ensures that fundamental rights are not disregarded completely. For example, torture or arbitrary arrest and detention are prohibited without exception. In practice, there is difficulty in enforcing these constitutional provisions.

ECONOMY

Under the new 1993 constitution, the Seychelles has tried to open up the country for business. In legal terms, it is now easy for citizens to establish their own private enterprises, and there is special assistance for small businesses from state and parastate authorities.

After a Marxist economic approach during the 1970s and 1980s, privatization of state-run companies is now at the top of the political agenda. However, the public sector still is the dominant factor in terms of employment.

RELIGIOUS COMMUNITIES

Freedom of religion or belief, which is guaranteed as a human right, also involves rights for religious communities. The government respects these rights in full. There is no state religion. All public authorities must remain strictly neutral in their relations with religious communities. These communities regulate and administer their affairs independently within the limits of the laws that apply to all.

There are tax-free privileges for religious communities. In order to be entitled to these privileges, the communities have to register with a state authority, but there is no obligation to register.

Despite the separation of religions and the state there are areas in which they cooperate. For example, there is program time for the different religious groups on the national television channel.

MILITARY DEFENSE AND STATE OF EMERGENCY

There is a defense force. It includes the presidential protection unit, the coast guard, and a national guard. The armed forces are primarily used for civil purposes, such as dealing with vessel incidents and environmental protection tasks. There is no conscription.

AMENDMENTS TO THE CONSTITUTION

The constitution can be changed by a two-thirds vote of the members of the parliament. Certain fundamental provisions may be changed only when 60 percent of all voters have agreed in a referendum.

PRIMARY SOURCES

Constitution in English (extracts). Available online. URL: http://www.chr.up.ac.za/hr_docs/countries/seychelles. html. Accessed on June 27, 2006.

Constitution in French: *Constitution des Seychelles.* Available online. URL: http://droit.francophonie. org/doc/html/sc/con/fr/1993/1993dfsccofr1.html. Accessed on June 27, 2006.

SECONDARY SOURCES

George Bennet, *Seychelles,* World Bibliographical Series. Vol. 153. Oxford, Clio Press, 1993.

Raphael Kaplinsky, "Prospering at the Periphery: A Special Case—the Seychelles." In *African Islands and Enclaves,* edited by Robin Cohen. Beverly Hills, Calif.: Sage Publications, 1983.

Robert Stock, *Africa South of the Sahara.* New York: Guilford Press, 1995.

Michael Blumenstock

SIERRA LEONE

At-a-Glance

OFFICIAL NAME
Republic of Sierra Leone

CAPITAL
Freetown

POPULATION
5,883,889 (2005 est.)

SIZE
27,699 sq. mi. (71,740 sq. km)

LANGUAGES
English (official, regular use limited to literate minority), Mende (in the south), Temne (in the north), Krio (English-based Creole, spoken by the descendants of freed Jamaican slaves, spoken by 10% of the population but understood by 95%)

RELIGIONS
Muslim 60%, indigenous beliefs 30%, Christian 10%

NATIONAL OR ETHNIC COMPOSITION
20 native African tribes 89%, Creole 10%, other (refugees from Liberia, small numbers of Europeans, Lebanese, Pakistanis, and Indians) 1%

DATE OF INDEPENDENCE OR CREATION
April 27, 1961

TYPE OF GOVERNMENT
Constitutional democracy

TYPE OF STATE
Centralist state

TYPE OF LEGISLATURE
Unicameral parliament

DATE OF CONSTITUTION
October 1, 1991

DATE OF LAST AMENDMENT
January 25, 2002

Sierra Leone is a centralistic state and a constitutional democracy. The constitution provides a separation of executive, legislative, and judicial powers. The fundamental set of human rights is guaranteed. To ensure that the constitution is respected the Supreme Court of Sierra Leone has jurisdiction over constitutional disputes.

The president of the republic is the head of state, the central political figure, and head of the executive administration. The legislative power lies with the unicameral parliament as the representative body of the people. The elections for parliament and the office of the president are secret, equal, general, and direct. The renewed pluralistic system of political parties has strong political influence.

Religious freedom is assured for the individual as well as religious communities. The economic system outlined in the constitution is that of a market economy with social responsibility.

CONSTITUTIONAL HISTORY

On April 27, 1961, Sierra Leone, the former British colony founded for freed slaves, became an independent state and a member of the Commonwealth. After gaining independence the country suffered years of political instability, with numerous government changes and military coups. In 1978 the dominant party—the All People Congress—set up a one-party system.

A new constitution was enacted in 1991, and with it Sierra Leone restored a multiparty system. The constitution was suspended twice after that, but a civil government was reinstated in 1998.

Between 1991 and 2002 a civil war between the government and the Revolutionary United Front resulted in the death of tens of thousands and the displacement of more than 2 million people, many of whom are still refugees in neighboring countries. With the support of the United Nations (UN) peacekeeping forces, some fighting groups were disarmed. The government has slowly continued to reestablish its authority. Most UN missions ended in early 2005.

FORM AND IMPACT OF THE CONSTITUTION

Sierra Leone has a written constitution, codified in a single document that takes precedence over all other national law. The wide range of customary law may have to be adapted with modifications and exceptions to make it conform with the constitution.

Since the constitution was suspended for many years, its impact in political life still has to grow. Recent developments, however, show a generally stronger commitment to compliance with the constitution.

BASIC ORGANIZATIONAL STRUCTURE

Sierra Leone is a centralistic state with four administrative divisions. Alongside the formal political authorities, tribal culture retains great impact. In response, 12 seats in parliament are reserved for tribal chiefs. Tribal influence shows itself especially in the diversity of customary law, which can differ widely in the region.

LEADING CONSTITUTIONAL PRINCIPLES

The governmental system provided for by the constitution is that of a constitutional democracy. Executive, legislative, and judicial powers are separate and bound by the rule of law. The judiciary is independent.

The constitution of Sierra Leone defines political, economic, and social objectives to ensure that Sierra Leone is a democracy, a republic, and a state that respects its social responsibilities.

CONSTITUTIONAL BODIES

The president of the republic with the cabinet, and the unicameral parliament, are the predominant organs provided for in the constitution. Other important constitutional bodies include the Supreme Court of Sierra Leone.

The President of the Republic

The president of the republic of Sierra Leone is the head of state as well as the head of the administration and the dominant figure in politics. The president serves a five-year term and can be reelected only once. Presidential

elections are direct, general, and public and by secret vote. The president appoints the cabinet of ministers with the approval of parliament. The cabinet supports the executive functions of the president.

The Cabinet

The cabinet determines the general policy of the administration. It consists of the president, the vice president, and the ministers. The cabinet ministers are collectively responsible before the parliament for any advice given to the president or any action taken by a cabinet minister.

The Parliament

Parliament is the main representative organ of the people and is the supreme legislative power. Most of the at least 60 members of parliament are elected directly for a term of five years in a general and secret balloting process. Alongside the elected members are 12 seats filled by tribal chiefs.

The Lawmaking Process

As the main mode of exercising its legislative powers, parliament passes laws in the form of acts of parliament, which must be signed by the president to go into force.

The president may refuse to sign. He or she must return the unsigned bill to parliament along with the reasons for the refusal. To override a presidential refusal the bill needs the support of at least two-thirds of the members of parliament.

The Judiciary

The independence of the judiciary is granted by the constitution. The highest court is the Supreme Court of Sierra Leone, which performs two functions: It is the final court of appeal for all inferior courts (Court of Appeal, High Court of Justice, and traditional courts). In addition, it has exclusive jurisdiction over constitutional disputes.

THE ELECTION PROCESS

There is universal suffrage for all citizens over the age of 18. Eligibility to run for office depends on proficiency in speaking English; the minimal age is 21 years to stand for parliament and 40 years to stand for the presidency.

POLITICAL PARTIES

Sierra Leone has a pluralistic system of political parties. To participate in political life a party has to apply for registration to the Political Party Registration Commission, and must fulfill certain conditions described in the constitution. No party may be based on exclusive ethnic or tribal support.

Political parties play an important role not only in public life and in parliament but also in the presidential elections, since a presidential candidate must be nominated by a political party, and the president must be a member of that party.

CITIZENSHIP

The requirements for citizenship are set out in the Sierra Leone Citizenship Act 1973. Citizenship is primarily acquired by birth. A child acquires citizenship if his or her father or grandfather is a Sierra Leonean citizen Citizenship can also be acquired by descent through the maternal line, provided that the mother is a Sierra Leonean citizen and that the child did not acquire any other nationality by birth in a foreign country.

FUNDAMENTAL RIGHTS

The constitution guarantees the traditional basic set of human rights and civil liberties. All public forces are bound by these rights and enforcement is guaranteed through the Supreme Court. The rights of accused persons are described very explicitly by the constitution, whereas other rights are mentioned in a general manner.

Impact and Functions of Fundamental Rights

As a result of massive human rights abuses during the civil war the impact of fundamental rights is a work in progress. The pardons granted under the Lomé Peace Accord did not apply to human rights abuses perpetrated during the period of civil conflict. A special court was set up by the United Nations at the request of the Sierra Leonean government to try those most responsible for crimes against humanity, war crimes, and other serious violations of international law committed since November 30, 1996.

Sierra Leone has experienced many forms of discrimination against Liberians and other foreigners and ethnic groups during its long-running wars. Noncitizens cannot stand for public office and cannot own land. Women are governed by customary law, which frequently discriminates against them. But new laws that are under discussion should change these situations for the better.

Limitations to Fundamental Rights

Each fundamental right guaranteed in the constitution has its own catalogue of reasons that could justify its limitation. The most common reasons are the needs of defense, public safety, public order, morality, and health.

All these possible limitations, however, face a limit themselves, since the constitution does not allow a fundamental right to be reduced to an extent that cannot be reasonably justified in a democratic society.

ECONOMY

The constitution of Sierra Leone does not favor a specific economic system. A section on economic objectives calls for control of the economy to ensure maximal welfare and freedom for every citizen. However, these goals are not enforceable before a court.

On the other hand, the right of every person to participate in any economic activity is guaranteed. Likewise, there are fundamental rights such as the freedom of property and the right to form associations, which can be restricted for the greater good. All this adds up to a system of social responsibility in the framework of a relatively free market.

RELIGIOUS COMMUNITIES

Freedom of thought and religion is guaranteed as a human right. This provision includes the religious communities, which have an explicit right to provide religious instruction. Apart from that guarantee they do not enjoy special rights or treatment. The constitution does not regulate or proclaim a specific system for the relationship between the state and the religious communities.

MILITARY DEFENSE AND STATE OF EMERGENCY

The military of Sierra Leone consists only of professional soldiers. There is no general conscription, but all men over the age of 18 are allowed to volunteer.

The purposes of the armed forces are not specifically outlined in the constitution. It is the responsibility of the Defense Council to administer and maintain the military. This council consists of the president, the vice president, the chief of defense staff, the commanders of the armed forces, and two other persons appointed by the president. Final decision lies with the president acting on the advice of the Defense Council. Only in the case of a formal declaration of war does the president need ratification from parliament.

Under Article 29 the president can declare a state of public emergency and can then act without restrictions. The parliament can invalidate such a declaration by a two-thirds vote.

No private person can be forced to participate in a military tribunal.

AMENDMENTS TO THE CONSTITUTION

To alter the existing constitution, a proposed change must undergo three readings in the House of Representatives. In the final reading it must be approved by at least two-thirds of all members. Parts of the constitution specified

in Article 108 (3) can only be changed by a popular referendum, with not less than two-thirds of all valid votes in
favor. It is also possible to enact a new constitution under
the procedures described previously.

PRIMARY SOURCES

Constitution in English. Available online. URL: http://
www.statehouse-sl.org/constitution/. Accessed on September 1, 2005.

SECONDARY SOURCES

Christoph Heyns, *Human Rights Law in Africa*. Vol. 2,
Domestic Human Rights Law in Africa. Leiden, The
Netherlands: Martinus Nijhoff, 2004 (with reference
materials available online. URL: http://www.chr.
up.ac.za/. Accessed on July 16, 2005).

Anja-Isabel Bohnen

SINGAPORE

At-a-Glance

OFFICIAL NAME
Republic of Singapore

CAPITAL
Not applicable

POPULATION
4,353,900 (resident population, 2004 est.); 3,263,200 (citizens/permanent residents, 2000 est)

SIZE
263 sq. mi. (682 sq. km)

LANGUAGES
Malay (national and official language), English (administrative and official language), Chinese (official language), Tamil (official language)

RELIGIONS
Buddhism (citizens, permanent residents, 2000) 42.5%, Islam 14.9%, Christian 14.6%, Taoism/traditional Chinese beliefs 8.5%, Hinduism 4.0%, unaffiliated or other 15.5%

NATIONAL OR ETHNIC COMPOSITION
Chinese 76.8%, (citizens, permanent residents, 2000) Malay 13.9%, Indian 7.9%, other 1.4%

DATE OF INDEPENDENCE OR CREATION
August 9, 1965

TYPE OF GOVERNMENT
Parliamentary democracy

TYPE OF STATE
Unitary state

TYPE OF LEGISLATURE
Unicameral parliament

DATE OF CONSTITUTION
December 22, 1965 (retroactive to August 9, 1965)

DATE OF LAST AMENDMENT
April 19, 2004

CONSTITUTIONAL HISTORY

The modern history of Singapore can be traced to 1819, when Sir Stamford Raffles claimed this small island for the British East India Company. From 1826 Singapore, and Malacca and Penang, in present-day Malaysia, were jointly administered as the Straits Settlements, but when the East India Company was abolished in 1858, the British colonial government in India assumed immediate supervision of the Straits Settlements. This state of affairs lasted until 1867, when the Straits Settlements were transferred to the British Colonial Office. Singapore was administered as part of the Straits Settlements until the onset of World War II (1939–45). In February 1942, the British in Singapore surrendered to the Japanese invading forces, who ruled until their surrender in 1945.

After the British regained control of Singapore, they decided that the Straits Settlement would be dissolved and Singapore administered as a separate Crown colony with its own constitution; that policy took effect in 1948. In 1953, the Rendel Commission was appointed by the British government to recommend changes in the constitution of the colony of Singapore. Recommendations from the commission eventually culminated in the implantation of a new constitution, known popularly as the Rendel Constitution in 1955. Under this constitution, the legislative council was converted into a 32-member assembly, with 25 elected members, of whom six elected members would hold ministerial positions in the Council of Ministers, with the leader of the largest party in the assembly appointed as chief minister. However, British appointed officials would retain the key ministerial portfolios of finance, administration, internal security, and law; this reservation of power in British hands posed a grave obstacle to the advancement of democratic self-rule in Singapore.

In 1956, a constitutional mission led by the first chief minister of Singapore, David Marshall, held discussions with officials from the colonial office in search of a compromise constitutional model. The negotiations failed and Marshall resigned as chief minister. A second delegation was led by Marshall's successor, Lim Yew Hock. A compromise was reached this time, and the terms of a new constitution were finalized in a subsequent mission in 1958.

The British Parliament then passed the State of Singapore Act in 1958, formally transforming the colony into a self-governing state. A new constitution was now passed in Singapore; the office of the Yang di-Pertuan Negara replaced the governor as the constitutional head of state, and a new legislative assembly was established, composed of 51 elected members and headed by a prime minister. The British government retained control over defense and external affairs.

The People's Action Party (PAP) won 43 of the 51 seats in the first general elections, and its leader, Lee Kuan Yew, became Singapore's first prime minister in 1959. Soon after, the PAP started campaigning for a merger with its immediate northern neighbor, the Federation of Malaya. This move was prompted by the Singapore government's desire to achieve political independence from the British and to anchor Singapore's economic survival to a rich hinterland.

The proposals for a new federation were accepted by the British government on condition that the military bases in Singapore remain under British control and that the citizens of the respective territories vote in favor of the merger. In Singapore, 71 percent of voters supported merger. Under the Malaysia agreement concluded in July 1963, the State of Singapore and the colonies of North Borneo and Sarawak would join the existing states of the Federation of Malaya to form the Federation of Malaysia. The central government in Malaysia would manage Singapore's internal security, defense, and foreign affairs, but its daily administration would be left to its own separate administration and legislature. A new state constitution was granted to Singapore in 1963 to put in effect the changes introduced in the Malaysia Agreement, and Singapore formally joined the federation in September 1963.

The merger proved to be short-lived as relations between Singapore and the central government soon soured over the perceived interference of the People's Action Party in federal politics and Singapore's apparent lack of compliance with federal mandates. Internal politics within the federation were played out against a turbulent background of communist and communalistic threats, which eventually convinced the Malaysian prime minister, Tunku Abdul Rahman, to expel Singapore from the federation in August 1965.

After expulsion and the concurrent proclamation of independence, the Singapore Parliament amended its state constitution to reflect its new sovereign status. The Republic of Singapore Independence Act (RSIA) vested the legislative and executive powers relinquished by Malaysia in Singapore's executive and legislature. It also made certain provisions of the Malaysian Federal Constitution applicable in Singapore.

Singapore has been a member of the British Commonwealth of Nations since independence in 1965 and is a founding member state of the Association of Southeast Asian Nations (ASEAN). Singapore is committed to greater economic integration within the region and is a strong proponent of regional security and stability.

FORM AND IMPACT OF THE CONSTITUTION

Singapore has a written constitution that is currently codified in a single document. A constitutional amendment was passed in 1979 to allow the attorney general of Singapore to consolidate the various preexisting constitutional documents into a single composite form. Customary rules of international law are considered to be part of the laws of Singapore only if they are not inconsistent with any acts of Parliament. Treaties entered into by the Singapore government form part of Singapore's laws only if Parliament subsequently passes enabling legislation.

The Singapore government generally does not engage in activities that lack a formal legal basis in the constitution. This does not imply that the constitution directly constrains government conduct. First of all, the constitution can be amended by a two-thirds parliamentary majority, and the ruling party, the People's Action Party, has enjoyed a much larger majority in Parliament since independence. Second, the courts have exercised great judicial self-restraint in constitutional adjudication and have generally deferred to legislative wisdom when the constitutionality of ordinary legislation is challenged.

More difficult to assess is the indirect impact on government policy of the values set out in the constitution and their implicit connection to the wider discourse of human rights. Some recent policy changes, such as the hiring of gays in the civil service and the extension of medical benefits for married civil servants to women, which in some jurisdictions might have been prompted by constitutional litigation, were initiated by the government without direction from the Singapore courts and, particularly in the former case, in spite of vocal opposition from some communities.

BASIC ORGANIZATIONAL STRUCTURE

Singapore is a unitary state.

LEADING CONSTITUTIONAL PRINCIPLES

Singapore's system of government is a British Westminster style parliamentary democracy. The legislative, executive, and judicial branches are formally separate, although the cabinet is typically composed of elected members of Parliament.

The constitution is the supreme law, and any law inconsistent with it is void to the extent of the inconsistency. The judicial power is expressly vested in the Supreme Court and subordinate courts. The constitution guarantees the sovereignty of Singapore, enumerates fundamental liberties, and sets out the powers of the three branches of government as well as the public service, the Council of Presidential Advisers, and the Presidential Council for Minority Rights. It contains provisions governing the status of citizenship, public finances, and emergency powers.

Singapore has been described as a quasi-secular state. Although there is no official state religion, the government is required by Article 152 of the constitution "constantly to care for the interests of the racial and religious minorities in Singapore" and to "recognize the special position of the Malays, who are the indigenous people of Singapore." Among its constitutional obligations to the minority Malays is its responsibility "to protect, safeguard, support, foster and promote" their interests, including their religious interests.

CONSTITUTIONAL BODIES

The main constitutional organs are the president, the Council of Presidential Advisers, the prime minister and cabinet, Parliament, the Presidential Council for Minority Rights, and the judiciary.

The President

The president is the head of state of the Republic of Singapore and, by constitutional amendment in 1991, is now an elected official serving a term of six years. The role is largely ceremonial, but the office does carry certain executive powers as safeguards against the abuse of authority. The president may withhold assent to any bill passed by Parliament that draws upon the national financial reserves. He or she may veto key appointments such as Supreme Court judges, the attorney general, the chief of the defense force, and statutory board members. The president's veto is only absolute if it is exercised in tandem with the recommendations of the Council of Presidential Advisers. Otherwise, the veto may be overridden by a two-thirds parliamentary majority.

Council of Presidential Advisers

The function of the Council of Presidential Advisers is to make recommendations to the president on the exercise of the discretionary veto powers conferred under the constitution. The council is composed of six members appointed for a term of six years.

The Prime Minister and Cabinet

The prime minister is the head of the administration in Singapore and is assisted by the cabinet of ministers. All ministers are members of Parliament, and they serve for the legislative period of the current Parliament. The president appoints as prime minister the member of Parliament who in his or her judgment commands the confidence of the majority of the members of Parliament; the prime minister is thus usually the leader of the ruling party in Parliament. The cabinet ministers are appointed by the president on the prime minister's advice.

Parliament

Parliament is the unicameral legislative body of Singapore. Theoretically, it serves as a check on executive authority as ministers can be held accountable to the house in legislative debates. Nevertheless, party leaders can compel their members to vote along party lines by invoking the party whip. Thus, although members may object vigorously to legislative bills introduced in Parliament, they nevertheless have to vote with the party when party discipline is enforced. Thus, in effect, the prime minister and cabinet set the legislative agenda in Parliament by ensuring that the parliamentary majority backbenchers under their control comply with the ruling government's stance.

Aside from the elected members of Parliament, the constitution provides for up to six nonconstituency members, composed of defeated opposition party candidates who garnered the highest percentage of the popular vote (but not less than 15 percent of the total number of votes in the constituency), and up to nine nominated members, who are nonpartisan citizens who have distinguished themselves in various fields and are appointed by the president on the recommendation of a parliamentary Special Select Committee. Both categories were introduced by the administration ruling government to raise the level of parliamentary debates and to entrench wider representation of political views in Parliament. Both groups have voting rights in Parliament, but they may not vote on budget or appropriations bills, bills to amend the constitution, motions of no confidence in the government, or motions to remove the president from office.

The Lawmaking Process

The enactment of legislation falls within the purview of Parliament. A legislative bill may be introduced by either a private member of Parliament or a minister.

The bill has three readings. No questions are posed in the first reading. On the second reading, a vote is taken after a round of debate. If the bill passes the second reading, a parliamentary Select Committee usually peruses the bill in detail and may recommend amendments. At the third reading, the amendments are put to a vote in the house, and if they are accepted, the bill is deemed to be passed.

After a bill has been passed by Parliament, a copy is provided to the Presidential Council for Minority Rights, which determines whether it contains any discriminatory measures against minority racial groups. If no such adverse ruling is made, the bill is presented to the president for assent. The bill becomes law when the president assents and it is published in the *Parliamentary Gazette.*

Subsidiary legislation consists of regulations, orders, notifications, by-laws, and other instruments made under the authority of an act of Parliament or other lawful authority. Subsidiary legislation must be presented to Parliament, is normally published in the *Gazette,* and unless provided otherwise goes into effect on the date of publication.

Presidential Council for Minority Rights

The Presidential Council for Minority Rights engages in legislative review and highlights parliamentary bills that contain discriminatory measures against minority racial groups. If the council issues an adverse report, the impugned bill may not be presented to the president for assent unless reaffirmed by two-thirds of Parliament. To date, the Presidential Council for Minority Rights has never made an adverse ruling on any parliamentary bill.

The Judiciary

The constitution expressly vests judicial power in the Supreme Court and the subordinate courts of Singapore. The Supreme Court, which comprises a permanent three-member Court of Appeal and a High Court, can invalidate legislation if it is inconsistent with the constitution.

Judicial independence is secured under the constitution to the extent that a Supreme Court judge has tenure until the age of 65, and the judge's remuneration may not be adversely altered post appointment. However, a Supreme Court judge's term may be extended contractually by the government beyond that age. In 2004, the 77-year-old chief justice had a further two-year contract renewal until 2006. The constitution also permits the appointment of temporary judicial commissioners to serve on the Supreme Court bench for short periods, so as to facilitate the disposal of cases. The lower court judges do not have tenure. They may be transferred between appointments in the executive and judicial branches by a Judicial Service Commission headed by the chief justice.

THE ELECTION PROCESS AND POLITICAL PARTICIPATION

Every Singaporean citizen above the age of 21 is generally eligible to vote in both the parliamentary and the presidential elections. Voting is compulsory.

Parliamentary Elections

Generally, a Singapore citizen who attains the age of 21 may stand for parliamentary elections. Since 1963, all electoral campaign periods have been restricted to the statutory minimum of nine days. Electoral boundaries are altered and redrawn before every election by the Electoral Boundaries Review Committee, a body of civil servants, answerable only to the prime minister's office.

Singapore uses the "first-past-the-post" parliamentary electoral system; that is, the political candidate who secures the highest vote in a constituency takes its seat. Thus, even though the opposition has consistently obtained at least 20 percent of the popular vote at every election since the country's independence, they have never won more than 5 percent of the elected seats in Parliament.

In 1988, the government introduced a Group Representation Constituency scheme, under which most members of Parliament are now elected as a slate of four to six members rather than facing off in one-on-one challenges. The stated reason for this change was to entrench minority representation in Parliament by constitutionally mandating that every team has to field at least one minority candidate. The People's Action Party has been astute in reaping collateral benefits from this arrangement by fielding newcomers on slates with strong ministerial candidates, thus securing a renewal of People's Action Party talent in Parliament. However, not all political parties have been able to run a slate of candidates in these super-constituencies, and in the 2001 parliamentary elections, only 29 of the 84 seats in Parliament were contested.

Presidential Elections

The constitution places very stringent limits on the qualifications of a presidential candidate. The candidate must have held key public office appointments such as cabinet minister or chief justice or managed a company with a paid-up capital of at least $100 million. The Presidential Elections Committee may in its discretion make exceptions if it believes that the prospective candidate has occupied comparable positions of responsibility in other organizations.

Because of the stringency of the selection criteria, in the last election of 2005, the incumbent president, S. R. Nathan, a former civil servant benefiting from the endorsement of the People's Action Party, was certified by the Presidential Election Committee as the only candidate qualified to contest the presidency. He was thus elected to office once again without receiving any affirmation at the ballot box.

POLITICAL PARTIES

The incumbent ruling party, the People's Action Party, has enjoyed almost absolute political hegemony in Parliament since 1968. In every election since independence, it has managed to secure at least 95 percent of the elected seats.

Other political parties active in Singapore include the Democratic Progressive Party, the Singapore Democratic Alliance, the Singapore Democratic Party, and the Workers' Party of Singapore. While there are more than 20 registered political parties in Singapore, few are consistently active in contesting elections. The ineffectiveness of the rival political parties to launch a credible opposition to the incumbent is thought by some to stem from their limited resources and their inability to project a coherent ideological alternative to the People's Action Party's meritocratic but paternalistic vision of good government, thereby restricting the choices available in fact to the electorate.

Under the Societies Act, the government can ban any political party if it believes that it is being used for purposes prejudicial to public peace and good order in Singapore. Political parties that do not confine their membership to Singapore citizens or have affiliations with any organization outside Singapore that is deemed contrary to Singapore's national interest may also be dissolved by the government.

CITIZENSHIP

Generally, a person who is born in Singapore can acquire citizenship unless neither parent is Singaporean. After a recent constitutional amendment in 2004, a person born outside Singapore may acquire Singapore citizenship if either parent is Singaporean. Prior to this amendment, citizenship by descent could only be attained if the child's father were Singaporean.

FUNDAMENTAL RIGHTS

Fundamental rights are set out in Part 4 of the constitution, which guarantees, subject to various limits, such rights as liberty of the person, freedom from slavery or forced labor, the right not to be punished retrospectively, the right to equality before and equal protection of the law, the right not to be banished, as well as freedom of speech, assembly, association, and religion. Most of these rights are guaranteed to "persons," but some are guaranteed only to "citizens," such as the right not to be banished, and the freedom of speech, assembly, and association.

Impact and Function of Fundamental Rights

The Singapore courts have historically been deferential to the legislature in constitutional cases, and there are few cases in which the courts have used the power of judicial review to invalidate legislation. In a rare recent case, the High Court struck down a penal provision in the Prevention of Corruption Act applicable only to citizens for violating the equality provisions in the constitution, but its decision was quickly reversed by the Court of Appeal on a subsequent constitutional reference. The courts have tended to interpret constitutional limitation clauses ex-

pansively, allowing the government considerable latitude in lawmaking.

Commentators on Singapore constitutional law observe that the judicial approach to constitutional interpretation is consistent with a communitarian rather than individualist ideology, a formal rather than substantive conception of the rule of law, and a particularistic rather than universal conception of values.

The communitarian strand in the constitutional jurisprudence stresses that the interests of the larger society, which find expression in the legal concepts of public order and morality, generally take precedence over the rights of individuals.

A formal conception of the rule of law, also described as "rule *by* law," can also be found in the constitutional jurisprudence. For instance, in a 1995 judicial pronouncement on the constitutional implications of the "death-row phenomenon" in Singapore, the court declared that any law "which provides for the deprivation of a person's life or liberty, is valid and binding so long as it is validly passed by Parliament," and the court "is not concerned with whether it is also fair, just and reasonable as well."

Finally, the Singapore courts have often held that "conditions local to Singapore" justify departures from the interpretive approach to constitutional rights adopted by foreign constitutional courts. These judicial references to local conditions echo the government's approach to cultural values, as reflected in its 1991 White Paper, "Shared Values." This official policy document maintains that a "major difference between Asian and Western values is the balance each strikes between the individual and the community," and that, on the whole, "Asian societies emphasize the interests of the community while Western societies stress the rights of the individual."

Limitations to Fundamental Rights

Many of the rights such as the rights to speech, assembly, and association are subject to internal limitation clauses. For example, the right to freedom of speech and expression is subject to the ability of Parliament to impose "such restrictions as it considers necessary or expedient in the interest of the security of Singapore or any part thereof, friendly relations with other countries, public order or morality and restrictions designed to protect the privileges of Parliament or to prevent contempt of court, defamation or incitement to any offence."

ECONOMY

The Singapore constitution does not specify an economic system nor provide for economic or property rights, but the economic system in Singapore can be described as a free-market economy, with some state investment in key sectors, such as transportation, banking and financial services, telecommunications and media, energy and resources, infrastructure and engineering, and pharmaceuticals and biotechnology.

RELIGIOUS COMMUNITIES

Singapore is a multireligious state with significant proportions of Buddhists, Muslims, Christians, Taoists, and Hindus. Freedom of religion is guaranteed in the constitution and encompasses the right to profess, practice, and propagate one's religion and the right not to be "compelled to pay any tax the proceeds of which are specially allocated in whole or in part for the purposes of a religion other than his own." Freedom of religion also encompasses the right not to receive instruction in or to take part in any ceremony or act of worship of a religion other than one's own.

Apart from individual rights, the constitution also grants to religious groups the right to manage their own religious affairs; establish and maintain institutions for religious or charitable purposes; acquire, own, and administer property; and establish and maintain institutions for the education and instruction of children in their own religion. As mentioned earlier, the Singapore government is required by the constitution to protect the interests of religious minorities and, in particular, to "protect, safeguard, support, foster" and promote the religious interests of its minority Malay community. The government has actively supported the Muslim community in Singapore, including support for *madrasahs* (religious schools), but it does restrict the wearing of the *tudung* (a headscarf worn by some female Muslim students) in public schools. The constitutionality of this ban has not been considered by the courts.

MILITARY AND DEFENSE AND STATE OF EMERGENCY

Singapore's military forces are subjected to civilian control by the minister of defense, a member of the cabinet. Singapore currently requires all men above the age of 18 to serve 24 months of full-time national service, typically with the armed forces or alternatively with the police or civil defense force. This compulsory national service is expressly exempted from the constitutional prohibition against forced labor. Jehovah's Witnesses, who object to military service, were deregistered as a religious community in 1972 and are considered an unlawful society. The constitutionality of deregistering this group and banning its publications has been upheld by the courts on the ground that the propagation and practice of this religion are deemed prejudicial to national security and thus contrary to public order.

The constitution makes provision for legislation against subversion. In this context, the constitution actually permits Parliament to pass legislation that is inconsistent with constitutionally enshrined fundamental liberties, as long as the law explicitly states that "action has been taken or threatened by any substantial body of persons, whether inside or outside Singapore" that might cause certain enumerated forms of violence or unrest, or which is "prejudicial to the security of Singapore."

One example of such legislation is the Internal Security Act, which can be traced back to colonial legislation passed during the communist insurgency in Malaya in the 1950s and 1960s. Under this legislation, the state may arrest and detain without trial persons suspected of "acting in any manner prejudicial to the security of Singapore." It was used, in the months after the September 11, 2001, terrorist attacks in the United States, against suspected members of Jemaah Islamiyah, a militant group that is alleged to have been plotting to bomb several targets in Singapore and has been linked to terrorist attacks in the region.

Persons detained under the Internal Security Act are accorded some basic due process rights and are permitted to make representations to an advisory board, whose recommendations are nonbinding on the government unless supported by the president. In 1990, in response to a court decision that expanded the scope of judicial view of detentions under the Internal Security Act, the constitution was amended to allow the scope of judicial review to be set by the legislation itself. The Internal Security Act was concurrently amended in an attempt to limit judicial review of acts done and decisions made under its authority, ostensibly in matters of procedural compliance alone.

The constitution also allows the president to issue a Proclamation of Emergency if he or she is satisfied that a grave emergency exists whereby the security or economic life of Singapore is threatened. A proclamation of emergency allows the president, if satisfied that immediate action is required and until such time as Parliament is able to sit, to promulgate ordinances that have the force of law. Once it is able to sit, Parliament can either annul the proclamation or, if it appears necessary by reason of the emergency, use a simplified process to create laws that are inconsistent with the constitution. The emergency measures cannot, however, be inconsistent with constitutional provisions relating to religion, citizenship, or language. Six months after the proclamation of emergency ceases to be in force, any laws made under it that could not otherwise have been made would also cease to have any force.

AMENDMENTS TO THE CONSTITUTION

As a general rule, the constitution can be amended by an act of Parliament supported by not less than two-thirds of the total number of the elected members of Parliament. However, any amendment to Part 3 of the constitution (which requires that any transfer of powers or relinquishment of control to the police or armed forces must be put before a national referendum) must itself be supported by at least two-thirds of the votes cast in a national referendum.

A 1991 amendment to the constitution, which as of early 2006 was not yet in force, would require that any amendment to fundamental provisions in the constitution, such as the amendment clause itself, fundamental liberties, and certain specified powers of the president, have the support not only of a two-thirds majority in Parliament, but also of at least two-thirds of the votes cast in a national referendum. The government currently has no immediate plans to put this provision in force.

PRIMARY SOURCES
Constitution in English. Available online. URL: http://statutes.agc.gov.sg/. Accessed on August 8, 2005.

SECONDARY SOURCES
Kevin Y. L. Tan, ed., *The Singapore Legal System,* 2d ed. Singapore: Singapore University Press, 1999.
Kevin Y. L. Tan and Thio Li-ann, *Constitutional Law in Malaysia and Singapore.* 2d ed. Singapore: Butterworths, 1997.

Victor V. Ramraj and Po-Jen Yap

SLOVAKIA

At-a-Glance

OFFICIAL NAME
Slovak Republic

CAPITAL
Bratislava

POPULATION
5,402,547 (2005 est.)

SIZE
18,932 sq. mi. (49,035 sq. km)

LANGUAGES
Slovak

RELIGIONS
Catholic 73%, Lutheran 6.9%, Calvinist 2%, Orthodox Christian 0.9%, Jehovah's Witnesses 0.4%, Methodist 0.1%, Baptist 0.1%, other (including Jewish) 3.5%, unaffiliated 13%

NATIONAL OR ETHNIC COMPOSITION
Slovak 85.6%, Hungarian 10.8%, other (Roma and Sinti, Czech, Ruthenian, and German) 3.6%

DATE OF INDEPENDENCE OR CREATION
January 1, 1993

TYPE OF GOVERNMENT
Parliamentary democracy

TYPE OF STATE
Unitary state

TYPE OF LEGISLATURE
Unicameral parliament

DATE OF CONSTITUTION
September 1, 1992

DATE OF LAST AMENDMENT
May 26, 2004

The Slovak Republic is a parliamentary democracy based on the rule of law with a strict division of executive, legislative, and judicial powers. The head of state is the president, whose functions are mostly representative. The Constitutional Court is an independent judicial authority with a mandate to protect the constitution.

The Slovak Republic is not bound by any official ideology or religion, although the constitution takes into consideration the spiritual heritage of Saint Cyril and Saint Methodius, who introduced Christianity to the Slavonic people in the ninth century. Freedom of thought, conscience, religion, and belief is guaranteed by the constitution.

The legal system of Slovakia is built on a clear division between the rights of citizens and those of the state. Everyone may claim his or her rights by procedures established by law in an independent and impartial process.

Fundamental rights are guaranteed in the Slovak Republic to everyone regardless of sex, race, color, language, belief or religion, political affiliation or other conviction, national or social origin, nationality or ethnic origin, property, descent, or any other status. Citizens exercise the right to vote through universal, equal, and direct suffrage by secret ballot.

The economy in Slovakia is based on the principles of a socially and ecologically oriented market economy.

CONSTITUTIONAL HISTORY

The favorable natural conditions of Slovakia made early human settlements possible. The remains of many Stone Age settlements have been discovered in Slovakia. During the Bronze Age Slovakia was a crossroads of many tribes and ethnic groups. The Slavic tribes arrived in the fifth and the sixth centuries C.E., when the oldest Slavic national unit—Samo's Empire—appeared. By the end of the eighth century, there were two princedoms on the territory of Slovakia: Pribina's Princedom in Nitra and Mojmir's Princedom in western Slovakia and southern Moravia. The two states were under united rule in the years 813 to 833 C.E., laying the foundations of the Great Moravian Empire, a powerful barrier against Frankish expansionism.

On the invitation of a Great Moravian ruler, Cyril and Methodius traveled from Byzantium in 863 C.E. and translated liturgical books from Latin and Greek into Old Slavonic. They developed the linguistic standard of the language Old Slavonic and devised the first Slavonic alphabet. Saint Cyril and Saint Methodius are considered to be the cornerstone of Slovak Christian identity, as cited in the Slovak constitution.

At the beginning of the 10th century, the Great Moravian Empire disintegrated as a result of the Hun invasion and pressure from the Frankish Empire. Slovakia became part of the early Hungarian state. In the following centuries the country went through very hard times—the Tatar invasion (1241) and the Turkish invasion (1526). The Turkish occupation lasted for 150 years. Nearly four centuries of Habsburg rule were punctuated by antifeudal and anti-Habsburg uprisings. A Slovak national revival in language and culture began in the 19th century. In the revolutionary years of 1848–49, Slovaks joined other suppressed peoples in the struggle for national emancipation from the Austro-Hungarian monarchy, but without any success.

The founding of the Czechoslovak Republic in 1918 after World War I (1914–18) satisfied the common aspirations of Czechs and Slovaks for independence from the Habsburg Empire. Czechoslovakia was the only east-central European country to remain a parliamentary democracy from 1918 to 1938. After the 1938 Treaty of Munich, the Czech regions were partly forcibly absorbed into Germany and partly transformed into a German protectorate. The Slovak region was transformed into a new entity called the Slovak State. It was recognized by a majority of states of the international community.

After the defeat of the Germans and the reunification of Czechoslovakia in 1945 (except a part of eastern Slovakia, annexed to the Soviet Union), the Czechs and Slovaks held elections in 1946. In Slovakia, the Democratic Party won the elections, but the Czechoslovak Communist Party won 38 percent of the total votes in Czechoslovakia and seized power in February 1948. The next four decades were characterized by strict Communist rule. The period was interrupted only briefly in the year 1968 by political, social, and economic reforms in an effort to create "socialism with a human face." The military invasion and occupation of Czechoslovakia on August 21, 1968, by Soviet, Hungarian, Bulgarian, East German, and Polish troops destroyed any hope for democracy in the country for the next 20 years.

The more than 40 years of communism and Soviet domination were years of suffering for many people, many of them clerics and lay supporters of the Catholic Church. Quiet resistance continued, however, often focused around the church.

On November 17, 1989, a series of public protests known as the Velvet Revolution began, leading to the downfall of communist rule in Czechoslovakia. A transitional government was formed in December 1989, and the first free elections since 1948 took place in June 1990. In 1992, negotiations on the new federal constitution deadlocked over the issue of Slovak autonomy, and in the second half of 1992 an agreement was reached to divide Czechoslovakia peacefully. On January 1, 1993, the Czech Republic and the Slovak Republic were simultaneously and peacefully founded. Both states attained immediate recognition from the United States and their European neighbors.

Slovakia was accepted into the United Nations, the Council of Europe, the North Atlantic Treaty Organization (NATO), and other international governmental organizations. Slovakia became a member of the European Union on May 1, 2004.

FORM AND IMPACT OF THE CONSTITUTION

The Slovak constitution is codified in a single written document, called the Constitution of the Slovak Republic. It has priority over all laws and international treaties valid in Slovakia, including European law; however, this legal question has not yet been resolved satisfactorily by juridical doctrine.

Courts, especially the Constitutional Court, implement all laws and treaties in accordance with the constitution, which is also the main legal source of fundamental values of the society.

BASIC ORGANIZATIONAL STRUCTURE

The territory of Slovakia is integral and indivisible. The capital of Slovakia is Bratislava. Only a constitutional law may change the borders of Slovakia. Reacting to new transatlantic and European challenges of recent history, Slovakia may, at its own discretion, enter into a union with other states.

A constitutional law, confirmed by a referendum, is required before entry into or secession from such a union. The constitution does, however, permit Slovakia to transfer the exercise of a part of its powers to the European Communities and the European Union. Legally binding acts of the European Communities and of the European Union have precedence over laws of Slovakia. Slovakia may also join an organization of mutual collective security for the purpose of maintaining peace, security, and democratic order, under conditions established by an international treaty.

As a principle, Slovakia supports the national consciousness and cultural identity of Slovaks living abroad, their institutions established to achieve this goal, and their relations with the homeland. The basic unit of territorial self-administration is the municipality.

LEADING CONSTITUTIONAL PRINCIPLES

The system of government is a parliamentarian democracy with a strong division of the executive, legislative, and judicial powers, based on checks and balances. The judiciary is independent and includes a Constitutional Court. Slovakia is a sovereign, democratic, and pluralistic state and is governed by the rule of law. It is not bound to any ideology or religion.

Slovakia acknowledges and adheres to general rules of international law, international treaties by which it is bound, and its other international obligations. The state power derives from the citizens, who exercise it directly or through their elected representatives. Slovakia is a social state, meaning that government is mandated to act to ensure a minimal standard of living to every resident of Slovakia.

State bodies may act solely on the basis of the constitution and within its scope. Their actions are governed by procedures specified by law. Everyone may do what is not forbidden by law, and no one may be forced to do what the law does not enjoin. The Slovak language is the official language of Slovakia.

Protection of the environment is a constitutional principle.

CONSTITUTIONAL BODIES

The executive power is represented by the president of Slovakia and the administration led by its prime minister. The legislative power is represented by the National Council. The judicial power is represented by the Constitutional Court, the office of the public prosecutor, and a system of general courts. The main independent control bodies are the Supreme Audit Office and the public defender of rights (ombudsperson).

The President of the Slovak Republic

The head of the Slovak Republic is the president. The president represents the country externally and internally, and he or she ensures the regular operation of constitutional bodies. The president performs the duties of the office according to his or her conscience and convictions and is not bound by orders from anyone.

The president may ask the Constitutional Court to review the constitutionality of a negotiated international treaty, a process for which the consent of the National Council of Slovakia is also necessary. The president receives, appoints, and recalls heads of diplomatic missions. The president convenes the opening session of the National Council of Slovakia and, in cases stated in the constitution, may dissolve the National Council. The president signs laws and can return laws to the National Council with objections, appoints and removes the prime minister and other members of the cabinet and charges them with the direction of ministries, and appoints and recalls principal officials and judges. The president can remit or mitigate sentences imposed by criminal courts and expunge sentences in the form of individual pardon or amnesty. The president is also the commander in chief of the armed forces and can declare war on the basis of a decision of the National Council. The president can call referenda.

A citizen of Slovakia eligible to vote who has attained 40 years of age may be elected president. The president may not serve more than two consecutive terms.

Citizens of Slovakia choose the president for a five-year term in direct elections by secret ballot. Candidates for president can be nominated by at least 15 members of parliament or by at least 15,000 citizens who have the right to vote for the National Council. A candidate needs an absolute majority of valid votes to win; in an eventual second round the greatest number of valid votes is needed.

The Administration

The administration or cabinet is the supreme executive body of the Slovak Republic. It consists of the prime minister, deputy prime ministers, and ministers. The prime minister is appointed and recalled by the president. The president appoints and recalls other members of the cabinet on the basis of the prime minister's recommendations. The administration is obliged to present itself to the National Council, submit its program, and ask for a vote of confidence. The administration is responsible to the National Council for the exercise of governmental powers and is subject to a vote of no confidence at any time.

Any cabinet resolution requires the consent of an absolute majority of all its members. The cabinet decides as a body on draft laws and regulations, on measures to promote the government's economic and social programs, on the draft budget and the final state budgetary account, and on other fundamental issues of internal and foreign policy.

The National Council

The National Council of the Slovak Republic is the country's sole legislative body. It consists of 150 members of parliament, elected for a four-year term. Members are expected to exercise their mandates individually and according to their conscience and conviction. No party orders can bind them. The members of parliament are elected by universal, equal, and direct suffrage by secret ballot.

The chief powers of the National Council are to adopt the constitution, constitutional laws, and other laws and to supervise their implementation. The National Council can approve or repudiate treaties on the union of Slovakia with other states. It decides on proposals for referenda.

No member of parliament can be prosecuted for any vote in the National Council or in its committees, even after expiration of his or her mandate. Members of parliament cannot be prosecuted for any statements made during their term in the National Council, even after their mandate expires. No member of parliament can be prosecuted, sanctioned by any disciplinary measure, or held in pretrial detention without approval of the National Council.

The Lawmaking Process

A bill may be introduced directly by the administration, a deputy, or a committee of the parliament.

Certain international treaties have precedence over all other laws. These include treaties on human rights and fundamental freedoms, treaties for whose exercise a law is not necessary, and treaties that directly confer rights or impose duties on natural persons or legal persons (e.g., corporations) and were legally ratified and promulgated.

The president signs and promulgates laws. He or she has the power to refuse to sign and return the bill to the National Council with comments up to 15 days after receiving it. The act must then be approved by parliament a second time in order to become law. The president also declares referendums.

To approve the most important international treaties, and to reconfirm a law returned by the president, an absolute majority of all members of parliament is required. A three-fifths majority vote is required for adopting or amending the constitution, passing a constitutional law, ratifying an international treaty concerning territorial matters or certain EU matters, declaring a plebiscite on the recall of the president, prosecuting the president, or declaring war on another state.

A constitutional law on joining a union with other states or seceding from it must be confirmed by a referendum. A referendum may also be used to decide on other crucial issues of public interest. No issues of fundamental rights and freedoms, taxes, duties, or the state budget may be decided by a referendum.

The Judiciary

The judicial system is composed of the Supreme Court of the Slovak Republic and other courts. The president appoints and recalls judges on the recommendation of the Judiciary Council; they are appointed without time restrictions.

The Constitutional Court is an independent judicial authority with a mandate to review the conformity of laws with the constitution. If the court finds that laws or regulations violate the constitution, they loose effect and the issuing body then has six months to harmonize them with the constitution, with constitutional laws, or with valid international treaties. If they fail to do so, these laws or regulations, or their unconstitutional provisions, cease to be valid.

The Constitutional Court also decides disputes over competency between the central state administrative bodies and complaints of the bodies of territorial self-administration against unconstitutional or unlawful decision. The court also hears claims by natural or legal persons of infringement of their fundamental rights or freedoms.

The Constitutional Court makes final decisions on verifying disputed mandates of members of parliament; validating elections for the president, the National Council, and local self-government bodies; and validating referenda and plebiscites on the recall of the president. It also issues final rulings on whether political parties or movements should be suspended or dissolved on the basis of nonconformity with constitutional and other laws.

When the president has been charged by the National Council with willful infringement of the constitution or treason, the Constitutional Court makes the final verdict. The court can also review the constitutionality of declarations of a state of exception or a state of emergency, and of the measures taken during those states.

The Constitutional Court is composed of 13 judges, who are appointed by the president for 12-year terms on the recommendation of the National Council.

THE ELECTION PROCESS

All Slovaks over the age of 18 have the right to vote. Members of parliament are elected by universal, equal, and direct suffrage by secret ballot. Any citizen who has the right to vote, has attained 21 years of age, and has permanent residency in Slovakia is eligible to be elected to the National Council.

POLITICAL PARTIES

Slovakia has a pluralistic system of political parties as a basic principle of the democratic system described in the constitution. The internal structure and all the activities of political parties are regulated by law. Parties are primarily self-financed.

The party that wins the most seats in parliamentary elections is delegated by the president to constitute the administration. If it fails to do so, the president then turns to the party that finished second.

CITIZENSHIP

Slovak citizenship is primarily acquired by birth (*ius sanguinis*) and may also be acquired by adoption or voluntarily as regulated by laws and international agreements. No one may be deprived of citizenship against his or her will.

FUNDAMENTAL RIGHTS

The constitution distinguishes among fundamental rights and freedoms, political rights, and the rights of national minorities and ethnic groups. It also provides economic, social, and cultural rights, as well as the right to protection of the environment and of one's cultural heritage. Judicial and other legal protections are guaranteed. The right to life is considered the most important human right. Human life is declared to be worthy of protection even before birth. The death penalty is prohibited.

More specifically, the constitution proclaims that everyone has the right to maintain and protect his or her dignity, honor, reputation, and good name; to be free of unjustified interference in private and family life; and to be protected against unjustified collection, disclosure, and other misuse of personal data. Everyone has the right to own property, and the rights of all property owners must be uniformly construed and equally protected by law. The right of inheritance is guaranteed. Expropriation or other restrictions on property rights may be imposed only to the extent necessary, in the public interest, in a legal fashion, and for just compensation. Secrecy of letters and other communications and of personal data is guaranteed. Freedom of movement and residence is guaranteed. No one can be forced to perform military service if it is contrary to his or her conscience or religion.

Impact and Functions of Fundamental Rights

The Constitution of Slovakia provides that all human beings are free and equal in dignity and in rights. Their fundamental rights and freedoms are sanctioned, inalienable, imprescriptible, irreversible, and covered by the right to judicial protection.

Everyone may claim his or her rights by law at an independent and impartial court or, in cases provided by law, at another public authority. Any person who claims his or her rights have been denied by a decision of a body of public administration may go to court to have the legality of the decision reviewed, save otherwise provided by a law.

Everyone has the right to compensation for damage caused by an unlawful decision of a court or other public authority, or by improper official procedure. Everyone has the right to have his or her case tried publicly without undue delay, to be present at the proceedings, and to comment on any evidence given therein. The public may be excluded only in cases specified by law.

Thus, the Slovak system of human rights provides a classic, wide, and precise constitutional structure based on stable principles, both conservative and liberal in nature, that reflect the impact of Christian culture. Fundamental rights are guaranteed in Slovakia to everyone regardless of sex, race, color, language, belief and religion, political affiliation or other conviction, national or social origin, nationality or ethnic origin, property, descent, or any other status. Everyone has the right to decide freely of which national group he or she is a member. No injury may be inflicted on anyone because of exercising his or her fundamental rights and freedoms.

Limitations to Fundamental Rights

Limitations of fundamental rights and freedoms have to be based on a law under the conditions set out in the constitution. Legal restrictions of fundamental rights and freedoms are applied equally in all cases fulfilling the specified conditions. When imposing restrictions on fundamental rights and freedoms, respect must be given to the essence and meaning of these rights and freedoms, and such restrictions may be used only for the purpose specified in the law.

Freedom of thought, conscience, religion, and belief is the most sensitive area of possible limitations. According to the constitutional doctrine, these rights have so-called absolute character; only their expressions have relative character and may be limited by law. The exercise of these rights may be restricted only by law, and the restriction must be necessary to any democratic society for the protection of public order, health, and morals or the protection of the rights and freedoms of others.

ECONOMY

The economy in Slovakia is based on the principles of a socially and ecologically oriented market economy. Slovakia protects and encourages economic competition.

The National Bank of Slovakia is an independent central bank. It may, within the scope of its legally endowed powers, issue generally binding legal regulations.

RELIGIOUS COMMUNITIES

There are 16 registered religious communities and churches, all with the right to subvention from the state budget. They are structured and function independently, within the bounds of the law. The relations between the state and religious communities are regulated by the constitution and laws, although bilateral international or national agreements have been in recent years considered to be the most convenient and precise instrument for this purpose. The 2000 Basic Treaty between Slovakia and the Holy See and several connected international or national agreements concluded with the Holy See as well as with other registered churches and religious communities complement a united and effective system of mutual relations between state and church. Of the inhabitants of the republic 72 percent are members of the Roman Catholic Church.

Freedom of thought, conscience, religion, and belief is guaranteed, including the right to change religion or belief and the right to refrain from a religious affiliation. Everyone has the right to express his or her mind publicly and has the right to manifest freely his or her religion or belief either alone or in association with others, privately or publicly, in worship, religious acts, ceremonies, or teaching. Churches and ecclesiastical communities administer their own affairs; in particular, they establish their bodies, appoint clerics, provide for theological education, and establish religious orders and other clerical institutions independently of state authorities.

MILITARY DEFENSE AND STATE OF EMERGENCY

War is declared by the president, subject to the support of a three-fifths majority of all members of parliament. This may take place if the country is attacked or as a result of obligations deriving from international treaties. The president also concludes peace.

The president may, upon the recommendation of the administration, order a mobilization of the military forces or declare a state of exception or a state of emergency. He or she also declares their termination. A constitutional law defines the restrictions to fundamental rights and freedoms, and the extent of citizens' duties, that may be necessary in times of war, a state of war, a state of exception, or a state of emergency.

AMENDMENTS TO THE CONSTITUTION

For the purpose of adopting or amending the constitution or a constitutional law, the consent of a three-fifths majority of all members of parliament is required.

PRIMARY SOURCES

Constitution in English. Available online. URL: http://www.concourt.sk/A/A_ustava/ustava_a.pdf. Accessed on August 7, 2005.
Constitution in Slovak. Available online. URL: http://www.concourt.sk/S/s_index.htm. Accessed on June 28, 2006.
Constitution in Slovak: Ján Drgonec, *Ústava Slovenskej republiky—Komentár*. Bratislava: Heuréka, 2004.

Marek Šmid

SLOVENIA

At-a-Glance

OFFICIAL NAME
Republic of Slovenia

CAPITAL
Ljubljana

POPULATION
1,964,036 (2005 est.)

SIZE
7,827 sq. mi. (20,273 sq. km)

LANGUAGES
Slovenian

RELIGIONS
Catholic 58%, Muslim 2.4%, Serbian Orthodox 2.3%, unaffiliated or other 37.30%

NATIONAL OR ETHNIC COMPOSITION
Slovenian 83%, Serbian 2%, Croatian 1.8%, Bosnian 1.1%, other (largely Muslim as ethnic entity, Hungarian, Macedonian, Montenegrin, Italian, and Roma) 12.1%

DATE OF INDEPENDENCE OR CREATION
June 25, 1991

TYPE OF GOVERNMENT
Parliamentary democracy

TYPE OF STATE
Unitary state

TYPE OF LEGISLATURE
Bicameral parliament

DATE OF CONSTITUTION
December 23, 1991

DATE OF LAST AMENDMENT
June 15, 2004

Slovenia is a parliamentary democracy based on the rule of law with a clear division of executive, legislative, and judicial powers. It is organized as a unitary state; although the 193 communes have local authorities, the country has a strong central government. The constitution provides for far-reaching guarantees of human rights that are widely respected by the public authorities; if a violation of the constitution does occur in individual cases, there are effective remedies enforceable by an independent judiciary, which includes a strong and visible Constitutional Court.

The president of the republic is the head of state, but his or her function is mostly representative. The central political figure is the president of the government. The president of the republic depends on the parliament as the representative body of the people. Free, equal, general, and direct elections of the members of parliament are guaranteed. A pluralistic system of political parties has intense political impact.

Religious freedom is guaranteed and state and religious communities are separate. The economic system can be described as a social market economy. The military is subject to the civil government in terms of law and fact.

CONSTITUTIONAL HISTORY

Slovenians are the westernmost Slavs in Europe. They settled the eastern Alpine area in the second half of the sixth century C.E., covering an area three times larger than today's Slovenia, with its center north of the Karavanken Mountains. Their name indicates close cultural and ethnic links with the peoples of Moravia, Slovakia, and Slavonia.

The Slovenian dukedom of Carantania, the oldest Slavic state entity, appeared in the first half of the seventh century; it was a part of Samo's tribal union to the north, which ended in 658. The Slovenians were included in the missionary activities of Saint Cyril and Saint Methodius. With the arrival of the Magyars and the creation of their state at the end of the ninth century these links were weakened.

Carantania survived as a significant entity until 1414; its duke was elected and enthroned in a special ceremony performed exclusively in the Slovenian language. This unique ceremony was known to the French legal scholar Jean Bodin and through him to Thomas Jefferson. Carantania fell under the dominance of Bavarians and Franks in the mid-eighth century, and the Slovenians lost their tribal self-government in 828.

The region became divided into provinces under Habsburg rule, each with its own political, legal, military, and even religious life until 1918. Slovenians lived for more than half a millennium divided among the provinces of Styria, Carinthia, Carniola, Gorizia, Istria, and Trieste. Of these provinces, only Carniola and Gorizia were predominantly Slovenian. Instead of an ethnic consciousness, a provincial consciousness that was strongly supported by the nobility developed.

Slovenians were the first Slavs to accept Christianity, undoubtedly the most important cultural legacy of antiquity. It was spread mainly from Aquilea with the help of the Salzburg and Freising dioceses. The Brižinski Monuments testify to the consolidation of Christianity. These Slovenian religious texts were written in a single manuscript before 1000 C.E. and represent the oldest Slavic text in Latin transcription. An important basis for further Slovenian cultural development was the printing of the first Slovenian book in 1550 and a translation of the Bible, both provided by Protestantism. The arrival of the Jesuits during the Counter-Reformation generated the founding of secondary schools and colleges in the capitals of the provinces.

For most of their history, Slovenians were referred to by their non-Slavic neighbors with a variety of names, such as Slavs, Winds, and Wends, or by their province names, such as Carniolians and Styrians. The provincial identification of the Slovenians was newly affirmed in the second half of the 18th century, when a national renaissance based on raising the social status of the Slovenian language and its use in all areas of life emerged.

Unlike the majority of other European nations, Slovenians defended their national rights from the standpoint of natural law. Their national movement reached its peak in the revolutionary year of 1848. A central demand of the revolutionaries was restructure of the old provinces in order to unify the Slovenians into a Kingdom of Slovenia with its own national assembly; it was the most radical of the national demands then put forward within the Austrian Empire. The revolutionaries also demanded that Slovenian be the official language in all fields of public life.

The Slovenians kept these demands alive, reiterating them in particular at the national *tabors* (meetings) in 1868–71, where up to 30,000 people gathered. The political parties that emerged after 1890 supported the claims as well. In this way the basic political principles on which the independent Slovenian state was born in 1991 were established.

Thus, by the time of World War I (1914–18), the Slovenians were a modern European nation, with a national culture comparable to that of other western and central European nations. This was achieved without the financial help or guidance of national or provincial government institutions.

After the war, a short-lived state was formed on the Slovenian, Croat, and Serb territories of the former Austria-Hungary. It soon merged with the Kingdom of Serbia and Montenegro to form the Kingdom of Serbs, Croats, and Slovenians on December 1, 1918, later renamed the Kingdom of Yugoslavia. However, more than one-third of the Slovenian population lived in areas annexed by Italy, where they suffered national persecution under fascism, or were included in the Austrian Republic, where the Carinthian Slovenians also faced a rapid worsening of national conditions. The greatest achievement of the Slovenians in Yugoslavia was undoubtedly the founding of the Slovenian University in Ljubljana in 1919 as well as other major cultural institutions. The language of instruction in all schools was Slovenian.

World War II (1939–45) began with the annexation of all Slovenian territory by Germany, Italy, and Hungary, who all aimed to eliminate the Slovenians as a nation. The Communist Party weakened the national resistance, provoking a civil war. After the end of World War II the democratic opposition was eliminated and half a century of one-party rule followed.

Slovenia became the most developed of the federal republics inside Yugoslavia. Nevertheless, there was growing sentiment to secede from Yugoslavia and establish an independent national state; in economic and social terms the country was lagging behind neighboring Italy and Austria, and Slovenian cultural identity was threatened by Yugoslav centralism. In the end, the predominant factor was a desire for freedom and democracy after the worldwide collapse of communism.

The public desire for independence was first expressed in the plebiscite of December 23, 1990. On June 25, 1991, the Slovenian parliament declared independence and adopted the Basic Constitutional Charter on the Sovereignty and Independence of the Republic of Slovenia. After only 10 days of resistance from the Yugoslav army, a peace agreement was reached, thus paving the way for national sovereignty and international recognition. The constitution of the Republic of Slovenia was adopted on December 23, 1991, by the Assembly of the Republic of Slovenia.

Slovenia is a state of all its citizens based on the right of the Slovenian nation to self-determination. Besides ethnic Slovenians, members of the Italian and Hungarian national communities live as indigenous inhabitants in Slovenia, while Slovenians also live as indigenous inhabitants of Italy, Austria, and Hungary.

Slovenia joined the North Atlantic Treaty Organization (NATO) in 2004 and became a member state of the

European Union on May 1, 2004. As such, Slovenia participates in an increasingly intense integration process of the European nations that seeks to ensure peace, stability, and prosperity across the continent.

FORM AND IMPACT OF THE CONSTITUTION

Slovenia has a written constitution that takes precedence over all other national law. International law must be in accordance with the constitution to be applicable within Slovenia. Only the law of the European Union has precedence over the Slovenian constitution—and only as long as it does not contradict the constitution's basic principles.

The constitution of Slovenia is significant not only for the legal system of the country, but also as a source of fundamental values for the functioning of society. All law must comply with the provisions of the constitution. The Constitutional Court is strict and powerful in implementing constitutional law.

BASIC ORGANIZATIONAL STRUCTURE

Administratively, the state is structured into 60 administrative units, linked directly with the central government. There are no independent regions in Slovenia, but local government is widespread. The citizens of the local communities elect mayors and other members of local political bodies. There are 193 local communities, which vary considerably in size—the smallest with fewer than 1,000 inhabitants and the largest, Slovenia's capital, Ljubljana, with 270,000 inhabitants. The local communities can make their own decisions on quite a number of issues, among which local urban and land planning is the most important.

LEADING CONSTITUTIONAL PRINCIPLES

Slovenia's system of government is a parliamentary democracy. There is a strong division of the executive, legislative, and judicial powers, based on checks and balances. The judiciary is independent and includes a Constitutional Court. On the national level, political participation is rather strictly shaped as an indirect, representative democracy. Direct democracy, whereby people decide directly on the relevant issues by means of a referendum, is also used.

The Slovenian constitutional system is defined by a number of leading principles: Slovenia is a democracy, a republic, and a social state, and it is based on the rule of law. The principle of republican government simply means that there shall be no monarchy. The principle of a social state means that government must take action to ensure a minimal standard of living to every citizen. Rule of law is of decisive impact. All state actions impairing the rights of the people must have a basis in parliamentary law, and the judiciary must be independent and effective.

Further structural principles are implicitly contained in the constitution: Religious freedom, separation of the state and religion, a commitment to protecting human rights and fundamental freedoms, protection of the human person and its dignity, the right to privacy and personality rights, the right to private property and inheritance, and the protection of a healthy living environment and of the natural and cultural heritage are all constitutional principles.

The constitution mandates direct application of ratified and published international agreements such as the European Convention on Human Rights and Fundamental Freedoms, the Universal Declaration of Human Rights, and the International Covenant on Civil and Political Rights.

CONSTITUTIONAL BODIES

The predominant bodies provided for in the constitution are the president of the republic; the administration; the parliament, which includes the National Assembly (Državni Zbor) and the National Council (Državni Svet); and the judiciary, which includes the Constitutional Court, the Supreme Court, and the judicial council. A number of other bodies complete this list, such as the court of audit and the ombudsperson.

The President of the Republic

The president of the republic is the head of state and represents the republic in international affairs; he or she is the commander in chief of its defense forces. The president issues the call for elections to the National Assembly and proposes to the National Assembly a candidate for president of the administration. The president of the republic promulgates laws. The president also appoints and recalls ambassadors and other state officials where provided for by law. The president of the republic has the right to grant clemency.

The political position of the president of the republic is limited, as most of these duties are largely representative. The impact depends largely on the president's personal charisma. This relative lack of political power enables the president to be representative of the whole of the Slovenian nation.

The president of the republic is chosen by direct elections for a five-year term and may be elected for a maximum of two consecutive terms.

The Federal Administration

The administration (cabinet) is the political nerve center of Slovenia. It consists of the president of the administration and the cabinet ministers. The president of the administration is the head of the executive branch of government. The candidate is proposed by the president of the republic and needs to be endorsed by parliament (National Assembly).

The president of the cabinet and the cabinet ministers serve for the legislative period of the National Assembly (i.e., four years), unless dismissed early in a vote of no confidence. Each newly elected National Assembly must go through the process of electing a president of the cabinet by majority vote.

The constitutional powers of the office generally make the president of the cabinet the dominant figure in Slovenian politics. Once elected, the president of the cabinet can only be dismissed if a majority of the assembly chooses a replacement. This provision tends to weaken parliament somewhat; the general political fact is that the majority in parliament backs the administration and stands against the parliamentary minority.

The National Assembly

The Slovenian National Assembly (Državni Zbor) is the central representative organ of the people at the state level. As a legislative body, it cooperates with a number of other constitutional organs, especially the National Council (Državni Svet), in which the social, economic, professional, and local interests are represented. In terms of the legislative process, the National Assembly and the National Council can be regarded as two chambers of parliament; however, the position of the first is far more influential.

The National Assembly also elects the president of the cabinet and its other members and monitors the administration. The members of the National Assembly have the right to put questions to the cabinet and any cabinet minister can be cited to appear before parliament. The National Assembly also elects the members of the Constitutional Court and the judges of all other courts, the state prosecutor, the members of the court of audit, and the ombudsperson.

An important right of the deputies that helps to ensure their independence is parliamentary privilege. This gives them far-reaching protection against legal action or other negative consequences arising from their votes or statements in parliament. Only with the permission of the National Assembly may a member of parliament be arrested, be subjected to any criminal prosecution, or have his or her personal freedom limited—unless the deputy is arrested in the course of committing a crime that has a penalty of five years or more.

The National Assembly consists of 88 deputies, plus one deputy each allocated to the indigenous Italian and Hungarian national communities. Its period of office, the legislative term, is four years. The deputies are elected in a general, equal, direct, free, and secret balloting process.

The National Council

The 40 members of the National Council represent the diverse social, economic, professional, and local interests of the country. Local interests choose 22 of the members; the others represent employers, employees, farmers, independent professionals, and noncommercial interests.

Members are elected indirectly by various communities and chambers for a term of five years. The council participates in legislation at the national level. It may propose laws to the National Assembly and can force the National Assembly to reconsider a law it has already passed.

The Lawmaking Process

The right to introduce a bill belongs to the cabinet, every member of the National Assembly, and the National Council. When the National Assembly passes a bill, it is sent to the National Council. The council may raise objections, but if these are rejected by the National Assembly, the bill can pass into law without its consent. For the law to take effect, the president of the republic must promulgate it.

The Judiciary

The judiciary in Slovenia is independent of the executive and legislative branches and is a powerful factor in legal life. Judges are elected to permanent office by the National Assembly on the recommendation of the Judicial Council.

There are three different branches of courts according to the legal nature of the matter. There are courts of general jurisdiction (mainly for civil and criminal cases), specialized courts for administrative matters, and specialized courts for social and labor law. The single national Supreme Court sits at the apex of all three branches.

The court of ultimate appeal is the Constitutional Court, which ranks above the Supreme Court and deals exclusively with constitutional disputes. It consists of nine judges, who elect a president from among their own number for a term of three years.

The importance of this court arises from the requirement that all exercise of state power must be in compliance with the constitution. The court can declare acts of parliament void on the basis that they are unconstitutional. A complaint can be taken before the court by any person on the basis of an allegation that the state has infringed one of his or her fundamental rights.

THE ELECTION PROCESS

All citizens of Slovenia over the age of 18 have both the right to stand for election and the right to vote in the elections.

Parliamentary Elections

The members of parliament (the National Assembly) are elected on the basis of proportional representation. Subject to certain exceptions (for example, to provide for indigenous national minorities), a party must win at least 4 percent of all votes to gain seats in the National Assembly. In 2004, eight national political parties were represented.

POLITICAL PARTIES

Slovenia has a pluralistic system of political parties. The multiparty system is a basic structure of the constitutional order. The parties constitute a fundamental element of public life that helps to form the political will of the people. Their internal structure must be in accordance with democratic principles and is subject to review by the Constitutional Court. They must be primarily self-financing, relying on membership fees and donations. Limited additional financing from public funds is guaranteed, in proportion to the parties' votes in national and local elections.

The Constitutional Court has not banned any parties in the short history of the Republic of Slovenia. A political party can be deemed unconstitutional only if it or its adherents try to impair or eliminate the free democratic basis of the country or threaten the existence of the republic.

CITIZENSHIP

Slovenian citizenship is primarily acquired by birth, based on *ius sanguinis*. A child acquires Slovenian citizenship if one of his or her parents is a Slovenian citizen. It is of no relevance where a child is born.

FUNDAMENTAL RIGHTS

The constitution defines fundamental rights in its second chapter and emphasizes the fundamental importance of the rights of the individual. Fundamental rights are of foundational importance for the state and constitution. The Slovenian constitution guarantees the traditional classic set of human rights and includes social human rights, such as the right to work and the right to education.

The starting point is the guarantee to protect human rights and fundamental freedoms in Article 5. Numerous specific rights are enumerated. These rights have binding force for the legislature, the executive, and the judiciary as directly applicable law.

The rights guaranteed by the constitution can be classified either as freedom rights or as equality rights. Article 35 protects the right to privacy and personality rights including the free development of the personality. This fundamental right functions as a general freedom right.

The general equal treatment clause is contained in Article 14, which guarantees that all persons are equal before the law. This fundamental right is a catchall for a number of specific equality provisions such as the guarantee of equality of men and women and the equality of voting rights. Another special equality right is provided in Article 14: "In Slovenia everyone shall be guaranteed equal human rights irrespective of national origin, race, sex, language, religion, political or other conviction, material standing, birth, education, social status, or any other personal circumstance."

The constitution distinguishes between general human rights and a much smaller number of rights reserved for Slovenians only, the so-called Slovenians' rights. Examples of general human rights are freedom of belief, freedom of opinion, equality rights, protection of human personality and dignity, rights of children, freedom of education, the right to assembly and association, and protection of property. Slovenians' rights include the right to vote in national elections, to participate either directly or through elected representatives in the management of public affairs, to file petitions, and to pursue other initiatives of general significance. Slovenians have a right to social security, and no Slovenian citizen may be extradited to a foreign country.

Impact and Functions of Fundamental Rights

Human rights are of fundamental importance and permeate all areas of the law. In the interpretation and application of all law, the value judgments contained in the fundamental rights must be given effect. Thus, even in relations between individuals, human dignity may not be violated, and freedom and equality must be respected in all circumstances.

The functions that are ascribed to the rights are correspondingly numerous. Fundamental rights are first of all defensive rights. This means that the state may not interfere with the legal position of the individual unless there is special reason to do so.

Apart from their defensive function, fundamental rights also traditionally involve the right to participate in the democratic political process. To a carefully limited extent, a certain positive dimension entitling an individual to services from the state is also recognized. Insofar as this is practical, the state has a duty to ensure that circumstances conducive to the exercise of the fundamental rights are created.

Finally, fundamental rights are also a guarantee of organization and due process. The state must provide appropriate organizational and procedural structures to ensure the prompt and effective protection of fundamental rights.

Limitations to Fundamental Rights

The fundamental rights specified in the constitution are not without limits. The Slovenian constitution specifies such possible limits, which are based on specific needs of the public and the rights of others. On the other hand, no fundamental right may be disregarded completely. Each limit to a fundamental right faces limits itself. One of the most important of the "limitation limits" is the principle of proportionality, which gives expression to the idea that all laws must be reasonable, and that any limitation must be in proportion to the goal of the state action in question. The principle of proportionality permeates the entire legal order.

Article 15 provides that the fundamental rights shall be limited by the rights of others only in such cases as are provided for by the constitution. Judicial protection of fundamental rights and the right to obtain redress for the violation of such rights and freedoms shall be guaranteed. No fundamental right granted by laws currently in effect may be restricted on the grounds that the constitution itself does not recognize that right or recognizes it to a lesser extent.

Specially protected fundamental rights (human life and dignity, prohibition of torture, presumption of innocence, fair trial in criminal proceedings, and freedom of belief) can never be suspended, even temporarily and even in wartime. Other constitutional rights may be suspended or restricted temporarily during a state of war or emergency. These lesser constitutional rights can only be suspended in a nondiscriminatory way for the duration of the state of emergency or war and to the minimal extent required.

ECONOMY

The Slovenian constitution does not specify an economic system. On the other hand, certain basic provisions of the constitution provide a set of conditions that have to be met while structuring the economic system.

The constitution protects freedom of property and the right of inheritance. Also protected are freedom of occupation or profession, general personal freedom, and the right to form associations, partnerships, and corporations. The right to form associations in order to safeguard and improve working and economic conditions is guaranteed to every individual and all corporations and professions. This right guarantees autonomy of trade unions and employer associations in labor bargaining.

Slovenia is also defined by the constitution as a social state, providing for minimal social standards. The constitution allows ownership rights to real estate to be revoked or limited in the public interest with the provision of compensation under conditions established by law.

Taken as a whole, the Slovenian economic system can be described as a social market economy. It combines aspects of social responsibility with market freedom.

RELIGIOUS COMMUNITIES

Freedom of religion or belief, which is guaranteed as a human right, also involves rights for the religious communities. There is no established state church, and all public authorities must remain strictly neutral in relations with religious communities. Religions must be treated equally. Nonreligious philosophies of life are accorded the same status as religious views. All churches and religious communities are corporations under private law.

The relations between the state and churches and the legal position of religious communities are based on the following constitutional principles: (1) separation of the state and religious communities, (2) equality of religious communities, and (3) free activity of religious communities within the framework of the laws. Freedom of conscience and belief is provided for under Article 41 with three provisions: the assurance of freedom of conscience (and the right to profess freely one's religion and other self-definitions in private and public) as a positive entitlement; the right for a person not to have any religious or other beliefs or not to manifest such, as a negative entitlement; and the right of parents to determine their children's religious and moral upbringing in accordance with their beliefs.

As a special aspect of freedom of conscience, the constitution provides for the right of parents to give their children a moral and religious upbringing in accordance with their beliefs. Religious and moral guidance given to a child must be appropriate to his or her age and maturity. The guidance must also be consistent with the child's free conscience and religious and other beliefs or convictions.

The right of conscientious objection is also protected by the constitution, in such circumstances as are determined by statute. This right can be limited only by the rights of others and in certain situations enumerated in the constitution. Today, conscientious objection is allowed only in two areas: state defense and medical operations. Two constitutional provisions regulate religious relations among individuals: It is prohibited to incite religious discrimination and inflame religious hatred and intolerance, or to discriminate on the basis of religion or other belief.

Separation and neutrality do not preclude the state from cooperating in common endeavors with churches and religious communities as it does with other organizations of civil society. The modern state actively participates in various social fields in which religious communities perform a variety of tasks; the state, in supporting and promoting various activities in society, cannot ignore or exclude religion.

The tension between the demands of state neutrality in religious affairs and the need to recognize the positive social contributions of religious communities is particularly acute in Slovenia, where the law relating to freedom of religion is still developing. Although the 1991 constitution assures religious freedom, the constitutional interpretations and legislation affecting religious communities are not always in line with modern trends in church-state separation.

Although the 1991 constitution was initially interpreted to favor religion, it has been more recently interpreted under principles of an ultrastrict regime of church-state separation. However, a new Religious Freedom Act acknowledges religious needs of both society and individuals and provides detailed regulations that are accordant to the principle of tolerance toward religion that can be drawn from the constitution. Church and state can be separated, yet they may at the same time cooperate in many ways in order to realize a welfare state principle.

MILITARY DEFENSE AND STATE OF EMERGENCY

The administration is responsible for creating and maintaining the national defense. The state maintains a policy of peace and an ethic of nonaggression. The Republic of Slovenia has obliged itself by international treaties not to produce nuclear, biological, or chemical weapons.

Citizens who because of their religious, philosophical, or humanitarian beliefs are not willing to perform military duty are assured the opportunity of participating in the defense of the state in some other manner. In Slovenia, general conscription was abandoned in 2002 and replaced by a professional military who serve for fixed periods or for life.

The military always remains subject to civil government. The National Assembly decides on the use of the defense forces. The commander in chief is the president of the republic.

AMENDMENTS TO THE CONSTITUTION

The constitution can only be changed if two-thirds of the members of the National Assembly vote in favor.

PRIMARY SOURCES

Constitution in English. Available online. URLs: http://www.dz-rs.si/index.php?id=351&docid=25&showdoc=1. Accessed on June 28, 2006.

Constitution in Slovenian. Available online. URL: http://www.dz-rs.si/. Accessed on August 19, 2005.

SECONDARY SOURCES

Arne Mavčič, "The Constitutional Law of Slovenia." In *International Encyclopaedia of Laws, Constitutional Law,* edited by André Alen, Supplement 28. The Hague/London/Boston: Kluwer Law International, 1998.

Janko Prunk, "The Origins of an Independent Slovenia." In *Making a New Nation: The Formation of Slovenia,* edited by Danica Fink-Hafner and John R. Robbins: 29. Aldershot, England/Brookfield, Vt.: Dartmouth, 1997.

"Short Constitutional History of Slovenia." Available online. URL: http://www.oefre.unibe.ch/law/icl/. Accessed on July 20, 2005.

Lovro Šturm

SOLOMON ISLANDS

At-a-Glance

OFFICIAL NAME
Solomon Islands

CAPITAL
Honiara

POPULATION
409,000 (2005 est.)

SIZE
Land area of 10,954 sq. mi. (28,370 sq. km), on 26 islands and several hundred small islets spread over a sea area of 517,377 sq. mi. (1,340,000 sq. km)

LANGUAGES
Official: English and Pidgin, about 65 vernacular languages and dialects

RELIGIONS
Church of Melanesia or Anglican 35%, Roman Catholic 20%, South Seas Evangelical Church 18%, United Church 11%, Seventh-Day Adventist Church

10%, other religions (traditional religion, Bahá'í, Jehovah's Witnesses) 6%

NATIONAL OR ETHNIC COMPOSITION
Melanesian 94.2%, Polynesian 4%, Micronesian 1.4%, European 0.4%, Chinese 0.1%

DATE OF INDEPENDENCE OR CREATION
July 7, 1978

TYPE OF GOVERNMENT
Parliamentary democracy

TYPE OF STATE
Sovereign democratic state

TYPE OF LEGISLATURE
Unicameral parliament

DATE OF CONSTITUTION
May 31, 1978

DATE OF LAST AMENDMENT
May 23, 2001

In 1978 Solomon Islands emerged from a period of dependency on the United Kingdom to become a sovereign state. Independence was achieved peaceably, as part of the decolonization process in the southwest Pacific. The independence constitution was appended to the Solomon Islands Independence Order 1978 (UK) rather than enacted locally. The constitution established a parliamentary democracy based on universal suffrage, a British Westminster style system of responsible government, and a separation of powers. The constitution is the supreme law and of great importance at a national level, but it has little relevance outside the capital and provincial centers. In rural areas, society still operates on a traditional basis and customary beliefs and practices remain strong.

CONSTITUTIONAL HISTORY

Solomon Islands was probably settled by explorers from Southeast Asia and New Guinea some time before 200 B.C.E. The islands were "rediscovered" by the Spanish in 1568 and European exploration continued until the 1800s. There was no concept of central or regional government at this time. The inhabitants were grouped together in small communities under the control of local "big men" or chiefs. In 1843 the southern islands of the Solomon chain became a British protectorate. In 1885, Germany declared a protectorate over the northern islands. About five years later, the German protectorate, except Buka and Bougainville, was transferred to Britain in exchange for recognition of German interests in Western Samoa. The Pacific Order in Council 1893 (UK) provided the basis of government. In 1960, the country's first constitution was put in force by a British order, which established a legislative council. This council was presided over by the high commissioner for the Western Pacific. Elected members were introduced in 1965, and in 1967 a legislative council and an executive council were introduced. In 1970, a new constitution, replacing the two councils with a single governing council, took force. Legislative functions were vested in the council, while executive functions were shared among committees, responsible to the council. For the first time, the majority of members were elected. In 1974 the British Solomon Islands Order 1974 (UK) introduced a Westminster style constitution, replacing the governing council with a council of ministers and a legislative assembly.

In 1975, a constitutional committee was appointed to seek local views on a draft independence constitution, based on the framework of the 1974 constitution. The committee's report was completed in March 1976, but its approval was frustrated by a change of government. Amended proposals were eventually approved by the legislative assembly. In September 1977, a delegation from Solomon Islands traveled to England for a constitutional conference to agree on the final provisions. Independence was finally achieved in 1978, when the Constitution of Solomon Islands, 1978, repealed and replaced the 1974 constitution. The constitution was appended to the Solomon Islands Independence Order 1978 (UK).

The constitution is currently under review and is likely to be replaced by a federal constitution within the near future.

FORM AND IMPACT OF THE CONSTITUTION

The constitution is contained in a single instrument, the Constitution of Solomon Islands, 1978. However, the Westminster system that it introduced is surrounded by a number of practices and conventions that are largely unwritten, such as party politics and the principle of responsible government. It is doubtful whether these concepts have translated well into the context of Solomon Islands society. Although the constitution is the supreme law and of great importance at a national level, it has little relevance outside a few urban centers. In rural areas, allegiance is owed to a clan or tribes made of family groups sharing a common language and culture.

In July 2003, an Australian-led armed intervention force arrived in Solomon Islands at the request of the government, after armed conflict between competing rebel groups—the Malaita Eagle Force and the Isatabu Freedom Movement. A reduced force remains. A reform program has been created as part of the peace process. This includes constitutional, legislative, political, and structural reform. The intention is to introduce a "homegrown" federal system of government. The new federal constitution is to be based on five principles, namely, inclusive development, the rule of law, transparency, accountability, and fiscal responsibility.

BASIC ORGANIZATIONAL STRUCTURE

The constitution provides for the division of the country into Honiara City and Provinces for the purpose of local government, which is limited to a list of matters specified by legislation. The local government system is governed by the Provincial Government Act 1997. The limited devolution provided for by the existing system of provincial government is inadequate to cater to the large numbers of people who live in remote areas. The central government has been accused of neglecting rural areas. In remote villages, the churches have provided the only link between the remote and unfamiliar Western style of government and the traditional authority of chiefs. In many areas they are the only provider of basic services, such as clinics and schools. In this way, the churches have become a surrogate local authority in some areas and a powerful political force in the country as a whole.

LEADING CONSTITUTIONAL PRINCIPLES

Solomon Islands is a sovereign democratic state with Queen Elizabeth II of England and her successors as head of state, acting through the governor-general. The Westminster system, including the separation of powers among the legislature, executive, and judiciary, is embedded in the constitution. The constitution establishes a central system of parliamentary democracy based on universal suffrage. Solomon Islands is a secular state, but it is founded on Christian principles, reflected in the reference to God in the preamble to the constitution. There is no one dominant church, and, although some religions have regional strongholds, Christianity seems to have acted as a uniting force. Solomon Islands is an independent member of the Commonwealth.

CONSTITUTIONAL BODIES

The most important constitutional bodies and offices are the National Parliament, the governor-general, the prime minister and cabinet, the judiciary, and the ombudsperson.

The National Parliament

The constitution establishes a single-chamber National Parliament, consisting of one member elected from each constituency. Parliament has a life of four years from the date of the first sitting after any general election, after which it stands dissolved. A general election must be held within four months of every dissolution of the National Parliament. Parliament may make laws for the peace, order, and good government of Solomon Islands.

The Governor-General

Executive authority is vested in the governor-general as representative of the head of state, who is the queen of England. The governor-general is appointed for a term of five years by the head of state on the advice of Parliament, from among persons qualified for election as a member of the National Parliament. The governor-general may be removed from office only by the head of state, acting on the advice of Parliament supported by the votes of at least two-thirds of all the members. The governor-general acts on the advice of the cabinet and is kept informed of the general conduct of government by the prime minister.

The Prime Minister

The prime minister is elected as head of the government from and by the members of the National Parliament. The office becomes vacant if a motion of no confidence is passed; after a general election, when the members of Parliament meet to elect a new prime minister; if the prime minister ceases to be a member of Parliament; if he or she is elected as speaker or deputy speaker; or upon resignation.

The Cabinet

The cabinet consists of the prime minister and other ministers. It is collectively responsible to the National Parliament. Ministers are appointed by the governor-general, on the advice of the prime minister, from among members of Parliament. The constitution provides for a maximum of 11 ministers in addition to the prime minister. This number may be increased by Parliament and this power has been exercised to increase the maximal number to 20. The number of ministers was reduced to 10 in 2002 in an attempt to reduce costs.

The Judiciary

The judiciary is independent of the executive and legislature and plays an important role in making, interpreting, and applying the law. The constitution establishes a high court with unlimited original jurisdiction and a court of appeal. Judicial independence is buttressed by appointment's being made on the advice of the judicial and legal services commission, which is established under the constitution, and by conferring of tenure until the age of 60. Removal is by the governor-general and is only permitted on the grounds of inability to discharge the functions of office or misbehavior, on the recommendation of a tribunal made up of current or former holders of high judicial office within the Commonwealth.

The judiciary exercises a power of judicial review of governmental action. The courts' authority to intervene on the grounds of lack of jurisdiction or breach of the principles of natural justice has been held by the courts to override any provisions in legislation meant to prevent such intervention.

The Ombudsman

The ombudsperson's office is established by the constitution and supplementary legislation—the Ombudsman (Further Provision) Act 1980. The ombudsperson's jurisdiction extends to investigation of conduct of government departments, statutory bodies, and provincial and local government, subject to specific exceptions. The ombudsperson is appointed for a maximal term of five years by the governor-general after consultation with the speaker of the National Parliament and the chairs of the public service commission and the judicial and legal services commission. Removal is by the governor-general and subject to the same restrictions that apply to judges.

The Lawmaking Process

The sources of law provided by the constitution are, in descending order of importance, acts of Solomon Islands' Parliament; United Kingdom acts of general application in force on January 1, 1961 (if there is no local legislation on point); customary law (on an equal footing with United Kingdom acts); the principles of common law and equity in force in England on July 7, 1978 (if they are appropriate to the circumstances of Solomon Islands and are not inconsistent with written laws or custom), and as subsequently developed by the courts of Solomon Islands.

Acts take the form of bills, which are required to pass through three readings in the National Parliament. After a bill has been passed, it must be presented to the governor-general for assent on behalf of the head of state, before becoming law. Laws must then be published in the government gazette before they begin operation. Parliament may postpone the going into operation of any law and may make laws, other than criminal laws, with retrospective effect.

THE ELECTION PROCESS AND POLITICAL PARTICIPATION

All citizens aged 18 or over are entitled to register to vote in the constituency in which they ordinarily reside. Voting is not compulsory. Only citizens over 21 are eligible to stand for election.

POLITICAL PARTIES

The introduced system includes party politics, but it is doubtful whether this concept has translated well into the context of Solomon Islands society. Generally, the weakness of the party system has resulted in government by unstable parliamentary coalitions. Party allegiances and government leadership often change, and frequent votes of no confidence merely highlight the lack of confidence in the system as a whole.

CITIZENSHIP

At independence, all indigenous Solomon Islanders automatically became citizens, as did any person born in Solomon Islands before independence who had two grandparents indigenous to Papua New Guinea or Vanuatu. Any child of a Solomon Islands citizen automatically becomes a citizen on birth. Dual citizenship is not permitted and any citizen of Solomon Islands who is a national of some other country automatically ceases to be a Solomon Islands citizen unless he or she renounces the other citizenship within a specified period. Noncitizens may not reside or work in Solomon Islands without a permit. Some professions and trades are reserved for Solomon Islands citizens.

FUNDAMENTAL RIGHTS

The constitution of Solomon Islands incorporates a bill of rights based on the United Nations Universal Declaration of Human Rights 1948 and the Council of Europe's Convention for the Protection of Human Rights and Fundamental Freedoms, 1950. The bill of rights recognizes the following fundamental rights and freedoms: the right to life, liberty, and protection from slavery and forced labor; the right to protection from inhuman treatment; the right to protection from deprivation of property; the right to protection of privacy of the home and other property; the right to protection from the law for persons charged with a criminal offense and, in more limited terms, to persons involved in civil cases; the right to freedom of conscience, of expression, of assembly and association, and of movement; and the right to protection from discrimination on the grounds of race, place of origin, political opinions, color, creed, or sex.

Fundamental rights are subject to a number of detailed exceptions. A provision exempts any laws that provide for the application of customary law from challenges based on discrimination.

ECONOMY

The constitution does not specify a particular economic system.

RELIGIOUS COMMUNITIES

The constitution contains a guarantee of freedom of religion, under the banner of "protection of freedom of conscience." Freedom of expression, which includes the right to express religious views, is also constitutionally protected.

In theory, 96% of Solomon Islanders are Christian, mostly organized into five major churches. The Baha'i faith and Jehovah's Witnesses also have a visible presence in Solomon Islands. There are a small number of Hindus and Muslims in the country, but neither group has an established place of worship. Traditional religion is still practiced and customary rituals often take place alongside or in combination with Christian worship.

MILITARY DEFENSE AND STATE OF EMERGENCY

Solomon Islands does not have its own military force, but relies on the police force and prison service to assist in the enforcement of law and order. The absence of a military

presence was very significant during the recent armed conflict and the government was eventually forced to ask its neighbors for assistance.

AMENDMENTS TO THE CONSTITUTION

The constitution may be amended by the National Parliament provided that notice of the amending bill has been given to the speaker at least four weeks before its first reading, and that the bill is clearly represented as a bill to alter the constitution. Generally, a special majority of two-thirds of the members is required. However, three-quarters of the members' votes are required to amend many provisions, including those governing amendment of the constitution, protection of fundamental rights and freedoms, the legal system, the ombudsperson, the establishment and composition of the National Parliament and electoral issues, the auditor-general, and miscellaneous provisions that relate to any of the preceding matters. The constitution may also be suspended or repealed by the same process.

PRIMARY SOURCES

Constitution of Solomon Islands 1978, appended to Solomon Islands Independence Order 1978 (UK), in English. Available online. URL: http://www.paclii. org/sb/legis/consol_act/toc-C.html. Accessed on July 17, 2005.

Governor General v. Mamaloni (unreported, Court of Appeal, Solomon Islands, *Civ App* 3/1993, 5 November 1993).

Minister for Provincial Government v. Guadalcanal Provincial Assembly (unreported, Court of Appeal, Solomon Islands, *Law Reports of the Commonwealth* (CAC) 3/97, July 11, 1997).

Ulufa'alu v. the Attorney General and Others [2002] LRC 1 at 28 to 37.

Loumia v. DPP [1985/6] *Solomon Islands Law Reports* (SILR) 158 at 169.

SECONDARY SOURCES

Jennifer Corrin Care, "Constitutional Challenges in Solomon Islands." *Queensland University of Technology Law and Justice Journal* 5 (1989): 145.

Jennifer Corrin Care and Kenneth Brown, "More on Democratic Fundamentals in the Solomon Islands: *The Minister for Provincial Government v. Guadalcanal Provincial Assembly.*" *Victoria University of Wellington Law Review* 32, no. 3 (2001): 653.

Jennifer Corrin Care, Teresa Newton, and Donald Paterson, Chapter 5. In *Introduction to South Pacific Law*. London: Cavendish Press, 1999.

John Nonggor, "Solomon Islands." In *South Pacific Island Legal Systems,* edited by Michael Ntumy. Honolulu: University of Hawaii Press, 1993.

Jennifer Corrin Care

SOMALIA

At-a-Glance

OFFICIAL NAME
Somalia

CAPITAL
Mogadishu

POPULATION
8,304,601 (July 2004 est.)

SIZE
246,201 sq. mi. (637,657 sq. km)

LANGUAGES
Somali (official), Arabic, Italian, English

RELIGIONS
Sunni Muslim

NATIONAL OR ETHNIC COMPOSITION
Somali 85%, Bantu and other non-Somali (including Arabs, 30,000) 15%

DATE OF INDEPENDENCE OR CREATION
July 1, 1960

TYPE OF GOVERNMENT
Transitional parliamentary government

TYPE OF STATE
Federal state

TYPE OF LEGISLATURE
Unicameral National Assembly

DATE OF CONSTITUTION
1960 and 2004 (Somaliland 2001)

DATE OF LAST AMENDMENT
No amendment

Somalia is often described as a failed state. At the time of writing the Transitional Government does not control the country. The inauguration of the new Somali president in October 2004 took place in Nairobi, the capital of Kenya, not in Mogadishu, the capital of Somalia.

The northern part of the country, Somaliland, has existed as a de facto independent state, with its own constitution, since Somalia collapsed in 1991 but has not been recognized by the outside world. To the extent that the Transitional Government is not in control of the rest of the country, power rests with local clans.

A new transitional charter, building on the 1960 constitution, was adopted by the feuding clans in February 2004 after peace talks that started in Kenya in 2002. It provides for a Federal Republic of Somalia. At the time of writing it seemed unlikely that Somaliland would join such a federation.

CONSTITUTIONAL HISTORY

Somalia was formed as a merger of the newly independent British and Italian Somaliland colonies in 1960. A constitution adopted the same year provided for a unitary state. In 1979, Siad Barre took over power and a new constitution was adopted. He was ousted in 1991, when the 1979 constitution was suspended. With the exception of the northern part of the country (former British Somaliland), the country descended into chaos.

In 2000, a transitional administration was appointed by a 245-member transitional parliament made up of clan representatives who had met for peace negotiations in Djibouti. The Transitional Federal Charter of the Somali Republic (the Charter) was adopted in February 2004. The 1960 constitution is applicable to issues not covered by and not inconsistent with the Charter. The Charter will remain in force until the adoption of a new constitution.

The constitution of the Republic of Somaliland was adopted in a referendum on May 31, 2001.

FORM AND IMPACT OF THE CONSTITUTION

As the government is not in full control of the country, the impact of the constitutional framework is at the time of writing very limited.

BASIC ORGANIZATIONAL STRUCTURE

The Charter provides for a federal state. Somalia is historically divided into 18 regions (*gobolka*). A state comprises a number of regions that have voluntarily joined to form a state. The Somali Republic shall comprise the transitional federal government, state governments, and regional administrations.

LEADING CONSTITUTIONAL PRINCIPLES

A new constitution will be adopted at the end of the transitional period. It is at the time of writing unclear whether the latest attempt with a transitional government will prove successful. A parliamentary system has been put in place, but no direct elections have been held. The constitutional calls for protection of human rights, but the judicial system that would be needed to enforce these rights remains in tatters.

CONSTITUTIONAL BODIES

The Charter provides for the following main federal bodies: the parliament, the president, the council of ministers led by the prime minister, and the Supreme Court.

The Parliament

The single-chamber 275-member parliament represents the legislative power of the transitional federal government. The Charter mandates that at least 12 percent of the members must be women. The current members were selected by the various clans in Somalia present at the negotiations in Kenya. Representatives of Somaliland refused to participate in this process. The parliament was inaugurated in Nairobi in August 2004, although only 214 members of parliament had been selected at the time.

A member of parliament must be a Somali citizen over 25 years old, of good character and sound mind. The term of the transitional federal parliament is five years, after which elections will be held for a new parliament under a new constitution.

Among the functions of the parliament are adopting legislation and the annual budget.

The Lawmaking Process

According to the charter, a law that is passed by parliament is presented to the president for assent. When the president refuses to assent, parliament reconsiders the law and takes into account the comments of the president. It either approves the recommendations or resubmits the law to the president without doing so. However, approval of the law in its original form requires a vote of 65 percent of all members of parliament. A law goes into operation once it is published in the official bulletin.

The President

The president is elected by parliament. The president is the head of state, commander in chief of the armed forces, and a symbol of national unity. The president must be a Muslim Somali citizen over 40 years old, the child of Somali citizens, and cannot be married to a foreigner. The president must be of sound mind and good character. The term of office is four years.

The Council of Ministers

The Council of Ministers is led by the prime minister, who is appointed by the president. The ministers are appointed from among the members of parliament. The Council of Ministers develops government policy and implements national budgets, prepares and initiates government legislation for introduction to the parliament, implements and administers acts of parliament, and coordinates the functions of government ministries.

The Judiciary

When the state collapsed in 1991, the courts closed as well. Conflict resolution has thereafter taken the form of either clan-based arbitration or the application of Islamic law (sharia).

The Charter provides for a judiciary independent of the legislative and executive branches of government. Judges are to be appointed by the president acting on the advice of the Judicial Service Council. The Charter provides for a Supreme Court, a Court of Appeal, and other courts established by law. No extraordinary or special tribunals shall be established, with the exception of military tribunals, with the competence to try military offenses committed by members of the armed forces.

THE ELECTION PROCESS

Every citizen over the age of 18 has the right to vote. Elections are not envisaged until after the end of the five-year transition period and the adoption of a new constitution. The Charter details the requirements for standing for the various state offices.

POLITICAL PARTIES

The Charter states that the transitional government shall encourage the formation of political parties. Political parties of a military or tribal nature are prohibited.

CITIZENSHIP

To acquire Somali citizenship a person must be of Somali origin and have been born in Somalia or have a father who is a citizen of Somalia.

FUNDAMENTAL RIGHTS

Chapter 5 of the Charter (Articles 14–27) is entitled Protection of the Fundamental Rights and Freedoms of the People. The rights protected mainly relate to civil and political rights, but labor rights are also protected.

Impact and Functions of Fundamental Rights

It will take time to establish a functioning court system that will be able to enforce the rights enshrined in the Charter. A state that is in full control of the country is a first requirement in guaranteeing the quite extensive rights protection that exists in the Charter read together with the 1960 constitution.

Limitations to Fundamental Rights

Freedom of expression may be proscribed by law for the purpose of safeguarding public morals and public security.

ECONOMY

The Charter states that the economy shall be based on free enterprise.

RELIGIOUS COMMUNITIES

Islam is the state religion. All Somali citizens have the right to equal protection and equal benefit of the law without distinction of religion. This entails the full and equal enjoyment of all rights and freedoms.

MILITARY DEFENSE AND STATE OF EMERGENCY

The Charter provides that the Somali Republic shall have a national armed force consisting of the army and the police. The armed forces have the duty to abide by and preserve the Charter, the laws of the land, and the unity of the country. As the Charter defines the territory of Somalia to include Somaliland and this entity at the time of writing refuses to join the federation, future armed conflict is highly probable.

AMENDMENTS TO THE CONSTITUTION

Amendments to the Charter can be made after a motion in parliament supported by at least one-third and passed by at least two-thirds of the members of parliament.

PRIMARY SOURCES
The Transitional Federal Charter of the Somali Republic. Available online. URL: http://www.iss.co.za/AF/profiles/Somalia/charterfeb04.pdf. Accessed on August 30, 2005.
Constitution in English. Available online. URL: http://www.somalilandforum.com/somaliland/constitution/revised_constitution.htm. Accessed on September 24, 2005.
Constitution in Somali. Available online. URL: http://www.somalilandforum.com/somaliland/constitution/dastuurka_jsl.htm. Accessed on July 20, 2005.

SECONDARY SOURCES
Harold D. Nelson, ed., *Somalia—a Country Study*. 3d ed. Washington, D.C.: United States Government Printing Office, 1983.
David Pearl, *A Textbook on Muslim Law*. London: Croom Helm, 1979.
Kenneth R. Redden, ed., "Somalia." In *Modern Legal Systems Cyclopedia*. Vol. 6. Buffalo, N.Y.: W.S. Hein, 1998.
Michael Schoiswohl, *Status and (Human Rights) Obligations of Non-Recognized de Facto Regimes in International Law: The Case of "Somaliland."* Leiden and Boston: Nijhoff, 2004.

Magnus Killander

SOUTH AFRICA

At-a-Glance

OFFICIAL NAME
Republic of South Africa

CAPITAL
Cape Town (legislative), Tshwane (administrative)

POPULATION
44,819,778 (2005 est.)

SIZE
470,606 sq. mi. (1,219,090 sq. km)

LANGUAGES
Afrikaans, English, isiNdebele, isiXhosa, isiZulu, Sepedi, Sesotho, Setswana, siSwati, Tshivenda, Xitsonga

RELIGIONS
Protestant (including Pentecostal and charismatic churches) 51.7%, African Independent Churches 23%, Catholic 7.1%, Islam 1.5%, Hindu 1.2%, African traditional beliefs 0.3%, Judaism 0.2%, no affiliation or affiliation not stated (majority probably traditional, indigenous religions) 15%

NATIONAL OR ETHNIC COMPOSITION
Black African 79.02%, Colored 8.91%, Indian or Asian 2.49%, white 9.58%

DATE OF INDEPENDENCE OR CREATION
April 27, 1994

TYPE OF GOVERNMENT
Parliamentary democracy

TYPE OF STATE
Cooperative federation

TYPE OF LEGISLATURE
Bicameral parliament

DATE OF CONSTITUTION
February 4, 1997

DATE OF LAST AMENDMENT
March 19, 2003

The Republic of South Africa is one sovereign democratic state, unitary in its conception, but with appreciable devolution of power to nine provinces and to local governments. It operates as a multiparty, parliamentary democracy, adhering to practices associated with regular, free, and fair elections.

The constitution states that human dignity, the achievement of equality, the advancement of human rights and freedoms, nonracism, nonsexism, supremacy of the constitution, and the rule of law are all founding values of the South African state. Extensive constitutional guarantees back these values and vouch for the division of executive, legislative, and judicial powers. Public authorities widely respect the constitution, and violations can effectively be remedied by an independent judiciary (spearheaded by a strong and visible Constitutional Court) and by a number of state institutions supporting and strengthening constitutional democracy. A president is the executive head of state, elected by and accountable to (but after election not a member of) the National Assembly.

The constitution guarantees freedom of religion, belief, and opinion, and religious communities operate independently of the organs of state. The economic system can best be described as a social market economy. National security is subject to civil legislative and executive authority and is designed to pursue and promote national and world peace.

CONSTITUTIONAL HISTORY

Homo sapiens and their immediate predecessors began to live in the south of Africa about 4 million years ago. The rudiments of the modern-day state were introduced in the mid-17th century.

On April 6, 1652, 175 officials and employees of the Dutch East Indian Company, mainly Dutch and German men, set foot at the Cape of Good Hope to establish a replenishment post for ships sailing back and forth between Europe and the East. This business venture was not intended to be a conventional colonial conquest, although in the end the company's regime at the Cape, characterized by minimalist and inefficient governance, lasted 143 years.

In 1795 Britain occupied the Cape as part of its tactics in the Napoleonic Wars. In 1803 the British handed the Cape back to the Batavian Republic, heir to a no-longer-extant Dutch East Indian Company. Three years of efficient administration followed. In 1806 the British finally occupied what henceforth became the Cape Colony.

The influx of Europeans caused a large-scale displacement of the indigenous Khoikhoi and San people, who had lived all over southern Africa for at least 10,000 years, and their traditional social organization was severely disrupted. From the late 1650s the import of slaves, mainly from the East, boosted the numbers of the colored population at the Cape.

During the last half of the 18th century white migrant farmers started moving inland, and over time the eastern frontier, about 500 miles from Cape Town, became a site of incessant conflict involving whites, Khoikhoi and San people, and black Africans (mainly Xhosa who had moved in from the north).

British rule in the Cape Colony introduced elements of a Westminster style of government, but Roman-Dutch law that entered with the initial arrivals from Europe remained the common law of the colony. The Cape's first elected parliament was inaugurated in 1853 and accountable government followed in 1872.

During the latter part of the 1830s white farmers on the eastern frontier, mainly descendants of the first European settlers, embarked on an organized migration to the north, accompanied by numbers of their colored laborers. These migrants or *voor-trekkers,* determined to free themselves of British rule, entered into conflict with powerful black African nations, such as the Ndebele and Zulu, who had previously subjugated many smaller black tribes in the interior. In the end the white migrants prevailed. The English, however, persisted in their efforts to exercise authority over the *trekkers,* and in 1843 Britain annexed the first republic established in Natal by the *trekkers.* The two other republics, the Transvaal and the Orange Free State, negotiated recognition of their independence in 1852 and 1854, respectively, and adopted constitutions. The benefits of these "progressive constitutions" remained restricted to white men, and political power was exclusively in the hands of the white, Dutch/Afrikaans-speaking population, known initially as *boers* (literally farmers) and later as Afrikaners.

The discovery of gold in the South African Republic in the 1880s rekindled the colonial interest of the British, and the South African, or Anglo-Boer, War of 1899–1902 resulted. The Free State joined forces with Transvaal, and when the English finally won the war, both *boer* republics became British colonies. On May 31, 1910, these two colonies, together with the Cape Colony and Natal, became the four provinces of a new Union of South Africa. The 1909 South Africa Act of the British Parliament served as the nonjusticiable constitution of this new Westminster type of state with its own sovereign parliament. In the two former *boer* republics the franchise was restricted to white men only, while in the Cape Colony and Natal limited numbers of black and colored men could vote, too.

Perennial tension between the English (imperialist) and Afrikaans (nationalist) segments of the white population in the political life of the 19th and early 20th centuries was second only to their shared condescension toward the non-European population. Since 1910 this latter section of the population has consisted primarily of blacks, constituting the vast majority of the overall population and made up of seven major ethnic groups. Another major group are the "coloreds," made up of descendants of the Khoikhoi and San, slaves, and people of mixed blood. Finally, the Asian section of the population consists mainly of Indians whose forebears entered Natal during the 19th century to work on the sugar plantations.

The union provided whites with an opportunity to assert their hegemony in a unitary state in which the sovereign will of Parliament would trump all law, including the constitution. The union government adopted legislation that discriminated against blacks and coloreds in various ways. For example, blacks' access to land was severely curtailed, as was their ability to hold their own in economic and social life. The limited black and colored vote in two provinces, which was entrenched in the constitution, was rescinded in 1936 and 1955, respectively.

The National Party government that took power in 1948 engineered a grand scheme of racial segregation, relying on its legislative and bureaucratic capacity. What the government called "separate development" was meant to provide each black ethnic group with its own independent homeland in which each group could rule itself. Among the majority of the population and in the rest of the world, however, this scheme earned the name *apartheid* (separation) and a reputation of racial discrimination and oppression.

During the late 1940s and 1950s liberation groups launched a campaign of defiance in which the African National Congress (ANC) played a major role. The ANC, founded in 1912 to voice black aspirations, had been transformed into a nonracial and activist liberation movement by the 1950s.

The defiance campaign met with severe repressive action from the authorities. In the early 1960s all the major liberation movements were banned and their leaders went either underground, into prison, or into exile. Without consulting the vast majority of the population, a constitution was adopted, turning South Africa into a republic on May 31, 1961, and retaining crucial features of the 1909 constitution, such as parliamentary sovereignty, nonjusticiability of the constitution, and the restriction of political rights to whites.

In the wake of this development, the liberation movements formed Umkhonto we Sizwe (Spear of the Nation) to wage a low-key armed struggle against the regime, mainly sabotaging government property. At the Rivonia trial in 1964 eight prominent leaders of Umkhonto, including Nelson Mandela, were sentenced to life imprisonment for sabotage and conspiracy to overthrow the government.

In 1976 thousands of schoolchildren took to the streets in Soweto, near Johannesburg, introducing a spate of unrest that spilled over into the 1980s. This turbulent decade saw local resistance movements join forces in the United Democratic Front and soldiers of Umkhonto we Sizwe, who had trained abroad, launch attacks in the country. International boycott campaigns designed to isolate the apartheid state were waged. The regime reacted harshly to this "total onslaught," and it transformed South Africa into a state essentially ruled by its security forces. At the same time the regime tried to win the goodwill of the Colored and Asian populations by including them in a tricameral parliament with racially separate chambers. The nonjusticiable constitution adopted in 1983 to effect this change retained the essentials of Westminster government with a few modest innovations. The majority of Coloreds and Asians rejected the new system.

Some blacks did accept the government's policy of "separate development," and four homelands opted for an "independence" recognized only by South Africa and the four homelands themselves. Some other homelands progressed to a fairly advanced stage of self-government.

On February 2, 1990, the then state president, F. W. de Klerk, announced that the liberation movements would no longer be banned and that political prisoners would be released. This policy paved the way for political negotiations. A multiparty negotiation process produced a transitional constitution late in 1993. This justiciable constitution was passed as a law of the then-existing Parliament, and it entered into force on April 27, 1994, the day when the first fully democratic elections in the history of South Africa began. The ANC achieved a resounding victory and Nelson Mandela became president.

The transitional or interim constitution provided for a bicameral parliament, the two houses of which, in joint session, constituted a Constitutional Assembly. It was charged with adopting, by a two-thirds majority, a final constitution in accordance with 34 principles contained in the interim constitution. The Constitutional Court established by the transitional constitution had to certify compliance with these principles. The court found instances of noncompliance, and the Constitutional Assembly redrafted the deficient provisions. The court thereupon certified what became the Constitution of the Republic of South Africa, 1996, which entered into force on February 4, 1997.

FORM AND IMPACT OF THE CONSTITUTION

South Africa has a written constitution, which in Section 2 proclaims that it is "the supreme law of the Republic; law or conduct inconsistent with it is invalid, and the obligations imposed by it must be fulfilled." International law must be consistent with the constitution to be applicable in South Africa.

The constitution is significant both for the legal system and as a source of fundamental values for the functioning of society. Under the judicial leadership of a powerful Constitutional Court, the implementation of the constitution over the short period of 10 years reshaped crucial facets of the legal system. It also had a considerable impact on social, economic, and political life. The court nonetheless heeds the exigencies of judicial self-restraint.

In short, the constitution plays a decisive role in the self-definition of an emerging nation.

BASIC ORGANIZATIONAL STRUCTURE

South Africa is a cooperative federation of nine provinces. The provincial borders do not always reflect historical actualities, and a sense of shared destiny is lacking in a number of instances. Moreover, the provinces differ considerably in geographic area, population size, and economic strength; however, their legislative and administrative powers are identical, and they are thus political equals.

South Africa's political history has not been conducive to federalism. In the quest to affirm white hegemony, the 1910 constitution created a unitary state with only modestly federalist features. In the heyday of apartheid, however, the regime resorted to a divide-and-rule strategy to balkanize the country, consigning blacks to homelands. Liberation movements thus began to regard territorially decentralized government with skepticism, claiming that only an undivided, nonracial South Africa would transcend the effects of apartheid's "divide-and-rule" tactics.

In the spirit of political compromise during the early 1990s, liberation movements, including the ANC, cautiously accepted some federalist arrangements. This compromise yielded a cooperative federation with constitutional arrangements sufficiently flexible to realize the key objectives of federalism in day-to-day political life.

Chapter 3 of the constitution states principles of "cooperative government," by which all national, provincial, and local government organs must work to preserve the integrity or "wholeness" of the republic. The constitution refers to the various tiers of government as *spheres* to emphasize that they are not hierarchical levels of authority.

The constitution authorizes each province to adopt its own constitution, subject to restrictions that prevent provincial constitutions from overriding the national constitution. The Constitutional Court must certify provincial constitutions' compliance with these restrictions. So far only one province has successfully adopted its own constitution.

The national constitution reserves certain legislative areas to the legislative competence of the province. Matters included in these areas are not particularly weighty, and in exceptional cases the national Parliament may overrule the provinces even in these areas. Other functional areas are within the legislative authority of both national and provincial legislatures, for example, education, health services, housing, and trade. Should there be a conflict in these latter areas, national legislation will override provincial legislation on certain conditions. These conditions are not very difficult to meet, but if they are not met, provincial legislation will prevail over national legislation.

Parliament has exclusive legislative competence in many areas. The National Council of Provinces, a second chamber of Parliament, gives the provinces a say in the enactment of national legislation.

The administrative competencies of the provinces are commensurate with their legislative powers. They have no judicial competencies.

The constitution provides a framework for local government. There are various types and categories of local governments elected by popular vote. Executive mayors who preside over local governments are elected indirectly.

LEADING CONSTITUTIONAL PRINCIPLES

South Africa is a parliamentary democracy. Its constitutional system is premised on certain leading principles such as supremacy of the constitution and cooperative federalism. Other principles are the separation of powers, the rule of law, democracy, and accountability.

Executive, legislative, and judicial powers are separated with checks and balances holding the various branches of government accountable to one another. The judiciary is independent and includes a Constitutional Court.

In a founding provision of the constitution, the rule of law is said to be a value on which the South African state is founded. So far *rule of law* has mostly been understood as a synonym for *legality:* The exercise of a public power is only legitimate when lawful. State powers can thus only be derived from the law, and their exercise is subject to control by the courts. Arbitrary decision making by authorities and self-help of citizens in violation of the law are forbidden. It remains for the Constitutional Court to explore other more substantive meanings of *rule of law.*

There are provisions for three kinds of democracy. First, representative democracy is manifested in constitutional guarantees that citizens can elect representatives in all three spheres of government. Second, popular participation in lawmaking, administrative decision making, and constitutional adjudication is possible. Third, entrenchment in the constitution of the right to assemble, picket, and petition paves the way for citizens to engage directly with authorities in the exercise of their democratic rights. Provision for referenda in the national and provincial spheres is a further example of direct democracy.

National security is subject to civil authority, and the pursuit and promotion of national and world peace are explicit constitutional objectives. The constitution also contains a set of basic values and principles that are to govern public administration. Finally, by entrenching, for example, religious and environmental rights, the constitution implicitly supports the principles of religious neutrality and protection of the environment, respectively.

CONSTITUTIONAL BODIES

The most prominent organs of state are the president and cabinet, Parliament, the Constitutional Court, and a number of institutions that support constitutional democracy.

The President

The president, elected by the National Assembly from among its members for a term of five years, is South Africa's head of state and head of the national executive branch. He or she will almost invariably be the leader of the majority party in the assembly. The president is enjoined to uphold, defend, and respect the constitution and to promote national unity.

Upon election, the president ceases to be a member of the National Assembly. No person may hold office as president for more than two terms. The National Assembly, with a two-thirds majority, may remove the president from office for a serious violation of the constitution or the law, serious misconduct, or inability to perform the functions of office.

The president is responsible for assenting to and signing into law legislation passed by Parliament, or for referring it back to the National Assembly for reconsideration of its constitutionality, or for referring it to the Constitutional Court for a decision on its constitutionality.

The president makes key appointments, such as a deputy president, cabinet ministers, deputy ministers, and judges. Other typical presidential tasks include receiving foreign diplomats, appointing South African diplomatic representatives, and pardoning or reprieving offenders.

The Executive Administration

The president exercises executive authority together with a cabinet that includes a deputy president and ministers whom the president appoints and can dismiss. The ministers' powers and functions are assigned by the president. The president may also appoint and dismiss deputy ministers. The executive powers include initiating and implementing legislation and developing and executing national policy.

Members of the cabinet, including deputy ministers, are accountable collectively and individually to Parliament for the exercise of their powers and the performance of their functions. Strict rules of conduct, contained in the constitution and in a code of ethics, apply to ministers and deputy ministers.

If, by majority vote, the National Assembly passes a motion of no confidence in the cabinet excluding the president, the president must reconstitute the cabinet. If the motion includes the president, the president, all other members of the cabinet, and all deputy ministers must resign.

Executive authority in a province is vested in a premier, who exercises this authority together with other members of an executive council. A municipality's executive authority pertains to local government matters listed in the constitution. A cabinet member can assign any of his or her powers or functions to a member of a provincial executive council or to a municipal council. When a province cannot or does not fulfill an executive obligation in terms of legislation or the constitution, the national executive may, on certain conditions, intervene.

Chapter 10 of the constitution lists values and principles that must govern public administration. A public service commission monitors and oversees the realization of these values.

Parliament

Parliament, consisting of a National Assembly and a National Council of Provinces, is the central representative organ of the people at the national level. It is the highest lawmaker in the republic. It is one of the three lawmaking bodies whose legislative authority is specified in the constitution; the other two are provincial legislatures and municipal councils.

Parliament's legislative authority enables it to amend the constitution, to pass legislation with regard to any matter except those within exclusive provincial competence, to intervene in provincial legislative processes, and to assign any of its lawmaking (but not constitution-making) powers to any legislative body in another sphere of government.

The National Assembly, elected for a period of five years, consists of no fewer than 350 and no more than 400 women and men. Every citizen qualified to vote for the National Assembly is eligible to be a member of the assembly, with some exceptions, such as paid public servants, unrehabilitated insolvents, people of unsound mind, and anyone sentenced to a term of imprisonment of more than 12 months without the option of a fine. A speaker and deputy speaker, both elected from among the members, preside over the National Assembly.

Most questions before the National Assembly are decided by a majority of the votes cast. In some instances, such as amending the constitution, enhanced majorities are required. A majority of the members must be present before a vote can be taken to pass or amend legislation. At least one-third of the members must be present before a vote can be taken on any other question.

The National Assembly may consider, pass, amend, or reject any legislation and initiate or prepare any legislation except money bills, which are initiated by the cabinet. The assembly is mandated to provide mechanisms to ensure that organs of the national executive branch are accountable to it, and to oversee the functioning of such organs. The president, cabinet ministers, and deputy ministers may speak in the assembly, but they have no vote.

The assembly determines and controls its internal arrangements, proceedings, and procedures. The constitution explicitly enjoins the National Assembly to ensure public access to and participation in its proceedings.

Cabinet members, deputy ministers, and members of the National Assembly enjoy parliamentary privilege. They are therefore not liable for what they say in, produce before, or submit to the assembly or any of its committees.

Members of the assembly are not legally bound to follow instructions from their parties, but political realities compel most members to do so. Legislation passed under the 1996 constitution provides limited opportunity for a member to defect to another party without compromising his or her membership of the assembly.

The National Council of Provinces represents the provinces, mainly by participating in the national legislative process and by providing a national forum for public consideration of issues affecting the provinces. It is composed of 10 delegates from each province, or 90 members in all. A delegation is headed by the premier of a province or someone designated by him or her, three other special delegates, and six permanent delegates of parties represented in the provincial legislature. The National Council of Provinces elects a chairperson and deputy chairperson from among the permanent delegates for a five-year term and one deputy chairperson for a one-year term. This latter deputy chairpersonship rotates among the provinces.

Organized local governments may designate part-time representatives of the different categories of municipalities in the National Council of Provinces. As many as 10 such representatives may participate when necessary in council proceedings, but none of them may vote.

The Lawmaking Process

A prospective law is introduced in the form of a bill and is usually accompanied by an explanatory memorandum. A cabinet member, a deputy minister, or a member or committee of the National Assembly may introduce a bill in the assembly, but only the cabinet member responsible for national financial matters may introduce money bills. Only a member or committee of the National Council of Provinces may introduce a bill in the National Council of Provinces.

Ordinary bills that do not affect the provinces must be passed by both houses of Parliament and then submitted to the president for his or her assent and signature. The same applies to money bills, but the procedures for passing them differ from those for ordinary bills. If the National Council of Provinces proposes amendments to or rejects a bill passed by the National Assembly, the bill is referred back to the assembly to adopt it with or without amendments or to allow it to lapse.

A parliamentary bill affecting the provinces or provincial interests may be introduced in either the National Assembly or in the National Council of Provinces. If the National Assembly passes such a bill, it must be referred to the National Council of Provinces. Should the two chambers be unable to agree on a bill, reconciliatory procedures involving a mediation committee follow. Ultimately, however, the National Assembly can pass the bill on its own, but then only with a two-thirds majority. Special procedures apply when a bill to amend the constitution is introduced.

A bill assented to and signed by the president becomes an act of Parliament, must be published promptly, and takes effect when published or on a date determined in terms of the act. In multilingual South Africa there may be versions of an act in different languages. However, only one version is signed by the president, and that copy is conclusive evidence of the provisions of an act.

A third of the members of the National Assembly may apply to the Constitutional Court for the abstract review of all or part of an act of Parliament. The court then tests the constitutionality of the impugned legislation with no reference to a particular event or set of facts.

Lawmaking procedures in provincial legislatures are akin to those in Parliament. The 1996 constitution treats municipal councils as original lawmakers. This means that municipal legislation is not subject to a substantially more far-reaching and intensive form of judicial review than national and provincial legislation, as was the case before 1994. Local legislation is nonetheless still subordinate to parliamentary and provincial legislation.

The Judiciary

The judicial authority of the republic is vested in independent courts subject only to the constitution and the law. Court orders and decisions are binding on all persons and organs of state.

A distinction of significance in the South African court structure is between high courts and lower or magistrates' courts. The various divisions of the high court function as courts of both first instance and appeal, and they have jurisdiction in geographical areas that more or less coincide with provincial borders. Magistrates' courts are only courts of first instance, with jurisdiction in districts and regions. The jurisdiction of magistrates' courts is restricted to less serious cases, and is rather limited as far as constitutional issues are concerned. There are also high and lower specialist courts for matters such as land claims, labor issues, and children's affairs.

The Supreme Court of Appeal handles only appeals and is the highest court in the country in all but constitutional matters. The Constitutional Court is the highest court in constitutional matters, and its president is the chief justice of the country. Generally speaking the Supreme Court of Appeal and high courts have jurisdiction in constitutional matters, but the Constitutional Court must confirm findings of these courts that legislation or conduct of the president is unconstitutional.

In some matters, only the Constitutional Court has jurisdiction. For example, disputes between organs of state, the abstract review of parliamentary and provincial legislation, and the constitutionality of amendments to the constitution must be determined by the Constitutional Court.

When judicial officers are appointed, the need for the judiciary to reflect broadly the racial and gender composition of South Africa must be considered. A Judicial Service Commission, representative of the different parties in Parliament, together with the judiciary and the various echelons of the legal profession, is actively involved in the appointment of judges.

The president, after consultation with the Judicial Service Commission, appoints both the chief justice and deputy chief justice as well as the president and deputy president of the Supreme Court of Appeal. The leaders of the parties in the National Assembly must be consulted about the appointment of a chief justice or deputy chief justice. All other judges of the Constitutional Court are appointed by the president (after consultation with the chief justice and the leaders of the parties represented in the National Assembly) from a list prepared by the Judicial Service Commission after public interviews of candidates. The list must contain three more names than the number of judges to be appointed. The president, acting on the advice of the Judicial Service Commission, appoints all other judges.

A judge must be a "fit and proper person." No academic or professional qualifications are required, but a judge must be "appropriately qualified." Constitutional judges must be South African citizens. Judges normally retire at a prescribed age (70 for Constitutional Court judges and 75 for others). A judge can, however, also be removed from office by the president on the grounds of gross misconduct, incapacity, or gross incompetence, after an investigation by the Judicial Service Commission and a request by two-thirds of the National Assembly.

A magistrate is appointed for a specific district or region by the minister of justice at the recommendation of a magistrates' commission representative of political and professional interest groups.

Institutions Supporting Constitutional Democracy

Chapter 9 of the constitution institutes six specialist institutions in support of constitutional democracy. These are the public protector, known elsewhere as ombudsperson; the South African Human Rights Commission; the Commission for the Promotion and Protection of the Rights of Cultural, Religious and Linguistic Communities; the Commission for Gender Equality; the Auditor-General; and the Electoral Commission. These institutions all became operational after national legislation put them in place, and they have made their influence felt to varying degrees.

THE ELECTION PROCESS AND POLITICAL PARTICIPATION

The constitution entrenches the right to free, fair, and regular elections for all legislative bodies. The right to vote may be qualified in exceptional circumstances, but applicable legislation has to be specific. In the absence of specific restrictions, all prisoners, for example, were found to have the right to vote in South Africa's 1999 elections.

Alluding to the disenfranchisement of the vast majority of the South African population in the past, the constitution mentions in three sections the significance of a common voter roll and highlights in its founding provisions the need for universal adult suffrage. The minimum voting age is 18 years.

The Election Process

Elections are called by the president and take place every five years. The members of the National Assembly, provincial legislatures, and municipal councils must all be elected in terms of a proportional representation system prescribed by national legislation. There are no individual constituencies except in the case of municipal councils, where provision is made for electoral wards.

General elections for the National Assembly and provincial legislatures usually take place on the same day. A voter casts separate votes for the National Assembly and the legislature of her or his province. There can be national as well as provincial party lists of candidates for the National Assembly.

A party need not win any minimal percentage of votes to gain seats in any legislative body. In 2004, 12 parties were represented in the National Assembly. All elections are managed and overseen by an Electoral Commission.

POLITICAL PARTIES

South Africa has a pluralistic system of political parties. Since 1994, there have been quite a number of different parties competing for the votes of the electorate. The constitution proclaims the multiparty system of democratic government one of the founding values of the South African state.

Incidentally to the freedom to make political choices, the constitution entrenches a package of rights particularly conducive to multiparty democracy. They are the rights to form and join a political party; to participate in the activities of, or recruit members for, a political party; and to campaign for a political party or cause. Moreover, the constitution mandates national legislation to help fund political parties that participate in national and provincial legislatures on an equitable and proportional basis.

No employee of the public service may be favored or prejudiced solely because that person supports a particular political party or cause. The security services are moreover forbidden to prejudice a political party interest that is legitimate in terms of the constitution or to further, in a partisan manner, any interest of a political party.

Since 1994, the ruling ANC has enjoyed a dominant position in South African politics. This dominance has not, however, thwarted or fatally inhibited free competition in the political arena or regular resort to compromise politics, which has become a feature of political life in South Africa since the constitutional negotiations of the 1990s.

CITIZENSHIP

The constitution lays the foundation for a common South African citizenship regulated in detail by national legislation. Citizenship is acquired, first, by birth in the country. Second, someone born outside South Africa can become a citizen by descent if either her or his parents is a South African citizen and the birth is registered according to South African law. Third, citizenship can be acquired by naturalization granted by the minister of home affairs on application. Marriage as such does not affect the citizenship of a person. A minor foreigner can be naturalized on application by a parent or guardian if the latter permanently and lawfully resides in South Africa.

The constitution entrenches a right not to be deprived of citizenship; however, this right is limited, and loss of citizenship is thus possible in certain circumstances. Acquiring citizenship of another state by voluntary and formal action while outside South Africa results in a loss of South African citizenship, as does service in the armed forces of an enemy state of which the person in question is also a citizen. Finally, there are certain instances in which the minister of home affairs can deprive a naturalized citizen or a South African citizen who is also a citizen of another country of South African citizenship.

FUNDAMENTAL RIGHTS

The advancement of human rights and freedoms is a founding value of the South African state. The constitution describes its bill of rights (Chapter 2), which enshrines a full catalogue of fundamental rights, as a cornerstone of democracy in South Africa. The basic values informing the bill of rights are human dignity, equality, and freedom, always mentioned in that sequence.

The South African constitution guarantees certain standard fundamental or human rights, such as the rights to life and privacy; freedom from slavery, servitude, and forced labor; and equality before, as well as equal protection and benefit of, the law. A number of classical freedom rights are also included, as are political rights, rights of association, and rights to demonstrate approval or disapproval of policies or of political and other action. Because of its contemporary origin, the bill of rights explicitly guarantees the rights to make decisions concerning reproduction and not to be subjected to medical experimentation. It also includes environmental rights, a right of access to information held by the state, and rights to just administrative action.

There is a guarantee for the "haves" against the arbitrary deprivation of property, while, for the "have nots" there are rights of access to socioeconomic benefits, such as adequate housing, health care, and sufficient food, water, and social security. Children's rights and certain rights to education have also been included.

The bill of rights applies to all law and binds the legislature, the executive, the judiciary, and all organs of state. It can also bind any natural or juristic person (other than an organ of state), taking into account the nature of a right and the nature of any duty imposed by the right. Direct horizontal application of the bill of rights is, in other words, possible in circumstances that are not explicitly defined in the constitution. A juristic person is entitled to fundamental rights to the extent required by the nature of the rights and the nature of that juristic person.

The right to equality enjoys extensive protection and includes entitlement to "measures designed to protect or advance persons, or categories of persons, disadvantaged by unfair discrimination." The constitution explicitly mentions 17 nonexhaustive grounds on which discrimination is forbidden, and included in these is "sexual orientation." This makes the South African constitution the first in the world to provide explicit protection for gays and lesbians.

Another feature of the bill of rights, apart from the fullness of the catalogue of rights it includes, is its detailed treatment of due process in criminal matters. In one of its earliest judgments, not applauded by the majority of South Africans, the Constitutional Court held that a law authorizing capital punishment was unconstitutional. As a result of constitutional review other aspects of criminal due process have also been refurbished, reformed, and aligned with internationally accepted standards and the latest developments in the field.

In general, fundamental rights are to benefit all who are in the country; certain rights, however, such as political rights, benefit citizens only. The Constitutional Court has, however, held that aliens who are permanent residents in South Africa are, under certain conditions, entitled to socioeconomic benefits derived from guarantees in the constitution.

Impact and Functions of Fundamental Rights

The state must respect, protect, promote, and fulfill the fundamental rights enshrined in the bill of rights. This provision places quite a far-reaching responsibility on the state that includes, but also extends well beyond, simply refraining from the overuse of state power. The promotion and fulfillment of some rights indeed require state intervention and the constructive use of state power.

When interpreting the bill of rights, a court, tribunal, or forum must promote the values that underlie an open and democratic society based on human dignity, equality, and freedom; must consider international law; and may consider foreign law. When interpreting legislation and developing the common law or customary law, every court, tribunal, or forum must promote the spirit, purport, and objects of the bill of rights. This latter requirement has opened the door for considerable judicial reforms of the existing law, in particular common law, through the mechanism of case law. The common law dealing with the scope of the state's duty to provide proactive protection to all whose safety has been entrusted to it has, for example, been transformed in this manner.

The constitution makes generous provision for standing to bring court actions for alleged infringements of or threats to fundamental rights. Any person whose rights have allegedly been infringed may seek appropriate relief, and so can anyone who is acting on behalf of such a person, who cannot act in her or his own name. Also eligible to bring a rights action are people who are acting as a member of, or in the interest of, a group or class of persons; any individual who is acting in the public interest; and any association that is acting in the interest of its members.

The Constitutional Court understands the bill of rights not merely as a catalogue of the "subjective" entitlements of the persons and institutions whose rights it enshrines, but also as an objective order of values informing an understanding and definition of various facets of constitutional democracy.

Limitations to Fundamental Rights

The fundamental rights enshrined in the bill of rights may all be limited, but may not be taken away completely. First, a right can be inherently limited. The rights to assemble, demonstrate, picket, and petition are, for example, only guaranteed for someone participating in these actions peacefully and unarmed. Similarly, the right to freedom of speech does not extend to hate speech. Second, rights can limit each other reciprocally. In the case of *crimen iniuria* (criminal insult), for example, the victim's right to the protection of human dignity limits the perpetrator's right to freedom of speech. Third, constitutional provisions that are not part of the bill of rights can limit rights. The right to be a candidate for public office is, for example, limited by minimal requirements for various offices.

Last, there is a general limitation clause in the bill of rights (Section 36) that authorizes limitations of rights by ordinary, "nonconstitutional," law provided that the following criteria are met: The law must be applicable to all similar cases in the same way; the limitation must be reasonable and justifiable in an open and democratic society based on human dignity, equality, and freedom, and the principle of proportionality must be heeded. The latter requirement takes into account the nature of the right, the importance of the purpose for which the right is limited, the nature and extent of the limitation, the relation between the limitation and its purpose, and the possibility that less restrictive means might achieve the stated purpose.

Rights may be suspended, that is, taken away temporarily, only during a state of emergency, which can be declared only when stringent requirements are met. Some rights cannot be suspended at all, namely, the rights to equality, life, and human dignity; the right not to be subjected to torture or cruel, inhuman, or degrading treatment or punishment; the right not to be subjected to slavery, servitude, and forced labor; some of the rights of children; and some of the rights of detained, arrested, and accused persons. Exceptional due process rights accrue to those detained under a state of emergency to compensate for the normal rights they lose.

ECONOMY

An economic system is not constitutionally specified, but crucial provisions of the constitution inevitably help shape the structure of the economy. The constitutional property clause in the bill of rights does not out-and-out guarantee a right to property but states that no one may be deprived of property except in terms of a law of general application, and that no law may permit arbitrary deprivation of property. Expropriation must be for a public purpose or in the public interest and must be subject to compensation.

The wording of the property clause has informed land reform legislation. This entails rectifying the consequences of past racial discrimination that resulted in the loss of or severely restricted access to land for many black and colored people.

Fundamental rights to freedom of association and to freedom of trade, occupation, and profession are entrenched in the bill of rights, as are basic rights of workers and employers.

Constitutional guarantees of access to adequate housing, health care, food, water, and social security charge South Africa with the responsibilities of a social state. Legislation and administrative action designed to realize minimal social standards are therefore justiciable. There are examples of cases in which the Constitutional Court has gone to some length to order executive state organs to fulfill rudimentary constitutional obligations in the socioeconomic arena. In one instance, organs of the executive branch were ordered to design and implement minimal standards for the provision of basic shelter to homeless people. In another instance the court ordered the national department of health to provide the drug Nevirapine to all pregnant women who had human immunodeficiency virus (HIV) and their babies at state hospitals in order to reduce the risk of mother-to-child transmission of HIV. The court thought that this was the minimum the department owed this category of people in order to comply with its constitutional duty to provide access to health care.

The South African economic system is best described as a social market economy. It combines accepted wisdom about both social responsibility of the state and a free-market economy.

RELIGIOUS COMMUNITIES

In South Africa "Everyone has the right to freedom of conscience, religion, thought, belief, and opinion" (Section 15). This guarantee is backed by a prohibition on unfair discrimination by the state against anyone on the grounds of religion, conscience, and belief. Constitutional protection of the freedom of speech does not extend to advocacy of hatred based on religion and incitement to cause harm.

There is no established state church in South Africa, and public authorities must remain neutral in their relations with religious communities. These communities regulate and administer their affairs independently within the limits of laws that apply to all. Nevertheless, there is no wall of separation between the state and these communities. The constitution envisages ways of protecting religion that advance the well-being of religious communities. The Commission for the Promotion and Protection of the Rights of Cultural, Religious, and Linguistic Communities, one of the constitution's state institutions supporting constitutional democracy, is enjoined to promote respect for the rights of religious communities. The commission is furthermore enjoined to promote and develop peace, friendship, humanity, tolerance, and national unity among religious communities, on the basis of equality, nondiscrimination, and free association.

Second, religious observances may be conducted at state or state-aided institutions in accordance with rules made by the appropriate public authorities, provided that these observances are conducted on an equitable basis and attendance at them is free and voluntary. Finally, the constitution caters to concerns of minority religious communities, Muslims and Hindus in particular, by envisaging statutory recognition of marriages concluded under a system of religious personal or family law.

MILITARY DEFENSE AND STATE OF EMERGENCY

The security services of the Republic of South Africa consist of a single defense force, a single police service, and intelligence services established in terms described by the constitution. National security, according to the constitution, must reflect the resolve of South Africans to live as equals and in peace and harmony, to be free of fear and want, and to seek a better life. A South African citizen is precluded from participating in any armed conflict other than that provided for in the constitution and in legislation. National security must be pursued in compliance with law, including international law, and is subject to the authority of Parliament and the national executive, in other words, civil government. Multiparty parliamentary committees oversee all security services.

The defense force is the only lawful military force in the republic. Other armed organizations or services may be established, but then only in terms of national legislation. The primary object of the force is to defend the country in accordance with the constitution and the principles of international law regulating the use of force. The president, as head of the national executive branch, is commander in chief of the defense force and appoints the military command; however, there is also a cabinet member responsible for defense, who directs a civilian secretariat for defense established by national legislation.

Only the president may authorize the deployment of the defense force, in cooperation with the police service, in defense of the republic or in fulfillment of an international obligation. The president must inform Parliament, promptly and in appropriate detail, of the reasons for employing the force, all places where it is being employed, the number of people involved, and the period for which the force is expected to be employed. If Parliament does not sit during the first seven days after the defense force is employed, the president must provide the specified information to an oversight committee.

The president is also the only one who may declare a state of national defense; once again, Parliament must be given information similar to that described. A declaration of a state of national defense lapses unless it is approved by Parliament within seven days. Such approval can also be obtained at an extraordinary sitting if need be.

A state of emergency, which is to be distinguished from a state of defense, may be declared only by an act of Parliament, and only when the life of the nation is threatened by war, invasion, general insurrection, disorder, natural disaster, or other public emergency. The declaration must be necessary to restore peace and order. Parliament has no right to indemnify the state or any person against any unlawful action taken in connection with the state of emergency.

In 1994 the system of conscription for white males ended. The defense force now consists of full-time profes-sional members and voluntary civilians. The Republic of South Africa, through international treaties, has undertaken not to produce or use atomic, biological, or chemical weapons.

AMENDMENTS TO THE CONSTITUTION

The constitution is more difficult to amend than ordinary acts of Parliament. The National Assembly can amend most sections of the constitution with a two-thirds majority. Amendments to the bill of rights (Chapter 2) require the support of at least six provinces in the National Council of Provinces, in addition to the two-thirds majority. The same applies to amendments of constitutional provisions that relate to the provinces or provincial matters. An amendment of the founding provisions in Section 1 of the constitution requires a 75 percent majority in the National Assembly and the support of six provinces in the National Council of Provinces.

In the first eight years of its existence there were 11 amendments to the constitution.

PRIMARY SOURCES

Constitution in English. Available online. URL: http://www.polity.org.za/html/govdocs/constitution/saconst.html?rebookmark=1. Accessed on August 29, 2005.

Constitution in English: *The Constitution of the Republic of South Africa.* Juta: Lansdowne, 2004.

SECONDARY SOURCES

Iain Currie and Johan De Waal, *The New Constitutional and Administrative Law.* Vol. 1, *Constitutional Law.* Lansdowne: Juta, 2001.

G. E. Devenish, "Constitutional Law." In *The Law of South Africa.* Vol. 5 pt. 3, 2d ed., edited by W. A. Joubert and J. A. Faris. Durban: LexisNexis Butterworths, 2004.

Ziyad Motala and Cyril Ramaphosa, *Constitutional Law: Analysis and Cases.* Oxford: Oxford University Press, 2002.

I. M. Rautenbach and E. F. J. Malherbe, *Constitutional Law.* 4th ed. Durban: LexisNexis Butterworths, 2004.

Lourens du Plessis

SPAIN

At-a-Glance

OFFICIAL NAME
Kingdom of Spain

CAPITAL
Madrid

POPULATION
42,717,068 (2005 est.)

SIZE
194,897 sq. mi. (504,782 sq. km)

LANGUAGES
Spanish (in some regions, second language, e.g., Catalan, Basque, Galician)

RELIGIONS
Catholic 80.3%, other Christian or other denominations 1.9%, nonbelievers 10.5%, atheists 5.2%, no details 2.1%

NATIONAL OR ETHNIC COMPOSITION
Spanish 93.7%, Latin American 1.9%, other (mostly Moroccan, British, Romanian, German, French, Italian, Portuguese) 4.4%

DATE OF INDEPENDENCE OR CREATION
Middle Ages

TYPE OF GOVERNMENT
Parliamentary monarchy

TYPE OF STATE
Quasi-federal state

TYPE OF LEGISLATURE
Bicameral parliament

DATE OF CONSTITUTION
December 27, 1978

DATE OF LAST (AND ONLY) AMENDMENT
August 27, 1992

Spain is a parliamentary monarchy based on the rule of law with a clear separation of the executive, legislative, and judicial powers. Over the course of the last three decades a process of rationalization has resulted in a move away from a centralist model toward a federal model. The constitution establishes a wide range of fundamental rights with highly sophisticated systems of jurisdictional protection. The Constitutional Court, apart from other functions, undertakes to protect these rights. After a period of authoritarian rule, the implementation of a constitution symbolizes the arrival of a fully democratic system.

The monarch is the head of state. He or she has no explicit political power but does, in addition to his or her symbolic function, exercise influence through advisory activities. The central figure of the political system is the prime minister. The prime minister is elected and removed from office by the lower house of parliament (Congreso de los Diputados). Free, egalitarian, general, and direct elections are held for the members of the lower house and for the majority of the upper house (Senado); some members of the upper house are elected by the regional parlia-

ments. The political parties are fully independent and are essential for the political life of the country.

Religious liberty is guaranteed. There is no official state religion, and there is a clear division between the church and the state. Public authorities cooperate with religious groupings. The economic system can be described as a social market economy. The armed forces are subject to civil control at all times.

CONSTITUTIONAL HISTORY

The Roman invasion of Spain began in 206 B.C.E. Complete integration into the empire took place in the year 212 C.E., when Roman citizenship was granted to all Hispanics. Although Spain officially remained part of the empire until the fall of Rome in 476, German tribes began to invade in 415; they eventually gained independence from Rome under the Visigoths. For over two centuries, Hispano-Romans and Visigoths coexisted under two distinct legal systems.

After 476 the Visigothic kings wielded undisputed rule over the entire territory, which increased or decreased with the fortunes of war. Although it did not encompass the entire Iberian Peninsula, the Visigothic Kingdom could be characterized as the Spanish kingdom in the sixth century. Power was held by a king, who was elected by a group of nobles and ecclesiastics. Numerous kings were deposed as a result of conspiracies or assassinations. A political institution of notable importance was that of the councils. In principle, they were ecclesiastical assemblies, but as the king convened them and participated in them, they functioned to limit royal power.

From a legal point of view, a key date was 654, when the *Liber Iudiciorum* (a book of legal rules) was applied to all residents. As of this date a somewhat unitarian legal system, which established a somewhat identifiable political entity, existed. Unification suffered a serious blow at the start of the eighth century, when the Moors took control of practically the entire Iberian territory. Soon afterward, the Spanish Reconquista movement began, not to end until 1492. The political organization of the Moors is unimportant to this history, as it bears no relation to the political-legal structure of the last several centuries. The small part of Iberia that was never subdued managed to reconquer the entire peninsula and impose its culture and legal ideas.

In Asturias in the north of Spain, Pelayo's proclamation as king in 718 can be seen as the beginning of the current dynastic succession. In other territories of northern Spain, kingdoms or independent counties arose.

As these entities grew at the expense of the Moors, a process of consolidation took gradual shape, via marriage and other dynastic manipulation. However, this did not necessarily produce a unification of legal systems or of political entities. One monarch may have ruled two kingdoms.

Throughout this period the monarchy was far from absolute. In general terms the monarch respected local laws, which were of common indigenous origin, with additional Roman and Germanic elements.

The culmination of this process occurred in the 15th century. The marriage of Isabel and Ferdinand united the Crowns of Castile and Aragon, which comprised practically all of the preexisting kingdoms and Crowns. Nevertheless, the final expulsion of the Moors in 1492 left behind a plurality of kingdoms, which were enlarged as Spain gained control of other land throughout Europe, such as Naples and Portugal. In addition, vast territories in America were integrated into the country in the following century by the descendents of Isabel and Ferdinand: their grandson, Carlos (Charles) V, and his son, Felipe (Philip) II. By this point Spain had become an independent political entity that controlled the entire Iberian Peninsula.

Although there was not yet an official Crown of Spain, because Isabel and Ferdinand, as well as their successors, maintained the individual titles (Castile, Leon, Aragon, Sicily, Granada, Toledo, Valencia, Galicia, Majorca, Seville, Sardinia, etc.), unification did indeed occur. Although over the course of the centuries since the pinnacle of Hispanic power during the times of Carlos V and Felipe II territories have been lost in Europe, America, Asia, Oceania, Africa, and even Iberia, the Spanish base has remained unchanged.

With notable changes over the course of the following centuries, including a change of dynasty from the Austrians to the Bourbons that did not alter the line of succession, a process of centralization and concentration of power in the monarch, known as absolutism, ensued. A most radical transition took place at the start of the 19th century, when Spanish constitutionalism emerged.

The system of absolute monarchy ceased in 1808 when the Spanish monarchs abdicated to Napoléon. The majority of the population refused to recognize Napoléon's brother as king and fought a guerrilla war supported by British forces against the French occupation. King Ferdinand VII, who had been exiled by the French in 1808, returned to the throne in 1814. He replaced the liberal 1812 constitution of Cádiz and introduced an absolute monarchy, which he was forced by military sedition to modify to more constitutional rule in 1820. Rising liberalism and interventions of the military in politics led to the proclamation of the republic in 1873 by the Cortes (parliament). It lasted only until 1975, when the monarchy was restored. It also remained in place when the general José Antonio Primo de Rivera in a coup d'état established a dictatorship in 1923. After Primo de Rivera's forced resignation in 1930, King Alfonso XIII, who had lost popularity because of his early support of the dictator, abdicated in 1931 and gave way to the Second Republic.

The Second Republic of Spain (1931–39) passed Spain's first modern constitution, which effected profound change in the legislative framework. Radical changes were imposed on economic and religious life, and political decentralization was furthered, all in an attempt to modernize Spain. These sudden changes, often poorly controlled, antagonized large sectors of the middle classes, the Roman Catholic Church, and the armed forces. A failed military coup d'etat triggered the outbreak of a bloody civil war (1936–39).

The conclusion of the civil war, with the victory of the military faction that had taken up arms against republican legality, was followed by the establishment of a unique political system. It would be simplistic to classify General Franco's regime as a one-man dictatorship.

Franco turned to nonmilitary factions to provide legitimacy, since he lacked a clear program of his own. He aligned himself with both the most reactionary Catholic attitudes, thus gaining the support of a large part of the Spanish Catholic hierarchy, as well as a radical political party that was clearly inspired by Nazism and fascism. The system that resulted, guided by a strong survival instinct, was at first undemocratic and unfree, but became more liberal in time. No single constitution as such was ever issued, but over the years a series of fundamental laws that were passed fulfilled that role and reflect this gradual liberalization, especially after the strong economic development in the 1950s.

Franco's constitutional framework did not outlast his death in 1975, when Juan Carlos de Bourbon, the person designated by Franco to be his successor with the title of king, began to make changes. He undertook to transform the autocratic system into a fully democratic one. This resulted in the renunciation by the monarch of the hereditary powers of the previous Franco regime and culminated in the ratification of the 1978 constitution, which established a parliamentary monarchy fully comparable with the most advanced systems in the world.

Spain is a member of both the United Nations and the North Atlantic Treaty Organization (NATO). It is also a member of the European Union and thus regards itself as subject to a process of the transfer of sovereignty to the union.

FORM AND IMPACT OF THE CONSTITUTION

The constitution is the sole text officially designated as such. No international agreements may be contrary to the constitution; should such an agreement be signed, the constitution would have to be amended. However, in relation to fundamental rights, the constitution itself establishes that it shall be interpreted in accordance with the Universal Declaration of Human Rights and other international treaties and declarations relating to them.

The constitution is the supreme source of law and takes precedence over other forms of legislation; no other legislation may contradict it. It establishes the system of the sources of law as well as the organization of the state, in addition to specifying a series of fundamental rights and establishing the mechanisms for their protection.

In addition to these strictly technical functions, the constitution fulfills a symbolic role in current society. It demonstrates the end of political confrontation among Spaniards and their dedication to maintaining a democratic system.

BASIC ORGANIZATIONAL STRUCTURE

The current constitution, starting as a centralized system of a Napoleonic nature that was the mainstay of Spanish constitutionalism for two centuries, lays the foundation for a process that will probably conclude with the establishment of a federal or quasi-federal system. It is an unfinished process and one that will therefore foreseeably change in the future.

On the basis of the constitution, 17 regions (Autonomous Communities), which in some cases correspond to former sovereign entities, were created. Their size and number of inhabitants vary greatly. Their jurisdictional powers reside in their statute of autonomy, which must be approved by the national parliament. Therefore, the powers held by the regions differ. Each region has its own parliament, which can legislate on matters within its competence.

The constitution reserves some areas as the exclusive concern of the central state, such as nationality, international relations, defense, administration of justice, and commercial, criminal, and employment legislation. Other matters, also stated in the constitution, may fall within the powers of the regions: for example, urban development, ports, agriculture, and fishing.

According to the constitution, regionalization is not obligatory; furthermore, it can be established in certain territories but not in others. For political reasons, however, the system was generalized and the entire national territory is split into regions. At first, the statutes of autonomy varied among regions, as did the powers they assumed. In 2004 the administration announced the start of a process to reform the statutes in order to increase the powers of the regions. However far the ongoing process extends, implementing it will not be easy. Given the complexity of today's society, everything is interrelated; even powers exclusive to the central state need the cooperation of the self-governing regions to translate them into practice.

Ironically, the decentralization process has proceeded hand in hand with a new kind of centralism based on the regions, as the smaller local entities have lost status. Although the system of 50 provinces established in the 19th century survives in the constitution, these entities have lost importance compared with the regions, which are usually made up of several provinces. With regard to municipal power, the situation is not very diverse. There are a little over 8,000 municipalities in Spain, each governed by a town council elected by the inhabitants and a mayor chosen by the council.

LEADING CONSTITUTIONAL PRINCIPLES

The first article of the constitution precisely establishes the basic constitutional principles: "1. Spain is hereby established as a social and democratic State, subject to the rule of law, which advocates freedom, justice, equality and political pluralism as highest values of its legal system; 2. National sovereignty belongs to the Spanish people, from whom all state powers emanate; 3. The political form of the Spanish State is the parliamentary monarchy."

In practice this means that Spain is governed by a system of parliamentary democracy with freely created political parties, in which there is a clear separation of legislative, executive, and judicial powers. There is a Constitutional Court with power to determine the constitutionality of laws and to protect fundamental rights.

The monarchical system entails that a king or queen fulfills the role of head of state. The monarch serves during his or her entire lifetime, unless the monarch renounces the throne, and is succeeded by his direct heir (generally his oldest son, but female succession is possible) according to strict rules contained in the constitution itself. The power of the monarch is limited to functions that are little more than symbolic.

The constitution's approach to human rights departs from the liberal model. It calls on public authorities to promote true liberty and equality by actively removing any obstacles to these goals.

CONSTITUTIONAL BODIES

The principal constitutional bodies are the Crown; the parliament, known as the Cortes Generales; the administration; and the judiciary, including the Constitutional Court.

The Crown

The monarch is the head of state. In constitutional terms the monarch "arbitrates and moderates the regular functioning of the institutions," but the monarch lacks real political power. Article 62 lists the monarch's functions as including but not limited to the following: to promulgate the laws, to dissolve parliament, to call elections, to propose a candidate for president of the government, to appoint governmental ministers, to make civil and military appointments, to exercise supreme command over the armed forces, and to exercise the right of clemency.

In all these functions, the monarch's powers are in fact limited, as he or she can perform them only at the initiative of other bodies. For example, the monarch appoints only ministers proposed by the president of the cabinet, promulgates only laws that are approved by parliament, and always proposes the leader of the party that receives the most votes in elections to be president of the cabinet. These other bodies bear the political responsibility for these actions.

In reality, the importance of the monarch, besides the representative function, lies in the way he or she exercises the functions of arbitration and moderation. The high-level experience and information available to the monarch frequently make his or her advice important to those in power.

The current monarch, Juan Carlos I de Bourbon, belongs to the dynasty that has reigned for many centuries. His oldest son, Felipe, will succeed him, unless judged unfit by parliament.

The Administration

The administration comprises the president of the cabinet (officially Council of Ministers), the vice presidents, and the cabinet ministers. Its responsibilities include managing domestic and foreign policy, civil and military administration, the exercise of the executive role, and legislative approval.

Although these responsibilities are exercised collectively by the cabinet, its president (equivalent to a prime minister) is the key figure in political life. The president of the cabinet is appointed by the king on the recommendation of a majority in the Congress, the lower house of parliament. The president nominates the vice presidents and governmental ministers who make up the cabinet; they are formally appointed by the monarch. The president may replace the cabinet with absolute freedom. The president can be any Spanish citizen of legal age, although traditionally he or she is a member of parliament.

The administration formally leaves office after the general elections or the resignation or death of the president, although it continues to function until the appointment of a new one. The president and cabinet can also be removed from office by a vote of no confidence, proposed by one-tenth of the Congress and supported by an appropriate majority. Any vote of no confidence must include the name of an alternative candidate for president, who is appointed by the monarch if the motion passes.

The Cortes Generales (Parliament)

Parliament (Cortes Generales or "General Courts" or National Assembly) exercises the legislative function and controls the actions of the government. It is made up of two houses, the Congress and the Senate.

Congress is composed of 350 members of parliament, who are elected through general, direct, free, and secret elections. The provinces constitute the electoral constituencies, and several members are elected from each on the basis of party lists.

A quorum is required before any important work can be done in the Congress. Some decisions are approved by simple majority and others by special majorities.

Both the president and the ministers may be required to appear and answer questions from members of parliament. Members are not formally required to follow instructions from their party or their electorate. In practice they tend to respect instructions from their parliamentary group, made up of members of the same party; the group has become the principal actor on the parliamentary stage. Select parliamentary committees can be set up to investigate any matter of public interest.

The Senate, or upper house, is intended to provide territorial representation. Currently, it is made up of four representatives from each province elected through general, free, direct, and secret elections by its citizens, as well as other representatives who are elected from among the members of the regional parliaments.

The function of the Senate is to provide additional control over the administration and the legislature. In the legislative sphere, the Senate may only propose amendments to laws approved by the Congress, which can accept or reject them at its discretion.

Both members of parliament and senators are elected for a period of four years, although they lose this status if the houses are dissolved by the king at the request of the president. Those senators chosen by the regional parliaments serve only until the next regional government election.

The Lawmaking Process

One of the essential functions of parliament is to create new laws. The initiative can originate in the cabinet, the Congress, the Senate, or, in certain cases, the regional parliaments.

A law can also be initiated through a petition that has at least 500,000 duly accredited signatures of citizens, although this procedure cannot be used in matters related to taxes, the Crown, and fundamental rights. In any case, it has never been used. In practice, the majority of laws are initiated by the cabinet.

Once proposed, the bill is debated at a plenary session of the Congress. If it is not rejected at that stage, a subcommittee is appointed to prepare a report, which is then debated by a committee. Upon approval by the committee, it is sent back to the plenary session, which submits it to the Senate if it is finally approved. During all these phases changes are made via the drafting of amendments. The process is repeated in a similar way in the Senate. If the text approved by the Senate is identical to that of the Congress then the law can be promulgated. If this is not the case, then it returns to the Congress in which a final decision on the language is made.

Approval of a law requires a simple majority with the sole exception of constitutional reforms and the so-called organic laws, which require an absolute majority—more than half of all members of each house. Organic laws are defined by the constitution as relating to fundamental rights, regional statutes of autonomy, and the general electoral system.

The Judiciary

The judiciary is independent of the legislative and executive branches. The constitution provides for a General Council of the Judicial Power, with authority in such areas as appointments, inspections, and discipline. Its members are appointed by parliament, but the majority of them must be judges or official state lawyers. Strictly speaking, the council does not form part of the judicial power, but rather is a governing body.

Jurisdiction is generally assigned according to subject matter and territory. There are specialized courts that deal with civil law, criminal law, administrative law, and company law. There are also various levels of courts that can review decisions made by lower courts in cases established by law.

The Supreme Court holds the highest position in the court system with jurisdiction over the entire national territory and over all matters, although it is composed of specialized divisions. The decisions of the Supreme Court not only apply to the case at hand; they also serve as precedents for any analogous cases that may arise in the future.

The Audiencia Nacional also has jurisdiction over the entire national territory, but at a lower level than the Supreme Court. It specializes in criminal matters that affect the whole country, such as terrorism, drug trafficking, and major economic offenses.

The Constitutional Court is not part of the judicial branch, yet it is of key importance in shaping some elements of Spanish law. It is the only body authorized to determine the constitutionality of laws. If the Constitutional Court decides that a law is unconstitutional, it cannot be applied. It also resolves disputes over territorial jurisdiction, between the central state and a region, or between two regions. Finally, it has a role in the protection of fundamental rights, given that any citizen who believes the ordinary courts of justice have not adequately protected him or her may appeal to it.

The Constitutional Court has 12 members, who are appointed for a nonrenewable period of nine years. Four are appointed by the Congress, four by the Senate, two by the General Council of the Judicial Power, and two by the administration.

THE ELECTION PROCESS

All Spanish citizens 18 years of age or older can vote and be candidates. In the case of municipal elections, a citizen of any member country of the European Union resident in Spain can vote or be a candidate. In any event, voters must be registered on the corresponding electoral roll.

The right to vote can be suspended by judicial ruling in certain cases, such as certain criminal convictions or mental imbalance. Members of certain professions, such as military personnel or judges, may not stand as candidates for election unless they leave their profession.

Parliamentary Elections

Elections to both houses of parliament—the Congress and the Senate—are held on the same date. Both are based on the provinces as the electoral constituency.

Each province has a constitutional minimal number of seats in the Congress and additional seats based on population. Each party presents a list of candidates; voters must choose the entire list. The electoral system is organized in order to make formation of parliamentary majorities easier; lists that receive most votes in each province take precedence.

Nearly all the provinces have four seats in the Senate. Voters choose three candidates from among all those on the ballot, presented in alphabetical (not party) order. The remainder of the senators are chosen by the regional parliaments from among their own members.

In practice, since the promulgation of the current constitution there has been a plurality of parties present in both houses. One of these had an absolute majority, another a simple majority that allowed it to form a government with the support of other groups. One center Right party, one center Left party, a minority Left party, and some regional parties account for nearly all the seats in both houses.

Regional and Local Elections

Each regional parliament has only one house. The electoral system is comparable to that for the Congress. With the exception of four regions, municipal elections are held on the same date as provincial elections. The two largest national parties are represented in all the regional parliaments, alongside regional parties in many cases. In some provinces, regional parties hold the majority.

POLITICAL PARTIES

The constitution establishes that "political parties are the expression of political pluralism; they contribute to the development and expression of the will of the people and are an essential instrument for political participation." They are a vital element of the political life of Spain. The constitution states that they must be organized on a democratic basis.

The number of registered parties is high, but only a few have a parliamentary presence, be it national or regional. Only such parties receive generous public financing, which is essential for their existence.

No party had been declared illegal in the recent history of Spain until 2004. That year a group was outlawed on charges of supporting the Basque terrorist network, which used violence and assassination to achieve Basque independence.

The importance of the political parties within the system is reflected in the voting behavior of members of parliament. Although members are legally free to vote as they wish, in fact rigid party discipline prevails, because parliamentary groups that usually identify themselves with political parties are the real actors on the parliamentary stage.

CITIZENSHIP

The criteria for the acquisition of nationality are not specified in the constitution, but rather in the Civil Code. Those persons whose father or mother is Spanish are considered to be Spanish, as are those born in Spain who lack any other nationality or whose father or mother was also born in Spain. The acquisition of nationality is also possible by governmental ruling. Dual nationality is an option, in some cases regulated by international treaties, particularly in the case of Latin Americans.

The constitution establishes that those who are Spaniards by origin, that is, by birth, cannot be deprived of their nationality.

FUNDAMENTAL RIGHTS

The constitution devotes almost 50 articles to the subject of fundamental rights and duties. The starting point is the definition of the dignity of the individual as "the foundation of political order and social harmony." Equality before the law is established, and the constitution expressly states that there can be no discrimination on grounds of birth, race, sex, religion, or ideas.

There is a wide-ranging list of rights, composed of traditionally held rights and those that have been incorporated in more recent times. Among those rights considered to be fundamental are religious liberty, freedom of movement and safety, inviolability of the home, secrecy of communications, free expression, the right to education, the right to form unions, and freedom of profession, association, and protest.

There is a constitutional obligation for the public authorities to "promote conditions so that the freedom and equality of the individual and of the groups in which he integrates himself are real and effective; and to remove those obstacles which may impede or complicate their fulfillment." In other words, we find ourselves in a promotional and not merely liberal state. The state must work proactively in order to allow equality and freedom to exist in good measure to allow the exercise of these fundamental rights.

Even more important are the mechanisms carefully designed to protect such rights. These mechanisms begin with the so-called organic laws, which regulate rights. Such laws require a special parliamentary majority for their approval, to ensure widespread agreement among the various political parties, thus impeding restrictive regulations.

The protection of rights in the courts is regulated by means of a specific procedure that is intended to be particularly fast and reliable, along with the option of appeal to the Constitutional Court. In addition, the constitution places rights among the items that are particularly complicated to amend. The constitution also establishes the office of ombudsperson (Defensor del Pueblo), who can supervise the activities of the administration and make sure it protects the exercise of human rights.

Apart from fundamental rights, the constitution refers to "guiding principles for social and economic policies." Among these are the protection of the family, social progress, equal distribution of income, and protection of health, the environment, and the artistic heritage. However, these principles merely act as a guide for the public authorities. There are no specific mechanisms to protect them, except those established by ordinary legislation.

Historically, fundamental rights were of an individual nature. However, the Constitutional Court has established with absolute clarity that groups of individuals can also be holders of such rights.

ECONOMY

The constitution recognizes a free-market economy, limited by the demands of the general economy and the general interest. State initiative in economic activities is also recognized, and the state may legally reserve the right to perform certain economic activities under a monopoly within the public sector, as well as to participate in private companies.

The state may also engage in economic planning. Private property and the right to inheritance are constitutionally recognized, but they may be regulated with an eye to their social function.

The idea of participation that is present in the whole constitutional text also appears in the specific field of economic activity. There is an Economic and Social Council composed of unions and professional and business organizations, among others.

In general, Spain's economy is typical of the social free-market model.

RELIGIOUS COMMUNITIES

Religious liberty is considered a fundamental right. There is no room for discrimination on grounds of religion. The constitution expressly states that no religion shall have national status; at the same time, it states that the state must establish a relationship of cooperation with the religious denominations.

The Roman Catholic Church is by far the predominant church. It has signed numerous agreements with the state, some with the status of international treaties (*concordats*). Three groups of minority denominations, Evangelicals, Jews, and Muslims, have also signed agreements with the state.

The Roman Catholic Church receives direct financing from the state, although of little significance. The church, as well as the other denominations that have signed agreements with the state, is entitled to tax allowances similar to those of other nonprofit organizations.

Religious education is taught as an optional subject in state schools. The Catholic Church is entitled to this teaching and to financing from the state; three minority religions may only receive financing in this respect if more than nine students at the same educational institution request such teaching.

The country's markedly Catholic past, and the numerical predominance of its followers today, means that the Catholic Church continues to receive favorable treatment in relation to other denominations. It is clear, however, that through scrupulous respect for religious liberty, a slow approximation to equal treatment is under way.

MILITARY DEFENSE AND STATE OF EMERGENCY

The constitution gives supreme command of the armed forces to the king, but the administration presides over the military; therefore, the function of the monarch is purely symbolic. Any declaration of war must be approved by parliament. The missions of the armed forces are stated in Article 8.3: "To guarantee the sovereignty and independence of Spain, to defend its territorial integrity and the constitutional order." This article means that, as a general rule, the armed forces do not intervene in the maintenance of domestic public order. This is the duty of a separate group, the security forces.

Military service is not obligatory; therefore, the armed forces are made up of volunteers. The members of the armed forces have a limited right of association and to membership in unions and are under no obligation to follow orders that are contrary to the constitution.

Aside from any declaration of war, the constitution allows for a state of emergency, which is probably intended to pertain to situations arising in wartime. This may be proposed only by the administration and must be approved by an absolute majority of the lower house of parliament. A state of emergency allows certain limitations in the exercise of specific rights, as specified in the constitution, and results in a form of militarization of the activity of the public authorities, although always subject to the control of the administration.

AMENDMENTS TO THE CONSTITUTION

Since the promulgation of the constitution, there has only been one amendment, to allow citizens of other European Union member states resident in Spain to stand as candidates in municipal elections.

A full revision of the constitution, or any amendment of articles that affect fundamental rights, the Crown, or the essential values of the constitution, is especially complicated. Such changes require approval by a two-thirds majority of each house of parliament, followed by new elections, followed by renewed two-thirds votes in each house. Finally, they must be approved in a national referendum. Obviously, this provision is meant to prevent any serious change that lacks widespread political and social support.

The remaining articles may be amended by three-fifths of each house of parliament. If one-tenth the members of either house request a referendum on the matter, it must be held.

PRIMARY SOURCES

Constitution in English, Spanish, and other languages. Available online. URL: http://www.congreso.es/. Accessed on August 6, 2005.
Constitution in Spanish: *Constitución Española*. Madrid: Boletín Oficial del Estado, 1999.
Constitution in English: Mariano Daranas Peláez, ed., *Constitution and Standing Orders*. Madrid: Congreso de los Diputados, 2004.

SECONDARY SOURCES

Elena Blanco Merino, *Spanish Legal System*. London: Sweet and Maxwell, 1996.
Charlotte Villiers, *The Spanish Legal Tradition. An Introduction to the Spanish Law and Legal System*. Brookfield, Vt.: Ashgate, 1999.

Iván C. Ibán

SRI LANKA

At-a-Glance

OFFICIAL NAME
The Democratic Socialist Republic of Sri Lanka

CAPITAL
Sri Jayewardenepura Kotte (legislative and administrative capital), Colombo (commercial)

POPULATION
20,064,776 (2005 est.)

SIZE
25,332 sq. mi. (65,610 sq. km)

LANGUAGES
Sinhala (official and national) 74%, Tamil (national) 18%, other (including English) 8%

RELIGIONS
Buddhist 69.1%, Sunni Muslim 7.6%, Hindu 7.1%, Christian (predominantly Roman Catholic) 6.2%, unspecified 10% (2001)

NATIONAL OR ETHNIC COMPOSITION
Sinhalese 73.8%, Sri Lankan Moors 7.2%, Indian Tamil 4.6%, Sri Lankan Tamil 3.9%, other (including Eurasians, Malay, Burgher descendants of union of Dutch and the local people, Veddha indigenous inhabitants) 0.5%, unspecified 10% (2001)

DATE OF INDEPENDENCE OR CREATION
February 4, 1948

TYPE OF GOVERNMENT
Mixed parliamentary/presidential democracy

TYPE OF STATE
Unitary state

TYPE OF LEGISLATURE
Unicameral parliament

DATE OF CONSTITUTION
August 16, 1978

DATE OF LAST AMENDMENT
September 25, 2001

Sri Lanka has a mixed presidential and parliamentary system of government. According to the constitution, there is a division of executive, legislative, and judicial powers.

Organized as a unitary state, Sri Lanka is made up of nine provinces and 25 administrative districts. The constitution prohibits the establishment of a separate state within the territory of Sri Lanka. Human rights, including specific language rights, are provided for by the constitution. There is a Supreme Court.

The powerful president is the head of state and the chief of the executive, but he or she can be reelected only once. The president appoints and dismisses the prime minister and the other cabinet ministers. The president and the cabinet of ministers are responsible to parliament.

Sri Lanka has had high levels of political violence since its independence, largely the result of ethnic clashes. The government has declared numerous states of emergency. Nevertheless, there is a multiparty system and the country enjoys relative political stability. The Sri Lankan electoral system enables voters to express preferences among candidates.

The constitution accords Buddhism "foremost place"; however, it is not recognized as the state religion. The economic system can be described as a social market economy. The military is subject to the civil government.

CONSTITUTIONAL HISTORY

Sri Lanka was known as Ceylon until 1972. From its earliest recorded history, the island had a multiethnic society. By the fifth century B.C.E. Sinhalese and Tamils had immigrated from different parts of India. The early political history of the territory is largely a chronicle of the rise and fall of individual kingdoms such as those at Anuradhapura and Polunaruwa.

The island was primarily inhabited by Sinhalese, Tamils, Veddha, and descendants of Arab seafarers when the Portuguese arrived in 1505, followed by the Dutch in 1658. The king of Kandy was the last of the native rulers of the territory. In 1815, the British defeated the king and created the Crown Colony of Ceylon. In 1931, the British granted limited self-rule and a universal franchise to the colony. Ceylon became independent in 1948.

The first constitution since independence, the 1948 Soulbery Constitution, was contained in several documents and included a governor-general. The first republican constitution was promulgated in 1972. In 1978, a presidential system was established as part of the second republican constitution. This constitution was amended several times and is still in force today.

In 1983, the Tamil United Liberation Front members of parliament were asked to renounce their objective for a separate Tamil state; however, they refused. Militant Tamils, including the Liberation Tigers of Tamil Eelam (LTTE), then started armed action, which developed into a civil war.

During the 1990s, several attempts were made to create a new constitution and to resolve the ethnic conflict. In 2000, the president presented a constitutional bill to parliament. The bill was not put for vote as it was clear that it would not muster the two-thirds majority. Instead, the 1978 constitution was amended and a Constitutional Council established.

In 2002, the government and Tamil Tiger leaders agreed on an internationally monitored cease-fire. The ban on the Tamil Tigers was formally lifted and they subsequently abandoned their ambitions for a separate state, settling instead for regional autonomy.

FORM AND IMPACT OF THE CONSTITUTION

Sri Lanka has a written constitution called the Constitution of the Democratic Socialist Republic of Sri Lanka. It consists of 172 articles and nine schedules; it has been amended several times.

The constitution takes precedence over all other national law. International law must be in accordance with the constitution to be applicable within Sri Lanka. The state is obliged to "endeavor to foster respect for international law and treaty obligations in dealings among nations."

BASIC ORGANIZATIONAL STRUCTURE

Sri Lanka is a unitary state made up of nine provinces, 25 administrative districts, and territorial waters. For each province there are an elected provincial council and a governor, who is appointed by the president.

Article 157A reads: "No person shall, directly or indirectly, in or outside Sri Lanka, support, espouse, promote, finance, encourage or advocate the establishment of a separate state within the territory of Sri Lanka."

LEADING CONSTITUTIONAL PRINCIPLES

Sri Lanka's system of government is a mixed parliamentary and presidential democracy. According to the constitution, there is a division of the executive, legislative, and judicial powers. The judiciary is independent.

Sri Lanka is defined as a free, sovereign, independent, and democratic socialist republic. The constitutional bodies are "pledged" by a large number of directive principles of state policy in Chapter 6, such as the general policy to establish a democratic socialist society. This includes the "full realization" of fundamental rights and freedoms and the "complete eradication of illiteracy." The provisions of this chapter, however, do not confer rights or obligations. They are not enforceable in any court.

CONSTITUTIONAL BODIES

The predominant bodies provided for in the constitution are the president, the cabinet ministers, parliament, and the Supreme Court. A number of other bodies complete this list, such as a parliamentary ombudsperson and a Constitutional Council.

The President

Executive power is vested in the president of the republic, who is both the chief of state and the head of the executive branch of government.

The president appoints and dismisses the prime minister and the other cabinet ministers. Major public officeholders such as the attorney-general and the heads of the armed forces, are appointed by the president. However, candidates for certain commissions may only be appointed with the approval of the Constitutional Council. The president summons and prorogues (adjourns) parliament. She or he may also dissolve parliament at any time except during the first year of its term.

The president is responsible to parliament and can be impeached by the legislature. The president holds office for a term of six years and can be reelected only once.

The Cabinet of Ministers

The president as the chief executive appoints as prime minister the member of parliament most likely to have the confidence of parliament. The huge cabinet is collectively responsible and answerable to parliament. Political tensions between the powerful president and the prime minister may arise, especially if they are members of different political camps.

The Parliament

Parliament has the power to make laws, including laws amending the constitution. It consists of 225 members and is elected for a term of six years.

If parliament rejects the official statement of government policy, rejects the budget, or passes a vote of no confidence in the cabinet, the latter is dismissed by the president, who then appoints another cabinet.

The Lawmaking Process

Every bill has to be published in the official gazette before it is placed on the parliament's agenda. A bill becomes a law when the certificate of the parliament's speaker is endorsed thereon. When the cabinet submits a bill for a referendum, it becomes a law when the president has certified that it was approved by the people.

Bills judged "inconsistent with the constitution" by the Supreme Court cannot become law unless they are approved by a two-thirds majority in parliament.

The Judiciary

The judicial power is exercised through courts, tribunals, and institutions established by the constitution. There are a Supreme Court, a Court of Appeal, and a number of regional high courts and courts of the first instance. The constitution underlines the independence of the judiciary.

Constitutional jurisdiction is exercised by the Supreme Court, which enjoys limited power to review the constitutionality of bills and acts of parliament. The Supreme Court also has the sole and exclusive jurisdiction over alleged violations of fundamental rights by state actions.

The Constitutional Council

The Constitutional Council is not a body of the judiciary, but approves candidates who are recommended by the president for independent commissions on such matters as elections, police, and the public service. The council is composed of 10 people, including the prime minister, the Speaker, and the leader of the opposition in parliament. The other seven members are appointed by the president. Five of these members need to be nominated by the prime minister and the leader of the opposition. Three of these five members should be representatives of the ethnic minorities.

In practice, the council often remains dysfunctional because of the way candidates are chosen. Even if the president and the prime minister should belong to the same political camp, there may be a disagreement between the president and the leader of the opposition. One side accuses the other of uncooperativeness and the process becomes deadlocked.

THE ELECTION PROCESS AND POLITICAL PARTICIPATION

All Sri Lankans over the age of 18 have the right to vote in the elections or a referendum and to stand for elections. A referendum can be held on matters of national importance; one must be held for certain bills that amend the constitution. Elections are free, equal, and secret.

Parliamentary Elections

Voters cast their vote (1) for a party and (2) for up to three candidates listed by that party in their electoral district. This means that voters cannot vote for candidates of another party, once they have endorsed a party. The seats won by each party are distributed among their candidates according to the number of preferences they receive. Proportional representation is diluted by a constitutional provision that grants the first seat to the party that receives the largest percentage of votes in that district. It is diluted, because the party gets this "bonus" seat in addition to those gained through proportional representation. Some seats are allocated on a proportional basis from national party lists.

Presidential Elections

A presidential candidate needs to be 30 years of age. Voters cast multiple votes in order of preference. If no candidate has an absolute majority of first preferences, all candidates except the two leaders are eliminated, and second or third preferences are distributed to these candidates to ensure a majority winner.

POLITICAL PARTIES

Sri Lanka has a multiparty democracy. It enjoys considerable stability despite relatively high levels of political violence. Two major parties, the United National Party (UNP) and the Sri Lanka Freedom Party (SLFP), have generally alternated rule.

CITIZENSHIP

Sri Lankan citizenship is primarily acquired by birth; that is, a child acquires Sri Lankan citizenship if the parents are Sri Lankan citizens. If the child is born in wedlock, the father must be Sri Lankan; otherwise it is the mother who must be Sri Lankan.

FUNDAMENTAL RIGHTS

The Sri Lankan constitution guarantees a set of liberal human rights. This set does not include the right to life;

however, this right is listed in the 2000 draft constitution. The 1978 constitution also acknowledges the existence of language rights in Chapter 4.

The chapter on fundamental rights takes freedom of thought, conscience, and religion as a starting point. The general equal treatment clause is contained in Article 12, which guarantees that all persons are equal before the law. No citizen can be subject to discrimination on the grounds of race, religion, language, caste, sex, political opinion, or place of birth. In practice, caste-based factions still exist in all modern institutions, including political parties.

Social human rights are somewhat underrepresented. However, social issues are addressed in the chapter on directive principles of state policy.

Impact and Functions of Fundamental Rights

The preamble promises "freedom, equality, justice, [and] fundamental human rights" to everybody. The constitution primarily entrusts the Supreme Court with the legal protection of fundamental rights. The Supreme Court has at times used international treaties as interpretive guides when there was ambiguity in statutory or constitutional provisions. For example, in the case of *Mrs. W. M. K. de Silva v. Chairman, Ceylon Fertilizer Corporation* (1989), the court referred to the definition of *torture* as adopted by the General Assembly of the United Nations in Resolution 3452 (XXX) of December 9, 1975, to assist in the interpretation of Article 11 of the Sri Lankan constitution, which prohibits torture.

Other mechanisms aim at strengthening fundamental rights such as a parliamentary ombudsperson. However, human rights violations by public authorities continue to be reported.

Limitations to Fundamental Rights

There are a variety of limitation clauses in Article 15. Besides the common restrictions in the interests of "public order" or "respect for the rights and freedoms of others," some rights may also be restricted in the interests of "national security," "racial and religious harmony," or "national economy."

ECONOMY

Some of the directive principles of state policy address economic issues. According to the constitution, the democratic socialist state pursues an economic system that does not result in the concentration of wealth, but in social security and welfare. In practice, Sri Lanka has abandoned socialist economic policies in exchange for market-oriented ones. Taken as a whole, the Sri Lankan economic system can be described as a social market economy.

RELIGIOUS COMMUNITIES

Although the constitution accords Buddhism the "foremost place," it is not recognized as the state religion. Every person is entitled to freedom of thought, conscience, and religion, and this right is generally respected in practice.

MILITARY DEFENSE AND STATE OF EMERGENCY

Recruitment to the ministry is solely on a voluntary basis and the minimal age for entry into the armed forces is 18 years.

Article 155 empowers the president of the republic to make emergency regulations under the Public Security Ordinance or under any other law relating to public security in force at the time. Such regulations may override all existing law except provisions of the constitution. The constitution provides for parliamentary monitoring of emergency powers. A proclamation of emergency would lapse after a period of 14 days unless approved by parliament. Sri Lanka has declared numerous states of emergency since its independence.

AMENDMENTS TO THE CONSTITUTION

An amendment bill needs to fulfill a number of formal requirements. The constitution can only be amended if two-thirds of all the members of parliament vote in favor of the change.

Some fundamental provisions, such as those regulating the president's and the parliament's term of office, require a popular referendum. The same applies to the very first chapters of the constitution ("The people, the state and sovereignty" and "Buddhism"), some fundamental rights (freedom of thought, conscience, and religion and freedom from torture), and the provision on amendments itself.

PRIMARY SOURCES

1978 Revised Constitution in English. Available online. URL: http://www.priu.gov.lk/Cons/1978Constitution/ CONTENTS.html. Accessed on June 28, 2006.

1978 Constitution in English (as amended in 2000): *Constitution of the Democratic Socialist Republic of Sri Lanka.* Colombo: Policy Research & Information Unit of the Presidential Secretariat, 2000.

2000 Draft Constitution: *An Act to Repeal and Replace the Constitution of the Socialist Republic of Sri Lanka (Bill No. 372).* Available online. URL: http:// www.priu.gov.lk/Cons/2000ConstitutionBill/ Index2000ConstitutionBill.html. Accessed on August 31, 2005.

SECONDARY SOURCES

Rohan Edrisinha, *Meeting Tamil Aspirations within a United Sri Lanka: Constitutional Options*. Sri Lanka: Centre for Policy Alternatives, 2001. Available online. URL: http://www.cpalanka.org. Accessed on August 12, 2005.

Wilhelm Geiger, *Mahavamsa: Great Chronicle of Ceylon*. New Delhi: Asian Educational Services, 1996.

Golden Jubilee of Sri Lanka Independence—50 Years of Parliament. Colombo: Parliament Secretariat Publication, 1998.

Rajendra Kalidan Wimala Goonesekere, *Fundamental Rights and the Constitution. A Casebook*. Colombo: Law and Society Trust, 1988.

Russell R. Ross and Andrea Matles Savada, *Sri Lanka—a Country Study*. Washington, D.C.: Library of Congress, 1988. Available online. URL: http://lcweb2.loc.gov/frd/cs/cshome.html. Accessed on July 22, 2005.

Jayampathy Wickremaratne, *Fundamental Rights in Sri Lanka*. New Delhi: Arnold, 1996.

Alfred Jeyaratnam Wilson, *The Gaullist System in Asia: The Constitution of Sri Lanka, 1978*. London: Macmillan, 1980.

Michael Rahe

SUDAN

At-a-Glance

OFFICIAL NAME
Republic of the Sudan

CAPITAL
Khartoum

POPULATION
39,148,162 (July 2004 est.)

SIZE
967,499 sq. mi. (2,505,810 sq. km)

LANGUAGES
Arabic (official), Nubian, Ta Bedawie, diverse Nilotic dialects, Nilo-Hamitic, Sudanic languages, English

RELIGIONS
Sunni Muslim 70% (in north), indigenous beliefs 25%, Christian 5% (mostly in south and Khartoum)

NATIONAL OR ETHNIC COMPOSITION
Black 52%, Arab 39%, Beja 6%, foreigners 2%, other 1%

DATE OF INDEPENDENCE OR CREATION
January 1, 1956

TYPE OF GOVERNMENT
Authoritarian regime, military junta in power from 1989

TYPE OF STATE
Federal state

TYPE OF LEGISLATURE
Unicameral parliament

DATE OF CONSTITUTION
Current constitution in force July 1, 1998; partially suspended December 12, 1999, by President Bashir

DATE OF LAST AMENDMENT
No amendment

Sudan is ruled by an authoritarian regime. A military junta took power in 1989; the current government is an alliance between the military and the National Congress Party (NCP) (formerly the National Islamic Front [NIF]). The constitution of Sudan proclaims it a federal state—it is in fact divided into 26 states—but the central government is very strong.

The constitution declares Islam to be the religion of the majority of Sudanese, and Islamic law (sharia) is recognized and enforced, but religious freedom is proclaimed nonetheless. The constitution provides for protection of human rights, but there are widespread human rights violations, as reported by international human rights groups, and public authorities do not always respect constitutional provisions. In theory, the courts are independent, but in reality there is executive interference in the judiciary.

The powers, duties, and terms of office of the president are defined in the constitution. The current president, Lieutenant General Umar Hassan Ahmad al Bashir, is the central political figure in Sudan. The constitution allows for formation of political parties, but the country has never had a free and fair election.

The constitution allows for a free-market economy. The military is under the command of the president.

CONSTITUTIONAL HISTORY

Sudan gained independence from Britain in 1956 under a provisional constitution, which paid little attention to the rights of the individual. Attempts were made to achieve a permanent constitution in the late 1950s, but these failed.

In 1964, the transitional constitution was reenacted with a few changes. In 1967, a Constituent Assembly attempted to draft a new constitution based on Islam, until Jaafar Mohamed Nimeiri seized power and issued a new constitution providing for a one-party state in 1969; this constitution provided for a few civil liberties.

After Nimeiri gained power, there was a move toward adoption of sharia. Nimeiri was overthrown in 1985 and the transitional government that took over adopted the

1964 constitution but did not make provision that it was the highest law in the country. A constituent assembly was established, and a multiparty system was established. Then, in 1989, a military coup d'etat put General al Bashir in office, where he has remained for over 15 years.

A national commission was formed in 1997 but was boycotted by some parties who were of the view that the government was undemocratic and a constitution would not be of much use. The national commission drafted a constitution that was adopted through a questionable referendum in 1998.

From the time of independence there has been tension between the Muslim, mainly Arab, north and the Christian and animist south, which is mainly black. This tension led to brutal wars between 1955 and 1972 and again since 1983; the death toll has been estimated at 1–3 million. Numerous attempts are being made to end this long-running conflict.

FORM AND IMPACT OF THE CONSTITUTION

Sudan has a written constitution that was adopted in 1998. The constitution sets out 18 guiding principles of the state. These principles are meant to guide state officials and lawmakers in performing their duties. The principles also address human rights. They are designed to shape the course of public life. The constitution guarantees judicial independence and separation of powers. Unfortunately, many of these principles have not been implemented in practice, and the constitution remains an ideal rather than a reality.

BASIC ORGANIZATIONAL STRUCTURE

Sudan is composed of 26 states known as *wilayat*. They differ in geographic size and population. All *wilayat* have identical legislative, administrative, and judicial powers, and each has its own state assembly. These assemblies have similar powers to those of the National Assembly, except that they may not ratify international agreements or treaties or make constitutional amendments. Members of the state assemblies are elected to office by procedures similar to those used in the election of National Assembly members; if the situation in a particular region of a *wilayat* precludes holding an election, the governor of the *wilayat* in question appoints a representative for that region.

LEADING CONSTITUTIONAL PRINCIPLES

The constitution of Sudan provides for a presidential system of government. There is a separation of powers of the executive, legislature, and judiciary.

The constitution has set out 18 principles that are to direct institutions and employees of government in the execution of their duties. These include that Sudan is a federal state, that God is supreme, that the country has a free-market economy, that all natural resources are public property, and that Islam is the religion of the majority and thus Muslims in public life should worship God and observe the Quran. Religion is therefore supposed to affect all the workings of government, including planning, laws, policies, politics, economics, and social and cultural activities.

CONSTITUTIONAL BODIES

The main constitutional bodies are the president, Council of Ministers, federal legislature (National Assembly), state legislature (state assemblies), and the judiciary, which has a Constitutional Court.

The President

The president is the highest sovereign authority of Sudan. The president is responsible for the armed forces; ensures the country's security; supervises foreign relations, the judiciary, and constitutional institutions; and mobilizes the country for development. The president is also responsible for appointing personnel in the federal offices created by the constitution. The president presides over the Council of Ministers, declares war, initiates amendments to the constitution, and represents Sudan in foreign relations. The president is elected for a five-year term by popular vote and can be reelected only once.

The Council of Ministers (Federal Administration)

The federal administration is formed under supervision of the president, who appoints the ministers. The ministers form the Council of Ministers, the highest federal authority in Sudan, whose decisions prevail over all other executive decisions. The president is the dominant figure in Sudan.

The National Assembly (Parliament)

The National Assembly is the representative body for the Sudanese people at the federal level. It is the legislative organ. Among other powers, it is supposed to represent the popular will in legislation, planning, and supervision of the executive. Its period of office is four years.

Seventy-five percent of the members of the National Assembly are supposed to be elected in direct general elections. The remaining 25 percent are elected in special or indirect elections by women and scientific and professional communities. If elections cannot be held in a particular region, then the president of Sudan can appoint a person to represent the region in question.

The State Assemblies

Every *wilayat* has a state assembly, wielding its legislative authority. The state assemblies have similar powers to those of the National Assembly, except that they may not ratify international agreements or treaties or make constitutional amendments. Members of the state assemblies are elected to office by the same procedures used to elect the National Assembly. If elections cannot be held in a region, the governor of the *wilayat* appoints the representative of that region.

The Lawmaking Process

One of the chief duties of the National Assembly is to pass legislation. The sources of the legislation are supposed to be sharia law, the constitution, and custom, which must all be taken into consideration when enacting any law. The lawmakers must also take into consideration public opinion and the work of scientists, intellectuals, and leaders.

Legislation may be initiated by the president, Council of Ministers, an individual minister, or an individual member of the National Assembly. Generally a bill has to go through four readings to be adopted. During this process amendments can be made, and the bill can be referred to specialized committees. Bills must be signed by the president to become law. If the president refuses, the National Assembly can override these objections by a two-thirds majority.

The Judiciary

The judiciary is in theory independent from the other arms of government, but in reality the executive exercises control. The judiciary is vested in a Judicial Authority. This body is supposed to undertake the administration of justice through adjudicating disputes and giving judgments in accordance with the constitution and the law. The Judicial Authority has a chief justice, who is the president of the highest federal court and of the Supreme Judicial Council. There are a high court, courts of appeal, and courts of first instance. The president of Sudan appoints the chief justice.

The highest court in Sudan is the Constitutional Court; it is independent of other courts. The chief justice and other judges of the Constitutional Court are appointed by the president and approved by the National Assembly. The court has power to review and rule on any matter concerning the execution of the constitution. It can interpret the constitution or other legal texts presented by the president. It can deal with cases involving protection of rights and with conflicts between state and federal authorities over their respective powers.

THE ELECTION PROCESS

The constitution provides for the establishment of an election commission to conduct both elections and referendums. The constitution does not specifically state the age at which Sudanese citizens become eligible voters.

POLITICAL PARTIES

The constitution of Sudan provides for the right of individuals to organize political activity, but it has no specific provision on the formation or the role of political parties.

CITIZENSHIP

Sudanese nationality is acquired by birth. Anyone born of a Sudanese mother or father has the inalienable right to Sudanese nationality. Also, anyone who has lived in Sudan during his or her youth has a right to Sudanese citizenship. The constitution has a vague provision that states that anyone who has lived in Sudan for several years has the right to Sudanese citizenship.

FUNDAMENTAL RIGHTS

Chapter 1 of the constitution sets out the rights of the individual; Chapter 2 sets out the responsibilities of the individual. The constitution guarantees a number of human rights that are internationally recognized.

Some of the rights that are protected under the constitution are the rights to life, liberty, equality, nationality, freedom of movement, freedom of religion and conscience, freedom of opinion and expression, freedom of association, right to property, and security of person. Any individual whose rights are violated and who has exhausted executive and administrative remedies may appeal to the Constitutional Court for protection. The Constitutional Court can annul any law or order that contravenes the constitution and order that the victim be compensated for the damage suffered.

The responsibilities of the citizens include the duty to be loyal to Sudan, defend the country, respect the constitution, protect public funds and property, and participate in economic activities and public development. These duties are general obligations governed by conscience, but in certain defined cases there can be penalties for noncompliance.

Impact and Functions of Fundamental Rights

Even though the constitution has set out fundamental human rights, the Sudanese authorities have often been accused of violating many of them, sometimes on a large scale.

Limitations to Fundamental Rights

Some of the fundamental rights stipulated in the constitution have limitations. For instance, the right to liberty and life has to be in accordance with the law. The right to life is further limited by allowing for the imposition of the death penalty. The right to religion and conscience has to be exercised in a manner that does not harm public order and must be carried out in accordance with the law. The freedoms of opinion, expression, and association have to be exercised in accordance with the law.

ECONOMY

One of the directive principles of the Sudanese constitution provides that the state should direct the growth of the national economy. This is to be accomplished by planning, taking into account labor, production, and the free exchange of goods. Monopoly and usury must be prevented, and self-sufficiency must be among the goals. Another directive principle provides that all natural resources are public property, and that the state must make plans to ensure the exploitation of these resources. The constitution provides for the right to property.

RELIGIOUS COMMUNITIES

The constitution of Sudan provides for religious freedom by stating that everyone has the right to freedom of religion and the right to manifest and disseminate his or her religion or belief in teaching, practice, and observance. However, the constitution gives greater weight to the Islamic faith. For instance, one of the directive principles states that supremacy in the state is to God, that sovereignty is practiced as worship to God. There is, therefore, no separation of religion from the state. Another directive principle states that those working in public life should worship God, and that Muslims in service in the state and public life should observe the Quran and the teachings of the Prophet Muhammad.

MILITARY DEFENSE AND STATE OF EMERGENCY

The Peoples' Armed Forces is the national military force. The constitution stipulates that its duty is to defend the country, preserve safety, participate in development, and guard the national interests and constitutional order. The constitution provides for what it terms the security forces, whose responsibility is to maintain peace in Sudan both internally and externally.

The constitution further provides for a popular defense force or volunteer force for the purposes of national defense. The popular defense force is under the command of the national armed forces or the police and promotes defense and security.

The president is responsible for all the armed forces and has to ensure the country's security.

The president can declare a state of emergency in the whole country or part of the country. Such a declaration has to be presented to the National Assembly within 15 days for approval. During a state of emergency, the president can suspend some individual rights. The president can also suspend the laws and powers of the *wilayat*. The president must submit all such exceptional measures to the National Assembly for approval; the assembly may amend, approve, or cancel them.

AMENDMENTS TO THE CONSTITUTION

The president or one-third of the National Assembly can propose amendments to the constitution. An amendment has to be approved by a two-thirds majority of members of the National Assembly. Certain amendments can only be made through a referendum—those that impact basic principles, including those that relate to sharia and freedom of conscience and religion and the principles that Sudan is a federal unitary government, that Sudan has a presidential system of government, that legislative authority is vested in the National Assembly, that the judiciary is independent, and that southern Sudan is governed by a transitional government. If an amendment affects any of these principles, it can only be adopted through a referendum approved by the majority of the voting population.

PRIMARY SOURCES
Constitution in English. Available online. URL: http://www.sudan.net/government/constitution/english.html. Accessed on September 11, 2005.
Constitution in Arabic. Available online. URL: http://www.pogar.org/countries/sudan/constitution.html. Accessed on August 27, 2005.

SECONDARY SOURCES
S. H. Amin, *Middle East Legal Systems*. Glasgow: Royston, 1985.
Ilias Bantekas and Hassan Abu-Sabeib, "Reconciliation of Islamic Law with Constitutionalism: The Protection of Human Rights in Sudan's New Constitution." *African Journal of International and Comparative Law* 12 (2000): 531–553.
Carolyn Fluehr-Lobban, *Islamic Law and Society in the Sudan*. London: Taylor & Francis, 1986.
Kenneth R. Redden, "Sudan." In *Modern Legal Systems Cyclopedia*. Vol. 6. Buffalo, N.Y.: William S. Hein, 1990.
"Sudan." Available online. URL: http://www.redress.org/studies/Sudan.pdf. Accessed on July 24, 2005.
"Sudan—a Country Study." Available online. URL: http://lcweb2.loc.gov/frd/cs/sdtoc.html. Accessed on July 23, 2005.
United Nations, "Core Document Forming Part of the Reports of States Parties: Sudan" (HRI/CORE/1/Add.99/Rev.1), 10 November 1999. Available online. URL: http://www.unhchr.ch/tbs/doc.nsf. Accessed on July 26, 2005.

Martin Nsibirwa

SURINAME

OFFICIAL NAME
The Republic of Suriname

CAPITAL
Paramaribo

POPULATION
436,935 (2005 est.)

SIZE
62,865 sq. mi. (162,820 sq. km)

LANGUAGES
Dutch (official language), Sranang Tongo (lingua franca), various other languages spoken

RELIGIONS
Hindu 27.4%, Muslim 19.6%, Roman Catholic 22.8%, Protestant 25.2%, indigenous beliefs 5%

NATIONAL OR ETHNIC COMPOSITION
Hindustani 37%, Creole 31%, Javanese 15%, Maroons 10%, Amerindian 2%, Chinese 2%, white 1%, other 2%

DATE OF INDEPENDENCE OR CREATION
November 25, 1975

TYPE OF GOVERNMENT
Constitutional democracy

TYPE OF STATE
Centralist state divided into 10 administrative districts

TYPE OF LEGISLATURE
Unicameral parliament

DATE OF CONSTITUTION
October 30, 1987

DATE OF LAST AMENDMENT
1992

A former Dutch colony, the independent Republic of Suriname has been transformed from a military dictatorship to a constitutional democracy based on the rule of law. Its constitution provides for a division of executive, legislative, and judicial powers.

The Republic of Suriname is a democratic state based on a governmental model comprising both parliamentary and presidential elements. The constitution, based on the principle of participatory democracy, enshrines fundamental civil and political rights as well as economic, social, and cultural rights, such as freedom of expression, freedom of assembly, freedom of religion, the right to work, and the right to education.

the legitimately elected government. In response to continuing pressure due to economic decline and mounting insurgencies, the military government organized free elections and drafted a new constitution. After public approval by plebiscite, the constitution entered into force on September 30, 1987.

After a second coup d'état, leading to another brief period of military rule between December 24, 1990, and May 25, 1991, the constitution was amended in 1992 to eradicate the military's powers to interfere with governmental authority, confining the armed forces to the protection of territorial integrity and thereby reducing threats of another coup d'état.

CONSTITUTIONAL HISTORY

After riots over unemployment and inflation, Suriname reached independence in 1975. Its first constitution was suspended on August 13, 1980, after a coup d'état removed

FORM AND IMPACT OF THE CONSTITUTION

The constitution of the Republic of Suriname is codified in a single document, constituting the primary source of law and taking precedence over all other national law. International law provisions governing relations between individuals are directly effective in Suriname; any other international legal provisions become effective only upon approval by the National Assembly. Once effective, international law takes precedence over domestic law, rendering any national legislation incompatible with it null and void.

BASIC ORGANIZATIONAL STRUCTURE

The Republic of Suriname is a centralist state, organized as a constitutional democracy. It consists of 10 administrative districts, each made up of several departments and headed by a district commissioner. A certain level of decentralization grants administrative and legislative powers to lower government bodies at those regional levels.

LEADING CONSTITUTIONAL PRINCIPLES

The system of government of Suriname is based on the principles of a democratic state, the participation of the people, respect for fundamental rights and freedoms, and self-determination of all peoples. The stated aims of any governmental activity are a just society, a national economy free of foreign intervention, national unity, and sovereignty.

CONSTITUTIONAL BODIES

The main constitutional bodies provided for in the constitution are the president and Council of State, the Council of Ministers, the National Assembly and People's Assembly, regional government bodies, and the Constitutional Court.

The President

The executive power is vested in the president, who simultaneously serves as head of state, head of the executive, and chair of both the Council of State and the Security Council. The National Assembly elects the president with a two-thirds majority for a period of five years.

The president's powers include the appointment of cabinet ministers, the development of foreign and national policy, direction of the Council of State's activities, and convocation and chairing of the Council of Ministers. The president is also the commander in chief of the armed forces. Unless the president resigns, he or she cannot be removed from office.

The Council of State, the composition and powers of which are regulated by law, advises the president. It acts as a constitutional watchdog, by guiding the government on proposed measures, suspending Council of Minister decrees incompatible with the constitution, and supervising the government's execution of National Assembly decisions.

The Administration

The president, together with the vice president and the Council of Ministers, forms the administration of Suriname. The administration determines all policies of the executive, draws up legislation, and is answerable to the National Assembly. The Council of Ministers, consisting of all cabinet ministers and deputy ministers, is the highest executive and administrative body of the government. It is primarily responsible for the execution of administration policies, as well as the drafting of laws and regulations.

The National Assembly

The National Assembly is the central representative organ of the people of Suriname. It consists of 51 members elected by a system of proportional representation for a term of five years. To prevent favoritism, members of the National Assembly may be neither related, up to the second degree, nor legally married to one another. Apart from its legislative powers, jointly exercised with the executive branch of government, the National Assembly must approve the administration's general socioeconomic and political program. It helps safeguard the constitution by supervising the work of the executive branch of the government. A People's Assembly, consisting of 869 local and district officials, as well as parliamentarians, may convene in certain cases specified by the constitution.

Regional Administration

The regional administration consists of district and department councils as well as a district commissioner. Their primary tasks include the preparation, creation, and execution of district and departmental development plans, as well as drafting of district laws and regulations.

The Lawmaking Process

Upon presentation of a draft bill by the executive branch of government, the National Assembly examines and publicly debates the draft. It may either pass it unchanged, amend it, or veto it. In any event, it is required to inform the president of its decision. Until the National Assembly reaches a decision, the president may withdraw the bill.

The constitution specifies certain subjects that are reserved to determination by law, such as constitutional amendments, declaration or termination of war and state of emergency, creation of a development council for national development, and determination of Suriname's territorial waters, continental shelf, and exclusive economic zone.

The Judiciary

Full independence of the judiciary is guaranteed by prohibition of any interference with court proceedings. There are two levels of jurisprudence, comprising the subdistrict court or cantonal court as the court of first instance and the High Court of Justice as an appeals court for all branches of the judiciary. While the constitution also envisages the creation of a constitutional court to deal exclusively with constitutional matters, it has not yet been established.

THE ELECTION PROCESS

The right to vote is granted to those who are above the age of 18 and hold Surinamese citizenship, unless their right to vote has been forfeited by virtue of lawful detention, insanity, or irrevocable judicial decision. The right to stand for office is granted to all Surinamese citizens who have reached the age of 21 and have not been deprived of their right to vote. All elections are held by secret ballot.

POLITICAL PARTIES

Since the end of military rule, Suriname has turned to a pluralistic system of political parties. The constitutionally guaranteed right to establish political parties is restricted only by constitutional requirements of transparency, internal democratic organization and compatibility with constitutional goals, national sovereignty, and democracy in general. Reflecting Suriname's diverse ethnic makeup, most political parties are defined along ethnic lines.

CITIZENSHIP

The constitution does not regulate Surinamese citizenship, leaving this area to be prescribed by law.

FUNDAMENTAL RIGHTS

Inspired by the Universal Declaration of Human Rights, the Constitution of the Republic of Suriname guarantees a wide range of civil and political as well as social, economic, and cultural rights, based on the overarching principle of equality and nondiscrimination. Civil and political rights include the right to life and liberty, freedom from torture and forced labor, the right to private and family life, the right to effective legal remedies, and freedom of religion, expression, political opinion, association, and assembly. Social, economic, and cultural rights include the right to work, labor and trade union rights, and the right to health, property, education and training, as well as the enjoyment of culture.

Impact and Functions of Fundamental Rights

The fundamental rights guaranteed in the constitution may be invoked in domestic courts in legal disputes governing the relationship between an individual and the government. They are supplemented by the direct application of the rights stated in the United Nations International Covenant on Civil and Political Rights (ICCPR), which takes precedence over domestic law and may be directly invoked before domestic courts. Unfortunately, respect for the fundamental rights of indigenous peoples and Maroons (descendants of slaves who freed themselves and founded well-organized communities in the 18th century) remains sporadic in practice, particularly with regard to land and property rights, nondiscrimination, and health, educational, and cultural rights.

Limitations to Fundamental Rights

Constitutionally guaranteed rights and freedoms may be restricted in the event of war, threat of war, state of siege, or state of emergency, or for reasons of state security, public order, and morality. However, a suspension of rights may only occur for a specified period and must be in compliance with international legal requirements, such as the principle of nonderogation from certain human rights as enshrined in the ICCPR (Article 4).

ECONOMY

The constitution lays out aspects of the Republic of Suriname's economic order, by prescribing a development plan to promote socioeconomic progress toward a just society. The government aims at shaping a national economy free of foreign intervention.

RELIGIOUS COMMUNITIES

The Constitution of the Republic of Suriname guarantees both freedom of religion and the right to association and assembly, thereby granting the full and free exercise of all faiths. The main religious groups—Christians, Hindus, and Muslims—freely and independently practice their religion in their respective places of worship. Despite constitutional references to the power of the Almighty, religion is clearly separated from the state and there is no recognized state religion.

MILITARY DEFENSE AND STATE OF EMERGENCY

The present constitution awards the military only one role: that of protecting national sovereignty and independence, as well as the rights and freedoms of its nationals. With the president as commander in chief, all military activities are governed by the rule of law.

Military service is obligatory for all male nationals of Suriname. However, in cases of physical disability or conscientious objection, military service may be replaced with civil service. No one enrolled in the service of the armed forces may hold office in government or any other public service.

Although the power both to declare and to end a state of emergency is vested in the president, it is subject to the consent of the National Assembly and limited to reasons provided for by law, such as the event or threat of war. During a state of emergency, the National Assembly may convoke the Security Council, consisting of the president, the chair of the National Assembly, the vice president, representatives of the Council of Ministers, the minister of justice, the armed forces, and the Suriname police corps. The Security Council is equipped with special powers to defend Suriname's external and domestic security.

AMENDMENTS TO THE CONSTITUTION

The power to amend the constitution is vested in the National Assembly, which may amend any provision of the constitution by passing a law containing the desired amendment by a majority vote of at least two-thirds of its members. Should this not be reached, the National Assembly may convene the People's Assembly to resolve the issue.

PRIMARY SOURCES

Constitution in English. Available online. URL: http://www.georgetown.edu/pdba/Constitutions/Suriname/english.html. Accessed on August 2, 2005.

SECONDARY SOURCES

Noelle Beatty, "Suriname." In *Overview of Culture, History, Economy and People*. Philadelphia: Chelsea House, 1997.

Concluding Observations of the Human Rights Committee: Suriname. 04/05/2004. CCPR/CO/80/SUR.

Ellen-Rose Kambel and Fergus MacKay, *The Rights of Indigenous Peoples and Maroons in Suriname*, International Work Group for Indigenous Affairs (IWGIA) Document No. 96. IWGIA: Copenhagen, 1999.

B. Sedoc-Dahlberg, ed., *The Dutch Caribbean: Old and New Connections, Economic and Political Conditions of the Netherlands Antilles, including Suriname and Aruba*. Amsterdam: Gordon & Breach, 1990.

Johanna Nelles

SWAZILAND

At-a-Glance

OFFICIAL NAME
Kingdom of Swaziland

CAPITAL
Mbabane

POPULATION
1,173,900 (2005 est.)

SIZE
6,704 sq. mi. (17,364 sq. km)

LANGUAGES
English and Siswati

RELIGIONS
Christian-African religion 100%

NATIONAL OR ETHNIC COMPOSITION
Swazi 100%

DATE OF INDEPENDENCE OR CREATION
September 6, 1968

TYPE OF GOVERNMENT
Parliamentary system

TYPE OF STATE
Unitary state

TYPE OF LEGISLATURE
Bicameral parliament

DATE OF CONSTITUTION
February 8, 2006

DATE OF LAST AMENDMENT
No amendment

Swaziland is a landlocked country that shares borders with Mozambique (105 km) and South Africa (430 km). It was founded by Bantu peoples from Mozambique in the 18th century and became a British protectorate when colonial rule was established in 1903. Swaziland was led to independence by Sobhuza II in 1968 and is now a dual monarchy with a king (King Mswati III since April 25, 1986) and queen mother.

The Kingdom of Swaziland operates under a parliamentary system lacking in respect for the rule of law and without a clear separation of the three arms of government: the executive, legislature, and judiciary. The kingdom is subdivided into four administrative regions with a strong central government.

Immediately after independence and operating under the Independence Westminster Constitution, Swaziland enjoyed a substantial degree of separation of powers, but this constitution was repealed on April 12, 1973, by King Sobhuza II.

King Mswati III is currently the head of state and a central political and traditional figure. The prime minister is the administrative head of the executive arm and is directly appointed by the king from among members of the dominant Dlamini clan, which forms the backbone of the monarchy. Members of Parliament are elected directly from constituencies into Parliament in what is called "election based on individual merit." Multiparty democracy is not allowed, and political parties remain banned since the repeal of the Independence Constitution in 1973.

Fundamental rights and freedoms are, in fact, not protected or guaranteed, and free political activity, including the right to associate and assemble peacefully, is not permitted. Leaders and members of opposition political organizations are constantly harassed, and political gatherings, rallies, demonstrations, and marches are forcefully dispersed by violent police and army personnel.

The judiciary lacks independence. Judges are appointed by the king on the advice of a Judicial Service Commission dominated by the king's appointees. Nevertheless, the judiciary has been under constant attack from the executive, which has refused to comply with and implement some of the judgments it has considered unfavorable.

The refusal to implement court judgments has led some members of the nation to flee into the Republic of South Africa. It is yet to be seen whether the damage done to the judicial system will be repaired.

CONSTITUTIONAL HISTORY

The Kingdom of Swaziland is a former British colony. On September 6, 1968, the kingdom gained independence through the Independence Constitution, and it became a sovereign state governed in accordance with the written constitution.

The Westminster-type constitution established a Parliament, executive, and judiciary. It created the office of the king as head of state. It provided in Chapter 2 for the protection of fundamental rights and individual freedoms, which included the right to life, personal liberty, protection from slavery and forced labor, protection from inhuman treatment, protection from deprivation of property, protection against arbitrary search or entry, freedom of conscience, freedom of expression, freedom of assembly and association, freedom of movement, and protection from discrimination. The Bill of Rights also provided for derogation and enforcement mechanisms.

The kingdom held three general elections. The 1964, 1967, and 1972 elections all were conducted under a multiparty electoral system.

It was the 1972 elections that turned the course of history when members of the opposition Ngwane National Liberatory Congress won parliamentary seats. This was the first time that there would be official opposition inside Parliament, because the opposition had not been victorious in previous elections.

After this development, the constitution was repealed on the questionable contention that it had caused growing unrest, insecurity, and dissatisfaction in the kingdom and that it had permitted the importation of undesirable political practices alien to, and incompatible with, the way of life of the Swazi nation.

Since that day, Swaziland has been without a comprehensive constitution save for the remnants that were retained, which did not include the Bill of Rights. The king has remained the absolute ruler, and proponents of democracy have been subjected to oppression and harassment.

Since the repeal of the Independence Constitution, there has been continuous agitation for constitutional reform. The establishment of the Tinkhundla Review Commission (TRC), Constitutional Review Commission, as well as the Constitution Drafting Committee (CDC) was not widely accepted, as the king himself chose all the members. Its mandate did not allow the participation of organized groups. At the end of the commission's term, the king appointed yet another body, called the Constitution Drafting Committee, which he mandated to draft a constitution suitable for Swaziland. This committee in May 2004 presented to the king a draft constitution, which was ratified by the king on July 26, 2005, and went into effect in 2006.

There is widespread doubt that it will resolve the country's constitutional and good governance problems.

FORM AND IMPACT OF THE CONSTITUTIONAL ARRANGEMENT

On July 26, 2005, Swaziland adopted a comprehensive constitution, or basic law. However, the document does not enjoy popular support and legitimacy across the spectrum of the Swazi society because of the manner in which it was done and the hostile political environment prevailing. Organized civil society groupings including political parties have disowned the constitution, contending that it does not reflect the true and genuine will and aspirations of the people. They continue to call and demand for the drawing of a constitution based on free and popular consensus. International law is not part of national law unless enacted by Parliament. Although Swaziland is a member state of the African Union and has ratified the major international and regional human rights instruments, such as the Universal Declaration of Human Rights, the African Charter on Human and Peoples' Rights, the International Covenant on Civil and Political Rights, and the International Covenant on Economic, Social and Cultural Rights, very little, if anything, has been done to comply with the standards set by these instruments.

BASIC ORGANIZATIONAL STRUCTURE

The kingdom is a unitary state divided into four administrative regions, which do not enjoy legislative and judicial competencies. The four regions correspond to Swaziland's geographic regions, which vary from 400 to 1,800 meters above sea level, each with its own climate and characteristics, which vary from tropical to near-temperate. The regions are part of the general governance with very limited autonomy since they are under the supervision of the central government. The central government is itself two-pronged. Traditional government bodies in Lobamba exercise more power than the conventional government in Mbabane.

As provided in the 1973 King's Proclamation and in the new constitution, all executive, legislative, and judicial power vests in the king. This position was reinstated by the 1992 Establishment of Parliament Order, which currently forms the basis for the creation of government but does not in any way depart from the provisions of the proclamation, as well as the new constitution, which five months from the day of adoption provides the fundamental law of the land.

CONSTITUTIONAL BODIES

In terms of the powers his majesty derives for himself under the King's Proclamation, powers that are not interfered with under the new constitution, he can appoint, in consultation with his appointed prime minister, the cabinet, 20 senators, and 10 members of the House of Assembly. The others are elected directly into Parliament on the basis of "individual merit," which excludes the participation of political groupings. On the advice of the Judicial Service Commission, the king appoints judges. He also appoints his advisers in the form of the King's Advisory Council and members of other bodies that perform constitutional functions.

The King's Advisory Council

The King's Advisory Council has the authority to advise the king on all matters. All of its members are appointed by the king, mostly from among princes, princesses, chiefs, and other Swazi citizens. It does not accommodate dissenting voices and is not amenable to criticism. It also is not transparent. It is based at the traditional capital, Lobamba. In most matters it is in conflict with the government, based in Mbabane.

The Lawmaking Process

Lawmaking power vests in the king and Parliament. Until 2000, when the Court of Appeal held that the king had no power to make law by decree, his majesty could adopt laws overriding even the laws adopted by Parliament, because a decree was superior to an act of Parliament.

Once parliament passes a bill, it is referred to the king for his assent, which he may withhold and refer the bill back to Parliament. The king can dissolve Parliament. This constitutional arrangement is not changed by the new constitution.

The Judiciary

The judiciary has become weak because of interference by the executive. The judiciary is made up of the magistracy, the High Court, and the Court of Appeal, which is the highest court. Judges are appointed by the king on the advice of the Judicial Service Commission, which is dominated by the king's appointees. In recent years, particularly from 2000 onward, judges have been subjected to harassment and intimidation; two High Court judges had to resign. The 2003 legal year operated without a Court of Appeal after many judges resigned in protest of the government's refusal to obey court judgments.

The new constitution also sets up a Human Rights Commission, a Public Administration Commission, and an Integrity Commission, which did not exist before. The powers of the Human Rights Commission are very limited when it comes to the exercise of power by the Crown.

THE ELECTION PROCESS

Swaziland has a political system based on Tinkhundla, a concept introduced by King Sobhuza II in 1978.

This system does not allow political activity or political parties. Elections are based on a concept of "individual merit." According to this system, an individual is elected into Parliament on the basis of his or her merit, without belonging to a political group but representing a constituency. All citizens over the age of 18 are entitled to vote.

POLITICAL PARTIES

There are no legal political parties in Swaziland. Even under the recently adopted constitution they remain banned.

CITIZENSHIP

Swazi citizenship is acquired by birth or registration. A child who has a Swazi father is a Swazi citizen, but the same is not true if only the mother is a Swazi citizen. The 2005 constitution creates a Citizenship Board and empowers it exclusively to decide questions of disputed nationality, thus limiting the jurisdiction of the courts in such matters.

FUNDAMENTAL RIGHTS AND FREEDOMS

Currently, fundamental rights and freedoms are not protected in fact. The new constitution, however, makes an attempt to provide for them, albeit in a limited way.

ECONOMY

Economic policies are drafted from time to time when a "new" government gains power or upon the renewal of a previous one. Generally, the country has a free-market economy.

The economy is based on subsistence agriculture, which occupies more than 60 percent of the population and contributes nearly 25 percent to the gross domestic product (GDP). Manufacturing accounts for another quarter of the GDP. Mining has declined in importance in recent years; high-grade iron ore deposits were depleted in 1978, and health concerns cut world demand for asbestos. Exports of sugar and forestry products are the main earners of hard currency. The country is heavily dependent on South Africa, from which it receives 90 percent of its imports and to which it sends about half of its exports.

RELIGIOUS COMMUNITIES

There are formal constitutional provisions for freedom of religion; the government generally respects it in practice.

MILITARY DEFENSE AND STATE OF EMERGENCY

The creation and maintenance of the armed forces are the responsibility of the government through the king, who is commander in chief. Recently, there has been a move to involve the army in services other than defending the country and the Tinkhundla system of government. In recent times, the army has shown signs of being politicized and has become intolerant of protestors who express a different view from that of the present regime.

The king has the power to declare a state of emergency, and the country has existed under a state of emergency since the repeal of the Independence Constitution on April 12, 1973.

AMENDMENTS TO THE REMNANTS OF THE CONSTITUTION

In the repealed constitution an amendment could be made only if two-thirds of the members of Parliament voted in favor in a joint sitting; the majority depended on whether or not the amendment was for a specially en-trenched provision, whereupon the amendment needed approval in a referendum. Once adopted by parliament the amendment requires the king to assent to it. This provision is essentially retained by the new constitution.

Until November 2001, when the Court of Appeal ruled that the king had no power to make law by decree, the king could himself amend his 1973 Proclamation, which stands as the supreme law of Swaziland. Since that judgment, there have been no amendments.

PRIMARY SOURCES

Constitution in English and Siswati summary. Available online. URL: http://www.constitution.org.sz/. Accessed on August 15, 2005.

SECONDARY SOURCES

"Government of Swaziland Website." Available online. URL: http://www.gov.sz/. Accessed on August 14, 2005.
Chris Maroleng, "Swaziland—the King's Constitution." *African Security Review* 12, no. 3 (2003). Available online. URL: http://www.iss.org.za/pubs/ASR/12No3/AWMaroleng.html. Accessed on July 29, 2005.

Thulani Maseko

SWEDEN

At-a-Glance

OFFICIAL NAME
Kingdom of Sweden

CAPITAL
Stockholm

POPULATION
9,006,405 (2005 est.)

SIZE
173,732 sq. mi. (449.963 sq. km)

LANGUAGES
Swedish; four minority languages (Finnish, Hebrew, Sami, and Finnish dialect spoken in the border region in the far north between Sweden and Finland)

RELIGION
Protestant 87%, other (Roman Catholic, Orthodox, Baptist, Muslim, Jewish, Buddhist) 13%

NATIONAL OR ETHNIC COMPOSITION
Swedish 80%, immigrants of various origins 20%

DATE OF INDEPENDENCE OR CREATION
June 6, 1523

TYPE OF GOVERNMENT
Parliamentary democracy

TYPE OF STATE
Unitary state

TYPE OF LEGISLATURE
Unicameral parliament

DATE OF CONSTITUTION
January 1, 1975; three other constitutional acts (1809, 1949, 1991)

DATE OF LAST AMENDMENT
November 27, 2002

Sweden is a parliamentary democracy based on popular sovereignty and the rule of law. The independence of the executive, legislative, and judicial powers is guaranteed through various provisions of the constitution, even though the principle of separation of powers was not a core value when the constitution was promulgated in the 1960s and 1970s. The political atmosphere in Sweden and the other Nordic countries was permeated with the idea of popular sovereignty, which was seen as the ideological basis of the successful welfare state. Later, in particular after January 1, 1995, when Sweden joined the European Union, the idea of separation of powers became more influential.

The parliament (Riksdag) consists of 349 members, sitting in one chamber. National elections take place every fourth year in September; elections for the 285 municipalities take place at the same time. The election system is strictly proportional. Each party that wins at least 4 percent of the votes in the country is represented in parliament.

Sweden is still a monarchy, although the tasks of the king are mainly representative. Political power rests with the parliament and, in particular, with the executive branch of the government. Within the executive, the prime minister has a very strong position.

The most important of the constitutional acts, Regeringsformen (The Instrument of Government), was enacted in 1974 and entered into force in 1975. Additionally, the 1809 Act of Succession, regulating the succession to the throne, and the 1949 Freedom of Press Act (which traces its origins to 1766) are both important parts of the Swedish constitutional heritage.

A number of important basic human rights are covered both by the Instrument of Government and by the European Convention of Human Rights, which has applied as domestic Swedish law since 1995. However, in general, the constitutional tradition in Sweden is weak, and it is only in the last decade that an increased interest in constitutional issues has become visible among scholars and the media.

CONSTITUTIONAL HISTORY

The first written Swedish constitution dates to the 14th century, the so-called Konungabalken (King's Act) of what is referred to as Magnus Eriksson's *landslag* (national law). The act contained rules on methods to elect kings and high officials and on the tasks of the council (*råd*), the government of the time.

Despite a few modifications, this basic "constitution" continued to apply at least in part until 1634, when the first Instrument of Government was enacted. The Instrument of Government was a very modern constitution for its time; it established the administrative features of the Swedish state that still largely exist. Because of the centralization of the administration, the main public authorities were regulated in the constitution. The relative strength of the administrative tradition compared with that of the constitutional tradition can be, in part, traced to this period.

It was under this constitution that an embryonic parliamentarism was developed for the first time. It was decided in 1660 that the four social classes (*stånd, ständer*)—aristocracy, clergy, merchants, and farmers—should form a parliament. This was the basis for Swedish parliamentarism until 1866, when a bicameral system was introduced. Nevertheless, autocracy prevailed for some time.

The next Instrument of Government, in 1720, emphasized the different functions of the state in a clearer way, and it was under this modernized constitution that political parties came into existence. The king had to govern the country according to the wishes of the council; he himself had two votes, but he had to bow to the will of the majority. It was also during this period that the concept of a constitutional law—more difficult to change than an ordinary law—took hold, and it became necessary to define which laws were constitutional. One of those so defined was the 1766 Freedom of Press Act, containing, among other elements, rules on public access to documents.

After yet another period of autocracy, the king had to resign in 1809, and a new constitution was established. This 1809 Instrument of Government formally remained in force until the end of 1974, by which time it had become the second-oldest written constitution in use anywhere in the world. This fact illustrates the peaceful development that the country has enjoyed for the last two centuries. However, some of the most important provisions in the 1809 constitution, such as the right of the king to govern the state alone, or his two votes in the highest court, gradually became obsolete. After the general democratic breakthrough of the early 1920s, most of the constitution was seen to have lost force and validity.

Under the 1809 constitution the executive power belonged to the king, and the legislative power was divided between parliament and king; up until a 1909 court reform, the king also held some judicial powers. A new Freedom of Press Act was introduced in 1810, as well as a new Parliamentary Regulation (Riksdagsordningen). That same year, the current Act of Succession was introduced; the same royal family (Bernadotte, of French origin) has held the throne since.

A new wave of constitutional reform began in the 1950s. The bicameral parliament was replaced by a one-chamber system in 1970, and the current constitution was enacted in 1975. Significant reforms were added in 1976, 1979, and 1994, in particular strengthening the protection of basic human rights. Nevertheless, the emphasis on popular sovereignty is still very strong. A core concept of the constitution is that all political power rests with parliament, representing the people. The monarchy has remained, but the king has been stripped of all formal powers, left with only purely representative functions.

From a general point of view, the most important constitutional change since 1974 is undoubtedly the accession to the European Union on January 1, 1995. The traditionally strong legislature suddenly lost some of its power, having to share its sovereignty with a supranational legislator. The incorporation of the European Convention on Human Rights into Swedish national law also contributed to a generally increased interest in constitutional issues.

FORM AND IMPACT OF THE CONSTITUTION

Sweden has four written constitutions, which date to 1810, 1949, 1974, and 1991, respectively. The constitutional system must be described as fairly modern, with the exception of some provisions in the Act of Succession (stating, for instance, that the monarch must be a follower of the pure evangelical belief). The constitution is fairly easy to change; a number of such changes have been introduced every four years, when general elections are held. This system does not promote respect for the constitution(s) as binding, superior law, although all four constitutions are formally of a higher rank than ordinary laws.

The idea of hierarchy of norms is acknowledged in the Swedish constitution and in the legal system, perhaps most clearly in Chapter 11, Article 14, of the constitution: "If a court or other public body finds that a provision conflicts with a rule of fundamental law or other superior statute, or finds that a procedure laid down in law has been disregarded in any important respect when the provision was made, the provision may not be applied." However, the statement continues, "If the provision has been approved by the Riksdag or by the Government, however, it shall be waived only if the error is manifest." This is another clear expression of the principle of popular sovereignty, with great practical consequences for the self-restraint shown, at times, by the courts when exercising judicial review.

International law does not become part of the national legal system and thus is not applicable before the national courts, unless it has been duly transformed and incorporated into national rules, either by transformation of a whole text, passage of new legislation, or some other method. The major exceptions are the laws of the European Union.

The four constitutional acts all still have at least some political relevance. The Act of Succession still regulates the way the throne is passed. The impacts of the Freedom of Press and Freedom of Speech Acts, respectively, are perhaps best seen in the rather strong position of the media in Swedish society and the privileged positions of writers and journalists in proceedings in which charges are brought against them. The Instrument of Government regulates the work and appointment of the parliament and the executive branch, as well as the election process. It also regulates the legislative process, the budget procedure, foreign relations, the position of the courts and other public authorities, and many other important issues. It must therefore be said to be of great political significance, although, at the same time, the idea that the constitution is the supreme source of law, against which all other legislative acts must be compared and measured, has never gained significant ground in Sweden.

BASIC ORGANIZATIONAL STRUCTURE

Sweden has a long history as a highly centralized state, and it remains so today.

LEADING CONSTITUTIONAL PRINCIPLES

Democracy in the form of popular sovereignty is the crucial feature of the Swedish constitution. The free formation of opinion is also very important; two separate constitutional laws are devoted entirely to issues related to freedom of speech. Free access to public documents leads to a far-reaching freedom of information, another key principle.

The Swedish constitutional system also relies on the rule of law in its formal sense, including legality, equality of all before the law, and predictability in the application of the law. The independence of the courts and public authorities is fiercely guarded. In fact, the prohibition against political intervention in administrative decision making is probably more far-reaching than in most democracies.

Sweden is a hereditary monarchy. The Act of Succession is the only part of the Swedish constitution that ignores freedom of religion, since the king or queen must "profess the pure evangelical faith, as adopted and explained in the unaltered Confession of Augsburg and in

the Resolution of the Uppsala meeting of the year 1593." Any member of the royal family who does not profess this faith is excluded from all rights of succession. Apart from that, Sweden is now a secular state with no official state religion. Freedom of religion and worship is guaranteed.

Local self-government and, in particular, municipal autonomy are important features of the Swedish constitution. However, the limits of this autonomy are unclear. The protection of human rights has been much reinforced since the Instrument of Government entered into force in 1974.

CONSTITUTIONAL BODIES

The main constitutional bodies are the parliament, the cabinet, and the judiciary.

Parliament

Parliament (Riksdag) consists of one single chamber of 349 members. Free secret and direct elections take place every fourth year, always on the third Sunday in September. The votes go to parties. Every Swedish citizen who has attained the age of 18 on or before election day is entitled to vote. Extraordinary elections for the Riksdag may be called by the cabinet, except for the first three months after an ordinary election, although this has not yet occurred. Municipal and regional elections take place at the same time as parliamentary election.

The country is divided into some 20 constituencies, which among then return 310 members. Seats are allocated to the constituencies on the basis of the size of their populations and divided among the parties within each constituency on the basis of proportional representation; there are 39 national adjustment seats, which are distributed among the parties so that the distribution of all the 349 seats is proportional to the total number of votes cast throughout the whole of the realm. Political parties that receive at least 4 percent of the votes cast throughout the whole realm are entitled to share in the distribution of seats. Also eligible are parties that receive fewer votes but at least 12 percent of those votes are cast in one single constituency.

Thus, compared with that of most other countries, the election system often makes for weak governmental administrations; Sweden has not had a majority administration since May 1981.

Cabinet

The prime minister is the dominant figure in the Swedish administration. He or she appoints the other ministers and can remove them at any time.

After every election, or when a prime minister has resigned for other reasons, the speaker of parliament consults representatives of each party group of the Riksdag and then presents a candidate for prime minister before the Riksdag. If more than half of the members of the Riksdag (i.e., 175) vote against the candidate, he or she is rejected; in any other case the candidate becomes prime minister. A possible world record was set in 1978, when Ola Ullsten became prime minister of a one-party liberal government after winning only 38 votes. Should the Riksdag reject the speaker's proposal four times (as has never happened yet), new Riksdag elections must be held.

The cabinet has collective and common responsibility for its decisions, which are made at cabinet meetings, where at least five ministers must be present. A declaration of no confidence requires the concurrence of more than half the total membership of the Riksdag. Should this happen to the prime minister, the whole cabinet is discharged.

The Lawmaking Process

A law is passed by a majority of the voting members of the Riksdag. However, the rules concerning legislation are among the most technical and complicated in the constitutional system.

Problems relating to the division of legislative authority between the parliament and the cabinet arise in many areas. The cabinet may make ordinances relating to matters other than taxes in a number of areas, such as the protection of life, health, or personal safety; the import or export of goods; public order; or education. The unclear rules create uncertainty as to when, how, and whether the cabinet may regulate a certain issue.

Of considerable importance is the so-called Law Council, or Council on Legislation. The rise of this formally weak but practically very influential judicial body must be understood in the light of the weak constitutional tradition and the absence of a separation of powers. Thus, it is seen as preferable to allow the council to give its opinion on draft legislation rather than to hand the matter over to the courts.

The Law Council includes justices or former justices of the two highest courts. It exists to pronounce opinions on draft legislation. Its opinions are sought out by the cabinet or by committees of the Riksdag. The council must be consulted about laws relating to freedom of the press or freedom of expression on the broadcast media, laws restricting the right of access to documents or other basic rights, and certain other laws relating to taxation, civil law, burdensome public law, or procedural law, unless the matter is without significance or would unduly delay the legislation. In practice, the opinions of the Law Council are quite influential; bills have been amended or even abandoned as a result of its opposition.

The Judiciary

The Supreme Court is the highest court of general jurisdiction, while the Supreme Administrative Court (Regeringsrätten) is the highest administrative court. The right to have a case tried by either of these courts may be restricted by law; in fact, those two courts deal only with issues that are of future, principled interest and may therefore be seen as precedents. Additional courts must be established by law. Any such court must have at least one permanent salaried judge, who may be removed from office only in very special cases.

No public authority, including the Riksdag, may determine how a court of law shall adjudicate an individual case or otherwise apply a rule of law in a particular case. Likewise, no public authority may determine the way an administrative body shall decide a particular case relating to the exercise of public authority vis-à-vis a private subject or a local authority, or relating to the application of law. Together with the rule that no judicial or administrative function may be performed by the Riksdag, except inasmuch as this follows from fundamental law or from the Riksdag Act, this constitutes an efficient body of rules aimed at protecting the independence of the courts and the public administration in general. These rules may also be seen as prohibiting legislation that covers individual cases or very specific situations.

The cabinet is responsible for appointing judges. Although in principle the cabinet looks only at objective factors such as merit and competence, the process is sometimes said to compromise the independence of judges. Particularly in relation to the highest courts, the cabinet is sometimes accused of appointing judges it knows and who have previously worked within the ministries.

An ombudsperson elected by the Riksdag supervises the implementation of laws and other statutes by public bodies, including courts. To that end, the ombudsperson may request opinions and information of any kind.

THE ELECTION PROCESS AND POLITICAL PARTICIPATION

Every Swedish citizen who is at least 18 years old on the day of the election is entitled to vote and may be a member or alternate member of the Riksdag. National referenda have taken place six times in Swedish history, for example, on the prohibition of alcoholic beverages in the 1920s (narrowly voted down) and for membership in the European Union in 1994 (supported). Local referenda take place more often, at the discretion of each municipality.

POLITICAL PARTIES

The Swedish party system is pluralistic, with seven parties represented in parliament after the 2002 elections and a number of other parties active at the local level. A political party is any association or group of voters that presents candidates for election under a particular designation. The main importance of the parties, from a legal point of view, is that they form the parliamentary basis for choosing a prime minister, who then chooses the members of the cabinet. Apart from that, no real formal responsibilities are placed within the hands of the political parties.

Swedish law does not provide for banning any political party, since freedom of association is understood to mean that parties or organizations as such may never be criminalized, only specific actions. Thus, members of parties inciting, for example, racial hatred, defamation, or violent actions may be prosecuted for those actions, but not the organizations as such. Freedom of association may be restricted only in respect to organizations whose activities are of a military or quasi-military nature or constitute persecution of a population group of a particular race, color, or ethnic origin.

Political parties are primarily financed by state subsidies. Private donations have played a minor role, although the parties are not obliged to reveal their exact sources of income. However, the contributions from the trade unions to the governing Social Democratic Party have long been controversial.

CITIZENSHIP

Citizenship is regulated by ordinary law. A major change took place in 2001, when the idea of dual citizenship was finally accepted in Swedish law. A debate on whether knowledge of the Swedish language should be a requirement for citizenship took place during the election campaign in 2002, but so far, this is not a requirement.

A child of a Swedish father or mother is a Swedish citizen. No citizen who is, or has previously been, domiciled in the realm may be deprived of his or her citizenship unless he or she becomes at the same time a citizen of another state, either with his or her own express consent or because he or she has taken up employment in the public service.

FUNDAMENTAL RIGHTS

According to Article 1 of the Instrument of Government, the right to exercise some basic, fundamental, civil, and political liberties, namely, the freedoms of expression, information, assembly, demonstration, association, and worship, is protected. As far as freedom of expression is concerned, two special constitutional laws regulate the exercise of this freedom in books, journals, and other media.

Negative liberties, such as the right not to divulge or reveal any opinions, are also protected. Capital and corporal punishment are prohibited, as are torture and similar actions. Protection against other physical violations, body searches, house searches, and other intrusions of privacy is guaranteed, although that guarantee is not unconditional.

There are also rights with somewhat weaker protection. They include the right of trade unions to strike and take part in industrial actions, the right to property, and copyright and intellectual property rights. This also applies to the right to trade and the free exercise of a profession, as well as the right of the Sami population to practice reindeer husbandry. All those rights exist unless otherwise provided in an act of law or some similar requirement; as a result, the value of their constitutional protection is somewhat doubtful.

Impact and Functions of Fundamental Rights

While certain fundamental rights apply regardless of nationality to both citizens and foreigners, some are reserved for citizens. Most rights are available to foreigners unless a special provision states otherwise. There are some rights that only apply to Swedish citizens; for example, a citizen is guaranteed that records in a public register may not be based, without consent, on political affiliation.

The character and the wording of fundamental rights generally make it clear that they apply only in relation to the government. The issue of whether they could also be applied in relation to other private persons has not been definitely resolved by the courts, although the answer today among Swedish lawyers would probably be no rather than yes. Swedish courts, in particular the Labor Court (Arbetsdomstolen), have left the door open to apply certain rights, such as the freedom of expression and the protection against bodily searches, in the private sector, notably against employers.

Sweden is often seen as a rather socialist country, with an advanced welfare system and a large public sector. This is typically attributed to the length of Social Democratic Party control; but nevertheless, the fundamental social and economic rights guaranteed in the Instrument of Government itself cannot be considered fairly generous. The right to free basic education for children and general access to the environment is mentioned, but the constitution's basic guarantees mainly concern classical rights protecting the private sphere against the public authorities. The main social and welfare rights are not legally binding. Instead, the personal, economic, and cultural welfare of the private person are but fundamental aims of public activity. It is incumbent upon the public institutions to secure the right to health, employment, housing, and education and to promote social care as well as sustainable development to ensure a good environment for present and future generations. There is thus no tendency in Sweden to anchor the welfare state by constitutional means.

What is even more striking are the weak constitutional tradition and the near-absence of judicial review. The emphasis on popular sovereignty is a much more distinctive trait of the Swedish constitution than any particular ideological tendency, even rights-based.

Limitations to Fundamental Rights

The protection of fundamental rights varies. Some of them are characterized as absolute, in the sense that they may never be limited, while others may be subject to limitations. Certain rights, such as providing for court proceedings to be open to the public, may be restricted by law or regulation. Restrictions or limitations may be imposed only to satisfy a purpose acceptable in a democratic society. They may never exceed what is necessary to achieve the purpose that occasioned it, nor carried so far as to constitute a threat to the free formation of opinion. Nor may any restriction be imposed solely on grounds of political, religious, cultural, or other ideology.

More detailed criteria exist for limiting freedoms of expression, information, assembly, demonstration, and association. Discrimination or unfavorable treatment in legislation of citizens due to race, color, ethnic origin, or gender is prohibited. However, discrimination on grounds of gender may be allowed as part of an effort to promote equality of men and women.

ECONOMY

It seems hard to claim, in a country with such a weak constitutional tradition as Sweden, that the constitution has any relevance to the economic life or plays any role in the daily transactions of business people. The absence of a strong constitutional tradition has also meant that there has not been great interest among economists in the importance of constitutional rules in general, or in the impact that constitutional rules may have on economic life.

The constitution does, however, contain rules on property and social protection, financial powers, taxation, and budget procedures. The rather high taxes in Sweden have no relation, as such, to the constitutional system, but result entirely from political decisions.

RELIGIOUS COMMUNITIES

Freedom of religion is total, although racial crimes, incitement to hatred, or other acts committed in the name of religion are punished in the ordinary manner. Sweden is a very secular state, where religion cannot be said to play any main part in most people's lives. The formerly strong bonds between the state and the church of Sweden are, since 2001, almost completely cut. Religious communities in general are treated in the same way as other associations and obey the same laws.

In the future, it is possible that the influence of new religious groups in the multicultural society will make religion a more important issue. At the moment, however, this does not seem to be the case.

MILITARY DEFENSE AND STATE OF EMERGENCY

The constitution contains very few rules on military defense. The most important is the provision that the cabi-net may commit the armed forces of the realm, or any part of them, to use force in order to repel an armed attack upon the realm. Swedish armed forces may also otherwise be committed to use force, or be dispatched abroad, provided that the Riksdag consents; that the action is permitted under an act of law; and that a duty to take such action follows from an international agreement or obligation that has been approved by the Riksdag. A state of war may not be declared without the consent of the Riksdag, although the government may authorize the armed forces to use force in accordance with international law in order to prevent violation of Swedish territory in times of peace or during a war between foreign states.

The constitution devotes a special chapter entirely to the circumstances of war and danger of war. Given that Sweden has not participated in a war since 1809, and that this constitution dates from 1974, these provisions have not merited much attention, in political or legal spheres.

Should the realm find itself at war or in danger of war, the cabinet or the speaker must convene the Riksdag in session, in Stockholm or at another convenient place. A special war delegation composed of members of different parties shall replace the Riksdag if necessary. Neither the Riksdag nor the cabinet may make decisions in occupied territory. The constitution includes other important rules, indicating, for instance, that during wartime the cabinet may decide by statute matters that should otherwise be decided by law, or that elections to the Riksdag should not take place unless the Riksdag itself decides so.

AMENDMENTS TO THE CONSTITUTION

The Swedish constitution(s) is easier to change than that of most other countries. Amendments only require two decisions, by a simple majority of the voting members of parliament, before and after a general election. Should a minority of one-third of the members of parliament demand, there is also the possibility of a referendum on a proposal concerning new or amended fundamental law. The result of such a referendum, which takes place on election day, is binding. So far, however, this procedure has never been invoked, possibly as a result of the tradition of consensus between the larger parties on any issues related to constitutional changes. The ease with which the constitutional laws can be amended, in combination with the existence of no fewer than four constitutional laws of which two are of a very technical character, leads to the occurrence of a significant number of constitutional changes every four years. This condition does not promote respect for the constitution as a special, fundamental kind of law.

A new committee revising the constitution has recently been summoned. It is projected to finish in 2008, with implementation envisaged for 2010.

PRIMARY SOURCES

Constitution in English. Available online. URL: http://www.riksdagen.se/templates/R_Page____6357.aspx. Accessed on September 9, 2005.

Constitution in Swedish. Available online. URL: http://www.riksdagen.se/templates/R_Page____4930.aspx. Accessed on September 8, 2005.

SECONDARY SOURCES

N. Berggren, N. Karlson, and J. Nergelius, eds., *Why Constitutions Matter.* Somerset, N.J.: Transaction Publishers, 2002.

Ulf Bernitz, *European Law in Sweden.* Stockholm: June 2002.

Michael Bogdan, ed., *Swedish Law in the New Millennium.* Stockholm: Norstedts, 2000.

Joakim Nergelius

SWITZERLAND

At-a-Glance

OFFICIAL NAME
Swiss Confederation (Confoederatio Helvetica)

CAPITAL
Berne

POPULATION
7,317,873; 1,463,574 (20%) foreign nationals (2000)

SIZE
15,943 sq. mi. (41,293 sq. km)

LANGUAGES
German 65%, French 18.4%, Italian 9.8%, Romansch 0.8%, other 6% (1997)

RELIGIONS
Roman Catholic 41.8%, Protestant 35.3%, Muslim 4.3%, other religious communities 3.2%, none 11.1%, no details 4.3%

NATIONAL OR ETHNIC COMPOSITION
German 65%, French 18%, Italian 10%, Romansch 1%, other 6%

DATE OF INDEPENDENCE OR CREATION
Founding of the Swiss Confederation (independence) August 1, 1291; federal state (Confederation) since 1848

TYPE OF GOVERNMENT
Constitutional democracy

TYPE OF STATE
Federal state

TYPE OF LEGISLATURE
Bicameral parliament

DATE OF CONSTITUTION
January 1, 2000

DATE OF LAST AMENDMENT
November 27, 2005

Switzerland is a parliamentary democracy with a clear division of executive, legislative, and judicial powers. By constitutional law, the state's activities are based on and limited by the rule of law. Switzerland is also obliged by the constitution to respect international law.

Organized as a confederation, Switzerland is made up of 26 sovereign cantons. Its federal constitution explicitly declares social goals and provides for far-reaching guarantees of human rights, the essence of which are declared inviolate by the constitution. The federal constitution is widely respected by the public authorities; if a violation of the constitution does occur, there are effective remedies for the individual that are enforceable by an independent judiciary. The judiciary includes a strong Federal Tribunal.

The federal president is not the head of state, because that position does not exist in Switzerland. The president only presides over the Federal Council. The presidency vice presidency rotate annually. The Federal Assembly elects the president and the vice president of the Swiss Confederation each year from among its members following the principle of seniority. The central political figures are the seven federal councilors, elected by the parliament for four-year terms; they are constitutionally obliged to make their decisions as a collective body.

Free, equal, general, and direct elections of Federal Assembly members are guaranteed. The pluralistic system of political parties has intense political impact.

The economic system can be described as a social economy. By constitutional law, Switzerland is obligated to respect the principle of economic freedom; ensure balanced economic development; protect consumers, employees, and the needy; and fight restrictions on competition.

The military is organized as a militia and is subject to the civil government in law and fact.

CONSTITUTIONAL HISTORY

Switzerland is regarded as having been founded in 1291, when the three valley communities of Uri, Schwyz, and Unterwalden (now divided into Nidwalden and Obwalden), the so-called Ur-Kantone, joined to struggle against the rule of the counts of Habsburg, who held the German imperial throne of the Holy Roman Empire and attempted to assert feudal rights in the area. The three communities signed the Letter of Alliance, agreeing to reject any administrative and judicial system imposed from outside. A citizen of each of these communities swore, in early August 1291 at a small meadow named Ruetli, the following oath: "We will be a one and only nation of brothers."

This led to the term *confederation* (in German translated as *Eidgenossenschaft*), which grew further with the adherence of the following cantons: Lucerne in 1332, Zurich in 1351, Glarus and Zug in 1352, Berne in 1353, Fribourg and Solothurn in 1481, Basel and Solothurn in 1501, and Appenzell in 1513. Switzerland's independence of the Holy Roman Empire and its neutrality were officially recognized in 1648 in the Treaty of Westphalia, which ended the Thirty Years War.

In 1798, the armies of the French Revolution conquered the Swiss territory and Napoléon Bonaparte, future emperor of France, unified Switzerland under the name of the Helvetic Republic. The Helvetic Republic was proclaimed and its new constitution confirmed on April 12, 1798, by 121 representatives of the territories Aargau, Basel, Berne, Fribourg, Léman (Vaud), Lucerne, Oberland, Schaffhausen, Solothurn, and Zurich. The new constitution was similar to that of the French Republic. The constitution, imposed on the territories and written by Napoléon, eliminated the federal tradition of Switzerland and established a bicameral parliament, an executive (the board of directors), and a supreme court of justice.

In addition, the Helvetic Republic gave up the traditional policy of neutrality and signed a Treaty of Alliance with France in August 1798. As a consequence of that decision Switzerland became a battleground: Austrian and Russian troops fought French troops on Swiss territories, with the aim of putting the country, or parts of it, under their own control. Throughout the five years of the Helvetic Republic, the country was very unstable politically, as centralists and federalists fought each other.

In 1802, a civil war (the so-called war of the sticks) led to the end of the Helvetic Republic. Napoléon Bonaparte intervened in October 1802 and managed to put an end to the civil war. Realizing that the Swiss people would never accept a centralist state and that it was in his interest to have Switzerland as an ally, Napoléon withdrew his occupying troops. Under his mediation a new constitution (the Mediation Act) was negotiated in March 1803. The Mediation Act, approved by the Swiss people, restored the Swiss Confederation. It gave most of the responsibility to 19 cantons. Six new cantons, Sankt Gallen, Grisons, Aargau, Thurgau, Ticino, and Vaud, were added to the existing 13 cantons.

Switzerland's final boundaries were established in 1815 at the Congress of Vienna, which also recognized the perpetual neutrality of Switzerland. All the European kings and statesmen, after defeating Napoléon, were interested in reducing the influence of France in Switzerland by guaranteeing Swiss neutrality. They also decided that Valais, Geneva, and Neuchâtel would become full members of the Swiss Confederation. Switzerland consisted herewith of 22 cantons, which recovered their sovereignty in all matters except foreign affairs.

The years between 1815 and 1830 are called the Restoration period. Each canton once again minted its own money, imposed taxes and customs, and introduced its own system of weights and measures.

Around 1830, a liberal renewal movement, the Regeneration, began in Switzerland. It demanded full democratic rights and equality between citizens in cities and the countryside. Within one year 12 cantons changed their constitution, established a representative government, abolished aristocratic rule and censorship of the press, and instituted freedom of trade and industry.

In 1847, another civil war broke out, this time between the Catholic and Protestant cantons (the Sonderbundskrieg); it lasted less than one month as General Henri Dufour, leading federal troops, managed to defeat the Catholic conservatives and to end the crisis before the European powers could intervene. The Sonderbundskrieg was the last armed conflict to occur on Swiss territory.

As a consequence of this civil war, in 1848 Switzerland adopted a federal constitution, which, modeled in part on the U.S. Constitution, is regarded as the main instrument for the foundation of modern Switzerland. The Swiss Confederation changed from a group of cantons to a united federal state.

The constitution of 1848 was completely revised in 1874, giving the central government more responsibilities, such as defense, trade, and legal matters. In 1971, the Swiss people voted for women's right to vote in federal elections and to hold federal office.

The last canton to join the confederation was the canton of Jura. In 1978, several French-speaking regions left the canton of Berne, attained independence, and formed the new canton, Jura.

The legal foundation of the Swiss Confederation is the new Federal Constitution of April 18, 1999. It entered into force on January 1, 2000.

FORM AND IMPACT OF THE CONSTITUTION

The Swiss constitution is codified in a single document. It is significant not only as the legal system of the country, but also as a source of fundamental values for the functioning of Swiss society. It is widely respected by the federal and cantonal authorities. All law must comply with the provisions of the federal constitution. Federal law takes precedence over contradicting cantonal law. The confederation and the cantons also must respect international law.

BASIC ORGANIZATIONAL STRUCTURE

Switzerland is a multiethnic, multilingual, and multireligious parliamentary democracy based on the diversity of its regions. It is a confederation of 26 autonomous cantons. Its present form was established by the 1848 constitution. Switzerland is one of the 23 federal states in the world, the second oldest after the United States of America. Its federal structure is based on three different political levels: the confederation; the 26 cantons, often referred to as the states; and the 2,873 municipalities.

The Confederation

Confederation is the term used in Switzerland to describe the central state. The confederation has authority in all areas in which it is empowered by the federal constitution, for example, in foreign and security policy, customs, and monetary affairs. It has power to pass nationally applicable legislation and controls certain other matters that are in the common interest of all Swiss citizens. Tasks that do not expressly fall within the domain of the confederation are left to the authority of the cantons. The cantons are sovereign, insofar as their sovereignty is not limited by the federal constitution, and they exercise all rights that are not transferred to the confederation.

International relations are a federal matter. According to the constitution, the confederation must strive to preserve the independence and welfare of Switzerland; it must also contribute to alleviation of need and poverty in the world and promotion of respect for human rights, democracy, the peaceful coexistence of nations, and the preservation of natural resources. It shall take into consideration the powers of the cantons and protect their interests.

Federal matters also include legislation in the fields of civil and criminal law and immigration, emigration, and asylum. The postal and telecommunication services as well as radio, television, and other forms of public telecasting of features and information are federal responsibilities. Weights and measures; the production, importation, refining, and sale of distilled spirits; and gambling and lotteries are federally regulated. Additional federal issues include the maintenance and use of the Swiss army, civil protection, transportation, nuclear energy, and fuel pipelines.

The Cantons

Article 1 of the Federal Constitution names the 26 Swiss cantons and guarantees their juridical existence by providing that the Swiss people and the cantons form the Swiss Confederation. A constitutional amendment is required to create or suppress a canton; it must be approved in a national referendum by a majority of votes as well as a majority of cantons.

The cantons differ considerably in geographic area, population size, and economic strength. According to Article 3 of the constitution, the cantons are sovereign insofar as their sovereignty is not limited by the federal constitution; they exercise all rights that are not transferred to the confederation.

Each canton has its own constitution, parliament, executive, and judiciary. According to Article 51 of the constitution, every canton shall adopt a democratic constitution, which must be approved by the people and must be subject to revision if a majority of the people so desire. The canton's legislatures and executives are of great importance, as are the courts. The courts of justice in Switzerland are cantonal, unless there is a final appeal to the Federal Tribunal.

The cantons retain attributes of sovereignty, such as their own procedural law system, the maintenance of law and order, the implementation of federal laws, fiscal autonomy, and the right to manage internal cantonal affairs. This is especially true in the fields of education and culture, the relationship between church and state, public health, commercial policy, taxation, and licensing of gambling. The cantons are also involved in town and country planning, which includes concerns such as the protection of nature and the cultural heritage, energy use in buildings, and the naturalization of foreigners. The cantons, however, no longer have any authority to make civil law and have only limited authority to make criminal law.

The cantons are also entitled to initiate legislation in the federal parliament.

The Local Authorities: The Municipalities

All the cantons are divided into autonomous municipalities or communes, of which there are currently 2,873. This number is declining, however, because of amalgamations of individual communes.

All Swiss people are first and foremost citizens of a commune. It is from this status that they automatically derive citizenship of a canton, and of the country as a whole. Foreigners who wish to become Swiss citizens must apply to the commune where they live.

The autonomy of the municipalities is guaranteed within the limits fixed by cantonal law. The confederation must take into account the possible consequences of its activities on the municipalities, in particular the special situation of cities, urbanized areas, and mountainous regions.

LEADING CONSTITUTIONAL PRINCIPLES

Switzerland is a parliamentary democracy and a confederation, with a strong division of the executive, legislative, and judicial powers, based on checks and balances. No individual may simultaneously belong to more than one of the three federal authorities—parliament, executive, and Supreme Court. The Swiss constitutional system is defined by a number of leading principles: democracy, rule of law, social welfare, and federalism.

State activity must be in the public interest and proportional to the goals pursued. State organs and officials must act in good faith, and the confederation and the cantons must respect international law. Fundamental rights must be realized throughout the legal system. Whoever exercises a function of the state must respect fundamental rights and contribute to their realization. The authorities shall also ensure that fundamental rights are respected in relationships between private parties, whenever the analogy is applicable.

Political rights protect the free opinion and expression of citizens. Various direct democracy instruments granted to the Swiss people and the cantons, such as popular initiatives, referenda, and political parties, are meant to contribute to the formation of the opinion and will of the people.

CONSTITUTIONAL BODIES

Switzerland has a unique political system. It is different from systems used in most countries, which are based on the dynamics between the administration in power and opposition parties. The Swiss system is based on consensus. National cohesion is achieved by involving the whole population in the decision-making process and by allowing citizens to participate in direct democracy.

The People and the Impact of Direct Democracy

Legislation cannot be vetoed by the executive or reviewed for constitutionality by the judiciary. However, all laws, with the exception of the budget, can be reviewed through a popular referendum before taking effect.

There are very few countries in which people have such far-reaching rights of direct democracy as in Switzerland. The long democratic tradition; the comparatively small size, in terms of both geography and population; and ultimately the high level of literacy and the diversity of media are critical in ensuring the proper functioning of this particular form of state.

Direct democracy has played a key role in shaping the modern Swiss political system. Yet one may question the actual impact of direct democracy on legislative issues that in other countries are the responsibility of elected representatives. On one hand, it could be argued that the impact of direct democracy has been limited. In the first century of using the initiative (1891–2004), only 14 initiatives were passed in Switzerland. Yet to consider this statistic alone ignores the considerable indirect impact

of direct democracy. Although the majority of initiatives fail, the fact that there has been an initiative, and therefore a campaign, increases publicity surrounding the issue in question and therefore the public's knowledge of it. This system may well increase pressure on the government to introduce measures dealing with the issue, even if the referendum itself is not successful. Thus many initiatives are filed but subsequently withdrawn when the government decides to act before an initiative reaches the referendum stage.

Another impact of the direct democracy mechanisms is that they force the government to seek a wider consensus regarding the statutory and constitutional measures that it seeks to introduce than it would in a purely representative system. In a representative system, the party of government may, in the absence of a large majority, have to develop cross-party consensus on an issue in order to ensure that the measure is approved. In the Swiss system, the possibility of an optional referendum forces the government to ensure consensus even with groups outside parliament to preclude the possibility that these groups will seek to overturn the new legislation.

Conversely, the significance of direct democracy in the Swiss system is often cited as the cause of the weakness of Swiss political parties and the relatively low significance attached to normal elections. Given the prominence of direct democracy, political parties are not solely responsible for controlling the federal agenda. In addition, direct democracy often raises cross-cutting issues on which members of political parties might not be in agreement.

The Legislative Authority

The Swiss parliament, the Federal Assembly, is the legislative authority of the country elected by Swiss citizens. Subject to the rights of the people and the cantons, it is the highest authority of the confederation. The Federal Assembly may be legally dissolved only after the adoption of a popular initiative calling for a total revision of the federal constitution.

The assembly consists of two chambers with equal powers—the National Council and the Council of States. The chambers legislate, approve treaties, vote on the budget and loans, and supervise the Federal Council and the administration. The bicameral parliamentary system was introduced in Switzerland to ensure that the larger cantons would not dominate the smaller ones.

Both chambers are directly elected by the people. The National Council is elected in accordance with federal rules and the Council of States according to provisions that differ from canton to canton. In both cases, the cantons form the constituencies.

The 200-member National Council represents the Swiss people as a whole. The individual cantons are represented in proportion to the number of their inhabitants, but there is at least one representative from each canton. The members of the National Council are elected by popular vote to serve four-year terms. The system of proportional representation, the distribution of seats according to the strength of the political parties, makes it possible for small political parties to win one or more seats in the National Council.

The Council of States represents the 26 cantons. Regardless of the size of the canton's population, 20 cantons each send two members to the Council of States, while the six cantons of Appenzell Outer Rhodes, Appenzell Inner Rhodes, Basel-City, Basel-Land, Nidwald, and Obwald send only one member each. The members of the Council of States also serve four-year terms. Only large parties are represented in the Council of States because in all the cantons, except in the canton of Jura, elections to the Council of States use the system of simple majority.

The Lawmaking Process
The process leading to the adoption of a new law is complex and often lengthy. It takes at least 12 months and in extreme cases can take up to 12 years. However, the number of laws adopted has increased greatly in recent years. On average, one new law or amendment enters into force each week.

A new law progresses through five stages: the initiative stage, the drafting stage, the verification stage, the final decision stage, the entry into force.

A bill may be initiated by an individual citizen or interest group, a member of parliament, an administrative department, a canton, or the Federal Council. To prepare a first draft, the Federal Council often sets up a committee of 10 to 20 members, including representatives of interested parties. The draft is then forwarded for consultation to the cantons, parties, associations, and other groups, who are all entitled to state their position and propose amendments. The federal administrative authorities then revise the draft and submit it to the Federal Council. The Federal Council verifies the text: It either refers it again for more detailed consideration or forwards it to the National Council and Council of States for parliamentary debate.

The Speakers of the chambers decide in which chamber the new law is to be debated first. A preparatory committee of the chamber concerned—which is generally one of the 12 permanent committees—discusses the text and presents its conclusions to the whole chamber.

The chamber has three options. First, it may regard the new law as superfluous and take no further action—in which case the text is shelved. Second, it may refer the text back to the Federal Council for revision. Third, it may discuss the law in detail and finally make a decision.

This procedure is repeated in the other chamber: The preparatory committee begins by examining the text adopted by the first chamber. The second chamber then considers the matter in plenary session. It has the same options as the first chamber.

If the decisions of the National Council and Council of States differ, a reconciliation procedure begins. If different versions of the new law still exist after three debates, the conciliation conference, consisting of members of the two committees who worked on the bill, is convened to seek a compromise, which is then submitted to the two chambers for a final vote.

The new law adopted by parliament enters into force unless a referendum is sought within 100 days. For it to be valid, the signature of 50,000 electors must be obtained in favor of a popular ballot. A public vote is compulsory for constitutional amendments, which must win in a majority of cantons.

The Executive Authority
Switzerland's executive branch consists of the seven members of the Federal Council, as well as the federal chancellor. The chancellor, while entitled to propose motions and to speak during the meetings of the Federal Council, has no vote. The Federal Chancellery is the general staff of the Federal Council. One member of the Federal Council is elected for just one year to be the federal president, and another member to be the federal vice president. Their function is mostly representative, and they each continue to administer their own department.

Switzerland has one of the most stable governments in the world. Changes in the Federal Council in practice only occur if a member resigns or dies. A federal councilor remains in office for the entire legislative period and usually serves during multiple assemblies. Every four years, after parliamentary elections, he or she, to remain in office, must submit to reelection by a majority vote, but this is mostly a formality.

The Federal Council, from 1959 to November 2003, was composed of a coalition of all four major parties (a system of power sharing known as concordance). According to the Zauberformel, the unwritten "magic formula," there were two members from the Radical Free Party, two from the Social Democratic Party, two from the Christian Democratic Party, and one from the Swiss People's Party.

This formula was broken after the 2003 elections, when the Swiss People's Party gained 26.9 percent of the vote and a plurality of seats in the National Council and demanded a second seat in the Federal Council. The Federal Assembly acceded to the demand, and a new magic formula was achieved. This was the first time in 131 years that a federal councilor standing for reelection was rejected by the legislative body. Additionally, the Federal Assembly prefers to elect a member of the same language group and sex to replace the resigning member of the Federal Council.

The seven members of the Federal Council, as do the federal chancellor and the members of the Federal Assembly, enjoy immunity.

Although each councilor heads one of the seven departments (ministries) and is responsible for preparing legislation in the field of its authority, the councilors are expected to act neither as individual ministers nor as representatives of their political party. Rather, they take collective *responsibility* for the decisions of the council.

Not only is there no head of state in the confederation, there is also no real opposition party. Another form of opposition exists, however. The proposals made by the Federal Council are often rejected by the Federal Assembly or by the Swiss people, but such a rejection does not lead to a government crisis, votes of confidence, or resignations, because the Federal Council as a body is not dependent on a parliamentary majority.

As the highest governing authority and the supreme executive authority of the confederation, the Federal Council is primarily responsible for the activities of government. It must continuously assess conditions that arise from developments in the state and society and from events at home and abroad. It must define the fundamental goals of state action and determine the resources needed to attain them, plan and coordinate government policy and ensure its implementation, and represent the confederation at home and abroad.

Furthermore, the Federal Council must regularly and systematically scrutinize the work of the federal administrative authorities in order to ensure their efficiency as well as the legality and practicality of their activities. The Federal Council itself takes administrative action only in exceptional cases.

The Federal Council also takes part in the legislative procedure by leading the preliminary proceedings of legislation, submitting federal laws and decrees to the Federal Assembly, and enacting regulations insofar as the federal constitution or federal law empowers it to do so. The council drafts the budget and the state accounts. It can also approve or reject cantonal decrees in certain controversial cases, as long as this is provided for in a federal decree and backed by a referendum.

The Judiciary

The administration of justice is primarily a cantonal function. The cantons dispense justice even when it concerns the application of federal statutes.

On the level of the confederation the Federal Tribunal, made up of the Federal Supreme Court, the Federal Criminal Court (since April 2004), the new Federal Administrative Court, and the independent Federal Insurance Court. The Federal Tribunal represents the highest judicial authority of the country, but its jurisdiction is limited. It is neither an American-type Supreme Court, nor a German Bundesverfassungsgericht, nor a French Conseil constitutionnel. It has no power to declare federal laws unconstitutional, though it may overturn cantonal legislation on those grounds.

Generally speaking, the Federal Tribunal is entrusted with the control of the unity of interpretation of federal law, especially to ensure the uniformity of the civil and criminal codes of the country. The Federal Supreme Court has 30 full-time and 30 part-time judges. The new Federal Criminal Court of first instance currently has 11 judges, and the Federal Insurance Court consists of 11 full-time and 11 part-time judges. The federal judges are elected by the united Federal Assembly on the basis of linguistic, regional, and party affiliation. The period of office lasts six years and the judges are eligible for reelection. In principle, the office is open to all Swiss citizens. No legal training is required under constitutional law, although it is in practice.

The Federal Supreme Court

The Federal Supreme Court has jurisdiction over complaints regarding the violation of constitutional rights or the violation of communal autonomy and other cantonal guarantees. It also hears complaints regarding the violation of international or intercantonal contracts, as well as public law disputes between the confederation and the cantons or between cantons.

On appeal, it reviews the decisions of the highest cantonal courts and other authorities of the confederation to ensure they are compatible with the applicable law. It is the highest court to rule on disputes concerning civil law, criminal law, and public and administrative law (disputes between persons and the state, between cantons, and between the confederation and the cantons).

The new Federal Criminal Court rules in first instance on criminal cases that fall within federal jurisdiction. The future Federal Administrative Court, which is expected to begin its duties in 2007, will replace the Supreme Federal Court in the field of appeals against acts of federal administrative authorities.

The Federal Insurance Court is considered to be an organizationally independent division of the Federal Supreme Court. Its 11 federal judges and 11 part-time judges are responsible for social insurance law as part of administrative law.

POLITICAL PARTIES

The federal constitution provides for political parties to help give form to the opinions and will of the people. A number of different political parties, competing for the favor and the votes of the public, exist in the country. In the 2003 elections, the four major parties gained the support of around 80 percent of the electorate.

CITIZENSHIP

Swiss citizenship is primarily acquired by birth. A child acquires Swiss citizenship if one of his or her parents is a Swiss citizen (*ius sanguinis*). It is of no relevance where a child is born.

Swiss citizenship is derived from membership in a Swiss commune. According to Article 37 of the federal constitution everyone who holds citizenship of a commune and of the canton to which it belongs has Swiss citizenship. It also provides that no one should enjoy privileges or suffer loss because of his or her citizenship. A foreigner can acquire Swiss citizenship by applying to the commune where he or she lives.

FUNDAMENTAL RIGHTS, CIVIL RIGHTS, AND SOCIAL GOALS

The federal constitution defines fundamental rights in Title 2, Fundamental Rights, Civil Rights and Social Goals, immediately after the general provisions. In doing so, the framers of the constitution have emphasized the fundamental importance of the rights of the people for the smooth functioning of the state and society.

Article 35 declares that the fundamental rights must be realized throughout the legal system. Everyone who performs any state function must respect fundamental rights and contribute to their realization. The authorities must also ensure that fundamental rights are respected in relations among private persons, whenever the analogy is applicable. Article 36 declares that the essence of fundamental rights is inviolable.

The Fundamental Rights

The federal constitution explicitly guarantees the following fundamental rights: human dignity; equality before the law; protection against arbitrariness and the principle of good faith; the right to life and personal freedom; protection of children and young people; the right to aid in distress; the right to privacy; the right to marriage and family; freedom of religion and conscience; freedom of opinion and information; freedom of the media; freedom of language; the right to basic education; freedom of science; freedom of art; freedom of assembly; freedom of association; freedom of residence; protection against expulsion, extradition, and removal by force; the right to property; economic freedom; freedom to form unions and the right to strike; general procedural guarantees; guarantee of access to a judge; guarantees in judicial proceedings; habeas corpus; rights in criminal procedures; and the right of petition.

Civil Rights

Article 34 of the constitution provides that political rights are guaranteed and that these guarantees protect the free formation of opinion by the citizens and the unaltered expression of their will.

Social Goals

The constitution requires the confederation and the cantons, while encouraging personal responsibility and private initiative, to strive to ensure that every person benefits from social security and necessary health care; every family as a community of adults and children is protected and encouraged; every person capable of working is able to sustain himself or herself through work under fair and adequate conditions; every person looking for housing shall find, for himself or herself and his or her family, appropriate housing at reasonable conditions; children, young people, and people of working age shall benefit from initial and continual education according to their abilities; children and young people shall be encouraged in their development to become independent and socially responsible persons, and they shall be supported in their social, cultural, and political integration. Every person shall be insured against the economic consequences of old age, disability, illness, accidents, unemployment, maternity, orphanhood, and widowhood. The confederation and the cantons shall strive to realize the social goals within the framework of their constitutional powers and with the means available to them.

Impact and Functions of Fundamental Rights

Social rights cannot be derived from the social goals, which do not confer any special rights to state services. These social goals remain a program to be followed by public authorities. Fundamental and civil rights, however, are directly applicable to every individual citizen. Fundamental rights, civil rights, and social goals are widely respected in Switzerland.

Limitations to Fundamental Rights

Any limitation of a fundamental right requires a legal basis, it must be justified by the public interest or the need to protect the fundamental rights of other persons, and it must be proportionate to the need. Serious limitations cannot be imposed unless expressly foreseen by statute. The essence of fundamental rights is inviolable.

ECONOMY

The Swiss economic system can be described as a social free-market economy. It combines aspects of social responsibility with market freedom. The constitution itself proclaims an economic system based on free competition. The legislature is thus free to structure the economy, but only according to a set of conditions provided by the framers. Switzerland is not explicitly defined by the constitution as a social state, but the constitution provides for minimal social standards.

RELIGIOUS COMMUNITIES

The federal constitution expressly guarantees complete freedom of religion or philosophical convictions. Everyone has the right to choose his or her religion or philosophical convictions freely and to profess them alone or in community with others. Everyone has the right to join or to belong to a religious community and to follow religious teachings. No person can be forced to join or belong to a religious community, to participate in a religious act, or to follow religious teachings.

No state church exists, but all cantons support, with public funds, at least one of the three traditional Christian denominations: Roman Catholic, Old Catholic, and Protestant, through the "church tax." Each individual may, however, choose not to contribute to church funding, by declaring that he or she does not wish to be a member of any of the three traditional denominations.

Article 72 of the federal constitution addresses the relation between church and state. The regulation of the relationship is considered a cantonal matter. The confederation and the cantons may, within the framework of their powers, take measures to maintain public peace among the members of the various religious communities.

Foreign missionaries must obtain a "religious worker" visa to work in the country. Requirements include proof that the foreigner would not displace a citizen from performing that job, that the foreign worker would be financially supported by the host organization, and that the country of origin of the religious worker also grants visas to Swiss religious workers.

Religion is taught in public schools. The doctrine presented depends on which religion predominates in the particular canton. However, those of different faiths are free to attend classes of their own creed during the class period. Atheists may also be excused from the classes. Additionally, parents may send their children to private religious schools or teach their children at home.

MILITARY DEFENSE AND CIVIL PROTECTION

According to Article 58 of the federal constitution, Switzerland shall have an army, organized in principle as a militia. The army shall contribute to the prevention of war and the maintenance of peace; it shall defend the country and protect the population. It shall lend support to the civil authorities to repel serious threats to internal security, to master other exceptional circumstances, or to perform additional tasks that statutes may provide.

In urgent cases, the Federal Council may mobilize troops. If it mobilizes more than 4,000 members of the armed forces for active duty, or if the mobilization is expected to last more than three weeks, the Federal Assembly must be convened without delay.

The use of the army is a federal matter. The cantons may engage their troops to maintain public order on their territory if the means of the civil authorities no longer suffice to deter serious threats to inner security. Legislation on the military and the organization, instruction, and equipment of the army is also a federal matter. Within the limits of federal law the cantons may form cantonal units, appoint and promote officers of such units, and furnish a portion of their clothing and equipment.

Every Swiss man must render military service. The law provides for an alternative service for conscientious objectors. Military service is voluntary for Swiss women. Swiss men who render neither military nor alternative service owe a tax. In 2003 Swiss voters approved the military reform project "Army XXI," according to which the size of the Swiss army will be drastically reduced and the mandatory term of service curtailed.

Legislation on civil defense is also a federal matter and has the purpose of protecting individuals and property against the consequences of armed conflicts. The confederation is authorized to legislate matters that concern the intervention of the armed forces in catastrophes and emergencies and has the right to impose mandatory civil defense service for men.

AMENDMENTS TO THE CONSTITUTION

Amendments to the federal constitution can be initiated through popular initiatives and are subject to a compulsory referendum. The initiative mechanism, as does the mechanism for a total revision of the constitution, requires 100,000 valid voters' signatures, collected within 18 months of the filing of the initiative.

A total revision of the federal constitution may be proposed by the people, by one of the two parliamentary chambers, or by the Federal Assembly as a whole. If the initiative emanates from the people, or if the chambers disagree, the people shall decide whether a total revision should be undertaken. Should the people accept a total revision, new elections to both chambers are held.

The government may not violate any mandatory provisions of international law. Similarly, no revision of the federal constitution may violate such provisions. The federal constitution, revised in whole or in part, shall enter into force as soon as it is accepted by the people and the cantons.

PRIMARY SOURCES
Constitution in English. Available online. URL: http://www.admin.ch; URL: http://www.swissemb.org/legal/const.pdf. Accessed on August 17, 2005.

The Federal Constitution in German, French, and Italian. Available online. URLs: http://www.admin.ch; URL: http://www.bundespublikationen.ch. Accessed on August 20, 2005.

SECONDARY SOURCES
Confoederatio Helvetica, The Federal Authorities of the Swiss Confederation, "The Political Structure of Switzerland." Available online. URL: http://www.

admin.ch/ch/e/schweiz/political.html. Accessed on July 2, 2005.

Confoederatio Helvetica, The Federal Authorities of the Swiss Confederation, "How Is a New Law Enacted?" Available online. URL: www.admin.ch/ch/e/gg/index.html. Accessed on August 9, 2005.

"Direct Democracy in Switzerland: The Players." Available online. URL: www.swissworld.org/dvd_rom/eng/direct_democracy-2004/content/involved/involved.html. Accessed on August 26, 2005.

"Direct Democracy in Switzerland: The Political System in Switzerland." Available online. URL: www.swissworld.org.dvd_rom/eng/direct_democracy_2004/content/politsystem/politsystem.html. Accessed on July 20, 2006.

"Direct Democracy in Switzerland: The Future." Available online. URL: http://www.swissworld.org/dvd_rom/eng/direct_democracy_2004/content/history/history.html. Accessed on August 15, 2005.

"Focus on Direct Democracy: Swiss Direct Democracy." Available online. URL: www.aceproject.org/focuson/direct_democracy/swiss.htm. Accessed on August 22, 2005.

"Government: The Smallest Political Division: The Commune." Available online. URL: http://www.swissworld.org/eng/index.html?siteSect=701&sid=4052 816&rubricId=1501.

"Nation-By-Nation: Switzerland." Available online. URL: http://www.nationbynation.com/Switzerland/Human.html. Accessed on August 4, 2005.

Cyrill P. Rigamonti, "The New Swiss Constitution and Reform of the Federal Judiciary." Available online. URL: http://jurist.law.pitt.edu/world/swisscor1.htm. Accessed on July 29, 2005.

The Swiss Confederation: A Brief Guide. Berne: Swiss Federal Chancellery, 2004.

Andreas Kley

SYRIA

At-a-Glance

OFFICIAL NAME
Syrian Arab Republic

CAPITAL
Damascus

POPULATION
18,016,000 (2005 est.)

SIZE
71,498 sq. mi. (185,180 sq. km)

LANGUAGES
Arabic (official); Kurdish, Armenian, Aramaic, Circassian widely understood; French, English understood

RELIGIONS
Islam (Sunni Muslim 72%, Alawite 11%, other Muslim communities 4%) 87%, Christian (Syrian Orthodox, Greek Orthodox, Armenian Orthodox, Copt, Protestant, Armenian Catholic, Chaldean Catholic Church, Maronite Church, Melkite Greek Catholic, Syrian Catholic, Roman Catholic) 8.5%, Druze 1.7%, Jewish, Yazidi, and other 2.8%

NATIONAL OR ETHNIC COMPOSITION
Arab 90.3%, Kurd, Armenian, and other 9.7%

DATE OF INDEPENDENCE OR CREATION
April 17, 1946 (from League of Nations mandate under French administration)

TYPE OF GOVERNMENT
Republic

TYPE OF STATE
Centralist state

TYPE OF LEGISLATURE
Unicameral People's Council

DATE OF CONSTITUTION
March 13, 1973

DATE OF LAST AMENDMENT
June 17, 2000

Syria's system of government is a presidential democracy. There is a written constitution that provides for a republican form of government and stipulates that the people are the ultimate source of national sovereignty. The president is vested with broad executive and legislative powers. There are very few checks on presidential authority. Syria has had 13 presidents since independence and two under the current constitution.

Syria is a centralist state, divided into governorates that enjoy little autonomy. The state is still constitutionally declared to be a member of the 1971 Federation of Arab Republics (FAR).

The president is the head of state, the chief executive, and the secretary of the ruling Baath Party. Ministers are responsible to the president of the republic. The prime minister enjoys only limited influence. While members of parliament are elected, there is no multiparty system and the electoral process does not attain certain democratic standards.

The constitution provides for guarantees of both generations of human rights. The Constitutional Court can be charged with reviewing the conformity of laws with the constitution.

The constitution provides for an economic system that is socialist. Syria has been reluctant to move toward a liberal market economy and privatization. Syria is not an Islamic state; however, the religion of the president of the republic must be Islam and Islamic jurisprudence is a main source of legislation. A state of emergency was proclaimed in 1963 and has not been lifted since. Justifying its official title, the "permanent" constitution of Syria has only been amended a few times since 1973.

CONSTITUTIONAL HISTORY

Syria is situated in what is broadly called the Middle East. The territory had been occupied successively by Canaanites, Phoenicians, Hebrews, Arameans, Assyrians, Babylonians, Persians, Greeks, Romans, Nabataeans, Byzantines, Arabs, and other groups before it was under the control of the Ottoman Turks in 1516.

When World War I (1914–18) broke out, the Ottoman Empire (centered in today's Turkey) sided with the German Empire and Austria-Hungary. The Allies, including the United States, France, the United Kingdom, and Russia, held out to the Arabs the hope of postwar independence in order to gain support against the Ottoman Empire. At the same time, Britain, France, and Russia signed the secret 1916 Sikes-Picot Agreement to divide the Middle East among them. In addition, the 1917 British Balfour Declaration promised the establishment of a national home for the Jewish people in the region.

The Ottoman Empire was defeated and an independent Arab Kingdom of Syria was established in 1920 under King Faysal of the Hashemite family (later king of Iraq and the brother of Jordan's King Abdullah). Its draft constitution was based generally on the Ottoman constitution of 1876. This was a last-minute attempt to foil the implementation of the Sikes-Picot Agreement. French troops occupied Syria later that year, after France had been given a mandate over the country by the League of Nations, an international organization founded after World War I. A mandate was a treaty between the league and the mandatory power, which was charged with establishing an independent administration for the long term. Under the Middle East mandates, the area that roughly now comprises Syria and Lebanon was assigned to France, and the area that now comprises Israel, the territories of the Palestinian Authority, and Jordan was assigned to the United Kingdom.

After the dissolution of Syria's Constituent Assembly, the French high commissioner issued a constitution on his own authority in 1930. The French territories were organized as a federation, within which each single state had its own constitution. Syrian nationalist groups forced the French to evacuate their troops in 1946, leaving the country in the hands of a republican government formed during the mandate.

With the proclamation of an independent state of Israel in 1948, a series of Arab-Israeli Wars began, several of them involving Syria. In 1948 Syria, together with Egypt, Iraq, Transjordan, Lebanon, and other Arab states, refused to accept the 1947 United Nations Partition Plan for Palestine and attacked Israel. After a year of fighting, separate cease-fire agreements were signed. The armistice line (Green Line) left Israel with more of the territory of mandatory Palestine than it had been assigned in the partition plan. The Gaza Strip and the West Bank of the Jordan were annexed by Egypt and Transjordan, respectively. Palestine ceased to exist as a political and administrative entity.

After the 1956 Suez War, the subsequent remilitarization of the Egyptian Sinai, and the closure of the Straits of Tiran, Israel attacked Egypt in 1967. In this 1967 Arab-Israeli War, Israel faced Egypt, Jordan, and Syria as allied enemies while other Arab states had already begun to mobilize their armed forces. As a result of the war, which lasted only six days, Israel annexed East Jerusalem (annexed previously by Transjordan) and gained control of the Sinai Peninsula (Egypt), the Gaza Strip, the West Bank, and the Syrian Golan Heights. The 1973 Arab-Israeli War, between a coalition led by Egypt and Syria and Israel, was a war to win back territory. It resulted in another cease-fire.

These external activities involving Syria were accompanied by internal political instability and a series of military coups, which began in 1949. The rise and fall of regimes were reflected by several rather short-lived constitutional documents. Syria became a unitary parliamentary state with the 1950 constitution. However, its democratic provisions were soon undermined by the military.

Planned mergers with other Arab states either were short-lived or did not materialize at all. In 1958, Egypt and Syria merged and adopted a provisional constitution for the United Arab Republic, but by 1961 Syria had already seceded, reestablishing itself as the Syrian Arab Republic and reinstituting the 1950 constitution. Members of the Arab Socialist Resurrection Party (Baath Party) initiated a takeover in 1963. The Baath Party, founded in the 1940s on the model of European nationalist movements, embraced secularism, socialism, and pan-Arab unity. It attracted many supporters in Iraq, Syria, Jordan, and Lebanon. In 1963, Egypt, and the now Baath-controlled Syria and Iraq, agreed on a referendum of unity and another draft constitution. This tripartite federation, however, did not materialize.

After Syria was defeated in the Six-Day War, conflicts emerged within the ruling Baath Party. Evidence for these conflicts included the 1970 retreat of Syrian army forces that had marched to support the Palestinian Liberation Army (PLA) in Jordan.

Minister of Defense Hafiz al-Assad took power in a bloodless military coup in 1970. The People's Council was chosen and a national referendum confirmed Assad as the new president. Proclaimed in 1971, the Federation of Arab Republics (FAR) was another attempt at political integration, this time consisting of Egypt, Libya, and Syria; it too, did not materialize.

In 1973, the current "permanent" Syrian constitution took effect and elections were held. This constitution resembled the 1971 Egyptian constitution and reaffirmed the ideological premise that Syria is a part of the "Arab nation." Syria was constitutionally declared to be a member of the FAR. In the late 1970s, insurrections against the secular Baath government by fundamentalist Sunni Muslims led to major clashes, and ultimately the destruction of the city of Hama in 1982.

Another Arab-Israeli war began in 1982, the Lebanon War. Israel attacked the Palestine Liberation Organization (PLO) and seized a "security zone" in the south, while Syrian and Muslim Lebanese forces occupied their own military zones in the country—Lebanese in the south, Syrians in the Beka'a Valley. Israel started to withdraw its forces in 1985 and completed the withdrawal in 2000.

After ongoing protests from the Lebanese people in 2005, Syria also withdrew from Lebanon troops that had been stationed there since 1976 when Syria intervened in the Lebanese civil war, first on behalf of the Maronite Christians and later switching to back Sunni Muslim groups. Syria is still formally at war with Israel, which still occupies the Golan Heights and imposes its jurisdiction there. The Syrian government maintains the state of emergency, proclaimed in 1963, which freezes several articles of the constitution.

Syria is a founding member of the League of Arab States (LAS).

FORM AND IMPACT OF THE CONSTITUTION

Syria's constitution is codified in a single document consisting of 156 articles. It tops the hierarchy of domestic norms. International treaties take precedence over national legislation. The Syrian constitution does not include any article that specifically declares itself, or the international treaties Syria has signed, as the supreme law of the state. However, Article 311 of the Syrian court procedure gives precedence to treaties, when it states that the "commitment to the above mentioned rules does not contravene provisions of treaties held between Syria and other states in this regard." The Supreme Constitutional Court examines and decides the constitutionality of laws, which can be referred to the court by a small number of official actors.

According to Article 3 of the constitution, Islamic jurisprudence is a, not *the*, main source of legislation.

Article 153 of the constitution stipulates that legislation in effect and issued before the proclamation of the constitution remains in effect until it is amended to be compatible with constitutional provisions. However, laws in force and issued before the declaration of the constitution that are not consistent with its articles have never been amended; the effect has been a freezing of certain constitutional articles, such as those related to the judiciary.

BASIC ORGANIZATIONAL STRUCTURE

Syria is a centralist state. It is divided administratively into 14 provinces, one of which is Damascus. The minister of the interior proposes governors, who are appointed by the cabinet. Each governor is assisted by an elected provincial council.

The constitution reaffirms the long-held premise that Syria is a part of the "Arab nation." Syria is still constitutionally declared a member of the 1971 FAR.

LEADING CONSTITUTIONAL PRINCIPLES

Syria's system of government is a presidential democracy. It is a republic. Sovereignty is vested in the people. Power is divided among the executive, legislative, and judicial branches. According to the constitution, the judiciary is independent and includes a constitutional court.

Chapter 1 contains basic political, economic, educational, and cultural principles. Article 1 reads: "The Syrian Arab Republic is a democratic, popular, socialist, and sovereign state. No part of its territory can be ceded. It is a member of the Union of the Arab Republics. The Syrian Arab region is part of the Arab homeland."

The constitution is also "based" on five major principles that are explained in the preamble. These principles can be summarized as follows: (1) the idea of an Arab revolution to achieve the Arab nation's aspiration for unity, freedom, and socialism; (2) the reality that the nation is divided and that collective defense is needed should certain dangers occur; (3) the march toward the establishment of a socialist order; (4) the citizens' freedom and popular democracy; and (5) the world liberation movement for freedom, independence, and progress. The constitution as a whole shall "serve as a guide for action to the Syrian people's masses so that they will continue the battle for liberation and construction." In the words of the former president, Hafiz al-Assad, the 1973 constitution was to be the first Arab constitution to make socialist nationalist thought its guiding principle.

CONSTITUTIONAL BODIES

The predominant bodies provided for in the constitution are the president of the republic and the cabinet, the People's Council, and the Supreme Constitutional Court.

The President of the Republic

The president is both the head of state and the chief executive officer of the executive administration.

The presidential candidate is proposed by the Arab Socialist Baath Party regional command and then nominated by parliament. The nominee must be confirmed for a seven-year term in a referendum. In practice, this person runs unopposed, as the current president did in 2000. The president is eligible for unlimited successive terms. A candidate for presidency must be an Arab Syrian Muslim and be over 34 years of age.

The president plays a key role in Syria's political life, thanks to the great range of executive and legislative powers attached to this office. The president appoints and dismisses the prime minister and the other cabinet ministers. Additionally, the president appoints top civil servants and military officers as well as the members of the Supreme Constitutional Court. Through consultation with the cabinet the president establishes the state's general policy and supervises its implementation.

The president can dissolve the People's Council after explaining his reasons. The constitution does not specify any grounds for dissolution, but the president may not dissolve it more than once for the same reason. Elections are held within 90 days of dissolution.

The president may also appoint an unlimited number of vice presidents. In practice, there are two, one with responsibility for political and foreign affairs, the other for internal and party affairs.

The Council of Ministers

The cabinet is the highest executive and administrative body. It consists of the prime minister (also known as the president of the Council of Ministers), the deputy prime ministers, and the cabinet ministers. The ministers are responsible to the president of the republic. A cabinet minister can also be a member of the People's Council.

As a result of the far-reaching powers of the president, the role of the prime minister is rather secondary.

The People's Council

The People's Council is part of the legislative authority. It has 250 members and is elected for four years. The term can be expanded by law only in a state of war.

Among others powers, it nominates the president of the republic, approves or amends laws (but does not initiate them), debates cabinet policy, and approves the budget. It may also withhold confidence in the cabinet or a cabinet minister.

A no confidence vote must be submitted by at least one-fifth of the members of the council. When confidence has been withheld from the whole cabinet, the prime minister must submit the cabinet's resignation to the president of the republic.

The president's liability to the assembly is limited to cases of high treason. A request for indictment requires at least one-third of the members; the indictment itself needs a two-thirds majority decision in an open vote at a special secret session.

The Lawmaking Process

The president may draft bills and submit them to the People's Council for approval. The president assumes legislative authority when the council is not in session, provided that all the legislation issued by him is referred to the council in its subsequent session. In certain cases of national interest the president can assume legislative authority even when the People's Council is in session.

The council can repeal or amend the legislation by a two-thirds majority of the members attending the session, provided their number is not less than the absolute majority and that the amendment or repeal does not have a retroactive effect. Therefore, the people's Council's power to nullify the decree is rather nominal. If the council does

not reject or amend the bill, it is considered approved without the need for any further vote.

Legislation issued by the president during the interim period between two councils is not referred to the council; it becomes permanent law.

The president promulgates the laws approved by the council. The president may veto these laws, within a month after receiving them, but must provide the reasons for the objection. If the council again approves them by a two-thirds majority, the president must promulgate them.

The draft budget must be transmitted to the council two months before the start of the fiscal year and must be approved to go into effect. After approval of the budget, the council can approve laws on new expenditures and revenues.

In practice, most Syrian laws are initiated by the administration and are adopted with little debate by a large majority.

The Judiciary

The Syrian judicial system is a synthesis of Ottoman, French, and Islamic laws. According to the constitution, the judicial authority is independent. The Council of State shall exercise administrative jurisdiction.

Syrian courts of general jurisdiction are divided into three levels. The first level consists of the magistrate courts, the courts of first instance, juvenile courts, and customs courts. The second level consists of courts for appeals, divided into civil and criminal chambers. The Court of Cassation is at the top level and has sections for civil, commercial, criminal, and personal status matters.

A separate court system exists for personal status cases. The law provides for sharia courts (for both Sunni and Shiite Muslims), Druze courts, and other religious courts (for Christians and Jews). In addition to the courts of regular jurisdiction and the personal status courts, Syria has several specialized court systems. These include military courts, economic security courts, a supreme state security court, and some administrative courts.

The State Supreme Security Court, established in 1968, operates under an order from the martial law governor. It is not committed to public trials and its rulings are irreversible; however, they must be endorsed by the president of the republic. Martial Field Courts, also established in 1968, examine crimes committed during time of war or during ordinary military operations if the minister of defense decides to refer the cases. Both courts were set up prior to the current constitution, and, according to reports by human rights organizations, these courts have exceeded their legal authority.

The Supreme Constitutional Court examines and decides on the constitutionality of laws, which a small number of official actors have the right to present to it. It cannot examine the constitutionality of a law passed by referendum. The court also has other duties, including jurisdiction over election disputes and the trial of the president of the republic. It is the president, however, who appoints all its members, to four-year, renewable terms; that may be the reason why the Supreme Constitutional Court is not a powerful actor in legal and political life.

THE ELECTION PROCESS AND POLITICAL PARTICIPATION

All Syrians above the age of 18 have the right to vote in elections. The president can hold public referenda on important issues that affect the country's highest interests. The results of the referenda are binding and effective on the date of their promulgation.

Parliamentary Elections

The members of the People's Council are elected by general, secret, direct, and equal ballot in accordance with the election law. The constitution requires that at least half the council members be workers and peasants. The election is held within 90 days of the date of the expiration of the previous council's term. According to the majority vote system, two candidates, one of whom is necessarily a worker or a peasant, are elected in each constituency.

The Baath Party and eight other smaller political parties compose the National Progressive Front (NPF), originally established in 1971. In the 2003 elections, the government allowed independent non-NPF candidates to run for just 83 seats in the People's Council. According to international observers, these elections could not be characterized as free and fair.

POLITICAL PARTIES

The National Progressive Front represents the only framework for legal political party participation for citizens. It remains dominated by the Baath Party and thus does not undermine the one-party character of the political system. It is the constitution itself that defines the Socialist Arab Baath Party as the leading party in society and the state.

The government has banned all political activities by Syrian Kurdish parties. A 1980 law imposed the death penalty for membership in the Muslim Brotherhood.

CITIZENSHIP

Syrian citizenship is primarily acquired by birth; a child acquires Syrian citizenship if one of his or her parents is a Syrian citizen. It is of no relevance where a child is born. Syrian citizenship is regulated by law. Special facilities are guaranteed for expatriates, their sons, and citizens of Arab counties.

FUNDAMENTAL RIGHTS

In Part 4, Freedoms, Rights and Public Duties, the constitution distinguishes between human rights that apply to every human being and those that apply to Syrian citizens only. The state protects the personal freedom of the citizens and safeguards their dignity and security. Citizens are equal before the law in their rights and duties. Freedom of expression and freedom of assembly are guaranteed for citizens. Work is a right and duty of every citizen. The state undertakes to provide work for all citizens. Freedom of religion is guaranteed for all.

Impact and Functions of the Fundamental Rights

The current decades-long state of emergency has had a negative impact on fundamental or human rights in Syria. The constitution prohibits arbitrary arrest and detention; however, because of the state of emergency, significant problems remain in practice. International human rights organizations constantly report serious human rights violations in Syria, such as arbitrary detention, disappearances, and torture.

Syria has ratified the 1966 International Covenant on Civil and Political Rights (ICCPR) and the International Covenant on Economic, Social, and Cultural Rights (ICESCR). Both have precedence over national legislation. These covenants require the state to provide immediate information as to which constitutional provisions have been suspended in a state of emergency. According to the covenants, certain rights, such as the right to life and freedom of thought, conscience, and religion, may not be suspended even then.

Human rights in Islam are rooted in the belief that God is the lawgiver and the source of all human rights. This widespread assumption is reflected, for instance, in the regional Arab Charter on Human Rights (ACHR), which was adopted by the Council of the League of Arab States in 1994. Compared to the 1966 covenants, which are explicitly mentioned in the Arab Charter on Human Rights, the latter reduced the number of rights that cannot be suspended in cases of emergency. The Arab Charter on Human Rights also includes the right of every state to enact laws further restricting the rights stipulated in it. This approach seems to contradict the stipulation of "inalienable" universal rights, irrespective of belief.

Limitations to Fundamental Rights

Apart from the state of emergency, the Syrian constitution allows other possible limitations to fundamental rights. Article 27 generally provides that "citizens exercise their rights and enjoy their freedoms in accordance with the law." Freedom to hold any religious rites is guaranteed only as far as it does not "disturb the public order."

ECONOMY

According to the constitution, the state economy is a planned socialist economy that seeks to end all forms of exploitation. It recognizes three categories of property. One category is the property of the people, which includes natural resources, public domains, nationalized enterprises, and state-run establishments. A second category consists of collective property, which includes assets owned by popular and professional organizations. Finally, there is private property. Individually owned property shall not be expropriated except for the public interest and in return for just compensation in accordance with the law.

President Asad has taken initiatives to ease state control over the economy. However, Syria is still very reluctant to move toward a liberal market economy and privatization.

RELIGIOUS COMMUNITIES

The constitution requires that the president be Muslim but does not declare Islam the state religion. Freedom of faith is guaranteed and the state generally respects all religions in terms of fact and of law. The current president himself is an Alawite and therefore belongs to a minority religious group, albeit one that exercises enormous influence in the government and military.

MILITARY DEFENSE AND STATE OF EMERGENCY

Conscription is compulsory for all Syrian males under the constitution. It requires all men above the age of 18 to perform military service for 30 months. Exemptions are available for students and only sons, or for reasons of health. Voluntary recruitment is open to men and women.

The president is the supreme commander of the army and the armed forces. The president can declare war and general mobilization and conclude peace after approval by the People's Council. Syria is formally still at war with Israel, which occupies the Golan Heights. The international community has repeatedly attempted to initiate peace negotiations.

The president can declare and terminate a state of emergency in a manner stated by law. On the basis of an emergency law, Syria's president announced the state of emergency by decree in 1963. The decree explicitly provided that it would "be submitted to the first meeting of the People's Council," that is, each term after a new government has been formed. The government has justified martial law by the state of war that continues with Israel and by continuing threats posed by terrorist groups. The state of emergency in Syria has thus become a permanent legal status rather than an exceptional one.

AMENDMENTS TO THE CONSTITUTION

The president, as well as a two-thirds majority of the People's Council, have the right to propose amendments to the constitution. Upon receipt of the proposal, the council establishes a special committee to investigate it. The amendment must be approved by a two-thirds majority and by the president of the republic.

Justifying its title, the "permanent" constitution of Syria has been amended very few times since 1973. The provision that the president must be of Islamic faith was one such amendment. Another, in 2000, reduced the mandatory minimal age of the president from 40 to 34 years.

PRIMARY SOURCES

1973 Constitution in English. Available online. URL: http://www.oefre.unibe.ch/law/icl/sy00000_.html. Accessed on July 28, 2005.

SECONDARY SOURCES

Moh'd Anjarini, "Law on the Emergency Status Issued upon the Legislative Decree No. 15." *Justice Journal* 1 (2001). Available online. URL: http://www.shrc.org.uk/data/aspx/d4/354.aspx. Accessed on September 13, 2005.

Nathan J. Brown, *Constitutions in a Nonconstitutional World—Arab Basic Laws and the Prospects for Accountable Government.* New York: State University of New York Press, 2002.

Bureau of Public Affairs, U.S. Department of State, "Background Note and Country Reports on Human Rights Practices and International Religious Freedom Report 2004." Available online. URL: http://www.state.gov/. Accessed on September 22, 2005.

Thomas Collello, ed., *Syria—a Country Study.* Washington, D.C.: United States Government Printing Office, 1988.

Steven Heydemann, *Authoritarianism in Syria: Institutions and Social Conflict 1946–1970.* Ithaca, N.Y.: Cornell University Press, 1999.

"The League of Arab States." Available online. URL: http://www.arableagueonline.org/. Accessed on September 6, 2005.

Syrian Human Rights Committee, "Jurisdiction Authority in Syria: Its Role in Protecting Human Rights." Available online. URL: http://www.shrc.org.uk/data/aspx/d5/1115.aspx. Accessed on September 20, 2005.

Syrian Human Rights Committee, "Report on the Human Rights Situation in Syria—over a 20-year Period 1979–1999." Available online. URL: http://www.shrc.org.uk/data/pdf/1275.pdf. Accessed on September 10, 2005.

United Nations Development Programme, "Constitutions of the Arab Region." Available online. URL: http://www.pogar.org/themes/constitution.asp. Accessed on September 8, 2005.

Michael Rahe

TAIWAN

At-a-Glance

OFFICIAL NAME
Republic of China, Taiwan

CAPITAL
Taipei

POPULATION
22,604,550 (end of 2003)

SIZE
13,887 sq. mi. (35,967 sq. km)

LANGUAGES
Mandarin Chinese (official), Taiwanese (Min), Hakka dialects

RELIGIONS
Buddhist, Confucian, and Taoist 93%, Christian 4.5%, other 2.5%

NATIONAL OR ETHNIC COMPOSITION
Taiwanese (including Hakka) 84%, mainland Chinese 14%, indigenous 2%

DATE OF INDEPENDENCE OR CREATION
January 1, 1912

TYPE OF GOVERNMENT
Republic

TYPE OF STATE
Unitary state

TYPE OF LEGISLATURE
Unicameral parliament

DATE OF CONSTITUTION
December 25, 1946

DATE OF LAST AMENDMENT
June 7, 2005

Taiwan is a republic with a strong presidency. Its current 1947 constitution was drafted for all of China, of which the island of Taiwan was a province. With the Communist takeover of the mainland the Chinese government and army retreated to Taiwan. The relationship of Taiwan with mainland China remains delicate today. Fundamental rights are protected by the constitution. State and religion are separated. Taiwan has a market-oriented economy.

CONSTITUTIONAL HISTORY

The island of Taiwan has been ruled as a part of China for several hundred years. Any discussion of its constitutional development must therefore begin with the history of constitutionalism in China. Taiwan was ruled by Japan from 1895 to 1945, but the Japanese occupation had no lasting effect on the political history of the island.

Constitutionalism in the modern sense emerged in China under the Qing (Ch'ing) dynasty (1644–1911/12 C.E.). The Sino-Japanese War (1894–95) was the final blow in a series of humiliating interventions in China by foreign powers. In 1905, the Qing dispatched five delegates to observe and study the Japanese constitutional monarchy, which had successfully built Japan into a powerful modern state. Upon their return, the delegates recommended that China adopt the Japanese model. In 1906 an imperial edict supporting the idea was issued.

In 1908, the government proclaimed the 23 Articles, the founding principles of constitutionalism, and set forth a nine-year implementation schedule or tutelage period. On October 10, 1911, the Wuhan (Wuchang) uprising began, ushering in the Xinhai Revolution, which overthrew the monarchy. In a final attempt at reform the Qing promulgated the 19 Tenets. In February 1912 the Qing court proclaimed the decree of abdication.

The Republic of China was proclaimed in 1911 by revolutionaries under the leadership of Sun Yat-sen (1866–1925). The new Republic of China adopted the 19 Tenets as its first constitutional document, though it remained largely a dead letter. In the elections to parliament the Nationalist Party (Kuomintang), made up largely of former revolutionaries, won a commanding majority. Several consecutive constitutions (1912, 1923, 1936, 1947) were passed. They introduced a number of Western constitutional principles such as the rights and duties of the people and a three-branch government. The 1947 constitution was based on Chinese constitutional ideas, with the addition of elements of the 1919 German Weimar constitution. Amended several times, it is the core of today's constitutional law of Taiwan. It includes a blanket human rights clause in Article 22.

Soon after the adoption of the national constitution, the Kuomintang led by Chiang Kai-shek were defeated in mainland China by the Communist Revolution and retreated to Taiwan, where it declared a Communist Rebellion Period and imposed martial law. The national constitution assumed a merely nominal existence, as the dictatorial presidency held total control over the exercise of power. This situation truly contradicted the spirit and legitimacy of democratic constitutional law.

It was only in 1991 that the period of the Communist Rebellion was officially terminated. The constitution was amended seven times from 1991 to 2005, successfully ending the era of dictatorship.

Taiwan is recognized as an independent state by a number of other states, but not by the United States. Taiwan's relationship to mainland China has remained politically delicate since the Beijing government claimed national supremacy over the island.

FORM AND IMPACT OF THE CONSTITUTION

The constitution is contained in one document together with Additional Articles. It takes precedence over all other national law. Framed for all of China under very different circumstances than those of today, it no longer reflects the actual needs of Taiwan.

In form, the constitution adopted the Five Power Constitution and division of powers theories of Sun Yat-sen, but in substance it implemented the cabinet system of the 1919 German constitution of the Weimar Republic.

BASIC ORGANIZATIONAL STRUCTURE

Taiwan is a unitary state structured in 16 counties and five municipalities. The 1947 constitution in theory applies to all of China including the mainland. In this framework, Taiwan has the status of a province. According to the con-stitution, "all levels of local government below the provincial level have self-government."

LEADING CONSTITUTIONAL PRINCIPLES

The constitution of Taiwan is based on the constitutional theory of Sun Yat-sen. It calls for a fivefold division of powers among the executive, legislative, judicial, control, and examination *yuan* (government bodies). The central government combines the cabinet and presidential systems of government.

CONSTITUTIONAL BODIES

The constitutional law of Taiwan establishes a complex framework with regard to the central organs, which mainly consist of the president, and the five branches of government, namely, the Executive Yuan, the Legislative Yuan, the Judicial Yuan, the Examination Yuan, and the Control Yuan. After seven constitutional revisions, the key to the system is the relationship among the president, the Executive Yuan, and the Legislative Yuan.

The President

The president is the head of state. He or she is directly elected by the people of the "free area" of the Republic of China. The president serves a four-year term and can be reelected to serve only one consecutive term. The president represents the state in foreign affairs and has supreme command of the army, navy, and air force. The president promulgates laws and issue mandates; declares martial law; appoints and dismisses the members of the Executive Yuan (with the cooperation of the Legislative Yuan) and other civil and military officers; confers honors and decorations; exercises the powers of amnesty, pardon, remission of sentence, and restitution of civil rights; and exercises the powers of concluding treaties, declaring war, and making peace.

The president may, within 10 days or passage by the Legislative Yuan of a no confidence vote against the president of the Executive Yuan, declare the dissolution of the Legislative Yuan after consulting its president. However, the president cannot dissolve the Legislative Yuan while martial law or an emergency decree is in effect.

The Executive Yuan

The Executive Yuan is the highest administrative organ of the state. It has a president (equivalent to a prime minister), a vice president, and a number of ministers, chairs of commissions, and ministers without portfolio. The president of the Executive Yuan is appointed by the president of the republic with the approval of the Legislative Yuan; the other cabinet members are appointed by the president of the republic upon the recommendation of the president of Executive Yuan.

The Legislative Yuan has the power to pass a motion of no confidence against the president of the Executive Yuan, who must then resign. However, after such passage, the Executive Yuan may ask the president of the republic to dissolve the Legislative Yuan. The existence of this option encourages the Legislative Yuan to act with caution with regard to motions of no confidence. The actual workings of the mechanisms depend on the decisions of the political parties.

The Judicial Yuan has noted, in a crucial ruling, that the constitution establishes a system of checks and balances between the president of the republic and the president of the Executive Yuan. The constitutional basis for this statement can be found in the articles pertaining to the issuance of emergency orders. Pursuant to current constitutional law, the Executive Yuan should be considered responsible to the Legislative Yuan rather than to the president of the republic, but this has not yet been fully implemented. In practice, the relationships among the president of the republic, the Executive Yuan, and the Legislative Yuan require clarification.

The Legislative Yuan

The Legislative Yuan is the highest legislative organ of the state; it exercises legislative power on behalf of the people. The Legislative Yuan has 225 (from December 2007 onward: 113) members. Some members are elected from a nationwide constituency and by Chinese citizens residing abroad, on the basis of proportional representation among political parties. The remainder are elected by popular vote in individual constituencies. Members of the Legislative Yuan serve a term of four years and are re-electable. The Legislative Yuan has a president and a vice president elected from among its members.

The Legislative Yuan has the power to decide by resolution matters such as statutory bills, budgetary bills, auditing reports, or bills concerning martial law, amnesty, declaration of war, conclusion of peace, treaties, and other important affairs of the state. It exercises the power of consent over the appointment of the president, vice president, and grand justices of the Judicial Yuan; the president, vice president, and members of the Examination Yuan; and the president, vice president, auditor general, and members of the Control Yuan.

The Lawmaking Process

Every bill, after it is passed by the Legislative Yuan, requires support from a majority in the cabinet or Executive Yuan. This dualist power structure allows for diverse political arrangements and shifts of powers among executive departments, subject to strict regulations.

Before the 1997 revision of the constitution, if the cabinet returned a bill to the Legislative Yuan for reconsideration, the latter needed a two-thirds majority vote to overrule the objection. Now it needs only a majority of all the members. This amendment will reduce the likelihood that the Executive Yuan will reject bills passed by the Legislative Yuan. The greatest hurdle for a system in which the president is head of administration as well as head of state will be the resistance of the Executive to implementation of bills passed by a Legislative Yuan under the control of a different political party.

The Judicial Yuan

The Judicial Yuan is the highest judicial organ of the state. It establishes subordinate organs, including courts of various instances, administrative courts, and the Committee on the Discipline of Public Functionaries. It is responsible for the trial of civil, criminal, and administrative cases and for the disciplinary punishment of public employees. The Judiciary Yuan is composed of 15 grand justices, including a president and a vice president selected from among them. Each grand justice of the Judicial Yuan serves an individual term of eight years and cannot serve another consecutive term. Grand justices are nominated and, subject to consent by the Legislative Yuan, appointed by the president of the republic. Among the grand justices nominated by the president in the year 2003, eight members, including the president and the vice president of the Judicial Yuan, will serve for four years. The remaining grand justices will serve for eight years. The Council of Grand Justices of the Judicial Yuan is responsible for interpreting the constitution.

The Examination Yuan

The Examination Yuan is the highest organ of the state dealing with the civil service. It is responsible for matters relating to screening of civil servants: their security of tenure, pecuniary aid in case of death, retirement, and old-age pension, as well as legal matters relating to the employment, discharge, official performance grading, salary scales, promotion and transfer, and awards and commendations of civil servants. These responsibilities are shared by the Ministry of Examination, the Ministry of Civil Service, the Civil Service Protection and Training Commission, and the Supervisory Board of the Public Service Pension Fund. The Examination Yuan comprises a president, a vice president, and 19 members, who serve six-year terms. They are all nominated and, with the consent of the Legislative Yuan, appointed by the president of the republic.

The Control Yuan

The Control Yuan is the highest control or audit organ of the state; it exercises powers of consent, impeachment, censure, and auditing. It is composed of 29 members, including a president and a vice president, who serve six-year terms. All of these are nominated and, with the consent of the Legislative Yuan, appointed by the president of the republic. The Control Yuan establishes the Ministry of Audit, responsible for auditing various public organs across the nation. The auditor general serves a term of office of six years and is nominated and, with the consent by the Legislative Yuan, appointed by the president of the republic.

THE ELECTION PROCESS

All Taiwanese above the age of 20 have the right to vote in the elections.

Members of the Legislative Yuan are elected by a mixed system of single nontransferable votes and by proportional representation. The president and the vice president are elected by direct vote of all citizens.

POLITICAL PARTIES

Taiwan has a pluralist system of political parties. The formerly overwhelming position of the Kuomintang Party has given way to make room for other important political parties in recent years. The grand justices of the Judicial Yuan also form a Constitutional Court to adjudicate matters relating to the dissolution of unconstitutional political parties.

CITIZENSHIP

Citizenship is primarily acquired by birth. The principle of *ius sanguinis* is applied. This means that a child acquires Taiwanese citizenship if one of his or her parents is, at the time of that child's birth, a Taiwanese citizen. It is of no relevance where a child is born.

FUNDAMENTAL RIGHTS

The constitution places strong emphasis on fundamental human rights: Articles 7 to 22 of Chapter 2 of the constitution all underline the importance of the protection of fundamental rights. The constitution guarantees a wide range of human rights. The general equal treatment clause is contained in Article 7, which guarantees that all citizens of the Republic of China are equal before the law, irrespective of their sex, religion, ethnic origin, class, or party affiliation. Article 8 guarantees personal freedom.

Impact and Function of Fundamental Rights

The executive government has taken steps to improve respect for human rights. Almost all restrictions on the press have ended, restrictions on personal freedoms have been relaxed, and the prohibition against organizing of new political parties has been lifted. Besides the fundamental rights already mentioned, Article 22 guarantees "all other freedoms and rights of the people," unless they are detrimental to social order or public welfare.

Limitations to Fundamental Rights

There is a general limitation clause, which provides that none of the freedoms and rights can be abridged by law except such laws as are necessary to prevent infringement upon the freedoms of others, to avert an imminent danger, to maintain social order, or to promote public welfare.

ECONOMY

The national economy is constitutionally based on the Principle of People's Livelihood. The constitution seeks to effect the equalization of land rights and regulate private capital in order to assure an equitable distribution of national wealth and sufficiency for the people's livelihood.

Private property is protected by the state. However, private wealth can be restricted, if it is deemed detrimental to the balanced development of national wealth and people's livelihood. Liberalization of the economy has diminished the dominant role of state-owned enterprises. Taken as a whole, the Taiwanese economic system can be described as a market-oriented economy.

RELIGIOUS COMMUNITIES

Freedom of religious belief is guaranteed. It is generally respected by the executive government in terms of law and fact. There is no state religion.

MILITARY DEFENSE AND STATE OF EMERGENCY

Citizens are constitutionally obliged to perform military service. General conscription requires all men to perform basic military service from January 1 of the year after they become 18 until December 31 of the year they become 40 years of age. Generally, men undergo 22 months of training. They may choose alternative nonmilitary national service instead.

The president is the supreme commander of the army, navy, and air force of the country. The Additional Articles to the Constitution of the Republic of China stipulate that the president may, by resolution of the Executive Yuan Council, issue emergency decrees and take all necessary measures to avert imminent danger affecting the security of the state or of the people, or to cope with any serious financial or economic crisis.

AMENDMENTS TO THE CONSTITUTION

The Legislative Yuan can amend the constitution on its own initiative. Upon proposal and by resolution of the Legislative Yuan, a bill to amend the constitution may be ratified by the majority of citizens through a referendum.

PRIMARY SOURCES

Constitution in Chinese. Available online. URL: http://www.president.gov.tw. Accessed on July 18, 2005.

Constitution in English: *Constitution, Republic of China.* Available online. URL: http://www.taiwandocuments.org/constitution01.htm. Accessed on September 15, 2005.

SECONDARY SOURCES

Bureau of Public Affairs, U.S. Department of State, "Background Note and Country Reports on Human Rights Practices and International Religious Freedom Report 2004." Available online. URL: http://www.state.gov/. Accessed on August 2, 2005.

The Constitution of the Republic of China: Its Brief Introduction and Text. The Secretariat of the Judicial Yuan of the Republic of China, 1975.

Thomas Benjamin Ginsburg, *Growing Constitutions Judicial Review in the New Democracies (Korea, Taiwan, China, Mongolia).* Berkeley: University of California, 1999.

"History of Constitutional Revisions in the Republic of China." Available online. URL: http://www.taiwandocuments.org/constitution07.htm. Accessed on August 25, 2005.

"Taiwan Documents Project." Available online. URL: http://www.taiwandocuments.org/. Accessed on September 29, 2005.

Tsi-Yang Chen

TAJIKISTAN

At-a-Glance

OFFICIAL NAME
Republic of Tajikistan

CAPITAL
Dushanbe

POPULATION
7,011,556 (July 2004 est.)

SIZE
55,251 sq. mi. (143,100 sq. km)

LANGUAGES
Tajik (official) and Russian (language of international communication)

RELIGIONS
Sunni Muslim 85%, Shia Muslim 5%, other 10% (2003 est.)

NATIONAL OR ETHNIC COMPOSITION
Tajik (including Islmaili Pomiri) 64.9%, Uzbek 25%, Russian 3.5%, other 6.6%

DATE OF INDEPENDENCE OR CREATION
September 9, 1991

TYPE OF GOVERNMENT
Authoritarian presidential regime

TYPE OF STATE
Centralistic state with federal elements

TYPE OF LEGISLATURE
Bicameral parliament

DATE OF CONSTITUTION
November 6, 1994

DATE OF LAST AMENDMENT
June 22, 2003

Tajikistan is a presidential autocracy with a strong president exercising control over executive, legislative, and judicial powers. The president appoints and dismisses the administration, the judges, and the members of the Majlisi Milli, the upper chamber of the parliament. Free, equal, direct, fair, and transparent elections are guaranteed by the constitution. However, none of the elections has met minimal democratic standards.

Tajikistan is made up of five provinces, including the city of Dushanbe and the Mountainous Badakhshan Autonomous Province. The constitution provides for fundamental human rights and allows individuals and government institutions to appeal to the Constitutional Court to protect those rights. Religious freedom and state noninterference in religious matters are guaranteed, but not implemented.

CONSTITUTIONAL HISTORY

According to the present-day Tajik leadership, the first Tajik state was the Persian-speaking Samanid Empire (875–999 C.E.), which ruled what is now Tajikistan and neighboring areas under the ruler Ismail Somoni, the "founding father" of the Tajik nation. In the early 13th century, the Tajik territory was incorporated into the realm of the Mongol conqueror Genghis Khan. After his death in 1227, Genghis Khan's empire was split among his sons. In the late 14th century, one of his relatives, Amir Timur (Tamerlane), conquered not only today's Tajik territory, but also vast parts of Russia, Persia, and Turkey. Starting from the 16th century Tajikistan was ruled as part of the Khanats of Kokand and Bukhara. After a series of attacks that began in the 1860s, during the "Great Game" between the British and the Russian Empires for supremacy in Central Asia, the Tajik people were under Russian rule, which continued after 1917 under Soviet auspices. In 1924, Tajikistan was styled an Autonomous Soviet Socialist Republic within Uzbekistan; in 1924 it was reorganized as a Soviet Socialist Republic. After the failure of the 1991 Moscow hardliners' coup, Tajikistan reluctantly declared its independence on September 9, 1991.

In 1992–97, a civil war pitted old-guard regionally based ruling elites against disenfranchised regions, liberal reformists, and Islamists loosely organized in the United Tajik Opposition (UTO). By 1997, the Tajik government and the UTO successfully negotiated a power-sharing peace accord, which was implemented in 2000.

On November 6, 1994, a new constitution was adopted by referendum to replace the 1978 constitution of the Tajik Socialist Soviet Republic and the 1977 constitution of the Soviet Union. The post-Soviet constitution was amended several times, most recently on June 22, 2003.

FORM AND IMPACT OF THE CONSTITUTION

Tajikistan has a written constitution, codified in a single document that takes precedence over all other national law. International law is a constituent part of the Tajik legal system and has precedence over Tajik laws.

BASIC ORGANIZATIONAL STRUCTURE

Tajikistan is a centralistic state, made up of five provinces (*viloyatlar*), including Dushanbe city and the Mountainous Badakhshan Autonomous Province. The provinces differ considerably in geographical area, population size, and economic strength.

The Mountainous Badakhshan Autonomous Province is an integral and indivisible part of the Republic of Tajikistan. Its territory cannot be changed without the consent of its own parliament; a right to secede from Tajikistan is not stipulated in the constitution.

Each province is governed by a chairperson of the *hukumat*, or province administration, who is appointed and dismissed by the president upon approval of the relevant local parliament. The chairperson of the *hukumat* is the president's representative, responsible before the higher executive bodies and assembly of the province.

LEADING CONSTITUTIONAL PRINCIPLES

Tajikistan's system of government is dominated by the president, who controls the executive, legislative, and judicial power. The judiciary is not fully independent.

The Tajik constitutional system is defined by a number of leading principles: state sovereignty, democracy, supremacy of the constitution and the law, separation of state and religion, and centralism. According to the constitution, Tajikistan is a social state; its policy is aimed at providing at least minimal living conditions for all.

Political participation is restricted, as key positions (e.g., chairpersons of *hukumats*) are appointed by the president. The lower chamber of the Tajik parliament and the parliaments of districts and towns are directly elected.

The rule of law is proclaimed. All state bodies, public associations, and citizens must act according to the constitution and the law. State and religion are separated.

CONSTITUTIONAL BODIES

The predominant bodies provided for in the constitution are the president; the administration; the bicameral parliament, the Supreme Assembly or Majlisi Oli; and the Constitutional Court.

The President

The president is the head of state and exercises the executive power. The president protects the constitution, laws, and the rights and freedoms of the citizens; guarantees the unity, national independence, territorial integrity, stability, and continuity of the state; ensures the functioning of the bodies of state power; and implements international treaties. The constitutional term of the president is seven years. The same person can be elected twice.

The president appoints and dismisses the prime minister and other ministers with the consent of the Supreme Assembly; the chairpersons of the provinces, districts, and towns with the approval of the relevant assembly; with the approval of the Ministry of Justice the president also appoints the prosecutor-general and the judges of all major courts.

The Administration

The administration implements the executive power. Formed by the president, it comprises the prime minister, the prime minister's deputies, cabinet ministers, and chairpersons of state committees.

The administration "ensures the successful leadership of economic, social, and spiritual spheres and the implementation of laws and decrees of the Supreme Assembly, and orders and decrees of the president of Tajikistan."

The Majlisi Oli (Parliament)

The Majlisi Oli, the Supreme Assembly, is the main representative body. It comprises two chambers—the National Assembly (lower chamber) and the Assembly of Representatives (upper chamber). The term of the Majlisi Oli is five years.

The Majlisi Namoyondagon is the lower chamber of the Majlisi Oli. It consists of 63 deputies, of whom 41 are elected in single-mandate constituencies and 22 are assigned to the parties on the basis of proportional representation. The Majlisi Namoyondagon sits permanently.

The Majlisi Milli is the upper chamber. It has 33 members, eight directly appointed by the president and 25 elected indirectly by the provincial assemblies. The Majlisi Milli acts on a convocational basis.

Besides adopting laws, both chambers share responsibility with the administration for defining the major directions of the republic's domestic and foreign policy; they adopt the state budget and confirm ministerial and presidential decisions. Whereas the Majlisi Namoyondagon has the prerogative of legislative initiative, the Majlisi Milli can either approve or veto its acts; the latter has power to fill key government positions.

The Lawmaking Process

The right of the legislative initiative belongs to the Majlisi Oli, the president, the administration, the Constitutional Court, the Supreme Court, the Supreme Economic Court, and the Assembly of People's Deputies of Badakhshan. A law legally goes into effect after it has been adopted by the Majlisi Namoyondagon, approved by the Majlisi Milli, signed by the president, and published in the media. If a law is rejected by the Majlisi Milli or the president, the Majlisi Namoyondagon can overturn the decision.

The Judiciary

The judicial system comprises the Constitutional Court, the Supreme Court, the Supreme Economic Court, the Military Court, and the Court of Badakhshan. All high-ranking judges are elected by the Majlisi Milli on the suggestion of the president. All lower-ranking judges are directly appointed and dismissed by the president on the suggestion of the Ministry of Justice. Their term of service is five years. According to the constitution, judges are independent and are subordinate only to the constitution and law. Interference in their activity is not permitted.

The Constitutional Court consists of seven judges, one of whom is a representative of the Badakhshan. It ranks at the same level as the Supreme Court, the Supreme Economic Court, the Military Court, and the Court of Badakhshan. It deals with constitutional disputes submitted by the government agencies with legislative initiative authority and individuals.

THE ELECTION PROCESS

All Tajik citizens over the age of 18 have the right to vote. Citizens who have been permanent residents in the country for at least seven years and have reached the age of 25 or 35, respectively, may stand for election to the Majlisi Namoyandagon and Majlisi Milli.

To be registered as a candidate in the presidential election, one has to be between the ages of 35 and 65, know the state language, and have lived on Tajik territory for the past 10 years. Citizens who have been judicially certified as insane, as well as those imprisoned upon verdict, may neither vote nor stand for election.

According to reports of international organizations, all elections held so far have fallen short of international election standards. They have lacked transparency, accountability, fairness, and secrecy.

POLITICAL PARTIES

The constitutional right to form political parties and other public associations is limited through provisions that ban organizations that encourage racism, nationalism, social and religious enmity, or hatred; or advocate the forcible overthrow of the constitutional structures; or form armed groups. Among the six registered political parties is the Islamic Revival Party. Several nonregistered political parties operate illegally in the underground.

CITIZENSHIP

On the day of adoption of the constitution, all people living on the territory of Tajikistan became Tajik citizens. Nowadays, Tajik citizenship is acquired at birth if one of the child's parents holds Tajik citizenship or, by an adult, after living on Tajik territory for five years.

FUNDAMENTAL RIGHTS

The constitution defines the fundamental rights of individuals and citizens in its second chapter. The traditional set of individual rights, and political, economic, and social rights are emphasized.

Impact and Functions of Fundamental Rights

According to the constitution, all Tajik citizens have equal rights and freedoms and are equal before the law, without discrimination by nationality, race, sex, language, religious belief, political persuasion, social status, knowledge, and property. Men and women enjoy equal rights. Citizens' rights and freedoms, established by constitution and laws, are not inalienable; they can be abolished by a constitutional change.

Limitations to Fundamental Rights

According to the constitution, the freedoms and rights of individuals and citizens are protected by the constitution, the laws of the republic, and international documents recognized by Tajikistan. Only a court decision may limit citizens' rights and freedoms.

ECONOMY

The constitution specifies that the economic system is based on various forms of ownership and structured by a set of conditions. Among them are the freedom of economic activity and entrepreneurship, equality of rights, and equality and legal protection of all forms of ownership. The constitution also defines social rights (to work, leisure, housing, health care, social security, and education).

RELIGIOUS COMMUNITIES

Freedom of religion or belief is guaranteed as a basic human right. According to the constitution, religious organizations and associations must be separate from the state and must not interfere with state affairs.

In reality, however, religion and state clearly interface in many ways. The government appoints the mufti as the supreme Muslim religious authority and controls nonstate religious associations such as Hizbut Tahrir. The religiously affiliated Islamic Revival Party is represented in parliament, and Islamists loosely organized in the United Tajik Opposition are included in the government.

MILITARY DEFENSE AND STATE OF EMERGENCY

The president is the chief commander of the armed forces, appointing and dismissing their commanders. The president also has the right to declare a state of war and a state of emergency, which must be approved by the Majlisi Oli.

A state of emergency may be declared as a temporary measure (not longer than three months) to ensure the security of citizens and the state when there is a direct threat to the rights and freedoms of citizens or to the independence or territorial integrity of the state and when natural disasters prevent the normal operations of the constitutional authorities. Even during a state of emergency, certain specified rights and freedoms may not be limited. The Supreme Assembly may be dispersed.

General conscription requires all men over the age of 18 to perform basic military service of 24 months. In addition, there are professional contract soldiers who serve for fixed periods in the Tajik army. The Tajik government has obliged itself by international treaties not to produce atomic, biological, or chemical weapons.

AMENDMENTS TO THE CONSTITUTION

The constitution can only be changed by referendum. Certain features are irrevocable, such as the form of public administration, territorial integrity, and the democratic, law-governed, and secular nature of the state.

PRIMARY SOURCES

Constitution of the Republic of Tajikistan, adopted on November 6, 1994, in English. Available online. URL: http://unpan1.un.org/intradoc/groups/public/documents/untc/unpan003670.htm. Accessed on September 4, 2005.

SECONDARY SOURCES

Nargis Bozorova, "Researching Tajik Law: A Guide to the Tajik Legal System." Available online. URL: http://www.llrx.com/features/tajik.htm. Accessed on June 29, 2006.

Mehmet Semith Gemalmaz, "Structure and Authority of the Judiciary within the Legal Order of the Tajikistan Republic." *Tilburg Foreign Law Review* 7, no. 4 (1998–9): 307–346.

Organization for Security and Co-operation in Europe, Centre in Dushanbe. Available online. URL: http://www.osce.org/tajikstan/. Accessed on June 29, 2006.

Marie-Carin von Gumppenberg

TANZANIA

At-a-Glance

OFFICIAL NAME
The United Republic of Tanzania

CAPITAL
Dodoma

POPULATION
34,569,2321 (2002 population census) with population density of 36 people per sq. km

SIZE
364,905 sq. mi. (945,100 sq. km)

LANGUAGES
Kiswahili (national and official), English (official)

RELIGIONS
Roman Catholic 50%, Islam 40%, Protestant 7%, traditional belief, Buddhism and other 3% (est.)

NATIONAL OR ETHNIC COMPOSITION
Approximately 130 Bantu ethnic groups 97%, Indian and Arab descendants 3%

DATE OF INDEPENDENCE OR CREATION
Tanganyika (December 9, 1961; republic December 9, 1962); Zanzibar (December 10, 1963, revolution January 12, 1964); United Republic of Tanzania (April 26, 1964, union of Tanganyika and Zanzibar)

TYPE OF GOVERNMENT
Parliamentary democracy

TYPE OF STATE
Unitary state

TYPE OF LEGISLATURE
Unicameral parliament

DATE OF CONSTITUTION
April 26, 1977, Constitution of the United Republic of Tanzania; 1985 Constitution of Zanzibar

DATE OF LAST AMENDMENT
April 6, 2005

The United Republic of Tanzania is a union of the two states of Tanganyika (on the mainland) and Zanzibar (on islands) founded on April 26, 1964. It is a parliamentary democracy and a unitary secular state. It is based on the rule of law with separation of executive, judicial, and legislative powers. The constitution is the supreme law of the land. The executive is accountable to the legislature and to the judiciary, which is independent.

The Constitution of the United Republic of Tanzania guarantees fundamental human rights. All public authorities are subject to the constitution. The Special Constitutional Court of the United Republic of Tanzania is established to protect human rights against violations. It is mandated to interpret the constitution.

Tanzania has been a multiparty democratic state since 1992 and has had a free-market economy since the 1990s. The military is subject to the civil government under the constitution.

CONSTITUTIONAL HISTORY

Tanzania was colonized in different phases. After the scramble for and partition of Africa that followed the 1884–85 Berlin Conference, Tanganyika fell under German colonial rule, and Zanzibar under British control. After World War I (1914–18) Britain took over Tanganyika as well. At the end of World War II (1939–45) Tanganyika became a United Nations Trust Territory under British control. By that time, Britain had imposed its own legal system.

Tanganyika gained independence with a Westminster system of government, whereby the head of the executive administration was the prime minister (Julius Kambarage Nyerere) while the head of state was the British monarch (Queen Elizabeth II). The people of Tanganyika soon declared a republic, which was inaugurated on December 9, 1962. With this change, Nyerere became president and head of state.

Zanzibar became independent of British rule on December 10, 1963. A month later, on January 12, 1964, a violent revolution overthrew the sultan and suspended the constitution of the State of Zanzibar. On April 26, 1964, the two independent states decided to form a union. The Articles of Union of Tanganyika and Zanzibar were to remain in effect in the new United Republic of Tanzania for one year. In 1965 the Interim Constitution of Tanzania was enacted. On April 26, 1977, the permanent constitution of the United Republic of Tanzania was enacted by the National Assembly. This basic law continues to apply in both parts of the union.

FORM AND IMPACT OF THE CONSTITUTION

The United Republic of Tanzania has a permanent written constitution codified in a single document called the Constitution (Katiba ya Jamhuri ya Muungano wa Tanzania). The constitution is the supreme law of the United Republic of Tanzania; any law inconsistent with it is declared null and void. All laws enacted must conform to the constitution, and international law must be in accordance with the constitution to be applied.

BASIC ORGANIZATIONAL STRUCTURE

Tanzania is divided into 26 administrative regions. There are 21 regions in Tanzania Mainland and five regions in Tanzania Zanzibar. Dar es Salaam is a distinct commercial city within Tanzania. The regions are subdivided into districts, divisions, wards, villages, and hamlets.

LEADING CONSTITUTIONAL PRINCIPLES

Tanzania is a sovereign united republic. It is guided by a number of principles: It is a democratic society, founded on the principles of freedom, justice, fraternity, and concord. Its government must adhere to the principles of democracy and socialism. The executive is accountable to a legislature composed of elected members who are representatives of the people. The judiciary is independent and dispenses justice without fear or favor, thereby ensuring that human rights are preserved and protected and that the duties of every person are faithfully discharged.

CONSTITUTIONAL BODIES

Tanzania has the following constitutional bodies: the executive (which comprises the president, vice president, prime minister, cabinet, and government); the legislature (the parliament, composed of the president and the National Assembly, or Bunge la Jamhuri); and the judiciary (Mahakama), which is independent in order to ensure separation of powers and checks and balances.

The Executive

The president is the head of state, the head of the executive administration, and the commander in chief of the armed forces. He or she is democratically elected to a five-year term of office and can be reelected for one more consecutive term. The vice president is the principal assistant to the president in all matters; in particular, the vice president assists the president in supervising the day-to-day implementation of union matters and performs all duties of the office of the president when the president is out of the country or is not functioning as president.

The president appoints a prime minister, who supervises the day-to-day functions and affairs of the executive administration. He or she also manages the executive's relations with the National Assembly.

The Legislature

Legislative power over all union matters, and of all matters concerning Tanzania Mainland, is vested in the parliament, which consists of two elements—the president and the National Assembly. The National Assembly is vested with powers to oversee and advise the executive administration on behalf of the people. The president may attend parliament but has no right to vote on any matter. The parliament is vested with the power to deliberate upon and ratify all treaties and agreements to which the United Republic is a party.

Legislative power in Tanzania Zanzibar is vested in the House of Representatives. If the House of Representatives enacts any matter that is within the legislative power of parliament, that law shall be null and void, and likewise if the National Assembly enacts any law on a matter within the purview of the House of Representatives, that law shall be null and void. There are specific union matters in which both Tanzania Mainland and Tanzania Zanzibar have jurisdiction and must cooperate. These include the constitution of Tanzania and the government of the United Republic, foreign affairs, defense and security, police, emergency powers, citizenship, immigration, external borrowing and trade, service in the government of the United Republic, income tax, ports, and all matters related to transport, mail, communication, higher education, industrial licensing and statistics, mineral resources, the National Examinations Council of Tanzania, the Court of Appeal of the United Republic, and registration of political parties. The legislature oversees the executive branch in the exercise of its duties.

The Lawmaking Process
The National Assembly is responsible for enacting laws for the United Republic of Tanzania. It does so by debat-

ing and passing bills that eventually have to be assented to by the president. The president can either approve or disapprove a bill passed by the assembly. In the latter case, the president returns the bill to the National Assembly together with a statement of his or her objections. The National Assembly must wait six months to resend the bill to the president; even then, it must pass the bill by a majority of two-thirds of all members of parliament. Then the president has two choices: to assent to the bill within 21 days or to dissolve parliament.

After the president's assent, the cabinet minister responsible for that matter gives notice of the law through the government *Gazette*. Cabinet ministers and others who have departmental responsibilities have the power under the constitution to make regulations that have the force of law. These need not go to the National Assembly.

The Judiciary

The judiciary is officially independent. The Court of Appeals of the United Republic of Tanzania is the supreme court of the country. There are High Courts both in Tanzania Zanzibar and Tanzania Mainland, with concurrent jurisdiction. The High Courts have original jurisdiction in all civil and criminal matters.

The Special Constitutional Court of the United Republic deals with constitutional and union matters. The court has the power to interpret the provisions of the constitution.

THE ELECTION PROCESS

Every citizen who has attained the age of 18 years is entitled to vote in any public election held in Tanzania. This right is subject to other provisions of the constitution.

POLITICAL PARTIES

The constitution guarantees a multiparty system. The multiparty system was first legalized in 1992, and the first multiparty election was held in 1995. Political parties are subject to registration; there are 14 political parties in Tanzania.

CITIZENSHIP

Citizenship in Tanzania is acquired by birth, naturalization, or affiliation. The Citizenship Act of 1995 specifies the conditions for granting, losing, and resuming citizenship.

FUNDAMENTAL RIGHTS

Chapter 3 of the constitution, Articles 12–24, enshrines the fundamental rights (the Bill of Rights). The Bill of Rights binds both individuals and state agencies.

The preamble to the constitution also mentions freedom, fraternity, justice, and concord as founding principles. The 1994 Basic Rights and Duties Enforcement Act was enacted to provide procedures for the enforcement of the fundamental rights.

Impact and Functions of Fundamental Rights

The United Republic of Tanzania is a democratic state. There is no democracy without fundamental rights. Thus, the fundamental rights are the core upon which the society is based, and the guarantee of good governance in line with the rule of law. A Commission on Human Rights and Good Governance has been established to promote these goals.

Limitations to Fundamental Rights

Human rights and freedoms as set out in the constitution have their reasonable limits. There is a general limitation clause (Article 30), which provides the parameters within which the fundamental rights may be enjoyed. Fundamental rights may be limited by the rights, reputation, and privacy of others; by the public interest in defense, safety, order, or public morality; or in the interest of ensuring the fair execution of justice.

ECONOMY

The constitution provides for a number of economic rights such as the right to property, the right to work with appropriate remuneration, and freedom of movement. Although there is no mention of a specific economic system, the current economic status of the United Republic of Tanzania is determined as a social market economy despite the principle of socialist democracy.

RELIGIOUS COMMUNITIES

The United Republic of Tanzania is a secular state. Everyone has the right to freedom of religion. Religious bodies manage their own affairs without interference from the state authorities.

MILITARY DEFENSE AND STATE OF EMERGENCY

The armed forces are responsible for the defense and security of the territory and the people of Tanzania, pursuant to the laws. Members of the defense and security forces are prohibited from joining any political parties, although they may vote in elections; this includes the police and the prison service as well as those in national service, whether on temporary or permanent terms.

The president, as commander in chief of the armed forces, has the power to declare war; he or she commands military operations connected with the defense of the United Republic, as well as rescue operations to save lives and property in times of emergency, whether within or outside the country. No one may establish a private armed force within the territory of the United Republic.

AMENDMENTS TO THE CONSTITUTION

Article 98 of the constitution specifies procedures for amending the constitution and certain other basic laws. Parliament enacts a law for amending the constitution by a vote of not less than two-thirds of all members of parliament from Tanzania Mainland and not less than two-thirds of all members of the parliament of Tanzania Zanzibar.

PRIMARY SOURCES

Constitution in English and Kiswahili. Available online. URL: http://www.tanzania.go.tz/constitutionf.html. Accessed on July 19, 2005.

Constitution of the United Republic of Tanzania. Dar es Salaam: Government Printer, 1998.

SECONDARY SOURCES

Legal and Human Rights Centre, Tanzania Human Rights Report 2003. Dar es Salaam: LHRC, 2004.

Harrison G. Mwakyembe, *Tanzania's Eighth Constitution Amendment and Its Implication on Constitutionalism, Democracy and the Union Questions*. Munster/Hamburg: LIT Verlag, 1995.

Chris Maina Peter, *Human Rights in Tanzania: Selected Cases and Materials*. Cologne: Rudiger Koppe Verlag, 1997.

"Tanzania National Parliament Website." Available online. URL: http://www.parliament.go.tz/bunge/index.asp. Accessed on June 29, 2006.

Chacha Bhoke

THAILAND

At-a-Glance

OFFICIAL NAME
Kingdom of Thailand

CAPITAL
Bangkok

POPULATION
65,444,371 (2005 est.)

SIZE
198,457 sq. mi. (514,000 sq. km)

LANGUAGES
Thai (official) and English; Chinese, Lao, Malay, and ethnic dialects (Mon-Khmer, Tibeto-Burman, and Miao-Yao)

RELIGIONS
Buddhist 95%, Muslim 3.8%, Christian 0.5%, other (including Hindu and Sikh) 0.3%, unaffiliated 0.4%

NATIONAL OR ETHNIC COMPOSITION
Thai 75%, Chinese 14%, other (including hill tribes such as Karen, Hmong, Mien, Lahu, Akha, and Lisu) 11%

DATE OF INDEPENDENCE OR CREATION
1238 (traditional founding date)

TYPE OF GOVERNMENT
Constitutional monarchy

TYPE OF STATE
Unitary state

TYPE OF LEGISLATURE
Bicameral parliament

DATE OF CONSTITUTION
October 11, 1997 (suspended on September 19, 2006)

DATE OF LAST AMENDMENT
No amendment

Thailand is a constitutional monarchy based on the rule of law with a clear division of executive, legislative, and judicial powers. Between 1932 and 2006, Thailand had 16 constitutions and 20 military coups.

Organized as a unitary state, it is made up of 76 provinces. The king is the head of state and appoints all ministers, but the king's function is mostly representative or symbolic. The strong prime minister is the chief executive. The prime minister must be appointed from among the members of the House of Representatives. The bicameral National Assembly consists of the Senate and the House of Representatives. The constitution includes a number of provisions designed to prevent conflicts of interest between public officials and private business. Thai constitutional law recognizes the significance of judicial independence. A constitutional court is charged with interpreting the constitution.

The constitution provides for far-reaching guarantees of human rights. However, civil rights are sometimes compromised by the discrepancy between government behavior and legal norms as well as by the authorities' selective application of established law. Thailand has achieved a pluralistic system of political parties and a well-differentiated system of interest groups. The economic system can be described as a social market economy. Religious freedom is guaranteed and Buddhism is the official religion of Thailand. According to the constitution, the military is subject to the civil government. However, following a military coup on September 19, 2006, the constitution was suspended.

CONSTITUTIONAL HISTORY

A unified Thai kingdom was well established by the mid-14th century C.E with the Kingdom of Sukothai. According to tradition, the city of Sukhothai was part of the Khmer Empire (centered in today's Cambodia) until 1238, when Thai chieftains seceded and established the Kingdom of Sukhothai (1238–1438). Its decline coincided with the rise of the Ayutthaya Kingdom in the south (1350–1767). Ayutthaya's system of government was based on the

Hindu concept of divine kingship; however, Theravada Buddhism was introduced as the official religion—to differentiate the kingdom from the neighboring Hindu kingdom of Angkor.

During the following centuries, a feudal system prevailed. By the 18th century the Kingdom of Siam (as the country was known until 1939) had become an absolute monarchy. The king is often referred to as Rama, from the Hindu deity.

Although the country was never formally taken over by any European colonial power, it began to open itself to Western powers in the 19th century. The process began with the 1855 Treaty of Friendship and Commerce with Great Britain.

In 1932, the absolute monarchy was abolished by a young Western-oriented political elite known as the promoters. A permanent constitution was promulgated that year (December 10 marks Constitution Day). It provided for a quasi-parliamentary regime in which the executive and legislative powers were vested in a unicameral legislature, the National Assembly. Suffrage was limited, and half the members of the assembly were appointed by the executive administration in power. Real power resided with the "promoters," who relied on backing from the army and the People's Party.

The first parliamentary elections in the history of Thailand were held in 1933. King Prajadhipok (Rama VII, 1925–35) abdicated two years later. His 10-year-old nephew, Ananda Mahidol (Rama VIII, 1935–46), was named king to succeed him, and a regency council was appointed to carry out the functions of the monarchy.

During World War II (1939–45), the country was governed by Prime Minister Phibun Songgram and his nationalist regime. It changed the name of the country to *Thailand,* which means "Land of the Free" (Muang Thai) in the Thai language. The pro-Japanese policy of the regime was opposed when Japanese forces started to occupy the country. Phibun was forced from office and replaced by the predominantly civilian government led by Pridi Bonomyong.

This government drafted a new constitution that established a bicameral legislature in 1946. The lower house was elected by popular vote and the upper house was elected by the lower house. The elections, which in fact preceded the formal enactment of the constitution, were the first in which political parties participated. The new constitution provided for a Constitutional Tribunal. This was a response to a famous Supreme Court judgment on the constitutionality of the War Criminal Act no. 1/2489, which had been enacted after the war. Before that decision, there was an ongoing debate as to which organization should be competent to consider the issue as to the constitutionality of a law. After the mysterious death of the king, who had recently returned from Europe, rumors spread and Prime Minister Pridi resigned.

The late king's younger brother, Bhumibol Adulyadej, Rama IX, succeeded to the throne. In the following years, Thailand saw a series of military coups d'état, the first with the return of Phibun to power. The 1949 constitution was suspended by the government and the 1932 constitution was declared in force again. A revised constitution was promulgated in February 1952, and elections were held for seats in the new, unicameral legislature. Nearly all the appointed members of parliament were army officers. Steps toward more democracy were stopped after university students protested against the elections, and a state of emergency was declared.

In 1973, students and workers again rallied in the streets to demand a more democratic constitution and genuine parliamentary elections. The king succeeded in negotiating a compromise, and a new constitution took force the following year.

Military power continued to limit parliamentary government. The 1978 constitution reestablished a bicameral legislature, in which the military-controlled Senate could block initiatives in important areas. Army rule ended in 1992 amid bloody fighting in the streets of Bangkok (known as Black May or Bloody May). In 1995, after having abolished absolute monarchy 60 years before, Thailand conducted its first genuine parliamentary elections free of military veto.

In 1997, a regionwide economic crisis accompanied the adoption of the current constitution. It was drafted by a 99-member Constitutional Assembly chosen by the National Assembly. Public consultation was an important aspect. Among the underlying problems to be addressed were the corruption and instability of civilian government. The constitution introduced proportional representation for some seats and established an independent election commission. It also strengthened the role of the prime minister, further separated executive and legislative functions, and reinforced a system of checks and balances.

Thailand is an active member of the regional Association of Southeast Asian Nations (ASEAN).

FORM AND IMPACT OF THE CONSTITUTION

Thailand has a written constitution, codified in a single document of 336 sections. Called the Constitution of the Kingdom of Thailand (or, informally, the people's constitution), it takes precedence over all other national law. The constitution is supplemented by eight obligatory organic laws to govern matters such as political parties and election procedures. International law must be in accordance with the constitution to be applicable within Thailand.

BASIC ORGANIZATIONAL STRUCTURE

Thailand is a unitary state made up of 76 provinces, called *changwat,* including the metropolitan area of Bangkok.

The provinces are administered by appointed governors (*phuwarachakan*) and divided into districts, subdistricts, and villages. Governors of the provinces are career civil servants appointed by the Ministry of Interior, whereas Bangkok's governor is popularly elected. The autonomy of the municipalities and the principle of self-government are constitutionally recognized.

LEADING CONSTITUTIONAL PRINCIPLES

The constitution takes five general principles as its starting point: First, Thailand is a unified and indivisible kingdom. It is a democracy, in which sovereignty resides with the people. People enjoy equal protection and are guaranteed the constitutionality of laws.

Chapter 5 of the constitution contains directive principles of state policy that serve as policy guides for legislation and the administration of state affairs. Among other provisions, they obligate the state to protect and uphold the institution of kingship and the independence and the integrity of its territories. The state maintains the armed forces, upholds the democratic regime of government, and fosters national development. The state is also directed to promote friendly relations with other countries and adopt the principle of nondiscrimination. Other directive principles urge the state to patronize and protect Buddhism as well as other religions, to promote and encourage public participation, and to prepare a political development plan.

CONSTITUTIONAL BODIES

Sovereignty belongs to the people of the nation, with the concurrence of the king (assisted by a Council of State), and exercised through the National Assembly, the Council of Ministers, and the courts, as stipulated by the constitution. Other constitutional bodies are the ombudspersons, the National Human Rights Commission, the National Anti-Corruption Commission, and the independent Election Commission.

The King

The king's sovereign power emanates from the people. The 1924 Palace Law on Succession provides for only male succession to the king. However, the constitution allows the king to change this law at will to make female succession possible in the future. The king is the head of state. The king exercises legislative power through parliament, executive power through the cabinet, and judicial power through the courts. The monarch is endowed with a formal power of assent and appointment; however, he is above partisan affairs and does not interfere in the decision-making process of the government.

The Buddhist king is expected to conform to the 10 principles of royal good governance derived from the teachings of the Lord Buddha. In practice, the current king exerts strong informal influence but has never used his constitutionally mandated power to veto legislation or dissolve parliament.

Royal succession is organized by the constitution and the 1924 Palace Law on Succession, which forbids a princess to inherit the throne. The king appoints his successor in accordance with the law on succession, which may only be amended by himself. However, if the king does not name his successor, the Council of State submits the name of the successor to the National Assembly and asks for approval. In this case (when the king does not name his successor) the Council of State may submit a name of a princess. The successor is then invited to ascend the throne and proclaimed by the president of the National Assembly.

The Council of State

The Council of State, or Privy Council, renders advice to the king, on his request, on all matters pertaining to monarchical functions. All 18 councilors are appointed by the king.

The Parliament

The bicameral National Assembly (Rathasapha) consists of the Senate and the House of Representatives. The Speaker of the House of Representatives is also the president of the National Assembly. The president of the Senate is the vice president of the National Assembly.

The National Assembly's main functions are to promulgate laws, to monitor the administration of state affairs, and to endorse or reject the administration's program.

Senate (Wuthisapha)

The Senate consists of 200 members, who, since 1977, are all elected by the people for a term of six years. The president of the Senate is elected for the full six-year term.

The main functions of the Senate are to scrutinize draft laws that have passed the House of Representatives and to sit together with the house to consider various important matters. It also monitors the administration, nominates persons for royal appointment such as the justices of the Constitutional Court, and has the power to impeach allegedly corrupt politicians. The Senate's monitoring powers are exercised through questioning, general debate, and the right to set up committees. Every senator has the right to question any minister on matters under the minister's responsibility. A motion for a general debate must be supported by three-fifths of the senators.

There are two categories of session, each lasting 120 days. During a legislative session only legislative work is permitted, on bills, government decrees, amendments to the constitution, and treaties. The Senate's supervisory function is restricted during these sessions; questions are permitted, but there may be no no confidence vote or motion of censure. Those matters can be dealt with during an ordinary session.

Under the 1997 constitution, the Senate has the duty to enact all of the required organic laws called for by the constitution within the time limits specified. If the House of Representatives is dissolved, full lawmaking authority passes to the Senate. The Senate cannot be dissolved.

House of Representatives (Sapha Phuthaen Ratsadon)

The House of Representatives consists of 500 members, who serve for a four-year term. Its main functions are to initiate and deliberate on draft laws, to scrutinize the budget, and to select the prime minister from among the members of parliament. It can also dismiss the prime minister or any cabinet minister, monitor the administration, and sit with the Senate to consider major matters, such as constitutional issues, important procedural matters, declarations of war or peace, and the ratification of international treaties.

The House of Representatives can hold a vote of no confidence in the prime minister. The motion requires the initial support of at least two-fifths of the total number of representatives, and it must include the name of a suitable replacement. To pass, the motion needs an absolute majority of representatives. If the motion is passed, the president of the House of Representatives submits the name of the person nominated to the king for appointment. Only one-fifth of the total number of representatives is required to initiate a vote of no confidence in individual cabinet ministers.

The dissolution of the House of Representatives is a royal prerogative. The royal decree must include the date when new general elections are to be held, which must be within 60 days. The king may dissolve the House of Representatives only once for the same reason.

The Council of Ministers

The Council of Ministers carries out the administration of state affairs. All ministers are appointed by the king.

The office of the prime minister is a central body and the nerve center of the administration. The latest constitution strengthens the office, so that the prime minister is less likely to need the support of a large coalition. The prime minister must be appointed from among the members of the House of Representatives.

Some of the key subdivisions of the Office of the Prime Minister are the Budget Bureau, the National Security Council, the Juridical Council, the National Economic and Social Development Board, the Board of Investment, and the Civil Service Commission.

The prime minister is assisted by deputy prime ministers and by a number of cabinet ministers who hold the portfolio of Minister to the Prime Minister's Office. The number of cabinet members is limited to 36.

Ministers are individually and collectively accountable to the House of Representatives and have to retain its confidence. The 1997 constitution requires all newly appointed cabinet members to resign from their parliamentary seats, in order to further separate the executive and legislative functions.

The constitution includes provisions to prevent conflicts of interest between elected officials and businesses. A minister may not own shares in a corporation. However, the constitution does not bar family members of politicians from owning these shares.

The Lawmaking Process
Bills are introduced either by the Council of Ministers or by members of the House of Representatives. The Senate does not have the right of initiative.

Both houses have to approve a bill. After a bill has been approved, the prime minister presents it to the king for signature within 20 days. It enters into force upon its publication in the *Government Gazette*.

In case of amendment by the Senate, the bill is sent back to the House of Representatives. If the House of Representatives accepts the amendments, the bill is sent to the king for signature; if not, a joint committee with equal representation of both chambers is set up.

If one of the two chambers rejects the conclusions of the joint committee, the bill is deferred. A deferred bill returns to the rejecting chamber, which reexamines it at the end of a period of 180 days. If the chamber now adopts either version by an absolute majority, the bill is considered to have been adopted by the National Assembly and is presented to the king for signature.

If the king refuses to assent within 90 days, the National Assembly can reaffirm it with a two-thirds majority of all members of both houses. The bill is then promulgated with or without the king's signature.

In ordinary affairs, the Senate has a period of 60 days to examine draft legislation; otherwise it is deemed to have adopted it. In budgetary affairs, the period is reduced to 30 days.

For certain types of legislation considered necessary for the administration of affairs of state, the Council of Ministers can demand a joint meeting of the two chambers to reconsider a bill that the House of Representatives declined to support. This mechanism of legislative arbitration is intended to prevent political bargaining by members of parliament who have been denied cabinet posts. The Council of Ministers is no longer compelled to resign, as was previously the convention if such bills failed to pass.

The Judiciary

The judiciary is composed of courts of first instance, courts of appeal, and the Supreme Court. The courts of first instance are trial courts of general jurisdiction (civil courts, criminal courts, provincial courts, and small claim courts), as well as special courts (the juvenile and Family Courts, the Labor Court, the Tax Court, the Intellectual Property and International Trade Court, the Bankruptcy

Court, and military courts). Appeals against judgments by courts of first instance can be filed with the Court of Appeals, subject to certain restrictions. The Supreme (Dika) Court can review and adjudicate all cases. Its judgments are final. Decisions of the Constitutional Court are not subject to review by the Supreme Court.

The Thai constitution recognizes judicial independence. For example, the Office of the Judiciary is an independent agency, no longer part of the Ministry of Justice; it is responsible for personnel and budget matters. Judges are independent in trial and adjudication.

The Constitutional Court, charged with interpreting the constitution, began operation in 1998. Its decisions are final and binding on the National Assembly, the Council of Ministers, the courts, and other state organizations. The scope of the Constitutional Court's powers is very broad. The court has the power to decide whether a bill or law, or any provision thereof, complies with the constitution, and it has the power to declare the law or provision void. The Constitutional Court also has the power to review the application of any pertinent law involved in any case before any court.

In 2004, the Constitutional Court upheld two antiterrorist decrees issued by the prime minister in 2003 that provided punishments ranging from fines to the death penalty. This was the first use of a constitutional provision that allows parliament to refer executive decrees to the Constitutional Court. Although the court has issued some controversial rulings that have split the justices into opposing camps, the vast majority of its rulings have been premised on a high degree of agreement. Apart from the king, the court enjoys the highest level of public esteem of all constitutional bodies.

The Election Commission

The Election Commission controls and conducts elections for the House of Representatives, the Senate, local assemblies, and local administrators. It also supervises referendums. The commission has the right to give orders to relevant officials, to conduct investigations, and even to order new elections when there is evidence that the polling stations had "not proceeded in an honest and fair manner."

The commission consists of a chair and four other commissioners appointed by the king with the advice of the Senate from among persons of evident political impartiality and integrity.

THE ELECTION PROCESS AND POLITICAL PARTICIPATION

The right to vote is granted to all those who have been Thai nationals for at least five years, are above the age of 18, and are registered in a constituency for 90 days or longer. Voting is compulsory.

The constitution includes several provisions for direct participation by citizens in the political process. For example, people can submit legislation to the parliament or ask the Senate to remove high officials. There can be a referendum initiated by the government, but it does not have any binding effect.

Parliamentary Elections

The constitution determines the general electoral framework. In addition, a 1998 organic law regulates elections to both chambers of the National Assembly.

Of the 500 members of the House of Representatives, 100 members are elected on a party list basis through proportional representation, and 400 are elected in single-member constituencies through a first-past-the-post majority vote. There is a constitutional hurdle of 5 percent of the total votes that has to be achieved by each party in order to win any of the 100 national seats. This mixed electoral system is called a parallel system.

Only Thai nationals by birth at least 25 years of age may stand for election to the House of Representatives. They must have graduated university (this is waived if they have been members of parliament before), and they must belong to a political party.

To stand for the Senate, a candidate must be at least 40 years of age, be a Thai citizen by birth, and hold a university degree. There is a single-vote majority system. Unlike in the House of Representatives, candidates may not be members of a political party. A senator can only be appointed a cabinet minister one year after the end of his or her senatorial term.

POLITICAL PARTIES

Thailand has had a pluralistic system of political parties since the 1946 constitution. The Communist Party is legally prohibited.

For many years, the parties were overshadowed by the military-bureaucratic elite. The perception that political parties were unworthy of trust was widespread. Although party politics received a major impetus from the student uprising of 1973, it has continued to suffer from long-standing deficiencies, such as patron-client relationships, especially in rural areas. In such relationships, several clients form a group, and a patron and the group are in turn subordinate to a higher-level patron. The organic law on political parties has attempted to deal with these problems. On the one hand, deficiencies remain and an organizationally stable party system has not taken firm root in the Thai society. On the other hand, Thailand has a well-differentiated system of interest groups, particularly in the nongovernmental organization (NGO) sector.

CITIZENSHIP

Thai citizenship is primarily acquired by birth, under the principle of *ius sanguinis*. A child acquires Thai citizenship if one of his or her parents is a Thai citizen. It is of no relevance where a child is born.

A foreigner can also acquire Thai citizenship if he or she legally resides in Thailand, has displayed good behavior, has a regular occupation, has a domicile in the Thai kingdom, and has knowledge of the Thai language. Dual citizenship is generally not recognized.

FUNDAMENTAL RIGHTS

Scattered throughout the constitution are guarantees of human rights and dignity, fundamental freedoms, and public participation in the democratic process. Chapters 3 and 4 call for protection of human dignity and of the rights and liberties of the Thai people. Chapter 5 lists the directive principles of state policies, which include compliance with the law, protection of rights and liberties, efficient administration of justice, and public participation.

A mechanism has been established to ensure respect for fundamental rights. Independent organizations, such as the National Human Rights Commission, provide checks and balances and monitor the compliance with the constitution.

The constitution provides for the full traditional set of human rights. The people are guaranteed freedom of expression, religion, movement, and association. Social rights, such as health care for the poor, pensions for the elderly without means of support, and guarantees of accessible facilities for the handicapped, are also addressed. Equal protection is a duty of the state in many respects: origin, race, language, sex, age, physical or health condition, personal status, economic or social standing, religious belief, education, or legitimate political views. Measures taken to eliminate obstacles to equality are not deemed to constitute unjust discrimination.

Thailand acceded to the International Covenant on Civil and Political Rights in 1997, and to the International Covenant on Economic, Social and Cultural Rights in 1999. Nevertheless, human rights activists are still concerned about a lack of protection for those defending human rights, the lack of rights for refugees, and the use of the death penalty, which is explicitly permitted by the 1997 constitution. The death penalty is regularly applied in Thailand, usually for murder, rape, or heroin trafficking.

Impact and Function of Fundamental Rights

The 1997 constitution is generally regarded as a benchmark in a reform process that began after Thailand's last military coup in 1991. This is reflected by the prominence of fundamental rights within the document. It is the first constitution in Thailand to link civil liberties to the idea of "human dignity." The Constitutional Court has a decisive role in protecting fundamental rights. While some decisions of the Constitutional Court have tended to enhance the fundamental rights of citizens, other decisions have promoted the authority of the state.

Fundamental rights can be defensive—preventing the state from interfering with the legal position of the individual, for example, in relation to individual freedom or property. Other rights entitle individuals to certain services from the state; for example, the state is required to provide 12 years of free education.

Fundamental rights also guarantee due process. The constitution allows for the detention of criminal suspects without a court order for 48 hours (instead of seven days under the earlier constitution). Unlike in other Asian countries, however, there is no direct access to higher courts on constitutional grounds in Thailand. This is a significant disadvantage for people who suffer human rights abuses. However, a person whose rights are violated can generally bring a lawsuit or defend himself or herself in the court.

The state in all its forms is constitutionally bound to uphold rights and liberties. Individuals also have some public duties, such as duty to defend the country. Unless or until the Constitutional Court decides otherwise, fundamental rights do not regulate relations among private individuals and legal persons in Thailand.

Those who stress the importance of defensive rights and due process tend to regard the constitution as the final result of the 1997 reform process. Others, however, consider the political guarantees in the constitution offer potential to continue and expand the reform process.

Limitations to Fundamental Rights

Section 28 contains a general limitation clause for fundamental rights. It states that a person can invoke his or her rights and liberties only insofar as such actions do not violate the rights and liberties of other persons or are not contrary to the constitution or good morals. Some sections contain specific limitation clauses, such as freedom of movement, which can be restricted by a law enacted to protect the security of the state, public order, public welfare, town and country planning, or welfare of youth. Another example is freedom of assembly: restrictions may explicitly be imposed when a state of emergency or martial law is declared.

There are also limitation limits, such as are stipulated in Section 29. A restriction cannot be imposed except by a law specifically enacted for the purpose and only "to the extent of necessity" and provided that it shall "not affect the essential substances" of such rights and liberties. This means that all state actions that affect the rights of people must be reasonable and there must not be any alternative that is less impairing.

ECONOMY

Some of the directive state principles in the constitution relate to the country's economy. The state is encouraged to provide for a system of labor relations, help people of working age obtain employment, and guarantee social security and fair wages. The state also encourages a free-market economic system. It does not engage in enterprises in competition with the private sector, except when necessary to ensure the security of the state, preserve the common interest, or provide public utilities. In sum, the economic system can be described as a social market economy.

RELIGIOUS COMMUNITIES

The king must be a Buddhist and is considered the upholder of the Buddhist religion and the upholder of all religions. Theravada Buddhism is the official religion of Thailand. The government permits religious diversity, and other major religions are represented. Spirit worship and animism are widely practiced.

The state constitutionally patronizes and protects Buddhism and other religions and promotes good understanding and harmony among followers of all religions. It also encourages the application of religious principles to create virtue and develop the quality of life.

MILITARY DEFENSE AND STATE OF EMERGENCY

Thai armed forces are composed of professional career soldiers and conscripts. Men who have reached the age of 20 are required to serve in the armed forces for two years. Every person has a constitutional duty to defend the country and to serve in the armed forces as provided for by law. The king holds the position of head of the Thai armed forces.

The constitution distinguishes among a state of emergency, martial law, and a state of war. A state of emergency is a declaration that may suspend certain normal functions of government. Martial law takes effect when a military authority takes control of the normal administration.

For the purpose of maintaining national or public safety or national economic security or averting public calamity, the king may issue an emergency decree, which has the force of an act of parliament, but only if the Council of Ministers finds the situation to constitute a case of emergency. Furthermore, the emergency decree must be approved by the National Assembly; if the assembly disapproves, the emergency decree lapses. During a state of emergency or martial law, restrictions on certain human rights are legally justified. For example, freedom of assembly and expression can be restricted, and forced labor is permitted.

The king has the prerogative legally to declare and lift the martial law. However, if necessary in a certain locality as a matter of urgency, the military authority also may declare martial law.

Violence in Thailand's southern, mainly Malay Muslim provinces has been steadily escalating since early 2004. Armed separatist groups have been active since the late 1960s. The origins of the current violence lie in historical grievances stemming from discrimination against the ethnic Malay Muslim population and attempts at forced assimilation by successive ethnic Thai Buddhist governments in Bangkok for almost a century. The government declared martial law. According to human rights reports, martial law has been in force in some areas for many years.

The king has the prerogative to declare war with the approval of the National Assembly. The declaration requires a majority of two-thirds of the total number of members of parliament.

AMENDMENTS TO THE CONSTITUTION

Draft constitutional legislation can be proposed by the Council of Ministers or by one-third of the total number of members of the House of Representatives. It can be proposed by members of the Senate and the House of Representatives if it is supported by one-third of the total number of members of both chambers.

The National Assembly examines the amendment in a joint sitting of both chambers and uses three readings. First, at least one half of the total number of the members of the assembly must vote in favor of the amendment in principle. The second reading examines the articles individually and requires only a simple majority vote. The third reading takes place 15 days after the second reading and requires an absolute majority of all the members in each chamber.

PRIMARY SOURCES
Constitution in English. Available online. URL: http://www.parliament.go.th/files/library/b05-b.htm. Accessed on September 18, 2005.
Constitution in Thai. Available online. URL: http://www.parliament.go.th/files/library/t-b05-b.htm. Accessed on August 13, 2005.
"Constitution of the Kingdom of Thailand." *Government Gazette* 114, pt. 559, Section 185-6 (October 11,1997).

SECONDARY SOURCES
Asian Legal Resource Centre, "Written Statements to the 61st Session of the CHR." Available online. URL: http://www.alrc.net/. Accessed on September 9, 2005.
Bureau of Public Affairs, U.S. Department of State, "Background Note and Country Reports on Human Rights Practices and International Religious Freedom Report 2004." Available online. URL: http://www.state.gov/. Accessed on August 26, 2005.
James Klein, *The Constitution of the Kingdom of Thailand, 1997: A Blueprint for Participatory Democracy*, Working Paper Series no. 8. San Francisco: The Asia Foundation, 1998.
"Legislative Acts." Available online. URL: http://www.krisdika.go.th/home.jsp. Accessed on August 20, 2005.
Bowornsak Uwanno and Wayne D. Burns, "The Thai Constitution of 1997: Sources and Process." *University of British Columbia Law Review* 32, no. 2 (1998): 227–233.

Michael Rahe

TOGO

At-a-Glance

OFFICIAL NAME
Republic of Togo

CAPITAL
Lomé

POPULATION
5,429,299 (2003)

SIZE
21,924 sq. mi. (56,785 sq. km)

LANGUAGES
French (official language), Ewé, Gurma, Kabiyé, Kotokoli

RELIGIONS
Christian 30%, Muslim 15%, traditional more than 50%

NATIONAL OR ETHNIC COMPOSITION
More than 30 social groups; Ewé (south), Gurma and Kabiyé (north) most important

DATE OF INDEPENDENCE OR CREATION
April 27, 1960

TYPE OF GOVERNMENT
Presidential regime

TYPE OF STATE
Unitary state

TYPE OF LEGISLATURE
Bicameral parliament

DATE OF CONSTITUTION
September 27, 1992

DATE OF LAST AMENDMENT
February 6, 2005

Since the 1990s, the Republic of Togo has begun implementing democracy, under political pressure from a worldwide movement backed by Western countries in general and the European Union in particular. The constitution sets up a presidential regime with some checks and balances, including the referendum, which can be initiated by the people, in such conditions as are prescribed by the constitution.

There is no specific economic system set up in the constitution. State and religion are separated.

CONSTITUTIONAL HISTORY

In 1884, Germany made Togoland a protectorate, establishing borders with the neighboring French and British territories. After World War I (1914–18), the country was divided between France and the United Kingdom under the League of Nations Mandate system; after World War II (1939–45) the two territories were placed under the United Nations trusteeship system, under the same rulers. The British territory was eventually merged with its newly independent neighbor, Ghana, the former British colony of the Gold Coast. The French area became an independent country on April 27, 1960, with Sylvanus Olympio as its first president.

In January 1963, Olympio was assassinated in a military coup led by Eyadéma Gnassingbe, who named himself president after a second coup in 1967, a post he held until his death in February 2005.

Upon the president's death his son, Faure Gnassingbe, assumed the presidency with the support of the ruling single party and the army; he was endorsed by the National Assembly with the help of some manipulations of the constitution. Pressure from African and international organizations forced him to resign, but he was then elected in the April 2005 presidential elections.

FORM AND IMPACT OF THE CONSTITUTION

The constitution of the Republic of Togo is one written document, comprising 159 articles. It establishes that international law will prevail over national law subject to the principle of reciprocity in international relations. The constitution recognizes human rights, although those provisions are not always implemented in practice.

BASIC ORGANIZATIONAL STRUCTURE

Togo is a unitary state.

LEADING CONSTITUTIONAL PRINCIPLES

The leading principles established in the constitution are the protection of rights and duties, political pluralism, and rule of law. Rights are also recognized for legal persons. The constitution also establishes a right of civil disobedience (Article 45). With regard to religion, the preamble makes a reference to God, as does the oath read out by a newly elected president.

CONSTITUTIONAL BODIES

The main constitutional organs are the president, the executive administration, parliament, and the judiciary, including a constitutional court.

The President

The president is the head of state and the head of the army. The president is elected through direct, secret, and universal ballot, for a five-year renewable term. The president presides over meetings of executive administration. The president has the right to promulgate acts adopted by the National Assembly. The president also has the power to dissolve the National Assembly, after consultation with the prime minister and the president of the National Assembly.

In case the Constitutional Court has declared the presidency vacant, the president of the National Assembly assumes the position in the interim, while an election is organized within 60 days.

The Executive Administration

The executive administration is composed of the prime minister, cabinet ministers, and secretaries of state, as deemed appropriate by the prime minister. The prime minister, appointed by the president, appoints the other members of the cabinet. The executive administration is responsible before the National Assembly.

The Parliament

The parliament is composed of the National Assembly and the Senate. The assembly deputies are elected through a secret, direct, and universal ballot for five-year terms. The function of the senators is to represent local communities; one-third are appointed by the president. Their term is also set at five years. However, the Senate has never actually been established. The assembly has legislative power. Deputies share the legislative initiative with the executive administration, adopt legislation, and exercise control over the executive. The number of deputies is established by legislation; the current number is 81.

The Lawmaking Process

Parliament meets twice a year for its ordinary sessions, which last not more than three months each. Legislative initiative is shared by the deputies and the cabinet. According to the constitution, the senators merely comment on legislation before it is voted upon by the assembly. A simple majority is usually sufficient to pass a law.

The Judiciary

The independence of the judiciary is provided for in the constitution, which establishes a Supreme Court as well as appeals courts and tribunals. The constitution also establishes the independence of the judges and requires that they be guided only by the law. The Supreme Court is the highest court in Togo to hear all matters related to the administration and individuals. It is composed of two chambers: one for civil and criminal litigations, one for administrative disputes. The High Court of Justice is composed of the presidents of the two chambers of the Supreme Court and four deputies of the National Assembly. It has jurisdiction over the president, the members of the executive administration, and the judges of the Supreme Court.

The Constitutional Court

The role of the Constitutional Court is to ensure that any law adopted by parliament is in conformity with the constitution, and that human rights are protected. It is composed of nine judges, three appointed by the president of the republic, three by the National Assembly, and three by the Senate for a renewable term of seven years. The president appoints the president of the Constitutional Court for a term of seven years.

In any case before an ordinary court, an argument of nonconformity to the constitution can be raised. The Constitutional Court must make a ruling on the matter before the original court may dispose of the principal matter.

THE ELECTION PROCESS

All Togolese above 18 years of age have the right to vote, unless they are banned from exercising their civil and political rights for reasons based on the law. Candidates for the presidential elections must be at least 35 years old.

POLITICAL PARTIES

Political parties are allowed insofar as they are in conformity with the principles stated in the constitution, especially concerning human rights and freedoms. In practice, the opposition parties have suffered a degree of harassment from the administration.

CITIZENSHIP

Citizenship is a matter of law. Nationality is acquired by birth or marriage. A child who has one Togolese parent is Togolese, unless he or she chooses not to acquire citizenship.

FUNDAMENTAL RIGHTS

The constitution establishes a system of human rights protection, with the Constitutional Court having formal jurisdiction. There is reference in the preamble to the African Charter on Human and Peoples' Rights, the Universal Declaration on Human Rights, and other international legal materials. In practice, however, there have been continuous violations of human rights and disregard for the rule of law by the administration, according to nongovernmental organizations and international rights groups.

For example, in February 2005, when President Eyadéma Gnassingbe died, the ruling party chose not to conform to the constitution by letting the president of the National Assembly become interim president. Instead the majority of deputies, who are members of the ruling party, decided to amend the constitution in violation of Article 144, which establishes the amendment procedure. Such manipulation permitted Faure Gnassingbe, son of the deceased president, to be appointed interim president. Only under international pressure did the ruling party relent and allow the constitutional procedures to be applied.

Impact and Function of Fundamental Rights

Human rights have been the major issue in the political and social development of Togo since 1990. The constitution highlights those rights and provides for judicial protection, but no clear provisions determine the jurisdictional procedures for such protection.

The constitution provides for two organs related to human rights protection. One is the National Commission of Human Rights, whose 17 members are elected by the National Assembly for a term of four years. The other is the ombudsperson, whose objective is to resolve disputes between individuals and the administration. The ombudsperson is appointed by the Council of Ministers for a term of three years.

Limitations to Fundamental Rights

The only limitations of human rights are the duties of individuals and national security. In practice, the government routinely infringes individual and collective rights by claiming that national security and the public order are at risk.

ECONOMY

The constitution does not stipulate a specific economic system but provides for the protection of economic rights.

RELIGIOUS COMMUNITIES

Freedom of religion or belief is recognized in the constitution, and there is separation between the state and religion.

MILITARY DEFENSE AND STATE OF EMERGENCY

The president of the republic is the head of the armed forces. Any member of the armed forces who wants to run in the presidential election must first resign from the service. Defending the state is an obligation for all citizens, and the constitution provides for compulsory military service. However, the National Assembly has not adopted any legislation to implement this provision as yet. The constitution obliges all Togolese to engage in civil disobedience if a military coup takes place.

AMENDMENTS TO THE CONSTITUTION

Either the president of the republic or one-fifth of the deputies in the National Assembly may propose amendments to the constitution. A vote of four-fifths of the National Assembly is needed to approve the amendment. If the amendment is supported by two-thirds of the National Assembly but fails to reach the four-fifths threshold, it is submitted to a referendum. During an interim presidency or a threat to the country's territorial integrity, amendments are prohibited. The republican form of the regime and the principle of secularism (*laïcité*) cannot be amended.

PRIMARY SOURCES
Constitution in English (extracts). Available online. URL: http://www.chr.up.ac.za/hr_docs/constitutions/docs/Togo(english%20summary)%20(rev).doc. Accessed on September 25, 2005.

Constitution in French. Available online. URL: http://droit.francophonie.org/doc/html/tg/con/fr/2002/2002dftgco1.html. Accessed on September 13, 2005.

SECONDARY SOURCES

Roland Adjovi, "Togo, un changement anticonstitutionnel savant et un nouveau test pour l'Union Africaine." In *Actualité et Droit International.* Février 2005. Available online. URL: http://www.ridi.org/adi/articles/2005/200502adj.pdf. Accessed on August 8, 2005.

Bureau of Public Affairs, U.S. Department of State, "Background Note and Country Reports on Human Rights Practices and International Religious Freedom Report 2004." Available online. URL: http://www.state.gov/. Accessed on August 30, 2005.

"National Commission of Human Rights." Available online. URL: http://www.cndh.netcom.tg. Accessed on August 10, 2005.

"Republic of Togo." Available online. URL: http://www.republicoftogo.com. Accessed on September 16, 2005.

Roland Adjovi

TONGA

At-a-Glance

OFFICIAL NAME
Kingdom of Tonga

CAPITAL
Nuku'alofa

POPULATION
97,784 (2005 est.)

SIZE
288 sq. mi. (747 sq. km) land size

LANGUAGES
Tongan, English

RELIGIONS
Protestant 70%, Roman Catholic 25%, other
(Anglican, Seventh Day Adventist, Church of Jesus
Christ of Latter-day Saints, Pentecostal, Baha'i,
Muslim) 5%

NATIONAL OR ETHNIC COMPOSITION
Tongan

DATE OF INDEPENDENCE OR CREATION
June 4, 1862

TYPE OF GOVERNMENT
Constitutional monarchy

TYPE OF STATE
Unitary state

TYPE OF LEGISLATURE
Unicameral parliament

DATE OF CONSTITUTION
November 4, 1875

DATE OF LAST AMENDMENT
October 16, 2003

Tonga is the only remaining kingdom in the Pacific Ocean. Its constitution is the third-oldest constitution in the world, in force since 1875. From time to time, when new circumstances arise, including international events, the constitution is amended to take those factors into account. The country has found it economically more practicable to follow the amendment path than totally replace the constitution.

The latest amendments to the constitution in 2003 were restrictions on freedom of speech in cases of threats against national security, the morality of the state, or traditional culture and values. The constitution embodies what transpired in the past and safeguards Tonga from being a victim of lawlessness and social disorder.

The ongoing vitality of the constitution guarantees the sovereignty of the Kingdom of Tonga. It has in essence upheld the peace and welfare of the Tongans in the past and, Tongans believe, will do so long into the future.

CONSTITUTIONAL HISTORY

Prior to 1875, Tonga was divided and ruled by a number of local tribal chiefs in their respective area. It was not un-

til 1845 that Taufa'ahau Tupou I, who adopted the English ruling title of George, unified Tonga and became its first king. He proclaimed the Emancipation Edict in 1862, abolishing slavery of commoners to the traditional chiefs and granting them freedom from servitude to chiefs and kings. This edict eventually led to the enactment of the constitution in 1875, as a guarantee of the reforms that had been achieved over the years.

The king's achievement in maintaining a unified kingdom for decades won him the title among historians of the father of modern Tonga, or the grand old man of the Pacific. His lineage still rules Tonga.

The 19th century was marked throughout the Pacific region by the encroachment of European colonial rule in all the neighboring Pacific Islands. George Tupou I looked for means to secure Tonga's sovereignty against the European threat. With the help of missionaries, especially Shirley Baker, George Tupou I understood that only by enacting a written constitution could he prevent the Europeans from colonizing his country.

A draft of a written constitution was submitted to the king, who modified it to fit local circumstances. He convened a council of tribal chiefs as a parliament in November 1875. On November 4 the council approved the document and it became the constitution of Tonga.

That constitution was a beacon for smaller and less powerful states. It legitimized the right of the Kingdom of Tonga to be recognized worldwide as an independent state. It also provided legal guidelines by which the kingdom could be ruled.

FORM AND IMPACT OF THE CONSTITUTION

Tonga has a written constitution that is the supreme law of the kingdom. Any other laws that are in conflict with it are null and void to the extent of the inconsistencies. Other laws also refer to international conventions.

BASIC ORGANIZATIONAL STRUCTURE

Tonga is composed of three main island groups: Tongatapu, Ha'apai, and Vava'u. The island groups differ in size. The main administrative center is situated in the main island group, Tongatapu. It has attracted local migration from the other two island groups and is the site of the capital, Nuku'alofa. The royal family's main residence is also in Nuku'alofa. The king with the consent of the cabinet appoints governors to Ha'apai and Vava'u. These governors are responsible for ensuring that the law is applied in the respective district.

LEADING CONSTITUTIONAL PRINCIPLES

Tonga is a constitutional monarchy. The constitution sets down the framework in which the kingdom should be governed, and the king rules according to what is stated in the constitution. The constitution sets out a separation of powers among the executive, legislative, and judiciary branches.

CONSTITUTIONAL BODIES

The constitution sets out the throne of Tonga and its order of succession. It also provides for a Privy Council and a Cabinet and specifies their respective powers and responsibilities.

The King

The monarch (referred to as king in the constitution) is a part of the executive. The monarch has prerogatives such as appointing cabinet ministers, including the prime min-ister; appointing the privy councilors; and appointing the Speaker of the Legislative Assembly.

The monarch is the commander in chief of the army and navy, but he or she may not declare war without the consent of the Legislative Assembly. The monarch may enter into treaties with other states only on the consent of the Legislative Assembly.

Succession of the throne goes to the eldest male child. In the absence of any male issue, succession can go to the eldest female child. In case of a vacancy of the line of succession, the nobles of the realm must select a new line of kings.

The Privy Council

The Privy Council acts as adviser to the king, who appoints all its members, most of whom are Cabinet ministers and governors. The members serve at the king's pleasure. Whenever the word "king" appears in any official document it is interpreted to refer to the King in Council.

The Cabinet

The Cabinet ministers are appointed by the king. They are not accountable to the Legislative Assembly; however, they must present an annual report to the Legislative Assembly every year. Their appointments can be terminated by the king at any time.

The Legislature

The legislature is known in Tonga as the Legislative Assembly. It is here where the peoples' representatives, the nobles' representative, Cabinet ministers, and the royal governors of the outer island groups meet to enact laws. These laws must be sanctioned by the king in person or are void.

There are nine representatives for the people in the Legislative Assembly.

The thirty-three nobles in the kingdom make up a class of their own. They elect nine members from among their peers, using the same geographic distributions as the people's representatives.

The Lawmaking Process

When the Legislative Assembly has agreed upon any bill that has been read and voted for by a majority three times, the bill is presented to the king for his sanction. All laws must be sanctioned by the king in person or they will be postponed until the next sitting of the assembly.

The Judiciary

The judiciary comprises the Court of Appeal, the Supreme Court, the Land Court, and the Police Magistrate Court. The Court of Appeal is made up of three judges; they sit only once a year in Tonga. There are only two Supreme

Court judges in Tonga. They also sit in the Land Court and are assisted by local assessors. The police magistrates are localized and are evenly located throughout the kingdom.

The jurisdictions of the courts are clearly defined, with the Court of Appeal as the highest court of law in the kingdom. The chief justice is the president of the Court of Appeal.

THE ELECTION PROCESS

All Tongans over the age of 21 have the right to vote in the general election. Any Tongan can stand for candidacy but must be supported by a certain number of votes, before that person can be registered as a candidate.

POLITICAL PARTIES

The election to the Legislative Assembly in 2005 was distinguished by the registration of a new political party with a candidate of its own. That candidate was elected in an election process held shortly after the general elections.

CITIZENSHIP

Tongan citizenship is acquired by birth. Any child born of a Tongan father automatically becomes a citizen. In the past decade Tonga introduced a system of naturalization. A foreigner who holds a Tongan passport and has lived in Tonga for five consecutive years can become a Tongan *subject*. The subjects cannot fully exercise the rights of a Tongan *citizen*. A Tongan citizen can inherit property according to Tongan laws; a Tongan subject cannot.

FUNDAMENTAL RIGHTS

Clause 1 of the constitution states that every Tongan is free and at liberty to do whatever he or she wants to do with her or his property. No laws whatsoever can take away such freedom from the Tongans.

There are other rights such as freedom of speech, freedom of religion, and the sacredness of the Sabbath day. The constitution guarantees that no laws shall take away those rights. However, there are certain limitations imposed on those rights. In relation to freedom of speech, the media must use as regulatory principles national security, nondefamation, protection of the king and the royal family, official secrets, public order, morality, privileges of the Legislative Assembly, and avoid contempt of court.

Freedom of religion allows free association of people to form religious groups in Tonga. Keeping the Sabbath sacred is a requirement of the constitution. It does not involve a total prohibition of work on Sabbath, but rather a requirement of decent behavior and outward observance of the Sabbath. Sabbath in Tonga is on Sunday.

These principles were incorporated into the constitution so that these rights can be exercised in a reasonable manner.

ECONOMY

The constitution guarantees freedom of property and due compensation from the government in case of expropriation of land. Agricultural products can be mortgaged by farmers in their loans, but these mortgages cannot be enforced against them. This restriction reflects the importance of agriculture, the predominant economic activity in Tonga.

RELIGIOUS COMMUNITIES

Freedom of religion is provided for in the constitution, which does not establish any national church. However, it is commonly perceived in Tonga that the Free Wesleyan Church of Tonga is the main national church, since it is the church of the royal family. However, there is a clear separation between the government and the church.

Several of the churches in Tonga have formed a council of churches as a nongovernmental organization of mutual cooperation.

MILITARY DEFENSE AND STATE OF EMERGENCY

The king is the commander in chief of the army. The king can declare martial law in Tonga. The army remains subject to the civil laws of the kingdom, except in times of martial law.

AMENDMENTS TO THE CONSTITUTION

Any provision of the constitution can be amended by the Legislative Assembly, but in general a unanimous vote is required. Certain provisions, however, such as the succession to the throne of Tonga, can be amended by the nobles' representatives alone.

An amendment has to be passed three times by the assembly before it can be submitted to the king for the king to assent.

PRIMARY SOURCES

Constitution in English. Available online. URL: http://www.paclii.org/to/legis/consol_act/cot238/. Accessed on June 29, 2006.

SECONDARY SOURCES

Rodney C. Hills, *Tonga's Constitution and the Changing State*. Canberra: Research School of Pacific Studies, Australian National University, 1991.

S. Latukefu, *Church and State in Tonga: The Wesleyan Methodist Missionaries and Political Development, 1822–1875*. Canberra: Australian National University Press, 1974.

'O. Mâhina, "Emancipation in Tonga: Yesterday and Today." Speech given at Sir Edmund Hillary Collegiate, Otara, New Zealand, June 11, 2004. Available online. URL: http://www.tonfon.to. Accessed on July 22, 2005.

"Tongan Government Website." Available online. URL: http://www.pmo.gov.to. Accessed on August 5, 2005.

'Ofa Pouono

TRINIDAD AND TOBAGO

At-a-Glance

OFFICIAL NAME
Republic of Trinidad and Tobago

CAPITAL
Port-of-Spain

POPULATION
1,096,585 (2005 est.)

SIZE
1,980 sq. mi. (5,128 sq. km)

LANGUAGES
English

RELIGIONS
Roman Catholic 29.4%, Hindu 23.8%, Anglican
10.7%, Muslim 5.8%, Presbyterian 3.4%, other 26.9%

NATIONAL OR ETHNIC COMPOSITION
East Indian (immigrants from northern India) 40.3%,

Afro 39.5%, mixed 18.4%, white 0.6%, Chinese or
other 1.2%

DATE OF INDEPENDENCE OR CREATION
August 31, 1962

TYPE OF GOVERNMENT
Parliamentary democracy

TYPE OF STATE
Unitary state

TYPE OF LEGISLATURE
Bicameral parliament

DATE OF CONSTITUTION
August 1, 1976

DATE OF LAST AMENDMENT
November 2, 2000

Trinidad and Tobago is a parliamentary democracy within the British Commonwealth of Nations. The country is a republic and organized as a unitary state. Executive, judiciary, and legislative powers are separated. Fundamental rights enjoy constitutional protection; in case of their violation, effective measures of redress exist.

The executive head of state is the elected president. Political power is exercised by the cabinet, headed by the prime minister. The cabinet relies on parliamentary support. In Parliament, the members of the House of Representatives are elected by popular vote. The members of the Senate are appointed by the president. The party system is pluralistic.

Freedom of conscience is guaranteed. The state is not affiliated with any religious group. The constitution protects the enjoyment of private property.

CONSTITUTIONAL HISTORY

Trinidad and Tobago emerged for the first time as a single entity in 1889 when Tobago became a ward of Trinidad.

Even though the economy on both islands relied on sugarcane plantations operated with African slaves, their history was quite different.

Trinidad had been ruled by Spain for more than 300 years when it became a British Crown colony in 1802. When slavery was abolished in the empire in 1834–38, large numbers of northern Indian laborers immigrated to work on the plantations and replaced the former slaves. The division between these two ethnic groups is still visible until today in the country's society.

Tobago changed hands many times between different European nations and was ultimately acquired by Britain in 1814. At that time, a legislative assembly existed, providing representation for a few landowners. This assembly was abolished in 1877.

When the islands were united in 1890, they became a Crown colony. They were ruled by a royal governor with virtually autocratic powers and a Legislative Council that was fully appointed by the British Crown.

The first steps toward increased self-government were taken in 1925, when limited elections for a few seats in the Legislative Council were held. The franchise was then based on property and the electorate was very small. The first elections under universal adult suffrage were held in 1946.

From 1958 until 1962, Trinidad and Tobago formed part of the West Indies Federation, which attempted to unite 10 British island colonies in the Caribbean to provide more self-determination.

When the West Indies Federation was dissolved in 1962, Trinidad and Tobago achieved its independence as a constitutional monarchy within the Commonwealth of Nations, following years of negotiation with the British Crown. Executive head of state became the queen of England, represented by an appointed governor-general.

In 1976, the current constitution came into force. It substituted the office of the governor-general with that of a president elected by parliament. Trinidad and Tobago became a republic.

Following Tobago's call for more autonomy, the Tobago House of Assembly was created in 1980 to deal with local affairs.

FORM AND IMPACT OF THE CONSTITUTION

The constitution is enshrined in Act 4 of 1976. It is the supreme law of Trinidad and Tobago and prevails over any other law made by Parliament.

BASIC ORGANIZATIONAL STRUCTURE

Trinidad and Tobago is a unitary state. There are seven counties and four municipalities on Trinidad, but they have no powers under the constitution. For historical reasons, Tobago is a ward of Trinidad. It has its own council for self-administrative purposes, the Tobago House of Assembly.

LEADING CONSTITUTIONAL PRINCIPLES

The country is a parliamentary democracy within the Commonwealth of Nations and a republic. There is a clear division of powers among the legislative, the executive, and the judiciary, and an adequate system of constitutional checks and balances exists. The judiciary is independent. Protection of individual fundamental rights is guaranteed.

CONSTITUTIONAL BODIES

The principal constitutional bodies are the president, the Parliament, and the cabinet.

The President

The executive head of state is the president. The holder of the office is elected by a special Electoral College composed of the two houses of Parliament. The president's term of office is five years. The president may be removed from office by a majority of two-thirds of all the members of each house of Parliament.

The president appoints the prime minister, the ministers, and the senators; exercises the power of pardon; and is the commander in chief of the armed forces. When exercising these powers, the president acts on the advice of the cabinet. However, the duty to act on constitutional advice is not legally enforceable, and the president is not constitutionally barred from political partisanship. This system led to several constitutional crises in 2000 and 2001 over the removal of some government-appointed senators and their replacement by other personalities.

The Parliament of Trinidad and Tobago

The Parliament of Trinidad and Tobago is based on the British Westminster model. It is composed of the president, the Senate, and the House of Representatives.

The House of Representatives has at present 36 members elected in general elections. At least two of the constituencies are granted to Tobago to secure representation of the smaller island's interests.

The Senate consists of 31 senators, all appointed by the president. Sixteen are appointed on the advice of the prime minister and six on the advice of the leader of the opposition. Nine senators are appointed at the president's discretion from among outstanding persons in the community.

The Parliament's term of office has a duration of five years.

The Lawmaking Process

Laws are made by both houses of Parliament. General legislative bills may be introduced in either house and require the approval of a majority of votes in both houses. The House of Representatives may, however, ultimately override the rejection of a bill by the Senate. To its entry into force the president's formal assent is required.

Money bills regulating issues of public finance may only be introduced to the House of Representatives. They may ultimately be passed without the Senate's consent.

The Cabinet for Trinidad and Tobago

The cabinet for Trinidad and Tobago has authority for the general direction and control of the executive. It is headed by the prime minister. The president appoints as prime minister that member of the House of Representatives who commands the support of the majority of its members. The other ministers are appointed from among the members of either house of Parliament.

The cabinet is collectively responsible for its actions to Parliament and may be voted out of office by a vote of no confidence.

The Judiciary

The legal system of Trinidad and Tobago is modeled on the British legal system. The judiciary is independent of the legislative and the executive.

The constitution establishes a Supreme Court of Judicature for Trinidad and Tobago, which includes a High Court of Justice and a Court of Appeal. The chief justice presides in both courts.

The High Court is the court of original jurisdiction for civil and criminal matters. It also has jurisdiction for allegations of violations of fundamental rights and for constitutional disputes over the validity of the appointment of senators and the Speaker of the House of Representatives. The High Court's decisions may be appealed in the Court of Appeal. The Court of Appeal has exclusive constitutional jurisdiction for decisions on a candidate's qualification for eligibility as president.

The court of last instance is the Judicial Committee of the Privy Council in London. In recent years, the Judicial Committee has had to decide regularly on cases of death row prisoners. In 2003, the Judicial Committee ruled that the mandatory death sentence for murder without consideration of extenuating circumstances violated the constitution.

THE ELECTION PROCESS

Any citizen of Trinidad and Tobago aged 18 or older is eligible to vote or to run for office as a member of the House of Representatives. Candidates must have resided in Trinidad and Tobago for a minimum of two years immediately before the election. Holders of a public office or a post in the country's police or military are disqualified from being members of Parliament.

Elections to the House of Representatives are secret. Constituencies are won by simple majority of votes.

POLITICAL PARTIES

The system of political parties in Trinidad and Tobago is pluralistic. Party politics run along ethnic lines, reflecting the partitioning of the society. The two parties currently represented in the House of Representatives are the People's National Movement (PNM), dominated by Afro-Trinidadians, and the United National Congress (UNC), whose followers are largely Indo-Trinidadians.

CITIZENSHIP

Generally, every person born on the territory of Trinidad and Tobago or as a child to a citizen of Trinidad and Tobago holds the country's citizenship.

FUNDAMENTAL RIGHTS

The constitution protects individual fundamental rights in Sections 4 and 5. The rights granted are exclusively liberal rights, such as the protection of life and liberty, freedom of religion, and private property. The constitution particularly emphasizes protection against discrimination on grounds of race, origin, color, religion, or sex.

Fundamental rights may be limited by acts of Parliament. Such an act must explicitly highlight the inconsistency with fundamental rights. It has to be approved by three-fifths of both houses of Parliament and must be shown to be reasonably justifiable. Redress for violations of fundamental rights may be sought in the High Court.

Generally, fundamental rights and freedoms are respected by the government. However, international human rights groups continuously draw attention to the conditions in state prisons and the treatment of police detainees. Trinidad and Tobago withdrew its ratification of the American Convention on Human Rights in 1999.

ECONOMY

Trinidad and Tobago's economy is market based. The constitution provides for the protection of private property.

RELIGIOUS COMMUNITIES

The constitution grants freedom of conscience, religious belief, and observance. The state is secular. Religious groups have the same rights and obligations as most legal entities. In recent years, the government has strengthened legal prohibitions against religious discrimination by amending legislation to remove certain discriminatory religious references.

MILITARY DEFENSE AND STATE OF EMERGENCY

The military is headed by the president of Trinidad and Tobago as the commander in chief. The armed forces are made up of volunteers, and there is no conscription.

A state of emergency has to be declared by the president. During this period, the president may issue orders and instructions to deal with the situation, including limiting individual fundamental rights and freedoms. The proclamation may be revoked or extended at any time by the House of Representatives.

AMENDMENTS TO THE CONSTITUTION

Legislative bills that provide for amendments of the constitution or alterations of any of the constitution's provisions require strong parliamentary support. The majority required depends on the particular section to be changed. Alterations of the fundamental rights and freedoms, for example, need the support of at least two-thirds of all the members of the Senate and the House of Representatives. Changes in the president's immunity from civil and criminal proceedings, or in Parliament's powers to alter the constitution, need an even higher majority of three-fourths of the votes of all the members of both houses.

PRIMARY SOURCES

Constitution in English. Available online. URL: http://www.ttparliament.org/Docs/constitution/ttconst.pdf. Accessed on August 7, 2005.

SECONDARY SOURCES

Ken Handley, "President versus Prime Minister." *Quadrant Magazine* 18, no. 6 (2003): 22. Available online. URL: http://www.quadrant.org.au/php/archive_details_list.php?article_id=235. Accessed on April 26, 2005.

Larissa Zabel

TUNISIA

At-a-Glance

OFFICIAL NAME
Republic of Tunisia

CAPITAL
Tunis

POPULATION
9,974,722 (2005 est.)

SIZE
63,170 sq. mi. (163,610 sq. km)

LANGUAGES
Arabic, French

RELIGIONS
Muslim 98%, Christian 1%, Jewish less than 1%

NATIONAL OR ETHNIC COMPOSITION
Arab-Berber 98%, European 1%, other 1%

DATE OF INDEPENDENCE OR CREATION
March 20, 1956

TYPE OF GOVERNMENT
Parliamentary democracy (presidential preeminence)

TYPE OF STATE
Unitary state

TYPE OF LEGISLATURE
Bicameral parliament

DATE OF CONSTITUTION
June 1, 1959

DATE OF LAST AMENDMENT
May 13, 2003

Tunisia is a presidential democracy based on the rule of law with a clear division of executive, legislative, and judicial powers. It is divided into 23 governorates, each headed by a governor appointed by the president. The constitution of Tunisia guarantees the inviolability of the human person and freedom of conscience and protects the free exercise of beliefs, with reservation that they not disturb the public order. The freedoms of opinion, expression, the press, publication, assembly, and association are also guaranteed and exercised within the conditions defined by the law.

The Tunisian constitution guarantees the inviolability of the home, the privacy of correspondence, and the right to move freely in the interior of the territory, to leave it, and to establish one's domicile within the limits established by the law.

The president of Tunisia is the head of state. The president is the guarantor of national independence, of the integrity of the territory, of respect for the constitution and the laws, and of the execution of treaties. The president watches over the regular functioning of the constitutional public powers and assures the continuity of the state.

The president of Tunisia is assisted by an executive administration directed by a prime minister.

Religious freedom is guaranteed and state and religious communities are separated. The economic system can be described as a social market economy. The military is subject to the civil government in terms of law and fact. By constitutional law, Tunisia is obliged to contribute to world peace.

CONSTITUTIONAL HISTORY

In the early centuries of the Islamic period, beginning in the seventh and eighth centuries C.E., Tunisia was called Ifriqiyah. The Arabs conquered Tunisia in 647 C.E. In 1230, a separate Tunisian dynasty was established by the Hafsids. Tunisia was incorporated in 1574 into the Ottoman Empire, an arrangement that formally lasted until 1922. In reality, Tunisia was long an autonomous state.

In 1860, a constitution (or *destour*), which in theory limited the authority of the monarch, was promulgated. In 1888, the Treaty of Bardo effectively established a

French protectorate over the country. This treaty made no reference to a protectorate; it stated that the military occupation was temporary and would end the moment there was evidence that the Tunisian administration was capable of reestablishing law and order in the country.

In 1920, the Destour Party confronted the *bey* (or governor) and the French government with a document demanding the establishment of a constitutional form of government in which Tunisians would possess the same rights as Europeans.

In 1951, France permitted a government that had nationalist sympathies to take office. In July 1954 the French premier, Pierre Mendès-France, promised complete autonomy to Tunisia, subject to a negotiated agreement. In June 1955, an agreement was finally signed by the Tunisian delegates, even though it imposed strict limits on Tunisia in the fields of foreign policy, education, defense, and finance.

In March 1956, France granted full independence to Tunisia and a republic was declared with Habib Bourguiba as president. In 1957 Bourguiba formally ended the nominal rule of the former Ottoman beys. In June 1959, the country adopted a constitution modeled on the French system, which established the basic outline of the highly centralized presidential system that continues today.

In 1975, the Chamber of Deputies unanimously bestowed the presidency for life on the sick and aging Habib Bourguiba, who centralized power under his progressive but increasingly personalized rule. In 1987, Bourguiba was deposed by his prime minister, Zayn al-Abidin bin Ali (Ben Ali). He promised greater democratic openness and respect for human rights, signing a "national pact" with opposition parties. However, the ruling party, renamed the Rassemblement Constitutionnel Démocratique (Constitutional Democratic Rally [RCD]), continued to dominate the political scene. Ben Ali ran for reelection unopposed in 1989 and 1994 and won the 1999 elections facing two weak opponents. Citizens still do not have full political freedom.

A constitutional amendment, approved in 2002 in a referendum, permitted the president to run for more than two terms, and in 2004 Ben Ali was reelected with 95 percent of the vote; he again faced only token opposition. The landslide victories of Ben Ali and the government party were marked by intimidation and credible accusations of vote rigging.

FORM AND IMPACT OF THE CONSTITUTION

Tunisia has a written constitution, codified in a single document called the Basic Law, which takes precedence over all other national law. International law must be in accordance with the constitution to be applicable within Tunisia. Treaties enter into force only after their ratification and provided they are applied by the other party. Treaties ratified by the president and approved by the Chamber of Deputies have higher authority than ordinary laws.

BASIC ORGANIZATIONAL STRUCTURE

The Tunisian state structure is made up of three levels: central, intermediate, and local.

At the central level, there are 21 ministries, organized into general directorates in accordance with the French administrative model.

The intermediate level includes 23 governorates, which have political representation at the central government level. Each governorate is headed by a governor, who is appointed by the president.

In 2002, the Council of Regions was created. This is a consultative body charged with suggesting to the president and the prime minister action that would give local administrations increased financial and decision-making autonomy.

The local level revolves around municipalities. Each municipality is headed by a president elected for a five-year term.

LEADING CONSTITUTIONAL PRINCIPLES

Tunisia's system of government is a parliamentary democracy. There is a division of the executive, legislative, and judicial powers, based on checks and balances. The judiciary is independent and includes a constitutional court.

The Tunisian constitutional system is defined by a number of leading principles: Tunisia is a democracy, a republic, and a social state, and it is based on the rule of law. The 2002 constitutional reform consecrated the principles of rule of law and pluralism, and the values of solidarity, tolerance, and liberty. At the same time that it promotes political and civil rights, Tunisia endeavors to guarantee the social, economic, and cultural rights of its citizens.

The Tunisian constitution does not allow the exploitation of religion or race for political purposes. It states in Article 8 that "a political party must not be based, at the level of its principles, objectives, activities and programs, upon a religion, language, race, gender or region."

The preamble of the constitution commits Tunisia to promote world peace, to consolidate national unity, and to remain faithful to human values that constitute the common heritage of peoples. These values include human dignity, justice, liberty, and a striving for peace, progress, and free cooperation among nations. The constitution obliges Tunisia to take an active part in the integration of the Maghreb (the North African states).

CONSTITUTIONAL BODIES

The predominant bodies provided for in the constitution are the president; the prime minister and the cabinet ministers; the parliament, formed by the Chamber of Deputies and the Chamber of Councilors; and the judiciary. A number of other bodies, such as the Economic and Social Council, complete this list.

The President

As head of state, the president is the guarantor of national independence and the integrity of the territory. The president upholds respect for the constitution and the laws, supervises the execution of treaties, monitors the regular functioning of the constitutional public bodies, and assures the continuity of the state.

The president is elected for five years by universal, free, direct, and secret suffrage. Elections take place within the last 30 days of the previous term of office. A candidate for the presidency must be a Tunisian who does not carry any other nationality and whose father, mother, and paternal and maternal grandfathers were of uninterrupted Tunisian nationality. The candidate must also be a Muslim between the ages of 40 and 70 on the day of submitting his or her candidacy, whose civil and political rights have not been curbed for any legal reason. The declaration of candidacy is recorded in a special register before a commission composed of the president and four other members. This commission rules on the validity of the candidacies and proclaims the result of the election.

The president is the supreme commander of the armed forces. He or she accredits the diplomatic representatives of foreign powers, ratifies treaties, and declares war and concludes peace with the approval of the parliament. The president also exercises the right of pardon.

The president promulgates constitutional, organic, or ordinary laws and ensures their publication in the *Official Journal of the Tunisian Republic.* The president of the republic may return the bill to the national parliament for a second reading. If the bill is adopted by the national parliament with a majority of two-thirds of its members, the law must be promulgated and published. The president may submit to a referendum any bill relating to the organization of the public powers or seeking to ratify a treaty that, without being contrary to the constitution, may affect the functioning of the institutions.

As head of the executive branch, the president directs the general policy of the nation, defines its fundamental options, and informs the national parliament accordingly. The president watches over the execution of the laws and exercises the general regulatory power, which he or she may delegate in whole or in part to the prime minister. The president appoints the highest civil and military officers on the recommendation of the executive administration.

In case the presidency of the republic becomes vacant as a result of death, resignation, total incapacity, or a rul-

ing by the Constitutional Council that the president is unfit for office, the president of the national parliament becomes interim president for a maximum of 60 days until a new president is elected for a full five-year term. The interim president may not be a candidate for the presidency and may not call a referendum, dismiss the executive administration, or dissolve the national parliament. During this period, a motion of censure against the executive government cannot be presented. During the same period, presidential elections are organized to elect a new president of the republic for a term of five years. The new president may dissolve the national parliament and organize early legislative elections.

The Executive Administration

The administration puts into effect the general policy of the nation. It is responsible to the president of the republic, who appoints the prime minister and, on the suggestion of the prime minister, the other members of the executive administration. The president can dismiss the executive administration or any of its members at his or her discretion or on the recommendation of the prime minister.

The president presides over the Council of Ministers; in his or her absence the prime minister presides. The prime minister directs and coordinates the work of the executive administration. Decrees of a regulatory character are countersigned by the prime minister and the interested member of the executive government.

Parliament may dismiss the executive administration by a motion of censure, on grounds that it is not following the general policy and fundamental options stated in its program. The motion must initially be supported by at least half the members of parliament and needs a two-thirds majority of the deputies to pass.

The Parliament

The Tunisian parliament is the central representative organ of the people. It is composed of the Chamber of Deputies and the Chamber of Councilors.

The members of the Chamber of Deputies (Majlis al-Nuwaab) are elected by universal, free, direct, and secret suffrage for a five-year term. Any voter born of a Tunisian father who is at least 25 years of age on the day of submission of his or her candidacy is eligible for election to the national parliament.

The Chamber of Councilors is composed of councils whose number shall not exceed that of two-thirds of the members of the Chamber of Deputies. The majority of councilors represent regions: One or two seats are allocated to each governorate (depending on its population); the elected members of the local authorities choose the advisers from among themselves by a secret ballot. One-third of the councilors are elected at the national level from among various social sectors: employers, farmers, and workers. Enough candidates are nominated by the relevant professional organizations to provide voters with a choice. Seats are distributed equally among the concerned sectors. The candidates must have the appropriate qualifications in the sector they are to represent.

The remaining members of the Chamber of Councilors are appointed by the president of the republic from among prominent figures and holders of positions of responsibility at the national level. Once elected, councilors must not be bound by local or sectoral interests.

The term of office for the members of the Chamber of Councilors is six years. Half of its composition is renewed every three years.

The Chamber of Deputies is elected for a period of five years. If war or imminent peril makes a new election impossible, the mandate of the Chamber of Deputies is extended by a law until it is possible to proceed with the elections.

The Chamber of Deputies meets each year in ordinary session from October to July. However, the first session of every newly elected legislature begins in November. During the vacation, the Chamber of Deputies may meet in extraordinary sessions at the request of the president or the majority of deputies.

No member of the Chamber of Deputies or the Chamber of Councilors can be arrested or prosecuted for the duration of his or her mandate for a crime or misdemeanor as long as the Chamber of Deputies or the Chamber of Councilors has not lifted the immunity. However, in the event of a flagrant offense, arrest is permitted, though the relevant chamber must be informed without delay.

The president has power to dissolve the Chamber of Deputies if it passes a second motion of censure during the same legislative period. New elections must be called within 30 days.

The Lawmaking Process

The right to introduce a bill is possessed equally by the president of the republic and by the deputies. However, priority is given to bills presented by the president.

The parliament may authorize the president to issue decree laws within a fixed time limit and for a specific purpose. They must be submitted for ratification to the parliament upon expiration of that time limit.

Organic and ordinary laws are passed by the parliament by absolute majority. A draft organic law may not be submitted for deliberation by the parliament until after the expiration of a period of 15 days from its filing.

The budget must be voted on by December 31. If by that date the national parliament has not made a decision, the provisions of the financial bill may be implemented by decree, in three-month renewable installments.

Once a bill has been passed by the parliament, it must be countersigned by the president and promulgated.

The Judiciary

The judiciary in Tunisia is independent of the executive and legislative branches and is a powerful factor in legal life. Sharia courts were abolished in 1956; since then Tunisia has had a single unified judiciary structure. Magistrates are appointed by presidential decree upon the recommendation of the Superior Judicial Council.

The Superior Judicial Council serves as the administrative authority of the judiciary, which is actually administered by the Ministry of Justice. The council is presided over by the president of the republic and is composed of senior jurors. The current judicial system has civil, criminal, and administrative departments.

At the base of the Tunisian judicial structure are the 51 district courts, in which a single judge hears each case. The jurisdiction of the district courts extends to civil cases of lesser value, as well as cases related to issues of labor and nationality, civil affairs, personal estate actions, actions in recovery, and injunctions to pay.

The courts of first instance serve as the appellate courts for the district courts. There is a court of first instance in each region of the country. Each court is composed of a three-judge panel. The courts of first instance are empowered to hear all commercial and civil cases, irrespective of the monetary value of the claim.

The appeal courts serve as the appellate courts for decisions made in the courts of first instance. The three appeals courts are located in Tunis, Sousse, and Sfax.

The Supreme Court or Court of Cassation is located in Tunis and serves as the final court of appeals. The court has one criminal and three civil divisions.

The district courts have jurisdiction to hear all misdemeanor cases. The courts of first instance hears all other criminal cases except felonies. A grand jury first hears felony crimes. Once a judge issues an indictment based on the grand jury proceedings, the case is submitted to the criminal court division of the appeals court. The criminal division of the Court of Cassation serves as the final appellate court for criminal matters.

The High Court meets in a case of high treason committed by a member of the executive government.

THE ELECTION PROCESS

According to the constitution and electoral code, all Tunisians over the age of 18 have the right to vote in the election: "Suffrage is universal, free, direct, and secret." Citizens naturalized for more than five years can also vote, as can Tunisians living abroad who have registered in their embassy or consulate and have received their electoral card.

A National Monitor for Presidential and Legislative Elections has been established to control the electoral process. This body includes personalities known for their autonomy. The Constitutional Council approves the applications of presidential candidates and validates the results of elections.

Each presidential candidate and each list of candidates to legislative elections receives government funding to finance the campaign. During the electoral campaign, candidates are all offered equal time to speak to voters on national radio and television.

Parliamentary Elections

A candidate to the Chamber of Deputies must be the child of at least one Tunisian parent and must be 23 years of age. Candidates are excluded if they have been convicted of a serious crime, are involved in undischarged bankruptcy, are insane, or are active members of the armed and security forces. The renewable term of office is five years.

Individual candidates and those running independently can advertise in the press and other media. Campaigning is allowed for only two weeks preceding the election.

A candidate to the Chamber of Councilors must be born of a Tunisian father or mother, be at least 40 years of age on the day of submitting the candidacy, and have the right to vote. Concurrent membership of the Chamber of Deputies and of the Chamber of Councilors is not allowed.

The authorities must inform the voters where to vote at least seven days in advance of an election. No military or security forces can be present in the polling stations during voting without special permission, and voters cannot be armed.

POLITICAL PARTIES

Tunisia has a "pluralistic system" of political parties. In 1981, Bourguiba authorized the legal formation of opposition political parties, indicating a possible shift in the direction of democracy, and multiparty legislative elections were held for the first time in 1981. By 1986, six opposition parties had legal status.

The 1980s was largely characterized by popular unrest and labor difficulties, as well as a search for the aged Bourguiba's successor. In November 1987, amid widespread unrest and growing support for Islamism, Bourguiba was declared mentally unfit to rule and was removed from office. He was succeeded by General Zine el-Abidine Ben Ali, whom he had appointed as prime minister a month earlier.

Ben Ali initially moved toward liberal reforms, but after the 1989 elections, he instituted repressive measures against Islamist activists. During the 1994 election campaign, the government arrested political dissidents and barred the Islamic party Al Nahda from participation.

In 1994 Ben Ali gained 99 percent of the vote and the RDI won all 141 seats in the legislature. In 1999, Ben Ali was again reelected with nearly 100 percent of the vote; he faced a token challenge from two opposition candidates.

CITIZENSHIP

Tunisian citizenship is primarily acquired by birth. The principles of *ius sanguinis* and *ius soli* are both applied.

Anyone who has a Tunisian father obtains Tunisian nationality automatically wherever he or she is born. Anyone who has a foreign father and a Tunisian mother must be born in the country to acquire nationality automatically. If born abroad, such a child can acquire Tunisian nationality only if his or her parents make the request.

A foreigner whose father and grandfather were born in Tunisia can become Tunisian. This right, however, is not granted to foreigners whose ascending maternal ancestors alone were born in Tunisia.

FUNDAMENTAL RIGHTS

The Tunisian constitution guarantees the inviolability of the human person and freedom of conscience and protects the free exercise of beliefs, with reservation that they not disturb the public order. The liberties of opinion, expression, the press, publication, assembly, and association are also guaranteed and exercised within the conditions defined by law.

The Tunisian constitution guarantees the inviolability of the home and the secrecy of correspondence and the right to move freely in the interior of the territory, to leave it, and to establish one's domicile within the limits established by the law. The right to form unions is also guaranteed.

The general equal treatment clause is contained in Article 6, which guarantees that all persons are equal before the law.

Every accused person is presumed innocent until his or her guilt is established in accordance with a procedure offering guarantees indispensable for defense. The sentence is personal and cannot be pronounced except by virtue of an existing law.

Impact and Functions of Fundamental Rights

The preamble of the Tunisian constitution states that the republican regime is "the best guarantee for the respect of human rights, for the establishment of equality among citizens in terms of rights and duties, and for the achievement of the country's prosperity through economic development and use of the nation's riches for the benefit of the people." It also characterizes it as "the most effective way of protecting the family and ensuring the citizens' right to work, health care and education."

Limitations to Fundamental Rights

The fundamental rights specified in the constitution are not without limits. The Tunisian constitution stipulates possible limitations according to specific needs of the public and to the rights of others. Article 7 states: "The citizens exercise the plenitude of their rights in the forms and conditions established by the law. The exercise of these rights cannot be limited except by a law enacted for the protection of others, the respect for the public order, the national defense, the development of the economy, and social progress." On the other hand, no fundamental right may be disregarded completely. Each limit to a fundamental right faces limits itself.

ECONOMY

The Tunisian constitution does not specify an economic system.

The fundamental rights protect the freedom of property and the freedom of occupation or profession, general personal freedom, as well as the right to form associations, partnerships, and corporations.

RELIGIOUS COMMUNITIES

Freedom of religion or belief, which is guaranteed as a human right, also involves rights for the religious communities.

Islam is the state religion. The constitution provides for the free exercise of other religions that do not disturb the public order, and the government generally observes and enforces this right.

The government recognizes all Christian and Jewish religious organizations that were established before independence in 1956 but does not permit Christian groups to establish new churches. The government also partially subsidizes the Jewish community.

The government controls and subsidizes mosques and pays the salaries of prayer leaders. The president appoints the grand mufti of the republic. The 1988 law on mosques provides that only personnel appointed by the government may lead activities in mosques and stipulates that mosques must remain closed except during prayer times and other authorized religious ceremonies, such as marriages or funerals. New mosques may be built in accordance with national urban planning regulations but become the property of the state.

MILITARY DEFENSE AND STATE OF EMERGENCY

In case of imminent peril menacing the institutions of the republic or the security and independence of the country or obstructing the regular functioning of the public powers, the president of the republic may take the exceptional measures necessitated by the circumstances, after consultation with the prime minister and the president of the national parliament.

During this period, the president of the republic may not dissolve the national parliament, and no motion of censure may be presented against the executive government. These measures cease to have effect as soon as the circumstances that produced them end. The president of the republic must address a message to the national parliament on this subject.

AMENDMENTS TO THE CONSTITUTION

An amendment to the constitution can be proposed only by the president of the republic or by one-third of the members of the Chamber of Deputies, provided the amendment does not undermine the republican form of the state.

The Chamber of Deputies studies the proposed revision after a resolution adopted by an absolute majority, after identification of the purpose of the amendment and its study by an ad hoc committee. The president of the republic may put to a referendum proposals for revision of the constitution; he or she submits the draft amendment of the constitution to the people after it has been adopted by an absolute majority of the Chamber of Deputies upon a single reading. If that route is not taken, the draft amendment of the constitution can be adopted by the Chamber of Deputies by a two-thirds majority upon two readings; the second reading takes place at least three months after the first.

PRIMARY SOURCES

Constitution in English. Available online. URL: http://www.chr.up.ac.za/hr_docs/constitutions/docs/TunisiaC(rev).doc. Accessed on September 22, 2005.

Constitution in French. Available online. URL: http://droit.francophonie.org/doc/html/tn/con/fr/1999/1999dftncofr1.html. Accessed on August 16, 2005.

Constitution in Arabic. Available online. URL: http://www.chambredeputes.tn/a_constit.html. Accessed on July 22, 2005.

SECONDARY SOURCES

Andrew Borowiec, *Modern Tunisia: A Democratic Apprenticeship*. Westport, Conn.: Praeger, 1998.

Michel Camau and Vincent Geisser, *Le syndrome autoritaire: politique en Tunisie de Bourguiba à Ben Ali*. Paris: Presses de Sciences pol, 2003.

Dwight L. Ling, *Tunisia: From Protectorate to Republic*. Bloomington: Indiana University Press, 1967.

C. H. Moore, *Tunisia since Independence: The Dynamics of One-Party Government*. Berkeley: University of California Press, 1965.

Ezzeddine Moudoud, *Modernization, the State, and Regional Disparity in Developing Countries: Tunisia in Historical Perspective, 1881–1982*. Boulder, Colo.: Westview Press, 1989.

Harold D. Nelson, ed., *Tunisia—a Country Study*. 3d ed. Washington, D.C.: United States Government Printing Office, 1988.

Dahmène Touchent

TURKEY

At-a-Glance

OFFICIAL NAME
Republic of Turkey

CAPITAL
Ankara

POPULATION
67,803,927 (2000)

SIZE
301,384 sq. mi. (780,580 sq. km)

LANGUAGES
Turkish (official), Kurdish, Arabic, Armenian, Greek

RELIGIONS
Muslim (mostly Sunni) 99.8%, other (Greek Orthodox, Armenian Gregorian, Catholic, Syriac Orthodox, Jewish) 0.2%

NATIONAL OR ETHNIC COMPOSITION
Turkish 80%, other (Kurdish, Greek, Armenian, Syriac, Jewish, Georgian, Lazian, Circassian, Bosnian, Arab) 20%

DATE OF INDEPENDENCE OR CREATION
October 29, 1923

TYPE OF GOVERNMENT
Parliamentary democracy

TYPE OF STATE
Unitary state

TYPE OF LEGISLATURE
Unicameral parliament

DATE OF CONSTITUTION
November 7, 1982

DATE OF LAST AMENDMENT
June 21, 2005

The Turkish republic is a parliamentary democracy based on the division of powers. Its fundamental principles are the rule of law, secularism, a social state, and respect for human rights. It is organized as a unitary state, and the central government monopolizes political power. The local administrations do not exercise power independently of it.

The predominant bodies provided for in the constitution are the Turkish Grand National Assembly, the president of the republic, the Council of Ministers, and the Constitutional Court. The assembly makes, amends, and repeals laws and controls the executive and the budget. Free, equal, general, and direct elections of the members of parliament are guaranteed.

The president of the republic is the head of the state. In this capacity, he or she represents the Republic of Turkey and the unity of the Turkish nation. The Council of Ministers, composed of the prime minister and the ministers, is the other branch of the executive power. The independence of the judiciary of the legislative and executive powers is safeguarded. The Constitutional Court examines the constitutionality of laws and ensures respect for human rights. Individual, political, and social rights and freedoms are secured by the constitution. The economic system is a social market economy. The constitution describes political parties as indispensable elements of the democratic political life.

CONSTITUTIONAL HISTORY

The Ottoman Empire ruled today's Turkey through the 14th century. A constitutional monarchy was first established by the constitution of 1876, which established a bicameral parliament, one of whose chambers, the Meclis-i Mebusan, was elected by the people. The other chamber, the Meclis-i Ayan, was appointed by the sultan. The legislative process was designed so that the sultan's decisions always prevailed. The administration was appointed by the sultan and was responsible directly and solely to him.

The transition to a genuine parliamentarian system occurred with the 1909 constitutional amendment, but it was soon supplanted by the one-party rule of the Union and Progress (İttihad ve Terakki) Party.

The 1921 constitution, considered a step to republican government, fused the legislative, executive, and partly the judicial powers under parliament, which presided over the War of Independence. The 1924 constitution followed the proclamation of the republic; it was directly inspired by the French Revolution and Enlightment philosophy, which exerted a considerable influence on Mustafa Kemal Atatürk, founder of the republic.

The multiparty system gained momentum in the first years of the 1924 constitution, until the so-called Law on the Establishment of Peace (Takriri Sükun Kanunu) opened the way to the authoritarian one-party rule of the People's Republican Party (Cumhuriyet Halk Partisi [CHP]), which lasted until 1946, when a multiparty system was reestablished. The Democratic Party (Demokrat Parti [DP]) gained a majority in parliament; its behavior—it considered itself to be the only representative of national sovereignty, and it deviated from the secular ideology of the republic—provoked the coup of May 27, 1960, which in turn led to the 1961 constitution.

The 1961 constitution created a social rule of law and guaranteed fundamental rights and freedoms. During the 20 years it remained in force, Turkey gained wide experience with democratic institutions. Perhaps the most important advances were the establishment of the Constitutional Court, full judicial control over the administration, full independence of the judiciary, and autonomy of universities and state broadcasting agencies. Individual and collective rights and freedoms, particularly the rights of labor unions, were effectively guaranteed.

The same constitution established the National Security Council, limited to a solely advisory capacity. As terrorist activities gained momentum, a movement favoring direct or indirect intervention in politics grew within the army. After several failed coup attempts and a military-dominated regime in 1971 and 1973, the army took full power on September 12, 1980.

The military regime lasted until the end of 1983. Its authoritarian vision shaped the current, 1982 constitution. However, that constitution has been amended several times, most significantly in 1995, 2001, and 2004. The latter two reforms are part of the process of harmonization with European Union (EU) standards, in preparation for membership in the EU.

There were institutional and practical reasons behind the emergence of the armed forces as an important actor in the country's politics, even under civilian administrations. The National Security Council still occupies an important place in the Turkish constitutional political system, although the amendments of 2001 gave its civilian members a majority for the first time. The 2004 amendments strengthened the powers of the Audit Court to monitor state property in the possession of the armed forces.

FORM AND IMPACT OF THE CONSTITUTION

Turkey has a written constitution, codified in a single document that has supremacy over all other laws. The revolutionary laws, annexed at the end of the constitution, have a special semiconstitutional status since they cannot be challenged on grounds of unconstitutionality. Likewise, international treaties duly put into effect have the force of ordinary law but cannot be appealed to the Constitutional Court. The 2004 amendment provides that in cases of conflict between national law and ratified international treaties on fundamental rights and liberties, the treaty takes precedence. Thus, international human rights treaties are superior to national law; whether they outrank the constitution is yet to be determined. Apart from these exceptions, all legal norms (laws, ordinances, regulations, etc.) must comply with the provisions of the constitution.

BASIC ORGANIZATIONAL STRUCTURE

The Turkish republic is a unitary state. The central government monopolizes political power and determines the powers allocated to local administrations. The powers, structure, and boundaries of the local units can be changed by the central government unilaterally. According to the Constitutional Court, the principle of the unitary state is not compatible with regional autonomy and self-government or with federalism.

The executive authority is, however, based on local as well as central administration. Turkey is divided into provinces on the basis of geographical features, economic conditions, and public service requirements; provinces are further divided into administrative districts.

The local units are public corporate entities established to meet the common local needs of the inhabitants of provinces, municipal districts, and villages. Their decision-making organs are elected by the people. The central administration has the power of administrative trusteeship over the local units. Stronger decentralization in local government is a pressing need. However, all reform initiatives in this field have failed for fear that such evolution could foster ethnic secessionist or Islamic fundamentalist tendencies in various local units.

LEADING CONSTITUTIONAL PRINCIPLES

The Turkish state is a democratic, secular, and social republic governed by the rule of law, respecting human rights and loyal to the nationalism of Atatürk. It constitutes, with its territory and nation, an indivisible entity.

The constitutional provisions relating to the form of the state as a republic, to the characteristics of the republic, and to its indivisibility cannot be amended.

Secularism occupies a prominent position. It is directly inspired by the French model of *laïcité* and based on a separation between the religious sphere and the political one. In the terms of the preamble, there can be no role whatsoever for sacred religious feelings in state affairs and politics. Secularism has been the spearhead of the modernization process of the republic. Even today, the judiciary and particularly the constitutional court play a zealous role in defending this principle.

The fundamental aims and duties of the state are to safeguard the independence and integrity of the Turkish nation: indivisible, republican, and democratic; to ensure the welfare, peace, and happiness of the individual and society; to strive for the removal of political, social, and economic obstacles to the fundamental rights and freedoms of the individual in a manner compatible with the principles of justice, the social state, and the rule of law; and to provide the conditions required for the development of the individual's material and spiritual existence.

Sovereignty is vested fully and unconditionally in the nation, which exercises it through the authorized organs as prescribed by the principles in the constitution. The right to exercise sovereignty cannot be delegated to any individual, group, or class. No person or agency can exercise any state authority that does not emanate from the constitution.

The principle of separation of powers is a prime feature of the Turkish constitution. The constitution implies a parliamentary system based on the principle of the collaboration of executive and legislative institutions of government. The judiciary, however, is entirely independent.

CONSTITUTIONAL BODIES

The predominant bodies provided for in the constitution are the Turkish Grand National Assembly (the parliament), the president of the republic, the Council of Ministers, and the Constitutional Court.

The Turkish Grand National Assembly

The Turkish Grand National Assembly is the legislative organ in Turkey. According to the constitution, legislative authority cannot be delegated to any other branch of government. The Turkish Grand National Assembly is composed of 550 deputies elected by direct universal suffrage.

The term of the assembly is five years. However, the assembly may decide to hold new elections any time before the termination of its regular term. The president of the republic can also call new elections when (1) the Council of Ministers does not receive a vote of confidence or is compelled to resign by a vote of no confidence, and (2) a new Council of Ministers cannot be formed within 45 days, or (3) the new Council of Ministers does not re-

ceive a vote of confidence within 45 days. The president can also call new elections if a new Council of Ministers cannot be formed within 45 days after the resignation of the prime minister or within 45 days after the election of the presiding members of the newly elected assembly. The assembly is dissolved automatically if the president of the republic has not been elected by the assembly even in the fourth ballot.

The members of the assembly enjoy the classical parliamentary privileges. They cannot be held liable for votes cast, speeches made, and opinions expressed in the course of legislative activities or for disclosure of those activities outside the legislature. The constitution provides that no members of the assembly can be arrested, interrogated, detained, or tried unless the assembly decides otherwise. If the assembly decides to remove a member's freedom from arrest, he or she can appeal to the Constitutional Court on the grounds that the removal is contrary to the constitution, law, or the rules and procedures of the assembly.

The most important functions of the assembly are to make, amend, and repeal laws. Its other important role is to control the executive and the budget. The assembly can force a cabinet member to resign by withholding its confidence, and it can exercise its supervisory power by motions of censure, questions, parliamentary investigations, general debates, and parliamentary inquiries.

The motion of censure is the most powerful instrument of the legislative control of the executive. A motion of censure may be tabled either on behalf of a political party group or by the signature of at least 20 deputies. In the debate about the motion, only one of the signatories to the motion, one deputy from each political party group, and the prime minister or one minister on behalf of the Council of Ministers may take the floor. In order to unseat the Council of Ministers or a minister, an absolute majority of the total number of members voting is required.

A question is a request for information addressed to the prime minister or to individual ministers to be answered orally or in writing on behalf of the Council of Ministers. A parliamentary investigation is conducted to obtain information on a specific subject. A general debate is the consideration of a specific subject relating to the community and the activities of the state at the plenary sessions of the assembly. Parliamentary inquiries may be initiated by a decision of the assembly to ascertain criminal responsibility of the prime minister or individual ministers in matters connected with their office. The inquiry is carried out by a parliamentary commission composed of 15 members. The decision to take a person to court is taken by secret ballot and requires an absolute majority of the total number of members. In the case of impeachment the prime minister or minister is tried by the Constitutional Court, called the Supreme Court when it exercises this power.

The budgetary powers of the assembly are set by the constitution with a detailed timetable. An annual budget bill is submitted to the assembly by the Council of Ministers at least 75 days before the beginning of every new fiscal year. A rejection of the budget by the assembly is considered as a vote of censure against the Council of Ministers.

The President of the Republic

Executive power is exercised by the president of the republic and the Council of Ministers in conformity with the constitution and the law. The president of the republic is the head of the state. In this capacity he or she represents the Republic of Turkey and the unity of the Turkish nation and ensures the implementation of the constitution and the regular and harmonious functioning of the organs of state.

The president of the republic is elected for a term of seven years by the Turkish Grand National Assembly. A candidate for the post must be a Turkish citizen over 40 years of age who has completed higher education and is eligible to be a deputy; he or she may be a sitting deputy. In order to secure impartiality, the constitution provides that the president of the republic cannot be elected for a second term; if the president-elect is a member of a party, he or she must leave the party; if the president-elect is a deputy, he or she must resign that post.

The president of the republic is elected by a two-thirds majority of the total number of members of the assembly by secret ballot. If a two-thirds majority of the total number of members cannot be obtained in the first two ballots, a third ballot is held and the candidate who receives the absolute majority is elected. If an absolute majority is not obtained in the third ballot, a fourth ballot is held between the top two third ballot candidates. If a president is still not elected by an absolute majority, new general elections for the assembly are held immediately.

The president is not politically responsible for his or her actions connected with the office. Therefore, all presidential decrees must be countersigned by the prime minister and the ministers concerned, who bear the political responsibility. Thus, in formal terms the executive functions are exercised by the Council of Ministers.

The president of the republic is not responsible even in criminal matters connected with his or her office. Here, too, the responsibility is assumed by the prime minister and the ministers concerned. The president of the republic may be impeached only for high treason, at the request of at least one-third of the total number of members of the Turkish Grand National Assembly and by the decision of at least three-fourths.

The constitution contains a long list of presidential powers and classifies them according to their legislative, executive, and judicial functions. Among the legislative powers are promulgating laws, returning laws to the Turkish Grand National Assembly for reconsideration, submitting proposed constitutional amendments to referendum, appealing to the Constitutional Court to annul laws or provisions of laws or other norms, and calling new elections for the assembly.

In the executive capacity, the president appoints the prime minister and has the power to accept his or her resignation. The president appoints and dismisses ministers on the proposal of the prime minister, summons the Council of Ministers whenever he or she deems it necessary and presides over its sessions, ratifies and promulgates international treaties, and summons and presides over the National Security Council. The president also has the power to proclaim martial law or a state of emergency; can issue decrees that have the force of law, in accordance with the decisions of the Council of Ministers; and appoints members of the Higher Education Council and rectors of universities.

The president appoints the members of the Constitutional Court, one-fourth of the members of the Council of State, the chief public prosecutor and the deputy chief public prosecutor of the High Court of Appeals, and the members of the Military High Court of Appeals, the Supreme Military Administrative Court, and the Supreme Council of Judges and Public Prosecutors.

In spite of this long list of competences, to which others can be added, the president of the republic is not the head of state as in presidential or semipresidential systems. Most of these powers are formal and not substantive; they may be exercised only upon the recommendation or prior action of another body or require the participation of the prime minister or other ministers.

The Council of Ministers

The other major organ of the executive branch is the Council of Ministers, composed of the prime minister and the other ministers. The prime minister is appointed by the president of the republic from among the members of the Turkish Grand National Assembly. The ministers are nominated by the prime minister and appointed by the president of the republic from among the members of the assembly or those eligible for election as deputies. They can be dismissed by the president of the republic upon the proposal of the prime minister when deemed necessary.

The completed list of members of the Council of Ministers is submitted to the assembly for a vote of confidence. A simple majority is sufficient for approval.

The prime minister, as chairperson of the Council of Ministers, ensures cooperation among the ministers and supervises the implementation of the administration's general policy. He or she ensures that the ministers exercise their functions in accordance with the constitution and laws, may take corrective measures to this end, and may propose to the president the dismissal of a minister. The prime minister is normally the leader of the majority party in the Turkish Grand National Assembly and has the support of the assembly.

In spite of the considerable powers of the president of the republic, the prime minister is the effective head of the executive. However, the prime minister has to maintain a good relationship with the president, who can stymie the administration by refusing to sign executive decrees.

All ministers assume both collective responsibility for the general policy of the administration and individual responsibility for the actions of their own ministry. No individual minister can stay in office if the Council of Ministers falls as a result of a vote of no confidence. By contrast, the assembly can vote a motion of censure to unseat an individual minister.

The Lawmaking Process

The Turkish Grand National Assembly enacts, amends, and repeals laws. The Council of Ministers and deputies are empowered to introduce laws.

The assembly convenes with at least one-third of the total number of its members and adopts laws by an absolute majority of those present; however, the quorum for enactment of a law can under no circumstances be less than a quarter plus one of the total number of members.

The laws adopted by the assembly are promulgated by the president of the republic within 15 days. The president may, within the same period, return a law for reconsideration, but if the assembly readopts the law without any change, the president must promulgate it.

The Judiciary

The judicial power is mainly exercised by courts of justice (civil and criminal), administrative courts, and military courts. Decisions by lower courts are examined by higher courts. The higher courts in Turkey are the Court of Cassation (final appeal), the Council of State, the Military Court of Cassation, the High Military Administrative Court of Appeals, the Court of Jurisdictional Disputes, the Audit Court, and the Constitutional Court.

The Court of Cassation is the last instance for reviewing decisions of courts of justice, the Council of State is the last instance for reviewing decisions of administrative courts, and the Military Court of Cassation is the last instance for reviewing decisions of military courts.

Some specialized courts prescribed by law act as both first and last instance in their limited field. The High Military Administrative Court of Appeals is the court of first and last instance for disputes that arise from administrative acts involving military personnel, even if such acts were carried out by civil authorities. In disputes that arise from the obligation to perform military service, there is no condition that the person concerned be a member of the military body. The Jurisdictional Court of Disputes is empowered to deliver final judgments in disputes among courts of justice, administrative courts, and military courts concerning their jurisdiction and decisions.

The Audit Court is charged with auditing, on behalf of the Turkish Grand National Assembly, all the accounts relating to the revenue, expenditure, and property of government departments financed by the general and subsidiary budgets. It makes final decisions on the acts and accounts of the responsible officials.

The Constitutional Court examines the constitutionality, in respect of both form and substance, of laws, decrees that have the force of law, and the rules of procedure of the Turkish Grand National Assembly. Constitutional amendments can be examined and verified only with regard to their form. However, no action can be taken before the Constitutional Court alleging the unconstitutionality as to the form or substance of decrees that have the force of law issued during a state of emergency or martial law or in time of war. In addition, international treaties cannot be taken before the Constitutional Court on grounds of unconstitutionality.

The Constitutional Court is composed of 11 regular and four substitute members. The president of the republic appoints all the members of the court, but the majority of the candidates (seven regular and three substitute members) are nominated by other high courts. The president of the republic also appoints one member from a list of three candidates nominated by the Higher Education Council from among members of the teaching staff of institutions of higher education and three members and one substitute member from among senior administrative officers and lawyers. The Constitutional Court has complete independence of the legislative and executive branch.

Access to the Constitutional Court is gained through two processes: An annulment action can be instituted by the president of the republic, parliamentary groups of the party in power and of the main opposition party, or a minimum of one-fifth of the total number of members of the Turkish National Assembly. The annulment action must be initiated within 60 days of the promulgation of the law in question in the official gazette. Secondly, any first instance court may dispute the constitutionality of a law to the Constitutional Court, subject to no time limitation. The first instance court which is trying a case may submit its appeal even before the parties raise an issue of unconstitutionality, or when one of the parties raises the issue during proceedings it may submit the appeal if it is convinced of the seriousness of the claim. Proceedings are delayed until the Constitutional Court can render its decision.

Any law, decree, or parliamentary rule annulled by the court ceases to have effect from the date the annulment is published in the official gazette.

THE ELECTION PROCESS AND POLITICAL PARTICIPATION

Elections for the Turkish Grand National Assembly are held every five years. Every Turk over the age of 30 who has completed primary education and has not been sentenced for serious offenses is eligible to be a deputy.

In conformity with the conditions set forth in the law, all Turkish citizens over 18 years of age have the right to vote, to be elected (to certain posts), to engage in political activities independently or in a political party, and to take part in a referendum.

Elections and referenda are held under the direction and supervision of the Supreme Election Council, a judicial body, in accordance with the principles of free, equal, secret, direct, and universal suffrage and public counting of votes. The Supreme Election Council supervises all election and campaign procedures, investigates disputes, and makes final decisions on all irregularities, complaints, and objections.

The constitution does not specify the system of elections to the Turkish Grand National Assembly. These are regulated by the Election of Deputies Law, which introduced the d'Hondt version of proportional representation. This method secures advantages for the small political parties and thus leads to a greater variety of opinions in the assembly. The large number of parties, however, can make it harder to fashion a Council of Ministers and win a vote of confidence. To counteract that tendency, the election law now requires a national threshold of 10 percent; parties that receive less than 10 percent of the votes nationally are not assigned any seats in the assembly. The system strongly favors the larger parties, and there have been discussions about lowering the threshold to 5 percent.

POLITICAL PARTIES

The 1982 constitution describes the democratic regime as a party democracy and classifies political parties as indispensable elements of the democratic political life.

Citizens over 18 have the right to form political parties and, in accordance with established procedures, to join and withdraw from them. Judges and prosecutors, members of higher judicial organs, civil servants not considered to be laborers by virtue of the services they perform, members of the armed forces, and students who are not yet in higher education institutions cannot be members of political parties.

Political parties can be formed without prior permission. The state provides financial assistance to the political parties, as regulated by law, and specifies procedures related to membership fees and donations. The activities, internal regulations, and operation of political parties have to be in line with democratic principles. Political parties cannot engage in commercial activities.

The statutes and programs, as well as the activities, of political parties must not be in conflict with the independence of the state, its indivisible integrity with the territory and people, human rights, the principles of equality and rule of law, sovereignty of the nation, and the principles of the democratic and secular republic. They must not aim to protect or establish class or group dictatorship or dictatorship of any kind; nor may they incite citizens to crime.

When it is established that the statute, program, or activities of a political party violate the principles mentioned, the Constitutional Court can dissolve it. The office of the chief public prosecutor must first file a suit to that effect.

CITIZENSHIP

Everyone bound to the Turkish state through the bond of citizenship is a Turk. The child of a Turkish father or a Turkish mother acquires Turkish citizenship. Citizenship can also be acquired under conditions stipulated by law, such as marriage or a decision of the Council of Ministers, and can be forfeited only in cases determined by law. No Turk is deprived of citizenship unless he or she commits an act incompatible with loyalty to the motherland, such as desertion from military service or escape abroad subsequent to a judicial condemnation for crimes against the security of the state. No citizen can be extradited because of a crime, except for the fulfillment of the obligations required by the International Criminal Court.

FUNDAMENTAL RIGHTS

Fundamental rights and freedoms are considered inviolable and inalienable.

Individual rights and freedoms are categorized as follows: right to life and right to protection and development of one's material and spiritual being; prohibition of forced labor; right to liberty and security; protection of private life and inviolability of the domicile; freedom of communication; freedom of residence and movement; freedom of religion and conscience, thought and opinion, expression and dissemination of thought; freedom of science and the arts; freedom of the press; freedom of association; property rights; and guarantees of lawful judgment.

A number of social and economic rights and duties are also guaranteed: protection of the family; right and duty of training and education; fair utilization of the coasts; land ownership; protection of agriculture, animal husbandry; and persons engaged in these activities; due compensation for expropriation, nationalization, and privatization; the right and duty to work, guarantees for working conditions, and the right to rest and leisure; the right to organize labor unions and engage in collective bargaining, strikes, and lockouts; guarantee of fair wage; the rights to health, environment, and housing; protection of youth; the right to social security; conservation of historical, cultural, and natural wealth; and protection of arts and artists.

Social rights first entered Turkish constitutional life with the 1961 constitution, which was highly advanced for its time. The 1982 constitution might be seen as a regression of social rights, or as an attempt to reconcile social justice concerns with the requirements of the capitalist economy.

As for political rights and duties, the constitution guarantees the right to vote, to be elected, to petition, and to engage in political activity and includes some provisions related to political parties. It protects the right to enter public service or the national service and imposes the obligation to pay taxes.

Impact and Functions of Fundamental Rights

The Turkish constitution is capable of being interpreted in a manner that would allow the state or its rulers to restrict or even destroy the fundamental rights and freedoms embodied in the constitution. Nevertheless, in practice many of these rights have undergone a process of entrenchment in the recent era.

As far back as 1987 Turkey recognized the right of individuals to appeal to the European Court of Human Rights. The court's judgments have had a huge influence on the Turkish law, necessitating the amendment of several laws and even of some provisions of the constitution. Turkey has recently ratified the United Nations Human Rights Conventions of 1966 but does not recognize the jurisdiction of the Human Rights Committee. Human rights questions play a major role in the relationship between Turkey and the European Union; every year, a considerable part of the annual report of the European Union about Turkey as a candidate for membership is devoted to human rights issues.

Limitations to Fundamental Rights

Fundamental rights and freedoms may be restricted only by law and in conformity with the reasons mentioned in the constitution and without infringing upon their essence. These restrictions must not be in conflict with the letter or spirit of the constitution or the requirements of the democratic order, the secular republic, or the principle of proportionality.

The rights and freedoms embodied in the constitution may not be exercised with the aim of violating the indivisible integrity of the state with its territory and nation, or endangering the existence of the democratic and secular order of the Turkish republic, based on human rights.

In times of war, mobilization, martial law, or state of emergency, the exercise of fundamental rights and freedoms can be partially or entirely suspended, to the extent required by the exigencies of the situation. In no case may obligations under international law be violated. Even under such circumstances, the individual's right to life and the integrity of his or her material and spiritual being are inviolable except when death occurs through lawful acts of warfare; no one may be compelled to reveal his or her religion, conscience, thought, or opinion or be accused on account of them; offenses and penalties may not be made retroactive; nor may anyone be held guilty until so proved by a court judgment.

The fundamental rights and freedoms of noncitizens may be restricted by law in a manner consistent with international law.

ECONOMY

The constitution of Turkey does not impose a specific economic system. Taking certain provisions into consideration, however, it can be said that the constitution implies a preference for a social market economy.

According to the constitution, everyone has the right to own and inherit property and the freedom to work and conclude contracts in the field of his or her choice. The constitution also safeguards the freedom to establish private enterprises. However, these rights can be restricted in order to secure the public interest and the principle of a social state. For instance, the right to property may be limited by law only in view of the public interest. The state can take measures to ensure that private enterprises operate in accordance with national economic requirements and social objectives and in conditions of security and stability.

In addition, the constitution obliges the state to engage in planning to accommodate economic, social, and cultural developments and to supervise markets. The rapid, balanced, and harmonious development of industry and agriculture throughout the country and the efficient use of national resources are the duties of the state. The state must also ensure and promote the sound, orderly functioning of the money, credit, capital, goods, and services markets. It must also prevent the formation of monopolies and cartels, in practice or by agreement.

RELIGIOUS COMMUNITIES

The right to freedom of conscience, religious belief, and conviction, as well as the right to perform acts of worship, religious services, and ceremonies, are placed under constitutional protection. No one may be compelled to worship or to participate in religious ceremonies and rites, to reveal religious beliefs and convictions, or be blamed or accused because of his or her religious beliefs and convictions. No one is allowed to exploit or abuse religion or religious feelings or things held sacred by religion for the purpose of personal or political influence. No one may attempt to base the fundamental, social, economic, political, and legal order of the state on religious tenets, even partially.

The relationship between state and religion is based upon a staunch secularism and a regime of total separation. Legal institutions are particularly hostile to the interference of religion. Nevertheless, a disposition of the 1982 constitution, though highly criticized, introduced a system of compulsory education and instruction in religion and ethics in the curricula of primary and secondary schools. These courses are conducted under state supervision and control. Other religious education and instruction is subject to the individual's own desire, and in the case of minors, to the request of their legal representatives.

Another element inconsistent with the secular conception of state is the department of religious affairs, which is within the general administration and exercises its duties prescribed in its particular law. In principle, this public entity must function in accordance with the principles of secularism, removed from all political views and ideas and aimed at national solidarity and integrity.

In practice, the department, charged to ensure the whole society's religious needs, represents only the Sunni version of Islam.

There is no legal practice of registration or "recognition of religions" as in many European countries. The non-Muslim religious institutions are organized in the form of foundations that enjoy the guarantees granted by the 1923 Treaty of Lausanne, which is considered the founding act of the republic. The Treaty of Lausanne confines the concept of minority to the non-Muslim minorities and provides a set of freedoms and rights for non-Muslim citizens as well as non-Muslim institutions. The status of non-Muslim institutions has been, however, quite problematic and influenced by the vicissitudes of international politics. Recently, in the context of the harmonization of laws with the European Union legal system, a reform considerably improved the legal status of non-Muslim institutions and facilitated the acquisition of land property and the construction of new houses of worship.

MILITARY DEFENSE AND STATE OF EMERGENCY

The power to authorize a declaration of war or to allow foreign armed forces to be stationed in Turkey is vested in the Turkish Grand National Assembly whether the assembly is adjourned and in recess or in session. If the country is subjected to sudden armed aggression and an immediate decision about the deployment of armed force thus becomes imperative, the president of the republic can mobilize the Turkish armed forces.

The office of commander in chief is considered inseparable from the Turkish Grand National Assembly and is represented by the president of the republic. The Council of Ministers is responsible to the assembly for national security and for the preparation of the armed forces for the defense of the country. The chief of the general staff is the actual commander of the armed forces and, in time of war, exercises the duties of commander in chief on behalf of the president of the republic. The chief of the general staff is appointed by the president of the republic, at the proposal of the Council of Ministers; the chief is responsible to the prime minister.

The National Security Council is composed of the prime minister; the chief of the general staff; deputy prime ministers; the ministers of justice, national defense, internal affairs, and foreign affairs; the commanders of the army, navy, and air forces; and the general commander of the gendarmerie, and is presided over by the president of the republic.

The National Security Council submits advisory decisions to the Council of Ministers. It works to ensure the necessary coordination of the civil and military organs with regard to the formulation, establishment, and implementation of the national security policy of the state.

In the event of natural disaster, dangerous epidemic disease, or a severe economic crisis, the Council of Ministers, presided over by the president of the republic, may declare a state of emergency for a period not exceeding six months. In the event of serious indications of widespread acts of violence aimed at the destruction of the free democratic order or fundamental rights and freedoms, or in case of a serious deterioration of public order as a result of acts of violence, the decision is made after consultation with the National Security Council.

In the event of a declaration of a state of emergency, the decision must be submitted immediately to the Grand National Assembly for approval. At the request of the Council of Ministers, the assembly may extend the duration of the state of emergency for a maximum of four months or may lift it altogether.

During the state of emergency, the Council of Ministers, presided over by the president of the republic, may issue decrees that have the force of law on matters necessitated by the state of emergency. These decrees are published in the official gazette and are submitted to the Grand National Assembly on the same day for approval; the time limit and procedure for their approval by the assembly are specified in the rules of procedure.

The Council of Ministers, presided over by the president of the republic and after consultation with the National Security Council, may declare martial law for a period not exceeding six months. This is possible only in the event of widespread acts of violence that are more dangerous than the cases necessitating a state of emergency and that are aimed at the destruction of the free democratic order or the fundamental rights and freedoms embodied in the constitution. Martial law is also possible in the event of war, the emergence of a situation necessitating war, an uprising, the spread of violent and strong rebellious actions against the motherland and the republic, or widespread acts of violence of either internal or external origin threatening the indivisibility of the country and the nation. This decision is submitted for approval to the assembly on the same day. If the assembly is in recess, it is assembled immediately. The assembly may reduce or extend the period of martial law or lift it.

During the period of martial law the Council of Ministers, presided over by the president of the republic, may issue decrees that have the force of law. These decrees are submitted for approval to the Grand National Assembly on the same day. Extension of the period of martial law, for a maximum of four months each time, requires a decision by the assembly. In the event of a state of war, the limit of four months does not apply.

Military service is compulsory and its term is 15 months. Neither conscientious objection nor substitution of civil service is allowed.

AMENDMENTS TO THE CONSTITUTION

The constitution of Turkey is not a flexible constitution. According to Article 4, the provisions contained in the first three articles cannot be amended nor their amendment be proposed. Article 1 states that "the state of Turkey is a republic." Article 2 describes the republic as "a democratic, secular, and social state governed by the rule of law in accordance with the concepts of social peace, national solidarity and justice, respectful of human rights, committed to Atatürk nationalism, and based on the fundamental principles set forth in the preamble." Article 3 states that "the Turkish state is an indivisible whole with its territory and nation. Its language is Turkish. Its Flag is composed of a white crescent and star on a red background, in the manner prescribed by law. Its national anthem is the Independence March. Its capital is Ankara."

The remaining provisions of the constitution can be amended in accordance with a complicated procedure. The amendment must be proposed by at least one-third of the total number of members of the Turkish Grand National Assembly. If the proposal is adopted by at least three-fifths but less than two-thirds of the total number of members of the assembly, the president of the republic may either return the amendment to the assembly for further consideration or submit it to a referendum. If the assembly adopts the proposal by a majority of at least two-thirds, the president may either ratify it, return it to the assembly for further consideration, or submit it to an optional referendum. If the assembly readopts the bill by a majority of at least two-thirds upon further consideration, the president of the republic still has the option of submitting it to a referendum.

Amendments submitted to referendum require the approval of more than half of the valid votes cast.

Despite the rigidity of the procedure, many amendments have been approved between 1987 and the current time. The provisions relating to fundamental rights and freedoms have been amended several times in order to eliminate the authoritarian character of the 1982 constitution and to effect greater conformity with liberal democracy.

PRIMARY SOURCES

Constitution in English. Available online. URLs: http://www.constitution.org/cons/turkey/turk_cons.htm; http://www.oefre.unibe.ch/law/icl/tu00000_.html. Accessed on September 17, 2005.
Constitution in Turkish. Available online. URL: http://www.tbmm.gov.tr. Accessed on September 5, 2005.

SECONDARY SOURCES

Tuðrul Ansay and D. Wallace, *Introduction to Turkish Law.* 3d ed. Deventer, Netherlands: Kluwer Law and Taxation, 1987.
Kudret Guven, *General Principles of Turkish Law.* Ankara: Gazi Kitabevi, 1996.
S. Kili, "Turkish Constitutional Developments: An Appraisal." *Capital University Law Review* 21 (1992): 1059–1078.
———, *Turkish Constitutional Developments and Assembly Debates on the Constitutions of 1924 and 1961.* Istanbul: Robert College Research Centre, 1971.
I. Özay, *Legitimacy of the Constitutional Court's Constitutional Jurisdiction,* edited by the Constitutional Court of Turkey, 75–83. Ankara, 1993.
Y. G. Özden, "30th Anniversary of the Turkish Constitutional Court: Opening Speech of the Court's President, Y. G. Özden." *Human Rights Review* 1, no. 2 (1992): 7–17.
Sibel İnceoğlu, "Turkey." *Yearbook of Islamic and Middle Eastern Law* 4 (1997/98): 455–461; Sibel İnceoğlu, "Turkey." *Yearbook of Islamic and Middle Eastern Law* 5 (1998/99): 453–459.
Aydoðan Özman and A. Lale Sirmen, "The Legal System of Turkey." In *Modern Legal Systems Cyclopedia,* edited by William S. Redden, 599–636. Vol. 5. Buffalo, N.Y.: William S. Hein, 1985.
F. Saglam, "General Framework of the Fundamental Rights and Freedoms under the 1982 Constitution." *Turkish Yearbook of Human Rights* 14 (1992): 3–23.
M. Turhan, "Parlamentarism or Presidentialism? Constitutional Choices for Turkey." In *A. U. Siyasal Bilgiler Facultesi Dergisi* 47 (1992): 153–168.
Seref Unal, *Turkish Legal System and the Protection of Human Rights.* Sam Papers No. 3/99. Ankara: Ministry of Foreign Affairs Center for Strategic Research, 1999.
Engin Ural, *Handbook of Turkish Law.* 4th ed. Ankara: Milet Publishing, 1997.

Emre Öktem and Sibel İnceoğlu

TURKMENISTAN

At-a-Glance

OFFICIAL NAME
Turkmenistan

CAPITAL
Ashgabat

POPULATION
6,408,600 (June 1, 2004)

SIZE
188,456 sq. mi. (488,100 sq. km)

LANGUAGES
Turkmen 72%, Russian 12%, Uzbek 9%, other 7%

RELIGIONS
Muslim 89%, Eastern Orthodox 9%, other 2%

NATIONAL OR ETHNIC COMPOSITION
Turkmen 85%, Uzbek 5%, Russian 4%, other 6% (2004)

DATE OF INDEPENDENCE OR CREATION
October 27, 1991

TYPE OF GOVERNMENT
Presidential republic

TYPE OF STATE
Unitary state

TYPE OF LEGISLATURE
Unicameral parliament

DATE OF CONSTITUTION
May 18, 1992

DATE OF LAST AMENDMENT
August 15, 2003

Turkmenistan is a presidential republic. Since independence from the Soviet Union in 1991, Turkmenistan has proclaimed a policy of permanent neutrality. Turkmenistan is a unitary state and has a written constitution, which was adopted in 1992.

The Turkmen constitution establishes the basic organizational structure of the state and the principles on which it is based. It enumerates fundamental rights and freedoms of citizens and stipulates the essence of state governance.

CONSTITUTIONAL HISTORY

In the middle of the 1850s the territory of Turkmenistan, populated by numerous separate tribes, was absorbed by the Russian Empire, and Russian laws and state institutions were introduced. In the 1920s, the country was incorporated into the Communist "new Russia," and in 1924 it became a founding member of the Union of Soviet Socialist Republics. Turkmenistan was one of the 15 republics until 1991, when the Soviet Union dissolved.

On October 27, 1991, Turkmenistan proclaimed its independence and became a sovereign state. On March 2, 1992, Turkmenistan joined the United Nations, in which on December 12, 1995, the permanent neutrality of Turkmenistan was supported by a resolution of the General Assembly.

Turkmenistan adopted a new, liberal constitution on May 18, 1992. Several amendments have been introduced since then, including the abolition of the death penalty and the proclamation of neutrality.

A significant revision of the constitution was undertaken in 2003 and approved on August 15 that year by the National Council, the supreme state body. Most amendments pertained to the new role and status of the National Council, as the fourth branch of state power superior to the classical legislative, executive, and judicial branches.

A number of legal difficulties still await adequate constitutional solutions. This condition suggests that the ongoing process of constitutional and legal reforms in the country has not yet been completed.

Turkmenistan is a member of the United Nations, the Commonwealth of Independent States, the Economic

Cooperation Organization, the Organization for Security and Cooperation in Europe, and a number of other regional and global organizations.

FORM AND IMPACT OF THE CONSTITUTION

Turkmenistan has a written constitution, codified in a single document. The principles and provisions of the constitution take precedence over all other national law. Laws that contradict the constitution are considered null and void. The constitution clearly acknowledges that because Turkmenistan is a fully admitted member of the world community it recognizes the priority and precedence of the universally accepted norms of international law. The international agreements that Turkmenistan signed and duly ratified have direct effect on national law, and the provisions of international treaties must be incorporated in explicit state laws.

BASIC ORGANIZATIONAL STRUCTURE

Turkmenistan's administrative and territorial structure is that of a unitary state. It is made up of five provinces (velayats) and 65 districts (etraps). The constitution explicitly grants province status to some cities (such as Ashgabat) and district status to some others. The governors of provinces, districts, cities, and towns are appointed by the president for a term of five years. Smaller towns and settlements elect local self-government bodies (gengesh).

LEADING CONSTITUTIONAL PRINCIPLES

Turkmenistan's system of government is a presidential republic. In addition to the executive, legislative, and judicial powers, there is a fourth power, called the National Council (Halk Maslahaty). Although the basic law of Turkmenistan acknowledges checks and balances among the four powers, the Halk Maslahaty takes precedence over the other three. The judiciary is independent.

The leading principles set forth in the Turkmen constitution are that Turkmenistan is a democracy, adheres to the rule of law, and is a secular state. Turkmenistan also has a unique status of permanent positive neutrality that was recognized and supported by the United Nations (UN) General Assembly in 1995. The constitution proclaims neutrality as the basis for the internal and external policies of the country. The constitution spells out that the bearer of the sovereignty and the only source of the state authority is the people of Turkmenistan.

CONSTITUTIONAL BODIES

The predominant constitutional organs are the National Council, the president, the Parliament (Mejlis), the cabinet of ministers, and the Supreme Court.

The National Council (Halk Maslahaty)

The National Council is a permanent organ and the highest representative body of the people. It is the state's supreme authority and government. The National Council consists of 2,507 members and includes the president of the republic; the members of parliament; the chairperson of the Supreme Court; the prosecutor-general; the members of the cabinet of ministers; the governors of all provinces, districts, cities, and towns; representatives of various public and government organizations; and 64 elected National Council deputies.

The National Council adopts and amends the constitution and constitutional laws, calls nationwide referenda, and schedules presidential and parliamentary elections. Council meetings are convened not less than once a year by the council's chair, who is elected in an open vote by two-thirds of the members of the council for a five-year-term.

The President

The president is the head of state and of the executive branch and is the highest official in the country. Within the limits of the constitution, the president exercises the following discretionary powers: The president implements the constitution and laws; leads the external politics of the country; appoints members of the cabinet of ministers; signs laws, decrees, and presidential instructions; and serves as commander in chief of the armed forces of Turkmenistan.

The president is elected in an open, direct election for a five-year-term and may be reelected with no limit. Candidates must be citizens of Turkmenistan, ethnic Turkmen, and 40 to 70 years old. President Saparmurat Niyazov, who has governed since 1990, is the absolutely central political figure of the country.

The Parliament (Mejlis)

The Parliament of Turkmenistan is the state's legislative body. It is unicameral and consists of 50 members who are elected for a five-year term. The Parliament can be dissolved by a decision of the National Council or a nationwide referendum, by self-dissolution, or by the president if the Parliament fails to form its mandated governmental bodies. Members of Parliament elect a chair from among themselves.

The Parliament exercises the following constitutional powers: It adopts, interprets, and amends laws; adopts the state budget; supervises and observes elections; institutes state awards; and determines the conformity of normative acts adopted by the administration to the constitution. In case of conflict of interests between the Parliament and the cabinet of ministers, these are resolved by the president. Members of Parliament enjoy immunities that may be removed only by a decision of the Parliament.

The Cabinet of Ministers

The cabinet of ministers of Turkmenistan is the chief executive and guiding body of the state. The president of the republic presides over its meetings. The body is formed by the president. The cabinet of ministers supervises the implementation of the laws, of presidential decrees, and of decisions of the National Council. It administers the country's economic and social development policies, monitors the functioning of government institutions and organizations, and implements the country's external economic policies.

The Lawmaking Process

A law is initially drafted in the relevant committee of Parliament. If it is adopted in the plenary, it is sent to the president for approval. The president has the right to veto the law. If vetoed, the law goes back to Parliament. In case the Parliament readopts the law by no less than two-thirds of the members, the president shall sign the law.

The Judiciary

In accordance with the constitutional requirements, the judiciary serves to protect the rights and freedoms of the citizens. The judiciary is independent, and justice is executed only by courts. The highest judicial body is the Supreme Court, followed by the courts of provinces and districts. There are no constitutional courts or military courts. Judges for all courts are appointed by the president for a five-year term. Unfortunately, the judiciary has not played much of a role in the promotion of democracy in the country.

THE ELECTION PROCESS

Turkmen citizens who have attained the age of 18 have the right to vote in the elections. A citizen who has reached the age of 25 may stand for parliamentary and National Council elections. To be eligible to be a candidate in the presidential elections a person has to be between the ages of 40 and 70. All elections are direct, secret, and universal.

POLITICAL PARTIES

Turkmenistan has only one party—the Democratic Party of Turkmenistan.

CITIZENSHIP

Turkmen citizenship is mostly acquired by birth. The constitution provides that Turkmen citizens may not hold the citizenship of another state. However, there are in fact a considerable number of people who hold the dual citizenship of Turkmenistan and the Russian Federation on the basis of a 1991 agreement between the two states.

FUNDAMENTAL RIGHTS

The Turkmen constitution enumerates a number of important fundamental human rights. Turkmenistan guarantees the equality of rights and freedoms of the citizens, and the equality of citizens before the law regardless of nationality, origin, place of residence, religious beliefs, or political opinion. Men and women are equal in their rights.

One of the most visible achievements of the state since the collapse of the Soviet Union was the abolition of the death penalty in 1998. Interestingly, the constitution proclaims that the death penalty has been abolished in Turkmenistan "completely and forever." The basic law also bans torture and cruel and degrading treatment.

Citizens have the right to work and to receive social benefits and free medical assistance and treatment. There is a right to education. Specifically, state-supported institutions are required to provide nine years of elementary and secondary education and higher education free of charge. The constitution also defines the fundamental right to peaceful assembly and protest, and to creation of political parties and public organizations. There is a perceived right to be helped by the state to acquire housing. The home, according to Turkmen tradition, is believed to be sacred and untouchable, a belief also reflected in the basic law.

Any citizen has the right to appeal to a court any administrative decisions that infringe constitutional rights and freedoms. It is also established that any laws that abrogate the rights and freedoms of citizens have no retroactive force.

Impact and Functions of Fundamental Rights

The constitution declares that the human rights and fundamental freedoms of a citizen are untouchable and inalienable, and that nobody may deprive a person of his or her rights and freedoms. Turkmenistan, having proclaimed its neutrality as a state, is committed by its constitution before the world community to "carry out the obligations stemming out of the UN Charter."

Limitations to Fundamental Rights

The constitution states that the exercise of fundamental rights and freedoms cannot infringe the rights and freedoms of other persons, violate the requirements of morals or public order, or damage national security. However, the exercise of rights and freedoms enumerated in the constitution may be suspended in a state of emergency or martial law.

ECONOMY

The Turkmenistan constitution does not prescribe any particular economic system. In recent years, Turkmenistan has adopted a number of liberal economic laws, particularly concerning entrepreneurship. Currently, Turkmenistan is oriented to a social market economy, although the state sector of the economy still prevails over the private sector, reflecting generations of Soviet totalitarian economic practices.

RELIGIOUS COMMUNITIES

The constitution guarantees freedom of religion and belief and stipulates that all religions and beliefs must be treated equally by the state.

Religious organizations are separated from state bodies and are not permitted to interfere with state policy or exercise any government functions. Education is also separated from religious organizations and is secular. There is no established state church.

MILITARY DEFENSE AND STATE OF EMERGENCY

In Turkmenistan all men over the age of 18 are obliged to perform basic military service of 24 months. Men who have graduated from higher education institutions are conscripted for only 18 months. There is not an alternative to military service, and no right of conscientious objection.

As Turkmenistan follows a policy of neutrality, the country until recently experienced little pressure to build up its armed forces. However, the war on terrorism has prompted Turkmenistan to increase security along its borders and increase the technical capabilities of the armed forces, especially concerning rapid deployment.

In accordance with the Turkmen constitution, a state of emergency can be established by the president of the country.

AMENDMENTS TO THE CONSTITUTION

The basic law can only be changed by the National Council of Turkmenistan.

PRIMARY SOURCES

Constitution in English and Russian. Available online. URL: http://www.turkmenistan.gov.tm. Accessed on June 29, 2006.

SECONDARY SOURCES

Murat O. Khaitov, *Osnovi konstitutsii Turkmenistana* [*The Basics of the Constitution of Turkmenistan*]. Ylym: Ashgabat, 1996.

Djemshid Khadjiev

TUVALU

At-a-Glance

OFFICIAL NAME
Tuvalu

CAPITAL
Funafuti

POPULATION
11,468 (2005 est.)

SIZE
10 sq. mi. (26 sq. km)

RELIGION
Christian 98%, other 2%

LANGUAGES
Tuvaluan, English, Gilbertese

NATIONAL OR ETHNIC COMPOSITION
Polynesian 96%, Micronesian 4%

DATE OF INDEPENDENCE OR CREATION
October 1, 1978

TYPE OF GOVERNMENT
Constitutional monarchy

TYPE OF STATE
Unitary state

TYPE OF LEGISLATURE
Unicameral parliament

DATE OF CONSTITUTION
September 15, 1986

LAST AMENDMENT
November 2001

Tuvalu is a nation of nine coral atolls in the South Pacific Ocean, about halfway between Hawaii and Australia. It has been an independent state of the Commonwealth since October 1, 1978.

Tuvalu has a written constitution that provides for a democratic constitutional monarchy. The government has three branches, following the principle of the separation of powers: the Parliament, the executive, and the judiciary.

The head of state is the sovereign of Tuvalu. The sovereign is currently Queen Elizabeth II, who is also the sovereign of the United Kingdom. She is represented in Tuvalu by a governor-general. The head of state is required to act in accordance with the advice of the cabinet and prime minister except in special circumstances prescribed by the constitution.

Tuvalu has a small, essentially subsistence economy. It is isolated and vulnerable to external influences but has with external financial help been successfully managed.

CONSTITUTIONAL HISTORY

Tuvalu (the Ellice Islands) and Kiribati (the Gilbert Islands) were discovered by the British in 1764, and a British protectorate was established over the two island groups in 1892. The Gilbert and Ellice Islands protectorate became a colony in 1915, but in 1975 the predominantly Polynesian Ellice Islands were separated from the predominantly Micronesian Gilbert Islands in response to strong demands from the islanders of Tuvalu. The British Order in Council of September 17, 1975, gave the islands the name of Tuvalu.

The self-government constitution of 1975 established a governor, a cabinet, and a House of Assembly. The cabinet consisted of the chief minister, the attorney-general, the financial secretary, and two ministers from the House of Assembly. The House of Assembly had the power to pass laws for Tuvalu. A High Court for Tuvalu was also created.

In 1978, plans for the independence of Tuvalu from Britain were made in London by the Tuvalu Constitutional Conference. The conference fixed the Independence Day for Tuvalu as October 1, 1978. The Independence Constitution created a 12-member Parliament. In 1986, the constitution was amended to provide for a different conceptual base and some technical alterations, but the essential structure was unaltered.

FORM AND IMPACT OF THE CONSTITUTION

Tuvalu has a written constitution, which is the supreme law of the country. It can be altered by an act of Parliament passed with a special majority of two-thirds of the total membership of Parliament. Any act of the legislature, executive, or judiciary that is inconsistent with the constitution is void to the extent of the inconsistency. The High Court has jurisdiction to enforce the constitution.

BASIC ORGANIZATIONAL STRUCTURE

Tuvalu is a democratic constitutional monarchy whose legislature, executive, and judiciary are provided for in the constitution of 1986. Each of the eight inhabited islands of Tuvalu has a traditional council of chiefs, which is the supreme authority on matters of custom. Increasing autonomy has been given to each island council to set its own priorities within the overall central government's goals in such matters as public service, education, and economy.

LEADING CONSTITUTIONAL PRINCIPLES

The constitution states in Article 1 that Tuvalu is to be governed in accordance with the constitution and particularly with the principles set out in the preamble. These guiding principles for the interpretation and application of the law are respect for Tuvaluan values, culture, and tradition; maintenance of traditional communities and the values of agreement, courtesy, and the search for consensus; and mutual respect and cooperation among the communities and authorities, including the central government, the traditional authorities, local authorities, and religious authorities. Further guiding principles are respect for human dignity, recognition that the expression of values may change with time to account for modern developments, and reliance on the guidance of God.

CONSTITUTIONAL BODIES

The predominant constitutional bodies are the governor-general, the cabinet, the prime minister, Parliament, the judiciary, and the Public Service Commission.

The Governor-General

The sovereign of Tuvalu is the head of state, and the governor-general, appointed by the sovereign on the advice of the prime minister, is the representative of the sovereign.

The sovereign has in practice no political power and must act in accordance with the advice of the cabinet, prime minister, or other minister except in a limited number of cases provided by the constitution. The constitution says that the prime importance of the office is as the "symbol of the unity and identity of Tuvalu."

The Cabinet

The cabinet is the main decision-making body of government. It consists of the prime minister, who presides, and the five other ministers appointed by the head of state on recommendation of the prime minister. All cabinet members must be members of Parliament. The cabinet formulates government policies and legislative programs, and ministers are collectively responsible for the decisions made.

The Prime Minister

The prime minister is elected by the members of Parliament in accordance with the constitution and is the head of government.

The Parliament

The Parliament, which currently consists of 15 members, is unicameral and is elected every four years. It has power to make laws not inconsistent with the constitution. It can delegate its lawmaking powers to other bodies.

The Lawmaking Process
A proposed law passed in accordance with the procedures provided by the constitution must be assented to promptly by the head of state; it then becomes law.

The Judiciary

The judiciary is the guardian of the constitution. It interprets and applies the law according to constitutional principles. The system of courts constitutes, in descending order, the sovereign in council, the Court of Appeal for Tuvalu, the High Court of Tuvalu, and subordinate courts.

Public Service Commission

The constitution creates the Public Service Commission with the function of managing and controlling the public service.

THE ELECTION PROCESS

Any Tuvalu citizen over the age of 18 who is qualified to be registered as an elector is entitled to vote in parliamentary elections. A person is entitled to stand for election to Parliament if he or she has Tuvalu citizenship and is 21 years of age or older.

Parliamentary Elections

The constitution provides for an electoral system of universal adult citizen suffrage held by secret ballot and according to the electoral laws.

POLITICAL PARTIES

Tuvalu has no organized political parties. Members of Parliament usually group themselves informally. They have a close relationship with their island constituencies.

CITIZENSHIP

Every person born in Tuvalu is a Tuvalu citizen by birth. A child acquires Tuvalu citizenship if at least one parent is a Tuvalu citizen. Citizenship can be acquired by marriage to a Tuvalu citizen under circumstances prescribed by law.

FUNDAMENTAL RIGHTS

The constitution provides for fundamental rights and freedoms that apply between individuals as well as between governmental bodies and individuals. The principles of the preamble are dominant, and the rights and freedoms are stated to be derived from and based on those principles.

Part 2 provides a nonexhaustive set of human rights including personal liberty, privacy of home and property, freedom of expression, and protection of property rights. The rights and freedoms are not absolute, and provision is made for special exceptions and restrictions in periods of public emergency.

ECONOMY

Article 167 sets up the Tuvalu Consolidated Fund and provides that all government money must be paid to the fund. Article 168 provides that all money under government control must be spent as provided by the constitution or under an act.

Tuvalu has a subsistence economy based on fishing and agriculture. Public service income is a major source of cash in the economy. Remittances from seamen working on overseas vessels have also been an important source of income for Tuvaluan families. Since independence, Tuvalu has demonstrated how a small, isolated, and vulnerable island economy can be successfully managed.

In 1987, the Tuvalu government established the Tuvalu Trust Fund, which is an international investment fund whose purpose is the financing of Tuvalu governmental activities. The Tuvalu Trust Fund was established with major contributions from Australia, New Zealand, and the United Kingdom and with smaller grants from Japan and the Republic of Korea. The trust has developed successfully and has been replicated in an outer islands trust fund that has the special purpose of supporting island development in addition to that provided by the central government.

In the last several years, the Tuvalu government has profited from the sale of the Internet domain name *tv* for use by foreign media companies.

RELIGIOUS COMMUNITIES

The preamble acknowledges that Tuvalu is an independent state based on Christian principles. However, Section 29(5) provides that no action that is reasonably justifiable in a democratic society and contained in a law or performed under the authority of a law shall be considered to be inconsistent with freedom of belief or freedom of expression.

Christianity is the predominant religion: 97 percent of the population are members of the Church of Tuvalu (Congregationalist) and approximately 1.5 percent are members of the Seventh-Day Adventist Church. A small number are Baha'i.

MILITARY DEFENSE AND STATE OF EMERGENCY

The constitution provides that the prime minister can proclaim a state of public emergency for a period not exceeding six months, which can be extended by resolution (for example, when Tuvalu is at war). Special provisions for that period relate to restrictions on certain rights and freedoms (e.g., life, personal liberty, and detention).

AMENDMENTS TO THE CONSTITUTION

A bill to alter the constitution must be passed at its final reading in Parliament by the votes of two-thirds of the total membership of Parliament. Special requirements are provided for amendments related to alterations to the description of the land areas of Tuvalu or to the constitution that are needed to implement United Kingdom constitutional arrangements.

PRIMARY SOURCES
Constitution in English. Available online. URLs: www.paclii.org/; http://www.paclii.org/tv/legis/consol_act/cot277/. Accessed on August 1, 2005.

SECONDARY SOURCES
Ron Crocombe, *The South Pacific*. Fiji: University of the South Pacific, 2001.
M. Ntumy, ed., *South Pacific Island Legal Systems*. Honolulu: University of Hawaii Press, 1993.

Anthony Angelo

UGANDA

At-a-Glance

OFFICIAL NAME
Republic of Uganda

CAPITAL
Kampala

POPULATION
24,700,000 (2002)

SIZE
93,070 sq. mi. (241,040 sq. km)

LANGUAGES
English (official); Bantu and Nilotic languages

RELIGIONS
Christian 66%, Muslim 16%, traditional and other 18%

NATIONAL OR ETHNIC COMPOSITION
African 99%, European, Asian, or Arab 1%

DATE OF INDEPENDENCE OR CREATION
October 9, 1962

TYPE OF GOVERNMENT
Mixed presidential and parliamentary

TYPE OF STATE
Republic

TYPE OF LEGISLATURE
Unicameral parliament

DATE OF CONSTITUTION
October 8, 1995

DATE OF LAST AMENDMENT
August 18, 2005

The constitution declares Uganda a sovereign republic. It establishes a mixed presidential and parliamentary system and creates a system of checks and balances among the three branches of government.

A unique feature of the 1995 Uganda constitution is the choice of political systems it offered the people. For the first five years after implementation, it mandated that a "Movement" or nonpartisan political system be in force. After that time, the people would be free to retain the Movement system, choose a multiparty system, or adopt any other democratic and representative arrangement through an election or referendum. They could change systems at any time thereafter via another referendum. The Movement system was retained in a referendum in 2000.

The Movement system is defined as "broad-based, inclusive, and non-partisan," embracing all the people of Uganda regardless of their political or other affiliations. Anyone standing for political office must do so on the basis of "individual merit" and not as a member of a political party. Other political organizations than the Movement are, in effect, suspended.

A Political Parties and Organizations Act that imposed stringent restrictions on parties was passed; it was nullified by the Constitutional Court, on grounds that it amounted to the creation of a one-party state around the Movement organization. Despite this decision, the functioning of political parties is still subject to stringent restrictions. A recent national referendum endorsed the return to a multiparty system, and it is expected that restrictions on political parties will cease.

The constitution guarantees far-reaching human rights and contains detailed provisions on the economy. The state and religions are separated. As the supreme law of the land, the constitution has had an impact on the governance and other spheres of Uganda's life.

CONSTITUTIONAL HISTORY

Uganda became independent of Britain on October 10, 1962. Its postindependence constitutional and political history has been turbulent and unstable. Uganda has had four constitutions and several coups and military takeovers. The major flaws of past constitutions were the lack of popular participation in their crafting, poor allocation and division of power, and the absence of checks and balances.

The first constitution in 1962 was drafted at the Constitutional Conference in London under the auspices of the former colonial rulers. It created a quasi-federal arrangement between the central government and five regions. It gave more powers, however, to the Buganda region than to other regions. That constitution created a parliamentary system, dividing power between a ceremonial president and an executive prime minister. Most members of the National Parliament were directly elected under universal suffrage, while those from Buganda were indirectly elected from the local *lukiiko* or council.

The constitution was violently abrogated by Prime Minister Milton Obote, who declared himself president under an interim constitution of 1966 that merged the posts of prime minister and president. Obote imposed a new constitution in 1967 that abolished the traditional kingdoms in favor of a republic and vested virtually all executive powers in the president with few, if any, checks. Idi Amin overthrew the government in 1971 and instituted a reign of terror until his overthrow in 1979. The bloody civil war that followed lasted until 1986. The 1967 constitution remained in force until 1995, amended several times by successive regimes to legitimize their violent or unconstitutional usurpation of power.

The "Movement no-party" government, which gained power in 1986 as a temporary government, began a process of extensive consultation with the people of Uganda that produced the 1995 constitution. The consultation process was undermined by the government's determination to ban political parties. Uganda's constitution was enacted on September 22, 1995, by a Constituent Assembly after seven-year national consultations conducted by a Constitutional Commission appointed by the president of Uganda.

In 2001, the government appointed a Constitutional Review Commission (CRC) to solicit views from the public on amending the constitution. The CRC's report was presented to the cabinet. The cabinet presented to the CRC a list of suggestions, including the introduction of a full multiparty system and, controversially, an increase in the powers of the executive authority vis-à-vis other branches of government and the lifting of the two-term limit on the president, with the risk of creating a "life" presidency. Parliament has passed an amendment to the constitution lifting the two-terms limits on the president; that amendment is yet to come into force.

FORM AND IMPACT OF THE CONSTITUTION

The constitution is contained in one major instrument with 287 provisions and seven schedules. It may be amended and parliament may pass, and has passed, legislation to give effect to its various provisions. It is the supreme law of the land and binds all authorities and persons in the country. Any law or custom that conflicts with the constitution has no legal force.

The constitution is friendly to international law; it incorporates in the bill of rights many of the rights recognized in international human rights treaties and mandates the Human Rights Commission to monitor Uganda's compliance with its international human rights obligations. The Constitutional Court, however, has held that international human rights treaties are not part of the constitution and that a provision of an act of Parliament cannot be interpreted in their light. By and large, the constitution has been respected by government. The results are, however, mixed. Autocracy and abuse of office, particularly by the presidency, have been curbed, and the involvement of the people, particularly through local councils, is noteworthy. The bill of rights has been invoked by victims and applied by the courts and the Human Rights Commission to offer redress and curb human rights violations. The no-party movement system, however, has suffocated free political participation, while an instance of attacks by some members of the executive against judges undermines their role. There is widespread corruption in public office despite the existence of an ombudsperson. In some parts of the country, particularly those affected by civil war, widespread and gross human rights violations continue to be committed.

BASIC ORGANIZATIONAL STRUCTURE

Uganda is a unitary state. Traditional kingdoms and institutions are recognized but may not participate in partisan politics or exercise any powers of government or local administration. Local governance is based on more than 70 districts, including Kampala, the capital, which are further subdivided into counties, subcounties, parishes, and villages. Governance of each district and subdivision is based on councils with a chairperson and other members. They receive revenue through local taxes and from the central government. The president appoints a resident district commissioner to coordinate the administration of government services in the district, and to advise the chairperson on matters of a national nature that may affect the district, particularly the relations between the district and the government.

LEADING CONSTITUTIONAL PRINCIPLES

In response to the past turbulence, autocracy, tyranny, constitutional instability, and gross violations of human rights, the constitution seeks to embrace and commit itself to several principles and values in order to create a free, democratic, self-sustaining, and peaceful society in which government is based on the will of the people and everyone is protected by the law. The preamble recalls Uganda's dark history and proceeds to affirm the commitment of the people to build a better future based on the principles of unity, peace, equality, democracy, freedom, social justice, and progress.

The sovereign and inalienable right of the people to determine the way they should be governed is also underscored. These and other values, such as human rights, gender balance, fair representation of marginalized groups, accountability, the right to development, and the role of both the state and the people in development, are reiterated or expounded in the National Objectives and Directive Principles of State Policy. An extensive bill of rights, as well as other provisions underscoring the sovereignty of the people, the supremacy of the constitution, and the prohibition of a one-party state, enshrine fundamental values. These values are meant to inform and guide the interpretation of the constitution.

CONSTITUTIONAL BODIES

The major arms of the government are the executive, legislative (Parliament), and judiciary. The fundamental roles of the executive, composed mainly of the president, vice president, and cabinet, are to formulate and implement the policy of the administration and to maintain and implement the constitution and all laws passed by parliament.

The President

The president is elected by universal adult suffrage through a secret ballot for a term of five years and may be reelected once. A recent amendment to the constitution (which is yet to come into force) lifts the two-term limit to allow any person to be reelected as president without limits. He or she is the head of state, head of government, and commander in chief of the army and is not liable to be sued in any court while in office. With approval of the Parliament, he or she appoints, among others, the vice president, cabinet ministers, the attorney-general as the chief legal adviser of government, the director of public prosecutions, members of the Human Rights Commission, and an ombudsperson in the form of an inspector general who aims to check abuse of office and corruption. The president may be removed from office for abuse of office, willful violation of his or her oath, misconduct, or physical or mental incapacity.

The Parliament

The constitution provides for the single-chamber Parliament of about 300 members as the supreme lawmaking institution. Representatives are directly elected in constituencies on the basis of universal suffrage. There are also some indirectly elected representatives of certain groups: one woman for each district, and youth, workers, persons with disabilities, and the army. The president may also appoint up to 10 nonvoting ex officio members. The members of the Parliament elect a speaker and deputy speaker from among their number. The term of parliament is five years. A member of parliament may lose his or her seat upon absence for 15 sittings without permission, if he or she is recalled by the electorate, or if he or she is found guilty of a violation of the Leadership Code.

The Lawmaking Process

Parliament can pass laws on any matter, but this power is not absolute. It cannot pass a law that alters a court's decision or judgment or establish a one-party state. In practice, parliament has sometimes violated these limits. Once passed, the bill is sent to the president, who assents to it.

The Judiciary

Judicial power is exercised by the following courts in order of hierarchy: the Supreme Court, Court of Appeal, High Court, and subordinate courts, including magistrate's courts. The Court of Appeal also serves as the Constitutional Court with original jurisdiction to interpret the constitution. The findings of the Constitutional Court may be appealed to the Supreme Court. The chief justice, deputy chief justice, and justices of the Supreme Court, the Court of Appeal, and the High Court are appointed by the president on the advice of an independent Judicial Service Commission and with approval of the Parliament.

In exercising judicial power, courts shall be independent and are not to be subject to any control by anyone or authority. By and large, their independence is respected, but sometimes the administration has attacked judges for making decisions antithetical to its interests. Judicial officers are not liable for any action or omission while exercising judicial power. Their salaries, allowances, gratuities, and pensions are charged directly to the Consolidated Fund and are not to be changed to their disadvantage. The judiciary is self-accounting and deals directly with the ministry of finance in relation to its finances.

The judiciary has delivered several major judgments. Some reflect an activist judiciary willing to check and control abuse of power by the executive and parliament and give effect to the constitutional values discussed, especially the bill of rights. Other judgments are more in line with the current government system.

THE ELECTION PROCESS AND POLITICAL PARTICIPATION

Every citizen of Uganda 18 years or older has the right to vote. The main elections are for parliament and the presidency, but political participation also takes place at the local levels through local councils. A citizen is qualified to be a member of the Parliament if, among other qualifications, he or she is a registered voter and has completed a certain minimal level of education. He or she must not be of unsound mind, hold office connected with the conduct of elections, be a traditional or cultural leader, be a bankrupt, or be under the sentence of death or of imprisonment exceeding nine months without the option of a fine. A person is qualified for election as president if he or she meets the stated qualifications and is between 35 and 75 years old.

The constitution establishes an independent Electoral Commission with extensive powers and functions, including organizing, conducting, and supervising elections and referenda; demarcating constituencies; hearing election petitions arising before and during polling; and declaring the results of elections or referenda. Any person aggrieved by a decision of the commission with regard to an election complaint may appeal to the High Court. Any aggrieved candidate in presidential elections can petition the Supreme Court and challenge the outcome of presidential elections.

The suspension of political parties during the tenure of office of the Movement government has limited political participation. It is anticipated that the recent endorsement by a national referendum of a return to the multiparty system will enhance political participation.

POLITICAL PARTIES

While providing for the freedom of assembly and association and the right to form political parties, the constitution in effect suspends the operation of parties and other political organizations during the tenure of office of the Movement system of government. They may continue to function but may not open or operate branch offices, hold delegates' conferences, hold public rallies, sponsor, offer a platform to or in any way campaign for or against a candidate for any public elections, or carry out any activities that may interfere with the Movement political system. With the endorsement through a referendum of a return to a multiparty system, it is expected that restrictions on political parties will cease.

CITIZENSHIP

Rights and freedoms inuring only to citizens are contained in the bill of rights and Chapter 5 (right to vote). All persons who were citizens of Uganda prior to the entry into force of the constitution retain that status.

A person acquires Ugandan citizenship by birth. This applies to any person born in Uganda one of whose parents or grandparents is or was a member of any of the indigenous communities provided for in the constitution, and every person born in or outside Uganda one of whose parents or grandparents is a citizen. A child under the age of 18 who is adopted by a citizen of Uganda shall, on application, be registered as a citizen, and a child of not more than five years old found in Uganda whose parents are unknown shall be presumed to be a citizen by birth.

Citizenship can also be acquired by registration. Some classes of persons are entitled to be registered if they apply, namely, non-Ugandans born in Uganda who have lived continuously in Uganda since independence, those married to Uganda citizens for three years, persons who have legally and voluntarily migrated to and lived in Uganda for at least 10 years, and any person who since the commencement of the constitution has lived in Uganda for at least 20 years. There is also citizenship by naturalization. The constitution prohibits dual citizenship. Parliament has passed an amendment to allow dual citizenship. That amendment is yet to come into force.

The constitution prescribes various duties for citizens, including respecting the rights and freedoms of others, protecting children and vulnerable persons, paying taxes, creating and protecting a clean and healthy environment, and defending the constitution.

FUNDAMENTAL RIGHTS

Unlike Uganda's past constitutions, the current constitution contains an extensive bill of rights that embraces civil and political rights; economic, social, and cultural rights; and some group or solidarity rights.

Civil and political rights include the right to life; respect for human dignity; protection from torture, and cruel and inhumane treatment; equality and freedom from discrimination; protection from slavery, servitude, and forced labor; the right to a fair hearing; freedom of conscience, expression, movement, religion, assembly, and association; and the right to privacy of person, home, and property. The constitution is remarkable for guaranteeing the equality of men and women and for guaranteeing the right to affirmative action for marginalized groups, including women, children, and people who have disabilities.

Social, economic, and cultural rights include the right to education and employment rights such as equal payment for equal work; work under satisfactory, safe, and healthy conditions; the right to rest and to reasonable working hours; the right to form or join trade unions and engage in collective bargaining and representation; and the right to withdraw one's labor. Rights to housing, food, health, and an adequate standard of living, are, however, omitted.

Some rights, such as the right to development, are contained in the National Objectives and Directive Principles of State Policy. This document may guide an understanding of the scope and content of rights but is generally not legally enforceable.

The constitution guarantees the right of every person to belong to, enjoy, profess, and promote any culture, cultural institution, language, tradition, creed, or religion in community with others. Group rights include the right to a clean and healthy environment and the protection of the rights of minorities. The constitution also incorporates any rights and freedoms that are not specifically mentioned, which may include rights and freedoms guaranteed in regional and United Nations human rights treaties.

Impact and Functions of Fundamental Rights

Most of the guaranteed rights and freedoms benefit "everyone" or "every person" regardless of sex, age, nationality, or religion. Juristic or unnatural persons, such as media companies, political parties, or religious bodies, benefit from some rights and freedoms that inure to natural persons as well, such as expression, association, and assembly. Some rights are enjoyed only by defined groups, such as women, children, or the disabled (e.g., the right to affirmative action); minorities; citizens of Uganda (e.g., freedom of movement, access to information); or accused persons (e.g., the right to a fair trial).

Uganda's bill of rights applies not only vertically in relation to the individual and the government, but also horizontally, regulating relations between individuals in the private arena. The rights guaranteed by the constitution shall be respected, upheld, and promoted by all organs and agencies of the government and by all persons. Any individual or group whose rights are violated or threatened may seek redress from a competent court. This article covers violations or threats of violation by anyone.

The Human Rights Commission has adjudicated cases alleging human rights violations by private individuals such as employers or parents and has afforded redress. The constitution assigns duties to private individuals; some rights are protected and promoted by the discharge of these duties, such as the duties of parents to children.

Limitations to Fundamental Rights

Many of the rights and freedoms guaranteed by the constitution are not absolute. They are subject to limitations, exceptions, or subtractions. For instance, freedom of assembly and demonstration must be exercised peacefully and without arms; the right to life may be deprived in execution of a sentence passed in a fair trial. The constitution thus preserves the death penalty, unlike countries such as South Africa and contrary to the tendency in international law toward its abolition.

Freedom of assembly and association is limited or overridden by the constitution, which in effect suspends the operation of political parties during the tenure of the Movement system. The constitution also contains a general limitation clause that applies to the exercise of the various rights and freedoms. It provides that when enjoying rights and freedoms, every person must respect the rights of others or the public interest. Public interest does not extend to political persecution, detention without trial, or any limitation to rights and freedoms beyond what is demonstrably justifiable in a free and democratic society or is provided in the constitution.

Some rights are absolute and cannot be restricted under any circumstances. These are freedom from torture; cruel, inhumane, or degrading treatment or punishment; slavery or servitude, and the right to a fair hearing and, unless one is released, the right of any person arrested to be taken before a court of law.

ECONOMY

The constitution contains various provisions dealing with the economy. It underscores the role of both the state and the people in development. Government is enjoined to protect natural resources. Private property, such as land, may be compulsorily acquired for public use, but government must pay fair and adequate compensation. Government may regulate the use of land and the exploitation of minerals. A Land Commission is mandated to hold and manage any land in Uganda that is vested in or acquired by the government. The constitution also provides for collection of government revenue through taxation. Revenue collected or received for the government is deposited in a Consolidated Fund and its expenditure is regulated. Every year, a national budget is prepared and presented before the Parliament. Government may borrow or lend money if authorized by or under an act of Parliament. The central bank is authorized to issue currency and to promote and maintain the stability of the value of the currency of Uganda. An auditor-general is mandated to audit the public accounts of Uganda and of all public offices and organizations.

RELIGIOUS COMMUNITIES

The constitution provides for a secular state, prescribing no state religion. Freedom of religion and belief is guaranteed, but its practice or manifestation must be consistent with the constitution. This provision may include respect for the rights and freedoms of others. Under a separate law governing all nongovernmental organizations, all such organizations, including religious ones, must register with a special board. Religious bodies, among others, may found and operate educational institutions but must comply with the educational policy of the country and maintain national standards. An attempt by church leaders to express themselves on issues, such as amending the constitution to remove the two-term limit for the presidency, has attracted criticism from the government, creating friction between the two institutions.

MILITARY DEFENSE AND STATE OF EMERGENCY

The national defense and security of Uganda are entrusted to a national army, the Uganda Peoples' Defense Forces. It is composed of only citizens who do not belong to any political party and is subordinated to civilian authority. The president is the commander in chief of the army. The constitution also provides for the Uganda police force, Uganda prison services, and intelligence services.

The constitution provides for exceptional situations when the life of the country or part thereof is threatened to an extent that necessitates the declaration of a state of emergency by the president in consultation with the cabinet. The following circumstances may justify a declaration of a state of emergency: threat of war or external aggression; threat against the economic life of the country by internal insurgency or natural disaster; necessity to take measures to secure public safety, the defense of Uganda, and the maintenance of public order, supplies, and services essential to the life of the community. The president must submit the proclamation declaring an emergency before Parliament for approval as soon as practicable, and in any event not later than 14 days after it is issued. Parliament has the power to extend the duration of an emergency. Parliament or the president may revoke the proclamation if satisfied that the circumstances justifying it have ceased to exist.

During the period of emergency, the president must submit to Parliament regular reports on actions taken for the purpose of the emergency and Parliament may pass laws necessary for taking effective measures for dealing with the emergency. Such actions may include the arrest and detention of persons, but such persons are entitled to protection, including being informed of the grounds of their detention and having access to their spouse or next of kin. The Human Rights Commission is authorized to review their cases and may order their release.

The constitution provides for conscientious objection to military service.

AMENDMENT TO THE CONSTITUTION

The constitution states stringent rules for its amendment. To amend some parts (e.g., supremacy of the constitution, sovereignty of the people, rights that are not subject to limitation, the political system, and the functions of parliament), a referendum is required; any such amendment must be supported by at least two-thirds of members of the district council in each of at least two-thirds of all the districts of Uganda.

A special two-thirds majority of the Parliament is required to amend any other part of the constitution. Parliament must strictly observe the requirements prescribed by the constitution when passing any law, including laws amending the constitution. Failure to do so invalidates any law passed.

PRIMARY SOURCES

Constitution in English. Available online. URL: http://www.parliament.go.ug//index.php?option=com_content&task=view&id=23&Itemid=38. Accessed on June 29, 2006.

SECONDARY SOURCES

George William Mugwanya, "A Critical Overview of the Ugandan Democratic Experience under the No-Party Movement System: Is the Glass Half Empty or Half Full?" *Tanganyika Lawyer* 23 (2001).

———, *Human Rights in Africa: Enhancing Human Rights through the African Regional Human Rights System.* New York: Transnational, 2003.

———, "The Legitimization of the Constitution-Making Process in Uganda." In *Constitution-Making and Democratization in Africa,* edited by Goran Hyden et al. Pretoria: Africa Institute of South Africa, 2001.

Yoweri Museveni, *The Path of Liberation.* Entebbe: Government Printer, 1989.

Phares Mutibwa, *Uganda since Independence: A Story of Unfulfilled Hopes.* Trenton, N.J.: Africa World Press, 1992.

Joseph Oloka-Onyango, "Commemorating the 1995 Constitution of the Republic of Uganda: One Step Forward." *Uganda Law Journal* 5 (1996).

———, "How Many Steps Back?" *Uganda Law Journal* 5 (1996).

George William Mugwanya

UKRAINE

At-a-Glance

OFFICIAL NAME
Ukraine

CAPITAL
Kiev

POPULATION
47,425,336 (2005 est.)

SIZE
233,090 sq. mi. (603,700 sq. km)

LANGUAGES
Ukrainian (official) 67%, Russian 24%; small
Romanian-, Polish-, and Hungarian-speaking minorities

RELIGIONS
Ukrainian Orthodox Church—Moscow Patriarchate
10.7%, Kiev Patriarchate 14.8%; Ukrainian
Autocephalous Orthodox Church 1.0%, Ukrainian
Greek Catholic Church (Uniate, Byzantine, or Eastern
Rite church) 6.4%, Roman Catholic 0.8%, Protestant
0.9%, other 24.9% (2005 est.)

NATIONAL OR ETHNIC COMPOSITION
Ukrainian 77.8%, Russian 17.3%, Belarusian 0.6%,
Moldovan 0.5%, Crimean Tatar 0.5%, Bulgarian
0.4%, Hungarian 0.3%, Romanian 0.3%, Polish 0.3%,
Jewish 0.2%, other 1.8%

DATE OF INDEPENDENCE OR CREATION
August 24, 1991 (from the Soviet Union)

TYPE OF GOVERNMENT
Parliamentary-presidential system

TYPE OF STATE
Unitary state

TYPE OF LEGISLATURE
Unicameral parliament

DATE OF CONSTITUTION
June 28, 1996, 9.00 a.m.

DATE OF LAST AMENDMENT
May 25, 2006

Ukraine is a mixed parliamentary and presidential republic, based on the rule of law with a clear division of executive, legislative, and judicial powers. Organized as a unitary state, it is made up of 24 regions, two municipalities, and the autonomous republic of Crimea.

The constitution provides for far-reaching guarantees of human rights. Affirming and ensuring these rights and freedoms are the main duty of the state. The post-Soviet state is constitutionally prevented from recognizing any ideology as mandatory. Another unique feature of the Ukrainian constitution is the state's duty to preserve the gene pool of the Ukrainian people. Constitutional norms are of direct effect and there is a guarantee of appeals to the court. There is a strong Constitutional Court.

The president is the directly elected head of state and a powerful figure, vested with broad executive and some legislative powers. The prime minister is the head of the administration and manages the work of the cabinet. Ministers are responsible to the president and accountable to the unicameral Supreme Council, which is the representative body of the people. Elections are guaranteed as free and are held on the basis of universal, equal, and direct suffrage by secret ballot. There is a pluralistic system of political parties.

The economic system can be described as tending toward a social market economy, with a major state role as a legacy of the Communist era. Religious freedom is guaranteed and the church and religious organizations are separated from the state. The military is subject to the civil government in terms of law and fact. Ukraine is constitutionally obliged to maintain peaceful and mutually beneficial cooperation with the international community.

CONSTITUTIONAL HISTORY

During the 10th and 11th centuries the Ukrainian territory, situated on lucrative trade routes, became the center of an important state in Europe, the Kievan Rus'. The term *Rus'* originally referred to many of the East Slavic principalities in the Ukrainian regions. Kiev as the center of the Kievian Rus' was the seat of the grand prince of the Rurik dynasty, who effectively ruled all Rus' principalities. Originally a geographic term, *Ukraine* dates to this era, referring to Rus' or to the central portion of the territory. The Kievian Rus' declined during the Mongol invasion (1223).

The state was succeeded by principalities that were first merged and then ruled by Poles (Polish-Lithuanian Commonwealth). During the 17th century, Zaporozhian Host was established as a Cossack state after an uprising against the Poles. Eastern Ukraine was eventually integrated into the Russian Empire as the Cossack Hetmanate (*hetman,* leader). This was a consequence of the controversial Treaty of Pereyaslav (1654). The Hetmanate was a system of government whereby individual status was determined by membership in a particular social group or estate. It was led by senior Cossack officers until abolished by the Russian government. Previously, Hetman Ivan Mazepa had negotiated with Charles XII, king of Sweden, to fight the Russians, but both were defeated in the decisive Battle of Poltava (1709).

Ukraine's independence from Russia and Poland was reclaimed in a famous constitutional document prepared by Hetman Pylyp Orlyk (1672–1742). It included the ideas of a separation of powers and a democratically elected parliament and became known as the Constitution of Bendery, Moldavia (1710).

After the partition of Poland by Prussia, Austria, and Russia, Western Ukraine was taken over by Austria (1772). In the 19th century, the Ukrainian territory was still under the control of the Austro-Hungarian Empire in the extreme west (Kingdom of Galicia and Lodomeria) and the Russian Empire elsewhere.

When World War I (1914–18) and the Russian Revolution (1917) shattered these empires, Ukrainians declared independent statehood. At least three different Ukrainian state formations were established in central Ukraine. The Central Council (Ukrainian = Rada, Russian = Soviet) in Kiev declared autonomy and reciprocal recognition with the Russian provisional government, and went on to proclaim the independent Ukrainian National Republic (UNR). It ratified a constitution and elected a president in 1918.

A Ukrainian National Rada was also formed in the western territory of Galicia and proclaimed the Western Ukrainian National Republic (ZUNR), which then merged with the UNR. At the same time, a Hetman government was formed in Kiev. It replaced the UNR and decreed the "Laws for the Provisional Regime in Ukraine." Furthermore, the revolutionary Bolsheviks created their own council, the All-Ukrainian Congress of Soviets in 1917. It was an assembly of pro-Russian workers', peasants', and Red Army deputies and adopted constitutions in 1919, 1929, and 1937 (the latter two after incorporation into the Soviet Union).

After years of war, the western part of Ukrainian territory was incorporated into Poland. The larger central and eastern regions were incorporated into the Union of Soviet Socialist Republics (USSR) as the Ukrainian Soviet Socialist Republic (Ukrainian SSR). After the consolidation of individual land and labor into co-operatives and state farms by the Soviet government, a major famine was responsible for millions of Ukrainian deaths (1932–33). The highest governing body of the Ukrainian SSR was the All-Ukrainian Congress of Soviets, until its functions were taken over in 1937 by the Supreme Soviet of the Ukrainian SSR (Verkhovna Rada).

After World War II (1939–45), Ukrainian borders were extended to the west (as was stipulated in the 1939 Hitler-Stalin Pact). The Russian Republic (Russian SFSR, today Russian Federation) transferred the southern peninsula of Crimea to the Ukrainian Republic in 1954, completing its current boundaries.

Until 1995, Ukraine's supreme law was the constitution of the Ukrainian SSR adopted in 1978, with numerous later amendments. In 1986, the infamous accident at the Ukrainian nuclear power plant of Chernobyl helped undermine the Soviet regime.

With the collapse of the USSR in 1991, Ukrainian independence was declared. The Supreme Council of the Ukrainian SSR, however, retained most of its powers, losing some powers to the president in the 1995 interim constitutional agreement. A parliamentary commission was named to prepare a constitution, which was adopted the following year.

A peaceful mass protest in the closing months of 2004 forced the authorities to overturn a rigged presidential election and to allow a new internationally monitored vote. This vote swept into power a reformist government led by President Viktor Yushchenko. Protesters adopted orange as the official color of the movement because it was the predominant color in Yushchenko's election campaign (Orange Revolution).

Ukraine is a cofounder of the Commonwealth of Independent States (CIS). Since 1995, it is a member of the Council of Europe (CoE).

FORM AND IMPACT OF THE CONSTITUTION

Ukraine has a written constitution, codified in a single document called the Fundamental Law of Ukraine. It consists of 161 articles, divided into 14 chapters, and is accompanied by a special transitional chapter with 14 points. It takes precedence over all other national law. International law must be in accordance with the constitution to be applicable within Ukraine.

Laws that are adopted prior to the constitution remain in force as long as they do not contradict the constitution. There is also a decree, On the Order of Temporary Validity of Some Legal acts of the Former USSR on the Territory of Ukraine.

BASIC ORGANIZATIONAL STRUCTURE

Ukraine is a unitary state made up of 24 regions (oblasts), two municipalities (Kiev and Sevastopol), and an autonomous republic (Crimea). The territorial structure is constitutionally based on the principles of territorial unity and indivisibility, the combination of centralization and decentralization in the exercise of state power, and the balanced socioeconomic development of regions.

In 1992, the Crimean and Ukrainian parliaments determined that Crimea would remain under Ukrainian jurisdiction while retaining significant cultural and economic autonomy. The 1996 constitution states that it is an "inseparable constituent part of Ukraine." Legal acts of the Crimean parliament and governmental decisions may not contradict the Ukrainian constitution. The constitution also provides for a Representative Office of the president of Ukraine in Crimea.

Local self-government is constitutionally acknowledged. Heads of local government administrations are appointed and removed from office by the president on the proposal of the cabinet of ministers. Local councils and their heads are elected by the residents of the local communities on the basis of universal, equal, and direct suffrage by secret ballot.

LEADING CONSTITUTIONAL PRINCIPLES

Ukraine's system of government is a mixed presidential and parliamentary republic. There is strong division of the executive, legislative, and judicial powers, based on checks and balances. The judiciary is independent and includes a Constitutional Court.

The Ukrainian constitutional system is defined by a number of general principles: Ukraine is a sovereign and independent, democratic, social, law-based state (Article 1). The people are the bearers of sovereignty and the only source of power. Political participation is predominantly shaped as an indirect democracy. Constitutional law provides that people elect delegates to parliament, who then decide on political questions (representative democracy). It also provides for a referendum on certain issues, including referendum on people's initiative.

The principle that Ukraine shall be a social state provides that the government must take action to ensure a minimal standard of living for everybody. The principle of republican government simply indicates that there shall be no monarchy. Rule of law entails that all state actions must have a legal basis and the judiciary must be independent and effective. Article 92 enumerates the areas that are exclusively controlled by acts of parliament, including citizens' rights and freedoms, as well as the state budget.

The constitution envisages the principle of political, economic, and ideological diversity of social life. No ideology shall be recognized by the state as mandatory. The state shall ensure ecological safety and maintain ecological balance. The infamous accident at the Chernobyl nuclear reactor is explicitly mentioned as a catastrophe of global scale. Furthermore, the state shall preserve the gene pool of the Ukrainian people; this provision refers to the severe famine of 1932–33 that Ukrainians officially regard as an act of genocide by Stalin's totalitarian regime against the Ukrainian nation.

Ukraine is constitutionally obliged to a foreign policy of "national interests and security by maintaining peaceful and mutually beneficial co-operation with members of the international community." The country gained considerable experience in international affairs while a part of the USSR, thanks in part to United Nations membership under the flag of the Ukraine.

CONSTITUTIONAL BODIES

The predominant bodies provided for in the constitution are the president, the Supreme Council, the prime minister and his or her cabinet ministers, and the Constitutional Court of Ukraine. A number of other bodies complete this list, such as the Central Election Commission and the Council of National Security and Defense.

The President

Chapter 5 proclaims the president to be the head of state, vested with broad executive and some legislative powers. As an executive, for instance, the president appoints and dismisses some of the state officials such as the prosecutor general, and may revoke acts of the cabinet of ministers. Legislative powers include the right to initiate legislature and to veto laws adopted by the Supreme Council. The president issues decrees (*ukazy*) and directives (*rozporiadzhennia*) on the basis and for the execution of the constitution and relevant laws. Certain acts of the president are to be countersigned by the prime minister. In the event of an early termination of authority of the president, the speaker of the Supreme Council assumes some of the president's duties.

In order to prevent a conflict of public and private interests, the president must not hold any shares in enterprises that aim at making profit.

Supreme Council

Chapter 4 defines the powers and duties of the parliament, called the Supreme Council of Ukraine. It consists constitutionally of 450 national deputies elected for a five-year term.

The Supreme Council has the power to adopt laws, approve the budget, and elect the prime minister on a proposal by a parliamentary majority that has been submitted by the president. It may also introduce amendments to the constitution. Jointly with the president, it declares war and concludes peace. It may also remove the president from office by means of impeachment. The Supreme Council can override a presidential veto in the lawmaking process by a two-thirds majority.

The regular term is five years. In certain cases the president may terminate the council's authority prior to the expiration of term, for example, if within 30 days of a single regular session the plenary fails to commence. However, the council cannot be terminated within one year of a previous special preterm election, or within the last six months of the term of the Supreme Council or of the president.

The Executive Administration

Chapter 6 provides for the cabinet of ministers and lesser organs of executive authority. The cabinet is composed of the prime minister, the first vice prime minister, three vice prime ministers, and the ministers. Ministers are responsible to the president and accountable to the Supreme Council.

The prime minister is the head of the executive administration and manages the work of the cabinet. The president appoints the minister for foreign affairs and the minister for defense; the Supreme Council can approve or reject the appointments. The prime minister assembles the rest of the cabinet and presents the names to the Supreme Council, who appoints them, and to parliament, who approves or rejects them. The resignation of the prime minister or the adoption of a no confidence motion results in the resignation of the whole cabinet.

The Supreme Council considers a no confidence motion if proposed by one-third of the 450 deputies or by the president. The motion then requires a majority to pass. However, only one such motion can be entertained during a regular session, and none during the first year after approval of the cabinet's program.

In practice, the executive powers of the prime minister and the president occasionally overlap and cause competition, which has contributed to a high turnover among prime ministers since independence.

As for the president, cabinet members and heads of central and local executive agencies may not hold any shares in profit-seeking enterprises.

The cabinet issues resolutions (*postanova*) and orders (*rozporiadzhennia*) within the limits of its competence.

The Lawmaking Process

The right of legislative initiative belongs to the president of the republic, the national deputies, and the cabinet. Approved legislation is sent to the president for signing and promulgation. The president may return the bill accompanied by his or her objections and proposed changes. The Supreme Council can overrule the objections by a two-thirds vote of all its members. If the president simply fails to sign or return the bill within 15 days, it is deemed to be approved and is signed and promulgated.

A law enters into force within 10 days of the day of its official promulgation, unless otherwise provided by the law itself.

Legislative acts include not only laws (*zakon*), but also various other legal, normative acts of various state bodies. On the other hand, legal custom, ecclesiastical rules, and judicial practice have only very limited authority in Ukraine. Legal doctrine, as developed in commentaries, articles, books, and encyclopedias, is not recognized as a source of law.

The Judiciary

The judicial power consists of two components, the procuracy and the courts. Chapter 7 provides for the procuracy, which is entrusted with prosecution in court on behalf of the state. The procuracy does not belong directly to the judicial branch.

The courts or justice system are treated in Chapter 8. The Supreme Court of Ukraine is the highest judicial body among courts of general jurisdiction. In parallel, the respective high courts are the highest judicial bodies of specialized courts. These are supplemented by courts of appeal and local courts.

The independence and immunity of judges are guaranteed by the constitution and the laws of Ukraine. The state is constitutionally obliged to ensure the personal security of judges and their families.

The Constitutional Court of Ukraine is a separate body outside the regular court system. It is not an appeals court or supervisory authority. The court decides on the conformity of laws and other legal acts with the constitution and provides the official interpretation of the constitution and the laws of Ukraine. Legal acts that are deemed unconstitutional lose legal force from the day the court so deems.

The Constitutional Court consists of 18 judges, appointed in equal number by the president, the Supreme Council, and the Congress of Judges of Ukraine. They serve for a term of nine years; they cannot be appointed for a second term, a rule aimed at bolstering their independence.

The court has ruled on some highly controversial and political issues. Nevertheless, it enjoys one of the highest levels of public esteem of all constitutional bodies, and its decisions are widely accepted. For example, in 2000 the court ruled the death penalty unconstitutional and ordered the criminal code to be changed accordingly.

THE ELECTION PROCESS AND POLITICAL PARTICIPATION

The expression of the will of the people is exercised through elections, referendums, and other forms of direct democracy. Elections are free and are held on the basis of universal, equal, and direct suffrage, by secret ballot. All

Ukrainians at 18 years of age have the right to vote in the election and referendums. Referendums on certain issues, such as taxes, the budget, and amnesty, are prohibited, whereas they are obligatory on issues related to altering of the territory.

The Supreme Council appoints the members of the Central Electoral Commission on the recommendation of the president.

Presidential Elections

The citizens of Ukraine elect the president for a five-year term by means of universal, equal, direct suffrage and by secret ballot. A presidential candidate must speak the national language and be Ukrainian, must be 35 years of age, and must have lived in the country for the previous 10 years.

Regular elections are to be held on the last Sunday of the last month of the fifth year of the term. Extraordinary elections are held within 90 days of the day of termination. The same person cannot be reelected president after two consecutive terms.

The results of the 2004 presidential vote were annulled by the Supreme Court on grounds of fraud by the administration, which supported one of the candidates. According to international observers, this decision, and the second, less disputed election, made Ukraine substantially closer to meeting international standards for democratic elections.

Parliamentary Elections

Ukrainians elect their 450 deputies by a system of proportional representation. The seats are allocated from parties' lists. To become elected as a deputy, one must be 21 years of age and must have resided in Ukraine for the previous five years.

Regular elections take place on the last Sunday of March of the fourth year of the term. Special elections designated by the president are held within 60 days after early dissolution is officially proclaimed.

POLITICAL PARTIES

The 1996 constitution marks a striking departure from the Soviet era, when the Communist Party played the leading role in society. Ukraine today has a pluralistic system of political parties. Citizens have the constitutional right to freedom of association in political parties and public organizations. For the purpose of parliamentary elections, most parties form voting blocs, which provide greater representation than they would otherwise receive. Ukrainian law requires that a party must receive at least 3 percent of the vote in order to get any of the proportional representation seats.

Political parties can be constitutionally banned through a judicial procedure. This may happen if their program aims to end Ukraine's independence or territorial indivisibility; promote violent change of the constitutional order; undermine security; unlawfully seize state power; spread propaganda of war and of violence; incite ethnic, racial, or religious enmity; or threaten human rights, freedoms, or the health of the population.

CITIZENSHIP

Ukrainian citizenship is primarily acquired by birth. The principle of *ius sanguinis* is applied: A child acquires Ukrainian citizenship if at least one parent is a Ukrainian citizen, wherever the place of birth.

A foreigner can also acquire Ukrainian citizenship if he or she does not possess any foreign citizenship, has resided in Ukraine for at least five years, is able to function in the Ukrainian language, and is knowledgeable about the Ukrainian constitution. Dual citizenship is not recognized by the constitution. A citizen of Ukraine may not be deprived of citizenship, be expelled, or be surrendered to another state.

FUNDAMENTAL RIGHTS

According to Article 3 of the constitution, "[t]he human being, his or her life and health, honor and dignity, inviolability and security are recognized in Ukraine as the highest social value." Human rights and freedoms are the constitutional means to preserve this value, and the state is constitutionally obliged to do so. In fact, it is the "main duty of the state" to affirm and ensure human rights and freedoms.

Chapter 2 details the rights, freedoms, and duties of individuals and citizens. The Ukrainian constitution guarantees the full traditional set of human rights. Social human rights, such as the right to work or the right to an education, are strongly represented. The constitution states that its explicit list of rights is not exhaustive, thereby acknowledging that human rights are regarded as inalienable and based on natural law.

Article 21 explicitly links human rights to the idea of human dignity: "All people are free and equal in their dignity and rights. Human rights and freedoms are inalienable and inviolable." The constitution acknowledges that human rights are the basis of every community.

The rights guaranteed by the constitution can be classified either as freedom rights or as equality rights. Article 23 protects the free development of the personality and functions as a general guarantee of personal freedom in a broad sense. Article 24 contains a general equal treatment clause, which guarantees that all citizens are equal before the law. There can be no privileges or restrictions based on race, color, political, religious and other beliefs, sex, ethnic and social origin, property status, place of residence, linguistic, or other characteristics. Equality of the rights of women and men is ensured by a number of affirmative actions, such as efforts to create conditions that allow women to combine work and motherhood.

The constitution distinguishes between those rights that apply to everybody and those reserved for Ukrainian citizens. For instance, freedom of opinion or freedom of belief is guaranteed for everybody, whereas only citizens of Ukraine have the right to freedom of association in political parties.

Foreigners living in Ukraine are protected by the human rights specified in the constitution, including the right to the free development of personality. Foreigners and stateless persons may be granted asylum by the procedure established by law.

The International Covenant on Civil and Political Rights (ICCPR) and International Covenant on Economic, Social and Cultural Rights (ICESCR) were already in force in 1976, when Ukraine still was a republic of the USSR. These covenants influenced the rights language of the Ukrainian constitutions. Ukraine took on additional obligations to legislate stronger protections for human rights when it joined the Council of Europe.

Despite significant improvements, several human rights organizations regularly report abuses. Political activity by organized crime and connections between government officials and organized crime often blur the distinction between political and criminal acts and impede criminal investigations. For example, a killing of a prominent journalist in 2000 remains unresolved, as accusations continue that senior officials in the former government were implicated. Even the purported poisoning of Viktor Yushchenko when he was a presidential candidate in 2004 remains unresolved.

Impact and Functions of Fundamental Rights

According to the constitution, human rights are of fundamental importance. The success of the Ukrainian constitution will depend on the impact and functions of the rights in contains. In Ukraine, the day the constitution was adopted is a national holiday.

Fundamental rights are often considered defensive rights. The state must not interfere with the legal position of the individual unless there is a good reason to do so. Official bodies are obliged to act only "within the limits of authority" and in the manner envisaged by the constitution and the laws.

In the Ukrainian concept, however, the state itself is obliged to establish freedom as a positive reality.

Fundamental rights in Ukraine do involve the right to participate in the democratic political process. This especially applies to freedom of assembly, of the press, and of opinion. Citizens also have the right to participate (or not to participate) in a strike, to participate in elections, and to participate in the administration of state affairs and in the justice system.

Many fundamental rights entitle an individual to services from the state, such as the right to social protection, housing, an adequate standard of living, and medical care. In practice, some of these rights have remained unfulfilled for the many Ukrainians whose income is lower than the subsistence minimum.

Fundamental rights are also a guarantee of due process. A person in temporary custody must be taken to a court within 72 hours or immediately released.

The state in all its agencies is bound to uphold fundamental rights. Constitutional norms are of direct effect. Constitutional appeals based on the constitution are guaranteed. However, individuals are not entitled to appeal directly to the Constitutional Court. As a result, many of the enumerated rights and freedoms have remained purely theoretical.

Everyone is, however, entitled to appeal to the human rights commissioner of the Supreme Council for the protection of rights. The commissioner exercises parliamentary supervision over the observance of human and citizens' rights and freedoms. The commissioner can ask the Constitutional Court to consider the constitutionality of laws and regulations that may violate human rights.

Finally, everybody has the right to petition or appeal to all bodies of state power. These bodies are constitutionally obliged to consider the complaint and to provide a substantiated reply.

Limitations to Fundamental Rights

Constitutional rights are not without limits. There is no general limitation clause, but some rights are explicitly limited to protect the public interest and the rights of others.

For instance, freedom of expression can be restricted for a number of qualified reasons, such as national security, territorial indivisibility, public order, prevention of disturbances or crimes, protection of health, the reputation or rights of other persons, protection of confidential information, or support for the authority and impartiality of justice. Freedom of belief may be restricted, but only by a law in the interest of protecting public order, the health and morality of the population, or the rights and freedoms of other persons.

A large number of rights, such as the right to life, are explicitly declared as nonrestrictable even in a case of emergency.

Each limit to a fundamental right faces limits itself. The scope of rights and freedoms cannot be diminished by new laws or changes in the law; nor can constitutional rights and freedoms be abolished completely.

Another guarantee that limits the limitations is the requirement that everyone is guaranteed the right to know his or her rights and duties. All normative legal acts that determine the rights and duties of citizens must be brought to the notice of the population by the procedure established by laws. Normative legal acts can have no retroactive force, except when they mitigate or annul individual responsibility.

The constitution does not contain many provisions that explicitly aim at preventing the abuse of fundamental rights. There is a general principle, however, that no one can usurp state power. The military forces of the state may not be used by anyone to restrict the rights and freedoms of citizens or to try to overthrow the constitutional order, subvert the bodies of power, or obstruct their activity.

ECONOMY

The Ukrainian constitution no longer specifies any particular economic system. On the other hand, certain provisions act as guidelines for state action, in effect obliging the state to ensure a social orientation for the economy. While private property is guaranteed, it entails responsibilities; it may not be used to the detriment of the person and society. The foreign investment law allows anybody to purchase businesses and property. However, foreign and local investors must compete with a large number of favored state enterprises; they also complain about corruption and lax law enforcement against powerful economic oligarchs.

Taken altogether, the economic system can be described as a socially oriented market economy.

RELIGIOUS COMMUNITIES

Freedom of religion is legally guaranteed, although religious organizations are required to register with local authorities and with the central government. The dominant religions are the Ukrainian Orthodox Church and the Ukrainian Greek Catholic Church. The Ukrainian Orthodox Church is divided between a Moscow Patriarchy and an independent Kiev Patriarchy, which was established after Ukrainian independence in 1991.

The church and religious organizations in Ukraine are separate from the state and from the school system. No religion is recognized by the state as mandatory.

MILITARY DEFENSE AND STATE OF EMERGENCY

Defense of the motherland and of the independence and territorial indivisibility of Ukraine and respect for its state symbols are made constitutional duties of all Ukrainians. Males are subject to conscription from age 18, and women may volunteer for military service at age 19. Alternative or nonmilitary service is constitutionally acknowledged. Conscientious objectors can file a petition to be excluded from military service.

The president is commander in chief of the armed forces and head of the Council of National Security and Defense, which is the coordinating body and adviser to the president on issues of national security and defense.

In 2000, Ukraine adopted laws regulating future states of emergency and martial law, which are permitted by the constitution. Certain restrictions can be imposed during those times, for periods that must be specified. For instance, the state may execute certain expropriations, order citizens to perform certain work or services, and limit specified rights and freedoms.

A large number of rights are explicitly declared as nonrestrictable in Article 64. Furthermore, the constitution cannot be amended under conditions of martial law or a state of emergency.

AMENDMENTS TO THE CONSTITUTION

Chapter 8 provides for a two-stage process of amending the constitution. After the Supreme Council adopts an amendment by simple majority, it must be approved a second time at the next regular session of the council by two-thirds majority of the deputies. The procedure also requires the permission of the Constitutional Court. The constitution is thus more difficult to change than ordinary laws, but the degree of difficulty varies, depending on the chapter or article being amended.

A bill to amend ordinary provisions of the constitution may be submitted by either the president of the republic or one-third of all the members of the Supreme Council. It is then reviewed by the Constitutional Court for conformity to the constitution. In the first vote, a simple majority of the deputies is needed for passage; at the second session, it needs a two-thirds vote. If the amendment is not passed, it may not be reintroduced for at least a year.

Amendments to general principles (Chapter 1), elections and referendum (Chapter 3), or the amendment process itself (Chapter 13) can be introduced either by the president or by two-thirds of all the members of the Supreme Council. Furthermore, after approval by a two-thirds majority, it needs further approval by an all-Ukrainian referendum. If the amendment does not pass, it may not be reintroduced after until the next Supreme Council elections.

Certain matters are not subject to change at all. Articles 157 and 158 give the Constitutional Court authority to disallow any change that might abolish or restrict human and citizens' rights and freedoms or tend toward the liquidation of the independence or violation of the territorial indivisibility of Ukraine. Furthermore, no amendment may be passed during periods of martial law or state of emergency. Finally, a Supreme Council cannot amend the same provisions twice during one term.

A series of fundamental amendments were passed in 2004. They aimed to alter the balance of powers between the executive and legislative branches, in part by providing further grounds for the president to dissolve the Supreme Council. They extended the term of the Supreme Council to five years, established elections on a purely proportional basis, and allowed deputies to be removed when they leave their parliamentary faction. Other changes included reforms in local self-government and provisions to prevent conflicts of public and private interests.

The law was approved by a 90 percent majority in the council. Most of the amendments took effect on September 1, 2005. The remaining amendments will take effect on the day a new parliament assembles after the 2006 elections.

PRIMARY SOURCES

Constitution in English. Available online. URLs: http://www.rada.kiev.ua/const/conengl.htm; http://www.president.gov.ua/en/content/103_e.html. Accessed on August 22, 2005.

Constitution in Ukrainian (authentic text): *Konstytutsiia Ukrainy.* Kiev: Presa Ukrainy, 1997. Available online. URL: http://www.kmu.gov.ua/document/235538/Konstitution.zip. Accessed on September 16, 2005.

SECONDARY SOURCES

Bohdan A. Futey, "Comments on the Constitution of Ukraine." *East European Constitutional Review* 5, no. 2–3 (spring–summer 1996): 29–34.

Bureau of Public Affairs, U.S. Department of State, "Background Note and Country Reports on Human Rights Practices and International Religious Freedom Report 2004." Available online. URL: http://www.state.gov/. Accessed on August 28, 2005.

"The Constitution of Bendery in English," *Towards an Intellectual History of Ukraine: An Anthology of Ukrainian Thought from 1710–1995,* edited by Ralph Lindheim and George Luckyj, 53–64. Toronto: University of Toronto Press and the Shevchenko Scientific Society, 1996.

European Commission for Democracy through Law (Venice Commission), "Amendments to the Constitution of Ukraine, adopted on December 8, 2004." Available online. URL: www.venice.coe.int/. Accessed on September 16, 2005.

Kharkiv Group for Human Rights Protection, "Human Rights in the Constitution of Ukraine." Available online. URL: http://www.khpg.org/. Accessed on September 16, 2005.

Office for Democratic Institutions and Human Rights, *Final Report on the 2004 Presidential Election in Ukraine.* Warsaw: ODIHR, 2005. Available online. URL: http://www.osce.org/. Accessed on August 23, 2005.

Richard C. O. Rezie, "The Ukrainian Constitution: Interpretation of the Citizens' Rights." *Case Western Reserve Journal of International Law* 31 (winter 1999): 169–210; "Ukrainian Legislative Acts." Available online. URL: http://www.eastlaw.co.uk/. Accessed on September 25, 2005.

Michael Rahe and Lidiya Syvko

UNITED ARAB EMIRATES

At-a-Glance

OFFICIAL NAME
United Arab Emirates (UAE)

CAPITAL
Abu Dhabi

POPULATION
3,400,000 (2005 est.)

SIZE
30,000 sq. mi. (77,700 sq. km)

LANGUAGES
Arabic

RELIGION
Islam

NATIONAL OR ETHNIC COMPOSITION
Arab, Asian, Far Eastern

DATE OF INDEPENDENCE OR CREATION
December 2, 1971

TYPE OF GOVERNMENT
Monarchy

TYPE OF STATE
Federal state

TYPE OF LEGISLATURE
Unicameral *majlis* (council)

DATE OF CONSTITUTION
December 2, 1971

DATE OF LAST AMENDMENT
January 10, 2004

The United Arab Emirates (UAE) consists of a central government and seven federal states or emirates—Abu Dhabi, Dubai, Sharjah, Ras-al-Khaimah, Ajman, Umm-al-Quwain, and Fujairah. It is a member of the Arab League, the United Nations, and the Gulf Co-Operation Council (GCC).

The political system is dominated by a series of ruling families who have presided over the emirates since the beginning of the 19th century.

The UAE constitution was not designed to rationalize the distribution of power or to introduce a "representative democracy" within the federation. Instead it accepted the existing constitutional position of the rulers and provided certain legislative and political improvements.

CONSTITUTIONAL HISTORY

Britain's connection with the territories of the UAE may be traced back to 1820, when it concluded a peace treaty with 10 sheikhs or tribal chiefs. In 1853, after a series of short-term treaties, Britain imposed the Perpetual Maritime Truce

on the emirates, and the area became known as the "Trucial States." The final step in the British plan to control the Trucial States was taken in 1892, when the sheikhs signed the Exclusive Agreement, agreeing on behalf of themselves and their heirs "not to enter into any agreement or correspondence with any power other than Britain."

Britain's presence and its treaty arrangements effectively split the two major political units—the Qawasim and the Bani Yas confederations—into several smaller units. The final result that emerged by 1952 was a weak political mosaic of seven emirates.

In January 1968, the British prime minister, Harold Wilson, announced that British troops would be withdrawn from east of Suez by the end of 1971. The seven rulers of the Trucial States together with the rulers of Bahrain and Qatar met in Dubai on February 25–27, 1968, and announced an agreement to establish a new nine-member Union of Arab Emirates.

The addition of Bahrain and Qatar was not successful; on December 2, 1971, the United Arab Emirates, consisting only of the seven original emirates, was declared a new independent state. A constitution was established under the direct authority of the seven rulers. The constitution owes its authority to royal edict.

FORM AND IMPACT OF THE CONSTITUTION

The UAE constitution is contained in a single written document. A notable feature is its federal nature. The constitution largely preserved and legitimized the pre-1971 traditional government. The framers labeled the document a Provisional Constitution and set a five-year goal for drafting a permanent constitution. In 1996 the word *provisional* was removed from the title.

The federal government represents the state in the international arena. The central federal government has exclusive powers in the field of foreign policy. It concludes international agreements and treaties, appoints diplomatic representatives, and can declare war. The supremacy of the federal constitution and laws over local laws and legislation is guaranteed by the constitution.

BASIC ORGANIZATIONAL STRUCTURE

The UAE is a federal state composed of seven emirates, which differ considerably in geographical area, population, and economic size.

There is a division of functions between the federation and the states. The federation has a monopoly in certain areas with regard to lawmaking and executive functions. Individual states have been assigned legislative and administrative functions.

LEADING CONSTITUTIONAL PRINCIPLES

The UAE constitutional system is defined by a number of leading principles: The UAE is an Arab state, an Islamic state, and a federation. The constitution preserves the rule of law; yet there is no clear division between the legislative and executive powers. The constitution is unique—a modern quasi-democratic basic law that governs a traditional society rooted in its premodern history.

CONSTITUTIONAL BODIES

There are not three but rather five branches of power in the federation. They are the Supreme Council, the president of the union and the president's deputy, the Council of Ministers, the Federal National Council (FNC), and the judiciary. The constitution was modeled neither on a parliamentary nor on a presidential system.

THE SUPREME COUNCIL

The Supreme Council consists of the rulers of the seven emirates. It forms the general policy of the union, sanctions the federal laws, ratifies international agreements and treaties, and approves the appointment or resignation of the prime minister, the president, and the judges of the Supreme Court. It retains vast powers in the legislative and executive realms.

Decisions in the Supreme Council on substantive matters need a majority of five, of whom two must be from Abu Dhabi and Dubai.

The Federal President

The federal president and the president's deputy are elected for a five-year term from among the members of the Supreme Council. There is no limit on reelection. The president is responsible for appointing the ministers and diplomatic representatives to foreign states.

The Council of Ministers

The Council of Ministers heads the administration of the federation. It consists of the prime minister, the prime minister's deputy, and a number of ministers. Ministers are forbidden to engage in commercial, professional, or financial affairs; to be a party to commercial dealings with the union; or to be a member of the board of directors of any financial or commercial institution. The ministers while in office are forbidden to hold any post in local government or the Federal National Council.

The Federal National Council

The Federal National Council (FNC) consists of 40 seats proportionally distributed among the emirates according to their influence, affluence, and population. Its term of office is two years.

The constitution provides that each emirate shall be free to determine the method of selection of its representatives in the FNC. All of the emirates have chosen to appoint their representatives instead of electing them.

The Lawmaking Process

Under the UAE constitution, the legislative process passes through four stages: the initiation of a bill, debate and discussion, ratification, and promulgation.

The Council of Ministers holds a monopoly over initiating a bill. The constitution restricts the role of the FNC in the debate and discussion of bills introduced by the Council of Ministers. No bill may become a law without the consent of the Supreme Council.

The Judiciary

The federal judiciary functions at three levels: the courts of first instance, the appeals courts, and the Supreme

Court. Local justice is administered in either civil or sharia courts.

The Supreme Court is composed of a president and a number of judges, not to exceed five. The judges are appointed by the president with the consent of the Supreme Council. Supreme Court judges are immune from dismissal during their term of office. The constitution permits the local authorities in the emirates to transfer all judicial matters to the federal courts if they so choose. Five emirates have taken advantage of this provision; the remaining two (Dubai and Ras al-Kaimah) retain their local courts.

THE ELECTION PROCESS

The traditional form of political participation in the UAE consists of consultations between the ruler and prominent public figures. There are no elections.

POLITICAL PARTIES

There are no political parties in the country.

CITIZENSHIP

Original citizens are those who acquired citizenship through *jus sanguinis*—a child born to a UAE father acquires citizenship regardless of the place of birth. Under certain circumstances a child can have UAE original citizenship if he or she is born to a UAE mother.

Naturalized citizens are those who have met certain conditions established by law. An applicant for UAE citizenship must have lived in the country for a long period; the residency period required by the law varies. A naturalized person must also relinquish his or her previous nationality.

FUNDAMENTAL RIGHTS

Most international human rights norms are incorporated in the UAE constitution, including both individual liberties and social rights. The constitution regulates fundamental rights in its second and third chapters, in some 23 articles.

Human dignity and the right to safety, security, peace, and the enjoyment of individual freedoms are guaranteed in several clauses. The right of free movement and residence is also a basic right that has been secured for all citizens.

Impact and Functions of Fundamental Rights

The constitution gives legally binding effect to the fundamental rights. Since the constitution is the supreme law of the land, fundamental rights share this position.

Limitations to Fundamental Rights

The constitution of UAE contains several limitation clauses that give the government the discretion to regulate or restrict certain fundamental freedoms included therein. Such limitations may be related to public order, public morals, and national security.

ECONOMY

The UAE constitution does not specify an economic system. However, the economic system embodied in the constitution can be described as a social market economy. It safeguards community interests as well as the freedom of property, the freedom of occupation, and the freedom of association.

The right to work is a cornerstone of the progress achieved by the federation. Moreover, the constitution regulates the relationship between employers and employees, rendering this a responsibility of the state.

Natural resources are owned by the individual states, and not by the federation or by any individuals.

RELIGIOUS COMMUNITIES

The UAE constitution states in Article 7 that "Islam is the official religion of the Union. The Islamic sharia shall be a main source of legislation in the Union." Sharia (Islamic law) is recognized as *a* main but not *the* main or *only* source of legislation in the country. Most federal laws, such as civil and penal laws, criminal procedures, and personal status laws, are based upon Islamic jurisprudence.

Freedom of religion or belief is guaranteed as a human right, as is freedom of worship, in accordance with the established customs. No Islamic communities regulate and administer their affairs independently.

MILITARY DEFENSE AND STATE OF EMERGENCY

The creation and maintenance of armed forces for defense are a responsibility of the federal government. There is no general conscription in the UAE. All members of the military are professional soldiers who serve for life.

The military is subject to civil government. The federal president is the head of the armed forces.

AMENDMENTS TO THE CONSTITUTION

The constitution is rigid; in other words, it cannot be amended as simply as ordinary legislation; certain key points are entrenched.

The constitutional body that has the right to issue constitutional amendments is the Supreme Council. The constitution insists that the "topmost interest of the Union," a term that is somewhat vague, must be consulted before any constitutional amendment is made. As a final safeguard, a special two-thirds majority in the Federal National Council is required to pass the amendment.

PRIMARY SOURCES

Constitution in English. Available online. URL: http://www.almajles.gov.ae/Front/eConstitutionSubjects.asp/. Accessed on August 24, 2005.

Constitution in Arabic. Available online. URL: http://www.almajles.gov.ae/index.asp. Accessed on June 29, 2006.

SECONDARY SOURCES

Frauke Heard-Bey, *From Trucial States to United Arab Emirates.* London: Longman Group, 1984.

Ali Mohammed Khalifa, *The United Arab Emirates: Unity in Fragmentation.* Boulder, Colo.: Westview Press, 1979.

Muhsin Khalil, *The Constitutional System of the United Arab Emirates.* Al Ain: UAE University Press, 1989.

Enver Koury, *The United Arab Emirates: Its Political System and Politics.* Hyattsville, Md.: Institute of Middle Eastern and North African Affairs, 1980.

Malcolm Peck, "Formation and Evolution of the Federation and Its Institutions." In *United Arab Emirates: A New Perspective,* edited by Ibrahim Al Abed and Peter Hellyer. London: Trident Press, 2001.

J. E. Peterson, "The Future of Federalism in the United Arab Emirates." In *Crosscurrents in the Gulf,* edited by H. Richard Sindelar and J. E. Peterson, 198–230. London: Routledge, 1988.

Mohamed A. Al Roken, "Human Rights under the Constitution of UAE." *Arab Law Quarterly* 12 part 1 (1997): 91–107.

Mohamed A. Al Roken

UNITED KINGDOM

At-a-Glance

OFFICIAL NAME
United Kingdom of Great Britain and Northern Ireland

CAPITAL
London

POPULATION
59,542,000 (2005 est.)

SIZE
92,248 sq. mi. (244,101 sq. km)

LANGUAGES
English, Welsh, Gaelic

RELIGIONS
Christian (Anglican 67.2%, Catholic 13.8%, all others 19%) 71.6%, Muslim 2.7%, Hindu 1.0%, Sikh 0.6%, Jewish 0.5%, other or none 23.6%

NATIONAL OR ETHNIC COMPOSITION
British white 87%, other white 3%, Asian 4%, black 2%, mixed, other, and unknown 4%

DATE OF INDEPENDENCE OR CREATION
Great Britain: May 1, 1707 (union of England and Scotland); United Kingdom: August 1, 1801 (union with Ireland)

TYPE OF GOVERNMENT
Constitutional monarchy

TYPE OF STATE
Unitary state with some devolved powers

TYPE OF LEGISLATURE
Bicameral parliament

DATE OF CONSTITUTION
No written constitution

The United Kingdom is unusual among major countries in having no written constitution. The country's constitutional arrangements are based on a large number of ordinary acts of Parliament and on "constitutional conventions" that have developed over the centuries and are still evolving. The last century has seen the creation of devolved assemblies in different parts of the United Kingdom, created again by ordinary acts of Parliament.

Formally, legislative and executive powers are vested in the reigning sovereign, who appoints the prime minister and other ministers, senior judges, and members of the House of Lords; the sovereign also summons and dissolves Parliament and is supreme governor of the Church of England. In practice, the constitutional conventions ensure that the queen acts almost wholly on the advice of the administration, which is formed to reflect the result of the elections to the House of Commons.

The absence of a written constitution entails that there is no constitutional court and no constitutional guarantees of human rights. Since 1999, the European Convention on Human Rights has been part of the law of the United Kingdom and has strengthened the powers of the courts, which have always been vigorous in checking any improper use of executive power.

CONSTITUTIONAL HISTORY

The major portion of the United Kingdom consists of the island of Great Britain. The southern part forms the Kingdom of England, unified under King Athelstan in about 927 C.E. The northern part is the Kingdom of Scotland, similarly unified under King Malcolm II in 1016 C.E. The Principality of Wales had its own native Welsh princes from early times, with Rhodri the Great ruling from 844 C.E. By the 13th century, Wales was under English rule, and it was formally united with England by the Act of Union of 1535. Since that date, England and Wales have for most purposes formed a single unit of government. In 1603, King James VI of Scotland inherited the English throne as King James I of England, but despite the union of the Crowns the two countries retained their own political institutions until 1707, when a single Parliament for the whole of Great Britain was established. Scotland retained its own legal system and its own established church (the Church of Scotland), but the principal features of constitutional practice post 1707 were clearly derived from the traditions developed in England.

The island of Ireland has had its own, troubled history. King Henry VIII of England declared himself king of Ireland in 1541, but the English controlled only parts of the country. A separate Irish parliament was created in the 18th century (still under British suzerainty) but was short-lived: Ireland was united with Great Britain to form the United Kingdom of Great Britain and Ireland in 1801. After the establishment of the Irish Free State in 1922, only the six counties of Northern Ireland remained in the United Kingdom.

The constitutional history of England is one of gradual transfer of royal power to more representative bodies. The origins of Parliament are to be found in the gathering of courtiers, judges, bishops, and others that had taken a recognizable shape by the 13th century and evolved into the House of Lords. An elected House of Commons emerged later, with the first speaker of that house appointed in 1377. Parliament met only when summoned by the king, and there were often intervals of some years between parliaments. However, the two houses and especially the Commons gradually asserted control over the grant of "supply," that is, the authorization of taxation to finance the work of government.

The relationship between the king and the Houses of Parliament was fundamentally changed as a result of three critical events in the 17th and 18th centuries. The first was the republican interlude between 1649 and 1660. The second was the overthrow of James II by Parliament in the so-called Glorious Revolution of 1688, which installed William III and Mary II as joint sovereigns the following year; their rule clearly depended on the will of the people as expressed by Parliament. Finally, in 1714, again by virtue of an act of Parliament, a German prince (George, elector of Hanover) succeeded to the British Crown. He was not fluent in English and so took a much-reduced part in the business of government. It was under William III and George I that the office of prime minister and the cabinet, drawn from the majority group in the House of Commons, first appeared.

Although this process produced the main features of the modern constitutional arrangements, a fully democratic system was yet to emerge. In the 19th century, representation in the Commons was reformed and the secret ballot introduced, but it was only in the 1920s that the franchise was extended to women. Finally, in 1999 the hereditary right of peers to sit in the House of Lords was removed. Thus, despite the absence of constitutional documents with their resounding statements of high principle, there did emerge a centralized, democratic state, respecting the rule of law and playing a leading part in the development of international law.

In recent decades, the centralization of power in Westminster (where Parliament meets) and Whitehall (the home of the civil service and government departments) has been thrown into reverse. Membership since 1972 in what is now the European Union has led to a significant transfer of power to European institutions, a development disliked by many in the United Kingdom. Within the United Kingdom itself, several regional parliamentary assemblies have emerged, with their own devolved powers and regional administration.

FORM AND IMPACT OF THE CONSTITUTION

The absence of a written constitution is a striking feature of the United Kingdom. In one sense it is a historical accident: the result of the slow evolution of the system of government in a group of islands whose boundaries are defined by geography, and the greater part of which has never had to declare its independence of any other state. It may also reflect, and help to maintain, an essentially pragmatic tradition in much of British intellectual life. If there is a theory of the British constitution, it is that of the sovereignty of Parliament: that Parliament has unlimited power, that no court can declare its acts void, and that no one Parliament can bind its successors.

There is, nonetheless, much public reference to the conventions of the constitution, for example, that the queen must invite the leader of the majority party in the House of Commons to form an administration. The effect of that particular convention is that the administration almost always controls the House of Commons, so there is a sense in which it is unrealistic to speak of the executive as subject to the legislature.

There are many conventions of lesser importance (for example, that legislation relating to the Church of England should be introduced into the church's own legislative body, the General Synod, rather than into Parliament). Some conventions are disputed (for example, that a cabinet minister should resign if a serious mistake is made by his or her officials, even if the minister is not personally implicated).

BASIC ORGANIZATIONAL STRUCTURE

The United Kingdom has a parliamentary rather than a presidential system. It is one of the conventions that ministers should be members of one or the other house of Parliament. Typically, in a cabinet of about 20 members, two or three ministers will be in the Lords and the rest in the Commons. Junior ministers are drawn from both houses, so that there is a responsible minister to answer questions in each house.

In times when the government party has a large majority in the Commons (such as the years after 1997), there is a tendency for ministers to adopt a more "presidential" style; there have even been occasions when the speaker of the House of Commons has publicly rebuked ministers for making important announcements to the media and not to the house. The House of Commons seeks to make ministers accountable by the daily question hour, by the ombudsperson system for complaints of maladministration, and by a series of select committees dealing with the affairs of each department. Those committees can summon witnesses, including ministers and civil servants from the department concerned, and their reports are often highly critical, even though the committees are dominated by administration supporters. The House of Lords has a similar system of committees but on broader themes, such as European affairs, and science and technology.

Although classified as a unitary rather than a federal state, the United Kingdom does consist of three distinct parts: (1) England and Wales (and for some purposes Wales may be seen as a distinct, fourth part); (2) Scotland; and (3) Northern Ireland. The United Kingdom Parliament in London can legislate for any part, but there are subordinate legislative assemblies in Scotland, Northern Ireland, and Wales, each with an executive headed by a first minister.

The events in Ireland in the early 1920s left Northern Ireland with its own bicameral parliament. After civil unrest in Northern Ireland, the local parliament was suspended and eventually replaced in 1999 by the unicameral Northern Ireland Assembly with a "power-sharing" executive representing all the major political parties. Certain matters were not devolved to the assembly, including police and security matters, criminal justice, international relations, and taxation; these remained the responsibility of the secretary of state for Northern Ireland, a U.K. cabinet minister. Continuing difficulties led to the repeated suspension of the assembly, with all ministerial responsibilities reverting to the secretary of state.

A unicameral Scottish Parliament was introduced in 1999. It has power to legislate on a range of topics including education, health, agriculture, and justice, and has limited taxation powers. Foreign affairs, defense, and national security remain a U.K. responsibility.

In the same year, the National Assembly for Wales (colloquially known as the Welsh Assembly) was established. It has responsibilities for what are essentially executive functions in certain areas, such as health, local government, and agriculture, but very limited legislative powers, essentially restricted to those items of secondary legislation that U.K. ministers can make in England.

In each part of the United Kingdom, there is a system of local government. The historic counties, each with a lord lieutenant representing the monarch and (in England) a high sheriff with ceremonial duties associated with the courts, remain the primary unit in much of England, where local government responsibilities are divided between county and district councils. In London and the major urban areas, these have been replaced by unitary authorities such as the 32 London Borough Councils. Wales, Scotland, and Northern Ireland also now have single-tier

systems. There are also parish or community councils in many small local areas. The major sources of income for all these local councils are the council tax levied on property in the area and grants from central government funds. Local government leaders frequently complain that their activities are more and more circumscribed by parliamentary legislation and ministerial guidelines, and that additional obligations placed on local authorities are not matched by increased grants to enable these obligations to be discharged. There are proposals for elected regional assemblies to assume some of the responsibilities of county councils, on the model of the Greater London Authority, which has strategic responsibilities for the whole London region.

It should be mentioned that some of the small islands within the geographical entity of the British Isles are not part of the United Kingdom, although the monarch is head of state and the U.K. government is responsible for defense and international relations. The Isle of Man has its own legislature, the Tynwald, the oldest parliament in the world with a continuous existence, and the two Bailiwicks of Guernsey and Jersey (in the Channel Islands) have assemblies known as the States. The remaining overseas dependent territories of the United Kingdom have their own constitutions and legislatures.

LEADING CONSTITUTIONAL PRINCIPLES

In the United Kingdom democracy and the rule of law are enshrined in constitutional practice, though not in any single document; however, some other characteristics of many constitutions are absent. There is no doctrine of the separation of powers: the lord chancellor and other senior judges sit in the House of Lords, of which the lord chancellor is Speaker, and the House of Lords is both part of the legislature and the highest court of appeal. The lord chancellor is also a cabinet minister, and so has a place in the executive, the legislature, and the judiciary. In 2003, controversial proposals were announced for the abolition of the office of lord chancellor and the transfer of the judicial functions of the lords to a new Supreme Court. At the time of writing (beginning of 2006) these proposals were still under consideration in Parliament.

CONSTITUTIONAL BODIES

The main state bodies are the Crown, the Privy Council, Parliament, and the cabinet.

The Crown

The monarchy retains its importance as a symbol of unity and a focus of loyalty. The monarch receives all major state papers, presides at the largely formal meetings of the

Privy Council, and receives the prime minister in a weekly private audience to receive and to give advice and information. There are from time to time suggestions that the system of honors awarded by the queen or king should be changed or abolished, but the monarchy remains very popular.

The monarchy is hereditary, under the system of male primogeniture, with male descendants of the sovereign taking precedence over female descendants, the senior line of descent always taking precedence over the junior line. So the male children of the sovereign succeed in preference to their older sisters.

The overthrow of King James II in 1688 was largely due to a fear that he might restore the Catholic faith, and in the following years Parliament was at pains to ensure the succession of Protestants to the throne. The Act of Settlement of 1700, which is still in force, declared Princess Sophia, electress of Hanover, as the next heir and provided for the succession to be to "the heirs of her body being protestants," excluding from succession to the throne anyone who "is are or shall be reconciled to or shall hold communion with the See or Church of Rome or shall profess the popish religion or shall marry a papist." Some members of the royal family have been excluded from the order of succession on this basis, but this provision has not affected anyone who had a realistic chance of inheriting the Crown.

The Privy Council

Apart from the monarchy itself, the most ancient part of the constitutional structure is the Privy Council, the successor of the inner council that advised the sovereign before the full development of cabinet government. It consists of several hundred persons, including all present and past cabinet ministers, other senior parliamentarians, senior judges, the archbishops of Canterbury and York, the bishop of London, and some other eminent individuals; membership is for life though there is power to remove an individual for some grave cause.

The Privy Council meets every few weeks, with a usual attendance of three or four cabinet ministers. Its meetings are traditionally conducted standing, a practice that no doubt helps ensure their brevity. The proceedings are almost entirely formal, as the monarch indicates approval of each item. The most important business is the making of orders-in-council, a form of secondary legislation made under statutory authority and considered too important to be dealt with by ministerial regulations.

The Privy Council has a number of "working" committees, the most important of which is the Judicial Committee: a court of law hearing appeals from the remaining overseas dependencies and some independent Commonwealth countries; it also has jurisdiction to resolve issues as to the powers of the devolved assemblies of Scotland, Wales, and Northern Ireland, to hear appeals in some ecclesiastical matters, and from some professional regulatory bodies. There is also a Universities Commit-

tee, dealing with the grant and amendment of charters and statutes to universities. Another committee deals with proposed legislation from the States of Guernsey or Jersey.

The Parliament

Technically, the United Kingdom Parliament consists of the sovereign and the two Houses. Legislation is enacted "by the Queen's most Excellent Majesty, by and with the advice and consent of the Lords Spiritual and Temporal, and Commons, in this present parliament assembled, and by the authority of the same." Each Parliament is formed after a general election to the House of Commons. Its maximal life is five years, but it is usually dissolved earlier at a time selected by the prime minister. There are annual sessions opened by the sovereign, normally in November of each year, and business unfinished at the end of one session (a few days before the opening of the next) must, in the absence of some special arrangement, begin again in the next session.

The House of Lords now consists of the 26 lords spiritual (the Anglican archbishops and bishops), 92 hereditary peers elected as an interim measure after the removal from the house of other hereditary peers in 1999, a number of judges appointed as lords of appeal and remaining peers for life, and an unlimited number (usually about 550) of other life peers. All are formally appointed by the monarch on the advice of the prime minister. Almost a third sit as crossbenchers, independent of any of the political parties; that and the life tenure of the members give the house a considerable degree of independence. The lord chancellor is currently the speaker, but the occupant of the woolsack, the seat for the presiding officer, has little control over debates, which are a matter for the house as a whole. Members are unpaid but have various expense allowances.

The House of Commons is wholly elected, with 659 members all representing single-member constituencies. In 2003, members received a pensionable annual salary of £56,000 and various expense allowances totaling up to £113,000 a year. The house elects its own Speaker. A cabinet minister serves as leader of the house, and the leader of the largest minority party becomes leader of the opposition. Most votes are subject to party "whips," but free votes are allowed on some matters. In any event, a member can vote as he or she wishes and defy party instructions; members may also change party allegiance without losing their seat.

There are a number of practices designed to ensure the integrity and probity of members. Members must declare their financial and other interests, a register of which is made public each year; a parliamentary commissioner for standards examines any alleged misconduct or impropriety; and the house has its own Committee on Standards and Privileges, which can discipline offending members. Similar arrangements apply in the other regional assemblies and local councils.

The Lawmaking Process

Bills may be introduced in either house of Parliament, by the responsible minister or by individual members. In each house, a bill receives a formal first reading and, if its principles are generally approved after debate, a second reading. It is then examined line by line by an appointed committee in the Commons or by the whole house in the Lords. The results are then reported to the house, and further amendments may be moved at this "report stage." Final approval is in the form of a vote on the third reading of the bill. The bill then goes to the other house and the process is repeated.

If, as is usually the case, the bill has been amended during its progress through the second house, the house in which it was first considered is asked whether it accepts the amendments. If it does not (for example, if the government uses its majority in the Commons to reverse decisions made in the Lords), the bill goes back to see whether the amendments are insisted upon. If there is no agreement, the bill falls at the end of the annual parliamentary session; there is no form of joint committee in which a compromise text can be negotiated.

It follows that the House of Lords can "block" a government bill. By a convention, this power is not used in the case of financial bills or when the government's proposals were clearly stated in its last election manifesto. In any event, if the House of Commons passes the same bill in two successive sessions, it may be presented for the royal assent without the endorsement of the House of Lords. The royal assent is the last formal stage; assent to a bill has not been withheld at any time during the last 300 years.

A large amount of legislation is in the form of statutory instruments: secondary legislation made by the sovereign-in-council or the relevant government minister in the exercise of a power conferred in an act of Parliament. In a typical year there may be some 40 acts of Parliament and over 3,000 statutory instruments. A small number of laws require that the statutory instruments issued under their authority must be laid before each house of Parliament in draft and approved by a vote in each house. The great majority of statutory instruments are simply reported to Parliament before they go into force; they may be blocked by a "negative resolution" of either house. Specialist committees scrutinize instruments that appear to raise issues of principle, but in practice very few indeed are objected to.

The Cabinet

Once the sovereign has invited a party leader to form a government as prime minister, usually after an election, it is for the new prime minister to select the other members of the cabinet and junior ministers. Cabinet ministers receive their seals of office from the monarch, but there is no requirement of parliamentary approval of the new cabinet or its program. Should a vote of "no confidence in Her Majesty's Government" be passed in the House of Commons, the government must either resign or advise the monarch to dissolve Parliament and call fresh elections.

The cabinet consists largely of secretaries of state for the various departments, with responsibilities determined by the prime minister. In recent years there has been a deputy prime minister, but this post is not formally established. The chancellor of the exchequer (effectively the minister of finance), the home secretary (responsible for matters such as the police and immigration policy), the foreign secretary, and until now the lord chancellor are seen as the senior ministers, but the prime minister is clearly the dominant figure. The cabinet usually meets weekly and has a number of standing committees, but the personality of the prime minister of the day determines whether decisions are genuinely decisions of the cabinet as such.

The Judiciary

In England and Wales there are High Court, circuit, and district judges appointed from the ranks of barristers (lawyers admitted to plead at the bar) and, less frequently, solicitors (lawyers with limited rights to practice before the courts). They preside over the civil courts (the High Court and the county courts) and the Crown Court, which deals with serious criminal cases. Lay magistrates, called justices of the peace, deal with minor criminal cases and some family cases. Appeals are heard by the Court of Appeal with a limited further appeal to the House of Lords. Northern Ireland has a similar but separate system.

Scotland has its own system of courts, with the same judges sitting in the Court of Session to deal with civil cases and in the High Court of Justiciary for criminal cases. Appeals lie to the Inner House of the Court of Session, with a limited further appeal to the House of Lords. Lower courts are presided over by sheriffs, each serving six geographical sheriffdoms.

Judges are appointed with full security of tenure until their retirement age, though powers do exist (but are rarely used) to remove a judge for incapacity or gross misconduct. The senior judges are treated with enormous respect: Every High Court judge becomes a knight or dame, and every Court of Session judge has the judicial title of lord. By a procedure known as judicial review, the judges can examine any administrative decision, for example, by a government minister, and can reverse any decision that is procedurally flawed or unreasonable. Ministers sometimes complain that the courts are frustrating their policies by such decisions, but respect for the judges and the rule of law overrules their complaints.

THE ELECTION PROCESS AND POLITICAL PARTICIPATION

The right to vote in parliamentary, local government, and European Parliament elections is given to anyone duly registered on the electoral roll for the relevant constituency. To be registered a person must be 18 years of age and a British citizen or a citizen of a Commonwealth country or the Republic of Ireland. Citizens of other EU countries may vote in local government and European Parliament elections. Convicted prisoners and members of the House of Lords have no vote. Voters must normally be resident in the constituency, but certain former residents living or serving in the armed forces abroad may also vote. In recent years, voting by post or via the Internet has been used on an experimental basis in selected areas. Voting is not compulsory; turnout for general elections has been falling in recent years and is now about 60 percent. The turnout in local government and European Parliament elections is much lower, typically 30 percent.

Elections to the House of Commons are conducted on the "first-past-the-post" system in single-member constituencies; the same system is used in most local government elections. Elections to the European Parliament are on a party list system with multimember constituencies. The Scottish Parliament, the Welsh Assembly, and the Greater London Assembly all have a dual system, with single-member constituencies and "additional members," the latter using the party list system. The Northern Ireland Assembly has multimember constituencies and uses the single transferable vote system, which is also used in the rest of Ireland.

There is no state funding for election campaigns, but there are tight limits on the amount that can be spent by any candidate: the figure varies with the size of the constituency, but in the 1997 election to the House of Commons it was about £40,000.

There is no regular practice of referendums, though several have been held under special acts of Parliament. Approval of the treaty for a European Union Constitution as drafted in 2004 will be the subject of a referendum.

POLITICAL PARTIES

The United Kingdom has a pluralistic system of political parties, which have no formal constitutional status. There is a system of registration of parties, but it exists mainly to protect the name and emblem of each party and to ensure proper financial control. It is only in recent times that the ballot papers for elections have identified the party allegiance of candidates. One consequence of registration is that it gives the registered party access to the times allocated for party political broadcasts on radio and television; these are typically five- or 10-minute broadcasts in the period before elections.

Since the early part of the 20th century there have been three major national parties: Labour, Conservative, and Liberal, now Liberal Democrat. The House of Commons also has members from regional parties: Plaid Cymru from Wales, the Scottish National Party, four Northern Ireland parties, and one or two Independents elected on particular issues. The United Kingdom Independence Party has seats in the European Parliament.

Parties represented in the House of Lords or the House of Commons receive some state financial support for their parliamentary work: The Conservative opposition received some £4 million in 2003–4, plus £500,000 for the expenses of the leader of the opposition's office.

The political parties have an influence that extends beyond their formal role. Appointment to public bodies, for example, health authorities serving local areas, is influenced by known party allegiance. Such appointments are not, however, formally political appointments, and a member's tenure survives any change in government.

CITIZENSHIP

The rules governing British nationality are very complex, with a number of categories resulting from the existence of dependent territories overseas. The principal type of citizenship, British citizen status, is enjoyed by anyone born in the United Kingdom, the Isle of Man, or the Channel Islands who has a parent who either (1) is a British citizen or (2) is or becomes settled in the United Kingdom. A child born overseas to a British citizen who was born in the United Kingdom also receives British citizen status. Persons in the other categories, such as British overseas territories citizens, can generally acquire full British citizenship by registration after a period of legal residence in the United Kingdom.

The principal significance of citizenship is associated with the right to reside permanently in the United Kingdom and to enter and leave it at will. The relationship between nationality and immigration law is, however, complex. For most purposes, Irish citizens and those from other European Union countries have rights very similar to those of British citizens.

FUNDAMENTAL RIGHTS

The absence of a written constitution necessarily means that there is no single legal document guaranteeing fundamental rights. The United Kingdom was an early party to the 1950 European Convention for the Protection of Human Rights and Fundamental Freedoms. This gave the right of access to the European Court of Human Rights, but since 1999 the convention has been incorporated in an act of Parliament and can be made the basis of claims in U.K. courts. There is no power to strike down an act of Parliament as inconsistent with the convention, but statutory instruments can be declared invalid on this basis. Legal provisions derived from the European Community have enhanced the law against discrimination on grounds of gender, age, race, and sexual orientation. These developments have had a considerable impact, but the absence of a constitution and a Constitutional Court means that there is little to say about the formal position of fundamental rights in U.K. law.

ECONOMY

Similarly, there can be no constitutional statements about the economy. The nationalization measures of the late 1940s and 1950s and the privatizations 20 years later raised no formal constitutional issues. If anything, financial institutions are being distanced from government: Interest rates are now set by the Monetary Policy Committee of the Bank of England; the Office of Fair Trading and the Office of Communications are examples of a growing number of regulatory bodies that enjoy some measure of independence.

RELIGIOUS COMMUNITIES

The United Kingdom now enjoys freedom of religion; the last restrictions on Roman Catholics were removed in the 19th century. That does not prevent, however, the existence of two established churches. There are an established church in England (the Church of England), of which the sovereign is supreme governor (but its associated Anglican churches in Wales and Northern Ireland have been disestablished), and an established church in Scotland (the Church of Scotland). The sovereign, supreme governor of an Episcopal church in the southern part of the kingdom, is a member of a reformed Presbyterian Church, the Church of Scotland, in the north.

The definition of the term *establishment* differs between the two countries. In Scotland, the church is declared by statutory law to have complete autonomy, while the Church of England is much more closely tied to the state. Its two archbishops and 24 other bishops sit in the House of Lords and its bishops are nominated by the sovereign on the advice of the prime minister. In practice, the church has real freedom. For example, the choice of bishops is restricted to those proposed by a church commission, and the General Synod of bishops and elected clergy and laity can enact legislation of equal force to acts of Parliament subject only to a single affirmative vote in each house of Parliament.

The churches play a fairly prominent part in public life despite the limited church attendance: Only some 3.5 million claim to be churchgoers. Each day's sitting of the House of Lords begins with prayers led by an Anglican bishop, and an Anglican priest performs a similar duty as speaker's chaplain in the Commons. The annual meeting of the General Assembly of the Church of Scotland is a significant national event. Hospitals, prisons, and the armed forces all have Christian chaplains paid for out of the relevant state budget, and provision is made for the spiritual needs of followers of other faiths. Particularly in rural areas, the parish church is the center of much community activity.

Neither of the two established churches receives funding from the state. There is no church tax, and the clergy must be paid, housed, and provided with pensions from the church's own resources. Church buildings are owned and maintained by the churches. The only exception is that repairs to churches listed as of historic or architectural interest are not subject to value-added tax at the usual rate, and various grants are made to pay for the repair of such churches, including the great cathedrals, and for the maintenance of redundant churches that are part of the architectural heritage.

All churches other than the two established churches and all groups of followers of other faiths are technically private charitable bodies, subject to the general law governing such bodies. There is no category of registered or recognized churches.

The churches, especially but not exclusively the two established churches, play a major part in the educational system, especially at primary school level (ages four to 11). Many schools are provided by a partnership of the church and the local education authority. There is provision for a daily act of worship in all schools; as some areas have a majority of children from non-Christian immigrant groups, the worship need not be exclusively Christian, but over the school year the predominant emphasis must be Christian. Religious education on a nondenominational Christian syllabus forms part of the basic school curriculum, though children may be withdrawn from those classes. Schools that have a distinctive religious foundation may teach on a denominational syllabus, and there are significant numbers of Anglican and Catholic schools that operate on this basis.

MILITARY DEFENSE AND STATE OF EMERGENCY

The sovereign is commander in chief of the Royal Navy, the army, and the Royal Air Force, but these standing forces are allowed only by act of Parliament and are controlled by the government through the secretary of state for defense. There is no compulsory military service. Total personnel in the forces number some 200,000 plus some 85,000 civilian support personnel. It is unclear whether the constitutional conventions require any parliamentary authorization of any major deployment of the forces outside the United Kingdom, but this has been sought in recent cases.

The administration has the right to take emergency powers when it finds that there is an event or situation that threatens serious damage to human welfare, the environment, or the security of the United Kingdom or any part of it. All these terms are closely defined, but include cases of disruption of the supply of money, food, water, energy, or fuel, or of services relating to health; contamination of land, water, or air with harmful biological, chemical, or radioactive matter, or flooding; war or armed conflict; and terrorism.

Where it is necessary to make new provision for the purpose of dealing with an actual or imminent emergency, the monarch may by order in council make emergency regulations; a senior minister may act if there would be serious delay in arranging a meeting of the Privy Council. Emergency regulations may make any provision that the person making the regulations thinks is for the purpose of preventing, controlling, or mitigating an aspect or effect of the emergency. They may deploy the armed forces; authorize the requisition, confiscation, or destruction of property (with or without compensation); prohibit or require movement to or from a specified place; prohibit assemblies of specified kinds; and prohibit travel and other specified activities. These powers were created in their present form in 2004; the earlier legislation had been used, apart from wartime, only to deal with the effects of serious industrial disputes.

AMENDMENTS TO THE CONSTITUTION

Since there is no written constitution, there is a continuing process of evolution in the workings of the political system. Some changes are brought about by formal means, for example, the changes in the composition of the upper House of Parliament, which were effected by statute. Others, often more subtle and gradual, may pass almost unnoticed until political leaders or commentators begin to identify a new constitutional convention.

PRIMARY SOURCES

Constitutional Law. Available online. URL: http://confinder.richmond.edu/uk.htm. Accessed on September 19, 2005.

SECONDARY SOURCES

A. W. Bradley and K. Ewing, *Constitutional and Administrative Law*. 13th ed. London: Longman, 2003.
R. J. Brazier, *Constitutional Practice*. 3d ed. Oxford: Oxford University Press, 1999.
V. Bogdanor, ed., *The British Constitution in the Twentieth Century*. Oxford: Oxford University Press, 2003.
D. Oliver, *Constitutional Reform in the United Kingdom*. Oxford: Oxford University Press, 2003.

David McClean

UNITED STATES

At-a-Glance

OFFICIAL NAME
United States of America

CAPITAL
Washington, D.C.

POPULATION
295,734,134 (2005 est.)

SIZE
3,679,192 sq. mi. (9,529,063 sq. km)

LANGUAGES
English

RELIGIONS
Christian 77.25%, Jewish 1.0%, Muslim 1.0%, Buddhist 0.38%, Hindu 0.27%, Native American 0.04%, Baha'i 0.03%, Taoist 0.01%, no religion/atheist and other 20.02%

NATIONAL OR ETHNIC COMPOSITION
White 81.7%, African American 12.9%, Asian 4.2%, Native American 1.0%, Native Hawaiian and Pacific Islander 0.2%

DATE OF INDEPENDENCE OR CREATION
July 4, 1776

TYPE OF GOVERNMENT
Representative democracy

TYPE OF STATE
Federal republic

TYPE OF LEGISLATURE
Bicameral congress

DATE OF CONSTITUTION
June 21, 1788

DATE OF LAST AMENDMENT
May 7, 1992

The United States of America is a federal state comprising 50 autonomous regional provinces, called states, plus the District of Columbia, which serves as the capital.

The federal legislature, called Congress, is made up of the Senate and the House of Representatives and is located in the Capitol Building in Washington, D.C. The president of the United States is head of the executive branch of the federal government. Executive functions of the federal government are executed through a number of departments. Executive departments are headed by a member of the cabinet, most of whom are called the secretary of the department concerned. (The attorney general, who heads the Department of Justice, is a notable exception.).

The judicial function at the federal level is executed by a hierarchy of federal courts, including district courts, circuit courts of appeal, and the United States Supreme Court. The Supreme Court, apart from its role as final appeals court, has jurisdiction to consider the constitutionality of laws and of executive acts and decisions, both at the federal and at the state level.

Each of the 50 states has its own constitution; legislature; executive government, headed by a governor; and court system. Leaving aside the institutions of local (municipal) government, state authority in the United States is consequently made up of 51 legislatures, systems of law, governmental structures, and judicial institutions.

The United States has a common law legal system based on English law, except, that is, Louisiana, which has in part a civil law system. Much of the common law has been superseded by legislative provisions. Common law crimes have all been replaced by statutory crimes, and criminal prosecutions can therefore no longer be based on the common law.

CONSTITUTIONAL HISTORY

The history of the United States begins with the discovery of the New World by Christopher Columbus (1451–1506), who set foot on the Caribbean islands off the coast of North America in 1492. Although an Italian by birth (as Christoforo Columbo), he sailed under the banner of Spain.

Columbus's three journeys to America opened the door for several European countries, notably England, France, Holland, Spain, and Portugal, to establish colonies in the Americas, some under the auspices of private corporations rather than the state.

The first permanent British settlement in North America was established in 1607 by Captain John Smith at Jamestown, Virginia. In 1620, a group of religiously motivated immigrants led by William Brewster and William Bradford, first known as Separatists but later as Pilgrims, crossed the Atlantic Ocean in the *Mayflower* and established a British colony at New Plymouth, Massachusetts. This settlement soon expanded to include all of what are now the New England states (Maine, New Hampshire, Vermont, Massachusetts, Rhode Island, and Connecticut).

Tensions between the motherland and the North American colonies emerged in the 18th century. The colonists lamented that though compelled by the British Parliament to pay taxes, they had no representation in the legislature. The conflict founded on the principle of "no taxation without representation" reached a peak with the Boston Tea Party of December 16, 1773, when a group of people disguised as Native Americans boarded three ships in Boston harbor and threw a valuable consignment of tea overboard in protest against the tea tax. The British authorities retaliated in 1774 by closing the harbor.

This led to a call for civil disobedience, which finally sparked the American Revolution (1775–83), during which 13 North American colonies on July 4, 1776, collectively declared themselves independent of British rule. Independence of the United States of America was recognized by Britain through the Treaty of Paris of September 3, 1783.

The newly established state extended its borders during the 18th and early 19th centuries, eventually to embrace the entire mainland of North America from the Atlantic Ocean in the east to the Pacific Ocean in the west and between the Gulf of Mexico and Mexico in the south and Canada in the north. New Amsterdam, a Dutch possession, was annexed by the English in 1664 and included in the original 13 states as the state of New York; through the Louisiana Purchase of 1803 the United States acquired from France a vast stretch of land that today includes all or part of the states of Louisiana, Missouri, Arkansas, Iowa, Nebraska, North Dakota, South Dakota, Montana, Minnesota, Kansas, New Mexico, Texas, Wyoming, Colorado, and Oklahoma; Florida was initially under Spanish rule, was ceded to England in 1763, was returned to Spain in 1783, and was finally purchased by the United States in 1819 to become the 27th state in 1845; after the Mexican War (1846–48), the United States acquired New Mexico and California and established a clear title to Texas; Utah was developed by members of the Church of Jesus Christ of Latter-day Saints (Mormons) in the mid-19th century and admitted to the union in 1896. Further states beyond the boundaries mentioned became part of the United States in the mid-20th century: Alaska, purchased from Russia in 1867, became a state in 1959, and Hawaii, which ceded itself to the United States in 1898, became the 50th state in 1959.

The unity of the United States was placed in peril by the American Civil War (1861–65) between the southern Confederate States of America and the (northern) Union states, better known in the southern states as the War between the States. Central to the tensions that culminated in the war was the question of slavery; a dispute that in part was fueled by a decision of the U.S. Supreme Court in the *Dred Scott* case of 1857 that held unconstitutional a law of Congress that prohibited slavery in a defined part of the United States. The Confederate States claimed jurisdiction in matters related to the institution of slavery and a right to secede from the union, while the Union states primarily opposed the right to secession but also favored emancipation of the slaves. Upon the election of Abraham Lincoln (1809–65) in 1861 as the 16th president of the United States, the Confederate States seceded from the union, and the newly elected president thereupon took military action to preserve the union. President Lincoln in 1863 announced the Emancipation Proclamation granting freedom to all slaves. The war cost the lives of 359,528 Union and 258,000 Confederate troops. In the end, the Union forces triumphed after the surrender by the Confederate commander, Robert E. Lee (1807–70), on April 9, 1865. Five days later, on April 14, President Lincoln was assassinated by a Confederate sympathizer.

In 1781, the 13 states in a first attempt to establish a national government ratified the Articles of Confederation. This constitutional instrument provided the national government with very little power and was for that reason quite impractical. The Articles of Confederation were superseded by the U.S. Constitution of 1788, which reflected a desire for more centralized political coordination. The Constitution was for that reason opposed by antifederalists.

The land now constituting the United States of America was at the time of European settlements occupied by numerous Native American tribes, who had lived in that part of the world for probably many millennia. It is believed that these peoples migrated to North America during the Ice Age when a geological land bridge connected Siberia and Alaska. Native American tribes are today largely located in reservations in Arizona, New Mexico, Utah, Oklahoma, Texas, Montana, Washington, North and South Dakota, and Wyoming by the terms of treaties concluded between the United States and several of the tribes. The Native Americans gained U.S. citizenship in 1924, but those living in a tribal setting are precluded from the protections afforded by the American Bill of Rights. Instead, they are protected from excesses of tribal authorities by the Indian Civil Rights Act of 1968. Though the civil rights of Native Americans are modeled on those listed in the U.S. Bill of Rights, their application is somewhat different.

The United States is a founding member of the United Nations Organization and of the North Atlantic Treaty

Organization. It is a permanent member of the Security Council of the United Nations and plays a leading role in international relations. It is a member of the Organization of American States and is as such subject to the jurisdiction of the Inter-American Commission on Human Rights.

The United States has ratified several international human rights conventions, namely, the Convention on the Prevention and Punishment of the Crime of Genocide (1948), the International Convention on the Elimination of All Forms of Racial Discrimination (1965), the International Covenant on Civil and Political Rights (1966), and the International Convention against Torture and Other Cruel, Inhuman or Degrading Treatment or Punishment (1984). It should be noted, though, that the United States subjected the ratification of those international instruments to a package of reservations, understandings, and declarations to ensure, among other points, that its international obligations will not require the United States to change any of its existing laws or practices. The United States is one of only two countries in the world that have not ratified the Convention on the Rights of the Child, although in 2003 it did ratify two protocols to that convention dealing with involvement of children in armed conflict and the prohibition of the sale of children, child prostitution, and child pornography.

FORM AND IMPACT OF THE CONSTITUTION

The Constitution of the United States is contained in a single document, which has the highest legal and political impact on the life of the nation.

Although the United States upholds a principle that renders judicial precedents binding on courts lower in status and generally controlling subsequent decisions of the same court (stare decisis), constitutional questions, ultimately the preserve of the U.S. Supreme Court, are considered always to be open to reinterpretation.

Justices of the U.S. Supreme Court have not upheld a consistent doctrine of statutory interpretation. Two major schools have emerged in this regard: the strict interpretationists and the revisionists.

Strict interpretationists emphasize the restrictions imposed on the judiciary by the actual language and history of the Constitution. An extreme brand of interpretationism has favored a literal construction of the Constitution. Another seeks to uncover the meaning of constitutional provisions as actually contemplated by the drafters at the time of their enactment. There is a general tendency among Supreme Court justices to subject at least the religion clauses of the First Amendment to such an "original intent" construction.

The most radical variety of revisionism, commonly referred to as judicial activism, reflects a desire to conform to major trends of public opinion and a commitment to respond to social injustices as perceived by the judges. In some instances, judicial activism ignores the drafters' original intent and reflects little regard for the actual wording of the Constitution.

Central to the idea of the rule of law as a basic principle of the U.S. legal system is the concept of legality: that the rights and duties of anyone subordinate to state authority, as well as the powers and responsibilities of governmental agencies, ought to be prescribed by, and executed subject to, clearly defined rules of law. The opposite of the rule of law in this sense is arbitrary powers of the repositories of state authority.

In principle, the legal system of the United States complies with the rule of law in the sense that all governmental powers, including those of the legislatures and executive institutions, must be exercised subject to the substantive and procedural provisions of the federal and state constitutions. On the other hand, the individual rights provisions of the United States Constitution clearly lack the measure of precision required by the legal certainty prong of the principle of legality. Given the wide powers of interpretation of courts of law that attend such generalities in statutory language (especially as construed by judicial activists), the United States Constitution is perhaps conducive to a gouvernement des juges, a government of judges, rather than to strict constitutionalism.

The president of the United States while in office can probably not be prosecuted for criminal conduct other than through impeachment and removal from office. The president furthermore enjoys sovereign immunity that precludes injunctions and civil actions for money damages based on acts committed while in office. However, the Nixon tapes case dramatically illustrated that even the president is not above the law, that the privilege of confidentiality of his conversations and correspondence "must be considered in light of our historic commitment to the rule of law" and weighed against "the inroads of such a privilege on the fair administration of criminal justice," and that "the legitimate needs of the judicial process may outweigh presidential privilege" (United States v. Nixon, 1974).

In terms of the Eleventh Amendment to the Constitution of the United States, a state enjoys sovereign immunity from "suits in law or equity" in federal courts commenced or prosecuted by a citizen of another state or of a foreign country. Under broader constitutional principles, the sovereign immunity of states extends further, to include all civil actions by private persons. Except for the power of Congress to enforce, by appropriate legislation, the provisions of the Fourteenth Amendment, the federal legislature cannot abrogate a state's sovereign immunity by affording a cause of action to private persons to bring suit against a state without the state's consent (Seminole Tribe of Florida v. Florida, 1996).

BASIC ORGANIZATIONAL STRUCTURE

The United States of America is made up of 50 autonomous states, plus the District of Columbia, which is the capital.

The United States also has several possessions outside its national borders that do not form part of the union as states. It upholds special relations with Puerto Rico, an island commonwealth in the West Indies, which was ceded to the United States after the Spanish-American War of 1898 and acquired commonwealth status with local self-government in 1952. The population is divided on the question whether the islands should become independent or be fully incorporated into the United States as a separate state. Other unincorporated territories of the United States include Guam, the Northern Mariana Islands, and the Virgin Islands.

The United States in 1788 selected for itself a federal constitution, described by Chief Justice Marshall as "the rare and difficult scheme of one general government, whose action extends over the whole, but which possesses only certain enumerated powers, and of numerous state governments, which retain and exercise all powers not delegated to the Union" (*Gibbons v. Ogden,* 1824).

Defining the powers of the federal government and vesting all residual powers in the states derived from a belief that the central governmental authorities were the ones that would most likely be inclined to abuse those powers. However, it emerged over the years that the states could also abuse their powers. In part for that reason perhaps, the federal structure envisioned by the founding fathers was considerably eroded. The power of Congress "[t]o regulate Commerce ... among the several States" (U.S. Constitution, art. 1, sec. 8, clause [3]) has thus been applied to justify federal jurisdiction over a wide range of issues that are not expressly mentioned among the enumerated powers of the Congress and may not be of an obviously commercial nature.

Federalism is probably more broadly practiced in the United States than in any other state in the world. The union and the 50 states are each regarded as distinct sovereign entities. In terms of the doctrine of multiple sovereignties, the legal systems of each political component constituting the United States are treated as distinct sovereign regimes.

The executive and legislative systems of the states in many respects resemble those operating at the federal level, including, for example, the institution of a single and separately elected head of government, called a governor. All the states but one (Nebraska) also have a bicameral legislature, with a state Senate and a state House of Representatives or Assembly.

The legislative process also resembles that applicable to federal legislation, and state legislation can also be vetoed by the executive. When a bill has been passed by the state legislature, the executive can return the bill with a veto message. If the executive does not sign the bill or return it with a message of disapproval, the bill becomes law after a prescribed number of days. If the legislature adjourns before the governor's time for signing the bill has expired, the bill does not become law unless it is signed by the governor.

The demarcation of functions between the federal and state governmental authorities is fraught with difficulties. The Constitution enumerates the specific powers of Congress, and in terms of the Tenth Amendment to the Constitution (1791), the powers not delegated to the federal executive and legislature vest in the states.

The question whether the Tenth Amendment can be invoked to invalidate congressional legislation that intrudes upon the states' "right to federalism" is controversial. Two different views seem to predominate in this regard, the one holding that the Tenth Amendment was not intended to limit the legislative powers of Congress but merely serves as a reminder that Congress can only legislate on matters stipulated in Article 1 of the Constitution, the other maintaining that the Tenth Amendment protects the sovereignty of states against intrusions by the federal legislature.

According to the first view, one cannot rely on the Tenth Amendment per se to contest the constitutionality of federal laws but must instead base one's case on the federal legislature's having exceeded the powers of Congress stipulated in the Constitution. The second view would have it that the Tenth Amendment does reserve a zone of powers for the states and can therefore be used to substantiate a finding of unconstitutionality of congressional legislation. At different times, the U.S. Supreme Court has supported one or the other of these two views. In recent times it has demonstrated a renewed leaning toward the second approach.

There has been a general tendency to extend federal powers over a fairly wide spectrum, relying mainly on the power of Congress "[t]o regulate Commerce . . . among the several States," as proclaimed in Article 1, section 8, clause [3]. Matters held to lie within the commerce clause included a wide range of subject matters, some of which have at best a remote effect on interstate commerce, such as racial discrimination in restaurants, hotels, and other public places. More recently, the U.S. Supreme Court, relying more on the Tenth Amendment, has tended toward restricting federal powers founded on the commerce clause in three distinct areas.

Congress cannot rely on the commerce clause to "commandeer" the governmental functions of the states. The U.S. Supreme Court therefore invalidated a provision in the Low-Level Radioactive Waste Policy Amendment Act (1985) that mandated states to "take title" to any privately owned hazardous waste within their borders that was not disposed of in accordance with requirements specified in the act (*New York v. United States,* 1992), as well as a federal law that required local sheriffs to conduct background checks on gun purchasers (*Prinz v. United States,* 1997).

Congress cannot rely on the commerce clause to regulate activities that have very little effect on interstate commerce or any sort of economic enterprise. The U.S. Supreme Court therefore declared unconstitutional the federal Gun-Free School Zones Act (1990), which prohibited the possession of a firearm in or near a school (*United States v. Lopez,* 1995), as well as the Violence against Women Act (1994), which rendered punishable "crimes of violence motivated by gender" (*United States v. Morrison*, 2000).

Congress cannot abrogate the sovereign immunity of states, which renders them immune from private suits for money damages, except when acting to enforce the Reconstruction amendments. The U.S. Supreme Court therefore invalidated provisions in the Indian Gaming Regulatory Act (1988) that (1) authorized Native American tribes to conduct certain gaming activities under the terms of agreements with state governments, (2) imposed a duty on states to negotiate such agreements, and (3) authorized a tribe to bring suit in a federal court to compel a state to comply with that duty (*Seminole Tribe of Florida v. Florida*, 1996). After this decision, the Court also held that Congress overstepped its powers when it authorized actions by private persons, even in state courts, for damages incurred through a state's violation of the Fair Labor Standards Act (1938) enacted under the commerce clause (*Alden v. Maine*, 1999).

In terms of the "full faith and credit clause" in the Constitution (art. 1, sec. 1), each state is obliged to respect and to uphold "the public Acts, Records, and judicial Proceedings of every other State." Federal legislation similarly requires federal courts to respect state acts, records, and judicial proceedings to the extent that they are valid in state courts. Recently, the question arose whether or not states would be bound to afford "full faith and credit" to same-sex marriages legally concluded in another state. The Defense of Marriage Act (1996) answered this question in the negative. A constitutional amendment to bar such marriages in any state failed in 2006.

LEADING CONSTITUTIONAL PRINCIPLES

The Declaration of Independence of July 4, 1776, spelled out the kind of social institution the United States of America aspired to become:

> We hold these truths to be self-evident: that all men are created equal; that they are endowed, by their Creator, with certain inalienable rights; that among these are life, liberty, and the pursuit of happiness. That to secure these rights, governments are instituted among men, deriving their just powers from the consent of the governed; that whenever any form of government becomes destructive of these ends, it is the right of the people to alter or abolish it, and to institute a new government, laying the foundation on such principles, and organizing its powers in such form, as to them shall seem likely to effect their safety and happiness.

The Constitution of the United States of America ratified in 1788 bears testimony of the founding fathers' distrust of the concentration of political power by the central government. The Constitution indeed differed from the earlier Articles of Confederation in being more conducive to centralized political coordination, but precautions to prevent the abuse of powers by the state remained a general characteristic of the American constitutional system.

The Constitution can be said to uphold the basic principles of representative democracy, separation of powers, federalism, the rule of law, and separation of church and state.

CONSTITUTIONAL BODIES

The predominant constitutional organs at the federal level are the federal executive administration, headed by the president and vice president; Congress as the federal legislature; and the U.S. Supreme Court. The courts, including the U.S. Supreme Court, have immense impact on the legal system.

The constitutional structure of the United States does indeed comply to a large degree with the contemporary notion of the separation of powers. It differentiates among the legislative, executive, and judicial components of state authority and applies the principle that persons serving in the one branch of state authority may not serve in any of the others. Members of the executive government are therefore disqualified from also being part of the legislature or the judiciary, and the same exclusionary rule applies to members of the other two branches.

However, the constitutional system of the United States ordains an elaborate system of checks and balances, which has resulted in a certain overlap of functions. The power of the president to veto congressional legislation, for instance, amounts to the performance of a legislative function by the head of the executive; the power of the Senate to impeach the president and members of the judiciary, to performance of judicial function by a legislative organ; the courts' power of substantive review, seen in conjunction with the sweeping language of the Constitution of the United States and of the constituent states, vests in the judiciary elaborate law- and rule-making powers.

The Federal Executive Government

The president of the United States is the executive head of government. The president appoints and presides over the cabinet, consisting of a secretary as the political head of each state department, or in the case of the department of justice, the attorney general. The president is commander in chief of the armed forces and of the militias of the states. The president enjoys executive privileges in respect of communications with advisers and may not be sued in civil proceedings for conduct while in office. The president can pardon offenses against the United States. The president enters into treaties with foreign governments, subject, however, to ratification by a two-thirds majority in the Senate. The president can enter into international agreements with another head of state, without Senate approval, although Congress decides what matters can be included in such agreements. The president annually delivers a state of the union address to Congress, outlining the administration's domestic and foreign policy for the coming year.

The major political parties (the Democratic Party and the Republican Party) designate their candidates for the presidency primarily via primary elections held in each state, or until a clear trend in favor of one candidate drives the others from the contest. Nothing prevents any person not associated with the major parties to present him- or herself for election to the presidency, although in most states it is difficult for such an independent to win a place on the ballot. In many states, the right to vote for a candidate of a particular party in primary elections is not limited to members of the party. The major parties nominate their candidates for president and vice president at a national convention convened after the primaries have been held.

The president is elected by an electoral college composed of representatives of the 50 states. The number of electors from each state equals the combined total of the state's representatives in the Senate and the House of Representatives; the latter number in turn depends on the state's population at the most recent decennial census. Though not required by law, by convention the electors cast the state's vote for the candidate who won the most votes there. In two states only, electors are chosen by congressional districts rather than statewide; the state's electoral votes may thus be split between two candidates.

The presidential candidate who receives an absolute majority in the electoral college is president. Because of the composition of the electoral college and the winner-takes-all system that applies in a vast majority of states, the person elected as president may not have the support of a majority of the voters who participated in the elections. Should no candidate receive an absolute majority (50 percent plus one) of the electoral votes, the president is elected by the House of Representatives from among the top three contenders for the presidency, with the representatives of each state casting only one vote.

The vice president is by a constitutional convention elected together with the president on one joint "ticket" and is nearly always a member of the same party.

The president and vice president hold office for a period of four years and can be reelected. However, the president can be reelected for only one further term of office. Should the president through death or otherwise vacate the office of head of state, the vice president automatically becomes the president for the unexpired term of the presidency.

The president and vice president may be removed from office on impeachment by the House of Representatives on grounds of "treason, bribery, and other high crimes and misdemeanors." The actual impeachment trial is conducted in the Senate. Conviction of the president requires a two-thirds majority of the senators present.

Impeachment proceedings have been brought against Presidents Andrew Johnson (1865–69) and William Jefferson Clinton (1993–2001). President Johnson's impeachment was based on the dismissal from office of the secretary of war, Edwin Stanton, in violation of a statute of Congress. He escaped conviction and removal from office by only one vote in the Senate. President Clinton's impeachment resulted from an affair the president had with a White House intern, Monica Lewinsky. He was acquitted in the Senate. In 1974, impeachment proceedings were also initiated against President Richard Nixon (1969–73) in the House of Representative's Judicial Committee, but he resigned before the house could put the matter to a vote. These proceedings were based on a cover-up by the president in the so-called Watergate scandal.

The Federal Legislature

The United States has a bicameral federal legislature, the Congress, which consists of an upper house, the Senate, and a lower house, the House of Representatives.

There are 100 senators: two for each state. Senators are elected by the electorate of the state that they represent in Congress. Each senator is elected to serve for a term of six years and can be reelected without limit. In order to ensure continuity, only one-third of the senators are subject to election every two years.

A senator must be at least 30 years of age, be a U.S. citizen for a period of no fewer than nine years, and be a resident of the state from which he or she is elected (though residency requirements vary between the states, almost vanishing in some cases). A candidate may be placed on the state ballot by either a major or a minor political party or present him- or herself for election as an independent candidate. If a candidate is opposed within the same party, primary elections are held to designate the party's candidate. Each voter has one vote, and the person who receives the most votes will be duly elected to the Senate.

The vice president of the United States is through the office president of the Senate. He or she has no vote in the Senate, unless there is a tie vote on any issue, in which event the vice president can cast a vote.

In impeachment proceedings, a decision to bring charges originates in the House of Representatives, but the Senate has sole power to try all impeachments. A decision of the Senate to impeach a president requires a two-thirds majority of all members present. Ratification of all treaties made by the United States also requires a two-thirds majority of all senators present. The Senate must give its consent for the appointment of ambassadors, other ministers and consuls, judges of the Supreme Court, and other officers of the United States by a simple majority.

The House of Representatives consists of 435 members, each serving for a period of two years. They can be reelected without limit. A representative must be at least 25 years of age, be a citizen of the United States for no fewer than seven years, and be resident in the state from which he or she is elected.

The number of seats in the House of Representatives allocated to each state depends on the state's population in the previous census (which is held every 10 years). Each state is divided into congressional districts based on the number of representatives of the particular state.

Nearly all representatives are elected from single-member districts within each state, which must be of equal population. "Gerrymandering" is the practice of demarcating electoral districts so as to benefit one party, often by concentrating the other party's votes in a handful of lopsided one-party districts. Gerrymandering has long been commonplace in state legislative as well as congressional districts; minority parties within each state have frequently called for nonpartisan commissions to take over the process.

Candidates for election to the House of Representatives may be members of one of the major political parties or a minor party or may run for office as independent candidates. Many states hold primary elections to designate candidates. Only voters registered in a particular congressional district may vote for a representative of that district in a primary or general election.

All laws with taxation implications must be introduced in the House of Representatives first. The House of Representatives must initiate impeachment proceedings, which then go before the Senate for adjudication.

The Federal Lawmaking Process

The Senate and the House of Representatives must approve federal laws in identical form. If the two houses pass different versions, consensus is sought via a "conference committee" with three to five members from each house. A compromise report may then be referred to both houses, which must both approve the compromise without amendment for the bill to pass.

Bills adopted by Congress are signed into law by the president of the United States, who may veto a bill adopted by Congress. Congress, in turn, can override a presidential veto by adopting the bill in a subsequent session with a two-thirds majority in both houses of Congress.

The Judiciary

The highest court in the United States is the U.S. Supreme Court. There are nine Supreme Court justices, comprising the chief justice and eight associate justices. They are appointed for life by the president of the United States and must be approved by the Senate. Supreme Court justices can be removed from office by impeachment for serious misconduct.

The Supreme Court hears appeals from decisions of the U.S. Court of Appeals and from the supreme courts of states. It also has appellate jurisdiction to resolve disputes between the executive and legislative branches of the federal government. The main focus of litigation in the U.S. Supreme Court concerns the interpretation of statutes and the constitutionality of legislation and of executive acts and decisions.

Federal courts lower in status are divided into district courts and courts of appeal. Judges of the federal courts are appointed for life by the president of the United States and must be approved by the Senate. They can be dismissed from office by impeachment for serious misconduct.

In 1968, a new lower tier was added to the federal court system, that of United States magistrates. Magistrates are appointed by the district judges of each district. They assist the district courts in the administration of justice by executing a variety of powers, such as issuing warrants, conducting preliminary examinations, and imposing conditions for the release on bail of a criminal defendant. They can also try misdemeanors, but the defendant can insist on being tried by the district court.

The states have their own court systems, comprising one or more trial courts (Indiana, Louisiana, and Michigan have two or more courts of general jurisdiction), intermediary courts of appeals (in 39 states), and supreme courts. These courts have jurisdiction in both civil and criminal cases.

There is a rich variety of systems in place to designate judges to state courts. In many states, judges, or some of them, are appointed by the governor; in other states they are elected by the voters.

Some states where judges are appointed have adopted the so-called merit plan or commission plan. Typically, a permanent, nonpartisan commission composed of both lawyers and nonlawyers recruits and screens persons to be considered for judicial appointment and forwards a list of several names to the executive, which appoints one person from the list to the judicial office. In most cases the appointee serves for a probation period of one or two years, upon which the appointee's name is submitted to the electorate in an unopposed ballet for confirmation. The question put to the electorate simply inquires whether the person concerned should be retained in office.

There are four states (California, Maine, New Hampshire, and New Jersey) where the governor appoints judges without inviting nominations from a commission. In three states (Hawaii, Louisiana, and Illinois) sitting judges appoint some of the newcomers to the bench. In Virginia, the legislature appoints all the judges.

In 21 states judges to the state supreme court are elected: eight of those in partisan elections and the remainder in nonpartisan elections. Of the 39 states that have intermediate courts of appeal, 17 have systems for the election of those judges, of which seven abide by partisan elections and 10 put candidates forward for election on a nonpartisan basis. As far as trial court judges are concerned, 13 states hold partisan elections for the designation of judges to those courts, and 17 prefer nonpartisan elections.

In most of the states one also finds a variety of special jurisdiction courts. The jurisdiction of those courts may in criminal matters be limited to preliminary proceedings or lesser offenses. A special jurisdiction court might be confined to a certain subject matter, such as water law.

Justices of the peace preside in civil matters in which the issue in dispute falls below a certain pecuniary limit.

Federal courts have limited subject matter jurisdiction in civil cases. In many cases, federal and state courts have concurrent jurisdiction, but there are several categories of civil cases in respect of which jurisdiction has been reserved by Congress for the federal courts, such as cases dealing with bankruptcy, copyright, or patent law. Besides their concurrent jurisdiction to hear civil matters, state courts have a substantial realm of exclusive jurisdiction in criminal cases.

Plaintiffs thus often have discretion to bring an action in either the federal or the state courts. If a case involves diversity jurisdiction—the plaintiff and the defendant reside in different states, or one party is a citizen of the United States while the other is a citizen of another country—or the case has "arisen" under federal law, either party to the dispute can place the case before the federal court. If the plaintiff has elected to proceed in a state court, the defendant may in almost all circumstances "remove" the case to the federal court.

The dual system of adjudication also applies to criminal cases. Federal courts have exclusive jurisdiction to hear criminal charges based on the law of nations (customary international law) or international crimes incorporated in the criminal code of the United States by implementing legislation. Federal courts have jurisdiction to try crimes enacted by Congress, while charges deriving from laws enacted by state legislatures must be brought in state courts. Federal crimes and state crimes do, however, overlap to a great degree. The dual system of criminal laws deriving from the federal structure of the United States has discreet implications for the rule against double jeopardy.

In the United States, the rule against double jeopardy precludes a subsequent prosecution "for the same crime," and not, as in many other jurisdictions, for the same conduct. American courts have interpreted the federal structure of the United States to afford to different states as against one another, and to the union as against a state or a state as against the union, separate sovereign status. The dual sovereignty doctrine has led the U.S. Supreme Court to decide that successive prosecutions by two states for the same conduct are not barred by the rule against double jeopardy, and that prosecution in the federal courts is not precluded by the conviction or acquittal of the same accused for the same conduct, or vice versa. As stated in *Heath v. Alabama*, 1985: "The dual sovereignty doctrine is founded on the common-law conception of crime as an offense against the sovereignty of the government. When a defendant in a single act violates the 'peace and dignity' of two sovereigns by breaking the laws of each, he or she has committed two distinct 'offenses.'"

Criminal procedure in the United States is founded on the adversarial system with the burden of producing evidence and of proof resting on the state. The rules of procedure and evidence are founded on basic principles of criminal justice (the due process of law) and require the state to prove the guilt of a defendant beyond reasonable doubt. The prosecutor has the discretion to press charges. The judge functions as an independent arbiter but must uphold the presumption of innocence that applies to all persons charged with criminal conduct. Many criminal cases are disposed of through plea bargaining, whereby the prosecution and defense counsel agree on a plea of guilty to be entered by the defendant and the punishment to be imposed for the offense, the latter subject to confirmation by the judge.

In many jurisdictions in the United States, courts hearing civil cases are entitled to award to a successful plaintiff punitive damages in addition to the damages awarded for actual pecuniary loss or compensation granted for harm suffered.

In civil cases, each party to the dispute may pay his or her own legal expenses irrespective of the outcome of the case. Alternatively, a contingency fee system relieves the plaintiff from paying legal fees but entitles legal counsel to a percentage of the award made by the court in favor of his or her client or upon reaching a favorable settlement of the dispute out of court. A reverse contingency fee would make the fee of counsel for the defendant dependent in whole or in part on the amount saved by his or her client, given his or her potential liability in the case.

Civil procedure in the United States also makes allowance for class actions that permit a single person or a small group of persons to take action in the interest of a larger group. A class action is only feasible if members of the group have the same cause of action and the legal and factual questions of the case are common to the class.

The system of civil procedure of the United States is also unique in that it applies the principle of universal jurisdiction to civil suits for compensation. By virtue of the Alien Tort Statute (2004), formerly the Alien Tort Claims Act (1789), federal courts have original jurisdiction to award damages to an alien for a tort committed by an alien in a foreign country in violation of the law of nations (customary international law) or of a treaty ratified by the United States.

THE ELECTION PROCESS AND POLITICAL PARTICIPATION

Representative government in a democratic polity rests on the assumptions that persons in authority ought to be designated by those subject to their power, and that a government that does not comply with the popular demands of the people may be deprived of its power in periodic elections.

In the United States special precautions prevail to uphold the essential components of democracy: universal suffrage irrespective of wealth, race, or gender; a free press and unrestrained canvassing of persons running for office to ensure the exercise of an informed choice by the voters; free and regular elections; equal weighting of votes; and accurate calculation of votes.

In the United States there are also instances of direct democracy. Referenda are held fairly regularly at the state level in conjunction with general elections to obtain the consent of the people for a (state) constitutional amendment or to gain popular support for state legislation or on matters of important public interest. A number of states, notably California, also apply the initiative, by which a certain percentage of voters proposes legislation stipulated in a proposition or compels a vote on the subject matter of the proposition by the state legislature or by the full electorate.

On the other hand, however, the power of courts of law—composed at the federal level and in some state courts of unelected judges who are not directly responsible to the people—to invalidate legislation and executive acts of democratically elected legislators and administrations might be seen as a decidedly undemocratic element within the governmental structures of the United States.

CITIZENSHIP

American law makes a distinction between citizens of the United States and nationals. All citizens are nationals, but not all nationals are citizens. Nationals are those who owe allegiance to the United States, including persons who are not citizens but were born in outlying possessions of the United States, such as Wake Island or Midway Island.

Citizenship derives from birth or naturalization. All persons born in the United States are citizens by birth of the United States. If a person has been born outside the territorial borders of the United States, that person becomes a U.S. citizen by birth if both parents are U.S. citizens. If one parent is a U.S. citizen and the other is a national but not a citizen, the child born in a foreign country becomes a citizen by birth if the citizen parent was physically present in the United States or in one of the outlying possessions for a continued period of one year prior to the child's birth. In cases of a child born out of wedlock in a foreign country, citizenship by birth attaches to the child if the mother was a U.S. citizen at the time of giving birth and had formerly been present in the United States or an outlying possession for a continued period of at least one year.

A child of non-U.S. citizens born in a foreign country can claim U.S. citizenship if the parents become naturalized, the child is taken to the United States before acquiring adult status, and the child upon becoming an adult claims U.S. citizenship.

A person can become a citizen of the United States through naturalization after having resided in the United States for a period of at least five years as an alien resident (someone who has permanent resident status). Naturalized citizens enjoy all the rights attaching to citizenship but one: A citizen through naturalization cannot become president of the United States.

The U.S. Constitution also attributes to U.S. citizens citizenship of a state, depending on the state where the person resides.

Citizens of the United States have a number of special rights, including the right to enter and to depart from the United States. Citizens therefore have a right to obtain a passport for travel abroad. The Unites States can prevent its citizens from traveling in hostile countries where such travel could endanger the safety of U.S. citizens.

Citizens traveling abroad retain the protection of the United States. If the U.S. citizen is arrested in a foreign country, the U.S. embassy in that country seeks to ensure that his or her rights are properly protected.

The primary obligations of citizens of the United States are loyalty and allegiance to the country.

Certain constitutional rights, such as the right to vote, are reserved for citizens of the United States. Other rights belong to every person, irrespective of nationality. It has been decided that individual rights protections afforded by the Fourteenth Amendment to the U.S. Constitution also apply to nondocumented (illegal) immigrants and that such persons cannot be treated as a "suspect class" merely because their presence in the United States is not legal (*Plyler v. Doe,* 1982).

In 1996, Congress enacted the Personal Responsibility and Work Opportunity Reconciliation Act, which granted elaborate welfare and public benefits, including child support, to aliens. Nondocumented aliens who are not "qualified aliens" as defined in the act are not eligible for "federal public benefits" but are, on the other hand, not precluded from benefits such as primary and secondary education.

FUNDAMENTAL RIGHTS

The 1789 Constitution is a cryptic document outlining purely formal matters such as the composition and legislative powers of Congress, the election and functions of the president, the institution and jurisdiction of courts of law, autonomy of the states and admission of new states to the union, amendment of the Constitution, and the status of international law in the United States.

In 1791, 10 amendments were added to the constitution and came to be known as the Bill of Rights. The substantive provisions of the Bill of Rights guarantee (1) certain freedoms, such as freedom of religion, freedom of speech, and freedom of the press; (2) certain rights, such as the right to assemble peaceably and the right to carry arms; (3) the absence of certain restrictions, such as the quartering of soldiers in a private dwelling without the consent of the owner, unreasonable searches and seizures, and the taking of property (expropriation) without just compensation; and (4) procedural rights associated with the due process of law, such as indictment by a grand jury, a jury trial in criminal and in some civil cases, the rule against double jeopardy, the privilege of not being compelled to be a witness against oneself, and finally the right in criminal cases to a speedy and public trial, to be tried by an impartial jury, to be informed of the nature and cause of the accusation, to be confronted by the witnesses for the prosecution, to have a compulsory procedure established for obtaining witnesses in favor of the accused, and not to be subjected to excessive fines or to cruel and unusual punishments.

The Ninth Amendment to the Constitution of the United States provides: "The enumeration in the Constitution, of certain rights, shall not be construed to deny or disparage others retained by the people." This provision must not be taken to create particular rights of the people but may serve as justification for the U.S. Supreme Court to define rights not expressly mentioned in the Constitution and constitutional amendments. The amendment has been invoked to proclaim a right to privacy as the basis for declaring unconstitutional a law that prohibited the use of contraceptives (*Griswold v. Connecticut,* 1965) and to proclaim the right of women to an abortion (*Roe v. Wade; Doe v. Bolton,* 1973).

American constitutional history has been blemished by institutionalized racial discrimination. Before the Civil War, slavery was widely practiced in the southern states. Slavery was abolished in the United States in 1865, but racial discrimination, including legally enforced segregation in public and private facilities, remained part of the American social, economic, and political structures for many more years.

Over the years, legislation in the form of Civil Rights Acts was enacted by Congress in an attempt to wipe out the remnants of slavery. The Civil Rights Act of 1866 was aimed at the so-called black codes of some southern states that were enacted to restrict the newly emancipated slaves in various ways. It enumerated the equal rights of citizens "of every race and color, without regard to any previous condition of slavery, or involuntary servitude," such as the right to enter into and enforce contracts, standing to institute civil actions, and the right to inherit, purchase, lease, sell, hold, and convey real and personal property. The Civil Rights Act of 1870 extended franchise rights in connection with a great variety of elections to all citizens "without distinction of race, color, or previous condition of servitude." The Civil Rights Act of 1871 (also known as the Ku Klux Klan act) promised criminal and private law sanctions for a variety of actions that would infringe a person's constitutional rights.

After the judgment of the U.S. Supreme Court in the case of *Plessy v. Ferguson* (1896), the doctrine of "separate but equal" was applied in public education to uphold the constitutionality of racially segregated schools until the U.S. Supreme Court in *Brown v. Board of Education* (1954) held that separate educational facilities were inherently unequal. This momentous decision set the tone for a concerted effort to eradicate all lingering manifestations of racism in the laws and practices of the United States. Those efforts included "bussing" of schoolchildren of a particular race to schools with a predominant enrollment of students from the other race and affirmative action programs designed to obliterate the persisting effects of past discrimination and to promote equal opportunities for disadvantaged sections of the community, by giving preferences in employment, education, contracts, and other social goods to disadvantaged groups.

Although great progress has been made over the years, racial differences in average levels of education, economic means, and living conditions are still evident. The issue has been complicated by the dramatic increase in racial and cultural diversity due to massive immigration from South America, the Caribbean, Asia, and Africa.

The American Civil War had a decisive influence on constitutional litigation in the United States. Prior to the end of the war, the Bill of Rights placed restrictions on the exercise of powers by federal authorities only. In consequence of the war, Congress enacted the Thirteenth Amendment (1865), Fourteenth Amendment (1868), and Fifteenth Amendment (1870), jointly known as the Reconstruction amendments, abolishing slavery; proclaiming the citizenship of all persons born or naturalized in the United States; outlawing the deprivation of life, liberty, or property without the due process of the law; proclaiming the equal protection of the laws; and guaranteeing the right to vote of all citizens irrespective of race, color, or previous condition of servitude.

These provisions were made applicable to the states. The U.S. Supreme Court in subsequent judgments "incorporated" most of the specific provisions of the Bill of Rights in the general language of the Fourteenth Amendment, prohibiting the states from abridging "the privileges or immunities of citizens of the United States," and from depriving "any person of life, liberty, or property, without the due process of the law." Certain provisions of the Bill of Rights have not been incorporated. The U.S. Supreme Court has decided against incorporation in the case of the right to carry arms, the right to a grand jury indictment in criminal cases, and the right to a jury trial in civil cases. The U.S. Supreme Court has thus far not made a ruling as to the incorporation of the right not to have troops quartered in one's home or the prohibition of excessive fines. Through incorporation, the other Bill of Rights provisions were made applicable to the states via the Fourteenth Amendment.

Impact and Functions of Fundamental Rights

Constitutional protection of human rights in the United States is in essence founded on a libertarian system, in which the First Amendment freedoms, notably freedom of speech, are of special significance. In case of a conflict between different constitutional rights and freedoms, the courts always attempt to "balance" those conflicting rights so as to give each a place in the Sun. However, should freedom of speech be in irreconcilable conflict with any other constitutional right, the former freedom trumps the other conflicting right. In terms of the doctrine of "preferred freedoms," the courts would find it easier to hold that legislation curtailing the First Amendment freedoms is unconstitutional than it would, for instance, if the economically qualified rights enunciated in the Fifth and Fourteenth Amendments (protecting property rights) were at stake.

The American Bill of Rights only affords protection to civil and political rights and does not contain express guarantees of the basic natural rights of the human person, such as the right to life and to human dignity. Under its federal system, the competence to deal with these matters is within the jurisdiction of states. Because of that, the United States has been condemned by the Inter-American Commission on Human Rights for not upholding the principle of equal treatment in respect of the most basic human rights and fundamental freedoms.

In 1803, in the case of *Marbury v. Madison,* the U.S. Supreme Court decided that it had the power of substantive review. In virtue of that power, which has been repeatedly reaffirmed and extended, both federal and state courts of law are competent to declare null and void legislation and acts and decisions of the executive found to be in violation of the federal and state constitutions, respectively.

Constitutional cases are brought before the U.S. Supreme Court by way of an appeal against the ruling of a court lower in status. However, the U.S. Supreme Court is not obliged to hear all cases. The U.S. Supreme Court must as a general rule grant certiorari for the case, that is, the case must be admitted to be argued before, and decided by, the Supreme Court, taking into account whether or not the matter appealed to the Court raises a "moot question," whether or not the matter is "ripe" for adjudication by the U.S. Supreme Court, and so on.

Limitations to Fundamental Rights

The rights and freedoms protected by the American Bill of Rights are drafted in general language without denoting any limitations to which those rights are to be subjected or specifying the circumstances in which limitations can be imposed. This matter is left entirely to the discretion of the U.S. Supreme Court.

ECONOMY

The United States upholds the essential principles of a free-market economy. In earlier times, the idea of a free-market economy was interpreted to limit drastically the role of federal and state authorities in the economic life of the nation. In *Lochner v. New York* (1905), the U.S. Supreme Court accordingly declared unconstitutional a state law that imposed maximal working hours for employees in a bakery on the grounds that it placed an undue limitation on freedom of contract. The Court held that freedom of contract could only be restricted to serve a legitimate "police power" (executive competence) for the protection of public health, public safety, or public morals, and that legislation curtailing freedom of contract would be carefully scrutinized to assure that it would not overstep this mark.

In consequence of the Depression of 1929, President Franklin D. Roosevelt (1933–45) introduced New Deal legislation, which put formerly unregulated aspects of the U.S. economy under federal control. As a mechanism to counteract the devastating consequences of the Depression, the legislative initiatives made provisions for employment in public works, low-interest farm loans, old age and unemployment insurance, prohibition of utilizing of child labor, protection of workers against unfair labor practices, encouragement of trade union membership, loans to local authorities to upgrade slum areas, and many more. In the period 1933–37, the U.S. Supreme Court invalidated many New Deal regulations.

However, in 1937 the majority in the Court changed to favor the New Deal initiative, and since then no federal or state law has been held unconstitutional on the grounds of the freedom of contract rationale. Roosevelt's New Deal policy (and similar initiatives that began earlier in the states) transformed the United States into a modern welfare state, whose government wields extensive regulatory powers over commerce, industry, and labor.

RELIGIOUS COMMUNITIES

The First Amendment to the Constitution of the United States of America provides, "Congress shall make no law respecting an establishment of religion, or prohibiting the free exercise thereof." The wording reflects the history of the colonies, many of them founded and peopled by dissenters fleeing persecution by established churches in Europe. Furthermore, no one church could claim majority status in the nation as a whole, as New England was largely Congregationalist, Pennsylvania Quaker and German Evangelical, Maryland Catholic, and the South Anglican.

The establishment clause and the free exercise clause embodied in this provision have been interpreted, in the words of Thomas Jefferson (1743–1826), to create a "wall of separation between church and state," which the United States Supreme Court has decided must be "kept high and impregnable" (*Everson v. Board of Education,* 1947).

In order to establish whether state action reflects the measure of religious neutrality required by the separation of church and state, the U.S. Supreme Court in the case of *Lemon v. Kurtzman* (1971) developed a three-prong test. In order to withstand constitutional scrutiny, the enactment in question (1) must serve a secular purpose, (2) must have a primary effect that neither advances nor inhibits religion, and (3) must avoid excessive governmental entanglement with religion.

MILITARY DEFENSE AND STATE OF EMERGENCY

The president of the United States is "Commander in Chief of the Army and Navy of the United States, and of the Militia of the several States, when called into actual Service of the United States" (art. II, sec. 2, clause [1]).

The Department of Defense includes the army, navy, air force, Marine Corps, and reserve units comprising 1 million volunteers. It has its headquarters in the Pentagon building in northern Virginia just outside Washington, D.C. It is headed by the secretary of defense.

The Joint Chiefs of Staff consists of a chair and vice chair, the chief of staff of the army, the chief of naval operations, the chief of staff of the U.S. Air Force, and the commandant of the Marine Corps. The chair is the principal military adviser of the president, the National Security Council, and the secretary of defense.

The Department of Defense is primarily responsible for providing military forces needed to protect the security of the United States against acts of aggression and civil unrest. After the terrorist attack of September 11, 2001, which, among other things, destroyed the World Trade Center in New York City, the Department of Defense reviewed some of its strategies for the protection of the United States from foreign militant threats. The president in 2001 created by executive order the Homeland Security Department to coordinate government efforts to protect the people of the United States against terrorist attacks. The executive order was subsequently endorsed by the Homeland Security Act of 2002. Since 2002, members of the national guard have been deployed to provide security at airports and border posts.

Congress enacted legislation authorizing the president "to use all necessary and appropriate force against those nations, organizations or persons he determines planned, authorized, committed, or aided the terrorist attacks ..., or harbored such organizations or persons" (Authorization for Use of Military Force, 2001). The military operations in Afghanistan that commenced toward the end of 2001 to topple the Taliban regime and against the al-Qaeda terrorist network led by Osama bin Laden was executed pursuant to this legislation.

Pursuant to the powers vested in the president by the same legislation, and in virtue of the office as commander in chief of the armed forces, the president may, by executive decree, proclaim a person to be an "enemy combatant," thereby condemning that person to indefinite detention and depriving him or her of constitutional protection. The U.S. Supreme Court did afford to those labeled enemy combatants the right to a hearing to produce evidence showing that they were not "enemy combatants" (*Hamdi v. Rumsfeld,* 2004).

The United States has become probably the most powerful military force in the history of humankind. Its military capabilities include one of the mightiest land and sea forces, an unprecedented arsenal of high-tech weaponry that includes nuclear weapons, and highly sophisticated strategic maneuverability. It is the most potent member state of the North Atlantic Treaty Organization (NATO) and, when required, a main contributor to the armed forces and peacekeeping operations of the United Nations.

The United States played a major role in the United Nations–sponsored military operations against Iraq in the Gulf War of 1991 that was sparked by the attempted annexation of Kuwait by Iraq. It was a main contributor to the NATO forces in the bombing campaign that commenced on March 24, 1999, against targets in Serbia and Montenegro in order to end the atrocities committed by Serbian forces against ethnic Albanians in Kosovo.

The United States has also proved willing to apply its military might, without United Nations or NATO authorization or concurrence, to topple what it perceived to be repressive regimes in countries that are of economic or strategic importance to the United States. On January 20, 2000, Senator Jesse Helms (Republican of North Carolina), at the time chair of the Foreign Relations Committee of the U.S. Senate, in a speech before the Security Council of the United Nations explained the so-called Reagan doctrine:

> In some cases, America has assisted freedom fighters around the world who are seeking to overthrow corrupt regimes. . . . We have provided weaponry, training and intelligence. And in other cases, the United States has intervened directly. And in other cases, such as in Central and Eastern Europe, we supported peaceful opposition movements with moral, financial and covert forms of support.
>
> The democratic expansion of freedom in the last decade of the 20th century is a direct result of those policies. In none of those cases, however, did the United States ask for, or receive, the approval of the United Nations to legitimize its actions.

In 1986, the International Court of Justice, in the case of *Nicaragua v. United States,* condemned the United States for affording military assistance, in violation of international law, to the contras—a militant group that sought to overthrow the government of Nicaragua. The "Reagan doctrine" seems to be the only credible explanation for the military invasion of Iraq by the United States on March 19, 2003, to topple the regime of Saddam Hussein.

The term *state of emergency* is reserved in the United States for situations prompted by a natural disaster. After an earthquake, tornado, flood, or similar catastrophe, proclamation of a state of emergency by the president in the region affected by the disaster authorizes the application of federal funds to provide relief to victims of the disaster.

Military intervention to deal with situations of military aggression or civil unrest or martial law on a national scale can be proclaimed by the president or by Congress. The president derives his or her authority from article II, section 2, clause [1] of the Constitution, which proclaims him or her to be commander in chief of the armed forces of the United States. The competence of Congress derives from article I, section 8, clause [15], which gives it the power "to provide for calling forth the Militia to execute the Laws of the Union, suppress Insurrections and repel Invasions." Governors have a similar competence to declare martial law within their respective states.

Martial law may include the use of military force; the authority of military personnel to make and enforce civil and criminal law; and the suspension of certain civil liberties, such as freedom of speech and of association, freedom of movement, and the writ of habeas corpus for challenging the legality of one's detention. In *Ex parte Merriman* (1861), the U.S. Supreme Court proclaimed its power to review the propriety of a declaration of martial law and held that only Congress can suspend the writ of habeas corpus.

Congress has never used its power to declare martial law. Martial law has only once been declared on a national scale, and once on a regional scale. During the Civil War, President Abraham Lincoln declared martial law, authorizing Union military forces to arrest persons and conduct trials. During World War II (1939–45), the Department of War implemented military law in all the states along the Pacific coast. Imposition of curfews to be observed by German and Italian aliens and by all persons of Japanese extraction was upheld in *Hirabayashi v. United States* (1945), and the random internment of people of Japanese extraction was declared lawful in *Korematsu v. United States* (1944).

After the attack by Japan on Pearl Harbor on December 9, 1941, Governor Joseph B. Poindexter declared martial law (subsequently approved by the president) in the Hawaiian Islands. All courts were closed, the writ of habeas corpus was suspended, and military personnel were authorized to arrest, try, and convict persons without the requirement to follow the rules of evidence. Military personnel conducting trials were furthermore not bound by sentencing laws. In *Duncan v. Kahanamoku* (1946), the U.S. Supreme Court decided that military tribunals could not assume jurisdiction over common crimes.

AMENDMENTS TO THE CONSTITUTION

The Constitution of the United States is said to be particularly inflexible in the sense that extraordinary and difficult to achieve procedural requirements must be satisfied for its formal amendment through the medium of legislation.

Under Article V, proposals to amend the Constitution must first be endorsed by a two-thirds majority in both houses of Congress. They must then be ratified by the legislatures of three-quarters of the states or by a constitutional convention in the same number of states. The convention method for the ratification of an amendment was only applied when the Twenty-first Amendment was adopted in 1933 to repeal the Eighteenth Amendment of 1919, which had prohibited the "manufacture, sale, or transportation" of intoxicating liquor in the United States.

An alternative method, never used, allows two-thirds of the state legislatures to petition Congress to call a national convention to propose amendments. Once proposed, they go back to the states for ratification, through either of the methods detailed.

A proposed constitutional amendment can stipulate the time within which ratification of the amendment must be finalized. If the prescribed number of state ratifications falls short of the three-fourths requirement by that date, the amendment does not become law. The Equal Rights Amendment proposed in 1972, which sought to outlaw discrimination based on sex, did not gain the required number of ratifications even after a 39-month extension expired on June 30, 1982. The Twenty-seventh Amendment, which regulates salary increases of members of Congress, was introduced in 1789 as part of the original Bill of Rights and only after 203 years had gained sufficient state ratifications to become law (1992).

Although the procedures attending the formal amendment of the Constitution render the constitutional system of the United States extremely inflexible, constitutional changes can be brought about by a system of interpretation that leaves ample scope for flexibility. The almost unbridled competence of the U.S. Supreme Court to reinterpret and to expand the general provisions of the Bill of Rights so as to accommodate the Court's evaluation of public opinion, changing circumstances, and current demands renders the constitution quite flexible.

PRIMARY SOURCES

Constitution. Available online. URL: http://usinfo.state.gov/usa/infousa/facts/funddocs/consteng.htm. Accessed on August 3, 2005.

SECONDARY SOURCES

Erwin Chemerinsky, *Constitutional Law: Principles and Policies.* New York: Aspen, 1997.
David S. Clark and Tugrul Ansay, eds., *Introduction to the Law of the United States.* 2d ed. The Hague/New York: Kluwer, 2002.

Johan D. van der Vyver

URUGUAY

At-a-Glance

OFFICIAL NAME
Oriental Republic of Uruguay

CAPITAL
Montevideo

POPULATION
3,399,000 (2005 est.)

SIZE
68,039 sq. mi. (176,220 sq. km)

LANGUAGES
Spanish

RELIGIONS
Catholic 66%, Jewish 1%, Protestant 2%. no religion 31%

NATIONAL OR ETHNIC COMPOSITION
White 88%, Mestizo 8%, black 4%, Amerindian practically nonexistent

DATE OF INDEPENDENCE OR CREATION
August 25, 1825

TYPE OF GOVERNMENT
Democratic republican

TYPE OF STATE
Unitary state with broad inner decentralization

TYPE OF LEGISLATURE
Bicameral parliament

DATE OF CONSTITUTION
November 27, 1966

DATE OF LAST AMENDMENT
October 31, 2004

The Uruguayan constitution, endorsed in a plebiscite in 1966 and effective since 1967, with four subsequent amendments (1989, 1994, 1997, and 2004), is a democratic constitution approved directly by a vast majority of the electoral body. Notwithstanding its amendments, this document, considered a model for South America in the 1960s, now often appears old-fashioned and difficult to apply to new realities.

CONSTITUTIONAL HISTORY

At the time of the Spanish colonization the territory of the present republic was almost uninhabited. A group of native tribes, generally related to the Guarani, lived in the country, the Charrúa the most important of them.

Although the Banda Oriental (the former name for Uruguay) belonged to the Spanish Crown, the first European settlement, Colonia del Sacramento, founded in 1680, was Portuguese. It was, however, quickly seized by Spanish troops.

Until 1811, the Banda Oriental was ruled by Spain. A governor was assigned to the city port of Montevideo, subordinated to the viceroy of the Río de la Plata, who was located in Buenos Aires, the capital of the viceroyalty. In 1811 a revolutionary movement coalesced around leaders called *caudillos,* especially José Gervasio Artigas (1764–1850).

Of Spanish descent, Artigas became the most important caudillo in the Banda Oriental, spreading his influence even to territories that now belong to the Argentine provinces of Santa Fe, Entre Ríos, Corrientes, and Córdoba. Artigas gave the revolutionary movement clear ideas that led to a confrontation not only with Spain and Portugal, but also with Buenos Aires. Artigas stood for independence from any European power and wanted to organize the Banda Oriental and the other provinces into a federal state similar to that of North America. He rejected the centralism of Buenos Aires and called for respect for human rights and for a democratic government elected by the people.

Independence from Spain was achieved in 1813, when a provisional government was installed under the guidance of Artigas. The Portuguese invaded the country in 1816, and after Brazil became independent of Portugal, Brazil ruled what now is Uruguay. An authentic national government followed between 1825 and 1828. In 1828, the Preliminary Peace Convention ended the armed conflict between Brazil and Argentina and called for an independent state in the conflicted territory of the old Banda Oriental. A new constitution became effective on July 18, 1830.

Nineteenth-century political life in Uruguay was highly complex, as it was in almost all South American countries. Under the pressure of international wars, such as the Great War (1839–52), which also involved Argentina, England, France, and Italy; internal revolts; coups d'état; and a sequence of military governments, the constitution was not seriously enforced.

In 1904 the last civil war, pitting the Colorado Party government of José Battle y Órdoñez (1856–1929) against the National (previously the Blanco) Party commanded by the caudillo Aparicio Saravia (1856–1904), took place; it ended with the latter's death. A Constitutional Convention in 1916 drafted a new constitution, which was ratified in a popular referendum and went into force in 1918.

As did its predecessor of 1830, the 1918 constitution called for a state of law and provided a presidential system with a clear division of executive, legislative, and judicial powers. The main difference between the two constitutions was that the 1918 version was actually enforced.

In 1933, Uruguay was hard hit by the world economic crisis. A new Constitutional Convention, even though no such body was foreseen in the 1918 constitution, created a new constitution, approved by a popular plebiscite in 1934, which generated many important changes. It turned to a more parliamentary system of government and strengthened the judiciary with the power to review the electoral process and annul government acts as unconstitutional when challenged. The constitution also laid the grounds for the present system of territorial decentralization and introduced economic, social, and cultural rights.

In 1942, still another new constitution ended the transition from a presidential to a parliamentary style of government and introduced the present Article 332, which states that constitutional provisions have direct impact even when due legal regulation has not yet been passed. A decade later, in 1952, yet another constitution was passed; it set up the collegiate National Council of Government as head of the executive power. The council was formed by nine members distributed as follows: six for the political party with the most votes in the elections and three for the party with the second-largest number of votes. This collegiate formula of government caused many problems and was replaced in 1966 by the constitution that is still in force today.

FORM AND IMPACT OF THE CONSTITUTION

The Uruguay constitution is a rigid one, difficult to change. It is contained in a single written document. Nowadays, there is full enforcement of the constitution, and its content is reasonably coincident with political practice. The constitution appears to have highest rank in the Uruguayan legal system. However, its relationship with international laws is not completely clear. Although constitutional regulations have higher rank than international law, methods for resolving contradictions between international and national laws are not clearly specified.

BASIC ORGANIZATIONAL STRUCTURE

The constitution creates a unitary state, with guaranteed territorial decentralization. Three levels of jurisdictions are established: national, departmental (with a superintendent and a departmental council), and local (with local authorities). The departmental governments have broad autonomous jurisdiction and have the authority to impose special taxes.

LEADING CONSTITUTIONAL PRINCIPLES

The constitution establishes a democratic government, acknowledging that the nation is the holder of sovereignty (Articles 4 and 82), which is exercised through the representative powers of government.

The system is based on a clear division of powers, in which the exercise of the legislative function belongs mainly to the legislative branch; there are no exceptions, and the executive is barred from issuing any form of delegated or emergency legislation. The judicial power is also largely exclusive, although there are constitutional exceptions, specifically the military justice system (Article 253), political trials (Articles 309, 312, 313, and 320), and the Electoral Court (Articles 77 and 322). The executive function belongs to the executive power.

The state is defined as nonreligious (unlike in the 1930 constitution, which acknowledged the Roman Catholic Church as the official religion), independent, and with a pacifist orientation (Article 6). Although the constitution is more than 35 years old, it can be considered to have founded a social democratic state based on the rule of law.

CONSTITUTIONAL BODIES

The main constitutional bodies are the two-chamber parliament, the executive administration, the president of the republic, and the judiciary.

The Parliament

At the national level, a bicameral legislature (including a Senate with 31 members and a Chamber of Deputies with 99), called the General Assembly, is elected directly by the people in a mandatory and secret ballot under a system of proportional representation. Senators are chosen in one constituency covering the entire national territory, while deputies are chosen with a mixed procedure that includes national and departmental constituencies.

The Executive Administration

The executive power functions differently than in other parliamentary systems in the world. As in other countries, it is composed of the president of the republic and cabinet ministers chosen by the president from among people who have parliamentary support. And as in other systems, many decisions are made by the Council of Ministers, a meeting of all the cabinet ministers presided over by the president of the republic (who has a double vote in case of a tie; in the case of tie votes the president has a double vote).

However, the system can also take action through individual "agreements" between the president and the cabinet minister or ministers who have jurisdiction on a matter requiring a decision. Certain matters are mandatorily reserved by the constitution to the Council of Ministers: a declaration of war, introduction of budget bills and financial reports, the introduction of bills that change the number of ministries, appointment and removal of directors of independent agencies, and delegation of jurisdiction.

The Presidency of the Republic

The presidency of the republic is, according to the most accepted doctrine, both a part of the executive power and independent of it. The president is elected directly by the people, in the same elections as are senators and deputies, by an absolute majority of the votes. If no presidential candidate obtains this majority, a second round must take place 30 days later between the two candidates who receive most votes in the first round.

The president has the ordinary jurisdiction of a parliamentary head of state: the internal and foreign representation of the state, the designation of the cabinet ministers, and the dissolution of parliament. The electoral system gives the president great legitimacy; he or she is the main political actor and the central figure of national political life.

The Lawmaking Process

It is the exclusive prerogative of the legislative power to make laws, although other organs have the power to pass bills. The executive has the authority to promulgate laws and the right to veto them and thus force their reconsideration; the deputies may overrule the veto by a qualified majority of three-fifths.

There are three different lawmaking procedures: the ordinary process; the process used when there is a declaration of "urgency," in which each chamber has less time to vote; the process of passing the five-year budget and the annual rendering of accounts.

In all these cases each chamber debates and votes separately. If the second chamber approves a different bill, the amended version goes back to the first chamber for reconsideration. If the disagreement persists, the General Assembly has to approve a version of the bill in joint session with two-thirds of the votes.

The Judiciary

The highest court is the Supreme Court of Justice. It has five members, who are elected by a majority of two-thirds of the General Assembly for a period of 10 years. The constitution establishes exclusive jurisdiction for the Supreme Court in matters such as declarations of unconstitutionality, prosecution of all violators of the constitution, admiralty cases, and cases related to international treaties. If a member of the Supreme Court violates the constitution or perpetrates another high crime, he or she is subject to impeachment. The constitution also provides for appellate courts and other courts to be established by law.

Judicial independence is guaranteed. The main problem faced by the Uruguayan judicial power is its inadequate budget. Economic problems that affect its functioning have become a tradition, as have the courts' repeated complaints on the subject.

THE ELECTION PROCESS AND POLITICAL PARTICIPATION

With reference to political participation, the constitution distinguishes three classes of individuals: citizens by birth, legal citizens (those who have acquired citizenship), and residents (noncitizens). The right to vote is granted both to citizens and to noncitizens. Voting is secret and obligatory.

There is a widespread range of matters subject to referenda and popular initiatives for laws. Electors who are not citizens are not allowed to vote in constitutional popular initiatives and constitutional plebiscites.

To be eligible to be president of the republic a person must be a citizen by birth and more than 35 years of age. To be a senator a person has to be a citizen by birth and more than 30 years of age or have been a legal citizen for at least 30 years.

POLITICAL PARTIES

Uruguay has a pluralistic system of political parties. The constitution promotes freedom in the creation and functioning of political parties in Article 77, which establishes that "the state will watch that the political parties enjoy the most ample freedom." The constitution also establishes obligations for the parties: to choose their authorities through democratic elections, to publicize their principles and organic structure, and to choose their candidates for the presidency of the republic through internal elections.

The Uruguayan constitution provides that in presidential election years the citizens can take part and vote in internal party elections organized by the Electoral Court, with the same suffrage guarantees as in presidential elections. A citizen can vote in the internal election of only one political party. This system secures great transparency in elections for presidential candidates.

CITIZENSHIP

Natural citizens are those born in the territory of the republic and the offspring of natural citizens born abroad who take up residence in the republic and register in the *Civic Register*. Legal citizens are those foreigners who request legal citizenship and who fulfill the requirements established in the constitution: the proof of a bond with the republic and other indications that the petitioner wants to reside in the country. The General Assembly can grant legal citizenship to those who have rendered outstanding service to the country.

FUNDAMENTAL RIGHTS

Section 2 of the constitution, Rights, Obligations, and Guarantees, deals with human rights. Chapter 1 enumerates the so-called individual rights or first-generation rights (such as the right to live, to work, and to have privacy; freedom of conscience, of religion, of enterprise, and of speech; physical freedom, freedom to travel, freedom of the press, the right to own property, and others). In Chapter 2 the economic, social, and cultural rights or second-generation rights appear (such as protection for the family, children, the disabled, and public health; the right to receive an education, the right to housing, to go on strike, and others), plus some third-generation rights, such as the preservation of the environment. The distribution of rights between the chapters is not perfect.

The constitution clearly reflects a belief in natural law. It acknowledges the existence of rights that precede the constitution and gives constitutional status to human rights even when they are not expressly established in the written text. According to Uruguayan constitutional law any right that is inherent to the human person or the republican way of government has constitutional status.

The principle of freedom is part of the foundation of the constitutional system, as expressed in Articles 7 and 10. Any limitation to fundamental rights must be written in law and must have a restricted interpretation. The principle of equality also appears as a fundamental part of the constitutional structure.

Impact and Functions of Fundamental Rights

Articles 7 and 72 oblige the government actively to protect fundamental rights. Article 332 provides that constitutional regulations go into force even if the supplemental legal regulations have not been passed.

Legal persons are also considered to be holders of fundamental rights. This provision gives standing to business companies to claim violations against their equal right.

Limitations to Fundamental Rights

According to the constitution there are three types of rights: those that preceded the constitution, which cannot be restrained; those established by the constitution that do not allow any limitation by law; and those established by the constitution that can be restricted by a law. In this latter case only a law (and no other type of regulation) can establish a valid limitation; the law must fulfill certain requirements such as being dictated by reasons of public interest or public order, safety, or hygiene.

ECONOMY

The constitution entails some provisions that, although not classified in a systematic way, can be considered as creating what is commonly known as the economic constitution. For example, it assumes the functioning of a free-market economy in the context of economic, social, and cultural human rights.

Article 51 states that the government must guide foreign trade. It also mandates decentralization policies in order to promote regional development and the general welfare.

RELIGIOUS COMMUNITIES

The constitution creates a secular state, stating in Article 5 that it has no religion. In the same regulation it is established that "in Uruguay the exercise of any religion is free." There are also far-reaching tax exemptions for religious activities.

MILITARY DEFENSE AND STATE OF EMERGENCY

Uruguay has a voluntary military service.

The constitution specifies three emergency situations that allow the use of special powers. In serious and unexpected cases of foreign attack or civil unrest the executive can exercise special emergency powers; its actions must be explained to the General Assembly within 24 hours.

In the event of high treason or conspiracy against the country, the protection of individual security can be temporarily interrupted but only in order to imprison criminals. Once imprisoned they can exercise their constitutional rights without exception.

In a state of war military courts can expand their jurisdiction. For example, they may try soldiers for the perpetration of ordinary crimes that in times of peace would be judged by regular courts.

AMENDMENTS TO THE CONSTITUTION

Article 331 provides four procedures for introducing amendments: "popular proposals" by 10 percent of the voters; "legislative proposals" by two-fifths of the members of the General Assembly; National Constitutional Conventions, with members elected in general elections; and constitutional laws, which must be approved by two-thirds of the members of each chamber of parliament. All the aforementioned procedures end with a popular plebiscite.

PRIMARY SOURCES

Constitution in English: A. P. Blaustein and G. H. Flanz, *Constitutions of the Countries of the World.* Dobbs Ferry, N.Y.: Oceana Publications, 1971.

Constitution in Spanish: *La Constitución Uruguaya.* Montevideo: Fundación de Cultura Universita-ria: 2004. Available online. URL: http://www. parlamento.gub.uy/palacio3/index1024.htm. Accessed on June 29, 2006.

SECONDARY SOURCES

Martin Risso Ferrand, *Derecho Constitucional.* Montevideo: Fundación de Cultura Universitaria, 2005.

Eduardo Esteva Gallicchio, *Lecciones de Derecho Constitucional.* Montevideo: Editión Revista Uruguaya de Derecho Constitucional y Político, 1981.

Justice Studies Center of the Americas, "Uruguay." In *Report on Judicial Systems in the Americas 2002–2003.* Santiago, Chile: Justice Studies Center of the Americas, 2003.

Justino Jiménez de Aréchaga, *La Constitución Nacional.* Montevideo: Edit. Senators Chamber, 1992–98.

José Korzeniak, *Primer Curso de Derecho Público: Derecho Constitucional.* Montevideo: Fundación de Cultura Universitaria, 2001.

Horacio Cassinelli Muñoz, *Derecho Público.* Montevideo: Fundación de Cultura Universitaria, 1999.

United Nations, "Core Document Forming Part of the Reports of States Parties: Uruguay" (HRI/CORE/1/Add.9/Rev.1), 30 September 1996. Available online. URL: http://www.unhchr.ch/tbs/doc.nsf. Accessed on September 28, 2005.

Uruguay—a Country Study. Washington, D.C.: United States Government Printing Office. Available online. URL: http://www.countrystudies.us/uruguay/62.htm. Accessed on September 28, 2005.

Martin Risso Ferrand

UZBEKISTAN

At-a-Glance

OFFICIAL NAME
Republic of Uzbekistan

CAPITAL
Tashkent

POPULATION
26,410,416 (2005 est.)

SIZE
172,742 sq. mi. (447,400 sq. km)

LANGUAGES
Uzbek 74.3%, Russian 14.2%, Tajik 4.4%, other 7.1%

RELIGIONS
Muslim (mostly Sunni) 88%, Eastern Orthodox 9%, other 3%

NATIONAL OR ETHNIC COMPOSITION
Uzbek 77%, Russian 5%, Tajik 5%, Kazakh 5%, Karakalpak 1%, Tatar 1.5%, other 5.5%

DATE OF INDEPENDENCE OR CREATION
September 1, 1991

TYPE OF GOVERNMENT
Authoritarian presidential regime

TYPE OF STATE
Centralistic state with federal elements

TYPE OF LEGISLATURE
Bicameral parliament

DATE OF CONSTITUTION
December 8, 1992

DATE OF LAST AMENDMENT
April 24, 2003

Uzbekistan is a presidential autocracy that has a strong president who exercises control over executive, legislative, and judicial powers. The president appoints and dismisses the administration, the judges, and the members of the Senate. Free, equal, direct, fair, and transparent elections are guaranteed by the constitution but have not been implemented. So far, all elections have failed to comply with international standards. There is no pluralistic political party system.

Uzbekistan is made up of 12 provinces, the city of Tashkent, and the Republic of Karakalpakstan. The constitution provides fundamental human rights; however, only selected government institutions, not individuals, may appeal before the Constitutional Court. Although religious freedom and state noninterference in religious matters are formally guaranteed, the state broadly suppresses nontraditional religious groups (e.g., Hizbut Tahrir, Jehovah's Witnesses).

CONSTITUTIONAL HISTORY

Over the centuries, the territory of Uzbekistan has been invaded by various foreign tribes and ethnic groups. In 651 C.E. Arabs started their invasion of Central Asia, conquering Bukhara in 709, Samarkand in 712, and Tashkent in 714. After 500 years of Arab domination, Bukhara and Samarkand were incorporated by the Mongol conqueror Genghis Khan. After his death in 1227, Genghis Khan's empire was split among his sons. In the late 14th century, one of his relatives, Amir Timur (Tamerlane), conquered not only what is today Uzbek territory, but also vast parts of what would become Russia, Persia, and Turkey. Samarkand was proclaimed his capital. Today's Uzbek leadership proclaims Amir Timur the founding "father" of the Uzbek nation-state. However, the name *Uzbek* was introduced later—when a group of Turkish nomadic tribes conquered today's Uzbek territory in the early 16th century. Their leader, Khan Uzbek, gave his name to the Turkish group, which later established the Khanates Bukhara, Khiva, and Kokand on Uzbek territory. When czarist troops conquered Central Asia in the 19th century, the epoch of the Uzbek khanates ended.

After the establishment of the Soviet Union in 1924, the Uzbek Socialist Soviet Republic was founded. After the failure of the Moscow hardliners' coup in 1991, Uzbekistan reluctantly declared its independence on August 31 of that year. On December 8, 1992, a new constitution was introduced, replacing the 1978 constitution of the Uzbek Socialist Soviet Republic and the 1977 constitution of the Soviet Union. The post-Soviet constitution was amended several times, most recently on April 24, 2003.

FORM AND IMPACT OF THE CONSTITUTION

Uzbekistan has a written constitution, codified in a single document that takes precedence over all other national law. There is no stipulation that international law must be in accordance with the constitution or take precedence over the Uzbek constitution. Often, Uzbek laws contradict the Uzbek constitution and/or international law.

BASIC ORGANIZATIONAL STRUCTURE

The constitution does not stipulate whether Uzbekistan is a federation or a centralistic state. The country is made up of 12 provinces (*viloyatlar*), Tashkent city, and the Republic of Karakalpakstan. The provinces differ considerably in geographical area, population size, and economic strength.

The provinces and Tashkent city are under the authority of the Uzbek constitution, whereas the Republic of Karakalpakstan has its own constitution. The Karakalpakstan constitution, however, must comply with the Uzbek constitution. Karakalpakstan has the right to secede from Uzbekistan on the basis of a Karakalpakstan-wide referendum held by its people.

The provinces and Tashkent city are governed by *khokims*, appointed and dismissed by the president. The *khokims* are expected to implement the laws, presidential decrees, and decisions of the higher bodies of state authority and to participate in the discussion of republic-wide and local matters.

LEADING CONSTITUTIONAL PRINCIPLES

Uzbekistan's system of government is dominated by the president, who controls the executive, legislative, and judicial powers. The judiciary is not fully independent.

The Uzbek constitutional system is defined by a number of leading principles: state sovereignty, democracy, supremacy of the constitution and the law, and a market economy. Political participation is restricted, as key positions (*khokims*) are appointed by the president. The lower chamber of the parliament, the Legislative Assembly, and the Kengashes, the parliaments of the regions, districts, and towns, are all directly elected. Rule of law is a fundamental principle. All state bodies, public associations, and citizens shall act according to the constitution and the law. State and religion are separated.

CONSTITUTIONAL BODIES

The predominant bodies provided for in the constitution are the president; the cabinet of ministers; the parliament, called Oliy Majlis, with its two chambers, the Legislative Assembly and the Senate; and the Constitutional Court.

The President

The president is the head of state and the executive power. He or she acts as "the guarantor of the rights and freedoms of the citizens, the constitution and the laws"; takes necessary measures to protect the sovereignty, security, and territorial integrity of the country; implements the legal decisions of the state; represents the republic in the country and abroad; and appoints and dismisses key governmental figures (prime minister, general prosecutor, judges, *khokims,* etc.). The president is directly elected for a seven-year term and can be reelected only once.

The Administration

The cabinet of ministers implements the executive power. Formed by the president, it is composed of the prime minister, the prime minister's deputies, ministers, and chairpersons of the state committees. It also includes the representative of the Republic of Karakalpakstan.

The cabinet of ministers shall "provide guidance for the efficient functioning of the economy, social, and spiritual areas, and execution of the laws, parliamentary decisions, presidential decrees, and resolutions."

The Oliy Majlis (Parliament)

The Oliy Majlis is the main representative body. It comprises two chambers—the Legislative Chamber and the Senate. The term of the Oliy Majlis is five years.

The Legislative Chamber consists of 120 deputies elected in single-mandate constituencies on a multiparty basis. The Senate has members from the Republic of Karakalpakstan, each of the 12 provinces, and Tashkent city. They are chosen, respectively, by the Jokarghy Kenes (parliament) of the Republic of Karakalpakstan and the *kengashes* (regional, district, and city parliaments), from among the local deputies. An additional 16 members of the Senate are appointed by the president.

In addition to the adoption of laws, both chambers share the responsibility for defining the direction of internal and external policy, approving the state budget, and confirming ministerial and presidential decisions. While the Legislative Chamber is responsible for initiating legislative, the Senate has been tasked predominantly with filling key government positions.

The Lawmaking Process

The right of legislative initiative belongs to the president, the Jokarghy Kenesh, the Legislative Chamber of the Oliy Majlis, the cabinet of ministers, the Constitutional Court, the Supreme Court, the Highest Economic Court, and the general prosecutor. A law takes effect after it has been adopted by the Legislative Chamber, approved by the Senate, signed by the president, and published in the media.

If the law is rejected by the Senate, a Conciliation Commission may be formed by the two chambers to structure a compromise, which must be approved by both chambers. The president has the right to return the law with objections to the Oliy Majlis, but not the right of veto.

The Judiciary

The judicial system in the Republic of Uzbekistan comprises the Constitutional Court, the Supreme Court, the Highest Economic Court, and the Supreme Civil and Criminal Court. All high-ranking judges are elected by the Senate at the recommendation of the president. All lower-ranking judges are directly appointed and dismissed by the president.

Consisting of 15 judges, the Constitutional Court ranks on a par with the Supreme Court, the Highest Economic Court, and the Supreme Civil and Criminal Court. It deals exclusively with constitutional disputes submitted by those government agencies that have power to initiate legislation. No individual complaints may be considered.

THE ELECTION PROCESS

All Uzbek citizens over the age of 18 have the right to vote in elections. Citizens who have reached the age of 25 by election day and have been permanently resident in Uzbekistan for not less than five years have the right to stand for parliamentary elections. To be registered as a candidate in presidential elections, one must have reached the age of 35, be fluent in the state language, and have lived no less than 10 years in Uzbek territory.

Citizens who have been judicially certified as insane, as well as those who are incarcerated, may neither vote nor be eligible for election. However, citizens whose verdict is outstanding may take part in the elections. According to reports of international organizations, none of the elections held so far has complied with international standards.

POLITICAL PARTIES

The constitutional right to form political parties, and any other public associations, is limited through provisions banning organizations that violate fundamental constitutional principles, aim at changing the constitution, advocate war, or stir up hostility in society. There is no party pluralism in Uzbekistan, as the five registered political parties were all created by the government. A handful of nonregistered political parties operate illegally. In general, political parties play no significant role in public life. Both registered and nonregistered parties are largely unknown in society.

CITIZENSHIP

Until May 1996, all people living on the territory of Uzbekistan were entitled to acquire Uzbek citizenship. Those who did not acquire Uzbek or any other citizenship became stateless. Today, Uzbek citizenship can be acquired by birth from a parent who holds Uzbek citizenship or after residence in Uzbek territory for more than five years.

FUNDAMENTAL RIGHTS

The constitution defines fundamental rights in its second chapter. Beyond the traditional set of individual rights, political, economic, and social rights are emphasized. In the third chapter, the relationship between the society and the individual is defined. The family, constituting the primary unit of society, has the right to state and societal protection.

Impact and Functions of Fundamental Rights

According to the constitution, all Uzbek citizens have equal rights and freedoms and are equal before the law, without discrimination based on sex, race, nationality, language, religion, social origin, conviction, or individual or social status. Citizens' rights and freedoms, established by the constitution and law, are not considered inalienable; they may be abolished by a constitutional change. Since 1995, an ombudsperson known as the plenipotentiary of Oliy Majlis of Uzbekistan on human rights is charged with monitoring the human rights situation in the country. In reality the office focuses mainly on violations of social and economic rights, not on fundamental human rights.

Limitations to Fundamental Rights

According to the constitution, only a court decision may limit citizens' rights and freedoms. Nevertheless, the executive and the law enforcement authorities may in practice limit citizens' rights and freedoms on their own initiative.

ECONOMY

The constitution specifies the economic system as an economy "evolving towards market relations," based on various forms of ownership. The constitution provides a set of conditions that must be met while structuring the economic system. Among them are freedom of economic activity, restricted only by consumers' rights, and equality of and legal protection for all forms of ownership. The constitution also defines social rights, including the right to work, to social security, to skilled medical care, and to education.

RELIGIOUS COMMUNITIES

Freedom of religion or belief is guaranteed as a basic human right. According to the constitution, religious organizations and associations shall be separated from the state and are equal before the law. The state shall not interfere with the activity of religious associations. However, it may prohibit public associations from advocating religious hostility, or political parties based on religious principles.

Despite the constitutional separation of religion and state, there are many areas in which the state interferes. The administration appoints the mufti, the supreme religious authority in the country, controls religious communities, and persecutes nonstate religious associations such as the moderate Islamist party Hizbut Tahrir.

MILITARY DEFENSE AND STATE OF EMERGENCY

The creation and maintenance of the armed forces for defense are the responsibility of the president. The armed forces may be used for the defense of the country and the security of the state. There is a Ministry of Emergency Situations to handle exceptional situations.

In Uzbekistan, general conscription requires all men over the age of 18 to perform basic military service of 12 months. There is alternative military service for conscientious objections, which takes 18 months. Women are not eligible for conscription but may serve as professional soldiers. Professional, contracted soldiers serve for fixed periods of up to five years.

The president serves as the supreme commander of the armed forces and appoints the high-ranking commanders. The president has the right to proclaim a state of emergency throughout Uzbekistan or in a particular area, in cases such as imminent outside threats, mass disturbances, or major catastrophes or epidemics. However, parliament must approve the proclamation within 24 hours.

The Uzbek government has obligated itself through international treaties not to produce atomic, biological, or chemical weapons.

AMENDMENTS TO THE CONSTITUTION

The constitution can only be changed by a law adopted by at least two-thirds of the deputies of both chambers of the Oliy Majlis, or by referendum. There are no restrictions on changing the constitution.

PRIMARY SOURCES

Constitution of the Republic of Uzbekistan of December 8, 1992, in English. Available online. URL: http://www.umid.uz/Main/Uzbekistan/Constitution/constitution.html. Accessed on August 9, 2005.

Constitutional Law of the Republic of Uzbekistan on the Legislative Chamber of the Oliy Majlis of the Republic of Uzbekistan, December 12, 2002.

Constitutional Law of the Republic of Uzbekistan on the Senate of the Oliy Majlis of the Republic of Uzbekistan, December 12, 2002.

Law on Introducing Amendments and Additions to the Constitution of the Republic of Uzbekistan, April 24, 2003. In Russian. Available online. URL: http://www.educasia.net/en/old_structure2/education_in_ca/legislation_and_policy_documents/ uzbekistan/law_constitution/document_view?month:int=5&year:int<0x003D >2005. Accessed on February 7, 2006.

SECONDARY SOURCES

Ilias Bantekas, *Law and Legal System of Uzbekistan.* Huntington, N.Y.: Juris, 2004.

Organization for Security and Co-operation in Europe, Centre in Tashkent. Available online. URL: http://www.osce.org/. Accessed on July 19, 2005.

United Nations, "Core Document Forming Part of the Reports of States Parties: Uzbekistan" (HRI/CORE/1/Add.129), 10 March 2004. Available online. URL: http://www.unhchr.ch/tbs/doc.nsf. Accessed on August 4, 2005.

Marie-Carin von Gumppenberg

VANUATU

At-a-Glance

OFFICIAL NAME
Republic of Vanuatu

CAPITAL
Port Vila

POPULATION
196,500 (2005 est.)

SIZE
4,587 sq. mi. (11,880 sq. km)

LANGUAGES
Bislama, English and French, and some 110 local
languages

RELIGIONS
Presbyterian 32%, Anglican 14%, Roman Catholic
13%, Seventh-Day Adventist 11%, other 24%,
indigenous 6%

NATIONAL OR ETHNIC COMPOSITION
Melanesian 98%, French, Vietnamese, Chinese, other
Pacific Islanders

DATE OF INDEPENDENCE
July 30, 1980

TYPE OF GOVERNMENT
Parliamentary democracy

TYPE OF STATE
Unitary state

TYPE OF LEGISLATURE
Unicameral parliament

DATE OF CONSTITUTION
July 30, 1980

DATE OF LAST AMENDMENT
June 27, 1983

Vanuatu is a republic with a parliamentary democratic
form of government, based on the rule of law and a
clear separation between the judicial branch of the state
and the executive and legislature. It is a unitary government, with six provinces that play, at present, a subordinate role in the government of the country.

There is a written constitution that contains a guarantee of fundamental human rights, which are enforceable
by the Supreme Court. The constitution also proclaims
certain fundamental duties, which are stated to be nonjusticiable. The constitution provides that the government shall be a parliamentary democracy on the British
model, and although the country is a republic, and the
head of state is a president, it does not follow the American or French model.

CONSTITUTIONAL HISTORY

During the 19th century the islands of the New Hebrides,
as they had been named by Captain James Cook, attracted

numbers of British settlers, especially from the British
colonies of Australia and New Zealand, and of French settlers, especially from the French colony of New Caledonia. In 1906, Britain and France agreed to establish a joint
sphere of influence in the New Hebrides. This arrangement was strengthened and fleshed out by the protocol
signed by the two countries in 1914, just before World
War I (1914–18), and ratified in 1922.

This joint sphere of influence, styled a condominium
(or more derisively, "pandemonium"), continued until
the 1970s. At that time, as a result of internal pressure
and a desire by Britain to withdraw from its holdings in
the Pacific Ocean, the country was granted independence
on July 30, 1980.

As a consequence of this history, the legal system is
quite complex. First, there is the constitution, which is
stated to be the supreme law of the country. Second, there
are the laws of Britain and France, written and unwritten,
imposed on their respective subjects during the time the
country was a condominium. Since independence, these
laws have been held to be applicable to every resident in

the country. Third, there are legislation enacted by the joint resident commissioners before independence, the legislation enacted by the parliament of Vanuatu since independence, and the subsidiary legislation authorized by such legislation. Finally, there are the customary laws of each island, which are stated by the constitution to be part of the law of the country.

FORM AND IMPACT OF THE CONSTITUTION

The constitution, which took effect on independence on July 30, 1980, is stated to be the supreme law of the country. Although the constitution does not expressly state so, the courts have held that legislation or executive action that is inconsistent with the constitution is void to the extent of the inconsistency.

The constitution also provides that the president may refer any bill that has been passed by parliament, and any regulation that has been made by the executive, to the Supreme Court for an opinion as to its constitutionality.

BASIC ORGANIZATIONAL STRUCTURE

Vanuatu is a unitary state, although the constitution declares that the republic recognizes the importance of decentralization. The Decentralization Act that parliament has enacted establishes two municipalities and six provinces but does not give them very extensive or independent powers, nor a very strong financial base.

LEADING CONSTITUTIONAL PRINCIPLES

Vanuatu's system of government is a republic based upon a national parliamentary democracy. The legislature, called Parliament, is a unicameral body. It is directly elected from multimember constituencies, in general elections that are organized by an independent electoral commission.

The executive is drawn from, and ultimately controllable by, the legislature. The actual administration of the country is carried out by a public service, which is politically neutral and controlled by an independent public service commission.

The judiciary is required by the constitution to be independent and politically neutral and is appointed by an independent judicial service commission.

Fundamental human rights are recognized by the constitution, and the Supreme Court has power to grant redress for any infringement of those rights. Fundamental duties are also recognized by the constitution, but these are stated to be nonjusticiable unless incorporated into a law.

Because much of the land in the country had been vested, during condominium times, in British or French settlers, the constitution states that all land in the country belongs to the customary owners and their descendants, except those areas that are owned by the government.

CONSTITUTIONAL BODIES

The main bodies established by the constitution are, in order of appearance in the constitution, as follows: the Parliament, the National Council of Chiefs, the president, the executive, the judiciary, the public service, and the ombudsperson.

The Parliament

The unicameral legislature is called the Parliament. It contains 52 members. General elections for parliament are to be held every four years, unless parliament is dissolved sooner on the basis of a resolution passed by parliament or a decision made by the Council of Ministers.

Parliament is authorized to make laws for the peace, order, and good government of Vanuatu. The courts have stated that they will not judicially review parliament's interpretation of those terms. Parliament's approval is required for the expenditure of public funds, and for the ratification of treaties. Parliament also has power, by an absolute majority of members, to remove the executive from office by passing a vote of no confidence in the prime minister.

The Lawmaking Process

Bills are introduced either by one or more members of parliament or by the prime minister or a minister. When a bill has been passed by parliament, it is presented to the president of the republic, who shall assent to it within two weeks. If the president considers the bill inconsistent with the constitution, he or she refers it to the Supreme Court for its opinion. The bill is not promulgated if the Supreme Court considers it inconsistent with a provision of the constitution.

The National Council of Chiefs

The National Council of Chiefs is stated to be composed of customary chiefs elected by their peers in district councils of chiefs. The council has an advisory role only. It can discuss all matters relating to custom and tradition and may make recommendations for the preservation and promotion of ni-Vanuatu culture and languages, that is, the culture and languages of the indigenous people of Vanuatu.

The President

The head of state of the republic of Vanuatu is the president, and that officer symbolizes the unity of the nation.

The president is elected by an electoral college that comprises all members of parliament and the chair of the provincial councils. A president may be removed by the same body, acting with a two-thirds majority, for gross misconduct or incapacity. Most of the powers given to the president by the constitution are required to be exercised on the advice of ministers.

The Executive

The executive power of the people of the republic of Vanuatu is vested in the prime minister, who is chosen by the members of Parliament from among their number, and the members of the Council of Ministers, who are appointed by, and dismissible by, the prime minister. The constitution reinforces the parliamentary nature of the executive by providing that members of Parliament who are appointed as ministers shall retain their membership in Parliament. In addition, the Council of Ministers is collectively responsible to Parliament and may be removed by a vote of no confidence in the prime minister passed by an absolute majority of the members of Parliament.

The Judiciary

The administration of justice is vested in the judiciary, who are required to resolve proceedings according to law, and, if there is no law available, then according to substantial justice, and whenever possible, according to custom. The judiciary is stated to comprise the chief justice, who is appointed by the president after consultation with the prime minister and the leader of the opposition, and other judges who are appointed by the Judicial Service Commission. Judges hold office until retirement and can be removed by the president only on grounds of criminal conviction, or a determination by the Judicial Service Commission of gross misconduct, incapacity, or professional incompetence.

The Supreme Court consists of the chief justice and three other judges. A court of appeal may be constituted by two or more judges of the Supreme Court. Magistrate's courts, which have jurisdiction over minor civil claims and criminal matters, are also established by legislation, as are island courts, which comprise three persons knowledgeable in local custom, at least one of whom must be a chief; they have only trivial jurisdiction. At present, island courts and magistrate's courts are not established on all islands.

The Public Service

The constitution provides that the public service owes allegiance to the constitution and the people of Vanuatu, and that only citizens of Vanuatu can be members of the public service. Members of the public service are appointed by, and dismissible by, an independent Public Service Commission.

The Ombudsman

The constitution establishes the post of an ombudsperson, who is empowered to conduct investigations into the conduct of any public servant, public authority, or ministerial department. Although the scope of investigation of the ombudsperson is wide, the power to take action upon those investigations is very limited; the ombudsperson may only make recommendations.

THE ELECTION PROCESS

The constitution requires that the Parliament must be elected on the basis of universal equal suffrage, available to all persons over the age of 18 years. Moreover, the electoral system must contain an element of proportional representation so as to ensure a fair representation of different political groups and opinions. The electoral system that has been adopted is that of multimember constituencies with a single nontransferable vote. There are at present 18 constituencies returning from one to seven members of Parliament, depending on their size. Political parties may be formed freely. All persons aged 25 and over are entitled to stand at elections.

POLITICAL PARTIES

There is no constitutional or legislative restriction on the formation of political parties. At the last general elections in 2004 there were some 31 political parties and 61 independent candidates standing for election.

CITIZENSHIP

Persons who automatically acquired citizenship at the time of independence were persons who had four grandparents indigenous to Vanuatu or were of Vanuatu ancestry and had no citizenship of another country. Persons of Vanuatu ancestry who had, at the date of independence, citizenship of another country were entitled, upon application within three months, to be registered as citizens. Citizens of another state may apply to become citizens by naturalization if they have lived continuously in the country for at least 10 years, provided they renounce the other citizenship. Vanuatu citizens who acquire citizenship of another country automatically lose Vanuatu citizenship, unless they renounce the other citizenship within three months.

FUNDAMENTAL RIGHTS AND DUTIES

The constitution recognizes the fundamental rights and freedoms of individuals, subject to respect for the rights and freedoms of others and subject to the legitimate public interest in defense, safety, public order, welfare, and health. The fundamental rights and freedoms are, within the specified limits, enforceable by the Supreme Court. The constitution also recognizes certain fundamental duties that are not enforceable by the courts, except to the extent that they are incorporated into law.

ECONOMY

Most of agriculture is subsistence, but there is commercial production of coconut products, beef, coffee and timber. Manufacturing is on a very small scale. Tourism is a very significant earner of foreign exchange, as are the finance center and offshore banking system.

RELIGIOUS COMMUNITIES

The constitution guarantees freedom of conscience and worship and nondiscrimination on grounds of religious or traditional beliefs. The largest religious denomination is Presbyterian, followed in size by the Anglican and Roman Catholic Churches, but there are also many adherents of the Assemblies of God and other Pentecostal groupings, the Seventh-Day Adventists, the Church of Christ, and Baha'i.

MILITARY DEFENSE AND STATE OF EMERGENCY

There is a paramilitary wing of the police, the Vanuatu Mobile Force, numbering some 200 persons, but no separate army. A state of emergency can be invoked by the Council of Ministers if the country is at war or if there is a natural calamity or to prevent a threat to, or to restore, public order.

AMENDMENTS TO THE CONSTITUTION

Amendments to most provisions of the constitution can be made by a bill passed by two-thirds of all the members of Parliament. Amendments of the more crucial provisions, however, require not only approval by two-thirds of the legislature, but also support by a majority of voters at a national referendum. This applies to the status of the languages, the electoral system, and the parliamentary system.

PRIMARY SOURCES
Constitution in English. Available online. URL: http://www.paclii.org/vu/legis/consol_act/cotrov406/. Accessed on June 29, 2006.

SECONDARY SOURCES
Don Paterson, "Vanuatu." In *South Pacific Island Legal Systems,* edited by M. Ntumy. Honolulu: University of Hawaii Press, 1993.

Don Paterson

VATICAN

At-a-Glance

OFFICIAL NAME
State of the Vatican City; Holy See

CAPITAL
Vatican City

POPULATION
792 (549 citizen, 243 resident)

SIZE
0.17 sq. mi. (0.44 sq. km)

LANGUAGES
Italian, Latin, German, French, English, and other languages

RELIGIONS
Catholic

NATIONAL OR ETHNIC COMPOSITION
Italian 42.4%, Swiss 23.2%, Polish 5%, Spanish 4.6%,
American 3.4%, French 2.7%, German 2.5%, Indian 2.5%, other (35 nationalities) 13.7%

DATE OF INDEPENDENCE OR CREATION
February 11, 1929

TYPE OF GOVERNMENT
Monarchy (elective)

TYPE OF STATE
Unitary state

TYPE OF LEGISLATURE
Unicameral (pontifical commission)

DATE OF CONSTITUTION
June 7, 1929

DATE OF LAST AMENDMENT
November 26, 2000

The State of the Vatican City, the smallest state in the world, is an enclave territory within the city of Rome placed under the authority of the Roman pontiff (the Holy See), the head of the Catholic Church. The state was established by the Lateran Treaty in 1929, concluded between the Holy See and Italy, in order to ensure to the pope absolute and evident independence and sovereignty, in the accomplishment of his worldwide mission, including all actions related to international relations. For this reason the State of the Vatican City, having such a particular character, cannot be considered separately from the Holy See and the Catholic Church.

The Vatican covers a geographical area smaller than the National Mall in Washington, D.C. It extends from the right bank of the Tiber River to a slight elevation (77.5 meters above see level) known as the Vatican Hill, the ancient location of a circus created by the emperor Caligula (37–41) and the site of a necropolis where Saint Peter, martyred during the reign of Nero (54–68), was buried. On this area the emperor Constantine (306–37) erected at the beginning of the fourth century the first Vatican Basilica, replaced by the present Saint Peter's Basilica built from the 15th to the 17th century.

One-third of the state's territory is occupied by palaces (e.g., the Apostolic Palace, the Vatican Library, the Vatican Secret Archives, and the Vatican Museum). The state is surrounded by the ancient Leonine Wall along the north, south, and west sides; the east boundary coincides with Saint Peter's Square, where the Colonnade of Bernini and a "white line" demarcate the border. According to the provisions of the Lateran Treaty, the square usually remains open to the public and is entrusted to the control of the Italian police forces, whereas the Vatican authorities and security forces have complete supervision of the square on the occasion of papal celebrations.

The sovereignty implemented by the Holy See over the Vatican state cannot be compared with that exercised until 1870 over the Papal States, some characteristics of which were comparable to ordinary state sovereignty. Nowadays, the purpose of the Vatican state is not that of guaranteeing the orderly existence and welfare of a population in a given territory. Rather, the state was created to ensure the absolute freedom and independence of the Holy See and to guarantee its authority over the Catholic Church in the world.

In this context it may be recalled what Pope Paul VI (1963–77), on October 4, 1965, said in his statement to the General Assembly of the United Nations: "You have before you a man like you: he is your brother, and among you, representatives of sovereign states, one of the smallest, invested he too, if thus it pleases you to consider us, with a minuscule, almost symbolic temporal sovereignty, all that he needs to be free to exercise his spiritual mission, and to assure whoever deals with him, that he is independent from every type of sovereignty of this world."

CONSTITUTIONAL HISTORY

The institution of the Vatican City state in 1929, with the conclusion of the Lateran Treaty between Italy and the Holy See, which legally settled the dispute known as the Questione Romana, did not represent a "beginning" of the temporal government exercised by the Holy See. The long-lasting fact of a territory in central Italy called the Patrimonium Sancti Petri and then the Papal States, or the States of the Church, saw the Holy See directly involved in activities proper to civil authorities as far as the government of a population in a given portion of territory was concerned. These states, formed over a period of 1,200 years, constituted a compact territory intended to guarantee the spiritual sovereignty of the pope and to prevent the association of the Catholic Church with any state and with a particular political commitment or position.

Various historical events had direct influence on the States of the Church, especially in more recent times, the French Revolution (starting in 1789); the Napoleonic campaign (1809–10), which led to the loss of territories; the Congress of Vienna (1815), which reestablished the pre-1789 borders; the occupation of the city of Rome by the Italian army on September 20, 1870; and its annexation to the Kingdom of Italy. The latter event caused the disappearance of the Papal States as Rome was proclaimed the capital of a united secular Italy.

The pope retreated into the Vatican Palace as a self-defined prisoner, refusing to cooperate with the Italian government, insisting on his old sovereignty and territorial rights. The conflict ended only with the Lateran Agreements that entered into force on June 7, 1929. These agreements comprised three international instruments: (1) the Lateran Treaty, which recognizes the absolute independence of the Holy See and inter alia created the Vatican City state under the full sovereignty of the pope; (2) a Concordat, regulating the situation of the Catholic Church and its institutions in Italy; (3) a Financial Convention, by which Italy gave to the Holy See a lump sum as a definitive settlement of the financial claims that followed the loss of the Papal States and of ecclesiastical properties.

With the Lateran Treaty the new state was officially established and became part of the international community. The Vatican state, indeed, was instituted as a "true" state from a formal point of view and therefore with all attributions proper to a state, including the existence of its own legal order formally distinct from (although based on) canon law, the legal system of the Catholic Church. Despite all this, the true function of the Vatican state is to be a guarantee for the independence of the Holy See, which exercises its own "sovereignty" over it.

FORM AND IMPACT OF THE CONSTITUTION

The State of the Vatican City lacks a formal constitution codified in a single document. However, one may refer to a collection of norms with constitutional value. In fact, the Lateran Treaty assumes the function of a source for norms about the nature and the purpose of the Vatican state, and it provides for many essential elements for the operation of the state.

Moreover, basic rules and fundamental principles are codified by six constituent laws, which entered into force on the same date as the Lateran Treaty: (1) the Fundamental Law of the Vatican City, as amended in 2001, which defines the character and the form of the state, the exercise of power, the public institutions, and their reciprocal relations; (2) the Law on the Source of the Legal Code, concerning the sources of the internal law of the state, establishing the links among the canon law, the laws and regulations issued by the Vatican authorities, and the laws issued by the Italian Kingdom or by the local government of Rome before June 8, 1929; (3) the Law on the Citizenship and Sojourn, which specifies the conditions to enjoy Vatican citizenship and the situation concerning the presence of any person in the state territory; (4) the Law on the Administrative Organization, with particular consideration of the power of officials and the regulation of contracts; (5) the Law on Economic, Commercial and Professional Organizations, which mainly defines the conditions of sale, purchase, and business enterprise; and (6) the Law on Public Security, which deals with subjects such as the Vatican state public order and the police. Finally, the 2002 Law on the Government of the Vatican state defines the structure, activities, and procedures of the Governatorato of the Vatican City, the central body that embraces the various administrative offices of the state.

BASIC ORGANIZATIONAL STRUCTURE

The State of the Vatican City is a unitary state with no internal administrative subdivisions, in part because of its small size.

LEADING CONSTITUTIONAL PRINCIPLES

The Vatican City, as a state, possesses certain peculiar characteristics, deriving from its special purpose.

A state is usually characterized—and consequently recognized—by sovereign authority, territory, population, and capacity to enter into relations with other states. The Vatican has indeed presented itself with a complete juridical and social organization, as a true state under the authority of the pope: "The Supreme Pontiff, Sovereign of the Vatican City State, has full legislative, judicial and executive powers". (Fundamental Law, Article 1). These same powers, during the "vacancy of the Apostolic See," when there is no pope, belong to the College of Cardinals, "which however will be able to only emanate legislative dispositions in emergency case, and this legislation may only be valid during the period of vacancy, unless confirmed at a later date by the Supreme Pontiff elected according to the rules of canon law" (Fundamental Law, Article 1.2).

It is important to emphasize that an independent territory is not absolutely indispensable to the institutional sovereignty of the Holy See, even in international law. The Vatican territory is but one of several political and juridical undertakings envisaged in the Lateran Treaty, as a means of support and symbol of the complete autonomy of the pope in the exercise of his spiritual mission. Given the limited extension of the territory, the treaty recognizes to the Holy See the full possession and property rights over some buildings and areas around the Vatican or in the city of Rome, according to the doctrine of extraterritoriality. These areas or buildings do not accommodate structures or offices of the Vatican state, but organs directly part of the Holy See as central government of the Catholic Church.

As stated in Article 4 of the Lateran Treaty, the recognition of the sovereignty and exclusive jurisdiction of the Holy See over the Vatican implies that there cannot be any interference whatsoever by foreign authorities and that within the Vatican City there will be no other authority than that of the Holy See. In fact, the power exercised by the Holy See over the Vatican state can be compared to that of a government over its territory and population. However, this similarity also entails deep contrast, given the singular nature and function of the Holy See in carrying out the universal mission of the Catholic Church.

This notion allows a further explanation of the subjective juridical qualification of "neutrality" of the Vatican state, as a consequence of an international obligation voluntarily assumed by the Holy See. Article 24 of the Lateran Treaty states: "The Holy See declares that it desires to take, and shall take, no part in any temporal rivalries between other States, nor in any international congresses called to settle such matters, save and except in the event of such parties making a mutual appeal to the pacific mission of the Holy See, the latter reserving in any event the right of exercising its moral and spiritual power."

The Vatican possesses independence and sovereignty not only with reference to its internal powers and domestic jurisdiction, but also in respect of international relations: conclusion of international treaties, relations with other states, participation in international meetings and conferences, and membership in intergovernmental organizations.

CONSTITUTIONAL BODIES

Different bodies, instituted by the constitutional norms or established by the laws in the Vatican City, have authority to perform functions relating to the exercise of power: the Pontifical Commission for Vatican City State, the president of the Pontifical Commission, the general counselor and the counselors of the state, the Governatorato, the Council of Directors, and the tribunals of the Vatican state.

These organs ordinarily achieve their tasks with delegated powers (the pope has full powers in the Vatican), also on the basis of specific internal regulations, with the exception of a few circumstances constitutionally recognized: above all the faculty of the supreme pontiff to retain some questions or cases for himself or for other instances such as legislative powers, or judicial powers. In matters of greater importance the organs exercising the legislative and executive powers must proceed in close cooperation with the Secretariat of State. The judicial power is exercised in the name of the supreme pontiff.

The Pontifical Commission for the State of the Vatican City

The Pontifical Commission Vatican City State consists of a cardinal president and other cardinals. At the moment they are seven, but no specific number is established. They are appointed by the pope for a five-year term. A secretary-general and a deputy secretary-general are also members of the commission; they participate in the meetings of the commission and collaborate, in a consultative status, in the decision process.

The main function of the Pontifical Commission is the exercise of legislative power. However, it also has executive powers, since it can examine issues of greater importance proposed to the commission by its president. In addition the commission has the exclusive power to issue general regulations, to approve the consolidated financial statement and the estimated budgets of yearly expenditures, and to submit them to the supreme pontiff.

The Lawmaking Process
The competence and the procedures that specifically involve the legislative function of the commission are explained through the special Regulation of the Pontifical Commission.

The supreme pontiff has the power to promulgate any legislation concerning the Vatican.

The President of the Pontifical Commission

The president of the Pontifical Commission, appointed by the pope, is the legal representative of the state in various matters, with the exclusion of questions related to international affairs. He exercises the executive power, according to the Fundamental Law and to other related norms and ordinances enforced in the Vatican legal system, particularly the 2001 Ordinance N°. CCCMXLVII on the competence of the president, secretary-general, and deputy secretary-general of the Pontifical Commission. The executive power of the president is implemented by issuing statutes, regulations, decrees, orders, and other lawful dispositions that must be confirmed by the commission within 90 days.

The whole activity of the state related to the exercise of the executive power is accomplished through different offices and structures, which are part of the Governatorato of the Vatican City. This entity is headed by the president of the commission, who, with the assistance of a secretary-general and a deputy secretary-general, has authority in the territory of the state as well as in the areas and buildings designated in the Lateran Treaty as "extraterritoriality zones" or "exempt buildings." In order to fulfill his functions the president is assisted by the Council of Directors, a special body composed of the heads of the different divisions and main offices of the Governatorato.

A special advisory function is assigned to the general counselor of the state and to the counselors of state in order to assist and to advise the Pontifical Commission and its president in the accomplishment of their legislative power, as well as "in other more relevant matters."

The Judiciary

The judicial power in the Vatican state is exercised according to the special 1987 Law on the Judiciary System. The court system is structured on three levels: (1) a single judge, who has primary jurisdiction on the matters conferred to him by law, relating to civil and criminal matters, and a court, composed of three judges dealing with cases not reserved for the single judge or prescribed by law; (2) a Court of Appeal, consisting of five members who sit in appeals that follow the verdicts adopted in the first instance; (3) a Court of Cassation (final appeal), composed of three cardinals authorized to receive and to examine petitions related to form or procedural defects in the proceedings of the lower courts.

Furthermore, with regard to juridical matters, given the particular situation of the Vatican, an enclave within the Italian territory, a special procedure of judicial cooperation has been established in the Lateran Treaty. Upon request of the Holy See in individual cases and also with a permanent delegation of power, Italian authorities take care of punishment of crimes committed in the Vatican City. In the case that the author of the crime has fled into Italian territory, the procedure against him or her is according to Italian law without any further requirements. The Holy See is obliged to hand over to the Italian state persons who have fled to the Vatican City charged with acts committed on Italian territory, considered criminal by the laws of both states. Analogous procedure applies to persons charged with crimes who flee into the extraterritorial zone under the jurisdiction of the Vatican, unless the authorities in charge of such property prefer to invite the Italian police to enter the premises and arrest the fugitives.

THE ELECTION PROCESS

The Vatican is an *elective monarchy:* The sovereign, the pope, is elected by the cardinals (with the exception of those who have reached their 80th birthday) gathered in the ancient institution of the Conclave with rules and procedures that have been established and defined by different formal decrees during history. At present, the conclave is functioning on the basis of the norms promulgated by Pope John Paul II on February 22, 1996, in the Apostolic Constitution Universi Dominici Gregis on the Vacancy of the Apostolic See and the Election of the Roman Pontiff. The contents of that instrument establish the government rules of the Catholic Church, and then of the Vatican state, in the transitional period, before the election of the new pope. They also establish the election procedures. For example, Article 62 states: "For the valid election of the Roman Pontiff two-thirds of the votes are required, calculated on the basis of the total number of electors present." The procedures of the election bring to light the importance that the norms of canon law have for the Vatican state: The Apostolic Constitution, in fact, is part of the legal system of the Catholic Church that affects the constitutional order of the Vatican.

POLITICAL PARTIES

As a result of the specific identity of the Vatican there are no political parties.

CITIZENSHIP

The population of the Vatican City does not constitute a national community—the Vatican constitutional law, in fact, makes no reference to nationality—but consists of persons subject to the power of the supreme pontiff. They are cardinals, dignitaries, senior officials, or all those persons who have at least a permanent residence in the Vatican according to special norms and procedures. Consequently the criteria generally accepted in order to confer citizenship (*ius sanguinis* or *ius soli*) are not taken into consideration by Vatican legislation.

Citizenship has a distinct feature that is acquired as a consequence of a particular relationship with the Holy

See (i.e., the diplomats and representative of the Holy See abroad) or with the Vatican state administration (i.e., function, regular employment, or permanent residence). This *ius officii* has no equivalent elsewhere.

FUNDAMENTAL RIGHTS

In the State of the Vatican City human rights are guaranteed and protected, respecting the provisions of canon law. It is evident from the very nature of the Catholic Church and from the spirit of its laws that the canon law rejects and condemns discrimination and violation of fundamental rights and that it has a positive attitude to promoting their implementation (Code of Canon Law, canons 741–43). According to the principle of fundamental equality, human persons all have the same rights and the same duties and possess the same legal capacity. In canon law, diversity does not result from differences in the legal status of persons in their being, but is determined by the diversity of vocations and the differences between roles.

Impact and Functions of Fundamental Rights

The conventions on human rights that have been ratified by the Holy See are implemented in the Vatican. In particular, the Convention on the Elimination of All Forms of Racial Discrimination (1966), of May 1, 1969; the Convention on the Rights of the Child (1989), of April 20, 1990; and the Convention against Torture and Other Cruel, Inhuman or Degrading Treatment or Punishment (1978), of June 26, 2002, have all been ratified.

A particular point arising from the examination of the laws mentioned concerns the supremacy of treaties over ordinary norms—that is, codes of canon law—and therefore prevailing of international law over domestic law. This explicitly establishes the primacy of international obligations contracted under treaties into which the Apostolic See has entered with states or other political entities.

Limitations to Fundamental Rights

The limitations to the exercise of the fundamental rights are those determined by law or by the particular situation of the State of the Vatican City. However, it is important to note that the conventions accepted by the Holy See are placed on a level higher than ordinary laws, subject to full respect of those areas of its own legislation "which are essentially within [its] domestic jurisdiction" (Article 2, paragraph 7, of the Charter of the United Nations). Such conventions assume the quality of standards in the law of the Holy See: "The canons of the Code do not abrogate, nor do they derogate from, agreements entered into by the Apostolic See with . . . civil entities; such agreements

therefore remain in force notwithstanding any contrary provisions of this Code" (can. 3).

ECONOMY

The Lateran Treaty confers on the Holy See the rights of exclusive property, considering the territory as a private domain. The Vatican is the unusual example of a "patrimonial sovereignty," as can be found in the concept of the Middle Ages of statehood. As a consequence of this constitutional principle, and according to the specific regulation of the Law on Citizenship and Sojourn and of the Law on Economic, Commercial and Professional Organizations, all people who have fixed residence in the Vatican City—ecclesiastics or laypersons—being subject to the sovereignty of the Holy See as a statehood authority, have no rights to the property of lands or buildings.

The finances of the state are constituted by contribution from different Catholic dioceses throughout the world, as well as the special annual collections known as Saint Peter's Pence. The income includes the sale of postage stamps, coins, medals, and tourist mementos; fees for admission to museums; and the sale of publications. The main categories of expenditure are salaries, pensions, fund reserves, preservation, and repairs of different buildings.

Vatican law is without any provisions regarding fiscal matters and therefore income taxes or tributes of any kind are not due by Vatican citizens or employers. When appropriate, only custom tariffs are established by special decree in order to regulate the imports of goods into territory under the jurisdiction of the Vatican authorities. Moreover, Italy exempts all persons who have fixed or partial employment in the Vatican state from taxes and fiscal duties.

RELIGIOUS COMMUNITIES

The Vatican state is based on Catholicism, as are its rules on citizenship. The issue of the status of different religious communities does not arise.

MILITARY DEFENSE AND STATE OF EMERGENCY

The Vatican state is constitutionally obliged to maintain its condition of neutrality and to implement the provisions of international treaties concluded by the Holy See on the behalf of the Vatican City, regarding production, detention, or use of conventional armaments as well as atomic, bacteriological, or chemical weapons.

The Swiss Guard Corps, founded in 1505 by Pope Julius II, is the only armed force existing in the Vatican City. In 1970, other military corps, the Noble Guard and the Palatine Guard, were dissolved. Unmarried Swiss males of

Catholic faith, between 19 and 30 years old, who have fulfilled their basic military training in the Swiss army form the Swiss Guard. They serve in this special body for a minimum of two years, with the possibility of extending service to a maximum of 25 years. The guard responsibilities include the protection and guarding of the pontiff, surveillance at the boundaries and entrances of the Vatican City, ceremonial honor guard, and security service.

A special police corps, the Gendarmeria, looks after security, public order, and the flow of vehicular traffic within state territory. If necessary, according to the Fundamental Law (Article 14), the president of the Pontifical Commission of the Vatican City may ask for assistance from the Swiss Guard.

AMENDMENTS TO THE CONSTITUTION

According to the Vatican legal system only the supreme pontiff can amend the Fundamental Law, and there is no specific rule for that process. Some of the constitutional laws are contained in the Lateran Treaty, whose amendment requires the agreement of the partner of the treaty, the Italian government.

PRIMARY SOURCES

Basic Law. "Legge Fondamentale dello Stato della Città del Vaticano [Fundamental Law of the State of Vatican City]." Available online. URL: http://www.vatican.va/news_services/press/documentazione/docs_index_en.htm. Accessed on June 29, 2006. (in Italian, German, Portuguese).

Lateran Treaty in English, February 11, 1929. Available online. URL: http://www.aloha.net/~mikesch/treaty.htm. Accessed on August 26, 2005.

SECONDARY SOURCES

Vincenzo Buonomo, "The Holy See in the Contemporary International Community: A Juridical Approach According to the International Law and Practice." In *Civitas et Justitia*. Vol. 2. Vatican City: Lateran University Press, 2004.

Hyginus E. Cardinale, *The Holy See and International Order.* Gerrards Cross, England: Colin Smythe, 1976.

"Vatican." *The Columbia Encyclopedia*. 6th ed. New York: Columbia University Press, 2004.

Vincenzo Buonomo

VENEZUELA

At-a-Glance

OFFICIAL NAME
Bolivarian Republic of Venezuela

CAPITAL
Caracas

POPULATION
24,390,000 (2005 est.)

SIZE
353,841 sq. mi. (916,445 sq. km)

LANGUAGES
Spanish and minority indigenous languages

RELIGIONS
Catholic 92%, other 8%

NATIONAL OR ETHNIC COMPOSITION
Half-caste 67%, white 21%, Afro-American
(descendants) 10%, indigenous peoples 2%

DATE OF INDEPENDENCE OR CREATION
July 5, 1811

TYPE OF GOVERNMENT
Presidential democracy

TYPE OF STATE
Federal state

TYPE OF LEGISLATURE
Unicameral parliament

DATE OF CONSTITUTION
December 30, 1999

DATE OF LAST AMENDMENT
No amendment

Venezuela is constitutionally defined as a democratic and social state of law and justice. Additionally, it is categorized as a decentralized federal state. However, the national government is highly privileged in assigning powers throughout the territorial levels of government; perhaps the truest categorization is a federal-central state.

The constitution is divided into the two fundamental texts: a dogmatic part, which includes an ample catalogue of rights and incorporates principles and obligations deriving from international law and human rights law; and an organic part, which covers the distribution of powers among the different political-territorial levels of government (national, state, and municipal), as well as the organization of public power and the fundamental aspects of the organization of states and municipalities. As regards the branches of national government, the classic tripartite division of legislative, executive, and judiciary powers has been expanded to include a citizenship branch and an electoral branch. The president is the chief of state and the executive government, elected through universal, direct, and secret vote. The constitutional design has been characterized by a marked presidentialist tendency.

CONSTITUTIONAL HISTORY

Venezuela's constitutional history begins with the approval of the first constitution in 1811, which was also the first Latin American national constitution. It was the turning point of a process leading toward the declaration of independence from the Kingdom of Spain. From that moment on an era was opened that has seen the promulgation of 26 constitutional texts to the present, with frequent interruptions of legal continuity by coups d'état or revolutions.

A global analysis of Venezuelan constitutional history leads to the recognition of two great polarities. One of these has been between the constitutional rule of law and an authoritarian state, the other between federalism and centralism.

Long periods of Venezuelan history have been under the yoke of the authoritarian model, characterized by total domination of the political scene by one leader or tyrant, who incarnated the fundamental values of the particular regime. In contrast, the constitutional state model was only in effect between 1830 and 1847; between 1864 and the beginnings of the 1870s; between 1936 and 1948; and then from 1958 until today.

The first constitution (1811) adopted the federal model, much influenced by the North American model and by the social reality of a country whose people were integrated at the province level. In 1830, the topic of state-hood was defined as a fundamental political decision, and a formula of compromise was adopted: a central-federal state. This system was in force until the end of the Federal War, which rampaged throughout the country for five years from 1859 until 1863, when a new constitution was promulgated, the 1864 constitution, which adopted a federal system that prevailed for the rest of the 19th century.

Thanks to Antonio Guzmán Blanco's autocracy, which began in the early 1870s, federalism did not entirely reflect institutional practice. During the first third of the 20th century, under the hegemony of Juan Vicente Gómez, ruler of one of Venezuela's longest dictatorships, the Venezuelan state was decidedly centralist, despite the fact that the 1925 constitution defined the country as a federation.

A historical constant in Venezuela's institutional evolution is the government's republican character, which has been maintained since 1811. Likewise, the predominant role of public rights and freedoms is manifest in all the constitutions. The institution of constitutional claims (*amparos*), which seeks to guarantee the validity and effectiveness of constitutional rights, points in the same direction.

The first Venezuelan constitutions of 1811, 1819, and 1821 were part of the independence process. Generals José Antonio Páez and José Tadeo Monagas and the liberal and conservative parties produced new constitutions in 1830, 1857, and 1858. Constitutions of the federative type and from Antonio Guzmán Blanco followed in 1864, 1874, 1888, 1891, and 1893. Again, a series of new constitutions was introduced by Cipriano Castro and Juan Vicente Gómez in 1901, 1904, 1909, 1914, 1922, 1925, 1928, 1929, and 1931. Those were followed by constitutions of transition toward democracy in 1936, 1945, and 1947, disrupted by the constitution of the Marcos Pérez Jiménez dictatorship in 1953. Finally, democratic constitutions were created in 1961 and 1999.

Most of the changes introduced between one constitution and the next were simple reforms or modifications. Using a more substantive criterion, the number of Venezuelan constitutions would be significantly reduced. The key documents were those of 1811, 1819, 1830, 1864, 1936, 1947, 1961, and 1999.

The 1961 constitution is of particular importance among the constitutions of democracy, both because of the long period in which it was in force (38 years) and because of its contents. This constitution was adopted after the fall of the military dictatorship of Marcos Pérez Jiménez. It was based on the Punto Fijo Covenant, signed on October 31, 1958, by the leaders of the three largest political parties. Thus the 1961 constitution was a product of a spirit of consensus, which was then made evident in the frequent use of compromise formulas in matters such as the country's economic system, in which socialist and liberal views joined on paper to form the state's economy.

A political system, under the lead of the Acción Democrática (AD) and the Social Christian Party (COPEI), emerged under the 1961 constitution and was labeled a partisan democracy. With the passage of time, the majority parties began to lose dynamism and social pull, and the important political decisions began to be adopted more and more by secret agreements between the leaders. Moreover, these political parties took hold of the country's institutions, including the administration of justice and even universities, professional associations, and labor unions. Furthermore, suspicion of corruption in the executive branch began to rise, while the economy fell from its artificial oil-derived prosperity.

In February 1989 the disorders known as El Caracazo broke out in the capital's suburbs and its poorest areas, as people ransacked supermarkets and other stores in protest against a rise in public transport prices. The violence was repressed with the use of excessive police and military force. As reform proposals made by a joint commission of congress in 1992 were not implemented, the political crisis deepened. Two attempted coups d'état, on February 4 and November 27, 1992, had popular support.

Promising to transform the political structure toward political and social democracy via a National Constituent Assembly, Hugo Chávez Frías, one of the military men who led the 1992 coup, was elected president in the 1998 elections.

The 1961 constitution did not provide for a Constituent Assembly, but several decisions of the Supreme Court of Justice cleared the way. By manipulating the election, the president's supporters managed to dominate the Constituent Assembly, immediately began to take over the legislative and judiciary branches in a revolutionary atmosphere, and quickly drafted a new constitution, which went into force on December 30, 1999.

Even after the approval of the constitution, the National Constituent Assembly continued to function, issuing a series of transitional decrees to govern until the new state organs could be constituted. It also designated the members of the National Legislative Commission (a transitional organ), as well as the justices of the new Supreme Tribunal of Justice, the prosecutor general, the ombudsperson, and the state comptroller. The unilateral designation of these senior authorities occurred outside the margin of the provisions of the new constitution.

FORM AND IMPACT OF THE CONSTITUTION

Venezuela has a written constitution, contained in a single document, the Constitution of the Bolivarian Republic of Venezuela. It has 350 articles, structured into nine titles.

There are discrepancies between the original version submitted to popular consultation through referendum; the text published in the *Official Gazette* of December 30, 1999; and a new version published March 24, 2000, which was the date when the constitutional text was reprinted. The version of March 24, 2000, contains the constitution's Exposition of Motives, which was never submitted to popular consultation and apparently was also never discussed or duly approved by the Constituent Assembly.

As provided in its Article 7, the constitution is the topmost norm and the basis of the juridical system; by implication therefore it has supremacy over all other legal norms. Moreover, this precept declares the constitution binding on all public powers and subjects of the law. In accordance with these provisions, ample powers are given to the Constitutional Chamber of the Supreme Tribunal of Justice and to other judicial organs in charge of protecting the constitution.

The constitution does not define any general guidelines as to the relationship between national and international law. However, the constitution is clear about human rights, and the economic integration of Latin America and the Caribbean. Distinctive features are the granting of constitutional hierarchy to the treaties and covenants on human rights ratified by Venezuela and the provision for their preferential application over the internal legal order as long as the international norms contain more favorable rights than those established in the constitution and national laws. The constitution also recognizes preferential application over national laws of norms dictated under the scope of Latin American and Caribbean integration agreements.

The constitution of the Bolivarian Republic of Venezuela is one of the nation's most publicized and best known to the common people. It was declared the symbol of the so-called Bolivarian Revolution, but it has also been invoked by the political opposition, to defend citizen participation and the rights it guarantees. Nevertheless, the constitution's significance has been reduced by the way that it has been interpreted frequently by the Constitutional Chamber of the Supreme Tribunal.

BASIC ORGANIZATIONAL STRUCTURE

Venezuela is a decentralized federal state. However, the constitution concentrates the highest authority in the "national public power," to a degree not compatible with the model of a federal state. Additionally, the constitution does not guarantee the boundaries of the current states, a role that is instead relegated to organic law. Moreover, parliament was made into a single chamber by eliminating the Senate, which had been based on territorial representation. Finally, the constitution does not provide for the participation of states in constitutional reform, as did the 1961 constitution. For these reasons, it has been said

that the 1999 constitution did not advance the decentralization process that had been developing under the derogated constitution.

There are presently 23 states, each of which is entitled to adopt its own constitution. These state constitutions can provide for the organization of municipalities and other local entities and their political-territorial division, subject to constitutional and national law; establish guidelines for the administration and investment of state resources; provide for state taxes, which are minimal; establish procedures for exploiting nonmetallic mineral resources not reserved to the federal state, such as salt and oyster beds; provide for the administration of uncultivated lands; and organize state police, subject to the provisions of national law. Moreover, state public services are covered in the state constitutions, as are state roads and national highways, commercial ports, and airports. There are also concurrent powers shared between states and the national government. These are governed by interlocking national and state laws.

States are divided into municipalities, which are the primary political unit in the national organization. Municipalities have separate legal personality and autonomy. Today, there are 335 municipalities throughout the country, and each elects its own government (mayors, councilpersons, and members of the community boards) autonomously. These authorities oversee matters under municipal jurisdiction, such as the provision and execution of domiciliary public services, territorial and urban delimitation, or historic patrimony. Municipal autonomy also includes the creation, collection, and investment of municipal income, which derives from tariffs for the use of municipal goods and services or taxes on local businesses. The constitution seeks to promote decentralization of state powers to the municipal level.

Finally, the 1999 constitution created a Federal Government Council to oversee decentralization and the transfer of powers. This council helps finance public investments that promote balanced regional development. However, this council has not yet been put into effect.

The city of Caracas is Venezuela's capital. Its metropolitan district has a complex structure. There is one metropolitan mayor, and one metropolitan town council, but there are many individual municipalities as well, with their own mayors and councils. All of these officials are elected by popular vote.

LEADING CONSTITUTIONAL PRINCIPLES

Venezuela is a free and independent republic, and a democratic and social state, based on the rule of law and justice. It is a federal decentralized state of a special kind. The constitution recognizes popular sovereignty as a fundamental principle. This sovereignty is expressed indirectly, through the election of the representatives who hold the seats of government, but it also manifests itself through direct means.

In that regard, the 1999 constitution is quite prolific in providing mechanisms for citizen participation, among which are consultative referenda, votes to recall officials, and referenda to abrogate or approve laws. There are also popular treaties or decrees with legal force; legislative, constitutional, and constituent initiative; and open councils and citizen assemblies. Organized civil society also has the right to participate in committees for the selection of nominees for the Supreme Tribunal of Justice (Judicial Nominations Committee) or members of the National Electoral Council (Electoral Nominations Committee), as well as for the selection of the ombudsperson, the prosecutor general, and the national comptroller (Citizen Power Nomination Evaluating Committee).

At the state and local levels, there are Councils for Public Planning and Policy, which are formed by local municipal and regional legislators and representatives of organized communities. Advocates of the 1999 constitution signal these features as its greatest achievement, since they represent the conversion of party-based representative democracy to a participatory democracy, in which the people are the protagonists of public decision making. In practice, these provisions have had little effect.

Another fundamental principle of the Venezuelan constitutional regime is the prevalence of human rights, which occupy an extensive part of the constitutional text.

Of the principles of public power, the most relevant is that of separation or division of powers. However, this separation is not absolute, as the various powers must collaborate.

CONSTITUTIONAL BODIES

The constitution provides for the following organs: the National Assembly; the national executive power, including the president of the republic, the executive vice president, and the secretaries; the judicial power, with the Supreme Tribunal of Justice at its head; the citizen branch, composed of the Ombudsperson's Office, the Prosecutor General's Office, and the National Comptroller's Office; and the electoral power topped by the Electoral National Council.

The President

The president is the chief of state and the chief of the executive. As chief of state, he or she oversees foreign relations and signs international treaties, covenants, and agreements. As chief of the executive government, the president designates and removes the executive vice president and the secretaries of the executive, allocates their responsibilities, presides over the Council of Secretaries, and administers the national budget.

The president can declare states of emergency and limit individual rights in cases provided by the constitution. The president can also adopt decrees with the force of law, whenever authorized to do so by an enabling law from the legislature, and draft regulations that develop laws. The president can also dissolve the National Assembly whenever the latter has removed three executive vice presidents as a result of censure votes within one session. The president is the commander in chief of the national armed forces, promotes officials from the rank of colonel or ship captain and upward, and can assign soldiers to official positions that would otherwise not be available to them. Finally, the president presides over the National Defense Council.

The presidential term is six years, with one consecutive reelection allowed. The president must be a Venezuelan-born person, have no other nationality, be over 30 years of age, have secular status, and have never been condemned by a final judicial decision. The president's mandate can be revoked by popular demand if, after the first half of the six-year period, no less than 20 percent of the registered voters request a recall vote. The president loses office if more voters support recall than voted for him or her in the election and if the number of voters in the recall election is at least 25 percent of registered voters.

The Parliament (National Assembly)

The National Assembly is a single-chamber parliament, elected in each federal entity through universal, direct, and secret voting. Additionally, each state elects three representatives, as do the indigenous peoples. At present, there are 165 representatives in the National Assembly.

The main functions of the National Assembly are to legislate on subject matters of national competence and on the operations of the various branches of public power and to exercise control over the executive. Additionally, parliament can propose amendments and reforms to the constitution, decree amnesty, discuss and approve the national budget, pass a censure vote on the vice president and secretaries of the executive, and authorize the executive branch to enter into contracts of national interest.

The assembly regularly works in two ordinary sessions, extending across most of the year, and can meet in special sessions as well, at its own or the president's summons. Drafts and reports are prepared by 15 permanent or temporary special committees. During recess, the National Assembly is run by the delegate committee, which is formed by the assembly's president, its vice presidents, and the presidents of each permanent committee.

Representatives must be Venezuelan, whether born or nationalized; must have lived in Venezuela for at least 15 years; be over 21 years of age; and have resided at least four consecutive years in the entity that they seek to represent before the date of the election. No major national, state, or municipal officer may run for representative.

Representatives of the National Assembly can be reelected for two consecutive terms, and they enjoy the privileges of immunity and inviolability of their privacy in the exercise of their functions. In order for them to be brought to trial, the Supreme Tribunal of Justice must authorize the trial by deciding favorably on a special merits trial petition.

The Lawmaking Process

There is one lawmaking procedure common to the various types of laws, though some categories have special quorum and majority requirements. The initiative for a bill can originate with the executive branch, any of the permanent commissions, the delegate committee; any three representatives, the Supreme Tribunal of Justice (laws referring to judicial organization and procedure), the electoral branch (on electoral matters), the citizen branch (laws pertaining to its organs), 0.1 percent of the total number of registered voters, and the state legislative councils (on matters related to state laws). Two discussions must be held at different sessions. The first is dedicated to the draft's motives, scope, and structure; the second is an article-by-article analysis. Once the legal draft is approved without amendments in the second discussion, it is considered a sanctioned law. If the president agrees with the content of the law, the president proceeds to its promulgation by signing it and orders its publication in the *Official Gazette*.

Organic laws are a different legislative category; laws are organic when the constitution designates them as such, or when they organize public powers, develop constitutional rights, or serve as a legal framework for other laws. Except those that are constitutionally designated as such, organic law drafts need the support of a two-thirds majority of the National Assembly before the first discussion. After this, the regular lawmaking process applies, except that draft organic laws must be sent to the Supreme Tribunal of Justice for a ruling on constitutionality.

Enabling laws authorize the president to legislate through decrees with the rank and force of law. These enabling laws must be approved by a qualified majority equivalent to three-fifths of all members. Their contents must include the purpose, guidelines, and framework of the subject matters delegated to the president for legislation, as well as the duration of the enablement.

Finally, there are base laws, which regulate the concurrent power of the national government and the states.

Bills that originate through popular initiative must be considered in the session immediately after their presentation to the assembly. Otherwise, the bill must be submitted to a popular referendum.

The Judiciary

The judiciary is formed by the Supreme Tribunal of Justice and the other tribunals and courts of the republic. The constitution blends the judiciary into the judicial system, which also includes the general prosecutor, the ombudsperson, and organs of criminal investigation; auxiliary and other judicial officers; penitentiaries, justices of the peace, arbitrators, citizens who participate in the administration of justice, and all lawyers authorized to practice law.

The Supreme Tribunal of Justice is not only the highest judicial court, but also the director, overseer, and administrator of the judiciary and the public defense system. The Supreme Tribunal includes six chambers: the Civil Cassation (appeals) Chamber, the Criminal Cassation Chamber, the Social Cassation Chamber, the Electoral Chamber, the Political-Administrative Chamber, and the Constitutional Chamber. Every chamber seats five justices, except the Constitutional Chamber, which seats seven. The Plenary Chamber is formed by all the justices of all the chambers to deal with special matters.

The Constitutional Chamber of the Supreme Tribunal of Justice can declare absolute or partial nullity of national laws and other public acts of national, state, municipal, or any other public authority that are contrary to the constitutional text. The chamber is the ultimate and supreme interpreter of the constitution, and its interpretative criteria are binding on every other chamber of the tribunal and the rest of the nation's courts.

The constitution expressly declares the independence of the judiciary, as well as the functional, financial, and administrative autonomy of the Supreme Tribunal of Justice, which commands at least 2 percent of the national budget allocated to the justice system. The tribunal drafts its own budget and that of the judiciary.

The constitution created a Judicial Nominations Committee staffed by the various civil society sectors, which compiles lists of potential candidates for supreme tribunal justices. This constitution also increased their term to 12 years, while prohibiting reelection.

Justices, judges, state attorneys, and public defenders are barred from political, partisan, collegiate, union, or any other such form of activism, as well as from conducting, whether personally or through third parties, any lucrative activity incompatible with their public functions.

Another innovation of the 1999 constitution is the recognition of indigenous justice, as long as its norms and procedures do not collide with the constitution, national laws, and public order. Furthermore, it foresees the creation of a justice of the peace system and the promotion of alternative means of conflict resolution.

In the area of organization of the judiciary, the constitution calls for a law to organize tribunals into judicial circuits and to create regional courts. However, this law has not yet been adopted. As regards grade or rank, the present judicial structure mandates that the Supreme Tribunal of Justice is followed in rank by superior courts or tribunals with jurisdiction over civil, commercial, and criminal matters, which receive appeals petitions in those areas. Immediately lower are first instance courts, some with civil and commercial jurisdiction, others with responsibility for criminal matters. Finally, there are municipal courts.

In addition, there are special courts and tribunals, such as courts for the protection of children and adolescents, tax courts, and administrative procedural tribunals.

In reality and practice, the judicial system differs substantially from what was foreseen in the 1999 constitution. The judiciary is today one of the weakest institutions within the Venezuelan rule of law. Despite compliance with certain formal aspects, the selection and designation of the supreme tribunal's justices have taken place in flagrant contradiction to the constitution, since there was never true citizen participation in the Judicial Nominations Committee, and political interest prevailed over institutional ends. Also, the vast majority of judges (almost 80 percent) were designated directly by the highest-ranking members of the judiciary, without the required public competition. They are called provisional or temporary judges, and this provisionary status exposes them to undue pressure from those who appointed them and have the power to remove them. Many lack the best qualifications, or even the right vocational background. Furthermore, disciplinary matters within the judiciary are still being decided on the basis of the 1999 transitory decree, since the legislature has not yet approved the Judges' Code of Ethics, and no disciplinary tribunals have been created to date.

Finally, despite the constitution's recognition of the right to access to justice, a large percentage of the country's population (the poor) still face important obstacles in the courts and tribunals. Notwithstanding, the recent reform of legal procedure in labor matters and the stimulation of alternative means for conflict resolution in this area of the law are positive signs.

The Citizen Branch

The Ombudsperson's Office, the Prosecutor General's Office, and the National Comptroller's Office form the so-called citizen branch, which is responsible for investigating and punishing any acts violating public ethics and administrative morals; overseeing the conduct of a good administration and the legality of the use of public resources; and promoting citizenship education. The branch has the power to issue warnings to public officials about faults in the exercise of their functions.

The Ombudsperson's Office is a novel institution for Venezuela. It is in charge of the defense and oversight of human rights and the protection of collective and diffuse interests of the citizenship. The Prosecutor General's Office is in charge of prosecuting all criminal actions in public action crimes, supervising criminal investigations, and ensuring respect for human rights in the judicial process. The comptroller general audits and supervises the national accounts, as well as public assets and resources.

Electoral Branch

The constitution considers election oversight as a branch of government. The electoral branch is overseen by the National Electoral Council, which organizes, administers, and oversees all acts related to the election of public officials by popular vote and all referenda.

THE ELECTION PROCESS AND POLITICAL PARTICIPATION

In order to be eligible for the highest positions in national government, a candidate must be a Venezuelan-born citizen. These positions are the presidency and the vice presidency; the presidency and vice presidency of the National Assembly; seats on the Supreme Tribunal of Justice; the presidency of the National Electoral Council; the attorney general, comptroller general, prosecutor general, and ombudsperson; the secretaries of defense, interior, justice, finance, energy and mining, and education; as well as state governor or mayor of frontier municipalities.

Also, the following government positions are subject to popular election: president, governor, mayor, National Assembly representative, State Legislative Council representative, municipal councilperson, and community council member. In the case of candidates to collegiate bodies (assembly, legislative councils, and municipal councils), the law provides a mixed voting system: Some are elected by single-member constituencies and others through proportional representation.

POLITICAL PARTIES

The constitution does not mention political parties directly, partly because of the discredit they suffered in the 1980s. Rather, the text uses a more ample concept, that of "organizations with political objectives." In practice, the weight of political participation still falls on the parties. The constitution does its best to ensure their democratic operations, in choosing their own officials and in nominating candidates for election.

There are many political parties and election groups. Nationally, there is the government party, Movimiento Quinta República (MVR), which occupies the majority of all popular representation positions; Acción Democrática (AD), which is one of the first political opposition parties; along with the Partido Socialcristiano (COPEI); the Socialist Movement (MAS); Primero Justicia; and Proyecto Venezuela.

CITIZENSHIP

Venezuelan nationality can be acquired by birth (originary) or upon compliance with certain prerequisites. Originary nationality is reserved to those who are born within the country to at least one Venezuelan parent, and to those who have at least one Venezuelan-born parent, outside Venezuelan territory, if they have established their residence in Venezuela or declare their will to acquire Venezuelan nationality. The same applies to those who have naturalized Venezuelan parents and are born outside Venezuelan territory but have established their residence within the country before becoming 18 years of age and have declared their desire to acquire Venezuelan nationality before turning 25.

Foreigners who have resided in the country for at least 10 years and comply with all the requirements of the naturalization process can acquire Venezuelan nationality. Foreigners from Spain, Portugal, Italy, Latin America, and Caribbean countries have a shorter, five-year residency requirement. Anyone who marries a Venezuelan can also acquire Venezuelan nationality five years after the wedding.

Any Venezuelan over 18 who registers in the permanent electoral registry and who is not subject to political inability or civil interdiction can exercise his or her political rights and duties and is considered a citizen. Naturalized Venezuelans have the same political rights, as long as they have entered the country before turning seven years old and have permanently resided within national territory until the age of 18.

FUNDAMENTAL RIGHTS

Title 3 of the constitution is dedicated to fundamental rights, which are subsumed under the international term *human rights*. Among the principles adopted from international law are progressiveness, which opposes any measures that might imply a retreat in the protection of rights, and the nondivisibility and interdependence of human rights, which prevent the sacrifice of one right to protect another.

There is also a general duty to investigate, punish, and repair human rights violations. In this context, amnesty laws that prevent the prosecution of human rights violations or crimes against humanity are prohibited. Moreover, these violations and crimes can only be investigated and prosecuted by judicial courts, and there is no statutory limitation on their prosecution.

Impact and Function of Fundamental Rights

The bill of rights in the constitution has an ample and open character. Its ampleness is reflected in the extensive and generous list of rights, including different types of rights. Following the terminology of international treaties, Venezuelans have civil and political rights, as well as economic, social, and cultural rights. The open character of the bill of rights is evidenced by the fact that the listing of constitutional rights is merely an enunciation and does not exclude other rights inherent to human nature, which do not need to be legislated upon in order to be effective. The rights guaranteed are binding primarily on the state, but they also bind private persons, who also have a general duty to respect the rights of others.

Human rights occupy a high place within the constitutional system since they have been declared superior values of the legal framework and the basis for the legitimacy of the government and the political regime. Unfortunately, the day-to-day impact of human rights in political and social life is still only partial. In matters related to politics or partisanship, rights have frequently been limited, sometimes with the support of the highest judicial levels, particularly rights such as freedom of expression, freedom of association, freedom to form workers' unions, freedom of conscience, and freedom of political participation.

In contrast, there has been progress in access to justice and the effectiveness of judicial remedies. Also, social rights have often been respected by official policies and judicial decisions.

Limitations to Fundamental Rights

As a general rule, constitutional rights are subject to limitations, which must be backed by a law and be necessary for the protection of other rights or of the public interest.

ECONOMY

The social-economic system can be qualified as a mixed system, oriented toward the development of a social market economy and inspired by the principles of social justice, economic freedom, private initiative, and free trade. The state owns all oil-related activities and those of other industries that are considered strategic to the development of the nation.

The constitution guarantees the right to private property, subject to restrictions established by law for the benefit of the public interest. Economic freedoms are also recognized, such as the freedom to work and the freedom to incorporate enterprises, commerce, and industries. The state is entitled to dictate measures to plan rationally and regulate the economy.

The state is multifaceted and active in the regulation, distribution, and development of various key sectors of the economy. It participates in the exploitation of certain resources, such as iron, aluminum, and hydrocarbons. In practice, however, the economy depends almost entirely on oil revenues, and thus on oil price fluctuations in the global market.

RELIGIOUS COMMUNITIES

In Venezuela, the state is nonconfessional, and freedom of religion and worship is guaranteed by the constitution. Every person can publicly and privately perform the rites of any religion he or she chooses, as long as it is not contrary to good manners, morals, or public order. No one can circumvent compliance with the law or prevent another person from exercising his or her rights on the basis of religious beliefs.

Roman Catholicism is by far the most professed religion. However, Muslim, Jewish, Evangelical, and Adventist communities also exist. The constitution protects the independence and autonomy of all religions. Civil legislation recognizes their legal personality, making them recipients of rights and duties. There is an Ecclesiastic Patronage Law, which protects the establishment and promotion of Catholicism throughout the country.

MILITARY DEFENSE AND STATE OF EMERGENCY

The National Armed Force is composed of the army, the navy, the air force, and the national guard. They are defined in the constitution as an essentially professional body, lacking a political role. However, the deletion of the words *apolitical and nondeliberative,* which existed in the previous constitution, has been interpreted as an attempt to politicize the armed forces and to place them at the service of a particular political project.

In any case, active members of the military are prohibited from running for office and from participating in acts of political propaganda or proselytism. The constitution is implicitly based on the premise that the military are subject to civil authority. In practice, there is a growing tendency to place active or retired military members in key positions of the central and decentralized administrations.

The National Armed Force is responsible for guaranteeing the nation's sovereignty, independence, and territorial integrity. They cooperate in maintaining internal order and participate in national development. This last role has raised fears that the role of the military may be abused, as it moves into the civil authority and, ultimately, politics.

The 1999 constitution eliminated mandatory military service as a general duty, by providing for the possibility of freely opting for civil service, which makes conscientious objection superfluous.

States of exception or emergency are regulated by the constitution and an organic law. The president is empowered to declare these states, but they must be ratified by the National Assembly and declared legal by the Supreme Tribunal of Justice. States of exception increase the powers of the executive branch and the military authorities, but they may not interrupt the operations of the organs of public power, or affect the subordination of military power to civil authority.

AMENDMENTS TO THE CONSTITUTION

The constitution provides for three means of change: amendments, reform, and national constituent assembly. Amendments are minor changes and as a general rule are overseen by the National Assembly and ratified by a referendum. A reform has a broader scope, but it does not alter the fundamental principles of the constitution. Reforms must be approved by the qualified majority of the representatives of the National Assembly. Finally, a National Constituent Assembly allows for the drafting of a new constitution. The constitution does not explicitly require a referendum to approve a new constitution, but such a requirement can be deduced from the fundamental principles and from the grant of constituent power to the people.

PRIMARY SOURCES

Constitution in English. Available online. URL: http://www.vheadline.com/printer_news.asp?id=6831. Accessed on September 29, 2005.

Constitution in Spanish. Available online. URLs: www.asambleanacional.gov.ve; http://www.tsj.gov.ve. Accessed on July 27, 2005.

"Constitución de la República Bolivariana de Venezuela" (official version in Spanish). *Gaceta Oficial de la República Bolivariana de Venezuela* (official gazette) no. 36.860 (December 1999).

SECONDARY SOURCES

Report on Justice, 2d ed. (2004–2005) *Venezuela* Available online. URL: http://www.cejamericas.org/reporte/muestra_pais.php?idioma=ingles&pais<0 x003D>VENEZUEL&tipreport=&seccion=0. Accessed on August 19, 2005.

Maria Isabel Fleury and Ruben Eduardo Lujan, "New Venezuelan Constitution," *International Legal Practitioner* 25 (2000): 60–63.

Gregory Wilpert, Venezuela's New Constitution. 2003. Available online. URL: http://www.venezuelanalysis.com/articles.php?artno=l003. Accessed on June 29, 2006.

Jesús María Casal Casal Hernández and Alma Chacón Hanson

VIETNAM

At-a-Glance

OFFICIAL NAME
Socialist Republic of Vietnam

CAPITAL
Hanoi

POPULATION
81,620,000 (2005 est.)

SIZE
127,259 sq. mi. (329,600 sq. km)

LANGUAGES
Vietnamese

RELIGIONS
Buddhist 50%, Catholic 25%, Caodaist 10%, Hoa Hao Buddhist 5%, other (largely of Muslim, Protestant) 10%

NATIONAL OR ETHNIC COMPOSITION
Vietnamese 84%, Chinese 2%, also Khmer, Cham

(remnant of once, great Indianized Champa Kingdom), and over 54 ethnolinguistic groups

DATE OF INDEPENDENCE OR CREATION
September 2, 1945

TYPE OF GOVERNMENT
State socialism

TYPE OF STATE
Unitary state

TYPE OF LEGISLATURE
Unicameral parliament

DATE OF CONSTITUTION
April 15, 1992

DATE OF LAST AMENDMENT
December 25, 2001

According to its constitution, Vietnam is a socialist republic based on principles of socialist legality and unity of power, with the National Assembly as the highest state organ. It is made up of 64 provinces and municipalities under a central authority. The constitution provides for far-reaching guarantees of human rights.

The president is the head of state, but his or her role is mostly ceremonial. The central political figure is the prime minister, the head of the executive government. The president and the prime minister are elected by the National Assembly. The constitution guarantees the free, equal, general, and direct election of members of the National Assembly.

The constitution upholds religious freedom, and religious communities and the state are separate. Vietnam promotes a multisectoral economy, which functions in accordance with market mechanisms under the management of the state. The military is subject, in fact and in law, to the civil government. The constitution declares that it is state policy to promote peace and friendship and expand its relations and cooperation with all countries in the world, regardless of political and social regime, on the basis of respect for each other's independence, sovereignty, and territorial integrity; noninterference in each other's internal affairs; equality; and mutual interest.

CONSTITUTIONAL HISTORY

Vietnam as an independent entity dates back to the early history of Southeast Asia. Around the fifth century B.C.E., the Dong Song culture, a unique and distinct civilization exhibiting a high level of technical and artistic skill and famed for rich bronze objects, emerged in northern Vietnam. Recent ethnological and archaeological studies have asserted the existence of a Hung dynastic period during the Van Lang (later Au Lac) Kingdom around 1000 B.C.E., In 200 B.C.E., the Au Lac Kingdom was invaded and annexed by the powerful Chinese Han Empire to the north, leading to a 10-century domination by China.

In the 10th century C.E., the Vietnamese built an independent state named Dai Viet. Centuries of war against the Chinese and Mongol Empires followed. In the middle of 19th century France began to encroach on the country, and before long Vietnam was transformed from a centralized state into a colonial one under French domination.

At the peak of the movement for national liberation, under the leadership of the Communist Party of Vietnam (then the Indochina Communist Party), headed by Ho Chi Minh, the National Congress of Representatives was convened in Tan Trao, Tuyen Quang province, on August 16, 1945. The congress agreed on launching the national general uprising proposed by the Indochina Communist Party. It issued a declaration calling on the people throughout the country to seize power and appointed a Committee for National Liberation, the Provisional Government. On September 2, 1945, Ho Chi Minh, on behalf of the Provisional Government, presented the Declaration of National Independence, proclaiming the birth of the Democratic Republic of Vietnam. In 1946, the first general elections were held throughout the country. For the first time in Vietnam's history, all Vietnamese citizens 18 years and older, regardless of gender, wealth, ethnic group, religion, or political opinion, could cast their votes to elect their own representatives to the National Assembly. Ho Chi Minh was elected president of the Democratic Republic of Vietnam, and on November 9, 1946, the National Assembly approved its first constitution.

After the formation of the Democratic Republic of Vietnam, France attempted to reassert control; the result was a renewed war of resistance that ended with the defeat of French forces at Dien Bien Phu on May 7, 1954, and eventually led to the Geneva Agreement on Vietnam signed in July 1954. According to this agreement the country was temporarily split along the 17th parallel into North Vietnam and South Vietnam and was to be reunified within two years (1956), following general elections held all over Vietnam. The elections, however, did not take place, as the southern part of Vietnam was placed under the control of, first, a pro-French and, later, a pro-American administration. This political situation led to the resurgence of the national movement with the goal of reunifying the country.

To help implement a socialist regime in the north of Vietnam and strengthen the base for the war against U.S. troops in the South, a new constitution was adopted in 1959. In 1973, the United States signed the Paris Peace Agreement and withdrew its troops from Vietnam.

After reunification with the South in 1975, Vietnam was renamed the Socialist Republic of Vietnam on July 2, 1976. A new constitution, establishing the political and economic system of the unified state, was adopted in 1980. The 1980 constitution followed the traditions of the 1946 and 1959 constitutions in recognizing the people's sovereignty, human rights, and unity of powers. New solutions, some based on the model of the Soviet Union, were introduced to aid the transition to socialism. For the first time the constitution declared Communist Party leadership of state and society. The economy was to be organized according to the socialist principles of a centrally planned economy and collectivization of land. A State Council (Hoi dong nha nuoc), which combined in a single institution two previous institutions, the presidency and the Standing Committee of the National Assembly, was created.

To restore an economy destroyed by years of war the government introduced free-market economic reforms in 1986, in the process of Doi Moi, or "all-around renovation." In June 1991, the Seventh Congress of the Communist Party of Vietnam reaffirmed its determination to pursue the renovation process and to maintain a foreign policy guided by the precept "Vietnam wants to be friends with all other countries in the international community for peace, independence and development." The 1992 constitution was promulgated to institutionalize the new policies of the Socialist Republic of Vietnam.

FORM AND IMPACT OF THE CONSTITUTION

Vietnam has a written constitution, codified in a single document, called the fundamental law of the state (Dao luat co ban), which has precedence over all other national law.

The constitution of Vietnam details the legal system of the country and establishes its values, and all other legal documents must conform to its provisions. The significance of the constitution, however, supersedes its legal implications in helping to shape the direction of the country's development and reaffirming Vietnam's policy of international peace, friendship, and cooperation.

BASIC ORGANIZATIONAL STRUCTURE

Vietnam is a unitary state divided into 64 provinces and cities under central authority. The central government, comprising a prime minister and the cabinet, is the highest administrative body of the land. It has the powers to implement the policies of the state and the duty to "ensure the effectiveness of the state apparatus from the center to the grassroots [and] respect for and implementation of the constitution and the law."

At provincial and local levels, elected people's councils choose people's committees to perform executive functions. Legislative and constitutional authority is vested in the popularly elected National Assembly, which selects from among its own members a president to serve as head of state. The highest judicial body is the Supreme People's Court, which supervises the work of people's courts and the Supreme People's Procuracy with people's procurators at provincial and district levels.

LEADING CONSTITUTIONAL PRINCIPLES

Vietnam's system of government is a socialist republic. On the one hand, the constitution clearly stipulates the legislative, executive, and judicial powers. However, Article 2 states that "state powers are unified and decentralized to state bodies, which shall coordinate with one another in the exercise of the legislative, executive, and judiciary powers." Thus, there is unity rather than separation of state powers. The National Assembly is the highest organ of state power. "However, in practice its function is limited, as it meets in only two brief sessions per year."

The Vietnam constitutional system is defined by a number of leading principles: Vietnam is governed by democratic centralism; it is an independent and sovereign country and "a law-governed socialist state of the people, by the people, and for the people."

According to Article 3 of the constitution, the state "guarantees and unceasingly promotes the people's mastery in all fields, and severely punishes all acts violating the interests of the motherland and the people; it strives to build a rich and strong country in which socialist justice prevails, and men have enough to eat and to wear, enjoy freedom, happiness, and all necessary conditions for complete development."

According to Article 4, the Communist Party of Vietnam—the only political party in the country—is the vanguard of the working class and the force leading the state and society. Its actions are based on Marxist-Leninist doctrine and Ho Chi Minh's teaching.

The constitution has provided a number of principles of the organization of the state. First is the principle of the unity of all nationalities living in the territory of Vietnam. According to this principle, the state must administer a policy of equality, solidarity, and mutual assistance among all nationalities and forbid all acts of national discrimination and division. Second, the principle of state accountability provides that all state organs, cadres, and employees must show respect for the people, devotedly serve them, and maintain close links with them; that all manifestations of bureaucratism, arrogance, arbitrariness, and corruption shall be vigorously opposed. Third, the principle of legality entails that the state shall exercise the administration of society by means of the law and thereby unceasingly strengthen socialist legality.

CONSTITUTIONAL BODIES

The main bodies defined in the constitution are the National Assembly, the president of the state, the prime minister, the People's Councils, the Supreme People's Court, and the Supreme People's Procuracy. Other bodies include the Standing Committee of the National Assembly, which functions as its permanent committee, and the National Defense and Security Council, which comprises the president of the state, the vice president, and others, who need not be members of the National Assembly.

The National Assembly (Parliament)

The constitution defines the National Assembly as "the highest representative organ of the people and the highest organ of state power" in Vietnam. The unicameral assembly has three main functions: creating legislation, formulating major domestic and foreign policies, and exercising supreme supervision over all activities of the state.

The National Assembly is not a full-time working body; it meets in two sessions of about two weeks duration per year. Therefore, the Standing Committee of the National Assembly has the predominant role in the functioning of the National Assembly and has considerable powers in preparing for and presiding over its sessions. The Standing Committee creates ordinances, which are decree laws on matters entrusted to it by the National Assembly, and exercises supervision and control over the activities of the executive government, the Supreme People's Court, and the Supreme Peoples' Procuracy in the period between National Assembly sessions. The Standing Committee of the National Assembly consists of the chair of the National Assembly, the vice chairs of the National Assembly, and members elected from among Assembly delegates, who cannot be members of the executive government at the same time.

The National Assembly is the only organ that has legislative powers. As such, it can make and amend the constitution, make and amend laws, and develop a program for creating laws and ordinances. Almost all of the laws passed by the National Assembly are initiated by the executive government. The National Assembly is a unicameral parliament. It elects, releases from duty, and removes from office the country's president and vice president, the chairman or chairwoman of the National Assembly, the vice chairpersons and members of the Standing Committee of the National Assembly, the prime minister, the chief justice of the Supreme People's Court, and the president of the Supreme People's Procuracy. The National Assembly exercises supreme control over conformity with the constitution, the law, and resolutions of the National Assembly and reviews the reports of the country's president, the Standing Committee of the National Assembly, the executive government, the Supreme People's Court, and the Supreme People's Procuracy.

The members of the National Assembly have the right to propose bills, make motions on laws before the National Assembly, and draft ordinances before the National Assembly Standing Committee. They also have the right to question the president of state, the National Assembly chairperson, the prime minister and other members of the executive government, the chief justice of the Supreme People's Court, and the president of the Supreme People's Procuracy.

An important right of the members of the National Assembly that helps to ensure their independence is parliamentary privilege. Deputies must not be detained or persecuted and their places of residence and work must not be searched without the consent of the National Assembly or of the National Assembly Standing Committee when the National Assembly is in recess. The only exception to this privilege occurs when a deputy is placed in custody when committing a crime, but the arrest must be immediately reported to the National Assembly or the National Assembly Standing Committee for consideration and decision.

At present, the National Assembly 11th Legislature consists of 498 deputies. Its period of office, the legislative term, is five years. The deputies are elected in a general, direct, free, equal, and secret balloting process.

The Executive Government

The government is the executive organ of the National Assembly, the highest organ of state administration of the Socialist Republic of Vietnam. The executive government is composed of the prime minister, the deputy prime ministers, the ministers, and other members. With the exception of the prime minister, its members are not necessarily members of the National Assembly. The prime minister is accountable to the National Assembly and reports to the assembly, its Standing Committee, and the country's president.

The constitutional powers of the prime minister are largely responsible for the prime minister's dominance in Vietnamese politics. The prime minister has considerable powers to direct the work of the executive government, shaping the policy of the government and its personnel.

The tenure of the executive government is the same as that of the National Assembly, i.e., five years. When the latter's tenure ends, the administration remains in office until the new legislature establishes a new administration.

The constitution stipulates that the ministers and the other executive government members shall be responsible to the prime minister and the National Assembly.

The constitution does not clearly stipulate the dismissal of the members of the executive government, although there is a clause in the law on organization of the National Assembly that the assembly can cast a vote of confidence for individuals who hold positions elected or ratified by the National Assembly. As such the members of the executive government can be subject to a vote of confidence at the proposal of the Standing Committee of the National Assembly.

The President of the State

The president is the head of state and represents the Socialist Republic of Vietnam internally and externally. The president promulgates the constitution, laws, and ordinances. The president is the commander in chief of the armed forces and the head of the National Defense and Security Council.

The president can propose to the National Assembly a motion to elect, release from duty, and remove from office the vice president, the prime minister, the chief justice of the Supreme People's Court, and the president of the Supreme People's Procuracy. The president formally appoints, releases from duty, and dismisses the deputy chief justices and judges of the Supreme People's Court, and the deputy president and procurators of the Supreme People's Procuracy. The president has the authority to proclaim a state of war, to proclaim an amnesty, to order a general or partial mobilization, and to proclaim a state of emergency throughout the country or in a specific region.

The country's president is elected by the National Assembly from among its members for a five-year term; he or she is responsible to the National Assembly and reports to it. The chairperson of the National Assembly of the new term proposes the candidate for election as president. There is no specific requirement of age to be elected as president.

The Lawmaking Process

One of the main duties of the National Assembly is to make the laws, in cooperation with various other constitutional organs. The constitution stipulates that the country's president, the Standing Committee of the National Assembly, the Nationalities Council and Committees of the National Assembly, the executive government, the Supreme People's Court, the Supreme People's Procuracy, the Vietnam Fatherland Front, and its member organizations may present draft laws to the National Assembly. Members of the National Assembly may present motions concerning laws and draft laws to the National Assembly. However, almost all of the laws passed by the National Assembly are initiated by the executive government.

Before they are submitted to the National Assembly for debate, all draft laws must be scrutinized by the Nationalities Council or Committees of the National Assembly. Laws must be approved by more than half the total membership of the National Assembly. Once a bill has been passed by the assembly, it must be signed by the National Assembly chairperson and must be promulgated by the country's president no later than 15 days after its adoption.

The Judiciary

The judiciary in Vietnam consists of the Supreme People's Court and the Supreme People's Procuracy. In Vietnam, there are four types of courts: the Supreme People's Court; the people's courts of the provinces and of cities directly under the central authority; the people's courts of the districts, towns, or cities under the provincial powers; and the military courts. In special circumstances, the National Assembly may establish special tribunals.

In Vietnam there is no constitutional court. The power to interpret the constitution, laws, and ordinances is vested in the Standing Committee of the National Assembly. On the other hand, an act of the

National Assembly cannot be declared void by the Supreme People's Court.

THE ELECTION PROCESS

All citizens of the Socialist Republic of Vietnam aged 18 or older, regardless of race, sex, social position, religion, education, occupation, or residency, have the right to vote, except mentally impaired people and those who are deprived of that right by law.

Parliamentary Elections

Every Vietnamese who is 21 or older has the right to stand for election to the National Assembly. To be elected to the assembly, the candidate must meet a number of requirements; for example, he or she must be loyal to the Socialist Republic of Vietnam, strive for national renovation, demonstrate moral and ethical qualification, abide by the laws, maintain close contact with the people, and deserve the people's trust.

POLITICAL PARTY

In the past Vietnam had a pluralist system of political parties, which included the Communist Party of Vietnam, the Democratic Party, and the Social Party. The Democratic Party, established on June 30, 1944, was a political organization of the nationalist bureaucracy and Vietnamese intelligentsia with the objective of fighting for national liberation and the people's happiness. The Social Party, formed on July 22, 1946, was a political organization of the progressive Vietnamese intelligentsia of the generation of the revolution. After the reunification of Vietnam in 1976, the two parties declared that they had fulfilled their objectives; they ceased to function in 1988.

At present, the Communist Party of Vietnam, founded on February 3, 1930, at the beginning of the national liberation movement, is the sole political party. Party policies are based on Marxist-Leninist doctrine and Ho Chi Minh's thought. The constitution acknowledges the role of the Communist Party of Vietnam as the force leading the state and society in Article 4. At the same time, the constitution states that all party organizations must operate within the framework of the constitution and the law.

CITIZENSHIP

Vietnamese citizenship is primarily acquired by birth. The principle of *ius sanguinis* is also applied; that is, a child acquires Vietnamese citizenship if one of his or her parents is a Vietnamese citizen, regardless of where a child is born.

FUNDAMENTAL RIGHTS

The constitution stipulates that in Vietnam human rights in the political, civic, economic, cultural, and social fields are respected. All citizens are equal before the law, and the citizen's rights are inseparable from his or her duties.

Political rights include the right to participate in the administration of the state and management of society, the right to petition the government, and the right to stand for elections. Economic rights include the right to work, freedom to conduct business, the right of lawful ownership, and the right of inheritance. Cultural and social rights include the right to education, the freedom to carry out scientific and technical research, and the right to housing. The constitution also emphasizes the citizen's right to freedom of opinion and speech, freedom of the press, the right to be informed, and the rights to assemble and to form associations.

Impact and Functions of Fundamental Rights

According to the constitution, human rights are of fundamental importance in Vietnam. First, they are defensive rights because the state may not interfere with the legal position of the individual unless there is special reason to do so. Further, the constitution declares that the state shall guarantee the rights of the citizen, and the citizen must fulfill his or her duties to the state and the society. The constitution explicitly mentions the responsibility of the state to protect children, ill and injured soldiers, and the family of fallen soldiers, and revolutionary martyrs.

A general equal-treatment clause in the constitution guarantees that male and female citizens have equal rights in political, economic, cultural, and social fields and in the family.

In addition, the constitution provides that no one shall be arrested in the absence of a ruling by the People's Court or a ruling or sanction of the People's Office of Procuracy except in cases of flagrant offences. Taking a person into or holding him or her in custody must be in accordance with the law. It is strictly forbidden to use any form of harassment, coercion, torture, or violation of honor and dignity against a citizen. The constitution states that no one shall be considered guilty and be subjected to punishment before the sentence of a court has taken full legal effect.

Limitations to Fundamental Rights

The fundamental rights specified in the constitution are not without limits. The constitution specifies such possible limitations in terms of the needs of the public and the rights of others.

ECONOMY

The constitution specifies that the Vietnamese economic system is a multicomponent commodity economy functioning in accordance with market mechanisms under the management of the state and with a socialist orientation. The constitution recognizes a system of ownership by the entire people, by collectives, and by private individuals.

The constitution prescribes that the state shall encourage foreign investment and guarantee the right to lawful ownership of interests by foreign organizations and individuals.

The constitution protects the citizens' right of lawful ownership and right of inheritance. Citizens enjoy freedom of enterprise and can set up enterprises of unrestricted scope in fields of activity that are beneficial to the country and to the people. The lawful property of individuals and organizations cannot be nationalized.

The aim of the state's economic policy is to make the people rich and the country strong by releasing all productive potential, developing all the talents of all components of the economy—the state sector, the collective sector, the private individual sector, the private capitalist sector, and the state capitalist sector in various forms—and by continuing to develop material and technical resources; broadening economic, scientific, and technical cooperation; and expanding relations with world markets.

RELIGIOUS COMMUNITIES

Vietnam is a multireligious state, which has more than 20 million believers, and more than 30,000 places of worship. Buddhism is the largest of the major world religions, with about 10 million followers. The second-largest religion is Catholicism, with about 6 million adherents. Protestantism is widespread throughout Vietnam, but the number of Protestants is not very large. In addition to these religions originating in other parts of the world, Vietnam has indigenous religions, such as the Cao Dai and Hoa Hao groups, whose holy places are in the city of Tay Ninh and the provinces of Chau Doc and An Giang in the Mekong Delta. The Vietnamese religions are united in the Vietnam Fatherland Front in order to cooperate to promote national sovereignty and reconstruction.

Vietnamese folk beliefs since ancient times consist of belief in fertility, worship of nature, and worship of humankind. Among the human-revering beliefs, the custom of worshiping ancestors is the most popular; it is a nearly universal belief of the Vietnamese (also called Dao Ong Ba in Cochin China). The Vietnamese choose the death day rather than the birthday to hold a commemorative anniversary for the deceased. Every family worships Tho cong, or the god of home, who takes care of the home and blesses the family. Every village worships its Thanh hoang, the god of the village, who protects and guides the whole village. The whole nation worships the first kings, sharing the common ancestors' death anniversary (the Ritual of Hung Temple).

Freedom of belief and of religion is guaranteed by the constitution as a human right. The constitution stipulates that anyone can follow any religion or follow none. All religions are equal before the law. Citizens, whatever their beliefs or religious attitudes, enjoy all civic rights and perform civic obligations.

Despite the separation of religion and the state, there remain many areas in which they cooperate, including recognition of religious organizations. According to the 2004 ordinance on beliefs and religions, the prime minister recognizes religious organizations that are active in more than one province and/or city under central authority; the chairperson of the people's committee of the province or city under central authority recognizes religious organizations that are active mainly in that province or city.

MILITARY DEFENSE AND STATE OF EMERGENCY

Creation and maintenance of armed forces are responsibilities of the national government. The constitution states that citizens must fulfill their military obligations to the national defense.

In Vietnam, general conscription requires all men above the age of 18 to perform basic military service of 18 months. In addition, there are professional soldiers who serve for fixed periods or for life. Women can volunteer.

The military always remains subject to civil government. The constitution states that the country's president is commander in chief of the armed forces.

AMENDMENTS TO THE CONSTITUTION

The fundamental law has been designed to be particularly difficult to change. It can only be changed by the National Assembly provided that at least two-thirds of the total members of the assembly shall approve an amendment to the constitution.

PRIMARY SOURCES

1992 Constitution in English. Available online. URL: http://www.vietnamembassy.us/learn_about_vietnam/politics/constitution. 2001 Law on organization of the National Assembly. Accessed on July 7, 2005.

SECONDARY SOURCES

Ngo Duc Manh, "Building Up a Legal Framework Aimed at Promoting and Developing a Socialist-Oriented Market-Driven Economy in Vietnam." In *Commercial Legal Development in Vietnam: Vietnamese and Foreign Commentaries,* edited by John Gillespie. Boston: Butterworth, 1997.
———, "On Further Renovation of Deliberation and Adoption of Legal Drafts." *Vietnam Law & Legal Forums* 8, no. 96 (August 2002):

Ngo Duc Manh

YEMEN

At-a-Glance

OFFICIAL NAME
Republic of Yemen

CAPITAL
Sanaa

POPULATION
19,721,643 (December 16, 2004 census)

SIZE
555,000 sq. km (official figure); since border settlements with neighboring countries, 460,000 sq. km in some studies and official documents

LANGUAGES
Arabic (official)

RELIGIONS
Islam (official religion; both Sunni and Zaidi), small minority of Jews

NATIONAL OR ETHNIC COMPOSITION
Predominantly Arab; also Afro-Arab, South Asian, European

DATE OF INDEPENDENCE OR CREATION
May 22, 1990 (Unification Day; 1918, North Yemen independence; 1967, South Yemen independence)

TYPE OF GOVERNMENT
Combination of parliamentary and presidential systems

TYPE OF STATE
Unitary state

TYPE OF LEGISLATURE
Unicameral parliament

DATE OF CONSTITUTION
May 16, 1990

DATE OF LAST AMENDMENT
April 27, 2001

Yemen is a unitary state with a president as the dominant figure in the political and institutional system. The legislative, executive, and judicial functions are not fully separated. Fundamental rights are guaranteed, though not completely respected in reality. Islam is the religion of the state. The constitution guarantees a free-market economy.

CONSTITUTIONAL HISTORY

The territory of Yemen has a long civilized history dating back to the ancient kingdoms of Mina (1200–650 B.C.E.) and Saba (750–115 B.C.E.). In the first century C.E., the Romans invaded the country, followed later by other regional powers such as Ethiopia and Persia. Yemen was known as Arabia Felix, or "Flourishing Arabia." Judaism and Christianity were the religions during this era.

In 628 C.E., Yemen adopted Islam and was subsumed under the rule of the Islamic caliphs. The Ottoman Turks occupied most of Yemen from 1538 to 1918. The British colonized the southern part of the country in 1839. From 1918 to 1990, Yemen was made up of two political entities. The North was ruled by an authoritarian imam until 1962, when a revolution established the Yemen Arab Republic. South Yemen, or Aden, remained a British colony until 1967, when it gained independence; three years later a radical regime took power and renamed the state the People's Democratic Republic of Yemen.

In North Yemen, from October 1962 onward, five different constitutions were promulgated. Four of them were officially provisional and frequently amended. The first permanent constitution was adopted on December 28, 1970. It established the first parliament, called the Consultative Council. It had 159 members, some appointed by the president and the others elected by general franchise. Elections were held in March 1971. However, political parties remained banned.

In the southern part of Yemen, a one-party system was established. After a period of instability (1967–70), the first constitution was introduced on November 30, 1970, and amended on October 31, 1987. The first parliament, called the People's Supreme Assembly, with 301 representatives, was formed in 1971.

In December 1981, the leaders of both countries signed a draft constitution for a United Yemen—with one state, one flag, and one people. This led to several further meetings and eventually resulted in the establishment of a joint Yemeni Council with representatives from both states to monitor progress toward unification. On December 1, 1989, a draft constitution for the unified state was published, to be ratified by both parliaments within six months and approved by a referendum.

On May 22, 1990, the Republic of Yemen was founded as the two political systems merged into one state. The unification of Yemen was achieved in a democratic way, and within a set of values and principles that have become permanent under the new constitution.

FORM AND IMPACT OF THE CONSTITUTION

The Republic of Yemen has a written constitution based on the principles of Islam and on the aims of the Yemeni revolutions of September 26 and October 14, 1962, which called for a democratic system based on political and intellectual pluralism.

BASIC ORGANIZATION STRUCTURE

Yemen is administratively divided into 21 governorates in addition to the capital city of Sanaa. The governorates in turn are divided into 352 districts comprising 2,082 subdistricts. According to the constitution, this division is based on the "principle of decentralization."

The governorates differ considerably in geographical area and population size. Each has its own representative council, all of whose members are elected except the chair, who is appointed by presidential decree and also acts as the governor. This structure applies also to the districts, each of which has an elected council and an appointed chair, who also serves as district director. This structure was organized under a local authority law, enacted to fulfill a constitutional mandate. The constitution considers the local authority as a third branch of the executive body of the government.

LEADING CONSTITUTIONAL PRINCIPLES

The leading principles are specified in the first two chapters of the constitution (Articles 1–60). The constitution defines Yemen as a republican and parliamentary democracy based on the rule of law. It does not make a clear division among executive, legislative, and judicial powers. However, it outlines certain tasks for the different authorities within the government. The Yemeni democratic system calls for a political and intellectual pluralism that guarantees freedom and personal liberties, human rights, and equal opportunities, under the law and the constitution.

Yemen's constitution provides for guarantees of human rights. In reality, however, they are not widely respected by the public authorities. If a violation of the constitution does occur in individual cases, there sometimes are no effective remedies enforceable by the judicial power.

The constitution has mandated the state to strengthen the economy on the basis of bilateral, regional, and international cooperation to advance mutual interests and strengthen peace. It also calls for stronger economic, administrative, and political structures that can apply enlightened and dynamic market mechanisms to support a larger role for the private sector.

CONSTITUTIONAL BODIES

The constitutional bodies, organized in the constitution according to their importance in constitutional theory, are the executive (which includes the president, cabinet ministers, and local authorities), the legislature (House of Representative), and the judiciary.

The Executive

The executive according to the Yemeni constitution consists of three branches organized as follows.

The president is the head of state. The president appoints the prime minister and forms the Shura Council (an advisory body). The president is also the head of the judiciary. The president has the ultimate responsibility to approve of government policies and strategies and oversee their proper implementation. The constitutional powers of the president reflect the fact that the president is the preeminent figure in Yemeni politics.

The president is elected for a seven-year term; he or she can be elected for two terms only.

According to the constitution, the Council of Ministers (cabinet) is the second branch of the executive. The prime minister is appointed by the president and forms the administration after consultation with the president. The Council of Ministers has the authority to set government policies and is empowered by the Parliament to issue by-laws and regulations. The constitution considers the Council of Ministers the highest executive and administrative body.

The local authority is considered to be the third branch of the executive. The main functions of the local authority are to raise funds and to plan and deliver services to the people according to the strategic targets set for their respective governorates and districts. This function includes caring for the poor.

The Shura Council

The Shura Council (*Al Showra*) consists of 110 members. It is a body of senior advisers, which reports directly to the president. This council conducts studies to aid the state in implementing its development strategies. It contributes to strengthening the democratic process and promoting public participation.

The members of the Shura Council are appointed by the president.

The House of Representatives

The House of Representatives (parliament) is the legislative body of the republic. It also approves, jointly with the Shura Council, the presidential candidates' nominations. The House of Representatives consists of 301 members, elected in general, direct, free, equal, and secret balloting.

The Lawmaking Process

One of the main duties of the Parliament is the passing of legislation. Both members of the Parliament and members of the Council of Ministers can propose bills for new or amended laws. Financial bills can be submitted only by the Council of Ministers or at least 20 percent of the members of the House of Representatives.

All proposed bills are referred to the relevant specialized committees of Parliament. Certain bills can only become law if they are passed by the majority of all members of Parliament. Before promulgating a law, the president may raise objections and return the law to the Parliament for reconsideration. However, if the bill is again adopted by Parliament, it can become law without the consent of the president.

The Judiciary

The judiciary is the third constituent body of the state enshrined in the constitution. The constitution guarantees the independence of the judiciary and further gives citizens the right to challenge any perceived absence of impartiality within the judiciary.

The judiciary has a high degree of authority and autonomy. The judiciary is considered by the constitution as an integrated system, and its structure of courts, responsibilities, and jurisdictions are determined by law. The constitution considers interference with the judiciary a crime.

THE ELECTION PROCESS

General, free, equal, and direct elections of the members of the House of Representatives, local authority councils,

and the president are guaranteed by the constitution. Article 43 guarantees the right to vote, to stand as an electoral candidate, and to express an opinion by referendum. All Yemenis over the age of 18, men and women, have both the right to stand for elections and the right to vote in them.

The Electoral Act makes no distinction between the genders, as both genders have legal competence.

POLITICAL PARTIES

A pluralistic system of political parties is guaranteed by the constitution. Multiparty parliamentary elections were held in 1993 and again in 1997 and 2003. The number of political parties increased rapidly to reach 22 in the 2003 elections.

The political parties law stipulates rules and procedures required for the formation of political organizations and parties, and the conduct of political activity. The constitution prohibits the misuse of governmental offices and public funds for the special interest of any specific party or political organization. According to the law, political parties can be banned only by a decision of the court.

CITIZENSHIP

Yemeni citizenship is primarily acquired at birth by children of a Yemeni father. An amendment to this law took place recently to allow the child of a Yemeni mother married to a foreigner to be treated as Yemeni until the child reaches maturity; at that time, the child may choose to be a Yemeni or to acquire the father's nationality.

The constitution guarantees that no Yemeni can be deprived of his or her citizenship. Once Yemeni nationality is acquired, it may not be withdrawn except in accordance with the law. The constitution does not allow the extradition of a Yemeni citizen to a foreign authority.

FUNDAMENTAL RIGHTS

The constitution of the Republic of Yemen recognizes the principle that all citizens are equal in accordance with Article 41, which stipulates that "all citizens have equal public rights and duties." Article 42 stipulates that citizens have the right to participate in political, economic, social, and cultural life. It also emphasizes that women are the sisters of men and have rights and duties guaranteed by the sharia and stipulated in law, as stated in Article 31.

The constitution guarantees the fundamental rights and duties of all citizens (Articles 41–61). It provides citizens with basic human rights, equal opportunities, education, freedom of movement within the state, social security, and health. Direct elections of the members of Parliament are guaranteed by the constitution.

Impact and Functions of Fundamental Rights

The constitution of the Republic of Yemen recognizes the principle that all citizens are equal, and it stipulates that citizens have the right to participate in the political, economic, social, and cultural life of the country. However, human rights are not respected in reality because of many factors, such as the impact of the tribal system on Yemeni society and culture and the neglected role of law enforcement. Some developments have been achieved in recent years in the field of human rights, but only limited progress has been made in freedom of expression and of the press.

ECONOMY

The constitution guarantees a free-market economy. It also permits lawful competition among the public, private, and cooperative sectors. The constitution mandates the government to strengthen the economic system, especially market mechanisms, through a larger role for the private sector.

RELIGIOUS COMMUNITIES

Islam is the religion of the state. The constitution guarantees religious freedom. It recognizes that residences, places of worship, and educational institutions have a sanctity that may not be violated by surveillance or search except in cases stipulated by the law.

Apart from the sanctity of houses of worship, the constitution makes no mention of the status of religious communities.

MILITARY DEFENSE AND STATE OF EMERGENCY

The constitution states that "establishing the armed forces is a responsibility of the state." The constitution also assures that such forces belong to all the people and their function is to protect the republic and to safeguard its territories and security. Establishing of armed forces or para-military groups by anyone else than the government for whatever purpose or under whatever name is prohibited by the constitution. The Yemeni constitution requires the military to be politically neutral.

The president is the head of the National Defense Council. The president of the republic, after the approval of the Parliament, has power to proclaim a state of emergency and summon public mobilization.

AMENDMENTS TO THE CONSTITUTION

Either the president or one-third of the members of Parliament can request a change or amendment to one or more articles of the constitution. The request must identify the article(s) that require(s) amendment as well as the reasons for such an amendment. In its first reading, an absolute majority is needed to agree that the amendment is justifiable in principle. The final reading requires a special majority of three-quarters of all the members.

If the motion is defeated, no request to amend the same article(s) may be submitted for a full year after that motion's defeat. Fundamental provisions of the constitution, listed in Article 158, require approval in a popular referendum, in addition to the three-quarters parliamentary support.

PRIMARY SOURCES

Constitution in English. Available online. URL: http://www.al-bab.com/yemen/gov/con94.htm. Accessed on August 21, 2005.

The Constitution of the Republic of Yemen: The Official Gazette. Sanaa: Ministry of legal Affairs, 2002 (original text is in Arabic).

SECONDARY SOURCES

H. A. al-Hubaishi, *Legal System and Basic Law in Yemen.* Worcester, England: Billing & Sons, 1988.

Mohamed Moghram, *Legal and Judicial System in Yemen.* Sanaa, 2003 (text and legal terms in English).

———, *Legal Framework of Civil Society in Yemen.* Taiz: HRTIC, 2003.

Mohamed Moghram

ZAMBIA

At-a-Glance

OFFICIAL NAME
Republic of Zambia

CAPITAL
Lusaka

POPULATION
10,462,436 (2005 est.)

SIZE
290,585 sq. mi. (752,614 sq. km)

LANGUAGES
English (official), major vernaculars Bemba, Kaonda, Lozi, Lunda, Luvale, Nyanja, Tonga, and about 70 other indigenous languages

RELIGIONS
Christian 50–75%, Muslim and Hindu 24–49%, indigenous beliefs 1%

NATIONAL OR ETHNIC COMPOSITION
African 98.7%, European 1.1%, other 0.2%

DATE OF INDEPENDENCE OR CREATION
October 24, 1964

TYPE OF GOVERNMENT
Mixed presidential and parliamentarian

TYPE OF STATE
Unitary state

TYPE OF LEGISLATURE
Unicameral parliament

DATE OF CONSTITUTION
August 24, 1991

DATE OF LAST AMENDMENT
May 28, 1996

Zambia has a constitutional system of government. It combines elements of presidential and parliamentary systems; it is based on the rule of law and on the constitution as supreme law of the land. The system embraces the separation of powers among the executive, the legislature, and the judiciary. Zambia is divided into nine provinces, whose administrations are accountable to the central government; it is not a federal state. The constitution provides for the protection of fundamental human rights, guaranteed under the Bill of Rights. Effective remedies exist for violations of human rights guaranteed under the constitution and are enforceable by an independent judiciary. Human rights are enforced in the High Court, in the Supreme Court, and by an independent Human Rights Commission.

The president is both head of state and head of the administration. The president is directly elected through a free, equal, and secret ballot process. Religious freedom is guaranteed, and state and religious communities are separated. The economic system may be described as an open market economy. The military is subject to the civil government in terms of law and practice. Zambia, as are most countries of the world, is obliged by its constitution to contribute to world peace.

CONSTITUTIONAL HISTORY

The area today known as Zambia was governed by a variety of local kings and rulers when, in 1890, agents of Cecil Rhodes's British South Africa Company made their appearance. They concluded treaties with several of the African leaders, including Lewanika, the Lozi king, and set up an administration for the region. The area was divided into the protectorates of Northwestern and Northeastern Rhodesia until 1911, when the two were joined to form Northern Rhodesia. In 1924, the British government took over the administration of the protectorate.

In 1953, the Federation of Rhodesia and Nyasaland was formed under a British initiative, combining Northern Rhodesia (now Zambia), Southern Rhodesia (now Zimbabwe), and Nyasaland (now Malawi). The capital was Salisbury (now Harare), Southern Rhodesia. The federation was also called the Central African Federation. Under an appointed governor-general, the federal government handled external affairs, defense, currency, intercolonial relations, and federal taxes for its constituent members, which, however, retained most of their former legislative structure.

The federation was dissolved on December 31, 1963, as decolonization gathered force in Africa. Kenneth Kaunda, a militant former schoolteacher, had formed a new party in 1959, the United National Independence Party (UNIP). He led a massive civil disobedience campaign in 1962, which earned Africans a larger voice in the affairs of the protectorate. On October 24, 1964, Northern Rhodesia became independent as the Republic of Zambia, with Kaunda as its first president. Kaunda ruled Zambia for a period of 27 years until 1991, when Frederick Chiluba, a trade unionist, was elected president under his party, the Movement for Multiparty Democracy (MMD), which won the majority of seats in the parliament.

Chiluba was reelected in 1996, after parliament passed a constitutional amendment preventing Kaunda from running for the presidency again. In the December 2001 elections, the MMD candidate, Levy Mwanawasa, was elected with less than 30 percent of the vote.

FORM AND IMPACT OF THE CONSTITUTION

Zambia has a written constitution, codified in a single document. The constitution takes precedence over all other laws. It is the supreme law of the land. Other laws, including international law, are applicable to the extent that they are not in conflict with the constitution.

BASIC ORGANIZATIONAL STRUCTURE

Zambia is a unitary state divided into nine provinces established under the constitution. The provincial administrations are subject to the control of the central government and have no legislative or judicial powers. The provinces differ in area, population, and economic strength. However, the same law governs their administration.

LEADING CONSTITUTIONAL PRINCIPLES

Zambia has a centralized system of government. The president is not only head of state but also head of the administration. Two chambers are provided for under the constitution, although the House of Chiefs (tribal leaders) was only established in November 2003. The role of the tribal leaders is not legislative, but merely advisory.

The constitutional principles that define the system include the idea of Zambia as a democracy and a republic based on the rule of law. At both national and local levels, participation is by way of indirect, representative democracy. All state actions that undermine the rights of the people must have their basis in the constitution.

CONSTITUTIONAL BODIES

The chief organs of government provided for in the constitution include the state president and the cabinet, parliament, and the judiciary. Others include the Permanent Human Rights Commission, the Anti-Corruption Commission, and the Drug Enforcement Commission.

The President

The president is elected directly by adult universal suffrage through secret ballot for a five-year term. The president is both head of state and head of the administration. Reelection is possible only once. The constitution provides for extensive powers for the president. The president is the dominant figure in Zambian politics.

The Administration

The president and the cabinet ministers together with their deputies form the administration. The president and the cabinet have the authority to determine the policy of the administration. The president appoints the cabinet ministers and their deputies.

The National Assembly (Parliament)

The Zambian National Assembly is the representative organ of the people and legislative body of the republic. By way of delegation local authorities may pass only by-laws with the approval of responsible ministers. The life of an elected parliament is five years. Members of Parliament are elected in a general direct, free, equal, and secret balloting process.

The Lawmaking Process

One of the functions of the National Assembly is to make laws. Most legislation is introduced by the cabinet, some by other members of Parliament. Legislation becomes law after the bills have been debated and approved by the National Assembly and assented to by the president.

The Judiciary

The judiciary is independent of the parliamentary and executive arms of the government. The highest court is the Supreme Court of Zambia, consisting of a bench of nine judges. The Supreme Court has unlimited jurisdiction and can hear appeals on all matters, including civil, criminal, administrative, labor, revenue, and social law, and, above all, constitutional matters.

THE ELECTION PROCESS AND POLITICAL PARTICIPATION

All Zambians who have attained the age of 18 have the right to vote in the elections. Those who are at least 21 have the right to stand for election as members of Parliament, and those who are at least 35 have the right to stand for election as president of the Republic of Zambia.

POLITICAL PARTIES

Zambia has a pluralist system of political parties. The multiparty system is provided for in the constitution and thus is a fundamental element of public life. Registered political parties may only be banned by an order of the High Court. They may be deregistered when they fail to comply with the law governing societies.

CITIZENSHIP

Zambian citizenship is primarily acquired by birth. This applies if either of the parents is a Zambian citizen irrespective of where the child is born. Citizenship may also be acquired through the process of naturalization or by registration.

FUNDAMENTAL RIGHTS

The constitution defines fundamental rights in its third chapter. The constitution guarantees traditional African rights, as long as they are not repugnant to natural justice or inconsistent with written law, the constitution itself, and civil liberties. The fundamental rights set out in Chapter 3 of the Zambian constitution have binding force on the legislature, the executive, and the judiciary as directly applicable law. All public authorities are bound by the constitution. The constitution guarantees rights to equality before the law.

Impact and Functions of Fundamental Rights

The constitution is the supreme law of the land, and all laws enacted and actions by those in authority must conform to the constitutional principles. The rights guaranteed under Chapter 3 of the constitution permeate all areas of the law. Fundamental importance is given to the rights guaranteed in the constitution in the interpretation and application of all laws and value judgments.

Limitation to Fundamental Rights

Fundamental rights are not absolute. They may be limited, but the limitation must be reasonable, justifiable, and proportional.

ECONOMY

The Zambian constitution does not specify an economic system. However, it does guarantee the ownership of property, freedom of occupation or profession, and freedom of assembly and association, including the right to form and belong to associations. The economic system is oriented toward an open market.

Despite progress in privatization and budgetary reform, Zambia's economic growth has remained below the rate necessary to reduce poverty significantly. Low mineral prices have slowed the benefits of privatizing the mining industry and have reduced incentives for further private investment in the sector. Zambia has, however, continued to cooperate with international bodies on programs to reduce poverty. The mining and refining of copper constitute by far the largest industry in the country, concentrated in the cities of the Copperbelt. Copper accounts for over 80 percent of foreign exchange. Cobalt, zinc, lead, gold, silver, gemstones, and coal are also mined. Manufacturing includes food products, beverages, textiles, construction materials, chemicals, and fertilizer. Hydroelectric plants, especially the one at Kariba Dam, supply most of Zambia's energy.

RELIGIOUS COMMUNITIES

Freedom of conscience and religion is guaranteed as a human right. This guarantee also includes rights for religious communities. There is no established state religion. All public authorities must by law remain neutral in their relations with religious communities, and all religions are equal. Religious communities conduct and regulate their affairs independently but within the law that applies to all.

MILITARY DEFENSE AND STATE OF EMERGENCY

The Zambian military is established under Part 7 of the constitution. It comprises the air force, army, and national service. The military is trained and commanded according to fixed organizational requirements and terms of service; it is governed by disciplinary rules and a clear chain of command. The three components together are called the Zambian Defense Force. Its functions are to preserve and defend the sovereignty and territorial integrity of Zambia, to cooperate with civilian authority in emergency situations such as natural disasters, to foster harmony and understanding between the Zambian Defense Force and civilians, and to engage in productive activities for the development of Zambia.

The military is nonpartisan and subordinate to the civilian authority. The head of state is also the commander in chief of the armed forces. The president can appoint and replace the commanders and is the head of the military chain of command, supported by civilian personnel who oversee the day-to-day activities of the armed forces through the Ministry of Defense.

AMENDMENTS TO THE CONSTITUTION

Most amendments to the constitution may be accomplished by a two-thirds majority of the members of parliament. However, certain parts, such as the Bill of Rights and Article 79 relating to the mode of adoption of the constitution, may only be amended by way of a referendum.

PRIMARY SOURCES

Constitution in English. Available online. URL: http://www.zamlii.ac.zm/const/1996/conact96.htm. Accessed on June 29, 2006. http://www.oefre.unibe.ch/law/icl/za__indx.html. Accessed on August 8, 2005.

SECONDARY SOURCES

Peter J. Burnell, "The Party System and Party Politics in Zambia—Continuities Past, Present and Future." *African Affairs* 100 (2001): 239–263.

Roger Chongwe, "The Constitution of Zambia: Its Strengths and Weaknesses." In *The State and Constitutionalism in Southern Africa,* edited by Owen Sichone: 51–64. Harare: SAPES Books, 1998.

"Eyes on Africa: Zambia History and General Information." Available online. URL: http://www.eyesonafrica.net/zambia. Accessed on August 13, 2005.

L. M. Habasonda, "The Military, Civil Society and Democracy in Zambia." *African Security Review* 11, no. 2 (2002): 227–238.

Abraham Mwansa

ZIMBABWE

At-a-Glance

OFFICIAL NAME
The Republic of Zimbabwe

CAPITAL
Harare

POPULATION
12,671,860 (July 2004 estimate)

SIZE
150,804 sq. mi. (390,580 sq. km)

LANGUAGES
English, Shona, Ndebele

RELIGIONS
Christian (various, with traditional influences) 75%, traditional religions 24%, Muslim and other 1%

NATIONAL OR ETHNIC COMPOSITION
Shona 82%, Ndebele 14%, other indigenous 2%, other (mixed, Asian, and European descent) 2%

DATE OF INDEPENDENCE OR CREATION
April 18, 1980

TYPE OF GOVERNMENT
Parliamentary democracy

TYPE OF STATE
Unitary state

TYPE OF LEGISLATURE
Unicameral parliament

DATE OF CONSTITUTION
December 21, 1979

DATE OF LAST AMENDMENT
May 2000

Zimbabwe is, theoretically, a parliamentary democracy with a clear division of executive, legislative, and judicial powers. The current constitution is a much-amended remnant of the 1979 constitution that ended the liberation war in Southern Rhodesia. Amendments made in the 1980s removed racist provisions that protected the undemocratic influence of a white minority, increased the power of the president, and replaced a bicameral parliament with a unicameral one. In the 1990s, amendments were made to limit civil and political rights after judicial decisions in their favor. In 2000, an amendment that gave the administration greater legal power to acquire privately owned land for resettlement was enacted.

For the first 20 years the administration respected the constitution to the extent that it obeyed judicial rulings that held that the administration had breached the constitution. However, the administration refused to enforce orders of the Supreme Court to evict illegal settlers from privately owned land between 2000 and 2001. Interference with the membership of the Supreme Court and the High Court and political pressure exerted on the magistrates' courts have damaged respect for the constitution and the independence of the judiciary.

In the late 1990s a parliamentary opposition that was strong enough to block amendments to the constitution, but not the passing of ordinary legislation, emerged.

CONSTITUTIONAL HISTORY

The area of present-day Zimbabwe was colonized by the British South Africa Company in the 1890s. The country was ruled by the company as Southern Rhodesia until 1923, when the British government gave limited self-rule to the white settlers. The period of administration by the company had seen the violent dispossession of the indigenous communities from their land, labor, and property. This process continued under minority white rule up to 1980.

In 1953, Southern Rhodesia entered the Federation of Rhodesia and Nyasaland with what are now Zambia and Malawi. The federation eventually failed when the political system's favoring of the white settlers of Southern Rhodesia became clear. In 1963 Britain granted a new constitution to Southern Rhodesia under continued white minority rule. That same year, Britain granted independence to Zambia and Malawi under majority African rule. Fearful that Britain would follow a similar path in Southern Rhodesia, the white government there declared independence as Rhodesia in 1965 and continued the political repression of the indigenous population. After a war of liberation fought from 1973 to 1979, Zimbabwe achieved its independence from Britain in 1980 under a negotiated constitution that established a parliamentary democracy.

In 2000, the Zimbabwean electorate rejected a constitution drafted by a Constitutional Commission appointed by the ruling administration. Although the draft was more liberal than the existing constitution, civil society objected that the administration had dominated the drafting process. In May 2000, immediately before parliamentary elections in which the governing party was expected to lose its constitutional majority, parliament amended the constitution to allow the executive greater power to acquire land for resettlement.

FORM AND IMPACT OF THE CONSTITUTION

Zimbabwe has a written constitution called the Constitution of Zimbabwe, which takes precedence over all other law, including common law, statutes, and customary international law. Customary international law is applicable in Zimbabwe to the extent that it does not contradict the constitution.

BASIC ORGANIZATIONAL STRUCTURE

Zimbabwe is a unitary state with a number of provinces nominally under the leadership of governors appointed by the executive. A parallel local administration includes councils, both rural and urban, elected by popular vote. However, administrative power lies with the central government and not the local government. Further, conflict between the Ministry of Local Government and urban councils dominated by the opposition has weakened the urban councils.

LEADING CONSTITUTIONAL PRINCIPLES

Zimbabwe's system of government is a parliamentary democracy. Although the president is not a member of parliament, all the cabinet ministers are. The judiciary is supposed to be independent, but its independence has been reduced in recent years as a result of forced resignations, intimidation, and political appointments. The result has been an increase in proadministration decisions, although most members of the judiciary continue to be professional and independent. The division of power has thus been eroded with the strengthening of the executive.

CONSTITUTIONAL BODIES

The predominant bodies provided for in the constitution are the president and the cabinet, parliament, and the judiciary.

The President

The president is the head of state and administration. The president appoints and dismisses all members of the cabinet, which together with the president constitutes the executive arm of government. Members of the cabinet must be members of parliament; however, having the right to appoint 12 members of parliament directly, the president can choose ministers who were never elected, place them in parliament, and fill the cabinet with unelected personnel.

The president is elected by universal suffrage for a six-year term and can be reelected. The president and the cabinet administer the country and determine which legislation is put before parliament. While the executive's control over parliament depends on its majority in parliament, direct and indirect appointments by the president make it easy for the executive to achieve such a majority.

The Parliament

The Zimbabwean parliament, the House of Assembly, is the legislative organ of the state and the representative of the constituencies set up under the constitution. Of the 150 members of parliament, 120 are elected every five years. Members of parliament are elected on a constituency roll in a secret ballot. However, accusations of electoral violence, voter intimidation, and vote rigging have made parliamentary and presidential elections subject to local and international condemnation. The president directly appoints 12 members of parliament and eight governors who have ex officio seats in parliament and appoints traditional leaders who select eight members to represent them in parliament.

The Lawmaking Process

Most legislation is enacted by the House of Assembly. Presidential approval is required before an act is promulgated. If parliament tries to force this approval, the president has the power to dismiss the body. Further, parliament passed an act granting the president power to enact emergency legislation. The act has been questioned as unconstitutional.

The Judiciary

The judiciary is appointed by the president on the recommendation of the Judicial Services Commission, a body created by the constitution and consisting of the chief justice and other members appointed by the president. The judiciary consists of a Supreme Court, which hears appeals and functions as the Constitutional Court; a High Court, which hears most serious civil and criminal cases; and the magistrate courts, which hear civil and criminal cases that are not considered serious enough for the High Court.

The executive may not fire a judge, who can only be legally removed after a panel of judges or legal practitioners nominated by the Law Society finds the judge guilty of misconduct. However, the de facto independence of the judiciary during the 1980s and 1990s was a result of executive choice rather than constitutional fact. After 1999 interference with the judiciary became common, and a new Supreme Court, more amenable to the executive, was constituted. The new bench has been markedly less proactive in protecting constitutionally enshrined civil and political rights, using technicalities to refuse to hear important matters. It has, however, been more willing to allow land reform.

Many earlier decisions by the Supreme Court enforcing constitutional rights continue in effect and continue to protect human rights in Zimbabwe; these include a decision that the administration could not force individuals to carry identification, and a ruling that allowed public demonstrations. However, legislation such as the Public Order and Security Act (which requires identification at police roadblocks and in the vicinity of crimes and allows police banning of demonstrations) appears to be in violation of the constitution but has not been overturned.

THE ELECTION PROCESS

All Zimbabweans over the age of 18 have both the right to stand for election to parliament and the right to vote in the election. All Zimbabweans over the age of 18 have the right to vote in a presidential election, but only a Zimbabwean citizen by birth or descent, and over the age of 40, can be elected president.

POLITICAL PARTIES

There is no constitutional restriction on the number of political parties. There is a strong opposition party represented in parliament, although it has indicated that it will boycott future elections.

CITIZENSHIP

Zimbabwean citizenship is primarily acquired by birth, although citizenship may also be acquired by registration (naturalization) or descent.

FUNDAMENTAL RIGHTS

The constitution of Zimbabwe guarantees fundamental rights and freedoms in Chapter 3. The constitution guarantees civil and political rights but not economic, social, and cultural rights. Sections 12 to 23 set out the specific rights, which include life, freedom from torture (amended to allow the imposition of the death penalty after extensive detention), freedom of association and expression, protection of private property (amended to facilitate acquisition of land for resettlement), and freedom from discrimination (amended to include sex and gender as prohibited grounds of discrimination). Section 24 allows direct access to the Supreme Court for remedy.

Impact and Functions of Fundamental Rights

While Zimbabwean legal and judicial thought has given centrality to fundamental rights and freedoms as protected in Chapter 3, the lack of popular participation in the drafting of the 1979 constitution has allowed some to refer to the rights protected as foreign imports. This has helped weaken the human rights culture in Zimbabwe, although the opposition continues to use rights language in its struggle for local and international support.

Limitations to Fundamental Rights

Fundamental rights and freedoms in the constitution are limited internally. The state is empowered to make laws that limit the rights in the interests of defense, public safety, public order, public morality, or public health, but only to the extent that the restriction is reasonably justifiable in a democratic society.

ECONOMY

The constitution of Zimbabwe does not determine the economic system that prevails in the country. However, in protecting private property and freedom of association, and ignoring economic, social, and cultural rights, the constitution predisposes the system toward a liberal market economy. However, massive violation of formal and informal property rights by the current administration, in both agricultural and urban areas, has severely undermined the free economy.

RELIGIOUS COMMUNITIES

There is no state religion and the formal divide between religion and state is maintained. All persons are entitled to practice their faith in freedom, subject to limitations for legitimate purposes. Freedom of conscience is protected as a fundamental right.

MILITARY DEFENSE AND STATE OF EMERGENCY

In a state of emergency, the state may, through an act of parliament, derogate from the list of fundamental rights that is set out in Schedule 2 to the constitution.

There is no compulsory military or national service in Zimbabwe. The military always remains technically subject to civil government, although in recent years members of the armed force and the police forces have made political speeches criticizing the opposition.

AMENDMENTS TO THE CONSTITUTION

The constitution of Zimbabwe may be amended by the vote of two-thirds of members of parliament.

PRIMARY SOURCES

Constitution in English. Available online. URL: http://www.nca.org.zw/COZ/coz_index.htm. Accessed on July 23, 2005.

SECONDARY SOURCES

S. Booysen, "The Dualities of Contemporary Zimbabwean Politics: Constitutionalism versus the Law of Power and the Land, 1999–2002." Available online. URL: http//web.africa.ufl.edu/asq/v7/v7i2a1.htm. Accessed on September 19, 2005.

"The CIA World Factbook—Zimbabwe." Available online. URL: http://www.cia.gov/cia/publications/factbook. Accessed on September 3, 2005.

John Hatchard, "Some Lessons on Constitution-Making from Zimbabwe." *Journal of African Law* 45, no. 2 (2001): 210–216.

Solomon Sacco

APPENDIX I
European Union

At-a-Glance

OFFICIAL NAME
European Union

CAPITAL
No capital. European Commission and Council have their seats in Brussels, Belgium; European Parliament has its seat in Strasbourg, France; European Court of Justice and Court of Auditors have their seats in Luxembourg.

POPULATION
461,500,000 (2006 est.)

SIZE
1,535,286 sq. mi. (3,976,372 sq. km)

LANGUAGES
21 official languages: Czech, Danish, Dutch, English, Estonian, Finnish, French, German, Greek, Hungarian, Italian, Latvian, Lithuanian, Maltese, Polish, Portuguese, Slovak, Slovene, Spanish, Swedish (Irish from January 1, 2007 onward); multitude of others

RELIGIONS
Roman Catholic 55.35%, Protestant 13.4%, Anglican 6.7%, Orthodox Christian 3.1%, Muslim 2.9%, Jewish 0.3%, other or none 18.25%

NATIONAL OR ETHNIC COMPOSITION
25 member states, many with several nationalities and ethnicities

DATE OF INDEPENDENCE OR CREATION
July 23, 1952 (ECSC), January 1, 1958 (EEC, EAEC), November 1, 1993 (EU)

TYPE OF GOVERNMENT
Supranational and intergovernmental democracy

TYPE OF INSTITUTION
Supranational, federal

TYPE OF LEGISLATURE
Executive and parliamentarian

DATE OF CONSTITUTION
Several documents since April 18, 1951; treaty establishing the European Union, November 1, 1993

DATE OF LAST AMENDMENT
May 1, 2004 (last accession treaty with 10 new member states)

The European Union is an entity consisting of a number of European states that have transferred a substantial amount of their powers onto that entity. Its powers are limited to those transferred on it. The European Union has 25 member states: Belgium, the Czech Republic, Denmark, Germany, Estonia, Greece, Spain, France, Ireland, Italy, Cyprus, Latvia, Lithuania, Luxembourg, Hungary, Malta, the Netherlands, Austria, Poland, Portugal, Slovenia, Slovakia, Finland, Sweden, and the United Kingdom. Any European state that respects the fundamental principles of the union may apply to become a member. These principles are liberty, democracy, respect for human rights and fundamental freedoms, and the rule of law, principles that are common to the member states.

The structures of the European Union are complex and often confusing. The European Union can be regarded as a roof on top of a building, this building consisting of communities and policies.

The European Union (EU) is founded on the European Community (EC), which was originally called the

European Economic Community (EEC), and on the European Atomic Energy Community (EAEC or EURATOM). It also consists of a Common Foreign and Security Policy as well as a Police and Judicial Cooperation in Criminal Matters, both of which establish institutional structures that provide for consultation and common policies of the member states in these fields.

In political practice, although technically not quite correct, people refer to the European Union to designate any one or all of those different communities and policies. The European Union must not be confused with the Council of Europe, an institution based on an international treaty among most European states including non-EU members such as Russia, Georgia, and Turkey. It is meant to promote democracy, the rule of law, and fundamental rights throughout Europe.

The European Community is the most important of the communities and policies under the roof of the European Union. A new constitution passed for the European Union in 2004 represents a further step in the process of European integration. This Constitution for Europe has to be ratified by all member states. This ratification process has been disturbed because referendums in the Netherlands and France did not approve the constitution.

The European Union acts through institutions of which the most important ones are the Council, in which the member states are represented; the parliament; the Commission, which can be seen as the executive branch of European government; and the European Court of Justice. There also is a Court of Auditors. The Economic and Social Committee in which societal groups are represented, and the Committee of the Regions representing regions and municipalities have mostly advisory functions.

The European Union protects fundamental rights in law and in fact. It promotes a social market economy by creating and maintaining a common market. The European Union is characterized by a process of integration heading for an ever closer union.

CONSTITUTIONAL HISTORY

Calls for a community of European states have a long history. They are based on a millennium-old common European culture and on a goal of ending the persistent and devastating wars among the European nations.

European unity became imminent after World War II (1939-45), when the British prime minister, Winston Churchill, called for a "United States of Europe." On a proposal by the French foreign minister, Robert Schumann, the six founding members, Belgium, France, the Federal Republic of Germany, Italy, Luxembourg, and the Netherlands, signed the Treaty of Paris on April 18, 1951, establishing the European Coal and Steel Community. This treaty was the first step toward the European Union in creating a pool for coal and steel production. These goods were regarded as being central to the ability to make war. From this it is obvious that the first and predominant idea

was to prevent further war among the founding states by installing mutual control over these key productions.

In a second step, the European Economic Community was founded by the Treaty of Rome on March 25, 1957, by the same six countries, heading for the step-by-step establishment of a common market. On the same day those states also signed the treaty establishing the European Atomic Energy Community for the promotion of nuclear industries for peaceful purposes.

The success of these three European communities in creating a common market and fruitful cooperation attracted new member states. The United Kingdom, Denmark, and Ireland became full members in 1973. Greenland, forming an autonomous part of Denmark, however, opted out of the communities in 1985. Norway, after having signed an accession treaty, decided in a referendum against membership in 1972, and again in 1994. Greece became a member of the communities in 1981; Spain and Portugal followed in 1986. Austria, Finland, and Sweden are members since 1995. The membership of the Federal Republic of Germany was extended to the territory of the former German Democratic Republic on its reunification with the Federal Republic of Germany in 1990. Ten new member states joined in 2004: Poland, Hungary, the Czech Republic, Slovakia, Lithuania, Latvia, Estonia, Slovenia, Cyprus, and Malta. Bulgaria and Romania are expected to join the European Union in 2007. Negotiations with Turkey and Croatia about their accession to the union are currently under way.

By way of many treaties of the member states in the course of their history, the European communities have achieved ever-closer union. Whereas initially each of the three communities had its own government organs, the 1965 Merger Treaty joined these powers in organs competent for all three communities. The 1985 Single European Act vested intensive powers in the European decision-making process in the European Parliament.

The 1992 Maastricht Treaty on European Union, signed in Maastricht, Netherlands, on February 7, 1992, established the European Union. After a somewhat difficult ratification process the European Union formally began to exist on November 1, 1993.

In 2000, the member states adopted the Charter of Fundamental Rights of the European Union, which, however, has not yet been given legally binding force, although it has important persuasive effect throughout the work of the European Union. The European Coal and Steel Community ceased to exist on July 23, 2002, while its remaining functions were taken over by the European Communities.

On October 29, 2004, the member states adopted a new Constitution for Europe, which will enter into force upon ratification by all member states. After referendums in France and the Netherlands decided against ratification, the ratification process was interrupted. New solutions are being looked for in order to overcome this difficult situation with the aim of final adoption of the new constitution.

If the process of ratification is successful, there will be one constitutional document instead of the numerous current documents. This single document would contribute further to the transparency of European Union decision making. The constitution will merge the European Community and the European Union in one new European Union.

The Constitution for Europe takes further steps in implementing democracy in its decision-making process by giving new powers to the European Parliament. The new constitution strengthens fundamental rights by giving directly binding force to the 2000 European Charter of Fundamental Rights, making it an integral part of the constitutional document. The constitution undertakes to contribute further to the development of a common foreign and security policy by providing for a European Union minister for foreign affairs. It makes its identity more visible by introducing the office of a president of the union.

FORM AND IMPACT OF THE CONSTITUTION

It is a controversial question whether the European Union has a constitution or not. There is not a single constitutional document. Some people say that only a state can have a constitution, and since the European Union is not a state, it cannot. From this perspective, even the 2004 Draft Constitution for Europe is not a constitution. However, a broader understanding of the term would allow one to consider that the basic structures of the treaties that formed the European Union are its constitution.

These founding documents are treaties of international law, as are the many treaties amending the founding treaties, the accession treaties, and the treaties creating special relationships with third countries. These international laws taken together are called primary community law. The institutions set up in these treaties can then adopt law, which is called secondary community law. This secondary community law may take the form of regulations of general application, binding in their entirety, and directly applicable within all member states. Secondary community law may also take the form of directives, which establish a result to be achieved by the member states within a given time. Each member state, however, can decide about the specific method and legal form to use in order to achieve this result. Finally there are decisions with binding effect on specific addressees, and recommendations and opinions without binding force.

This system of European legislation has far-reaching effects on the member states in harmonizing their legal systems. Community law takes precedence over member states' law in the specific cases in which it applies.

BASIC ORGANIZATIONAL STRUCTURE

The European Union is a supranational body that exercises its own sovereign powers within its member states.

Although the member states have transferred considerable sovereign powers to the union, they remain sovereign states. The member states are very diverse in size, economic strength, and political impact.

LEADING CONSTITUTIONAL PRINCIPLES

The European Union is founded on the principles of liberty, democracy, respect for human rights and fundamental freedoms, and the rule of law. It respects the national identities of its member states. The union has as its particular objectives promotion of economic and social progress through the creation of a territory without internal frontiers, implementation of a common foreign and security policy, strengthening of the protection of the rights and interests of the nationals of its member states, and maintenance and development of the union as an area of freedom, security, and justice.

The goal of the European Union is to create an ever closer union among the peoples of Europe; toward that end, the member states have transferred a substantial part of their sovereign powers to the European Communities.

The provisions on a common foreign and security policy empower the union to define and implement such a policy covering all areas of foreign and security policy. The treaty foresees greater consultation among the member states and the eventual adoption of common policy positions. The member states, however, will retain the last say in their foreign and security policies. The common policy is more a matter of intergovernmental cooperation than a policy of the union itself. The same applies to the provisions on police and judicial cooperation, for closer cooperation among police forces, customs authorities, and other agencies in the member states.

According to the principle of conferral, the European Union acts only within the limits of the powers conferred upon it by the treaties. Such powers cover major policy areas such as the single internal market, in which all obstacles to the free movement of persons, goods, capital, and services are being removed. There are common policies on agriculture, competition, taxation, immigration, social matters, culture, public health, industry, and research and technical development, and a customs union. Based in the European Community, the union also pursues environmental protection.

A number of member states have signed the 1995 Schengen Accord, which abolishes border controls on persons and goods between them. These states are Austria, Belgium, Denmark, Finland, France, Germany, Greece, Italy, Luxembourg, the Netherlands, Portugal, Spain, and Sweden. The non-EU members Iceland, Norway, and Switzerland have also joined in this accord.

One group of member states formed the Economic and Monetary Union in 1999, introducing the euro as the common currency. These are Austria, Belgium, Finland,

France, Germany, Greece, Ireland, Italy, Luxembourg, the Netherlands, Portugal, and Spain.

CONSTITUTIONAL BODIES

The major institutions through which the European Union acts are the European Council, the Council, the European Commission, the European Parliament, the Court of Justice, and the Court of Auditors. Also of considerable importance as advisory bodies are the Economic and Social Committee, representing societal groups, and the Committee of the Regions, in which territorial regions and municipalities are represented. The presidency of the European Union is held for a period of six months by one member state in a rotation system.

The European Council

The European Council comprises the heads of state or government of the member states and the president of the commission. It usually meets four times a year to provide the union with the necessary impetus for its development and to define its general political guidelines. It is a body distinct from the Council.

The Council

The Council is the predominant decision-making institution of the European Union. In the majority of cases, the Council shares this power of decision making with the parliament. The Council decides on matters of community legislation such as regulations and directives, ensures coordination of general economic policies and strategies of employment, and acts in all other matters provided for by the treaties.

The Council consists of a representative of each member state at ministerial level. It does not have specific permanent members, but the government ministers of the member states responsible for the area to be discussed in the Council meet for that purpose, in various configurations. Thus, if a question on agriculture is on the agenda, the government ministers for agriculture meet, or on a question of finances the government ministers of finance do so.

The voting system within the Council provides for a majority vote of the member states in cases such as budget and staff matters. For many questions, however, a qualified majority is needed. In this case the votes of the members are weighted according to the size of the member state. There is a minimal factor of 3 that applies for Malta; others, such as Luxembourg, Slovenia, Estonia, and Cyprus, are weighted by 4; some are weighted by 12, such as Hungary or Greece; France, the United Kingdom, Italy, and Germany all have a weight of 29.

Each member state occupies the presidency of the Council in a rotation system for a period of six months. The presidency coordinates the activities of the Council and usually sets priorities for the time of its office.

The European Commission

The European Commission, of 25 members, acts as the executive body of the union. It ensures the proper functioning and development of the common market. Its term of office is five years.

In a sense, the commission fills the role of a council of ministers in a parliamentary system, and its membership is assembled in a similar fashion, except that each member state is entitled to one seat. The Council, meeting in the composition of heads of state or government, nominates a candidate for president of the commission, analogously to a president's or monarch's nominating a prime minister. The nomination has to be approved by the European Parliament, as does a prime minister in most parliamentary systems. Then the Council in its normal composition, and by common accord with the nominee for president, adopts a list of persons whom it intends to appoint as members of the commission. The European Parliament votes on the nominated commission. If this vote is in favor, the members of the commission are appointed by the Council. The European Parliament can pass a motion of censure, by a two-thirds majority of the votes cast, representing a majority of all members of parliament; in that case, the commission must resign as a body.

The European Parliament

The European Parliament is the representative assembly within the European Union. It consists of representatives of the peoples of the member states. Although it has not yet acquired the normal status of parliaments in the member states, it has over time gained considerable powers and political impact. Its powers are to take part in decision making, to advise, to pronounce on a number of matters relating to the union's external relations, to adopt the budget in cooperation with the Council, and to supervise other institutions and bodies of the union.

The European Parliament has a maximum of 732 members. The number of seats allocated to each member state takes into account the size of its population. Malta has five seats; other countries such as Luxembourg, Cyprus, or Estonia have six seats; the Czech Republic or Portugal, 24; Poland, 54; France, Italy, and the United Kingdom, 78; and Germany, 99 seats. Representatives are elected for a term of five years.

The Legislative Process

The right of initiative for community legislation is vested only in the commission. However, the European Parliament by a majority vote of its members may ask the commission to submit proposals on matters on which parliament considers that an act of the community is needed. Also, the Council can make such a request. Such requests are often made.

Parliament takes part in legislating by the procedure of codecision with the Council, which is required in many matters, such as discrimination on grounds of nationality, free movement of workers, education, consumer protection, or environmental protection. If in these matters the Council and the European Parliament do not reach agreement, a Conciliation Committee is convened; unless both parties approve the proposed text, it is deemed not to have been approved. There are also cooperation matters such as the European Monetary Union. In these cases the European Parliament is heard but does not have a decisive vote.

The Judiciary

There are a Court of Justice and a Court of First Instance. They ensure that in the interpretation and application of the treaties the law is observed. The judiciary is independent. The Court of Justice consists of one judge for each member state, assisted by eight advocates general and a registrar. The Court of Justice has always been of high importance in promoting European integration.

THE ELECTION PROCESS

The electoral procedure to the European Parliament is determined by each member state. Throughout the union, there is a direct universal balloting process based on proportional representation.

Every citizen of the union residing in a member state of which he or she is not a national has the right to vote and to stand as a candidate at municipal elections in the member states in which he or she resides, under the same conditions as nationals of that state.

Every citizen of the union residing in a member state of which he or she is not a national also has the right to vote and to stand as a candidate in elections to the European Parliament. This applies also in member states in which he or she resides, and under the same conditions as nationals of that state.

POLITICAL PARTIES

Truly European political parties have not yet been established. However, within the European Parliament, political groups are formed by political parties existing within the member states that have common political convictions and objectives. There is a highly pluralist system of political parties throughout the European Union.

CITIZENSHIP

The European Union has established the citizenship of the union. Every person holding the nationality of a member state is a citizen of the union. Citizenship of the union complements and does not replace national citizenship.

Every citizen of the union has the right to move and reside freely within the territory of the member states, subject only to the limitations and conditions established by the treaties.

FUNDAMENTAL RIGHTS

The law of the European Union provides for a wide range of fundamental rights. The union is founded on the principle of respect for human rights and fundamental freedoms.

Within the scope of their application, the treaties prohibit any discrimination on grounds of nationality. European Union law also guarantees four specific freedoms according to its aim of integration: free movement of goods, free movement of persons, freedom to provide services, and free movement of capital and payments.

Those fundamental rights that form part of the constitutional traditions common to the member states are also fundamental rights valid in European Union law. The European Court of Justice has stated that it always is the highest level of protection of a fundamental right in any member state that constitutes what the constitutional traditions common to the member states require.

The union respects also those fundamental rights guaranteed by the 1950 European Convention for the Protection of Human Rights and Fundamental Freedoms, which are binding within European Union law. The European Union has also adopted the 2000 European Charter of Fundamental Rights. This is a concise declaration of fundamental rights, including social rights such as the right to work and to form trade unions. The charter also proclaims respect for the diversity of cultures, religions, and languages by the European Union.

Impact and Functions of Fundamental Rights

Fundamental rights guaranteed by the European Union have binding force only within the areas in which European Union law applies. Within that range, however, European Union law provides strong protections. This includes affirmative action. The Council may take appropriate action to combat discrimination based on sex, race or ethnic origin, religion or belief, disability, age, or sexual orientation. The European Court of Justice is a strong and vigilant institution that guarantees the implementation of fundamental rights.

The European Charter of Fundamental Rights has not yet obtained binding force. It remains a declaration of intent, not yet directly enforceable before a court. However, the European Court of Justice does take the charter into account as an expression of the constitutional traditions common to the member states.

The relationship between the protection of fundamental rights by European Union institutions and member states' courts is still an open question. Several constitutional courts of member states have declared that they would require a final say in whether European institutions have violated fundamental rights. However, they would do so only in a case of gross and unacceptable violation. No such case has occurred so far. The European Court of Justice insists that it and not the courts of the member states would have the final decision.

Limitations to Fundamental Rights

The union may restrict fundamental rights provided that these restrictions in fact correspond to objectives of general interest pursued by the union and that they do not constitute disproportionate and intolerable interference that infringes upon the very substance of the right guaranteed.

The limitation principles included in the 1950 European Convention of Human Rights are applied within European Union law. According to these principles certain fundamental rights are subject only to specifically qualified restrictions. They must be in accordance with the law and necessary in a democratic society pursuing certain specific legitimate interests, such as public safety, the prevention of disorder or crime, the protection of health or morals, or the protection of the rights and freedom of others.

ECONOMY

The treaties provide for a social market economy in a common market; for harmonious, balanced, and sustainable development; for a high level of employment and social protection; and for improvements in the standard of living and the quality of life.

RELIGIOUS COMMUNITIES

The European Union respects and does not prejudice the status of religious communities that they enjoy under member states' law. It equally respects the status of nonconfessional organizations. Religious freedom is guaranteed.

MILITARY DEFENSE AND STATE OF EMERGENCY

The European Union has no direct powers in military matters and commands no armed forces. It also does not provide for any state of emergency.

However, the provisions on a common foreign and security policy set out a number of basic objectives in the area of security policy. The most important of these objectives are to safeguard the common values, fundamental interests, independence, and integrity of the union; to strengthen the security of the union; to preserve peace and strengthen international security; to promote international cooperation; and to develop and consolidate democracy and the rule of law, and respect for human rights and fundamental freedoms. The treaty has set up a regime of consultation, information, and cooperation in matters of security policy. The union can adopt joint actions.

In a state of emergency according to member states' law the relevant member state has the right to adopt certain measures otherwise not permitted under European Union law, such as to prohibit the entry of goods or persons of other member states in its territory.

AMENDMENTS OF THE TREATIES

The treaties constituting the European Union, as international law treaties, can be changed by mutual consent of all member states, who thus have the role of a constituent assembly. The European Parliament does not have a decisive say in the procedure for amending the treaties. Amendments to the treaties and new treaties need ratification by the member states according to their internal law. In some member states referendums are needed, in others not.

PRIMARY SOURCES

The Treaty on European Union (consolidated version as applicable on November 1, 2004). Available online. URL:http://europa.eu.int/eur-lex/lex/en/treaties/dat/12002M/pdf/12002M_EN.pdf. Accessed on June 29, 2006.

Treaties in English. Available online. URL: http://europa.eu.int/eur-lex/lex/en/treaties/index.htm. Accessed on July 29, 2005.

2004 Draft Constitution in English. Available online. URL: http://europa.eu.int/constitution/en/allinone_en.htm. Accessed on September 8, 2005.

SECONDARY SOURCES

Case Reports. Available online. URL: http://europa.eu.int/eur-lex/en/search/search_case.html. Accessed on September 8, 2005.

Journals relevant in European integration research. Available online. URL: http://www.jeanmonnetprogram.org/TOC/index.php. Accessed on September 17, 2005.

Koen Lenaerts and Piet Van Nuffel, *Constitutional Law of the European Union*. 2d ed. London: Sweet & Maxwell, 2005 (parliamentary documents). Available online.

URL: http://www.europarl.eu.int/plenary/default_en.
htm. Accessed on August 27, 2005.
P. S. R. F. Mathijsen, *A Guide to European Union Law.* 8th ed.
London: Sweet & Maxwell, 2004.

Monitoring of the decision-making process of institutions.
Available online. URL: http://europa.eu.int/prelex/
apcnet.cfm?CL=en. Accessed on August 3, 2005.

Gerhard Robbers

APPENDIX II
Special Territories

Akrotiri

Akrotiri is a peninsula on the southwest coast of the island of Cyprus. It is an overseas territory of the United Kingdom. Akrotiri is administered by an administrator for the United Kingdom. This administrator is the same person as the commander of the British Forces Cyprus.

American Samoa

American Samoa is a group of islands in the South Pacific Ocean, east of the independent state of Samoa. American Samoa is an unorganized and unincorporated U.S. territory. American Samoa is administered by the Office of Insular Affairs in the U.S. Department of the Interior.

Anguilla

Anguilla is a Caribbean Island, east of Puerto Rico. It is an overseas territory of the United Kingdom. The British monarch is chief of state, represented by a governor. The governor appoints the chief minister and the cabinet ministers from among the elected members of the House of Assembly.

Antarctica

Most of the continent of Antarctica lies south of the Antarctic Circle. The Antarctic Treaty has more than 40 signatory nations and establishes a legal framework for managing the territory. Several nations maintain research stations on the continent.

Aruba

Aruba is an island of the Caribbean, north of Venezuela. It is an integral part of the Kingdom of the Netherlands. Aruba enjoys full autonomy in internal affairs. The Dutch government remains responsible for defense and foreign affairs.

Ashmore and Cartier Islands

Ashmore and Cartier Islands is a territory of Australia comprising a number of islands north of Australia in the Indian Ocean. Ashmore and Cartier Islands is administered by the Australian Department of Transport and Regional Services.

Baker Island

Baker Island is an atoll in the Pacific Ocean north of Australia. It is an unincorporated U.S. territory administered by the Fish and Wildlife Service of the U.S. Department of the Interior.

Bassas da India

Bassas da India is an atoll in the Indian Ocean, between Madagascar and Mozambique. It is an overseas possession of France. Bassas da India is administered by a high commissioner of France, who is resident in Réunion.

Bermuda

Bermuda is a group of islands in the North Atlantic Ocean. It is an overseas territory of the United Kingdom. Bermuda enjoys internal self-government. The British monarch is head of state, represented by a governor. The governor appoints the prime minister and on his or her nomination the cabinet ministers. The members of parliament are popularly elected and the leader of the majority is usually appointed prime minister.

Bouvet Island

Bouvet Island is an island in the South Atlantic Ocean, situated southwest of South Africa. It is a territory of Norway, administered by the Polar Department of the Ministry of Justice and Police.

British Indian Ocean Territory

The British Indian Ocean Territory is a group of islands south of India in the Indian Ocean. It is an overseas territory of the United Kingdom. The British Indian Ocean Territory is administered by a commissioner in the Foreign and Commonwealth Office. The United States and the United Kingdom run a joint military base on the most southerly island, Diego Garcia.

British Virgin Islands

British Virgin Islands is a group of islands in the Caribbean Sea, east of the U.S. Virgin Islands. It is an overseas territory of the United Kingdom enjoying internal self-government. The British monarch is head of state, represented by a governor. The leader of the majority of the popularly elected legislature is usually appointed chief minister by the governor, who also appoints the members of the Executive Council from among the members of the Legislative Council.

Cayman Islands

Cayman Islands is a group of islands in the Caribbean Sea, between Cuba and Honduras. It is an overseas territory of the United Kingdom. The British monarch is head of state, represented by a governor. After elections to the Legislative Assembly, the leader of the majority is appointed as leader of government business by the governor. The governor also appoints three members of the Executive Council; the other four members of the Executive Council are elected by the Legislative Assembly.

Christmas Island

Christmas Island is an island in the Indian Ocean, south of Indonesia. It is a territory of Australia. Christmas Island is administered by the Australian Department of Transport and Regional Services.

Clipperton Island

Clipperton Island is an island in the Pacific Ocean, southwest of Mexico. It is a possession of France. Clipperton Island is administered by a high commissioner of France residing in French Polynesia.

Cocos (Keeling) Islands

Cocos (Keeling) Islands is a group of islands in the Pacific Ocean, north of New Zealand. It is a territory of Australia. Cocos (Keeling) Islands is administered by the Australian Department of Transport and Regional Services.

Cook Islands

Cook Islands is a group of islands in the Pacific Ocean, north of New Zealand. It is a self-governing territory in free association with New Zealand. Cook Islands enjoys full self-government in internal affairs. External affairs and defense are administered by New Zealand in consultation with the Cook Islands.

Coral Sea Islands

Coral Sea Islands Territory is a group of islands in the Pacific Ocean, northeast of Australia. It is administered by the Australian Department of the Environment, Sport, and Territories.

Dhekelia

Dhekelia is a territory situated on the southeast coast of Cyprus. It is an overseas territory of the United Kingdom. Dhekelia is administered by an official who at the same time is the commander of the British Forces Cyprus.

Europa Island

Europa Island is an island in the Indian Ocean, west of Madagascar. It is a possession of France. Europa Island is administered by a high commissioner of France, who resides in Réunion.

Falkland Islands (Islas Malvinas)

Falkland Islands (Islas Malvinas) is a group of islands in the Atlantic Ocean, east of southern Argentina. It is an overseas territory of the United Kingdom. It enjoys internal self-government. Matters of defense and foreign affairs remain with the British government. The British monarch is head of state, represented by a governor. The Legislative Council consists of the governor, the chief executive, and the financial secretary as ex officio members and three other members elected by the Legislative Council. Falkland Islands (Islas Malvinas) is also claimed by Argentina.

Faroe Islands

Faroe Islands is a group of islands in the Atlantic Ocean, north of Great Britain. It is a part of the Kingdom of Denmark. Faroe Islands enjoys self-government, forming an overseas administrative division of Denmark. The Danish monarch is head of state, represented by a high commissioner. The leader of the majority in the popularly elected parliament is usually appointed prime minister.

French Guiana

French Guiana is a country in northern South America, between Brazil and Suriname. It is an overseas *département* of France.

French Polynesia

French Polynesia is a group of islands in the Pacific Ocean, between Australia and South America. It is an overseas land of France.

French Southern and Antarctic Lands

French Southern and Antarctic Lands is a group of islands in the Indian Ocean, among Africa, Antarctica, and Australia. It is an overseas territory of France.

Gibraltar

Gibraltar is a country in southwestern Europe on the southern coast of Spain. It is an overseas territory of the United Kingdom. The British monarch is head of state, represented by a governor and commander in chief. The leader of the majority of the elected House of Assembly is usually appointed chief minister. A council of ministers is appointed from among the members of the House of Assembly on consultation with the chief minister.

Glorioso Islands

Glorioso Islands is a group of islands in the Indian Ocean, northwest of Madagascar. It is an overseas possession of France. Glorioso Islands is administered by a high commissioner of France, who resides in Réunion.

Greenland

Greenland is an island in the Atlantic Ocean, northeast of Canada. It is an integral part of the Kingdom of Denmark. Greenland enjoys self-government as an overseas administrative division of Denmark. Greenland opted out of the European Union in 1985. The Danish monarch is head of state, represented by a high commissioner. The prime minister and the members of the cabinet are elected by the parliament according to the strength of the political parties.

Guadeloupe

Guadeloupe is a Caribbean island, southeast of Puerto Rico. It is an overseas *département* of France.

Guam

Guam is an island in the Pacific Ocean, between Hawaii and the Philippines. It is an organized but unincorporated territory of the United States. Guam has policy relations with the United States under the jurisdiction of the Office of Insular Affairs in the U.S. Department of the Interior.

Guernsey

Guernsey is an island in the Bristol Channel in Western Europe. It is a British Crown dependency. The British monarch is head of state, represented by a lieutenant governor and commander in chief. The States of Deliberation (parliament) is elected by a popular vote. The chief minister is elected by the States of Deliberation.

Heard Island and McDonald Islands

Heard Island and McDonald Islands is a group of islands in the Indian Ocean, between Madagascar and Antarctica. It is a territory of Australia. Heard Island and McDonald Islands is administered by the Australian Arctic Division of the Department of the Environment and Heritage.

Hong Kong

Hong Kong is a country in eastern Asia bordering China and the South China Sea. It is a special administrative region of China. Hong Kong is guaranteed internal autonomy by an agreement signed by China and the United Kingdom.

Howland Island

Howland Island is an island in the Pacific Ocean, between Hawaii and Australia. It is an unincorporated U.S. territory. Howland Island is administered by the Fish and Wildlife Service of the U.S. Department of the Interior.

Jan Mayen

Jan Mayen is an island northeast of Iceland, between the Norwegian Sea and the Greenland Sea. It is a territory of Norway. It is administered through the county governor of Nordland. This authority has been delegated to a station commander of the Norwegian Defense Communication Service.

Jarvis Island

Jarvis Island is an island in the South Pacific Ocean, about halfway between the Cook Islands and Hawaii. It is an unincorporated U.S. territory. Jarvis Island is administered by the Fish and Wildlife Service of the U.S. Department of the Interior.

Jersey

Jersey is an island in the English Channel, between the United Kingdom and France. It is a British Crown dependency. The British monarch is head of state, represented by a lieutenant governor, who is also the head of the executive branch of government. There is an Assembly of the States, which in its majority is popularly elected. Some members are appointed by the monarch.

Johnston Atoll

Johnston Atoll is a group of islands in the North Pacific Ocean, southeast of Hawaii. It is an unincorporated U.S. territory. Johnston Atoll is administered by the Pacific Air Forces at Hickam Air Force Base and the Fish and Wildlife Service of the U.S. Department of the Interior.

Juan de Nova Island

Juan de Nova Island is an island in the Indian Ocean, between Mozambique and Madagascar. It is a possession of France. Juan de Nova Island is administered by a high commissioner of France, who resides in Réunion.

Kingman Reef

Kingman Reef is a reef in the North Pacific Ocean, between Hawaii and American Samoa. It is an unincorporated U.S. territory. Kingman Reef is administered by the U.S. Fish and Wildlife Service of the Department of the Interior.

Macau

Macau is a territory in eastern Asia bordering the South China Sea. It is a special administrative region of China. China has promised that Macau, until 1999 administered by Portugal, will enjoy far-reaching internal autonomy and that China's socialist economic system will not be practiced in the territory.

Man, Isle of

The Isle of Man is an island in the Irish Sea, between Ireland and the United Kingdom. It is a British Crown dependency. The British monarch is the head of state, represented by a lieutenant governor. The chief minister as the head of the executive branch of government is elected by the bicameral parliament.

Martinique

Martinique is an island in the Caribbean Sea, north of Trinidad and Tobago. It is an overseas *département* of France.

Mayotte

Mayotte is an island in the Indian Ocean, between Madagascar and Mozambique. It is a territorial collectivity of France.

Midway Islands

Midway Islands is a group of islands in the Pacific Ocean, between Hawaii and Japan. It is an unincorporated U.S. territory administered by the Fish and Wildlife Service of the U.S. Department of the Interior.

Montserrat

Montserrat is an island in the Caribbean Sea, southeast of Puerto Rico. It is an overseas territory of the United Kingdom.

Navassa Island

Navassa Island is an island in the Caribbean Sea, west of Haiti. It is an unincorporated U.S. territory. Navassa Island is administered by the Fish and Wildlife Service of the U.S. Department of the Interior.

Netherlands Antilles

Netherlands Antilles are two island groups in the Caribbean Sea, east of Venezuela and east of the U.S. Virgin Islands. It is an autonomous country within the Kingdom of the Netherlands. Netherlands Antilles enjoys full autonomy in internal affairs. The Dutch government remains responsible for defense and foreign affairs.

New Caledonia

New Caledonia is a group of islands in the South Pacific Ocean, east of Australia. It is an overseas territory of France.

Niue

Niue is an island in the South Pacific Ocean, east of Tonga. It is a self-governing territory in free association with New Zealand. Niue is fully responsible for its internal affairs. The government of New Zealand remains responsible for external affairs and defense. These responsibilities are exercised only at the request of the government of Niue and confer no rights of control.

Norfolk Island

Norfolk Island is an island in the South Pacific Ocean, east of Australia. It is a territory of Australia. Commonwealth responsibilities on Norfolk Island are administered through the Australian Department of Environment, Sport, and Territories.

Northern Mariana Islands

Northern Mariana Islands is a group of islands in the North Pacific Ocean, between Hawaii and the Philippines. It is a commonwealth in political union with the United States. Federal funds to the Commonwealth are administered by the U.S. Department of the Interior, Office of Insular Affairs.

Palmyra Atoll

Palmyra Atoll is a group of islands in the North Pacific Ocean, between Hawaii and American Samoa. It is an incorporated U.S. territory. Palmyra is privately owned by the Nature Conservancy. However, it is administered by the Fish and Wildlife Service of the U.S. Department of the Interior. The Office of Insular Affairs of the U.S. Department of the Interior continues to administer nine excluded areas, which comprise certain islets and submerged lands.

Paracel Islands

Paracel Islands is a group of islands in the South China Sea. It is held by China, but also claimed by Vietnam and Taiwan.

Pitcairn Islands

Pitcairn Islands is a group of islands in the South Pacific Ocean. It is an overseas territory of the United Kingdom.

Puerto Rico

Puerto Rico is an island in the Caribbean Sea, east of the Dominican Republic. It is a commonwealth associated with the United States. The chief of state is the president of the United States. There is an elected governor, who appoints the cabinet with the consent of the popularly elected bicameral legislature.

Réunion

Réunion is an island in the Indian Ocean, east of Madagascar. It is an overseas *département* of France.

Saint Helena

Saint Helena is a group of islands in the South Atlantic Ocean, between South America and Africa. It is an overseas territory of the United Kingdom. The British monarch is head of state. The governor is appointed by the monarch and is the head of the executive branch of government. The Executive Council (cabinet) consists of the governor, nonelected members, and members elected by the unicameral legislature, which in turn is elected by popular vote.

Saint Pierre and Miquelon

Saint Pierre and Miquelon is a group of islands in the North Atlantic Ocean, south of Newfoundland, Canada. It is a self-governing territorial collectivity of France.

South Georgia and the South Sandwich Islands

South Georgia and the South Sandwich Islands is a group of islands in the South Atlantic Ocean, east of South America. It is an overseas territory of the United Kingdom, also claimed by Argentina. South Georgia and the South Sandwich Islands is administered from the Falkland Islands by a commissioner, who is also the governor of the Falkland Islands.

Spratly Islands

Spratly Islands is a group of islands in the South China Sea, between Vietnam and the Philippines. The more than 100 islands are in total or in part claimed by China, Taiwan, Vietnam, Malaysia, and the Philippines.

Svalbard

Svalbard is a group of islands in the Arctic Ocean, north of Norway. It is a territory of Norway. Svalbard is administered by the Polar Department of the Ministry of Justice through a governor residing in Spitzbergen.

Tokelau

Tokelau is a group of islands in the South Pacific Ocean, between Hawaii and New Zealand. It is a self-administering territory of New Zealand.

Tromelin Island

Tromelin Island is an island in the Indian Ocean, east of Madagascar. It is a possession of France. Tromelin Island is administered by a high commissioner of France, who resides in Réunion.

Turks and Caicos Islands

Turks and Caicos Islands are two groups of islands in the North Atlantic Ocean, north of Haiti. It is an overseas territory of the United Kingdom. The British monarch is head of state, represented by a governor. After election to the unicameral legislature the leader of the majority in parliament is usually appointed chief minister.

Virgin Islands

Virgin Islands is a group of islands in the Caribbean Sea, east of Puerto Rico. It is an organized, unincorporated U.S. territory. Policy relations with the United States are under the jurisdiction of the Office of Insular Affairs of the U.S. Department of the Interior.

Wake Island

Wake Island is a group of islands in the North Pacific Ocean, between Hawaii and the Northern Mariana Islands. It is an unincorporated U.S. territory. Wake Island is administered by the Department of the Interior.

Wallis and Futuna

Wallis and Futuna is a group of islands in the South Pacific Ocean, between Hawaii and New Zealand. It is an overseas territory of France. There is a unicameral Territorial Assembly elected by popular vote. The cabinet consists of three kings and three members appointed by the high administrator of France on the advice of the Territorial Assembly.

Western Sahara

Western Sahara is a territory in northern Africa, between Morocco and Mauritania, boarding the Atlantic Ocean. It is practically annexed by Morocco.

APPENDIX III
Glossary

absolute majority more than half of the number of qualified voters. In a parliament the absolute majority is more than half of the members of parliament regardless of whether they have participated in the actual voting or not.

absolutism a political doctrine or system in which the ruler has unlimited power; all legislative, executive, and judicial power is vested in the person of the ruler.

administration the leading body of the executive branch of government, especially in American English; composed of, e.g., a presidency and cabinet, or a prime minister and council of ministers.

administrative law law that regulates the powers of the executive branch of government; it controls the structure and functions of the administrative authorities and remedies against their abuse.

Allies, the the countries (United States, United Kingdom, Soviet Union, France, and many others) that fought together against the CENTRAL POWERS in World War I (1914–18) and against the AXIS powers (predominantly Nazi Germany, Fascist Italy, and the Empire of Japan) in World War II (1939–45).

amparo a proceeding before court in predominantly Spanish legal systems originally protecting against unlawful imprisonment and now extended to the protection of other fundamental rights.

annexation addition of a territory of a state or unorganized area to the territory of another state by a law.

bicameral consisting of two chambers or houses; used to describe many parliaments or legislatures; e.g., the bicameral Congress of the United States of America consists of the Senate and the House of Representatives.

Bolshevik Revolution the Russian Communist revolution of November 1917. The bolshevik (majority) faction of the Russian Social Democratic Party in 1903 developed into the Communist Party, known as the Bolsheviks.

cabinet the policymaking body at the top of the executive branch. It usually consists of a prime minister, cabinet ministers, and/or other department heads.

capitalism a system of economy based on private ownership and private economic enterprise.

Central Powers, the an alliance of the German, Austro-Hungarian, and Ottoman Empires with Bulgaria during World War I (1914–18). They fought against Russia in the east and France and the United Kingdom in the west of Europe, which are also referred to as the ALLIES.

checks and balances a principle of government organization in which each of the branches of government has powers to oversee or limit the other branches.

civil law the law governing the relationships between private persons; the law of private rights. It is usually distinguished from criminal law, administrative law, constitutional law, and other fields of law.

civil law systems those systems of law that have developed from the law of the Roman Empire in Europe. Civil law systems are usually distinguished from common law systems, which characterize Great Britain and many of its former dependencies, such as the United States.

cohabitation in the French political system, a situation in which the president and the prime minister are members of different political camps.

cold war the decades-long political conflict (c. 1946–90) between the capitalist powers led by the United States and the Communist powers led by the Soviet Union.

common law systems those systems of law that have developed from the legal culture of England. In common law systems, precedents deriving from court decisions are dominant over statute law. Common law systems are usually distinguished from the civil law systems that characterize the European Continent.

Commonwealth (of Nations) an association of independent states united by their common allegiance to a mother country. Usually the British Commonwealth of Nations.

concordat a treaty between a national government and an external religious group, usually the Roman Catholic Holy See, regulating religious affairs.

confederation a political system combining a group of independent states for permanent joint action, such as common defense.

constitutional in accordance with the constitution.

constitutional directive provisions in the constitution providing for an aim to be pursued by the authorities but not providing for a fundamental right of individuals.

constitutional law the field of law dealing with the constitution of a state or a similar entity.

constitutional monarchy a system of government headed by a monarch who is bound by a constitution. Constitutional monarchies developed in Europe in the late 18th and 19th centuries.

constructive motion of confidence a rule by which the holder of an office such as president, chancellor, or prime minister can only be removed from office through the election of a successor in the office. Contrary to a destructive motion of confidence, by which the holder of the office can be removed without immediate election of a successor.

co-optation election or selection to a body by vote of its own members.

corporative state a political system in which the government of a state depends on professional corporations or organizations.

coup d'état an overthrow of the government by means contrary to the constitution.

criminal law a field of law that relates to crimes.

Crown dependency a territory in possession of the British Crown, applied to overseas territories or colonies.

customary international law international law that develops by custom, i.e., by the accepted practice of states.

data protection the legal protection of a person's personal or professional data such as names, addresses, religion, or economic situation.

decree a special form of legal rule issued either by order of a ruler or by an ordinance enacted by a council or administrative body. Decrees usually have inferior rank to general laws.

decree law an ordinance or other authoritative decision with the force of a law. In many countries decree laws, when issued, need subsequent approval by parliament.

delegated legislation legislation by an executive authority empowered to do so by parliament.

democratic centralism a concept in communist theory by which the will of the people is expressed and often determined by a centralist government.

double standard test a method of judicial review used by the U.S. Supreme Court. While the court upholds legislation in the economic realm as long as it is supported by any rational basis, it scrutinizes governmental attempts to regulate or abridge other civil liberties rather closely.

encomienda a system of tributes to be paid by the Native American people, introduced to all the Spanish colonies by the 1512 Laws of Burgos.

entrenched provision a provision of a constitution that either can never be changed or requires an extraordinary procedure to change.

European Council one of the governing bodies of the European Union.

European Community the most important of the communities and policies under the roof of the European Union.

ex officio member one who is a member of a body by virtue of another office he or she holds.

executive the branch of a government that is responsible for the day-to-day activity of a state, formulation of its general policy, and execution and implementation of the laws.

extraterritoriality exemption from the application of the law of a state. Usually, a diplomatic mission of one state in another state is extraterritorial of that latter state.

federal state a nation-state in which government power is distributed between a national government and component provincial or state governments.

federation See FEDERAL STATE.

free development of the personality; often also: free development of the person A widespread human right that guarantees freedom of action and privacy.

feudalism a system of government widespread in medieval Europe in which a ruler divides territory among his or her followers, who render military service in exchange; in a wider sense, any system in which large landholders exercise government functions in their domains.

first-generation rights the set of fundamental rights that historically were the first to be generally protected, such as freedom of religion, protection against unfair arrest (habeas corpus), and right to a fair trial.

first past the post election in which only the candidate who receives the most votes in a constituency obtains a mandate.

fiscal of or relating to financial matters of government.

flagranti delicto in the very act of committing a crime; caught in the act.

fundamental rights basic rights of a person, generally guaranteed in constitutions; often divided into human rights and citizens' rights.

general international law the law governing the relations between states and other subjects of international law.

government in American English, the sum of all the organs through which a state exercises its authority and performs its functions—legislative, executive, and judicial. In England and many other states the term often refers to the body heading the executive branch (including the prime minister, cabinet, etc.), which in the United States is known as the administration.

habeas corpus the right of a citizen against illegal imprisonment.

Hashemite an Arab dynasty from the Hejaz region of Arabia, along the Red Sea, who provided kings to Iraq and Jordan in the 20th century. The Hashemites trace their ancestry from Hashem (died 510 C.E.), the great-grandfather of the Prophet Muhammad.

hierarchy of norms in a given legal system there are usually a variety of types of norms or legal requirements, which can be ranked in a hierarchy of precedence; usually the constitution has the highest rank (it prevails in any conflict with a lower norm); below that is ordinary or statute law; government regulations or ordinances are of still lower status, followed by other types of provisions.

impeachment conviction of misconduct normally leading to removal from office.

imperative mandate the rule that a representative has to vote in a given matter according to the will of his or her elector.

imperialism the policy of seeking control over (many) other nations.

imprescriptable inalienable, unable to be removed.

injunction order a decision granted by a court whereby one is required to do or to refrain from doing something.

incompatibility the legal inability to exercise an office while holding another office.

incorporated territory in the United States, a territory over which the U.S. Constitution applies in its entirety, as it does in the 50 states.

initiative the power or the right to introduce a bill of law in a parliament; the power to start the legislative process.

international law See GENERAL INTERNATIONAL LAW.

interpellation the act of formally putting in question in parliament a policy or an action of the executive branch of government.

ius officii the right or power of an office.

ius sanguinis: right of blood the rule of citizenship law that determines the citizenship of a person by the citizenship of his or her parents.

ius soli: the right of the soil in citizenship law the rule by which the citizenship of a person is determined by the place of birth.

judiciable enforceable in court.

judicial review the practice of courts to decide on the legality or constitutionality of an act or a matter.

judiciary the court system.

laicist (from the French term *laïc*) characterized by a complete, principled separation of state and religion.

law a specific kind of legal provision usually passed by a parliament. Law usually has a higher rank in the legal order than regulations, ordinances, or decrees. Often synonymous with *statutory act*.

legal person an entity that by law has full legal rights. An association or company can be a legal person and as such take part in legal transactions.

legislature the branch of government having the right to make laws.

liberal rights in most constitutional systems those fundamental rights characterized by preventing government from limiting the freedom of individuals. These liberal rights usually include freedom of speech, freedom of the press, freedom of religion and belief, freedom of association, freedom of assembly, and the right against unlawful imprisonment.

liberalism in most countries, a political philosophy insisting on the freedom of the individual and on limited government, especially in the economic and social spheres. Liberalism also describes a 19th-century European movement of economically independent citizens struggling to limit the power of monarchs and, often, of state churches; in the United States, liberals are the equivalent of social democrats in Europe.

margin of appreciation a widespread rule of law by which government authorities enjoy a certain freedom of judgment beyond what a court can claim; e.g., authorities can usually decide freely whether it is preferable to build a street with two or three lanes.

martial law suspension of the normal way of government and enforcement of the law by the military.

Muhammad (570–632 C.E.) the Arab founder and chief Prophet of the religion of Islam, whose preachings are the basis of Sharia, Islamic law.

negative rights in many constitutional systems negative rights are those fundamental rights that restrict government action; freedom of speech is a negative right in that it prevents government from censoring opinions. Negative rights are often opposed to positive rights—the right to be provided with a good or service by the government.

no confidence vote a vote in parliament declaring that parliament no longer supports a current administration; in many systems a no confidence vote means the dismissal of the administration.

ordinance a form of general rule ranking below parliamentary laws; usually issued by the president, the cabinet, an individual cabinet minister, or a local government body.

organic law in many constitutional systems a specific kind of parliamentary law with special constitutional relevance, usually requiring a special majority for its passage; organic laws often structure the government and are often called for in the text of the constitution.

organized territory under U.S. law a territory for which the U.S. Congress has enacted an organic act. Such organic acts usually include a Bill of Rights and rules about a government.

overseas collectivity in French law a territory of France not in mainland France with specially defined status.

overseas *département* in French law an ocean territory of France not in mainland France enjoying the same status as a metropolitan *département*.

overseas land in French law a territory of France not in mainland France with specially defined status.

overseas region in French law a territory of France not in mainland France enjoying the same status as a French metropolitan region. A metropolitan region is the largest territorial division within France and comprises several *départements*. Overseas regions are Guadeloupe, French Guiana, Martinique, and Réunion. Each of these regions also is an overseas *département*.

overseas territory in French law a territory of France not in mainland France with specially defined status. A similar status exists in the laws of several other countries.

parliament representative body of the people; parliaments are usually entrusted with the chief legislative power.

parliamentary system or parliamentarism a system of government in which the executive branch or administration is chosen by and can be dismissed by parliament, often via a vote of confidence.

peoples' rights in human rights law, a third-generation right enjoyed not by an individual but by one or more peoples; it can include language rights, rights to sustainable development, or protection for a threatened minority culture.

personal union different countries or territorial units governed by the same monarch.

plebiscite a referendum in which the voters directly approve or reject a law or any legal provision.

positive rights in many constitutional systems, positive rights give the citizens guaranteed access to a good or service from the government, such as free education, adequate housing, or work; often contrasted with negative rights.

Potsdam Declaration the 1945 Declaration in the German city of Potsdam (near Berlin) in which the Allied powers (United States, Great Britain, and the Soviet Union) decided on the future shape of Germany after World War II (1939–45).

preamble introductory part of a constitution or a law; usually states the basic principles or goals of the government.

preferential voting a system of voting in which the voter indicates his or her order of preference for each of the candidates. If no candidate receives the majority of first preferences, then the second and if necessary lower-order preferences can be added until a majority for one candidate is obtained.

presidential system a system of government in which the executive branch is elected separately from the legislative branch; often contrasted to cabinet government, which is usually a feature of parliamentarism.

primogeniture a rule by which the first-born son follows in a position; when the successor to a monarchical throne is chosen by primogeniture, the oldest son (or sometimes, the oldest child of either sex) inherits the Crown upon the monarch's death or abdication.

private law the law governing the relations between private individuals or corporations.

Privy Council a body of dignitaries and officials constituting an advisory council to the British monarch; usually functions through committees such as the judicial committee, which serves as court of last appeal in several present or former British colonies.

promulgate to pass (a law, a statute) into force.

proportional representation an electoral system in which party representation is proportionate to the overall share of the vote the party receives, either in the whole state or in any constituency.

proportionality a widespread principle of law requiring any legal act, action, or measure to be adequate to its purpose without any overreaching; it is often used to curb excesses when rights must be limited by law.

prorogue to adjourn a session of parliament.

public law the law governing the action of governments.

qualified majority a higher majority than a simple majority, i.e., more than just half plus one of those voting; a qualified majority may be as high as four-fifths for some purposes in some systems.

quorum the minimal number of members of a legislature or cabinet who must be present before a valid vote can be taken.

ratification the formal act of confirmation of an international treaty or constitutional amendment.

referendum a direct poll of all voters by which they may decide important matters, such as a constitutional amendment, a tax, or a change in the territory of a state.

regulation a legal rule ranking below parliamentary law. Regulations are usually issued by the administration and are often of a technical nature.

relative majority the majority of the actual votes casts. See absolute majority.

retroactive having effect on a past action; a retroactive law enters into force at a time before its enactment. A person may be prosecuted by a retroactive law for a crime committed before the law was passed.

retrospective affecting something in the past. A retrospective law affects situations that have since passed.

rule of law the principle that all government action should be based on a law; lawful government.

second-generation rights those fundamental rights that were historically recognized later than first-generation rights. They usually include social rights such as the right to work, to be educated, or to be provided with adequate housing.

semipresidential system (or mixed presidential-parliamentary system) a system of government in which the president has real and not merely symbolic functions, shared with an executive prime minister, who has some responsibility before the legislature.

sharia the body of Muslim sacred law based primarily on the Quran and other traditional sources traced back to the Prophet Muhammad.

Shiite follower of Shiism or Shia, a branch of Islam.

single transferable vote in systems of proportional representation the voter can rank candidates from different lists first, second, third, and so on, without being confined to the list of one party.

socialist legality a concept in communist theory by which the law has to be interpreted and applied according to the Marxist-Leninist revolutionary theory.

social market economy a national economy based on the idea of a free-market system tempered with ideas of social responsibility and welfare programs. In a social market economy freedom of enterprise usually is limited by a set of rights of employees such as pension rights, health insurance, and limitations on firings.

social rights Human or fundamental rights that guarantee basic prerequisites for life; often the right to work, the right to education, or the right to housing.

social state a concept of statehood in many constitutions by which government has to provide actively for the basic needs of life of the people; this can cover minimal standard of living or a system of social insurance.

sovereignty the foundational power in a government system, endowed with the last word on all matters. In most constitutional systems the people are the sovereign; sometimes—frequently in the past—sovereignty lies with the monarch, the state, or another entity.

statute law (also statutory law) law specified in statutes; usually a law enacted by the supreme legislative branch of a government.

subsidiarity the rule that a smaller or hierarchically lower entity (a community, a county) should decide a matter as long as it can reasonably do so; only when the lower entity is incapable of tackling a problem should the higher entity intervene.

Sunni follower of Sunnism, the larger of the two major branches of Islam.

supranational organization an organization of a number of states transferring part of their sovereign rights to that organization. The European Union is a supranational organization, which has sovereign powers directly over and within its member states.

suspensive veto the refusal by an executive to assent to a decision of parliament, without actually vetoing it. Often, the president of a country can refuse to sign a bill into law, but this refusal can be overridden by subsequent repeated passing of the law by parliament, and thus can only *suspend* the act.

third-generation rights those fundamental rights that have found wide constitutional protection most recently, usually entailing the rights of groups, such as minority protection, protection of cultures and languages, or the right to sustainable development of developing countries.

tutela action the right to act in court in favor of someone else.

two-round system (runoff system or double-ballot system) a system of election in which a candidate must receive an absolute majority to be elected. If no one achieves a majority in the first round, a second round is conducted, usually between the two candidates who have won the most votes in the first round. Often used in presidential elections.

Ulema a group of Muslim scholars and theologians who professionally study and elaborate the Muslim legal system.

unicameral having only one chamber or house; used of parliaments or other representative bodies.

unincorporated territory a territory under U.S. jurisdiction in which only select parts of the U.S. Constitution apply.

unitary state a state system without subdivisions of relevant independence; opposite of a federal state.

United Nations Partition Plan a 1947 plan to resolve the Arab-Jewish conflict in the British Mandate of Palestine, by partitioning the territory into Jewish and Arab states, with the Greater Jerusalem area (encompassing Bethlehem) under international control. The failure of this plan led to the 1948 Arab-Israeli War.

unorganized territory under U.S. law a U.S. territory possessed by the U.S. government that is not within any of the states of the union and has not been organized into a self-governing unit.

Velvet Revolution the period that brought about the bloodless overthrow of the Communist regime in Czechoslovakia (today the Czech Republic and the Slovak Republic).

Versailles, Treaty of the peace treaty that put an official end to World War I (1914–18) between the ALLIES and CENTRAL POWERS.

veto a rejection by the executive of a bill already passed by the legislature; if the president exercises the veto, the law cannot go into force (absolute veto) or has to be enacted again, sometimes with a special majority (suspensive veto).

vote of no confidence See NO CONFIDENCE VOTE.

Westminster type of government a type of government structured as the British system is, characterized by the predominant position of the prime minister and a weak division of powers.

writ a document usually issued by a court.

writ of mandamus order of a higher court to an inferior court.

Index